GROWING

Also of interest from the Urban Institute Press:

Work-Life Policies, edited by Ann C. Crouter and Alan Booth

Intergenerational Caregiving, edited by Alan Booth, Ann C. Crouter, Suzanne M. Bianchi, and Judith A. Seltzer

THE URBAN INSTITUTE PRESS
WASHINGTON, DC

GROWING UP HISPANIC

Health and Development of Children of Immigrants

Edited by
NANCY S. LANDALE, SUSAN McHALE,
and **ALAN BOOTH**

THE URBAN INSTITUTE PRESS
2100 M Street, N.W.
Washington, D.C. 20037

Library of Congress Cataloging-in-Publication Data

Growing up Hispanic : health and development of children of immigrants / edited by Nancy Landale, Susan McHale, and Alan Booth.
    p. cm.
 "Based on papers presented at the 16th Annual Penn State Symposium on Family Issues in October 2008"—Preface.
 Includes index.
 ISBN 978-0-87766-763-6 (alk. paper)
 1. Latin Americans—United States—Social conditions. 2. Children of immigrants—United States—Social conditions. 3. Hispanic American children—Social conditions. I. Landale, Nancy. II. McHale, Susan. III. Booth, Alan, 1935- IV. National Symposium on Family Issues (16th : 2008 : Pennsylvania State University)
 E184.S75G76 2009
 305.23089'68073—dc22

                                                              2010007948

Printed in the United States of America

13 12 11 10   1 2 3 4 5

Contents

PART III. **Schooling and the Development of Children and Youth in Hispanic Immigrant Families**

PART IV. **Access to Health Care and Well-Being of Children and Youth from Hispanic Immigrant Families**

Preface

O ne in five children in the United States has immigrant parents, and children of immigrant parents are the fastest-growing component of the child population. The development of these young children is critical for their life chances and for their long-term social and economic integration into U.S. society. The regional origins of immigrant families are diverse and must be recognized when studying the circumstances and experiences of children of immigrants. Given the high volume of immigration from Latin America, the focus of this volume is Hispanic children in immigrant families. They are a diverse group that is of growing importance because Hispanics constitute the largest ethnic minority group in the nation.

A range of challenges face immigrant children and their families. Negative sentiments toward immigrant families are the highest they have been in nearly a century. National immigration policy appears to be in a gridlock, but local policies are changing rapidly. Immigrant destinations have expanded to include both new metropolitan locations and rural areas. These and other changes have altered the social, political, and economic forces in host communities and the broader social contexts in which children develop. Thus, the study of children and youth in immigrant families is timely and important.

The contributions to *Growing Up Hispanic* are based on papers presented at the 16th Annual Penn State Symposium on Family Issues in

October 2008, "Development of Hispanic Children in Immigrant Families: Challenges and Prospects." This edited volume is the culmination of two days of stimulating presentations and discussions examining four arenas of research and policy that are significant in the development and well-being of children and youth in immigrant Hispanic families: (1) the social ecologies of children and youth in immigrant families, including the range of setting characteristics and the implications of such characteristics for child and youth well-being and development; (2) the role of families in children's successful adaptation to "host" environments; (3) the implications of the school and community contexts as well as education policies for children's school experiences and academic achievement; and (4) the roles of health care, social service provision, and health policies in children's mental health and well-being.

Each of the four parts in this volume includes a chapter by a lead author, followed by shorter chapters by discussants. Care has been taken to bring together perspectives from diverse disciplines in each part. The volume concludes with an integrative commentary.

Growing Up Hispanic begins with a comprehensive description by sociologist Richard Alba from the City University of New York and his colleagues from The University at Albany, State University of New York, of the residential environments in which Hispanic children live. Even though Hispanic children are only moderately segregated from white children, the neighborhoods in which they live have higher levels of poverty, more immigrants, fewer fluent English speakers, and a less-educated adult population. Among the many important themes addressed in this chapter are the implications of the recent residential dispersion of Hispanics for children's neighborhood environments.

Residential dispersion to new immigrant destination areas is further developed in two additional chapters in part I. Demographer and policy analyst Randy Capps from the Migration Policy Institute, along with his colleagues, and economist Stephen J. Trejo from the University of Texas at Austin emphasize that Hispanic children's neighborhood environments may be better in new destination areas because migration to such areas is primarily driven by job opportunities and better living conditions. Trejo also comments on the methodological challenges of estimating the causal impacts of residential integration and neighborhood quality on Hispanic children's outcomes. An additional perspective is provided by psychologist Stephen M. Quintana of the University of Wisconsin–Madison, who elaborates on the microdynamics of intergroup contact in different types of neighborhoods and their influence on youths' self-concepts.

Part II of the volume shifts from the neighborhood context to the family context. Drawing on social ecological and person-oriented approaches, Kimberly A. Updegraff and Adriana J. Umaña-Taylor from Arizona State University examine differences across families in *within-family* patterns of involvement in Mexican and Anglo cultures. They argue that cultural adaptation can best be understood as a family-level phenomenon. Also emphasizing a family perspective on culture and youth development, clinical psychologist Rosalie Corona of Virginia Commonwealth University draws attention to an understudied topic: the roles fathers and siblings play in Latino youth sexual health. Two additional chapters offer insights from a demographic perspective. Donald J. Hernandez of CUNY and his colleagues at the University at Albany, SUNY, document the resources and challenges faced by children in immigrant families, and Jennifer Van Hook of Penn State outlines fruitful potential areas of interdisciplinary exchange between demographers and child development scholars.

Beyond the family and the neighborhood, the school is the other major setting in which children live out their everyday lives. Part III of *Growing Up Hispanic* examines in detail the state of education among Hispanics in the United States. The lead chapter by Carola Suárez-Orozco, Francisco X. Gaytán, and Ha Yeon Kim, scholars of applied psychology at New York University, presents and interprets various indicators of educational performance among Hispanic youth from preschool to college. Extensive recommendations for research, practice, and policy are aimed at improving the limited educational prospects of Hispanic youth. Chapters by sociologist Katharine M. Donato of Vanderbilt University and political scientist Melissa Marschall of Rice University, and by Suet-ling Pong, education policy researcher at Penn State, also outline policies that may improve the bleak educational prospects of Hispanic youth. Importantly, both Donato and Marschall's chapter and a chapter by developmental psychologist Andrew J. Fuligni of the University of California, Los Angeles, emphasize the promise of policies that build on the strengths of Hispanic families to improve Hispanic youths' educational performance.

Part IV focuses on mental health and the services available to address mental health problems. Clinical psychologist Margarita Alegría and her colleagues at Harvard University address mental health service disparities, noting that availability of such services through schools is critical to access by impoverished populations. Chapters by sociologist and demographer

Deborah Roempke Graefe of Penn State and social psychologist and demographer Robert E. Roberts and community psychologist Catherine R. Roberts of the University of Texas, Houston, augment Alegría's recommendations for further research. Cheryl Anne Boyce, a clinical psychologist at the National Institute of Mental Health, expands the focus by framing disparities in mental health and education in terms of their implications for the broader society. Arguing that inequality is a burden that leaves society in debt, she provides recommendations to reduce service disparities.

The concluding chapter is an integrative commentary by Matthew Hall and Anna R. Soli, Penn State graduate students in the department of sociology and the department of human development and family studies, respectively. These authors provide a thorough summary and integration of the major themes addressed in the volume, with an emphasis on what we know, what we don't know, and where we should go from here.

Acknowledgments

The editors are grateful to the many organizations at Penn State that sponsored the 2008 Symposium on Family Issues and this resulting volume, including the Population Research Institute; the Children, Youth, and Families Consortium; the Prevention Research Center; the Center for Human Development and Family Research in Diverse Contexts; the Women's Studies Program; the College of Education; and the departments of labor studies and employment relations, human development and family studies, psychology, sociology, and rural sociology. The editors also gratefully acknowledge essential core financial support in the form of a five-year grant from the National Institute of Child Health and Human Development (NICHD), as well as guidance and advice from Christine Bachrach (Office of Behavioral and Social Sciences Research, National Institutes of Health), Rebecca Clark, Rosalind King, and Peggy McCardle of NICHD. The ongoing support of all these partners has enabled us to attract excellent scholars from a range of backgrounds and disciplines—the sort of group on whom the quality and integrity of the series depends.

A lively, interdisciplinary team of scholars from across the Penn State community meets with us annually to generate symposia topics and plans and is available throughout the year for brainstorming and problem solving. We appreciate their enthusiasm, intellectual support, and creative ideas. In the course of selecting speakers, symposium organizers consult with a wide range of people at other universities, NICHD, and other organizations so the most qualified people are identified and contacted about participating. We also sincerely thank Gordon De Jong, Mayra Y. Bámaca, Leif Jensen, and Pamela Farley Short for presiding over symposium sessions.

The many details that go into planning a symposium and producing a volume cannot be overestimated. In this regard, we are especially grateful for the assistance of our administrative staff, including Tara Murray and Sherry Yocum. Finally, we could not have accomplished this work without Carolyn Scott, whose organizational skills, commitment, and attention to the many details that go into organizing a good conference and edited book series make it possible for us to focus on the ideas.

Nancy S. Landale
Susan McHale
Alan Booth

PART I
The Social Contexts of Children and Youth in Hispanic Immigrant Families

1

Nowhere Near the Same
The Neighborhoods of Latino Children

Richard Alba, Nancy A. Denton, Donald J. Hernandez,
Ilir Disha, Brian McKenzie, and Jeffrey Napierala

Children depend on the resources of their neighborhoods more than adults do. The great majority of American children attend local schools and play with children who live near them (Lareau 2003). They walk and ride their bicycles on the streets around their homes and are thus exposed to the risks that prevail there, and many may glimpse the possibilities and limits of their own futures as they look at the older teenagers and young adults on those streets. Children become familiar with the worlds of adults through the grown-ups they encounter in their residential environments, not only their parents and other relatives, but also neighbors and the parents of friends.

The vulnerability of children to their residential environments is one reason the extensive literature on residential segregation looms so large in the investigation of ethno-racial inequalities in the United States. In terms of segregation, Latinos have often been seen as an in-between population: not as segregated as African Americans, but still substantially segregated from whites and with little sign of full residential integration in the near future. While African American segregation has been very slowly subsiding over time—falling during the 1990s, for example, from an average of 68.9 to 65.2 according to the index of dissimilarity—Hispanic segregation from whites increased slightly in the same period, from 50.7 to 51.6 (Logan, Stults, and Farley 2004). Latino segregation is especially high in some parts of the United States, such as the metropolitan regions of the Northeast, where segregation in general is extensive and the Latino population is dominated by groups, such as Dominicans and Puerto Ricans, with a visible admixture of African ancestry (Landale and Oropesa 2002; Rosenbaum and Friedman 2007).

One major influence on Hispanic residential patterns is the large scale of current Latin-American immigration. This plays a key role in maintaining the level of Hispanic segregation, since immigrants tend to go initially to areas where many people that share their ethnicity can be found. Starting in 1980, Hispanic segregation rose notably in several places with rapidly growing Latino immigrant populations, including Anaheim (12.9 percent increase by 2000), Atlanta (21.1 percent increase), Los Angeles (5.8 percent increase), Seattle (11.1 percent increase), and Washington, D.C. (16.1 percent increase) (Logan et al. 2004). As a consequence, many Hispanic children, but especially those in immigrant families, are growing up in immigrant-rich neighborhoods, surrounded by other children and adults who are relative newcomers to the society. Nevertheless, John Iceland's (2009) recent analysis finds that, over time, the integration of settled Hispanics tends to increase—for example, integration with U.S. natives is greater the longer that Hispanic immigrants have resided in the United States. His analysis thus implies that Latino neighborhoods experience considerable residential instability, as new immigrants arrive but some of the more settled ones leave for other places to live. Speaking to the intermediate situation of Hispanics, however, is that the residential integration found by Iceland involves greater co-residence with both whites and blacks.

The literature on Hispanic residential patterns raises many questions about the residential environments in which Hispanic children, especially those in immigrant families, are growing up: What are these residential environments like? How do they compare to the environment in which the average white child, or the average African American child, is found? What implications do the residential contexts of Hispanic children have for their life chances? Do these environments change as the position of their family does—in socioeconomic and other terms? Are the residential options for Hispanic families constrained by their racial and ethnic origins and/or their legal status?

In this chapter, we try to answer some of these questions with data from the 2000 Census that allow us to characterize in various ways the neighborhood environments of the children from different ethno-racial groups. The chapter grows out of a larger project on the social contexts of the children in immigrant families that is led by the first three authors. It represents a first cut into a large body of data and is limited by its reliance on aggregate data from census summary files. Nevertheless, since this is typically the primary data source for studies of residential patterns, we are not any more limited than most other studies. We will be able to answer satisfactorily some of the questions we have just posed, and the data we present and interpret will carry implications for the others.

What Do We Know about Hispanic Residential Patterns?

How we interpret statistical indicators of residential patterns is necessarily informed by the theoretical concepts that we use to understand such patterns more abstractly. The dominant conception of the settlement process for an immigrant-origin group remains the model of spatial assimilation, which originates in the era of mass immigration from Europe of a century ago (Massey 1985). The model presumes that the residential situation of relatively new arrivals lies in immigrant neighborhoods where they can draw upon the assistance of relatives and other immigrants with greater experience in the United States. These neighborhoods typically have limited resources and amenities compared with the neighborhoods in which middle-class natives live. Hence, as immigrant families climb the socioeconomic ladder and as their adult members acculturate, they tend to leave immigrant areas of settlement for better neighborhoods in which to live and raise children. Since the neighborhoods with the most desirable characteristics are frequently those in which members of the white majority also reside, the improvements that minority families seek in their residential contexts often bring them and their children into greater contact with the majority population. This residential mobility can extend over several generations.

To be sure, a model rooted in the residential patterns of the first half of the 20th century has some features that seem dated, but nevertheless some core expectations of the spatial-assimilation model appear applicable to contemporary immigrant-origin groups. As noted above, the recent analyses of John Iceland indicate that Latino residential patterns are consistent with some hypotheses of the model: namely, such variables as longer residence in the United States, birth in the United States, English fluency, and higher income are all associated with greater residential integration with whites. Similar findings have been reached with the locational-attainment models of Alba and Logan (e.g., Alba, Logan, and Stults 2000). They find that, under some conditions, Latinos live in the same, or equivalent, neighborhoods as their Anglo peers, the ultimate standard for spatial assimilation. This is true in particular of middle- and higher-income, light-skinned Latinos who speak only English at home. Darker-skinned Latinos, those who classify themselves racially as "other" or "black," do not have residential outcomes as favorable as "white" Latinos, although the differences between white and other Latinos are generally not large. Linguistic assimilation also has a sizable influence on the residential location of Hispanics.

Research that pays attention to the different national origins among Hispanics indicates that the appropriateness of the spatial assimilation model varies by subgroup. South, Crowder, and Chavez (2005b) find that the expectations of spatial assimilation fit Mexicans better than they do Cubans and Puerto Ricans and that the constraint of dark skin on residential location is particularly important for the latter two groups. However, in research on the ability of the members of different groups to leave high-poverty neighborhoods, the same researchers find that Mexicans, along with Puerto Ricans, have difficulties exiting from such neighborhoods that are as serious as those confronting African Americans (South, Crowder, and Chavez 2005a). For obvious reasons given the size of the Mexican American population, considerable effort has gone into studying its residential trajectories. Findings from the Immigration and Intergenerational Mobility in Los Angeles (IIMLA) study suggest that residential assimilation proceeds slowly in generational terms, and that Mexicans attain only in the fourth and later generations what the European ethnics managed by the third generation if not before (Brown 2007). The recent study by Telles and Ortiz (2008) of Los Angeles and San Antonio Mexican Americans originally surveyed in the mid-1960s and of their grown children confirms that even after several generations in the United States, Mexican Americans tend to live in neighborhoods that have relatively large numbers of other Hispanics. It also reveals, however, that mobility away from these regions is connected with much greater spatial assimilation.

Iceland's conclusion that residential integration occurs with blacks as well as with whites highlights the high variability in residential patterns of Hispanics. Spatial assimilation in the conventional sense of growing integration into the residential mainstream is not the only appropriate model, for Hispanics can also suffer from the barriers imposed by nonwhite race in U.S. society as well as those associated with recent immigration and undocumented status. The impact of race is evident in the high segregation levels that characterize some Hispanic groups from the Caribbean, such as Dominicans and Puerto Ricans (Denton and Massey 1989; Iceland and Nelson 2008; Massey and Bitterman 1985).

The variability in the residential incorporation of Latinos is suggested by the ambiguous role the suburbs have played for them. In the canonical statement of the spatial assimilation model, suburbia was identified as the landscape where segregation along ethno-racial lines was greatly reduced and integration into the residential mainstream largely accomplished. In fact, the presence of Latinos in suburbs where they are also home owners has surged in recent years (Alba et al. 1999; Myers 2007; Suro and Singer 2002). However, in many cases, they are residing in declining, inner-ring suburbs, which represent the extension of the conditions of inner-city neighborhoods beyond municipal boundaries (Holzer and Stoll 2007). For example, within the Chicago metropolitan region, the majority of Latinos now reside outside the central city, but most of these new suburbanites are concentrated in older inner-ring suburbs such as Aurora and Cicero (Newbold and Spindler 2001). Of the immigrant enclaves that have arisen in poorer suburbs, many are home to Latino populations, and new immigrants are frequently settling initially in them rather than in inner-city areas.

Another element that complicates the picture of the residential environments for Hispanic children is the spread of Latin American immigrants outside the traditional gateway zones and, in particular, their entry into new destination areas (Massey 2008; Suro and Singer 2002; Suro and Tafoya 2004; Zúñiga and Hernández-León 2005). This new geographical component came into sharp focus during the 1980s and 1990s, as the Hispanic populations in states like Georgia, North Carolina, and Oregon increased dramatically and surprisingly. The increases were especially strong in the Southeast, in metropolitan regions such as Atlanta and Raleigh-Durham. Much of the spread outside the traditional gateway areas involves Mexican immigrants and their children; as a consequence, the geographic dispersion of the Mexican immigrant population has increased to the point that Mexicans now have a national presence, as opposed to their previous regional one concentrated in the Southwest, California, and Illinois. The implications of the entry of many Mexican families into new destination areas for the contexts in which children are being raised have yet to be examined.

The Data We Bring to Bear

Our analyses are based on the data available in summary file 3 of the 2000 Census. Since these data report many characteristics of census tracts, including the numbers of children from different ethno-racial groups,[1] we are able to describe the features of the census tract, the unit we use to bound approximately a residential neighborhood, where the average child in a particular group resides. The averages we present are weighted according to the number of children from a particular group who reside in a tract. Hence, one can think of them as the conditions to which the average Hispanic, white, or black child is exposed by virtue of residential location.

We construct these averages for a sample of metropolitan regions chosen according to the needs of our larger project. The sample is focused in part on the neighborhoods where immigrants are concentrated, and so we have selected metropolitan regions that satisfy the condition that they contain at least 25,000 persons born in a country other than the United States (and who make up at least 1 percent of a metropolitan region's population). For the analyses presented here, we consider only those regions that satisfy this condition for one or more Latin American countries (with Puerto Rico included in this list).

The 54 regions that meet our requirements include 29 of the largest 50 metropolitan areas, and 16 of the largest 20. The set of areas included in the analysis encompasses a wide range of metropolitan characteristics related to sociodemographic composition, population size, region, and Latino settlement history. Large established destinations such as Los Angeles, Miami, and San Francisco are included. Several metropolitan areas are small regions in California such as Santa Rosa, Santa Cruz, Santa Barbara, and Stockton. A handful are long-standing Puerto Rican hubs, including New York, Philadelphia, and Hartford. Fort Lauderdale, Jersey City, and Miami are established Cuban areas of settlement. New Latino destinations such as Atlanta, Portland (Oregon), Charlotte, and Salt Lake City are also in our sample. Most metropolitan areas in the analysis have a sizable foreign-born Mexican population. For 37 of them, Mexicans are the sole Latino group that meets the 25,000 criterion.

Among the large metropolitan areas not included in the analysis are several older regions that formerly served as heavy manufacturing centers but have experienced population loss or stagnation (especially within central cities) throughout the latter half of the 20th century and into the 21st century—Cleveland and Detroit are examples. Our sample framework misses a few emerging Latino destinations that have experienced significant Latino growth in recent decades but have not gained a foreign-born population of at least 25,000 for any single Latino national-origin group (e.g., Nashville, Providence, and Oklahoma City). In a few regions, there is an immigrant group of this size, but it does not meet our secondary criterion of composing at least 1 percent of the total population (e.g., Minneapolis and Detroit).

Our sample takes in the regions where the great majorities of Hispanic children and children in Latin American immigrant families are growing up. The 54 regions are home to 69 percent of all Hispanic children in the nation and 75 percent of all the Hispanic children growing up in immigrant families. In fact, most Hispanic children in these regions, 61 percent, are living in families where one or both parents are immigrants.

Using geographical information system (GIS) procedures, we have identified the immigrant neighborhoods in these regions as clusters of adjacent tracts. We will describe these procedures later, but here we point out their relevance for identifying the conditions in the neighborhoods occupied by Hispanic children in immigrant families. Because we use summary file data, we cannot link children to their parents and determine whether they are growing up in immigrant-headed households. (In fact, we cannot even determine at the tract level how many of these children were born outside the United States.[2]) However, given the rather strong link between neighborhood context and the assimilation-related characteristics of individuals such as the adoption of English that has been detected in prior research (Alba et al. 2000), the conditions in immigrant-rich neighborhoods are a plausible approximation of those faced by the children growing up in Latin American immigrant households.

Despite our use of summary-file data, we are able—in, admittedly, a limited way—to examine the connection between family characteristics and those of the neighborhood of residence. This is because the third summary file presents some data specific to ethno-racial populations, such as the distribution of family income in each census tract for Hispanic, white, and black families. These data at the tract level are equivalent to micro-level data that contain a single variable for each micro unit—we have chosen income at the family level—along with aggregate variables that characterize the neighborhood and metropolitan environments in which the unit is located (see Alba and Logan 1992). Hence, these data allow us to conduct a limited form of locational analysis involving family income as a determinant of residential context. This kind of analysis tests a basic relationship anticipated by the spatial assimilation model. Since this relationship may vary across metropolitan region, we also take metropolitan-level variables into account and estimate hierarchical linear models (HLM).

We begin the analysis with an overview of segregation indices before turning to the characteristics of the neighborhoods in which the average children from different groups—we consider Hispanic, non-Hispanic white (abbreviated as "white" in what follows) and non-Hispanic black (or "black") children[3]—are living. We then analyze how these conditions change according to family income for these groups. In the next stage of the analysis, we limit our focus to Hispanic children and consider the neighborhood environments for children living in immigrant areas and those living outside them. This powerful distinction is then incorporated in our HLM models. In the final part of the analysis, we investigate the neighborhood environments for Hispanic children in different kinds of metropolitan regions—such as traditional gateway regions and new destination regions—drawing upon the classification developed by Suro and Singer (2002).

Patterns of Segregation

The frequent characterization of Latinos as an intermediate population for residential segregation is visible in the segregation values that we have computed for children and adults in our sample of 54 metropolitan regions (table 1.1). We distinguish between children and adults because segregation indices that obscure this distinction run the risk of registering as integration when the families of a minority group move into an area that the families of another group have exited, leaving behind households without children. Clearly, in focusing on the integration of children, we are interested in knowing whether they reside in the same area as the children of another group, not just its adults.

Hispanic children are less segregated from white children than are black youngsters, as one would expect from the entire volume of segregation research. However, the level of segregation from white children experienced by the average Hispanic child is 57.8, significantly above the average segregation index between Hispanics and whites reported by Iceland based on all metropolitan regions in the nation and bordering on the threshold generally considered to represent high segregation (60.0).

Table 1.1. Weighted Dissimilarity Indices (Multiplied by 100) for Children and Adults

	Total number in group	White children	Hispanic children	Black children	Asian children	White adults	Hispanic adults	Black adults	Asian adults
White children	13,940,588	—	56.0	68.5	49.1	16.0	55.2	66.7	47.1
Hispanic children	8,513,954	57.8	—	53.1	57.1	55.7	9.3	52.5	54.5
Black children	4,507,962	73.0	57.3	—	69.5	70.1	58.1	14.1	67.9
Asian children	1,712,792	51.8	55.4	63.6	—	49.9	53.2	62.0	18.1
White adults	50,374,889	16.3	53.4	66.2	48.3	—	50.3	62.2	42.3
Hispanic adults	16,318,768	55.5	10.0	55.3	55.6	52.4	—	52.4	51.1
Black adults	10,171,742	71.9	57.3	14.1	68.9	67.4	56.3	—	65.5
Asian adults	5,547,059	50.3	54.2	63.6	18.0	44.4	49.6	59.3	—

Source: Author calculations from summary file 3 of the 2000 Census.

Notes: Each cell shows the average dissimilarity index value from the point of view of the row group. That is, values are weighted averages across metropolitan regions, where the weight is the number of row-group members in each region. Consequently, the matrix is not symmetric.

Since the metropolitan regions we have chosen for our analysis all have a substantial presence of Latin American immigrants, the magnitude of Hispanic child segregation is perhaps not that surprising. It is, in the event, smaller than the segregation from white children experienced by black children, which at 73.0 appears very high. However, Hispanic children are more segregated from whites than are Asian children, who experience on average a level of 51.8. Iceland's finding of Hispanics' simultaneous integration with whites and blacks is echoed here, for the segregation value of Hispanic from black children, 53.1, is slightly lower than that of Hispanic from white children.

The segregation of Hispanic children from adults of different ethno-racial populations is very similar to the pattern just described in relation to other children; the values are nearly identical (e.g., an average value of 55.7 for Hispanic children in relation to white adults). Interestingly, children appear to be somewhat more segregated from each other along ethno-racial lines than adults are. While the reasons are not altogether clear, the pattern suggests that adults without children, especially whites, will tolerate residential proximity to members of other groups to a degree that is not true of families with children. For example, the average value of the index of segregation of Hispanic from white adults is 52.4, about 5 points below the comparable index value for children. A decline from the children's segregation levels of roughly the same magnitude holds for most other segregation indices among ethno-racial groups of adults.

These segregation values imply the possibility of diverse playmates for the average Hispanic child, certainly more so than is the case for white children. This conclusion is affirmed in the isolation and exposure indices that we present for children in table 1.2. To begin with, the isolation indices, reported in the diagonal of the table, show that Hispanic children are less isolated than white children. The average Hispanic child lives in a census tract where about half the children are Hispanic. This is a substantially lower level of isolation than that found in the neighborhood of the average white child, who lives where about 70 percent of the children are also white. Black children are also less isolated than white children. Their isolation index score is about the same as that of Hispanic children; however, if we take into account the smaller population of black children in the metropolitan regions under study, then relative to their population base their isolation is greater than that of Hispanic children.

In terms of non-co-ethnic children who live in the vicinity, the neighborhood of the average Hispanic child tilts strongly in the direction of

Table 1.2. Weighted Isolation and Exposure Indices (Multiplied by 100) for Children

	White children	Hispanic children	Black children	Other children
White children	69.9	15.3	6.1	8.7
Hispanic children	25.1	55.5	11.0	8.4
Black children	19.1	20.7	53.5	6.7

Source: Author calculations from summary file 3 of the 2000 Census.

Notes: Each cell shows the average neighborhood (census tract) exposure of the children in the row category to those in the column category; when the row and column categories are the same group, the cell reports the isolation index. Values are weighted averages across metropolitan regions, where the weight is the number of children in the row category in each region.

the white majority. That is, Anglo children outnumber black children by a margin of more than two to one. Correspondingly, in the neighborhood of the average white child, the proportion of Hispanic children is more than twice as great as that of black children. Only in the neighborhood of the average black child do we find something close to a balance in the composition of non-co-ethnic children: there, the proportions of white and Hispanic children are very similar. The contrast between the neighborhoods of black and Hispanic children in the composition of other groups of children suggests a direction for the integration of Hispanic families—toward neighborhoods where whites form a larger proportion of the population. This hint is one that we will track—and confirm—below.

Neighborhood Characteristics

While segregation indices can inform us about the degree to which members of different groups live in different neighborhoods, they cannot tell us directly about the "qualities" of the neighborhoods in which group members reside, whether these qualities are reflected in the risk of becoming a victim of a crime (or of becoming a criminal), attending good schools, or enjoying affluent playmates. Scholars often presume that the neighborhoods in which whites live have superior amenities and afford better life chances than do those in which minority groups typically reside. To the degree, then, that minority groups are segregated from the white majority, they are presumed to occupy neighborhoods with inferior qualities. But this assumption ought to be demonstrated empirically rather than simply taken as ironclad law.

Table 1.3, therefore, presents some average characteristics of the neighborhoods in which white, black, and Hispanic children reside. These weighted averages, once again, reflect the residential conditions in the 54 metropolitan regions on which our analysis focuses. At the level of the metropolitan region, each data point represents a weighted average of tract characteristics, where the weight is the number of a group's children residing in a tract; these data were then averaged across the regions using weights representing the numbers of a group's children in the different metropolitan regions. We can therefore think of them as characterizing the neighborhood (tract) environment of the average child in each group in our sample of regions.

The table displays the very clear separation in the qualities of the residential environment between white children and black and Hispanic children. While Hispanic children appear as intermediate between the racial segregation of blacks and the ideal of integration when we consider segregation indices, they are virtually indistinguishable from black children when we look at the kinds of neighborhoods in which they are found.

Some differences in neighborhood environment among the groups of children are unsurprising. In metropolitan regions that have received substantial immigration from Latin America, it goes almost without saying that many Latino children live in immigrant-rich neighborhoods, and this fact implies overall differences in ethno-racial composition, the presence of the foreign born, and the languages heard at home and on the street. In fact, 45 percent of the Hispanic children reside in census tracts that we have coded as parts of Latin American immigrant neighborhoods. Consequently, the average Hispanic child lives in a neighborhood where nearly 50 percent of the residents are Hispanic (see table 1.3). In addition, 33 percent of the residents are non-Hispanic whites, while only 11 percent are black. This ethno-racial profile differs substantially from that of the average non-Hispanic white child, who lives in a neighborhood where the great majority of residents (three-quarters) belong to his or her ethno-racial category. That child does share the neighborhood with a nontrivial presence of Hispanics, who make up one of every eight residents, but the presence of blacks is small. The profile of the average

Table 1.3. Average Neighborhood Characteristics of White, Hispanic, and Black Children

	White (N = 13,937,727)	Hispanic (N = 8,512,071)	Black (N = 4,506,382)
Ethno-racial composition (%)			
Non-Hispanic white	75.1	32.6	25.4
Hispanic	12.1	48.5	18.0
Non-Hispanic black	5.4	11.0	49.9
Immigration-related characteristics (%)			
Foreign born	13.0	30.7	17.8
Among foreign born, entering 1990–2000	35.9	41.4	42.1
Do not speak English fluently	8.1	27.6	12.2
Speak only English at home	80.5	49.0	75.1
Socioeconomic characteristics			
Median household income	$62,160	$39,944	$38,568
% in poverty	7.2	19.2	20.2
% in extreme poverty	3.4	8.6	10.4
% with income more than twice the poverty level	81.0	56.8	59.4
% of adults with post-secondary education	62.5	40.2	44.5
% in professional/ managerial occupations	39.9	24.0	27.0
Other characteristics (%)			
In overcrowded households	5.1	22.4	12.8
Home owners	73.0	51.1	50.5
16–19-year-olds who are idle high-school dropouts	2.6	6.7	5.8

Source: Author calculations from summary file 3 of the 2000 Census.

Hispanic child's neighborhood is closer to that of the average black child in these metropolitan areas, with the main difference being the higher percentage of African Americans and the lower percentage of Hispanic Americans in the neighborhoods of black children.

Latino children also live with larger numbers of the foreign born. About 30 percent of residents in the neighborhood of the average Hispanic child are immigrants, and over 40 percent of them are recently arrived, having come in the decade preceding the census. It follows that a high percentage of residents, about 50 percent, speaks a language other than English at home. A relatively high proportion, more than a quarter, is not fluent in English (which we define as speaking English less than "very well"). The neighborhood of the average white child presents the stronger contrast: about one in eight residents is an immigrant, and one in three of the foreign born arrived in the decade preceding the census; the overwhelming majority speak only English at home, and less than 10 percent of residents are not fluent in English. The neighborhoods in which black children are found are close to those of white children in these respects.

Equally momentous differences are evident in the socioeconomic character of neighborhoods. The median household income in the neighborhood where the average Hispanic child resides is nearly $40,000, barely more than that found in the neighborhood of the average black child. However, the average white child lives in a much more affluent neighborhood where the median household income is more than $60,000. The neighborhood of the average white child is thus more than 50 percent more affluent than that of the average Hispanic child. Correspondingly, 19 percent of the residents of the average Hispanic child's neighborhood live below the poverty level, and nearly half of them are in extreme poverty, surviving on incomes below half the poverty level. The figures are very similar, if a little higher, in the average black child's neighborhood. However, they are not even half as high in the neighborhood where the average white child is found. Even when the residents in the neighborhoods of Hispanic and black children have incomes above the poverty level, they are often precariously close to it—in the case of the average Hispanic child, less than 60 percent are in households with incomes more than twice the poverty level. In the case of the average white child, the figure is above 80 percent.

The adults whom a child may encounter also differ substantially across the neighborhoods of the average child from the three groups. Insofar as these adults provide role models for children, affecting their educational and occupational aspirations, we would expect differences in the transition to young adulthood to result from these exposures. Thus, nearly 40 percent of workers in the neighborhood of the average non-Hispanic white child are engaged in professional and managerial occupations, compared with 24 percent of workers in the neighborhood of the average Hispanic child (and a slightly higher figure for the neighborhood of the average black child). More than 60 percent of the adults in a white child's neighborhood have some postsecondary education, compared with 40 percent in an Hispanic child's neighborhood. The postsecondary education level in the neighborhood of the average black child is a bit higher, at 45 percent.

Differences in housing follow from the socioeconomic differentials. A very high percentage of households occupy their own homes in the neighborhood of the average white child—more than 70 percent. And a very small percentage, just 5 percent, is crowded, with more than one person per room. In the neighborhood of the average Hispanic child, the percentage of households that own their homes is substantially lower, around 50 percent, and the percentage of crowded households is, at 22 percent, much higher. The level of home ownership is similar in the neighborhood of the average black child, but that of overcrowding is significantly lower, roughly midway between the average white and Hispanic neighborhoods.

Locational Attainment: How Much Improvement with Socioeconomic Advance?

Most Hispanic children are growing up in neighborhoods that are quite different from those in which most white children are being raised. Since many Hispanic children are in immigrant-headed households and since the metropolitan areas on which we are focusing are themselves immigrant-rich, the aggregate differences in the character of neighborhoods are perhaps to be expected. An important question to ask is how much the neighborhoods of Hispanic children change if their families become more affluent. The model of spatial assimilation, on which many scholarly and lay predictions about residential improvements for immigrant-origin groups are based, anticipates that socioeconomic improvements lead to residential ones.

To address this question, we have constructed rather simple locational-attainment models, in which a series of census-tract characteristics provides the dependent variables. The goal of such models is to see how the characteristics of the neighborhood of residence depend upon the socio-economic, acculturation-related, and other characteristics of households containing children. However, our analyses are confined to the data from summary census files, and so therefore we are unable to construct elaborate models at the household level. Instead, we base the analysis on family income (expressed in units of $10,000), which is tabulated by major ethno-racial group in one of the summary files; this feature of the data allows us to drill down to the family level, as long as we do not include any other micro-level variables.[4] By using family income, we are eliminating non-family households from the analysis since, with rare exceptions, they do not contain children. However, many families are childless; but we cannot further improve the accuracy of our focus with aggregate census data.

Our analyses are multi-level because we need to take into account the potential for variations in residential patterns across metropolitan regions. We include three metropolitan-level variables: the percentage of the population that is foreign born, the percentage of the foreign born that immigrated during the 1990s, and the percentage of the population belonging to the same ethno-racial category as the family. These first two variables distinguish to some extent between those metropolitan areas that are well established as immigration gateways (e.g., Los Angeles) and those that have recently become destinations for large-scale immigrant flows (e.g., Atlanta). We estimate these multi-level models with hierarchical linear modeling procedures, in which both the intercept and the family-income coefficient can vary with the metropolitan-level variables.[5] Table 1.4 shows some key results for white, Hispanic, and black families.

As is to be expected, Hispanic and other families move away from concentrations of the foreign born as their income rises. Hispanic families with children, as table 1.3 showed, are more likely to reside in neighborhoods that also contain relatively high foreign-born proportions.[6] Consequently, the intercept in the corresponding locational-attainment model for Hispanic families is substantially higher than those in the white and black family models. The family-income coefficients in all three models are significantly negative: that is, as family incomes increases, the percent foreign born in the neighborhood of residence tends to decrease. The coefficient in the Hispanic model is larger than the others, indicating that the percent foreign born among the neighbors goes down more rapidly with increases in income among Hispanic families. Nevertheless, the differences among the coefficients are such

Table 1.4. Hierarchical Linear Model Analyses of Selected Neighborhood Characteristics According to Family Income and Metropolitan-Level Variables for White, Hispanic, and Black Families

	% White			% Hispanic			% Black		
	White	Hispanic	Black	White	Hispanic	Black	White	Hispanic	Black
Intercept	63.88***	37.02***	26.81***	21.30***	41.79***	24.72	6.26***	12.23***	40.25***
Income ($10,000 units)	0.66***	1.44***	1.28***	-0.48***	-1.16***	-0.54	-0.16***	-0.36***	-0.83***
MSA % foreign born	-0.01	-0.56**	-0.52***	-0.31*	0.09	0.38	-0.07	0.14	-0.14
MSA % 1990s immigrants	-0.01	0.23	0.73***	-0.33*	-0.36*	-0.45	0.36***	0.25	-0.37
MSA % co-ethnic	0.82***	-0.40**	-1.48***	-0.77***	0.96***	-1.01	-0.11*	-0.36***	2.83***
Income × % foreign born	0.00	-0.02	-0.03***	0.01	0.01	0.01	0.00	0.00	0.02*
Income × % 1990s immigrants	0.00	-0.02	0.00	0.00	0.02*	0.01	-0.01***	0.00	0.00
Income × % co-ethnic	-0.01***	-0.01	0.00	0.01**	-0.01	0.04	0.00	0.01***	-0.04***
Intraclass correlation	0.244	0.262	0.273	0.435	0.322	0.383	0.127	0.231	0.339

(continued)

Table 1.4. *(Continued)*

	% Foreign-Born			% Who Do Not Speak English Fluently			% Who Speak Only English		
	White	Hispanic	Black	White	Hispanic	Black	White	Hispanic	Black
Intercept	17.41***	29.40***	19.99***	12.46***	26.00***	15.64***	72.69***	53.43***	69.27***
Income ($10,000 units)	-0.22***	-0.56***	-0.14***	-0.30***	-0.77***	-0.37***	0.41***	0.98***	0.41***
MSA % foreign born	1.01***	1.16***	0.73***	0.47***	0.65***	0.46***	-0.74***	-0.82***	-0.77***
MSA % 1990s immigrants	0.02	0.06	0.02	0.00	-0.09	0.00	0.18*	0.42*	0.27*
MSA % co-ethnic	0.08***	-0.04	-0.33***	-0.08**	0.14*	-0.45***	0.31***	-0.40***	0.78***
Income × % foreign born	-0.01***	0.00	0.00	-0.01***	0.00	0.00	0.01	-0.02*	-0.01
Income × % 1990s immigrants	0.00	-0.01	-0.01	0.00	0.01	0.00	0.00	-0.02*	0.00
Income × % co-ethnic	0.00	-0.01*	0.03***	0.00	-0.01*	0.02***	0.00	0.01	-0.04***
Intraclass correlation	0.388	0.363	0.325	0.225	0.224	0.231	0.370	0.330	0.314

	Median Household Income			% below the Poverty Level			% of Adults with Postsecondary Educations		
	White	Hispanic	Black	White	Hispanic	Black	White	Hispanic	Black
Intercept	46,077***	36,723***	33,423***	11.04***	19.39***	22.40***	53.45***	40.08***	41.10***
Income ($10,000 units)	1,409***	1,396***	1,508***	-0.30***	-0.74***	-0.94***	1.02***	1.21***	1.24***
MSA % foreign born	597***	358**	153	-0.16*	-0.19	0.05	0.27	0.09	-0.02

MSA % 1990s immigrants	−66	−51	151	−0.05	−0.15	−0.22	−0.05	0.23	0.34*
MSA % co-ethnic	373**	−302***	−330*	−0.20***	0.21**	0.28*	0.17	−0.23*	−0.57***
Income × % foreign born	8	9	−5	0.01**	0.01*	0.01	−0.01*	−0.01	−0.01
Income × % 1990s immigrants	16	−8	−7	0.00	0.01*	0.01*	0.02***	−0.01	0.00
Income × % co-ethnic	−2	−12*	15*	0.01***	0.00	−0.02**	−0.01*	0.01	0.01
Intraclass correlation	0.209	0.225	0.201	0.213	0.208	0.136	0.169	0.168	0.183

	% in Professional and Managerial Occupations			% Overcrowded Households		
	White	Hispanic	Black	White	Hispanic	Black
Intercept	32.19***	23.17***	23.92***	8.62***	19.03***	15.16***
Income ($10,000 units)	0.87***	0.89***	0.85***	−0.27***	−0.65***	−0.50***
MSA % foreign born	0.29**	0.10	0.06	0.16**	0.44***	0.48***
MSA % 1990s immigrants	0.01	0.11	0.15	−0.05	−0.12	−0.07
MSA % co-ethnic	0.11	−0.13**	−0.21*	−0.12**	0.18*	−0.20*
Income × % foreign born	−0.01	0.00*	−0.01	0.00	−0.01	−0.01
Income × % 1990s immigrants	0.01***	0.00*	0.00	0.00	0.01	0.01
Income × % co-ethnic	−0.01*	0.00	0.01	0.00*	−0.01	0.01
Intraclass correlation	0.176	0.128	0.132	0.199	0.243	0.304

Source: Author calculations from summary file 3 of the 2000 Census.

MSA = metropolitan statistical area

p < .05; **p* < .01; ****p* < .001

that Hispanic families are unlikely to catch up to their white and black counterparts. Even a massive change in family income, of $100,000, would reduce the percentage of the foreign born among neighbors by just 6 percentage points, smaller than the differences in the intercepts.

The differences among the groups also depend on the metropolitan region. The high intraclass correlations (.33–.39) indicate that the variations across metropolitan regions account for a large portion of the variance in neighborhood context. The single most important regional characteristic is the overall percentage of the population that is foreign born. The higher this is, the higher the expected concentration of the foreign born in the neighborhood. This effect, however, is larger for Hispanic families, and the slope of income is no different for them in the metropolitan areas with higher percentages of the foreign born. This configuration implies that the difference in neighborhood conditions between Hispanic and other families is larger in such metropolitan areas even when Hispanic families possess high incomes.

With relatively minor variations, the same basic pattern characterizes other neighborhood characteristics related to the presence of immigrants. For instance, the percentage of residents who are monolingual English speakers is lower in the neighborhood of the average Hispanic family. As their income rises, Hispanic families tend to live in neighborhoods where they are surrounded by more English-only speakers. For every additional $10,000, the percentage of residents who speak only English rises by 1 point. It does not rise nearly as much with income among whites and blacks. Nevertheless, even at high family incomes, Hispanic families can be expected to reside in neighborhoods with lower percentages of English-only speakers.

In this case, the effects of metropolitan region initially seem complex, but they are reducible to a simple main finding. To begin with, the percentage of neighbors who speak only English at home declines in the neighborhoods of all three groups as the percentage of immigrants in the metropolitan region's population rises. Since these effects have roughly the same magnitude for all the groups, they do not contribute much to intergroup differences in neighborhood context. More relevant in that respect are the effects of the co-ethnic proportion of the region's population. For whites and blacks, the percentage of English-only neighbors increases as that proportion does; for Hispanics, the effect is in the reverse direction. Hispanic families who live in regions with high Hispanic-population concentrations will be exposed to fewer English-only households in their neighborhoods. A very similar paragraph to this one could be written about the percentage of neighbors who do not speak English fluently.

The ethno-racial composition of the neighborhoods where affluent Hispanic and black families reside differs from that where their poorer co-ethnics are found. For minority families, the percentage of their neighbors who are non-Hispanic whites rises sharply as their own incomes go up; correspondingly, the percentage belonging to their own ethno-racial category goes down. The percentage of non-Hispanic whites among neighbors differs greatly among families with low incomes from the three groups. The intercepts indicate that low-income white families still live in neighborhoods where whites are in the majority; the percentages of whites in the neighborhoods of low-income Hispanic and black families are only about half as high. However, the white percentage of the neighborhood rises more rapidly with family income among Hispanics and blacks than among whites. For Hispanics in particular, the coefficient of family income indicates an increment of 1.4 percentage points for every $10,000 of additional family income; this is more than twice the coefficient for white families. The metropolitan-level coefficients show that these differences depend unsurprisingly on the percentages of co-ethnics in the regional populations. In addition, the percentages of whites among neighbors are smaller for Hispanics and blacks in regions where the foreign born constitute a larger fraction of the population; the neighborhoods of whites are not affected in this way.

Almost the same pattern in reverse is found for the percentage of Hispanics among neighbors. At low income levels, Hispanic families reside in neighborhoods with relatively high percentages of co-ethnics, though on average these are not neighborhoods where Hispanics are in the majority. However, the Hispanic percentage drops by more than 1 point for every increment of $10,000 in the income of Hispanic families. Interestingly, although research based on segregation indices suggests that Hispanics integrate with blacks as well as with whites, the locational-attainment models indicate that the percentage of non-Hispanic blacks in the neighborhood is lower for Hispanic families with higher incomes (and is not high, in any event). The reduction in the number of black neighbors is even greater for black families, though in general black families live with many more black neighbors than the families of the other groups do.[7] These analyses demonstrate that, at higher income levels, Hispanic and black families live in neighborhoods that narrow the gap in ethno-racial composition from the neighborhoods in which most white families are found, but their neighborhoods remain nevertheless considerably more diverse.

The socioeconomic character of the neighborhood improves as the family incomes of Hispanics rise. However, even at high family income levels, Hispanics are in neighborhoods that contain fewer socioeconomic "resources" than those of their white counterparts. This difference is striking in what is probably the single best measure, median household income, which undoubtedly correlates with many hard-to-measure features of neighborhoods, from the safety of their streets to the quality of their schools. The intercepts in the white and Hispanic equations, which reflect the anticipated affluence of the neighborhood for families with no income, are about $10,000 apart. The slopes of family income are virtually identical, about $1,400 (per $10,000 increment in family income). They indicate that, although the neighborhoods of Hispanic families with higher incomes are correspondingly more affluent, they just keep pace with the improvements that white families experience in their neighborhood environments as their incomes go up. In short, Hispanic families do not catch up.

Interestingly, the locational impact of family income is slightly larger among blacks than among the other groups. However, their intercept indicates that, at low incomes, the socioeconomic character of the neighborhood is also less favorable (though not by much) than is the case among Hispanics. The higher slope among blacks thus indicates that, at higher incomes, they edge closer to Hispanics but hardly at all to whites. The affluence of the neighborhoods where black families reside is worse, however, in metropolitan regions where blacks form a higher percentage of the population, and a similar proposition holds for Hispanic families in regions where their group is larger in numbers. The affluence of the neighborhoods of white families, by contrast, improves when whites make up a larger percentage of the population.

The story differs somewhat when examining the level of poverty in the neighborhood environment, but the bottom-line conclusion—that high levels of income allow Hispanic families to improve their residential environments, but they are still located in less well-off neighborhoods than those in which similar white families reside—stands. As is indicated in the intercepts of the relevant equations, Hispanic and black families with low family incomes reside in neighborhoods that have substantially higher levels of poverty than is the case for similar white families. The slopes of the family-income coefficients indicate that the poverty level of the neighborhood goes down more quickly for minority families as their income rises. However, even when their family incomes are $100,000, minority families are still expected to be in neighborhoods with higher levels of poverty than similar white families encounter.

That the adults in the neighborhoods of even affluent Hispanic families are less likely to have postsecondary education or to be engaged in high-status occupations would seem to follow, and it does. Since these neighborhood characteristics exhibit patterns similar to those we have already described, we will only discuss one of them, the percentage of adult residents with some postsecondary education. The intercepts reveal that, even at low income levels, white families are advantaged in the educational attainment of their neighbors. All groups experience improvements in this level as their family income rises, according to the coefficients of the family-income variable; the improvements are in fact greater for Hispanics and blacks, but only modestly so. Accordingly, they do not catch up to white families.

This is also the conclusion from the two variables that characterize the general living conditions in a neighborhood, the percentage of households that own the homes they occupy and the percentage in overcrowded quarters. Taking the second as a suitable indicator, we find that, at low income levels, Hispanic families live in neighborhoods where a relatively high proportion of households are overcrowded. For a family with income between $0 and $10,000, this proportion is nearly one in five, much higher than is true for low-income white families and higher than is the case for black families. The slope of the family-income variable among Hispanics indicates that the proportion of overcrowded households declines more rapidly with increases in income among Hispanics than among the other groups. However, even Hispanic families with high incomes live in neighborhoods where overcrowding is more common than it is in the neighborhoods occupied by the average white family. An Hispanic family with an annual income of $100,000 is predicted to live in a neighborhood where about one of every eight households are overcrowded, a proportion higher than that found in neighborhood of low-income white families.

We have paid less attention to the metropolitan-level characteristics than to family income and the intercepts because, even though neighborhood contexts vary considerably across metropolitan regions, the pattern of the metropolitan-level variables is fairly consistent and does not contribute greatly to the story. For one thing, the dependence of the slope of income on metropolitan-level variables is typically minor in magnitude even when the relevant interaction terms are significant (which is often not the case). Thus, the main impacts of metropolitan variations are on the intercepts. In general, the neighborhood contexts in which Hispanic families live seem more distressed in metropolitan regions with higher proportions of foreign-born and/or Hispanic residents. The effects are felt by Hispanic families at all income levels since these metropolitan characteristics have little impact on the slope of income.

Immigrant-Rich Neighborhoods as Places

The metropolitan areas that we are analyzing, which have been selected because of their large foreign-born populations, all have neighborhoods where concentrations of immigrants from specific Latin-American countries reside. Undoubtedly, were we to parachute into every one of these regions, we would be able to find residents who could identify these neighborhoods for us by name. Not having that strategy available to us, we have resorted to a GIS procedure to identify them in a statistically consistent way (Mitchell 2005). Using the Anselin Moran's i statistic, it operates with the proportions that a specific country-of-origin group forms of the census tracts in a given metropolitan region. This statistic is a local indicator of spatial autocorrelation (LISA); here, it indicates the degree to which each census tract's proportional representation of a given group is similar to that of surrounding tracts, relative to the group's mean proportional representation of the entire metropolitan region. We include a census tract in a clustered ethnic residential area if its Moran's i statistic is significant at the 95 percent confidence level or better. We have found it necessary in some cases to make adjustments at the edges, to add bordering tracts that do not meet local Moran's i criterion but contain concentrations of an immigrant group that are equal or superior to the average for a cluster.

Based on this procedure, we have identified 320 Latin-American immigrant neighborhoods containing 4,162 census tracts. Every region in our sample possesses at least one such neighborhood, but the spatial distribution of the neighborhoods varies across regions. In a few regions, Latino immigrant clusters are restricted to the urban core. Within many established Latino immigrant gateways, however, long-standing centralized Latino immigrant neighborhoods such as East Los Angeles are accompanied now by Latino immigrant enclaves in more suburban environments, including such suburbs as Huntington Beach and Santa Ana (see figure 1.1). In the Northeast, many urban communities that have long

Figure 1.1. Latino Immigrant Neighborhoods in the Los Angeles Region

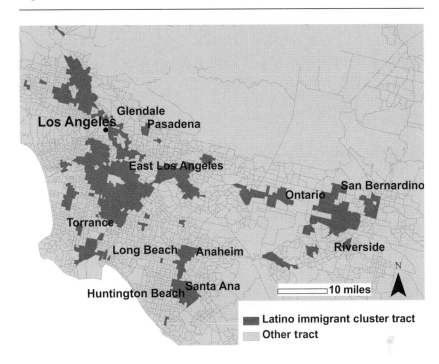

been areas of Puerto Rican concentration, including Manhattan's East Harlem neighborhood, are now also classified as areas of Mexican immigrant concentration. In several new Latino destination regions, a majority of Latino immigrant enclaves have formed outside the urban core. For example, sizable Latino communities have developed along the suburban periphery of Portland, Oregon, in the communities of Hillsborough and Forest Grove (figure 1.2). In Atlanta, a large portion of the rapidly growing Latino immigrant population has bypassed the central city to settle in the northeastern suburbs and several smaller suburban communities south of downtown, including College Park and Forest Park.

The proportion of the population of these neighborhoods that is Latino is closely linked to each region's Latino settlement history. In established Latino immigrant gateways such as Los Angeles, New York City, Chicago, and San Francisco, the presence of Latinos in the population of an immigrant-cluster tract generally exceeds 50 percent, whereas in several new Latino destinations, including Charlotte, Raleigh-Durham, and Seattle, Latinos make up less than 26 percent of the population of the

Figure 1.2. Latino Immigrant Neighborhoods in the Portland, Oregon, Region

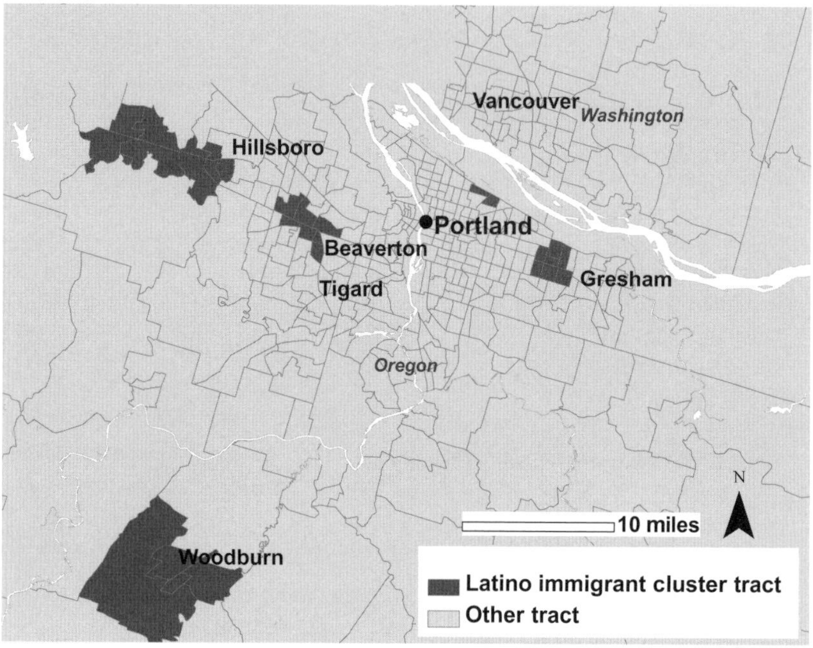

average immigrant-neighborhood tract. These residential patterns suggest that, in places where Latino immigrant clusters are only beginning to emerge, the spatial distribution of Latino immigrant neighborhoods is closely linked to local nuances in the spatial distribution of employment opportunity, affordable housing, and other ecological characteristics of the metropolitan area.

The majority of Hispanic children (55 percent) reside outside these immigrant neighborhoods; thus, 45 percent reside in them. Obviously, since our sample of metropolitan areas targets those with large numbers of immigrants, this latter percentage overstates how many Hispanic children in the nation as a whole live in neighborhoods where Latin-American immigrants are concentrated.

The differences between the residential contexts afforded by immigrant and nonimmigrant neighborhoods are very striking (table 1.5). The average conditions Hispanic children confront in immigrant neighborhoods are even further from those in which white children are found

Table 1.5. Average Neighborhood Characteristics of Hispanic Children in Immigrant versus Nonimmigrant Neighborhoods

	In immigrant clusters (N = 3,825,354)	In nonimmigrant clusters (N = 4,686,717)
Ethno-racial composition (%)		
Non-Hispanic white	15.5	46.5
Hispanic	67.8	32.7
Non-Hispanic black	10.8	11.2
Immigration-related characteristics (%)		
Foreign born	41.2	22.2
Among foreign born, entering 1990–2000	45.0	38.4
Do not speak English fluently	40.0	17.5
Speak only English at home	31.9	63.0
Socioeconomic characteristics		
Median household income	$32,600	$45,939
% in poverty	25.6	13.7
% in extreme poverty	11.4	6.3
% with income more than twice the poverty level	44.9	66.6
% of adults with postsecondary educations	27.9	50.2
% in professional/managerial occupations	16.6	29.9
Other characteristics (%)		
In overcrowded households	32.2	13.6
Home owners	41.1	59.4
16–19-year-olds who are idle high school dropouts	9.2	4.7

Source: Author calculations from summary file 3 of the 2000 Census.

than were the average neighborhood values for Hispanic children altogether. As residential contexts, the nonimmigrant neighborhoods in which Hispanic children live are in between those in which white children live and the immigrant neighborhoods. They differ from the neighborhoods in which black children are typically found.

Quite obviously, Hispanic children are exposed to very different levels of the foreign born among their neighbors in the two neighborhood types: for the average Hispanic child in an immigrant neighborhood, more than

40 percent of the neighbors are foreign born; for the equivalent child in a nonimmigrant neighborhood, the percentage is only half as high. Certain other differences follow as corollaries: the average Hispanic child in an immigrant neighborhood encounters many neighbors—40 percent of them—who do not speak English fluently; for the average child outside such a neighborhood, only 18 percent of the neighbors do not speak English fluently. Indeed, more than 60 percent of the neighbors outside an immigrant neighborhood speak only English at home, and just 25 percent speak Spanish at home (this is not shown in the table); in an immigrant neighborhood, the figures are almost reversed. The language environment that an Hispanic child encounters outside an immigrant neighborhood begins to approximate that found in the neighborhood of the average white child. There, 78 percent of the neighbors speak only English at home and 13 percent speak Spanish.

The ethno-racial compositions of the immigrant and nonimmigrant neighborhood types also differ. The Hispanic child in a nonimmigrant neighborhood encounters whites more than the members of any other group: nearly half the neighbors are non-Hispanic whites, and a third are Hispanics. For the child in an immigrant neighborhood, the neighbors are mainly other Hispanics, who constitute two-thirds of residents; non-Hispanic whites are a small minority, just a sixth of residents. The percentages of non-Hispanic blacks do not differ between the neighborhood types. In their ethno-racial composition, the nonimmigrant neighborhoods of Hispanic children are situated between the typical immigrant contexts of Hispanic children and the typical neighborhoods of white children, where three-quarters of the residents are also white. In this respect, the nonimmigrant areas also differ from the typical neighborhoods of black children, where just a quarter of residents are whites.

The socioeconomic environment for Hispanic children living outside immigrant neighborhoods represents a distinct improvement over that found in immigrant neighborhoods, but it remains far from that in the neighborhood of the typical white child. The average Hispanic child outside immigrant areas lives in a neighborhood whose median household income is $46,000, quite a bit higher than the $32,600 median income found in the immigrant neighborhood of the typical Hispanic child. Nevertheless, even outside immigrant areas, Hispanic children are living in neighborhoods that are considerably less affluent than the neighborhood of the average white child, where the median household income is $62,000. In addition, the immigrant neighborhood of the average Hispanic child is less affluent than that of the average black child, who lives in a neighborhood where the median household income is $38,600.

Hispanic children outside immigrant areas see much less poverty than do those living with many immigrants, but the poverty in the neighborhood of the average white child is least of all. Fourteen percent of households in the nonimmigrant area of the average Hispanic child are poor, and 6 percent are in extreme poverty (i.e., with household income below half of the poverty level). The comparable figures for the immigrant neighborhood of the average Hispanic child are almost twice as high, which makes them higher than those in the neighborhood of the average black child. By contrast, the average white child resides in a neighborhood where just 7 percent of households are classified as poor and just 3 percent are in extreme poverty.

The adults whom Hispanic children meet outside immigrants areas have much higher average levels of educational attainment than do those in immigrant areas. Half the adult neighbors of the average Hispanic child outside an immigrant area have some form of postsecondary education, compared with slightly more than 60 percent of the adults in the neighborhood of the average white child. However, just 28 percent of the adult neighbors of the average Hispanic child in an immigrant neighborhood have some level of education after high school, a figure substantially lower than that found in the neighborhood of the average black child (44 percent). A very similar ranking of neighborhoods occurs if we examine the percentage of adults engaged in professional and managerial occupations.

The differences between the conditions in immigrant neighborhoods and those in nonimmigrant areas shed considerable light on the environments in which the children of Latin-American immigrants are growing up. Much past research has shown that, with the possible exception of Dominicans and Puerto Ricans, the neighborhood environments of Hispanic families vary substantially with their assimilation-related characteristics, not just according to their socioeconomic variables. Thus, households where the adult members are U.S.-born or where they speak English fluently or have become monolingual English speakers tend to be located in better neighborhoods, as indexed, say, by the median household incomes of their neighbors. Because of the limitations imposed by data taken from summary tape files, we are not able to control effectively for these characteristics in ways that get at the living conditions of children. However, it is highly likely that residence in a nonimmigrant versus an immigrant area is strongly correlated with them, that the generational position of a household's adult members and their language characteristics are very predictive of whether it is located in an immigrant area. Hence, the characteristics of the immigrant-neighborhood context of Hispanic children are in all likelihood informative about the environments of children growing up in immigrant families.

In terms of the characteristics that we can measure in demographic data, these environments seem much more disadvantaged than are those in which other Hispanic children are found, and they may be worse on the whole than the environments in which black children typically grow up, even though the latter's families are very constrained in their residential options because of racial residential segregation (Sampson and Sharkey 2008). Granted, there may be benefits to immigrant families of living in an immigrant-rich neighborhood that we cannot measure, and these benefits may be relevant for children's health and social resources (Portes and Rumbaut 2001). Nevertheless, according to standard socioeconomic measures, the disadvantages seem stark, as one indicator to which we have not previously referenced illustrates: in the immigrant area of the average Hispanic child, 9 percent of the youth between the ages of 16 and 19 have dropped out of high school and are idle (that is, without employment). Many of these young people are likely to be hanging out on street corners with nothing to do. In the corresponding nonimmigrant area, the percentage is only half as high. In the neighborhood of the typical white child, the figure is less than 3 percent; in that of the typical black child, less than 6 percent. Indeed, pushing young people onto the street could be the overcrowding characteristic of the immigrant areas. In the immigrant neighborhood where the average Hispanic child resides, fully a third of households are overcrowded, compared with just over one-eighth in the equivalent nonimmigrant neighborhood. Overcrowding is much lower, just 5 percent, in the neighborhood of the average white child and lower also, 13 percent, in the neighborhood of the average black child.

Our findings also suggest caution regarding Iceland's conclusion that spatial assimilation for Hispanics brings about greater integration with black as well as white Americans. Perhaps this is the case for some Hispanic populations where African ancestry and black skin are common. For instance, in the metropolitan region centered on New York City, where Dominicans and Puerto Ricans are the two largest Hispanic groups, the percentage of African Americans among neighbors is somewhat higher for Hispanic children living outside immigrant areas than it is for those within them (however, the percentage of non-Hispanic whites among neighbors goes up even more for the children in nonimmigrant areas). Some other areas display the same pattern, though the differences tend to be small and the percentages of blacks among neighbors low. More generally, however, the residential environments of Hispanic children growing up outside immigrant enclaves resemble those of white children far more than they do those of African American children. This suggests—it does not prove, given the limits of our data—that the direction of spatial assimilation for Hispanic families is predominantly toward the white mainstream. There are still, of course, Hispanic families who are constrained residentially—because of skin color, say—and cannot easily pursue this trajectory. But our data appear to indicate that it is nevertheless rather common, even in metropolitan regions that have large Latin-American immigrant populations and therefore large Hispanic residential concentrations.

Locational Attainment and Latin-American Immigrant Neighborhoods

If the immigrant neighborhoods in which Hispanic children are growing up are as disadvantaged as appears to be the case, then it is crucial that their families have the opportunity to leave them. The spatial-assimilation model depicts this exit process as contingent on the characteristics of the adults in those families, especially on their socioeconomic situation, length of residence in the United States, and linguistic adjustment to the mainstream society. However, the process may also depend on the ethno-racial phenotypical features of those adults, since the immense literature on residential segregation establishes that the residential choices of dark-skinned Americans are constrained.

In this analysis, we are unable to represent this locational attainment as fully as we would like. As in our previous HLM analysis, we must limit our micro-level independent variable to family income. We represent residence in an immigrant-rich neighborhood as a dichotomous outcome, while controlling as before for some immigration-related characteristics of the metropolitan region.

The results (not shown in a table) indicate that Hispanic families with higher incomes are less likely to reside in immigrant areas, as one would expect from the spatial-assimilation model. However, the income-neighborhood link is moderate, and not as strong as one might anticipate. According to the full model, which includes the effects of metropolitan region, every increase of $10,000 in family income reduces the odds of residence in an immigrant neighborhood by about 10 percent, clearly a modest effect. Translated into a percentage difference, such an effect can be stated as follows: for the average Hispanic family (which has a .45 probability of residing in an immigrant neighborhood), an increase of $10,000 in family income reduces the likelihood of living in an immigrant neighborhood by 2.7 percentage points. Stated in this way the effect looks larger in general than the effects of income on other neighborhood variables. However, it is not linear, as they are. To reduce the odds of immigrant-neighborhood residence by half would require an increase of $70,000 in family income. But compared with this effect, those of metropolitan region are surprisingly small (and mostly nonsignificant). Nevertheless, in regions with many immigrants, the coefficient of family income is reduced: in other words, even at high incomes, Hispanic families have a relatively large "risk" of living in immigrant neighborhoods in these regions.

However, the plausible possibility that residence in a nonimmigrant area is a proxy for a bundle of assimilation-related characteristics, including U.S.-born parents, suggests that the relationship of family income to the characteristics of the neighborhood of residence may look quite different for Hispanic families in immigrant areas than for those outside them. We could be dealing with distinct populations, in other words. The results of HLM analyses that include neighborhood type as a second level (table 1.6) strongly sustain this conclusion.[8] (For the sake of simplicity and interpretability, we omit the metropolitan-level variables from this analysis.) These analyses further underscore the disadvantages associated with residence in an immigrant neighborhood for Hispanic families, and they spotlight the difficulties that Hispanic families, even more assimilated ones, confront in ever catching up to the advantaged contexts in which white families tend to live.

A good starting point is the median household income of the neighborhood (census tract) of residence. Since housing is purchased in a market, one would expect a strong relationship between family income and the income of neighboring households. The coefficients of the HLM model demonstrate what we already suspected: that, net of their incomes, Hispanic families in immigrant areas have less affluent neighbors than do

Table 1.6. Hierarchical Linear Model Analyses of Selected Neighborhood Characteristics by Hispanic Family Income and Neighborhood Type

	% white	% Hispanic	% black	% foreign born	% who do not speak English fluently	% who speak only English
Intercept	49.61***	30.06***	11.37***	20.72***	16.91***	65.65***
Income ($10,000 units)	1.09***	−0.71***	−0.39***	−0.34***	−0.46***	0.62***
Immigrant cluster	−26.13***	28.16***	0.16	13.68***	17.50***	−24.26***
Income × immigrant cluster	−0.78***	0.44***	0.29***	0.21***	0.20***	−0.42***
Intraclass correlation	0.561	0.656	0.337	0.58	0.573	0.643

	Median household income	% below poverty level	% of adults with postsecondary educations	% in professional and managerial occupations	% in overcrowded households
Intercept	39,433***	15.88***	47.39***	27.50***	12.34***
Income ($10,000 units)	1,350***	−0.59***	1.02***	0.79***	−0.41***
Immigrant cluster	−7,663***	9.41***	−16.73***	−9.84***	13.12***
Income × immigrant cluster	−885***	0.16**	−0.70***	−0.60***	0.15***
Intraclass correlation	0.377	0.448	0.718	0.381	0.574

* $p < .05$; ** $p < .01$; *** $p < .001$

those outside such areas. The coefficients also indicate that, for families within such areas as for those outside them, the affluence of the neighborhood improves as their own incomes rise. However, quite remarkably, the slope of that relationship is much lower for families within immigrant neighborhoods than for other Hispanic families. For the latter, every rise of $10,000 in family income is associated with an increase of almost $1,400 in the median household income of the neighborhood, while for the former, the improvement is less than $500. The higher coefficient for Hispanic families outside immigrant neighborhoods suggests that, as their incomes go up, they narrow somewhat the neighborhood-affluence gap that separates them from white families, but not by much, as things turn out. According to the coefficients in table 1.6, such a family with $100,000 in annual income would be expected to reside in a neighborhood where the median household income is about $53,000, well behind the median household income in the neighborhood of the average white child, though also well ahead of that on average in the immigrant-rich neighborhoods of Hispanic children.

The analysis of neighborhood affluence could serve as a paradigm for most other neighborhood characteristics. That is, in every case but one in table 1.6 (the percent non-Hispanic black among residents), the intercept for the families in immigrant neighborhoods indicates a more distressed neighborhood, or one more distant from the white mainstream, than is the case for other families. And, without exception, the income slopes for families in immigrant neighborhoods show less improvement as the economic situations of families gets better.

Nevertheless, it is important to underscore that Hispanic families that remain within immigrant areas are still able to move to better neighborhoods as their incomes rise. Consider in this respect the poverty level in the neighborhood. Families in immigrant-rich areas generally live with higher levels of poverty in their surroundings—the increment to the intercept (9.41 percentage points) associated with residence in such a neighborhood indicates this. However, for every additional $10,000 in income, the families in immigrant neighborhoods reduce the poverty level around them by .4 points (i.e., $-.59 + .16 = -.43$). This reduction is nevertheless smaller than that for families living outside immigrant neighborhoods, which is .6 points per $10,000. Even when their own incomes are relatively high, families in immigrant areas are living with much more poverty in their surroundings than are other Hispanic families.

Neighborhood Conditions in Immigration Gateways, New Destinations, and Other Metropolitan Regions

The dispersion of Latin-American immigrants and their families throughout the United States is one of the most prominent demographic patterns of recent decades and one that seems heavy with implications for the neighborhoods in which Hispanic children are being raised. In moving into regions such as Atlanta, where few Hispanics lived before 1980, immigrant families of necessity are entering neighborhoods where the presence of Hispanics is sparser than it is in regions with a long-established Hispanic presence. What sorts of neighborhoods are these?

To classify metropolitan regions by type, we have relied on the work of Suro and Singer (2002), who have developed a four-category typology based on the Hispanic presence among residents in 1980 and the rate of growth of the Hispanic population during the last two decades of the 20th century. Their four categories, which we also employ, are established Latino region (large presence in 1980, relatively slow growth since then), fast-growth Latino hub (large presence in 1980, fast growth since), new destination region (small presence in 1980, fast growth since), and places with a small Hispanic presence (small presence in 1980, slow growth since). Suro and Singer locate the top 100 metropolitan regions according to this scheme; for the handful of regions in our sample that are outside the top 100, we have classified them according to the criteria used by Suro and Singer.

Table 1.7 reports the average neighborhood characteristics for Hispanic children by metropolitan region and immigrant versus nonimmigrant neighborhood. What stands out is that the new destination regions provide rather different places to live than do the regions with a long-established Hispanic presence. For the latter, the rapidity of Hispanic population increase (i.e., the distinction between established regions and fast-growing hubs) makes little difference; and there are so few Hispanic children in the fourth type, the regions with little Hispanic presence, that it can be ignored here.

To begin with, Hispanic children are less likely to be growing up in an immigrant-rich neighborhood when they are located in a new destination area: only one-third are in neighborhoods that we have classified as part of immigrant clusters. More than half the children in established regions are in immigrant-rich neighborhoods, as are nearly 40 percent of children in fast-growing Latino hubs.

Table 1.7. Neighborhood Conditions for Hispanic Children by Type of Neighborhood and Metropolitan Area

	Immigrant Neighborhoods			
	Established areas (N = 2,256,039)	New destination areas (N = 432,352)	Fast-growing hubs (N = 1,066,587)	Other places (N = 70,376)
Ethno-racial composition (%)				
Non-Hispanic white	12.0	31.4	16.5	13.8
Hispanic	71.0	45.4	70.8	54.2
Non-Hispanic black	10.6	17.3	7.2	29.7
Immigration-related characteristics (%)				
Foreign born	43.9	31.1	41.2	16.3
Among foreign born, entering 1990–2000	41.6	54.4	48.0	50.4
Do not speak English fluently	41.8	28.7	41.4	27.4
Speak only English at home	27.8	50.3	32.4	43.8
Socioeconomic characteristics				
Median household income	$32,509	$36,760	$31,708	$23,467
% in poverty	26.1	19.6	26.2	36.9
% in extreme poverty	11.9	8.9	10.6	20.0
% with income more than twice the poverty level	45.1	54.7	40.9	37.4
% of adults with postsecondary education	28.0	35.7	25.2	20.4
% in professional/managerial occupations	17.3	20.1	13.9	15.9
Other characteristics (%)				
In overcrowded households	35.1	18.4	36.4	16.1
Home owners	38.0	47.1	44.9	43.9
16–19-year-olds who are idle high school dropouts	8.5	9.2	10.5	11.0

	Nonimmigrant Neighborhoods			
	Established areas (N = 2,071,928)	New destination areas (N = 823,699)	Fast-growing hubs (N = 1,690,722)	Other places (N = 100,368)
Ethno-racial composition (%)				
Non-Hispanic white	37.2	64.6	48.6	55.0
Hispanic	40.2	15.0	33.2	16.9
Non-Hispanic black	11.5	13.2	9.2	22.5
Immigration-related characteristics (%)				
Foreign born	27.2	16.0	19.3	19.8
Among foreign born, entering 1990–2000	35.8	44.3	38.5	41.3
Do not speak English fluently	21.6	10.7	16.0	14.3
Speak only English at home	54.5	76.8	66.3	71.6
Socioeconomic characteristics				
Median household income	$44,800	$49,627	$45,387	$48,481
% in poverty	15.4	10.6	14.0	12.3
% in extreme poverty	7.1	5.0	6.0	6.0
% with income more than twice the poverty level	64.7	73.5	65.3	72.1
% of adults with postsecondary educations	48.8	54.4	50.3	43.5
% in professional/managerial occupations	30.0	32.6	28.6	29.7
Other characteristics (%)				
In overcrowded households	16.3	6.7	14.0	7.2
Home owners	55.7	62.9	62.3	57.4
16–19-year-olds who are idle high school dropouts	4.6	4.2	5.0	3.7

Source: Author calculations from summary file 3 of the 2000 Census.

The classification of neighborhood type by metropolitan region type in table 1.7 spans a wide range of average neighborhood conditions. Consider, for example, the Latino percentage of a neighborhood. In both types of regions with a long-standing Hispanic presence, children growing up in immigrant areas live with neighbors who are also mostly Hispanic—about 70 percent. The neighbors are considerably more diverse for an Hispanic child growing up in an immigrant area in a new destination region, for on average only 45 percent of the residents are Hispanic. The same order of difference is found for children living outside immigrant-rich neighborhoods. In both types of long-standing-Hispanic regions, a large number, though not a majority, of residents are Hispanic; the figure goes as high as 40 percent on average in the established Hispanic regions (e.g., Los Angeles). In the new destination regions, Hispanic children outside an immigrant neighborhood live with few neighbors who are Hispanic, only 15 percent on average. A similar profile of differences is found for the share of neighbors that is foreign born, though the differences across the neighborhood/region classification are smaller.

The greater diversity in the neighborhoods in the new destination regions is weighted in the direction of much greater exposure to non-Hispanic whites and somewhat greater exposure to blacks. Even in the immigrant-rich neighborhoods of these regions, Hispanic children encounter many non-Hispanic whites: on average, a third of their neighbors are white and a sixth are black. The figures are about half as high for children in immigrant-rich neighborhoods of regions with a long-standing Hispanic presence. For children in new destination regions who are living in nonimmigrant neighborhoods, a substantial majority of their neighbors—almost two-thirds—are white, while about an eighth are black. Especially with non-Hispanic white neighbors, the figures are much lower in the regions with a long-standing Hispanic presence. In particular, the nonimmigrant neighborhoods in established Latino regions have relatively few Anglo residents—only a third. In terms of an ethno-racial profile, the *immigrant* areas in the new destination regions actually resemble the *nonimmigrant* areas in established Latino regions.

Other differences follow from what has already been described and thus do not need to be described in detail. Thus, the exposure of Hispanic children to neighbors who speak English fluently is very different in the neighborhoods of the new destination regions than it is in regions with a long-standing Hispanic presence. To take an extreme contrast:

only 11 percent of the neighbors of Hispanic children in nonimmigrant areas in new destination metropolitan areas fail to speak English with fluency, compared with more than 40 percent in the immigrant areas of regions with a long-standing Latino presence.

The socioeconomic conditions to which Hispanic children are exposed in new destination regions are also more favorable, though here the differences among region types are modest compared with the differences between neighborhood types within regions. Hispanic children living in the most affluent areas are residing outside immigrant neighborhoods in the new destination regions: the median household income in their tracts averages just about $50,000. Those living in the least affluent areas are residing in immigrant-rich neighborhoods in regions with a long-established Hispanic presence, where the median household income of the tract averages in the low $30,000s. While children in new destination regions tend to be in more affluent tracts, whether these are in immigrant neighborhoods or outside them, the biggest improvements are associated with changes in neighborhood type. Hispanic families that move outside immigrant areas but stay in the same region type improve the affluence of their surroundings by about $12,000 in median household income.

A number of other neighborhood characteristics closely track the pattern just described for census-tract affluence. For instance, poverty is much less common outside immigrant neighborhoods, but it is least of all in the nonimmigrant areas of the new destination regions. The Hispanic children living there are exposed to a level of poverty in their surroundings, about 10 percent, that comes close to the poverty rate in the neighborhood of the average white child (7 percent; see table 1.3). The poverty levels in the immigrant-rich neighborhoods of regions with a long-standing Hispanic presence are two-and-a-half times greater. Other differences of this sort are found for the percentages of adult neighbors with postsecondary educations or who are engaged in professional and managerial occupations.

We close this section with an observation about living conditions in the neighborhoods of new destination regions compared with those with a long-standing Hispanic presence. Residential crowding is very common in the immigrant-rich neighborhoods of long-standing Hispanic regions: more than a third of the households to which the children growing up there are exposed contain more than one person per room. The level of crowding is only half as high in the immigrant areas of the new destination regions. But outside the immigrant zones of these regions, Hispanic children are exposed to very low levels of household crowding: just 7 percent of neighboring households hold more than one person per room, a level that comes close to the conditions in the neighborhood of the average white child.

In conclusion, this portion of the analysis seems to sustain a conclusion that has been reached from examining the secondary migration patterns of Latin-American immigrants: namely, the dispersion of immigrants through the United States is motivated partly by a search for better living conditions.[9] On the whole, neighborhood conditions in new destination areas are considerably more favorable than are those in regions with a long-standing Hispanic presence. Families in new destination areas are more likely to be living outside immigrant barrios and in diverse neighborhoods that contain many whites. Under such circumstances, the characteristics of their neighborhoods improve substantially. To be sure, Hispanic families can also improve their neighborhood environments in regions of long-standing Hispanic presence by moving away from immigrant concentrations. But this is harder to do in these regions than in others.

One could argue, of course, that the more favorable neighborhood environments available in the new destinations areas represent only temporary improvements, that as the numbers of Hispanic immigrants in these regions increase, immigrant barrios will become more extensive and include larger portions of the Hispanic population, and that the neighborhood environments in which Hispanic children are typically being raised will deteriorate. That could be, but we do not think it should be taken as a certainty. We will have to await future developments.

Conclusion

Our survey of the neighborhood environments in which Latino children are growing up leads to some disturbing conclusions. Even though Hispanics on the whole are only moderately segregated from whites, the conditions in the neighborhoods where their children are being raised are on average much worse those confronting white children. This is not as paradoxical as it seems. For example, we have found that the neighbors of the average Hispanic child are disproportionately other Hispanics and frequently immigrants and others who do not speak English fluently. A high proportion of the adult neighbors does not have any education beyond high school, and relatively few engage in high-status professional and managerial occupations. The average household income is relatively low and the rate of poverty high. Overcrowded households are commonplace. In all these respects, the neighborhood of the average Hispanic child resembles that of the average black child, often taken as the standard for residential disadvantage in American society. Neighborhood conditions for both groups of children on the whole differ from the more comfortable circumstances in which white children typically live.

We have not been able to identify and analyze separately the children growing up in Latin-American immigrant households. However, based on locational-attainment studies of Hispanic residential patterns, it is plausible to think that the conditions in neighborhoods where Latin-American immigrants are concentrated approximate those to which most children in immigrant households are exposed. These neighborhoods are, on virtually all our measures, even more distressed than the neighborhoods in which the average Hispanic and black children are found. One measure of this distress is the relatively high percentage of 16–19-year-olds who are just hanging out, having dropped out of high school but not found employment. Even if there are benefits to living in these neighborhoods that we have not been able to measure, the percentage of older teenagers who are idle suggests that a high level of risk is present for children growing up in them.

To be sure, the spatial-assimilation model anticipates that immigrant families generally start out in very distressed neighborhoods. The better conditions visible to them in other neighborhoods are expected to act as a spur to improve their living circumstances as soon as their finances allow. We have found strong evidence that spatial assimilation continues to function in this way for Hispanic families, that the characteristics of their neighborhoods change as their income does. Further, living outside immigrant areas, which almost certainly increases in likelihood as length of residence and other indicators of settlement and assimilation do, is also associated with improved neighborhood environments. However, we do not find that, in terms of these environments, Hispanic children ever catch up to white children. Even when their families have high incomes, Hispanics appear to live in neighborhoods that are less favorable to development and integration than are those in which poor white children live. In this critical respect, our findings are different from those based on locational analyses of 1990 Census data; these appeared to indicate that some Hispanics attain neighborhood conditions like those of their white peers (Alba et al. 2000).

This raises a question that we cannot yet answer: Have conditions in the neighborhoods where Hispanic children live deteriorated over time? Or is our analysis limited because of the data that we have used, so we cannot detect the circumstances under which real spatial assimilation is achieved and Hispanic children are growing up in neighborhoods like those of their white counterparts? A straightforward argument can be constructed to support the hypothesis that the first question should be answered in the affirmative. The 1990s were a decade of high immigration; thus, in many immigrant-receiving metropolitan regions, immigrant residential enclaves expanded and, in all probability, became more homogenous (that is, containing fewer non-Latinos). This explanation is consistent with the effects of the metropolitan-level variables in our HLM analyses, which show that on the whole neighborhood conditions worsen for Hispanic children as the percentages of foreign-born and Hispanics in the regional population increase.

Yet it is very plausible that the second question should also be answered in the affirmative. The locational-attainment analyses of Alba and Logan demonstrate that Hispanic residential location is sensitive to numerous personal and household characteristics, not just income. Linguistic assimilation and skin color, for instance, both played important roles in determining the neighborhoods of Hispanics as of 1990. Moreover, we know from aggregate analyses of neighborhood ethno-racial composition that some Hispanics, but few African Americans, reside in white-dominated neighborhoods (Friedman 2008). What we cannot tell from these analyses is who such Hispanics are: for example, are they disproportionately Hispanics with European phenotypes, such as Argentinean and Chilean immigrants and their children? Are they very high income Hispanics, who may in some cases be paying a premium to reside in largely white neighborhoods, by living (for instance) with whites who are less affluent than they are? For answers, we will have to await a new stage of the current project, in which we will carry out locational-attainment analyses with the resources available at a research data center.

The important role of neighborhood type in our analysis also requires further comment and admission about what is unknown. We have argued based on our findings that Hispanic families can improve their living situations by moving to nonimmigrant neighborhoods. However, it is entirely possible that some Hispanic families cannot escape these areas even when their incomes place them comfortably above the poverty level. Apart from limited English proficiency, along with family and cultural loyalties that in principle could tie some families to immigrant neighborhoods, there is legal status. While we cannot be sure, we find it plausible that families where one or more adults lack legal status in the United States are more likely to stick to neighborhoods with many immigrants, where their presence is unlikely to attract notice. What our analysis does establish is that the children in these families, even when they have been born in the United States and are therefore citizens, are not only disadvantaged then by the lack of documentation of their parents, but also by the neighborhood environments in which they are growing up.

We close with the most hopeful sign in our data: the improvements in neighborhood environment that are achieved when Hispanic families move to new destination areas. In part, this occurs because they are then more likely to live outside immigrant enclaves. As Hispanics disperse around the country, more Hispanic children may be living in more diverse and more affluent neighborhoods. Of course, neighborhood conditions could deteriorate as the numbers of Hispanic families in some regions increase substantially and enclaves expand or are established. Nevertheless, we think that this finding is a sign of things to come—that the diversity in neighborhood environments that we have found across region and neighborhood types will come to be seen as more and more characteristic of Latinos. Mapping this diversity and untangling its implications will be a research task of major import for the future.

NOTES

The authors are grateful for the assistance of the Center for Social and Demographic Analysis at the University at Albany, SUNY, in data preparation and in particular for the help of Dr. Ruby Wang. The research reported here was supported financially by a grant from NICHD to the senior authors ("The social contexts of children of immigrants in the United States," 5R01HD049993-02).

1. The main groups we consider are Hispanics, non-Hispanic whites (sometimes called Anglos or whites) and non-Hispanic blacks (also called African Americans and blacks). Because of data limitations in the third summary file, the black group sometimes contains Hispanic blacks, as we subsequently explain.

2. In principle, we could obtain more detailed data about the characteristics of Hispanic children from the fourth summary file. However, data suppression is a major

problem in using this file, especially in integrated tracts where the number of Hispanics is small. Hence, we do not resort to it.

3. There is a definitional problem in the estimate of the number of African American children in the third summary file. The file reports the total number of persons of black race (alone, not in mixtures) by Hispanic origin. When it comes to children, however, we depend on a sex-by-age table that is reported only for persons of black race (alone), without the control for Hispanic origin. Therefore, in computing segregation indices, we have estimated the number of non-Hispanic black children by applying the overall percentage of blacks in a tract who are not Hispanic to the count of black children. This problem, incidentally, does not arise for non-Hispanic white children, since the file reports the sex-by-age table for non-Hispanic whites (white alone).

4. For all categories but the top one, we have coded the income intervals reported in summary file 3 with their midpoints. For the top category, containing families with $200,000 or more in annual income, we have supplied the arbitrarily chosen value of $225,000. Only a small percentage of the families in each group is found in this category.

5. The metropolitan-level variables have been centered around their weighted means over the metropolitan regions. However, family income has not been centered.

6. We present results here where the dependent variables (with the exception of median household income) take the form of percentages and thus can vary between 0 and 100. Because these variables are bounded, they violate the assumptions of linear regression analyses and are often transformed into unbounded forms by use of the logit transformation. We have conducted the same analyses with logit-transformed variables and found the results to be the same, apart from some minor details. Since the coefficients of dependent variables taking the form of percentages are readily interpretable, we present them here.

7. There is one difficulty in the data for the black locational-attainment analyses: the family income table for each tract in the third summary file on which our analysis depends includes Hispanic blacks. There is no easy solution to this problem, which we are convinced is a minor perturbation in the results.

8. Since neighborhood type and the dependent variables are both measured at the census tract, constructing these HLM analyses was not as simple as just adding the neighborhood-type indicator to the equation. To carry them out, we constructed a new level that combined neighborhood type with metropolitan area. That is, we divided each metropolitan region into two parts, the Latino immigrant-enclave portion and the remainder. This new level is then the second level in the analysis.

9. Mark Leach, "The Temporal and Spatial Dynamics of Mexican Migration and Earnings Inequality in the United States, 1990 to 2006," unpublished paper, department of agricultural economics and rural sociology, Pennsylvania State University.

REFERENCES

Alba, Richard, and John Logan. 1992. "Analyzing Locational Attainments: Constructing Individual-Level Regressions Using Aggregate Data." *Sociological Methods & Research* 20:367–97.

Alba, Richard, John Logan, and Brian Stults. 2000. "The Changing Neighborhood Contexts of the Immigrant Metropolis." *Social Forces* 79(2): 587–621.

Alba, Richard, John Logan, Brian Stults, Gilbert Marzan, and Wenquan Zhang. 1999. "Immigrant Groups in the Suburbs: A Reexamination of Suburbanization and Spatial Assimilation." *American Sociological Review* 64(3): 446–60.

Brown, Susan. 2007. "Delayed Spatial Assimilation: Multi-Generational Incorporation of the Mexican-Origin Population in Los Angeles." *City & Community* 6:193–209.

Denton, Nancy, and Douglas Massey. 1989. "Racial Identity among Caribbean Hispanics: The Effect of Double Minority Status on Residential Segregation." *American Sociological Review* 54(5): 790–808.

Friedman, Samantha. 2008. "Do Declines in Residential Segregation Mean Stable Neighborhood Racial Integration in Metropolitan America?" *Social Science Research* 37(3): 920–33.

Holzer, Harry, and Michael Stoll. 2007. "Where Workers Go, Do Jobs Follow? Metropolitan Labor Markets in the U.S., 1990–2000." Washington, DC: The Brookings Institution.

Iceland, John. 2009. *Coming Together or Living Apart? Immigration and the Racial and Ethnic Transformation of America's Neighborhoods.* Berkeley: University of California Press.

Iceland, John, and Kyle Anne Nelson. 2008. "Hispanic Segregation in Metropolitan America: Exploring the Multiple Forms of Spatial Assimilation." *American Sociological Review* 73(5): 741–65.

Landale, Nancy, and R. S. Oropesa. 2002. "White, Black, or Puerto Rican? Racial Self-Identification among Mainland and Island Puerto Ricans." *Social Forces* 81:231–54.

Lareau, Annette. 2003. *Unequal Childhoods: Class, Race, and Family Life.* Berkeley: University of California Press.

Logan, John, Brian Stults, and Reynolds Farley. 2004. "Segregation of Minorities in the Metropolis." *Demography* 41:1–22.

Massey, Douglas. 1985. "Ethnic Residential Segregation: A Theoretical Synthesis and Empirical Review." *Sociology and Social Research* 69:315–50.

———. 2008. *New Faces in New Places: The Changing Geography of American Immigration.* New York: Russell Sage Foundation.

Massey, Douglas, and Brooks Bitterman. 1985. "Explaining the Paradox of Puerto Rican Segregation." *Social Forces* 64(2): 306–31.

Mitchell, Andy. 2005. *The ESRI Guide to GIS Analysis. Volume 2: Spatial Measurements and Statistics.* Redlands, CA: ESRI Press.

Myers, Dowell. 2007. *Immigrants and Boomers: Forging a New Social Contract for the Future of America.* New York: Russell Sage Foundation.

Newbold, Bruce, and John Spindler. 2001. "Immigrant Settlement Patterns in Metropolitan Chicago." *Urban Studies* 38(11): 1903–19.

Portes, Alejandro, and Rubén Rumbaut. 2001. *Legacies: The Story of the Immigrant Second Generation.* Berkeley: University of California Press.

Rosenbaum, Emily, and Samantha Friedman. 2007. *The Housing Divide: How Generations of Immigrants Fare in New York's Housing Market.* New York: New York University Press.

Sampson, Robert, and Patrick Sharkey. 2008. "Neighborhood Selection and the Social Reproduction of Concentrated Racial Inequality." *Demography* 45(1): 1–29.

South, Scott, Kyle Crowder, and Erick Chavez. 2005a. "Exiting and Entering High-Poverty Neighborhoods: Latinos, Blacks, and Anglos Compared." *Social Forces* 84(2): 873–900.

———. 2005b. "Migration and Spatial Assimilation among U.S. Latinos: Classical versus Segmented Trajectories." *Demography* 43(3): 497–521.

Suro, Roberto, and Audrey Singer. 2002. "Latino Growth in Metropolitan America: Changing Patterns, New Locations." Washington, DC: The Brookings Institution.

Suro, Roberto, and Sonya Tafoya. 2004. "Dispersal and Concentration: Patterns of Latino Residential Settlement." Washington, DC: Pew Hispanic Center.

Telles, Edward, and Vilma Ortiz. 2008. *Generations of Exclusion: Mexican Americans, Assimilation, and Race.* New York: Russell Sage Foundation.

Zúñiga, Victor, and Rubén Hernández-León. 2005. *New Destinations: Mexican Immigration in the United States.* New York: Russell Sage Foundation.

2

Economic Integration of Latino Immigrants in New and Traditional Rural Destinations in the United States

Randy Capps, Heather Koball, and William Kandel

This chapter focuses on the integration of Latino immigrants in rural areas of the United States, based on research funded by the U.S. Department of Agriculture (USDA). There has been much debate in the literature over the nature and pace of integration in metropolitan areas—including the virtues and challenges of integration in ethnic enclaves of longer-term settlement versus newer destinations without long histories of settlement (Bump, Lowell, and Pettersen 2005; Crowley, Lichter, and Qian 2005). This chapter shifts the focus of research on immigrant integration to rural areas, which have been under-studied. It compares new rural destinations and those rural areas with longer, more traditional histories of immigrant settlement, as well as these two types of rural areas and metropolitan areas. This chapter focuses on economic measures of integration available in large-scale surveys such as the decennial census, although the research project also considered indicators of social integration.

The Growing Importance of Latino Immigrants to Rural Areas

The primary research imperative underlying the USDA project lies in the fact that Latino immigrants are the fastest growing group in rural America. Data since 2000 show large increases in the Latino population throughout all regions of the country (Guzmán and McConnell 2002). Rural Latino population growth rates have surpassed those of metropolitan areas, as well as those of all other racial and ethnic groups in metropolitan and nonmetropolitan areas (Kandel and Cromartie 2004). Latinos are dispersing to new destinations, most of which are in the Midwest and Southeast, and for the first time in U.S. history, half of all rural Latinos now live outside the traditional southwestern settlement region. Many rural Latino residents migrate from larger metropolitan areas in search of better-paying jobs, lower-cost housing, safer schools, and a higher quality of life (Fennelly 2005; Hernández-León and Zúñiga 2000). In turn, rural-based industries, such as meat processing and other manufacturing industries, have recruited workers to meet their rising demand for mostly low-skilled and low-paying jobs. The result has been widespread Latino population dispersion punctuated by concentration: while almost all 2,289 nonmetropolitan counties experienced Latino population growth during the 1990s, 30 percent of growth occurred in just 149 "rapid Hispanic growth" counties (Kandel and Cromartie 2004). Thus, patterns of concentration and dispersal somewhat mirror those in metropolitan areas, with Latino immigrants growing in number and concentration in traditional settlement areas but also dispersing to new rural communities throughout the country.

Like many metropolitan areas, rural areas have both benefitted from and experienced costs as a result of the infusion of new immigrant populations. Demographically, Latinos made up less than 6 percent of all nonmetropolitan residents in 2000, yet they accounted for 25 percent of all nonmetropolitan population growth between 1990 and 2000. More than 100 rural counties would have lost population during the 1990s without Latino in-migration (Kandel and Cromartie 2004). Such population infusions have reduced population losses and shored up rural workforces.

While Latinos typically fill jobs in rural areas that might otherwise disappear, Latino population growth also creates challenges for rural communities by altering and often increasing public expenditures for public schools, affordable housing, and other services. Recent Latino immigrants differ socio-demographically from rural native-born residents: on average, they are considerably younger, are less educated, speak little English, and frequently lack legal status, all of which hinder their socioeconomic incorporation and mobility (Parrado and Kandel 2008). Many rural communities are unprepared for the challenges presented by significant numbers of newcomers who seek inexpensive housing, require distinct social services, and struggle to learn English. These challenges have resulted in visible social and political conflict in rural communities, as documented in media reports and academic studies (for example, Zúñiga and Hernández-León 2005 and Millard and Chapa 2004).

Defining the Economic Integration of Latino Immigrants

While immigration policy is generally a federal responsibility, the challenge of immigrant integration often falls to states, local governments, and private entities in local communities. Inexperience with developing and implementing policies that address immigrant integration challenges new rural destinations compared with metropolitan areas and the rural Southwest that have lengthy immigrant histories and established immigrant communities (Bump et al. 2005; Crowley et al. 2005). The challenges are exemplified by a growing number of anti-immigrant measures enacted by state and local governments.[1]

The economic progress of immigrants is a perennial topic of academic debate (Borjas 2000). Prospects for Latinos in contemporary rural America hinge on the same mechanisms for social and economic mobility used by earlier generations of U.S. immigrants. These include acquiring work experience, English language skills, training and education, and legal status, as well as overcoming discrimination and prejudice. Policymakers and local officials must concern themselves increasingly with helping these new residents become integrated and effective citizens (Jones 2003). Rural places that ignore these issues may face the prospect of growing numbers of disadvantaged and marginalized residents who, in some areas, already compose a significant portion of employees, taxpayers, and citizens.

While the USDA study examined a broad range of integration indicators, this chapter focuses mostly on economic indicators. Economic opportunities have arguably driven most of the migration of Latinos to rural areas, but many Latino immigrants in rural areas remain poor because of low wages. In rural communities as in cities, most expenses incurred with newcomer populations are related to poverty and low socioeconomic status. Thus, it is important to understand whether Latino immigrants are experiencing economic incorporation and improvements in their living standards in rural areas.

The measures of economic integration considered in this chapter are based on the concept of economic security, broadly defined as full-time employment with a living wage. While labor force participation rates of immigrant Latinos exceed those of native-born residents, immigrants experience more inconsistent employment spells because many industries in which they concentrate offer unstable, seasonal, or part-time employment. In rural areas, 32 percent of Mexican immigrants have household incomes below the federal poverty level, over twice the rate of 14 percent for native-born rural residents (Donato, Tolbert, and Nucci 2005). Among employed adults, 46 percent of immigrant workers have employer-sponsored health insurance, compared with 59 percent of native-born workers (Fix, Zimmermann, and Passel 2001). Further, undocumented immigrants and recent legal immigrants are ineligible for public health insurance in most states (Zimmermann and Tumlin 1999). As a consequence, children of immigrants are twice as likely as children of native-born parents to lack health insurance (Capps 2001).

Low-wage work among immigrants is closely tied to their low educational attainment and limited English proficiency. Over the past two decades, the income of full-time workers with at least some college education has increased, while the income of full-time workers lacking college educations has declined (Koball and Douglas-Hall 2004). Nationally, 30 percent of immigrant workers lack high school degrees, and three-quarters of all workers without 9th grade educations are immigrants. Two-thirds of low-wage immigrant workers—those earning under twice the minimum wage—lack English proficiency, and the majority lack high school diplomas (Capps et al. 2003). Some research indicates that lack of English proficiency is more closely linked with poverty in immigrant families than either legal status or U.S. experience (Capps and Fix 2002).

The research described in this chapter focused on four measures of economic security provided by the decennial census and its more recent counterpart, the American Community Survey (ACS). These four measures are Latino immigrants' full-time employment rate, poverty rate, average hourly wage, and home ownership rate. These measures encapsulate both immediate patterns of work and returns from labor, as well as longer-term integration via economic advancement and acquisition of assets. Throughout the chapter, comparisons are made between Latino immigrants and native-born populations in rural areas, as well as among traditional rural destinations, new rural destinations, and metropolitan areas.

Data and Methods

The USDA study employed Public Use Microdata Sample (PUMS) 5 percent data from the 1990 decennial Census and 1 percent sample data from each of the 2005 and 2006 ACS (combined to yield a 2 percent sample). Datasets on immigrants in rural areas are limited, and some scholars note that recent surveys of immigrants do not provide the geographic information necessary to identify rural areas.[2] The decennial census, with its large sample size, is generally considered the best available data source for rural immigrants. Further, in 2000, the Census Bureau greatly increased its outreach efforts in communities with hard-to-enumerate populations, such as recent immigrants (Citro, Cork, and Norwood 2004). Additionally, the annual ACS PUMS 1 percent sample has been designed to replace the "long form" version of the decennial census and has the geographic detail necessary to identify rural areas.

Identifying Latino Immigrants

The Census and ACS data include the necessary information to identify Latino immigrants, including questions about respondents' nativity, place of birth, and Latino ethnicity. Additionally, the data include questions about the citizenship and year of entry of the foreign-born population, as well as the English proficiency of all household members. These data allow researchers to disaggregate foreign-born populations into groups that are better and not as well integrated (i.e., citizens versus noncitizens, recent immigrants versus longer-term residents, and English-proficient versus limited proficient adults).

Focus on Working-Age Adults

The analyses described in this chapter are limited to immigrants of working age (16 to 64) because the chapter focuses on economic integration measures that are valid primarily for this age group, and not for seniors or children.[3] In addition, it is typically adults in Latino immigrant families that decide to migrate to new rural areas, often based on employment opportunities. The 2 percent sample obtained by combining the 2005 and 2006 ACS yielded sample sizes of 6,173 Latino immigrants for new rural destinations, 6,786 for traditional rural destinations, and 201,953 for metropolitan areas.[4]

Identifying Rural Areas

With some manipulation, the data in the Census and ACS can be used to identify rural versus metropolitan areas. In the current study, rural areas are counties or groups of counties considered nonmetropolitan by the U.S. Census Bureau or by USDA's Economic Research Service (ERS). The lowest level of geography identified by the Census and ACS is the Public Use Microdata Area (PUMA), which in rural areas generally consists of groups of counties. In the PUMS data, most PUMAs are specified as either metropolitan or nonmetropolitan, although a few are mixed. The definition of rural areas employed by the study includes all PUMAs specified as nonmetropolitan as well as "mixed" PUMAs categorized by USDA or ERS as rural based on the characteristics of the underlying counties.

Defining Traditional versus New Rural Immigrant Destinations

Traditional and new rural destinations are defined at the state level. Traditional areas are those states where at least 10.3 percent of the population residing in rural areas in 1990 was Latino.[5] Thus defined, the traditional rural states are primarily in the Southwest: Arizona, California, Colorado, Hawaii, Nevada, New Mexico, and Texas (figure 2.1). New rural states are those with a growth rate in their rural Latino populations of 3.4 percentage points or higher between 1990 and 2006.[6] The new rural states are distributed across several regions: Delaware, Florida, Georgia, and North Carolina in the Southeast; Idaho, Oregon, and Washington in the Northwest; and Kansas and Nebraska in the Midwest.[7] The balance of rural counties fell into the "all other" states category.

The analyses in this chapter compare these traditional and new rural areas with each other, and compare both types of rural areas to metropolitan areas. Rural areas in lower growth and concentration states (i.e., the "all other" category) are not included in the analyses because of the relatively small numbers of Latino immigrants in these states.

In 2006, 7 percent of Latino immigrants lived in rural areas, with the balance living in metropolitan areas. Though the percentage of Latino immigrants living in rural areas was small, the number of Latino immigrants in these areas tripled between 1990 and 2006. As a result of rapid population growth in new rural destinations, the distribution of Latino immigrants across traditional and new destinations has become roughly

Figure 2.1. Categorization of States as Traditional versus New Rural Destinations

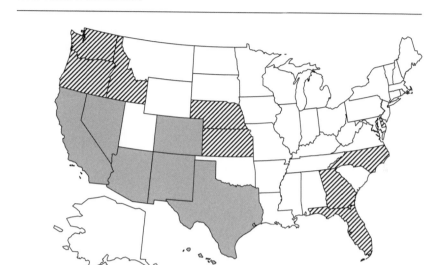

▣ Traditional rural destinations	(7)
▨ New rural destinations	(9)
▢ All other states	(34)

Source: Urban Institute tabulations of 1990 U.S. Census and 2005–06 American Community Survey data.

even: about 37 percent of Latino immigrants lived in each rural area type by 2006. The remaining 26 percent of rural immigrants lived in "all other" states with lower growth and smaller overall rural immigrant populations.

Economic Integration Measures

The analyses in the chapter focus on four measures of economic integration. Wages are expressed in dollars, but the three other measures are categorical:

1. **Full-time work:** The adult worked more than 1,750 hours (an average of at least 35 hours a week for 50 weeks) during the previous year (1989 for the 1990 Census and the average of 2004 and 2005 for the 2005–06 ACS). Full-time work status was measured only for those in the labor force.

2. **Wages:** Hourly wages for the most recent job were reported in the Census and ACS; only those adults with nonzero wages were included in the analysis.
3. **Poverty:** The adult lived in a family with annual income below the federal poverty level for families the size of the individual's family (during the previous year, as with the full-time work measure).
4. **Home ownership:** The adult lived in an owner-occupied home, as data on individual-level home ownership were not available in the ACS or Census.

Regression Modeling

After conducting descriptive analyses, regression models were developed using these four economic integration indicators as dependent variables. For wages, regression was conducted on the log of hourly wage. For the other three variables, logistic regression was conducted on the odds of the outcome (i.e., full-time work, family income below poverty level, or living in an owned home).

The primary explanatory variables in the regression models were the type of destination (traditional rural, new rural, metropolitan) and whether the adult was a Latino immigrant. Additional characteristics of Latino immigrants were considered as follows:

- **Length of U.S. residence:** Length of residence was determined by subtracting the year of entry of each foreign-born adult from the year of the survey. Residence was categorized as less than 5 years (the cutoff for citizenship eligibility), 5 to 10 years (up to twice the citizenship cutoff), and more than 10 years.
- **Citizenship:** The citizenship of foreign-born persons was reported in the Census and ACS.
- **Linguistic isolation:** The primary language spoken at home was reported as either English or another language. Individuals living in households where a language other than English was spoken were identified as speaking English very well, well, not well, or not at all. Linguistically isolated households are those where a language other than English was spoken and where no household member over age 13 spoke English very well.

Controls for gender, age, education, marital status, presence of a child in the household, and whether the respondent had moved in the previous year were included in all regression equations. Industry of employment was also included as a control in the full-time employment and wage models.

Findings

The USDA project included several levels of descriptive analysis for traditional versus new rural areas, between Latino immigrants and the general population, and for different periods (1990, 2000, and 2005–06). During the most recent period, the general demographic and social characteristics of Latino immigrants were compared across new rural, traditional rural, and metropolitan destinations. Compared with their counterparts in traditional rural and metropolitan areas, the Latino immigrants in new rural destinations were more likely to be men, younger, high school dropouts, short-term U.S. residents, and employed in manufacturing and agriculture (table 2.1).

Despite their relative youth, recency of arrival, and low formal educations, Latino immigrants in new-destination rural areas are faring similarly economically to immigrants in traditional destinations. In addition, economic integration indicators show improvements for Latino immigrants in both types of rural areas as well as metropolitan destinations over the period of study.

Full-time employment increased dramatically among Latino immigrants between 1990 and 2005–06. In 1990, 55 percent of Latino immigrants in new rural destinations were employed full time; by 2005–06, this share had risen to 69 percent (figure 2.2). Latino immigrants in traditional rural destinations and metropolitan areas experienced similarly dramatic increases in full-time employment, with rates increasing by over 10 percentage points in both locations.

Poverty rates among Latino immigrants declined during this time; however, given the substantial increase in full-time employment, the drop was small, particularly in new rural destinations and metropolitan areas. In new rural destinations, poverty declined only slightly from 29 to 27 percent between 1990 and 2005–06. Latino immigrants in traditional rural destinations experienced a much more dramatic decline in poverty from 38 to 28 percent, to reach near-parity with their counterparts in new rural destinations. The Latino immigrant poverty rate in metropolitan areas also declined, and it remained substantially below the levels for both types of rural areas.

Table 2.1. Demographic and Social Characteristics of Latino Immigrants, 2005–06 (percent)

	New rural destinations	Traditional rural destinations	Metropolitan areas
Male	60	53**	54**
Age			
16–24	22	16**	16**
25–44	60	55**	58**
45–64	18	29**	26**
Unmarried	40	31**	41
Education			
Less than 9th grade	44	40**	30**
9th to 12th grade	17	18**	16**
12th grade or more	38	42**	55**
Length of U.S. residence			
5 years or less	29	18**	21**
6 to 10 years	25	17**	20**
More than 10 years	47	65**	59**
Employment by industrial sector			
Manufacturing	27	14**	14**
Agriculture	22	15**	3**
Low-skill services	19	25**	32**
Construction	17	16**	19**
Other	10	16**	21**
Education/health services/ public admin.	5	14**	11**

Source: Mathematica Policy Research analysis of the 2005–06 American Community Survey.

Note: All analyses are restricted to Latino immigrants between the ages of 16 and 64.

**Characteristics are statistically significantly different from new destination areas at the .01 level.

Wages actually decreased slightly in new rural destinations between 1990 and 2005–06 (table 2.2), which may explain the small decline in poverty despite the large increase in full-time employment (shown in figure 2.2). Wages rose slightly in traditional rural areas but also fell in metropolitan areas.

Home ownership among Latino immigrants increased between 1990 and 2005–06 in all destination areas. In new rural areas, home ownership increased from 40 to 44 percent (figure 2.3). The largest increases

Figure 2.2. Full-Time Employment and Poverty Percentages for Latino Immigrants Age 16–64

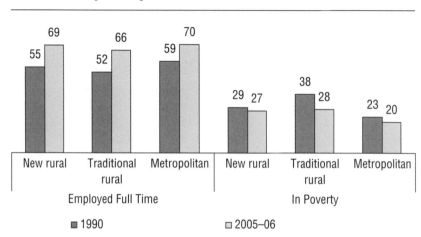

Source: Mathematica Policy Research tabulations of 1990 U.S. Census and 2005–06 American Community Survey data.

occurred in metropolitan areas, where home ownership rose from 37 to 46 percent. Latino immigrant home ownership also rose in traditional rural areas, where it was the highest in 2005–06 (59 percent).

These economic indicators show some improvements and some declines over time for immigrants in new rural destinations. Poverty there has declined only slightly, despite increases in full-time employment. Stagnating wages for Latino immigrants in all areas—rural and metropolitan—may continue to impede economic integration. Home ownership, however, appears to be increasing in both rural and metropolitan areas. Taken together, these descriptive analyses of economic indicators indicate that

Table 2.2. Median Hourly Wages for Latino Immigrants Age 16–64

	1990	2005–06
New rural destinations	$9.20	$9.03
Traditional rural destinations	$8.58	$9.49
Metropolitan areas	$11.46	$11.02

Source: Mathematica Policy Research tabulations of the 1990 U.S. Census and 2005–06 American Community Survey.

Figure 2.3. Home Ownership Percentages for Latino Immigrants Age 16–64

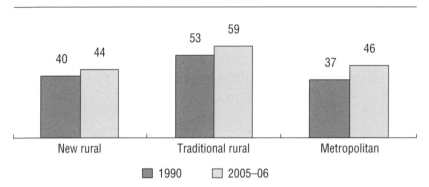

Source: Mathematica Policy Research tabulations of 1990 U.S. Census and 2005–06 American Community Survey data.

Latino immigrants in new rural areas are faring as well or almost as well as their counterparts in traditional rural and metropolitan areas, despite their disadvantages in terms of youth, recency of arrival, and schooling. Multivariate analysis is needed to disentangle the associations of these social and demographic characteristics from the associations of rural versus urban location on economic integration outcomes.

Logistic Regression on Full-Time Employment

Full-time employment rates—among adults age 16 to 64 who are employed—are similar for Latino immigrants and natives in both new and traditional rural areas, when controlling for other factors. Length of U.S. residence, citizenship, and linguistic isolation of rural immigrants also do not appear to affect their full-time employment versus natives (table 2.3). In metropolitan areas, immigrants with longer U.S. residency (of at least five years) and those who are U.S. citizens are more likely than natives to work full time, while those who are linguistically isolated are less likely to work full time.[8] The pattern is similar but not strong enough to be statistically significant in rural areas except for immigrants in new rural areas with 5–10 years of U.S. residency.[9] In no cases are immigrants *less likely* than natives to be working full time.

The regression analysis also indicates significant differences in full-time employment rates across industries, with the highest rates in manufacturing. In rural areas, workers in manufacturing industries are almost

Table 2.3. Odds Ratios of Full-Time Employment, Adults Age 16 to 64, 2005–06

	New rural destinations	Traditional rural destinations	Metropolitan areas
Immigrants by length of U.S. residence (versus natives)			
Less than 5 years	1.195	1.414	1.049
5 to 10 years	1.628**	1.225	1.366***
More than 10 years	1.025	1.263	1.246***
Citizens (versus noncitizens)	1.191	1.112	1.063**
Linguistically isolated	1.036	0.987	0.962*

Source: Mathematica Policy Research analysis of the 2005–06 American Community Survey.

Notes: The analyses include only respondents between the ages of 16 and 64 who were employed at the time of the survey. Linguistically isolated individuals live in households where no one over the age of 13 speaks English very well; the reference group is individuals living in households where at least one member over 13 speaks English very well. Controls for gender, age, education, marital status, presence of a child in the household, whether the respondent moved in the previous year, and industry of employment are included in all regression equations.

*Difference from native born is statistically significant at the .05 level.

**Difference from native born is statistically significant at the .01 level.

***Difference from native born is statistically significant at the .001 level.

three times as likely as workers in service industries to work full time (not shown), when controlling for other factors. Patterns are similar though not as striking for traditional rural destinations and metropolitan areas. Workers in service industries have the lowest relative odds of full-time employment—in rural as well as metropolitan areas.

Hourly Wages

Wage patterns show a significant disadvantage for immigrant versus native workers, a disadvantage that does not change with increasing U.S. residence but does decline with citizenship and English language proficiency. In new rural destinations, recent immigrants (those with less than five years of residence) have wages similar to natives, when controlling for other factors (table 2.4). But those with *longer* U.S. residency have wages that are slightly lower than those for natives. There is no such pattern for immigrants versus natives in traditional rural areas; wages of immigrants and natives seem close to equal in these areas. In metropolitan

Table 2.4. Log of Hourly Wages from OLS Regressions, Adults Age 16 to 64, 2005–06

	New rural destinations	Traditional rural destinations	Metropolitan areas
Immigrants by length of U.S. residence (versus natives)			
Less than 5 years	−0.081	0.054	−0.129***
5 to 10 years	−0.134***	0.035	−0.148***
More than 10 years	−0.073*	−0.032	−0.120***
Citizens (versus noncitizens)	0.075**	0.067*	0.116***
Linguistically isolated	−0.024	−0.070**	−0.105***

Source: Mathematica Policy Research analysis of the 2005–06 American Community Survey.

Notes: The analyses include only respondents between the ages of 16 and 64 who were employed at the time of the survey. Linguistically isolated individuals live in households where no one over the age of 13 speaks English very well; the reference group is individuals living in households where at least one member over 13 speaks English very well. Controls for gender, age, education, industry of employment, marital status, presence of a child in the household, and whether the respondent moved in the previous year are included in all regression equations.

*Difference from native born is statistically significant at the .05 level.

**Difference from native born is statistically significant at the .01 level.

***Difference from native born is statistically significant at the .001 level.

areas, there is a clear and consistent wage disadvantage of between 10 and 15 percent for immigrants regardless of their length of residency.[10] Linguistically isolated immigrants earn significantly less than natives in metropolitan areas and traditional destinations, but not in new rural areas. Citizens earn significantly more than noncitizens across all areas. These findings suggest that citizenship and English language proficiency are important predictors of immigrants' wages, in both rural and metropolitan areas. But the magnitude of the coefficients shows a greater impact of these factors in metropolitan than in rural areas. Thus rural areas—especially new rural areas—may offer immigrants who have not achieved citizenship or English proficiency better employment opportunities relative to the overall cost of living than metropolitan areas.

There are also significant differences in wages by industry of employment, just as there are for full-time employment rates. Workers in manufacturing, construction, education, and health and social services all earn significantly more than workers in services or agriculture in both rural and metropolitan destinations. In both new and traditional rural areas, education, health, and social service workers earn about 25 percent more than those employed in services; workers in construction earn about 20 percent more than service workers, all else equal (not shown). Workers employed in agriculture earn between 5 and 10 percent less than those in services.

Poverty Rates

Despite their lower wages, Latino immigrants actually have lower odds of poverty than natives, after controlling for citizenship, linguistic isolation, education, and other factors (table 2.5). The odds of poverty are lowest for the most recent immigrants, then rise over time to reach near-parity with natives in rural but not in metropolitan areas.[11] Citizens are only about two-thirds as likely to be poor as noncitizens in rural areas; in metropolitan areas, they are about three-quarters as likely to be poor. Linguistically isolated immigrants have significantly higher poverty rates across both rural and metropolitan areas than those who are not linguistically isolated.

Table 2.5. Logistic Regression Results, Odds Ratios of Family Income below Federal Poverty Level, Adults Age 16 to 64, 2005–06

	New rural destinations	Traditional rural destinations	Metropolitan areas
Immigrants by length of U.S. residency (versus natives)			
Less than 5 years	0.676*	0.660*	0.789***
5 to 10 years	0.696*	0.998	0.779***
More than 10 years	0.781	0.814	0.804***
Citizens (versus noncitizens)	0.648**	0.670***	0.712***
Linguistically isolated	1.223*	1.681***	1.691***

Source: Mathematica Policy Research analysis of the 2005–06 American Community Survey.

Notes: The analyses include only respondents between the ages of 16 and 64. Linguistically isolated individuals live in households where no one over the age of 13 speaks English very well; the reference group is individuals living in households where at least one member over 13 speaks English very well. Controls for gender, age, education, marital status, presence of a child in the household, and whether the respondent moved in the previous year are included in all regression equations.

*Difference from native born is statistically significant at the .05 level.

**Difference from native born is statistically significant at the .01 level.

***Difference from native born is statistically significant at the .001 level.

These results suggest that immigrants actually do better than natives in terms of poverty rates, once English proficiency, family structure, educational attainment, age, and other factors are controlled. The evidence suggests that their advantage in rural areas is somewhat greater than their advantage in urban areas at initial settlement, although this advantage erodes over time. Further, the official poverty level is not adjusted for geographic differences in the cost of living, so the lower cost of living in rural areas may be an additional buffer against poverty there.

Home Ownership

The results for home ownership also show positive signs for integration of immigrants over time, although here the results are strikingly different for rural and metropolitan areas. After controlling for other factors, recent immigrants are much less likely to live in their own homes than natives in both rural and metropolitan areas (table 2.6). The lower level of home

Table 2.6. Logistic Regression Results, Odds Ratios of Home Ownership, Adults Age 16 to 64, 2005–06

	New rural destinations	Traditional rural destinations	Metropolitan areas
Immigrants by length of U.S. residency (versus natives)			
Less than 5 years	0.272***	0.406***	0.356***
5 to 10 years	0.543***	0.914	0.534***
More than 10 years	1.099	1.353+	0.799***
Citizens (versus noncitizens)	1.295*	1.607***	1.724***
Linguistically isolated	0.453***	0.533***	0.450***

Source: Mathematica Policy Research analysis of the 2005–06 American Community Survey.

Notes: The analyses include only respondents between the ages of 16 and 64. Linguistically isolated individuals live in households where no one over the age of 13 speaks English very well; the reference group is individuals living in households where at least one member over 13 speaks English very well. Controls for gender, age, education, marital status, presence of a child in the household, and whether the respondent moved in the previous year are included in all regression equations.

+ Difference from native born is statistically significant at the .10 level.

*Difference from native born is statistically significant at the .05 level.

**Difference from native born is statistically significant at the .01 level.

***Difference from native born is statistically significant at the .001 level.

ownership among immigrants disappears after five years of U.S. residence in traditional rural areas and after 10 years of residence in new rural areas, but the disadvantage remains even after 10 years in metropolitan areas. Citizens are more likely than noncitizens to live in owned homes, while those who are linguistically isolated are *less* likely to live in owned homes; this pattern is consistent across both rural and metropolitan destinations. These findings suggest that, with longer U.S. residence, citizenship, English language acquisition, and education, immigrants are able to fully integrate in terms of residential permanence (i.e., home ownership) in rural areas, but not metropolitan areas. Lower housing costs in rural areas may be an important explanation for this pattern.

Discussion and Conclusions

The findings from our analysis suggest that employment, wages, and home ownership opportunities are major draws for rural areas, especially new destinations—at least during the most recent economic expansion. In 2006, Latino immigrants in both new and traditional rural areas were just as likely to find full-time employment as native-born adults, even if the immigrants had just arrived in the United States. Latino immigrants reached parity with natives in home ownership after five years in traditional rural destinations and 10 years in new rural destinations. Although there are some minor differences, wages for immigrants are nearly on par with those for natives in rural areas. In metropolitan areas, however, immigrants' wages and home ownership rates are consistently lower than those for natives. It is only in terms of the poverty rate—which is not adjusted for the higher cost of living in metropolitan areas—that immigrants appear to be doing better in cities than in the countryside.

The fact that Latino immigrants fare better relative to natives in rural than metropolitan areas has important implications for the well-being and development of their children. First, the higher home ownership rate of Latino immigrants in rural than metropolitan areas is not only a sign of their positive integration, but also a signal that the home environment may be more conducive to children's well-being. If immigrant parents in rural areas are able to afford better housing, or at least avoid the crowded conditions in many urban immigrant neighborhoods, this may offer children more stable living arrangements and more space for them to do their homework and conduct their own activities. Second, if Latino immigrants' wages are higher relative to the cost of living in rural than urban areas—which appears to be the case—then immigrant families in rural areas should experience relatively less stress in terms of affording food, housing, and the other necessities of life. This in turn could lower the stress levels of immigrant parents, benefitting them in their interactions with children. Third, the gap in income and poverty between immigrants and natives appears to be considerably smaller in rural than suburban areas. The high segregation levels of ethnic minorities—including Latino immigrants—in many American cities and suburbs result in large part from differences in their income levels and the high costs of urban housing. The high segregation of Latinos in U.S. cities has negative implications for the schooling, safety, and economic opportunities of their children, as Richard Alba and colleagues discuss in chapter 1 of this volume. But in rural areas, especially small towns, Latino immigrants are likely to experience less segregation and more access to better schools and safer neighborhoods. The lower living standards between immigrants and natives in rural compared with urban areas signals not only higher integration but also better conditions for childrearing.

On most integration measures considered in this chapter, immigrants fare as well or better in traditional than new rural areas. These findings suggest then, that while new rural areas may offer economic opportunities that are superior to metropolitan areas, the traditional areas may retain their luster. On the longer-term immigration measure—home ownership—immigrants fare much better in traditional than new rural areas. In terms of children's well-being, these findings suggest that traditional rural areas may be better places for raising immigrants' children, as housing conditions and segregation may be lower there. In other words, many conditions that advantage the well-being and development of Latino immigrants' children in rural areas generally appear to be more favorable in traditional than new rural areas. However, without a thorough analysis of Latino immigrant segregation in traditional versus new rural areas (or the quality of schools and other social institutions, for that matter), no firm conclusion can be drawn in this regard.

Citizenship and English proficiency appear to be very important factors across the board in promoting immigrant economic integration. Citizenship and English proficiency are associated with higher wages, lower poverty, and higher home ownership in all rural and metropolitan destinations. Thus the analysis of rural areas presented here echoes the findings of most work using national samples and based on studies of urban areas. Full-time employment is the only economic indicator on which citizenship and English proficiency do not appear to have much of an impact.

The current economic crisis threatens these avenues for immigrant integration. Although agriculture remains strong, two key industries for immigrant advancement in rural areas—construction and manufacturing—have been hard hit by the recession. Immigrants may no longer find the same employment opportunities in these industries that they found in 2006 (the last year in the data employed for this study), and their patterns of employment, migration, wages, and poverty could be affected. In fact, a recent study by the Pew Hispanic Center (Kochhar 2008a) has already shown declining employment and labor force participation for Latinos nationally between 2007 and 2008, and a second study (Kochhar 2008b) shows a decline in noncitizen immigrants' incomes during this period.

As of this writing, it seems that the current recession is deep and that the recovery will be long in coming. Due to the length and severity of the recession, some new rural destinations will likely see reversal—or at least significant slowdown—in immigration trends. Some immigrants may move from impacted industries into agriculture (which thus far has been spared from contracting employment), and this shift may reduce some immigrants' wages and increase their poverty. Alternatively, unemployment and poverty more generally may increase in rural immigrant communities. Credit is tighter than it was in 2006, making affording a home more difficult. Some immigrants who bought homes may have lost them to foreclosure, depending on whether they signed on to loan packages they could afford over the longer term. These short-term trends suggest that the significant advances observed for Latino immigrants on most economic integration measures from 1990 through 2005–06 may slow or even reverse.

If the gains Latino immigrants experienced in rural areas over the past 15–20 years are retarded or reversed by the current recession, then the development and well-being of their children may suffer. Many rural areas lack the intensive nonprofit and faith-based safety nets for immigrants that exist now in most major U.S. cities. New rural areas in particular have institutions with little experience settling newcomers and assisting them during tough times. The thin safety nets of rural communities—especially new immigrant destinations—may leave immigrants with little to fall back on if they lose their jobs during the recession. These safety nets are important because many Latino immigrants—especially those who are unauthorized—cannot access most public benefits and services. The current recession could lead to an exodus of immigrant families from some rural communities, and growing impoverishment with little social support among other families. The children in those immigrant families that stay behind and become impoverished may be at risk for considerable economic hardship and developmental difficulties in the coming years.

Policy Recommendations

In the short term, it will be important to keep employment and home ownership opportunities open for immigrants as well as natives in rural areas. And if poverty rises, more social assistance may be required. Even with the large economic stimulus package enacted in 2009, many immigrants—especially those without legal status—are ineligible for government assistance such as job retraining, unemployment, public benefits, and assistance to stay in their homes. It may fall on local rural communities to help immigrant families make it through difficult times as the economic crisis continues.

At the same time, economic contraction will likely increase competition between immigrants and natives for the same jobs, or at least increase the perception among the native-born population that such competition might occur. Native-born residents and community leaders are already wary of recent Latino populations in many new destination areas, and the backlash against Latino immigrants there may grow as economic conditions deteriorate. In this increasingly difficult climate, it is important for researchers, employers, community leaders, and others to carefully examine the evidence and discuss immigrants' economic contributions as well as their potential costs and competitive characteristics.

If the current economic crisis subsides and long-term growth returns, rural communities may again experience labor shortages and increasing demand for immigrant labor. The baby boom generation is beginning to retire, and record numbers of workers are nearing retirement age. Rural communities tend to be older than metropolitan areas and are especially susceptible to large-scale retirement and workforce contraction without immigration (Nelson, Nicholson, and Stege 2004; Salamon 2003). The types of industries located in many rural communities—construction, low-skilled manufacturing, agriculture, and mining (which may become a major growth industry domestically if the prices of oil and gas rebound)—

could with economic prosperity continue to drive the immigration of large numbers of poorly educated, linguistically isolated, and often unauthorized immigrants.

The analysis presented in this chapter suggests that Latino noncitizens (many of whom are unauthorized) and immigrants who are linguistically isolated have the most difficulty integrating economically. This suggests that two types of interventions could lead to more rapid and complete immigrant integration in rural areas.

First, the lack of legal status and citizenship of many Latino immigrants should be addressed. The unauthorized status of immigrants stands in the way of their integration for several reasons. Unauthorized immigrants are limited in the jobs they can find, the wages they are paid, and the conditions of those jobs relative to legal immigrants and citizens. Unauthorized immigrants are limited in their access to loans to buy homes and other goods because of lack of documentation. They are also subject to enforcement actions that can abruptly remove them from communities, even after years of hard work and economic progress. Only some form of immigration reform—either through permanent legalization or provision of temporary work permits—would help unauthorized immigrants overcome these disadvantages.

Even among those with legal status, Latino immigrants are less likely than other immigrants to apply for and achieve citizenship (Passel 2007; Fix, Passel, and Sucher 2003). Some states with large immigrant concentrations—Illinois and Massachusetts, for example—have initiatives to help immigrants become citizens. These states are usually traditional destinations with large metropolitan areas and small rural populations. Extending such citizenship services to states with large rural populations and new destination areas would help immigrants integrate economically. A stronger federal role in the promotion of citizenship could help reach immigrants in those rural areas where state and local resources are relatively scarce.

The second major area for policy intervention is in English language instruction. Our findings further support other research—usually using data on urban areas—that highlights the importance of English language proficiency for immigrant integration (Chiswick and Miller 1999). Investments in English language instruction for immigrants could pay off not only in increased wages and lower poverty, but also in longer-term social and civic incorporation. The challenges that immigrants' lack of English skills impose on local communities are one major factor cited by proponents of anti-immigrant initiatives and enforcement actions. Whether English instruction should be a federal, state, or local obligation would be a subject of further policy conversation. But as with other integration services, it is unlikely that some of the smaller rural communities would have the resources sufficient for such instruction.

NOTES

Funding for this project was provided by the Rural Development program of the National Institute of Food and Agriculture, USDA. The descriptive analyses included here were published previously by Mathematica Policy Research as briefs: "Integrating Latino Immigrants in New Rural Destinations," by Heather Koball, Randy Capps, William Kandel, Jamila Henderson, and Everett Henderson (November 2008), and "Social and Economic Integration of Latino Immigrants in New Rural Destinations," by Heather Koball, Randy Capps, William Kandel, Jamila Henderson, and Everett Henderson (November 2008). Randy Capps was a senior research associate at the Urban Institute and William Kandel was a sociologist with the USDA's Economic Research Service when the analyses underlying this chapter were produced.

1. Migration Policy Institute, "State Responses to Immigration: A Database of All State Legislation," http://www.migrationinformation.org/datahub/statelaws_home.cfm, accessed October 2, 2008.

2. Jenn Martin, project manager, New Immigrant Survey, e-mail correspondence with Heather Koball, December 2, 2005.

3. Adults age 16 to 64 made up 86 percent of all Latino immigrants in rural areas in 2005–06.

4. The sample size for the 1990 Census was considerably larger, as this was a 5 percent sample of the U.S. population. The ACS does not include data on people living in group quarters—for example, people living in college dormitories or prison facilities—and so we exclude group quarters populations from our analyses of both the Census and the ACS.

5. The cutoff for traditional areas of 10.3 percent was obtained by adding the mean share Latino in rural areas for all states in 1990 to half the standard deviation of this mean.

6. The same approach (the mean plus one-half standard deviation) was applied to the percentage point change in share Latino from 1990 to 2006 to identify rural new destination states.

7. States identified by this method as traditional and new destinations are generally consistent with those identified through other methods or studies. The primary differences in the current study are the categorizations of Hawaii as a traditional state and Florida as a new destination. Hawaii has a long-term Mexican immigrant population that has worked on the islands' plantations for more than a century. Florida is often considered a traditional metropolitan destination for Latino immigrants because of the high concentrations of Latinos in Miami; however, an examination of rural areas in Florida suggests that they have only recently become destinations for Latino immigrants.

8. A very small share of native-born adults is linguistically isolated. Thus, although the linguistic isolation measure was constructed for all adults—both immigrants and natives—it is only discussed for immigrants.

9. The significance tests employed here depend on sample size. Since the sample in metropolitan areas is much larger than in either type of rural area, in some cases similar odds ratios are significant for metropolitan but not rural areas. In these cases, it is likely that the patterns are similar for rural and metropolitan areas.

10. Wages appear to reach parity with natives after 6–10 years of residency in traditional rural areas, then decline somewhat with longer residency. However, the odds-ratio for immigrants with more than 10 years of residency is not statistically significant. Once again, the pattern is similar between rural and metropolitan areas, but the findings are only significant for immigrants with more than 10 years of residency in metropolitan areas—perhaps because of the larger sample size for this group.

11. Once again, the pattern of poverty rates by immigrants' U.S. residency are similar among rural and metropolitan areas. The relative odds of poverty versus natives for immigrants with more than 10 years of residency are similar across rural and metropolitan areas, but only the metropolitan odds ratio is significant; this may be the result of larger sample size for the metropolitan group.

REFERENCES

Borjas, George J. 2000. "The Economic Progress of Immigrants." In *Issues in the Economics of Immigration,* edited by George J. Borjas (15–49). Chicago: University of Chicago Press.

Bump, Micah M., B. Lindsay Lowell, and Silje Pettersen. 2005. "The Growth and Population Characteristics of Immigrants and Minorities in America's New Settlement States." In *Beyond the Gateway: Immigrants in a Changing America,* edited by Elzbieta M. Gozdziak and Susan F. Martin (19–53). Lanham, MD: Lexington Books.

Capps, Randy. 2001. "Hardship among Children of Immigrants: Findings from the 1999 National Survey of American Families." *Assessing the New Federalism* Policy Brief B-29. Washington, DC: The Urban Institute.

Capps, Randy, and Michael Fix. 2002. "Immigrant Well-Being in New York and Los Angeles." *Immigrant Families and Workers* Brief 1. Washington, DC: The Urban Institute.

Capps, Randy, Michael Fix, Jeffrey S. Passel, Jason Ost, and Dan Perez-Lopez. 2003. "A Profile of the Low-Wage Immigrant Workforce." *Immigrant Families and Workers* Brief 4. Washington, DC: The Urban Institute.

Chiswick, Barry S., and Paul W. Miller. 1999. "Language Skills and Earnings among Legalized Aliens." *Journal of Population Economics* 12(1): 63–91.

Citro, Constance F., Daniel L. Cork, and Janet L. Norwood, eds. 2004. *The 2000 Census: Counting under Adversity.* Panel to Review the 2000 Census. Washington, DC: National Academies Press.

Crowley, Martha L., Daniel T. Lichter, and Zhenchao Qian. 2005. "Beyond Gateway Cities: Economic Restructuring and Poverty among Mexican Immigrant Families and Children." Working Paper 05-07. Columbia, MO: Rural Poverty Research Center.

Donato, Katharine M., Charles Tolbert, and Alfred R. Nucci. 2005. "Changing Places, Changing Faces: What Do Internal Census Data Tell Us about Immigrant Settlement in Nonmetropolitan U.S. Areas?" Paper presented at the Russell Sage Foundation New Immigrant Destinations Conference, New York, February 3.

Fennelly, Katherine. 2005. "Latinos, Asians, and Africans in the Northstar State: New Immigrant Communities in Minnesota." In *Beyond the Gateway: Immigrants in a Changing America*, edited by Elzbieta M. Gozdziak and Susan F. Martin (111–36). Lanham, MD: Lexington Books.

Fix, Michael, Jeffrey S. Passel, and Kenneth Sucher. 2003. "Trends in Naturalization." *Immigrant Families and Workers* Brief 3. Washington, DC: The Urban Institute.

Fix, Michael, Wendy Zimmermann, and Jeffrey S. Passel. 2001. *The Integration of Immigrant Families in the United States*. Washington, DC: The Urban Institute.

Guzmán, Betsy, and Eileen Diaz McConnell. 2002. "The Hispanic Population: 1990–2000 Growth and Change." *Population Research and Policy Review* 21:109–28.

Hernández León, Rubén, and Victor Zúñiga. 2000. " 'Making Carpet by the Mile': The Emergence of a Mexican Immigrant Community in an Industrial Region of the U.S. Historic South." *Social Science Quarterly* 81(1): 49–66.

Jones, Gaytha. 2003. *Migrant Services Directory: Organizations and Resources*. Charleston, WV: ERIC Clearinghouse on Rural Education and Small Schools.

Kandel, William, and John Cromartie. 2004. *New Patterns of Hispanic Settlement in Rural America*. Rural Development Research Report 99. Washington, DC: U.S. Department of Agriculture, Economic Research Service.

Koball, Heather, and Ayana Douglas-Hall. 2004. "The Effects of Parental Education on Income." New York: National Center for Children in Poverty, Mailman School of Public Health, Columbia University.

Kochhar, Rakesh. 2008a. "Latino Workers in the Ongoing Recession: 2007 to 2008." Washington, DC: Pew Hispanic Center.

———. 2008b. "Sharp Decline in Income for Non-Citizen Immigrant Households, 2006–2007." Washington, DC: Pew Hispanic Center.

Millard, Ann V., and Jorge Chapa. 2004. *Apple Pie and Enchiladas: Latino Newcomers in the Rural Midwest*. Austin: University of Texas Press.

Nelson, Peter B., James P. Nicholson, and E. Hope Stege. 2004. "The Baby Boom and Nonmetropolitan Population Change, 1975–1990." *Growth and Change* 35(4): 525–44.

Parrado, Emilio, and William Kandel. 2008. "New Hispanic Migrant Destinations: A Tale of Two Industries." In *New Faces in New Places: The Changing Geography of American Immigration*, edited by Douglas S. Massey (99–123). New York: Russell Sage Foundation.

Passel, Jeffrey S. 2007. "Growing Share of Immigrants Choosing Naturalization." Washington, DC: Pew Hispanic Center.

Salamon, Sonya. 2003. *Newcomers to Old Towns: Suburbanization of the Heartland*. Chicago: University of Chicago Press.

Zimmermann, Wendy, and Karen C. Tumlin. 1999. *Patchwork Policies: State Assistance for Immigrants under Welfare Reform*. Assessing the New Federalism Occasional Paper 24. Washington, DC: The Urban Institute.

Zúñiga, Victor, and Rubén Hernández-León, eds. 2005. *New Destinations: Mexican Immigration in the United States*. New York: Russell Sage Foundation.

3

On the Intergenerational Mobility of U.S. Hispanics

Stephen J. Trejo

Historically, much of the socioeconomic mobility achieved by U.S. immigrant families has taken place across rather than within generations. For example, previous waves of predominantly unskilled immigrants, such as the Italians and the Irish, enjoyed substantial intergenerational progress that ultimately enabled their descendants to join the economic mainstream of American society, but this process took at least two or three generations to unfold (Alba and Nee 2003; Borjas 1994; Chiswick 1977; Farley 1990; Lieberson and Waters 1988; Neidert and Farley 1985; Perlmann 2005; Perlmann and Waldinger 1997). There is considerable skepticism, however, that assimilation and adaptation will operate similarly for the predominantly nonwhite immigrants who have entered the United States in increasing numbers over the past several decades (Gans 1992; Portes and Zhou 1993; Rumbaut 1994). Huntington (2004) voices a particularly strong version of such skepticism toward Hispanic immigration.

Professor Alba and his coauthors (chapter 1, this volume) provide an extraordinarily informative, insightful, and provocative analysis of the neighborhoods in which Hispanic children in the United States are growing up. This analysis illuminates the social, economic, and residential contexts in which mobility or stagnation will take place for the next generation of U.S. Hispanics. My discussion of their chapter is organized in three parts. First, I describe why Hispanics are an especially important group to study in this regard. Next, I offer a few comments directly related to the Alba chapter. Finally, I note how selective intermarriage and endogenous ethnic identification can make it difficult to track the socioeconomic attainment of the later-generation descendants of Hispanic immigrants.

Are Hispanics Unique among Immigrant Groups?

Figure 3.1 shows one dimension of educational mobility between the first and second generations for a large number of U.S. immigrant groups. Using 1994–2006 data from the Current Population Survey, high school dropout rates (i.e., the percentage of individuals with less than 12 years of schooling) were calculated for first- and second-generation men from the 51 source countries with reasonable sample sizes (at least 30 observations). Here, the first-generation men are foreign-born immigrants between the ages of 45 and 59. The second-generation men are U.S.-born children of immigrants, and they are between the ages of 25 and 39. The regression line plotted in the figure shows the central tendency of the relationship between the dropout rate of the second-generation men from a particular source country and that of their immigrant ancestors.

Figure 3.1 illustrates several important points regarding the intergenerational mobility of immigrant families in the United States. First, U.S. immigrants with the lowest skills (i.e., the highest dropout rates) originate predominately in Hispanic countries. Six of the seven countries with immigrant dropout rates above 40 percent are Spanish speaking (with Portugal the lone exception), as are 9 of the 11 countries with immigrant dropout rates exceeding 25 percent (with Haiti the other exception). Second, the relatively high dropout rates of Hispanics persist into the second generation, particularly for the two most populous Hispanic groups (Mexicans and Puerto Ricans) and for two of the fastest-growing groups (Salvadorans and Dominicans). Indeed, the dropout rates of second-generation Mexicans and Puerto Ricans are well above the regression line, suggesting that the large educational deficit of these U.S.-born Hispanics is not simply the result of their having poorly educated immigrant parents. As a frame of reference, consider the comparable dropout rates for young (i.e., age 25–39), non-Hispanic white and black men who are third generation or beyond (i.e., these men and both their parents were all born

Figure 3.1. Dropout Rates of First- and Second-Generation Men

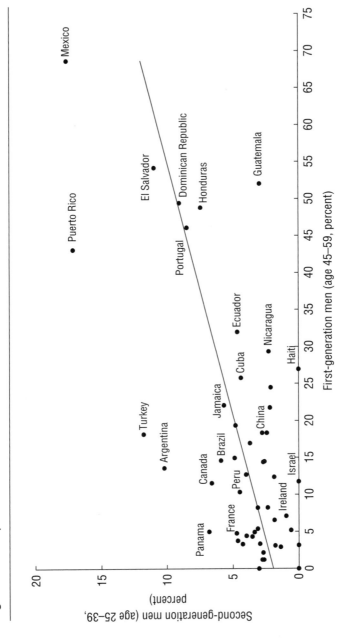

in the United States). These rates are 7 percent for whites and 10 percent for blacks. Therefore, by the second generation, young men from the vast majority of immigrant source countries already have lower dropout rates than the average American. The primary exceptions are second-generation men from some of the largest Hispanic groups.

Finally, there exists considerable diversity across Hispanic national origin groups in the educational attainment of both immigrants and their U.S.-born children. Among second-generation men, for example, Cubans, Ecuadorians, Guatemalans, and Nicaraguans have low dropout rates (all are below 5 percent), especially compared with what we would expect given the schooling levels of their immigrant fathers. This contrasts sharply with the very high dropout rates of second-generation Mexicans and Puerto Ricans (above 17 percent). The dropout rates of second-generation Salvadorans, Dominicans, and Hondurans fall between these two extremes (rates of 7–11 percent).

As a result, Hispanics assume a central role in current discussions of immigrant intergenerational progress and the outlook for the "new second generation," not just because Hispanics make up a large share of the U.S. immigrant population, but also because most indications of relative socioeconomic disadvantage among the children of U.S. immigrants vanish when Hispanics are excluded from the sample (Perlmann and Waldinger 1996, 1997). Therefore, to a great extent, concern about the long-term economic trajectory of immigrant families in the United States is concern about Hispanic-American families.[1]

Comments on the Alba Chapter

Let me now offer a few comments directed specifically at the analysis conducted by Alba and his coauthors. This analysis clearly shows that the typical Hispanic child grows up in a much less favorable neighborhood environment than does the typical Anglo child. An unresolved question, however, is what impact these neighborhoods ultimately have on the life chances of Hispanic children. In other words, is residential integration a root cause of Hispanic socioeconomic mobility, or is it merely a symptom of such mobility, or is it both at the same time? Important previous work on locational attainment by Alba, Logan, and various coauthors (for example, Alba and Logan 1993; Alba, Logan, and Stults 2000; and Alba et al. 1999) shows that residential integration is associated with other factors—such as income, education, and intermarriage—that could be driving Hispanic progress. What is the independent or causal effect of residential integration?

Of course, this question is very difficult to answer. A few studies by economists try, in different ways, to address the endogeneity of location choice when estimating the impacts of residential integration and neighborhood quality. One study, which focuses on the residential segregation of African Americans (Cutler and Glaeser 1997), finds that the estimated causal effects are similar to the partial correlations or associations obtained from descriptive analyses. However, in two other studies—one that investigates adult outcomes for individuals who grew up in Toronto public housing projects (Oreopoulos 2003) and another that examines the influence of ethnic enclaves on the labor market success of refugee immigrants to Sweden (Edin, Fredriksson, and Aslund 2003)—the estimated causal effects are very different from the partial correlations. Hopefully, future research will attempt to devise some way of estimating the causal impacts of residential integration and neighborhood quality for Hispanic children.

Alba and his coauthors show that the positive relationship between a family's income and the quality of the neighborhood in which it lives is much weaker for Hispanic families residing in heavily immigrant neighborhoods than for other Hispanic families. It is unclear how we should interpret this finding. Perhaps the primary pathway to a better neighborhood is to move out of immigrant enclaves, and family income is strongly predictive of such movement. In addition, Hispanic families with relatively high incomes who remain in immigrant neighborhoods may have unusually strong ties to their neighborhood (e.g., because of elderly parents, or a favorite church or school, or something else along these lines). For these reasons, it is difficult to know whether the relationship between family income and neighborhood quality truly differs for Hispanic families living in immigrant enclaves.

Related issues pertain to the intriguing finding that Hispanic neighborhoods in immigrant new destination regions tend to be more favorable than neighborhoods in traditional Hispanic regions. Why is this so, and what does it mean? Do the new destinations lack Hispanic cultural amenities and infrastructure that the traditional regions have accumulated through time and through Hispanic population density? If so, then perhaps Hispanics will choose to locate in new destination regions only if these neighborhoods possess compensating advantages in other dimensions; therefore, comparisons of neighborhood quality for Hispanics residing in new destination regions versus other regions might be confounded by selection on unobservable characteristics of the new destination neighborhoods and of the Hispanic families who choose to locate in them. Nevertheless, an interesting question for future research is whether the new destination neighborhoods will maintain their observed advantages as these areas adapt to the continuing influx of Hispanic immigrants.

All analyses in the Alba chapter are confined to metropolitan regions with a relatively high concentration of Hispanic immigrants. Given the goals of the chapter, focusing on these metropolitan regions makes sense, and almost 70 percent of U.S. Hispanic children reside in these regions. It is likely, however, that Hispanic children excluded from the analysis sample live in more advantaged neighborhoods than those included in the sample. As a result, the analysis omits one potentially important avenue for Hispanic socioeconomic mobility—movement out of Hispanic regions—and the residential disadvantage of the typical Hispanic family may be somewhat overstated.

In its concluding section, chapter 1 raises the provocative point that legal status might tie Hispanic families with undocumented parents (or other undocumented adults) to immigrant neighborhoods, and that the U.S.-born children in these families could be paying a price for this. We currently know very little about the intergenerational effects of legal status: how does growing up with an undocumented parent (or other family member) affect second-generation Hispanics? If suitable data could be found, this would be a fruitful topic for future research.

Intermarriage and Selective Ethnic Attrition

Frequent intermarriage is one of the strongest signals of social assimilation by an ethnic group with immigrant origins (Alba and Nee 2003; Gordon 1964). In addition, intermarriage is a key determinant of weakened and/or multiple ethnic attachments for future generations of the group (Hout and Goldstein 1994; Perlmann and Waters 2007). After a few generations in the United States, so much intermarriage had taken place among the descendants of earlier European immigrants that most white Americans could choose among multiple ancestries or ethnic identities (Alba 1990; Waters 1990). For such individuals, ethnicity has become subjective, situational, and largely symbolic, and the social boundaries between these ethnic groups have been almost completely erased.

Recently, Brian Duncan and I have begun to assess the potential empirical importance of selective ethnic attrition among Mexican Americans (Duncan and Trejo 2007, 2008, forthcoming). Specifically, we have investigated what factors influence whether individuals choose to identify themselves (or their children) as Mexican-origin, and how these ethnic choices may affect inferences about the socioeconomic attainment of later-generation Mexican Americans. Our work draws inspiration and insight from Professor Alba's long-standing and influential research on ethnic identity (e.g., Alba 1986, 1990) as well as from his recent paper (Alba and Islam 2009) that explores some of the same issues that we do for Mexican Americans.

Intermarriage has always been a fundamental source of ethnic flux and leakage in American society (Hout and Goldstein 1994; Lieberson and Waters 1988; Perlmann and Waters 2007). For Mexican Americans, Rosenfeld (2002, table 1) shows that intermarriage increased substantially between 1970 and 1980 and even more sharply between 1980 and 1990. As of 2000, more than a third of married, U.S.-born Mexicans have non-Mexican spouses (Duncan and Trejo 2007). Because it takes two Mexican-origin spouses to create an endogamous Mexican marriage, whereas a Mexican intermarriage requires only one Mexican-origin spouse, the observed rate of intermarriage implies that almost half of Mexican American marriages involve a non-Mexican spouse. Indeed, Perlmann and Waters (2004) argue that the proclivity for intermarriage by second-generation Mexicans today is similar to what was observed for second-generation Italians in the early 1900s. This argument has potentially provocative implications for ethnic attachment among future generations of Mexican Americans, because intermarriage became so commonplace for subsequent generations of Italian Americans that Alba (1986) characterized this group as entering the "twilight of ethnicity."

How does Mexican intermarriage influence the ethnic identification of the children produced by these marriages? Not surprisingly, virtually all children with two Mexican-origin parents are identified as Mexican in Census data, but about 30 percent of the children of intermarried Mexican Americans are not identified as Mexican. As this dynamic plays out across generations, it is likely that an increasingly small fraction of the descendants of Mexican immigrants continue to identify themselves as Mexican. In addition, this ethnic leakage is highly selective, because Mexican Americans who intermarry tend to have much higher education levels and earnings than Mexican Americans who do not intermarry. Consequently, available data for third- and higher-generation Mexicans, who usually can only be identified by their subjective responses to questions about Hispanic ethnicity, probably understate the socioeconomic attainment of this population. In effect, through the selective nature of intermarriage and ethnic identification, some of the most successful descendants of Mexican immigrants assimilate to such an extent that they fade from empirical observation. Unfortunately, although the direction of this measurement bias seems clear, we do not yet have a good idea of its magnitude.

For our purposes, the ideal dataset would include the family tree of each individual, enabling us to identify which individuals are descended from Mexican immigrants and how many generations have elapsed since that immigration took place. It would then be a simple matter to compare outcomes for this "true" population of Mexican descendants with the corresponding outcomes for a relevant reference group (e.g., non-Hispanic whites) and with those for the subset of Mexican descendants who continue to self-identify as Mexican-origin. Such an analysis would provide an unbiased assessment of the relative standing of the descendants of Mexican immigrants in the United States, and it would show how selective ethnic identification distorts estimated outcomes for this population when researchers are forced to rely on standard, self-reported measures of Mexican identity.

Following the 1970 Census, unusually detailed information of this sort was collected for a small sample of individuals with ancestors from a Spanish-speaking country. After each decennial U.S. census, selected respondents to the census long form are reinterviewed in order to check the accuracy and reliability of the census data. The 1970 Census was the first U.S. census to ask directly about Hispanic origin or descent, and therefore a primary objective of the 1970 Census Content Reinterview Study was to evaluate the quality of the responses to this new question (U.S. Bureau of the Census 1974). For this purpose, individuals in the reinterview survey were asked a series of questions regarding any ancestors they might have who were born in a Spanish-speaking country. Among those identified by the reinterview survey as having Hispanic ancestors, table 3.1 shows the share who had previously responded on the 1970 Census long form that they were of Hispanic "origin or descent."[2]

Overall, 76 percent of reinterview respondents with ancestors from a Spanish-speaking country had self-identified as Hispanic in the 1970 Census, but the correspondence between Hispanic ancestry in the reinterview and Hispanic identification in the census fades with the number

Table 3.1. Hispanic Identification of Individuals with Ancestors from a Spanish-Speaking Country, as Reported in the 1970 Census Content Reinterview Study

Hispanic ancestry classification in reinterview	% who identified as Hispanic in the Census	Sample size
Most recent ancestor from a Spanish-speaking country		
Respondent (i.e., 1st generation)	98.7	77
Parent(s) (i.e., 2nd generation)	83.3	90
Grandparent(s) (i.e., 3rd generation)	73.0	89
Great grandparent(s) (i.e., 4th generation)	44.4	27
Further back (i.e., 5th+ generations)	5.6	18
Hispanic ancestry on both sides of family	97.0	266
Hispanic ancestry on one side of family only	21.4	103
Father's side	20.5	44
Mother's side	22.0	59
All individuals with Hispanic ancestry	75.9	369

Source: U.S. Bureau of the Census (1974), table C.

Note: Information regarding the generation of the most recent ancestor from a Spanish-speaking country was missing for 68 respondents who nonetheless indicated that they had Hispanic ancestry on one or both sides of their family.

of generations since the respondent's Hispanic ancestors arrived in the United States. Virtually all (99 percent) first-generation immigrants born in a Spanish-speaking country identified as Hispanic in the census, but the rate of Hispanic identification dropped to 83 percent for the second generation, 73 percent for the third generation, 44 percent for the fourth generation, and all the way down to 6 percent for higher generations of Hispanics. Interestingly, intermarriage seems to play a central role in the loss of Hispanic identification. Almost everyone (97 percent) with Hispanic ancestors on both sides of their family identified as Hispanic in the census, whereas the corresponding rate was only 21 percent for those with Hispanic ancestors on just one side of their family. Given the small number of Hispanics in the reinterview sample (369 individuals reported having at least one ancestor from a Spanish-speaking country), the percentages in table 3.1 should be regarded with caution, especially those for the very small samples of Hispanics who are fourth generation or higher. Nonetheless, these data suggest that self-identified samples of U.S. Hispanics might omit a large proportion of later-generation individuals with Hispanic ancestors, and that intermarriage could be a fundamental source of such intergenerational ethnic attrition.

Unfortunately, the microdata underlying table 3.1 no longer exist, so we cannot use them to examine straightforwardly how selective ethnic attrition affects observed measures of intergenerational progress for Mexican Americans. Out of necessity, we instead have to pursue other strategies for trying to shed light on this issue. For example, using Current Population Survey data, we assess the influence of endogenous ethnicity by comparing an "objective" indicator of Mexican descent (based on the countries of birth of the respondent and his parents and grandparents) with the standard "subjective" measure of Mexican self-identification (based on the respondent's answer to the Hispanic origin question). For third-generation Mexican American youth (i.e., U.S.-born youth with two U.S.-born parents and at least one grandparent who was born in Mexico), we show that ethnic attrition is substantial (about 30 percent) and could produce significant downward bias in standard measures of attainment (such as dropping out from high school) that rely on ethnic self-identification rather than objective indicators of Mexican ancestry (Duncan and Trejo 2008).

NOTES

1. See Smith (2006), however, for a more optimistic take on the intergenerational schooling gains made by Hispanics.

2. The information in table 3.1 is reproduced from table C of U.S. Bureau of the Census (1974, p. 8).

REFERENCES

Alba, Richard D. 1986. *Italian Americans: Into the Twilight of Ethnicity*. Englewood Cliffs, NJ: Prentice-Hall.

———. 1990. *Ethnic Identity: The Transformation of White America*. New Haven, CT: Yale University Press.

Alba, Richard D., and Tariqul Islam. 2009. "The Case of the Disappearing Mexican Americans: An Ethnic-Identity Mystery." *Population Research and Policy Review* 28(2): 109–21.

Alba, Richard D., and John R. Logan. 1993. "Minority Proximity to Whites in Suburbs: An Individual-Level Analysis of Segregation." *American Journal of Sociology* 98(6): 1388–1427.

Alba, Richard D., and Victor Nee. 2003. *Rethinking the American Mainstream: Assimilation and Contemporary Immigration.* Cambridge, MA: Harvard University Press.

Alba, Richard D., John R. Logan, and Brian J. Stults. 2000. "The Changing Neighborhood Contexts of the Immigrant Metropolis." *Social Forces* 79(2): 587–621.

Alba, Richard D., John R. Logan, Brian J. Stults, Gilbert Marzan, and Wenquan Zhang. 1999. "Immigrant Groups in the Suburbs: A Reexamination of Suburbanization and Spatial Assimilation." *American Sociological Review* 64(3): 446–60.

Borjas, George J. 1994. "Long-Run Convergence of Ethnic Skill Differentials: The Children and Grandchildren of the Great Migration." *Industrial and Labor Relations Review* 47(4): 553–73.

Chiswick, Barry R. 1977. "Sons of Immigrants: Are They at an Earnings Disadvantage?" *American Economic Review* 67(1): 376–80.

Cutler, David M., and Edward L. Glaeser. 1997. "Are Ghettos Good or Bad?" *Quarterly Journal of Economics* 112(3): 827–72.

Duncan, Brian, and Stephen J. Trejo. 2007. "Ethnic Identification, Intermarriage, and Unmeasured Progress by Mexican Americans." In *Mexican Immigration to the United States,* edited by George J. Borjas (227–69). Chicago: University of Chicago Press.

———. 2008. "Intermarriage and the Intergenerational Transmission of Ethnic Identity and Human Capital for Mexican Americans." Manuscript. Austin: University of Texas.

———. Forthcoming. "Ancestry versus Ethnicity: The Complexity and Selectivity of Mexican Identification in the United States." *Research in Labor Economics.*

Edin, Per-Anders, Peter Fredriksson, and Olof Aslund. 2003. "Ethnic Enclaves and the Economic Success of Immigrants: Evidence from a Natural Experiment." *Quarterly Journal of Economics* 118(1): 329–57.

Farley, Reynolds. 1990. "Blacks, Hispanics, and White Ethnic Groups: Are Blacks Uniquely Disadvantaged?" *American Economic Review* 80(2): 237–41.

Gans, Herbert J. 1992. "Second-Generation Decline: Scenarios for the Economic and Ethnic Futures of the Post-1965 American Immigrants." *Ethnic and Racial Studies* 15(2): 173–92.

Gordon, Milton M. 1964. *Assimilation in American Life: The Role of Race, Religion, and National Origins.* New York: Oxford University Press.

Hout, Michael, and Joshua R. Goldstein. 1994. "How 4.5 Million Irish Immigrants Became 40 Million Irish Americans: Demographic and Subjective Aspects of the Ethnic Composition of White Americans." *American Sociological Review* 59(1): 64–82.

Huntington, Samuel P. 2004. *Who Are We? The Challenges to America's Identity.* New York: Simon and Schuster.

Lieberson, Stanley, and Mary C. Waters. 1998. *From Many Strands: Ethnic and Racial Groups in Contemporary America.* New York: Russell Sage Foundation.

Neidert, Lisa J., and Reynolds Farley. 1985. "Assimilation in the United States: An Analysis of Ethnic and Generation Differences in Status and Achievement." *American Sociological Review* 50(6): 840–50.

Oreopoulos, Philip. 2003. "The Long-Run Consequences of Living in a Poor Neighborhood." *Quarterly Journal of Economics* 118(4): 1533–75.

Perlmann, Joel. 2005. *Italians Then, Mexicans Now: Immigrant Origins and Second-Generation Progress, 1890–2000.* New York: Russell Sage Foundation.

Perlmann, Joel, and Roger Waldinger. 1996. "The Second Generation and the Children of the Native Born: Comparisons and Refinements." Working Paper 174. Annandale-on-Hudson, NY: Jerome Levy Economics Institute.

———. 1997. "Second Generation Decline? Children of Immigrants, Past and Present—A Reconsideration." *International Migration Review* 31(4): 893–922.

Perlmann, Joel, and Mary C. Waters. 2004. "Intermarriage Then and Now: Race, Generation, and the Changing Meaning of Marriage." In *Not Just Black and White: Historical and Contemporary Perspectives on Immigration, Race, and Ethnicity in the United States,* edited by Nancy Foner and George M. Fredrickson (262–77). New York: Russell Sage Foundation.

———. 2007. "Intermarriage and Multiple Identities." In *The New Americans: A Guide to Immigration Since 1965,* edited by Mary C. Waters and Reed Udea (110–23). Cambridge, MA: Harvard University Press.

Portes, Alejandro, and Min Zhou. 1993. "The New Second Generation: Segmented Assimilation and Its Variants among Post-1965 Immigrant Youth." *Annals of the American Academy of Political and Social Science* 530:74–96.

Rosenfeld, Michael J. 2002. "Measures of Assimilation in the Marriage Market: Mexican Americans 1970–1990." *Journal of Marriage and Family* 64(1): 152–62.

Rumbaut, Ruben G. 1994. "The Crucible Within: Ethnic Identity, Self-Esteem, and Segmented Assimilation among Children of Immigrants." *International Migration Review* 28(4): 748–94.

Smith, James P. 2006. "Immigrants and the Labor Market." *Journal of Labor Economics* 24(2): 203–33.

U.S. Bureau of the Census. 1974. *1970 Census of Population and Housing, Evaluation and Research Program: Accuracy of Data for Selected Population Characteristics as Measured by Reinterviews.* Washington, DC: U.S. Government Printing Office.

Waters, Mary C. 1990. *Ethnic Options: Choosing Identities in America.* Berkeley: University of California Press.

4

Psychological Implications of Demographic Trends in Latino Children's Neighborhoods

Stephen M. Quintana

D emographic growth of the Latino population has and will continue to influence the United States. This demographic pattern is
influential in regions of the country that have been traditional gateways
for Latino immigration, such as Texas, California, Florida, New York,
and Chicago. Even areas that had been relatively untouched by Latino
immigration, known as new destinations, such as the Midwest and rural
Southeast regions of the United States, are experiencing a significant
growth of Latino populations. In many of these areas, Latinos are the
fastest growing ethnic population (Bohon, Macpherson, and Atiles 2005).
The issue of Latino population growth has become nationalized in several
ways given the focus on immigration in 2006 and 2008 political campaigns
as well as the importance of Latino votes in the 2008 presidential elec-
tion: most states that switched from Republican to Democratic had significant Hispanic populations. To date, however, the focus of attention
has been on the impact of these demographic trends on the longer-term
residents in those regions—how life will change for them. In contrast,
there has been relatively little consideration of these trends' implications
for Latino families and children. For this chapter, I focus on the social
and psychological implications of these demographic trends for Latino
immigrant populations.

Intergroup Contact between Latinos and Anglos

As described by Alba and his coauthors (chapter 1, this volume), the growth of the Latino population has increased contact between Latino and Anglo populations. Although many immigrants from Latin America begin their U.S. residence in predominantly immigrant neighborhoods, Latino families are moving into Anglo neighborhoods. Alba describes the attractiveness of moving into Anglo neighborhoods based on greater access to social capital in the predominantly Anglo neighborhoods, not the least of which is proximity to good schools. Other demographic trends described by Alba suggest that Anglos may not appreciate and some may resent Latinos moving into their neighborhoods. Some Anglos are choosing to leave their neighborhoods as more Latinos move in.

Increased density of Latinos in neighborhoods often signals a decline in social capital of the neighborhood. Consequently, although Latinos may voluntarily move into Anglo neighborhoods, Anglos' contact with Latinos often occurs involuntarily. When Anglos have sufficient financial resources, they often choose to move away from ethnically integrated neighborhoods and move to predominately Anglo neighborhoods, frequently in suburban areas. "White flight," which is often associated with whites moving out as African Americans move into neighborhoods, also occurs in neighborhoods into which Latinos are moving (Crowder 2000; South, Crowder, and Pais 2008). Crowder and colleagues demonstrate that whites' decisions to leave neighborhoods are directly predicted by the density of the minority populations. Importantly, they demonstrate that the effect of anti-minority sentiments on white flight is independent of changes in neighborhood income or stability of residents in the neighborhood; these decisions are also not limited to the density of only African Americans but include the density of Latino and Asian neighbors.

Voluntary versus Involuntary Intergroup Contact

Research suggests that the voluntary or involuntary nature of intergroup contact influences the frame of reference that populations bring to that contact. Ogbu (1994) describes how immigrants who voluntarily have intergroup contact as an ethnic minority have a positive frame of reference toward these interactions. Cultural challenges that voluntary minorities experience, such as linguistic differences, are not resented by the voluntary minorities. Instead, cultural changes and other hardships concomitant with intergroup contact are viewed as part of seeking, for example, a better life that is reflected in access to good educations and higher incomes. Similarly, social conflict experienced by voluntary minorities is often not viewed as prejudice but as arising from the minority group's limitations in cultural skills, such as speaking the dominant language. Consequently, Latinos who voluntarily enter predominantly Anglo neighborhoods are seeking the benefits associated with these neighborhoods and may be willing to tolerate the cultural and social challenges they experience. Ogbu suggests that these sacrifices are often considered worth the benefits the immigrants are seeking.

Conversely, ethnic groups who become involuntarily involved in intergroup contact are described by Ogbu (1994) as having a negative frame of reference toward intergroup contact. Groups in this situation will often resent cultural challenges they experience as a result of the intergroup contact and view cultural differences as unnecessary inconveniences. Extending this theoretical principle to the Latino-Anglo intergroup contact, when Latinos move into Anglos' neighborhoods, the intergroup contact occurs voluntarily for Latinos but involuntarily for Anglos. Although Ogbu (1994) does not apply this voluntary/involuntary framework to ethnic majority groups, the principles seem applicable in light of the white flight described above. The propensity for white flight is one sign that some Anglos bring this negative frame of reference to their intergroup contact with Latinos. Additional signs are reflected, partly, in political opposition to bilingual education and social services to immigrants, which seem to result from the resentment that stems from the Anglos' intergroup contact with Latinos.

FBI statistics indicate that the United States has experienced rises in hate crimes perpetuated against Latinos, which is concomitant to increases in density of Latino immigrant populations.[1] The largest growth of hate crimes against Latinos occurs in the states that border Mexico, reflecting animosity toward Latino immigrants. These more egregious forms of racism underestimate the frequency of negative interactions that Latinos, especially immigrants, experience daily. Research on Anglo children reveals that they show consistent preference for other Anglos, relative to Latino children; on the other hand, Latino children show no such bias against Anglo children (Tropp and Prenovost 2008). Additional research indicates Anglo children show implicit racial bias against Latinos, but Latinos do not show the same bias against Anglo children, although both

Anglo and Latino children show bias against African Americans (Banaji et al. 2008). Further research suggests, however, when children are rejected based on ethnic status, they experience anxiety and negative attitudes toward the rejecting group (Nesdale 2008). Consequently, while Latinos may bring a positive frame of reference to intergroup contact, the positive orientation has its limits and will turn to resentment as the hostility from Anglos increases.

Conditions of Positive Intergroup Contact

Allport (1954) defined the conditions necessary for positive intergroup contact. These conditions include equal status between the ethnic groups, common goals, cooperative means of reaching these common goals, and authority. A fifth condition, added by Pettigrew (1998), includes the opportunity to form personal relationships and friendships. Positive contact is defined by Allport as that which results in positive attitudes and establishes the context by which ethnic prejudice can be reduced. When one or more of these conditions are absent, the intergroup contact will often involve stereotyping—that is, intergroup attitudes will not improve or may become worse, particularly when competition exists between these groups.

As chapter 1 in this volume makes clear, the Latinos that move into Anglo neighborhoods typically lack equal status, in terms of social class and social capital. This differential social class status undermines the opportunities for the intergroup contact to reduce the social distance between the ethnic groups as well as negative intergroup attitudes. Research documents intergroup tension and conflict between Latinos and Anglos (Marx 2008).

Critical Levels of Population Densities

Another important factor to consider when Latinos move into Anglo neighborhoods is the density of the Latino residents. Individual Anglo home owners will have varying degrees of tolerance for the density of Latinos and other racial groups moving into their neighborhoods before they take flight, often to predominately white suburbs. This flight to mostly white suburbs may further reinforce negative ethnic and racial attitudes. Namely, meta-analyses of school composition find that when there is only token representation of a minority group, children tend to increase their reliance on skin color and ethnic/racial classification to socially evaluate their peers; conversely, those who have at least 20–25 percent of their peers from a different ethnic heritage use racial or ethnic classification less often as basis for social evaluation (Tropp and Prenovost 2008). Interestingly, only Anglos in bilingual classrooms who are learning Spanish rate their Latino peers as more similar and rate the potential for friendship higher, relative to Anglos in ethnically mixed classrooms (e.g., greater than 23 percent of Latinos) where the Anglos are not learning Spanish or Anglos in classrooms with only token representation of Latinos (e.g., 7 percent of Latinos).

Just as there is a critical mass of same–ethnic group representation in the neighborhood for those in the majority to feel comfort, there is a critical mass for levels of comfort for ethnic minorities to feel they are socially accepted or to attain a similar social status. For example, although Latinos across all classrooms (token, ethnically mixed, and bilingual instruction) rate their Anglo peers equivalently to same-ethnicity peers and as having equal potential for friendships, Latinos do not rate themselves as similar to their Anglo peers. This result suggests that Latinos are willing to make friends with Anglo children despite some lack of similarity, and that Latinos perceive inequities in their own group relative to their Anglo peers (see Tropp and Prenovost 2008).

Additional interesting research on how the proportion of African Americans in classrooms affects the social status of students may have important implications for the proportion of Latinos in classroom. Specifically, Jackson and colleagues (2006) find that the critical mass before members of an ethnic minority group reach parity with whites in social status is more than 50 percent. That is, ratings of the desirability of making friends among white and African American peers favor white children until the representation of African Americans in the classroom is more than 67 percent. Moreover, parity is not reached based on perceptions of leadership qualities until African Americans are the overwhelming majority of classrooms (i.e., between 67 and 100 percent). The important point is that as Latino immigrants move into Anglo neighborhoods, the improvements in access to social capital are likely to come at some cost in social status for Latino children. Conversely, as the potential for parity for Latino children in social status increases, the access to social capital available in predominantly Anglo neighborhoods decreases.

Intergroup Contact between Latino Immigrants and Other Minority Groups

Many Latino immigrants move into neighborhoods that have long-standing Latino populations. Although, technically, immigrant and non-immigrant Latino subgroups are not ethnically different, intergroup conflict does occur between these two subgroups. In these situations, conflict can arise between the immigrant and nonimmigrant Latino groups. The conflict often focuses on the nonimmigrant Latinos attempting to distances themselves from the stereotypes associated with Latino immigrants (e.g., cultural values, speaking English with a Spanish accent), while the immigrant Latinos are unable to distance themselves from these same stereotypes; instead, immigrants pride themselves in their adherence to traditional Latino culture.

In a seminal publication, Matute-Bianchi (1991) eloquently describes social conflict among five Mexican subgroups found in a California high school: recent Mexican immigrants, Mexican-oriented, Mexican American, Chicano, and Cholo. She describes how these five subgroups are engaged in struggles and conflicts. Social identity theorists predict that special hostility may be manifest against ingroup members who violate group norms or in other ways compromise the groups' interests. Nonimmigrant Latinos who attempt to minimize the way in which they confirm negative stereotypes may feel that immigrants undermine these efforts and reinforce negative stereotypes. Analogously, immigrant Latinos may feel as if nonimmigrants fail to pride themselves in their cultural heritage—the derogatory term Cholo is applied to Mexican-heritage teenagers who have forgotten or lost their cultural heritage (Reyes 2006).

A neglected area of research has been the intergroup contact between African American and Latino populations. The research in chapter 1 suggests, however, that Latino groups are coming into increasing contact with African Americans. It is important to understand that despite both groups having a stigmatized minority status, Latinos moving into a neighborhood that has African American residents do not necessarily voluntarily engage in racial integration. Instead, residence in integrated black-Latino neighborhoods likely occurs out of economic necessity, rather than desire to live in racially mixed neighborhood.

There is relatively little research investigating black-Latino relationships. It is important to note that racial attitudes prevalent in Latin

America influence Latino immigrants. Mindiola, Niemann, and Rodriguez (2001) find that many Latino immigrant families bring negative stereotypes toward African Americans with them to the United States. Mindiola and colleagues find broad stereotypes of African Americans by Latinos, with the stereotyping stronger among Latino immigrants. They also find that African Americans hold stereotypes of Latinos groups. African Americans may support and further negative attitudes toward immigration rights and perceive competition between themselves and Latinos for resources (Watkins, Larson, and Sullivan 2007).

In general, neither Latinos nor African Americans are immune to the ethnic and racial stereotypes prevalent in the United States. Where Latinos and African Americans are competing for limited resources, stereotyping is seen as more likely (Mindiola et al. 2001). Nonetheless, when Anglos are present in contexts in which African Americans and Latinos interact, Latinos tend to prefer African Americans over Anglos as social partners (see Hamm 1998). Latinos prefer members of their own group as social partners over African Americans, particularly if there is a relatively large number of same-ethnic peers (Bellmore et al. 2007).

Conclusions

Neighborhood composition has important social and psychological implications for Latino children. When families move into predominantly Anglo neighborhoods, they can access social capital, and Latino children often have positive views toward their new Anglo peers. The reception they receive from their Anglo peers, however, may not be particularly welcoming. If Latinos have only token representation in Anglo neighborhoods and schools, Anglo peers are prone to maintaining ethnic bias. As Latinos increase in representation, they may feel more accepted by some of their Anglo peers, but they may be confronted with white flight from the neighborhood and diminished access to social capital. Even when Latinos have attained parity in numerical representation, they often hold lower social status relative to Anglo peers, which sets the stage for less-than-desirable intergroup conditions. Latinos also show some bias toward African American peers and even manifest intraethnic conflict between immigrants and nonimmigrant groups. Hence, demographic trends hold critical social and psychological implications for Latinos.

NOTE

1. U.S. Department of Justice, "Hate Crime Statistics," http://www.fbi.gov/ucr/hc2007/index.html.

REFERENCES

Allport, Gordon W. 1954. *The Nature of Prejudice*. Oxford: Addison-Wesley.

Banaji, Mahzarin R., Andrew S. Baron, Yarrow Dunham, and Kristina Olson. 2008. "The Development of Intergroup Social Cognition: Early Emergence, Implicit Nature, and Sensitivity to Group Status." In *Intergroup Attitudes and Relations in Childhood through Adulthood*, edited by Sheri R. Levy and Melanie Killen (197–236). New York: Oxford University Press.

Bellmore, Amy D., Adrienne Nishina, Melissa R. Witkow, Sandra Graham, and Jaana Juvonen. 2007. "The Influence of Classroom Ethnic Composition on Same- and Other-Ethnicity Peer Nominations in Middle School." *Social Development* 16(4): 720–40.

Bohon, Stephanie A., Heather Macpherson, and Jorge H. Atiles. 2005. "Educational Barriers for New Latinos in Georgia." *Journal of Latinos and Education* 4(1): 43–58.

Crowder, Kyle. 2000. "The Racial Context of White Mobility: An Individual-Level Assessment of the White Flight Hypothesis." *Social Science Research* 29(2): 223–57.

Hamm, Jill V. 1998. "Negotiating the Maze: Adolescents' Cross-Ethnic Peer Relations in Ethnically Diverse Schools." In *Making Friends: The Influences of Culture and Development*, edited by Luanna H. Meyer, Hyun-Sook Park, Marquita Grenot-Scheyer, Ilene S. Schwartz, and Beth Harry (243–61). Baltimore, MD: Paul H. Brookes Publishing.

Jackson, Melissa Faye, Joan M. Barth, Nicole Powell, and John E. Lochman. 2006. "Classroom Contextual Effects of Race on Children's Peer Nominations." *Child Development* 77(5): 1325–37.

Marx, Sherry. 2008. " 'Not Blending In': Latino Students in a Predominantly White School." *Hispanic Journal of Behavioral Sciences* 30(1): 69–88.

Matute-Bianchi, Maria E. 1991. "Situational Ethnicity and Patterns of School Performance among Immigrants and Non-Immigrant Mexican-Descent Students." In *Minority Status and Schooling: A Comparative Study of Immigrant and Involuntary Minorities*, edited by Margaret Gibson and John U. Ogbu (205–47). New York: Garland.

Mindiola, Tatcho, Yolanda Flores Niemann, and Néstor Rodriguez. 2001. *Black-Brown Relations and Stereotypes*. Austin: University of Texas Press.

Nesdale, Drew. 2008. "Peer Group Rejection and Children's Intergroup Prejudice." In *Intergroup Attitudes and Relations in Childhood through Adulthood*, edited by Sheri R. Levy and Melanie Killen (32–46). New York: Oxford University Press.

Ogbu, John U. 1994. "From Cultural Differences to Differences in Cultural Frame of Reference." In *Cross-Cultural Roots of Minority Child Development*, edited by Rodney R. Cocking and Patricia M. Greenfield (365–91). Hillsdale, NJ: Lawrence Erlbaum.

Pettigrew, Thomas F. 1998. "Intergroup Contact Theory." *Annual Review of Psychology* 49:65–85.

Reyes, Reynaldo III. 2006. "Cholo to 'Me': From Peripherality to Practicing Student Success for a Chicano Former Gang Member." *Urban Review* 38(2): 165–86.

South, Scott J., Kyle Crowder, and Jeremy Pais. 2008. "Inter-Neighborhood Migration and Spatial Assimilation in a Multi-Ethnic World: Comparing Latinos, Blacks, and Anglos." *Social Forces* 87(1): 415–43.

Tropp, Linda R., and Mary A. Prenovost. 2008. "Role of Intergroup Contact in Predicting Children's Interethnic Attitudes: Evidence from Meta-Analytic and Field Studies." In *Intergroup Attitudes and Relations in Childhood through Adulthood,* edited by Sheri R. Levy and Melanie Killen (236–48). New York: Oxford University Press.

Watkins, Natasha D., Reed W. Larson, and Patrick J. Sullivan. 2007. "Bridging Intergroup Difference in a Community Youth Program." *American Behavioral Scientist* 51(3): 380–402.

PART II
Structure and Process in Hispanic Immigrant Families and Their Implications for the Development of Children and Youth

5

Structure and Process in Mexican-Origin Families and Their Implications for Youth Development

Kimberly A. Updegraff and Adriana J. Umaña-Taylor

Hispanics are the largest and most rapidly growing ethnic minority group in the United States.[1] In fact, the United States is second only to Mexico in the size of its Hispanic population. In the United States, most of the Hispanic population is of Mexican origin: 66 percent, or 28.3 million individuals. In addition, the largest proportion of immigrant children is born to Mexican immigrants: 39 percent of all children born to immigrants in the United States are from Mexico, with no other single country representing more than 4 percent of immigrant children (Hernandez, Denton, and Macartney 2007). These trends underscore the importance of scientific investigations aimed at understanding the role of culture in youth development in this significant and growing segment of the U.S. population. This chapter examines the role of family members' cultural experiences in youth well-being in Mexican-origin families.

Adapting to a new culture and navigating between two different cultural contexts daily is a significant task for immigrant children and their parents. A true understanding of Mexican-origin families in the United States requires careful attention to the ways that their cultural backgrounds and experiences are linked to individual and family well-being and to how cultural processes interact with individual, developmental, family, and broader contextual factors. For researchers interested in studying immigrant families, the conceptualization and measurement of cultural factors has elicited criticism from scholars in a number of disciplines (e.g., Cabassa

2003; Hunt, Schneider, and Comer 2004; Rogler, Cortes, and Malgady 1991) and has posed significant challenges in efforts to understand the complex ways that culture shapes youth well-being.

Slightly over a decade ago, developmental scholars noted several limitations in research on ethnic minority youth (García Coll et al. 1996; McLoyd 1998). First, most studies relied on ethnic comparative research designs to investigate differences across groups in youth adjustment (García Coll et al. 1996; McLoyd 1998). In this body of work, ethnic minority families facing disadvantage (e.g., unemployment, poverty) typically were compared to more economically advantaged majority families. The focus on risk and pathology among ethnic minority youth and the confound between social class and cultural group membership in most ethnic comparative studies resulted in a developmental literature that emphasized deficits in ethnic minority children. Second, research on immigrant children was guided by theoretical frameworks (e.g., acculturative stress models) that directed researchers' attention to the negative implications of cultural adaptation processes (García Coll and Magnuson 1997; Gonzales et al. 2002; Laosa 1997). Finally, scholars note the lack of longitudinal designs (Fuligni 2001; Gonzales et al. 2002) and the failure of studies of cultural adaptation to incorporate developmental perspectives (García Coll and Magnuson 1997; Laosa 1997). The result has been a striking absence of literature on the role of culture in Hispanic youths' *normative* development, on sources of variability within cultural groups, and on how cultural and developmental factors interact. By complementing insights from ethnic-comparative research with ethnic-homogeneous designs, we are able to learn about the specific experiences and values that are pertinent to subgroups of ethnic minority families and to investigate how diversity within a particular group in cultural factors gives rise to variations in individual and family well-being.

Recent data suggest, however, that research on ethnic minority populations in child and adolescent development remains limited. In her review of articles published in *Child Development* and *Journal of Research on Adolescence* in 2007 and the first half of 2008, Umaña-Taylor (2009) notes that not a single study in *Child Development* and only two studies in *Journal of Research on Adolescence* (3.8 percent of empirical articles during this period) used ethnic-homogeneous research designs to study Hispanic youth. Hagen, Nelson, and Velissaris (2004) find that 5 to 10 percent of articles in two developmental journals focused on Hispanics, and fewer than 2 percent of those articles examined normative developmental processes. Longitudinal studies of ethnic minority youth that examine the connections between developing cultural orientations and experiences and well-being also are rare (Fuligni 2001; Gonzales et al. 2002; Hirschman 1997).

In this chapter, we provide examples from an ongoing study, the Juntos ("Together"): Families Raising Successful Teens Project, designed to investigate normative developmental and family processes in an ethnic-homogeneous sample of Mexican-origin families with adolescent siblings. Although we present cross-sectional data, our *within-family* design including siblings in early and middle/late adolescence allows us to consider potential interactions between culture and developmental factors.

Capturing the Role of Culture in Youths' Lives

Theoretical perspectives highlight the bidimensional nature of cultural adaptation processes and specify two independent and concurrent mechanisms (Bernal and Knight 1993; Berry 2003; Gonzales et al. 2002; Knight et al. forthcoming). *Acculturation* is the process of acquiring knowledge, behaviors, and values associated with the mainstream culture. In contrast, *enculturation* is the process of acquiring knowledge, behaviors, and values associated with the ethnic culture. In studying these two processes, researchers have moved away from conceptualizing cultural adaptation as falling along a single continuum to a view that individuals can adhere strongly to the ethnic culture and engage in traditional cultural practices while at the same time participating fully in the majority culture (Berry 2003; Gonzales et al. 2002; Knight et al. 1993; Phinney 1990). Although there is strong consensus that culture is multidimensional and multifaceted, empirical work continues to be limited by a focus on single dimensions and use of proxy measures such as language preference or generation status (Cabassa 2003; Gonzales et al. 2002; Rogler et al. 1991). Understanding the interrelations between different dimensions of culture (e.g., cultural background, cultural values, ethnic identity) is an important step in understanding the complex ways that culture is linked to youth well-being (Fuligni 2001; Gonzales et al. 2002).

Data from the Juntos Project offer the opportunity to examine how dimensions of culture that are typically used (e.g., national origin, nativity, generation status) are linked to dimensions of culture that are less often studied such as cultural values and involvement in culturally linked daily activities. A unique aspect of the Juntos Project is that, in addition to assessing global involvement in the ethnic and host culture (Cuéllar, Arnold, and González 1995), we use daily diary methods to capture time spent in different ethnic contexts and with different companions. Daily activities are the building blocks of development (Bronfenbrenner 1979; Weisner 1989); they provide opportunities for developing social ties, learning skills, and forming an identity (Bronfenbrenner 1979; Larson and Verma 1999; Silbereisen, Noack, and Eyferth 1986). We examine youths' involvement in culturally linked daily activities, including time spent with family (nuclear and extended kin), time spent in Mexican, non-Mexican, and ethnically heterogeneous peer contexts, and time spent in gender-typed activities (e.g., household tasks).

Between- and Within-Family Variations in Culture: Mothers, Fathers, Adolescents, and Siblings

A number of theoretical models highlight the importance of examining youths' cultural backgrounds and experiences within the broader contexts of their daily lives. Ecological models of human development direct our attention to interactions between individual and contextual factors in shaping interpersonal relationship processes and youth well-being and development and highlight the connections between youths' everyday contexts (such as family, peers, schools) and larger contextual forces (such as parents' work, culture; see Bronfenbrenner and Crouter 1983). Family systems theorists recognize the interdependence of families and highlight the importance of examining the connections among individual family members and their different relationships within families (Cox and Paley 2003).

We draw on these perspectives to argue for the importance of extending current research beyond a focus on how individual cultural factors (e.g., language use or preference, nativity, acculturation status) are linked to youth well-being to examine youths' cultural experiences *in combination with* those of other family members. Although some consideration has been given to the connections between parents' (particularly mothers') and adolescents' cultural experiences, exploring adolescents' cultural experiences in the context of their fathers' or siblings' is virtually nonexistent. Further, to our knowledge, no published studies have examined the connections among the cultural experiences and adjustment of Mexican-origin mothers, fathers, and multiple children within the same family.

Scholars have argued that discrepancies between parents and adolescents in their cultural behaviors, values, or orientations are important for understanding the experiences of immigrant families (Birman 2006; Portes and Rumbaut 2001; Szapocznik and Kurtines 1980, 1993). These ideas are consistent with a person-environment fit perspective (Eccles et al. 1993; Lerner and Lerner 1983), which highlights the importance of congruence across different facets of youths' lives. The sometimes conflicting values and traditions of the two cultures in which Hispanic youth spend their time (García Coll et al. 1996; Szapocznik and Kurtines 1993) mean that issues of congruence may be especially pertinent to understanding youth psychosocial functioning. In their work with Cuban Americans, Szapocznik and Kurtines (1980, 1993) propose that problems may arise when youth adapt to U.S. culture at a faster rate than their parents, resulting in strained parent-child relationships and, in turn, youth involvement in maladaptive behavior.

Birman (2006) reviews research on the implications of parent-child discrepancies in immigrant families for the quality of the parent-child relationship and conclude that the findings are inconsistent. She highlights three common approaches to studying parent-child acculturation gaps: (1) comparing immigrant- and native-born parent-youth relationships and inferring acculturation gaps, (2) measuring *perceived* dyadic discrepancies with information from a single family member, and (3) measuring *actual* discrepancies by incorporating information from multiple family members. Comparisons of actual versus perceived discrepancies in a study of Hispanic refugee parents and adolescents reveal that very few family members (5 percent) accurately estimate the other dyad members' acculturation status (Merali 2002). This pattern underscores the value of gathering data from multiple family members to assess discrepancies in their cultural experiences.

Despite the substantial interest in discrepancies between Hispanic parents and youth in their cultural adaptation, empirical work on this topic remains relatively rare (Gonzales et al. 2002). Notably uncommon are studies that measure discrepancies using data from multiple family members and that move beyond the mother-adolescent dyad to consider discrepancies between fathers and their children and between sisters and brothers. Further, empirical research on parent-child discrepancies most often focuses on a single dimension of culture or measure culture along a single continuum (Birman 2006; Gonzales et al. 2002). Using data from the Juntos Project, we extend prior work by using mothers', fathers', and adolescent siblings' ratings of involvement in Mexican and

Anglo culture using the Acculturation Rating Scale for Mexican Americans II, or ARSMA-II (Cuéllar et al. 1995), to assess the family cultural context. In particular, we examine the *constellation* of family members' involvement in Mexican and Anglo culture to identify families that are similar versus different across family members in their profiles.

Interactions between Individual Characteristics, Culture, and Context in Family Dynamics and Youth Well-Being

The family cultural context is one of many important settings in Mexican-origin youths' everyday lives. Ecologically oriented researchers underscore the importance of examining how individual characteristics and family and other social contexts *interact* to shape youth well-being. We consider both adolescents' and siblings' gender as potential factors that may interact with the family cultural context to explain youth development and well-being.

Gender is an organizing feature of family life in Mexican culture (Cauce and Domenech-Rodriguez 2002; Valenzuela 1999) and may have implications for the potentially different socialization experiences of girls versus boys, especially sisters versus brothers. Research on gender socialization processes in European American families (see McHale, Crouter, and Whiteman 2003 for a review), and more recently in Mexican American families (McHale et al. 2005), highlights the significant role of children's and their siblings' gender (or sibling dyad constellation) in shaping interpersonal relationships, roles, and activities. McHale and Crouter (1996) find that the combination of firstborn and secondborn siblings' gender in European American families is linked to paternal involvement, with fathers the most involved with boys in older brother-younger sister pairs. Using longitudinal data from the same sample of European American families, Crouter, Manke, and McHale (1995) find that when young adolescents have opposite-sex siblings, they spend increased time in dyadic activities with their same-sex parent during the transition to adolescence. Young adolescents' patterns of involvement in household tasks also are linked to adolescents' and their siblings' gender, with girls spending more time doing housework when they have brothers (Crouter et al. 2001). Together, these findings highlight the potential role of adolescents' and siblings' gender characteristics in shaping family dynamics and youth well-being. The current study allows us to take this analysis one step further by understanding whether the family cultural context has different implications for the well-being of girls versus boys and adolescents with sisters versus brothers.

The Juntos ("Together") Families Raising Successful Teens Project

The Juntos Project was designed to examine within-group variability in Mexican-origin families raising adolescent siblings in a southwestern metropolitan area of the United States. Participants were 246 Mexican-origin families recruited from public and Catholic schools in and around the greater Phoenix area in 2002 and 2003. Eligible families included those with a seventh grader and an older sibling (less than 21 years of age) living in the home with a biological mother and biological or long-term adoptive father (i.e., greater than 10 years). In addition, fathers had to be employed at least 20 hours a week for pay. Although only mothers were required to be of Mexican origin, 93 percent of fathers also reported Mexican ancestry.

Our sampling criteria and our focus on a local population mean that our sample was not designed to be representative of Mexican-origin families in general. Instead, the overall study goals directed our attention to two-parent families (so we could examine the role of fathers) with two siblings in a circumscribed age range (so we could compare the experiences of older and younger adolescents). Paternal employment was a criterion given our interest in the larger contexts within which family dynamics emerge and research documenting the role of work in defining parents' roles in Mexican-origin families (Baca Zinn 1980; Coltrane and Valdez 1993). These considerations directed our focus on a representative local sample with wide variability in socioeconomic status. Our design contrasts with those of other studies of families that often rely on one or two family members to provide information about family dynamics. Our approach highlights the perspectives of four family members while treating the family as the analytic unit; indeed, this study of 246 families could be conceptualized as an analysis of the experiences of 984 individuals.

To recruit families, letters and brochures describing the study (in both English and Spanish) were sent to families, and follow-up telephone calls were made by bilingual staff to determine eligibility and interest in participation. Families' names were obtained from junior high schools in five school districts and from five parochial schools. Schools were selected to represent a range of socioeconomic situations, with the proportion of students receiving free/reduced-price lunch varying from 8 to 82 percent across schools. Schools also differed in the percentage of students who were Hispanic (range of 6 to 63 percent for public junior high schools). Letters were sent to 1,851 families with a Hispanic seventh grader who was not learning disabled. For 438 families (24 percent), the contact information was incorrect and repeated attempts to find updated information through school personnel or public listings were unsuccessful. An additional 42 families (2.4 percent) moved between the initial screening and final recruitment contact, and 148 (8 percent) refused to be screened for eligibility. There were 421 eligible families (23 percent of the initial rosters and 32 percent of those we were able to contact and screen for eligibility). Of those 421 who were eligible, 284 (or 67 percent) agreed to participate, 95 (23 percent) refused, and we were unable to re-contact the remaining 42 families (10 percent). Interviews were completed by 246 families. Those who agreed but did not participate in the final sample ($n = 38$) were families that we were unable to locate to schedule the home interview, that were unwilling to participate when the interview team arrived at their home, or that were not home for repeated interview attempts.

Families represented a range of education and income levels, from poverty to upper class. The percentage of families whose incomes met the federal poverty level was 18.3 percent, a figure similar to the 18.6 percent of two-parent Mexican American families that met the federal poverty level in the county from which the sample was drawn (U.S. Census Bureau 2000). Median family income was $40,000. Mothers and fathers had completed an average of 10 years of education ($M = 10.34$; $SD = 3.74$ for mothers, and $M = 9.88$; $SD = 4.37$ for fathers). Mean ages were 39.0 years for mothers and 41.7 years for fathers. Most parents had been born outside the United States (71 percent of mothers and 69 percent of fathers); this subset of parents had lived in the United States an average of 12.4 ($SD = 8.9$) and 15.2 ($SD = 8.9$) years, for mothers and fathers, respectively. About two-thirds of the interviews with parents were conducted in Spanish. The total number of children living in the household averaged 3.39 ($SD = 1.20$; range = 2–8). Older siblings were 50 percent female ($n = 123$) and 15.70 ($SD = 1.6$) years old on average. Further, 47 percent had been born outside the United States, and 82 percent were interviewed in English. The younger siblings were 51 percent female ($n = 125$) and 12.8 ($SD = .58$)

years old on average. Of these youth, 38 percent had been born outside the United States, and 83 percent were interviewed in English.

This project involved intensive data collection with four family members, including home interviews conducted separately with mothers, fathers, and older and younger siblings. Family members also participated in seven nightly phone calls designed to gather information about youths' daily activities and companions, and parents' division of household tasks and child care. Families' addresses also were linked to census data using geographic information systems. A strength of this study is the detailed information about the family relationships, work experiences, cultural experiences, daily activities, and individual well-being of four family members. We capitalize on these strengths to provide a nuanced examination of how four family members' cultural involvement is linked to cultural values and behaviors and youth well-being.

Family as a Cultural Context

Our goal was to explore the potential differences across families in *within-family* patterns of cultural involvement using a pattern analytic approach (Cairns, Bergman, and Kagan 1998; Coatsworth et al. 2005; Magnusson 1998). Pattern analytic approaches are ideal for capturing profiles or patterns across a set of constructs or variables. Pattern analytic analyses offer different information than variable-oriented approaches by capturing patterns across a range of variables in a coherent or holistic way.

Our approach, measuring family members' patterns of cultural involvement using the four members' ratings of involvement in Mexican and Anglo culture (ARSMA-II; see Cuéllar et al. 1995), has both strengths and limitations. An advantage is that we move beyond what are typically referred to as "proxy" measures (e.g., nativity) and use a measure that assesses involvement in both the host and ethnic culture (e.g., language use, affiliations, ethnic label identification, food preferences). We also created profiles that represent the four family members' experiences, extending prior research by considering mothers, fathers, and two siblings in each family. This approach recognizes that each family member's cultural involvement must be understood within the broader context of other family members' cultural involvement. Consistent with the idea that cultural adaptation is multidimensional and multifaceted (Berry 2003; Cabassa 2003; Cuéllar et al. 1995), we also explore how these family profiles are related to other indices of culture, including background characteristics (e.g., years living in the United States, language use, nativity), cultural values (familism, traditional gender role attitudes), and culturally linked behaviors (e.g., time spent in different ethnic contexts, time spent with family, time spent doing housework). A limitation of our approach is that the ARSMA-II has a significant portion of language-based items and therefore is strongly related to language fluency. In addition, for parents in our sample, negative correlations between Mexican and Anglo orientation were strong suggesting that parents' cultural involvement fell along a single continuum.

Pattern Analytic Analyses

Using a cluster analytic approach (Bergman and El-Khouri 2002), we identified three different family-level patterns of cultural involvement. We used both older and younger siblings' ratings of involvement in Mexican and Anglo culture separately and the difference score of parents' Anglo involvement minus their Mexican involvement. As noted, the difference score was used for parents because of the high negative correlations between the Mexican and Anglo subscales for both mothers and fathers, suggesting that parents in this sample are either highly involved in Mexican culture or Anglo culture but not both.[2] The cluster solution was determined using both the explained error sums of squares to select the solution prior to a large decrease and the merging coefficients to identify a solution before a large increase (Aldenderfer and Blashfield 1984). Both indices suggested that the three-group solution was optimal. The three groups are depicted in figure 5.1 and labeled Mexican-oriented families, Anglo-oriented families, and Mexican/dual-involvement families.

Mexican-Oriented Group. In the Mexican-oriented cluster ($n = 47$), all four family members reported high levels of involvement in Mexican culture, youth reported low levels of Anglo involvement (as measured independently), and parents' low levels of Anglo involvement were reflected in the difference scores based on the ARSMA-II. By almost all cultural background characteristics we examined (see table 5.1), parents in this group had very strong ties to their Mexican backgrounds. All mothers and fathers were born in Mexico and spoke Spanish as their primary language. Parents in this group lived in the United States for the shortest time among parents born in Mexico. Older and younger siblings also had strong ties to Mexican culture. Siblings were more likely to be

Figure 5.1. Family Members' Mexican and Anglo Orientation by Family Cultural Group

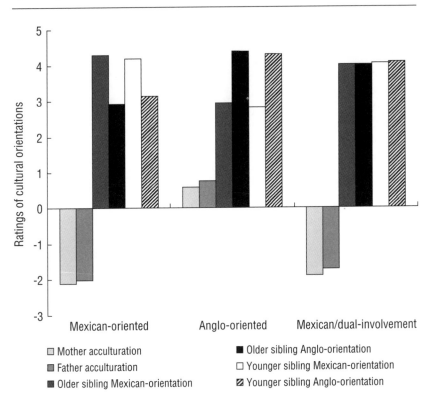

born in Mexico than the United States and were mostly first generation; parents, grandparents, and siblings were born in Mexico in more than 80 percent of these families. Siblings' language usage was more differentiated than parents', however, with 36 percent of older siblings and 40 percent of younger siblings speaking English as their primary language, and the remainder of siblings preferring Spanish. In this group, parents' economic and educational resources were more limited than those of parents in the Anglo-oriented group. Using census data, we found that families in the Mexican-oriented group had higher percentages of Hispanics and families in poverty in their neighborhoods than families in the Anglo-oriented group. The characteristics of these families are consistent with those of families residing in immigrant neighborhoods in established areas of migration in the United States (see Alba et al., chapter 1, this volume).

Table 5.1. Cultural, Family, and Neighborhood Characteristics by Family Cultural Group

	Mexican-oriented (n = 47)	Anglo-oriented (n = 83)	Mexican/dual-involvement (n = 114)
Cultural Background			
Percent Spanish speaking			
Mothers	100	11	93
Fathers	100	10	97
Older siblings	64	1	10
Younger siblings	60	0	9
Percent born in Mexico			
Mothers	100	21	96
Fathers	100	16	97
Older siblings	87	8	57
Younger siblings	83	6	47
Parents' years living in United States[a]	7.68 (5.92)	26.20 (11.43)	14.92 (6.48)
Education and Income			
Parents' education[b] (years)	8.44 (3.6)	12.88 (4.2)	8.92 (3.5)
Annual family income[b] ($)	30,100 (15,409)	77,936 (40,504)	53,550 (45,384)
Neighborhood Census Data			
Percent Latinos[b]	41.13	22.96	36.07
Percent of families in poverty[b]	12.31	6.11	11.00

Source: The Juntos ("Together") Families Raising Successful Teens Project.

a. Mexican-oriented, Anglo-oriented, and Mexican/dual-involvement families are significantly different from one another at $p < .05$.

b. Anglo-oriented families differ from both Mexican-oriented and Mexican/dual-involvement families at $p < .05$.

Anglo-Oriented Group. Parents and siblings in Anglo-oriented families ($n = 83$) reported high levels of involvement in U.S. culture based on the ARSMA-II and cultural background characteristics (table 5.1). The majority of older siblings, younger siblings, mothers, and fathers were born in the United States. Further, almost all siblings spoke primarily English, and the vast majority of parents did as well. Slightly more than three-quarters of siblings (77 percent) were from third- or fourth-generation families. The Mexico-born parents in this group had lived in the United

States significantly longer than the Mexico-born parents in the other two groups. These parents also described significantly more socioeconomic resources than parents in the other two groups, and they lived in neighborhoods with the lowest percentages of families in poverty and of Hispanic descent. Families in this group are similar in their profiles to families in non-immigrant neighborhoods in established areas of migration (chapter 1, this volume).

Mexican/Dual-Involvement Group. Families in this final group ($n=114$) included parents with high levels of Mexican cultural ties and siblings who were involved in both Mexican and Anglo culture based on their ARSMA-II ratings and cultural background indicators (see table 5.1). Most parents in this group were born in Mexico and spoke primarily Spanish. Parents reported living in the United States an average of 15 years, differing significantly from the other two groups in their length of time in the United States. Older siblings in these families were more likely to have been born in Mexico whereas younger siblings were more likely to have been born in the United States. Both siblings spoke English most often. Unlike sibling pairs in the other two groups, siblings in this group differed significantly from one another in their generation status with older siblings more likely to be classified as first-generation immigrants (60 percent) and younger siblings more likely to be classified as second-generation immigrants (56 percent). These families may be most commonly described as families where parents and older siblings were born in Mexico and migrated to the United States before the birth of younger siblings. Parents in this group did not differ significantly from parents in the Mexican-oriented group in their educational and economic resources or neighborhood characteristics. Thus, like Mexican-oriented families, these families also likely represent those residing in immigrant neighborhoods in established areas of migration (chapter 1, this volume).

Links between Family Cultural Groups and Culturally Oriented Values and Behaviors

Cultural adaptation frameworks highlight contact with and interaction between individuals from different cultural contexts as stimuli for changes in values and behaviors associated with both the ethnic and host culture (Berry 1980, 2003; Marín and Gamba 2003; Redfield, Linton, and

Herskovits 1936). Drawing on these ideas, indicators of involvement in a cultural setting, such as number of years living in a culture, generation status, and use of the host or ethnic language, are thought to represent opportunities that may lead to changes in individuals' cultural values and behaviors. An important, but rarely tested, assumption in acculturation research is that measures of cultural background or involvement reflect differences in family members' cultural values, attitudes, and behaviors (Gonzales et al. 2002; Marín and Gamba 2003). Yet, empirical evidence linking proxy measures of cultural involvement to cultural values and behaviors is limited. In the findings we describe now, we examine how these different family profiles are linked to family members' cultural values, including familism values and traditional gender role attitudes, and behaviors, such as time spent with nuclear and extended family members (i.e., family time), time spent with siblings, parents' division of paid work and household and childrearing responsibilities, and siblings' involvement in housework.

Family-Oriented Values and Behaviors

Familism, a key feature of Hispanic culture in general and Mexican American culture specifically (Marín and Marín 1991), is a multidimensional construct that includes both values and behaviors (e.g., Baca Zinn 1994; Sabogal et al. 1987). Familistic values emphasize family support, solidarity, and obligations, and familistic behaviors focus on involvement with nuclear and extended family. Anecdotal writings on the importance of familism for Mexican Americans have been substantiated by a growing body of empirical work. Sabogal and colleagues (1987), for example, find that Hispanic adults, including those of Mexican origin, endorse higher values of family support, obligations to family members, and using family members as referents than do individuals of European American descent. Focusing on an ethnically diverse sample of adolescents, Fuligni, Tseng, and Lam (1999) document that Mexican American adolescents (as well as those from other Hispanic backgrounds and Asian descent) place significantly greater value on family assistance, support, and future obligation than European American youth. Within-group analyses of Hispanics who differ in generation status reveal that values regarding family support do not differ across generations but that values regarding family obligations and the use of families as referents are stronger for Hispanic adults who are foreign born (Sabogal et al. 1987).

We explored family members' ratings of their familism values, using the 16-item familism scale of the Mexican American Cultural Values Scale (Knight et al. forthcoming), and time spent with nuclear and extended family and with siblings, using daily diary data, as indices of familism behaviors. We conducted mixed-model analyses of variance[3] with cluster group and older and younger siblings' gender as between-groups factors and family member as the within-groups factor. This approach allowed us to test whether differences across family cultural groups in family members' values and behaviors were similar or different for mothers, fathers, and adolescent siblings.

Several important patterns emerged in these analyses. First, highlighting the value of considering how the family cultural context may be *differentially* linked to family members' values, we found that the connections between family cultural group and family members' familism values differed for parents versus older siblings versus younger siblings. Both mothers and fathers reported significantly lower levels of familism values in the Anglo group than in the other two groups, supporting ideas that high levels of Mexican cultural involvement and strong ties to Mexico (the vast majority of these parents were born in Mexico and spoke only Spanish) are linked to a strong emphasis on family-oriented values (figure 5.2). Such a pattern is consistent with other data linking involvement in Mexican culture to strong family values (Sabogal et al. 1987).

The findings for siblings suggest a more complex pattern, however, and underscore a second theme: the possibility of interactions between developmental and cultural factors. The pattern for younger siblings, who are in early adolescence, revealed stronger familism values for siblings who were involved in *both* Mexican and Anglo culture (i.e., youth in the Mexican/dual-involvement group) than for youth who were described as Mexican-oriented. In early adolescence, when identity development and the formation of a value system is an emerging developmental task (Erikson 1968; Marcia 1994), youths' involvement in both cultures may lead to their recognition of the importance of culturally linked values, such as familism, and thus stronger adherence to these values than for youth whose involvement is primarily in Mexican culture. Youth who are primarily involved in Mexican culture, in contrast, may have fewer opportunities to compare the cultural value systems of the two different cultures. It is also possible that younger siblings in the Mexican/dual-involvement families, who have stronger connections to Anglo culture than older siblings, mothers, and fathers, may have strong family-oriented

Figure 5.2. Family Members' Reports of Familism Values
by Family Cultural Group

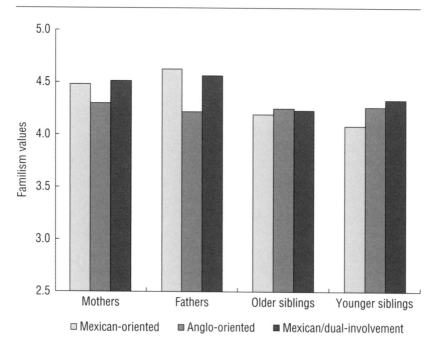

values because they assume a potentially important role in the family as
the eldest sibling who is knowledgeable about U.S. culture. That is, their
greater involvement in Anglo culture relative to older siblings and parents
means that they may negotiate educational, health care, and community
settings for other family members (e.g., language brokering). Although
socioeconomic resources also are highlighted in how strongly individuals rely on family members for support (Roosa et al. 2002), it is notable
that youth in the Mexican/dual-involvement and Mexican-oriented groups
did not differ in families' economic resources, educational levels, or indicators of neighborhood poverty (based on census data).

Older siblings reported similar levels of familism values, regardless of
the family cultural context. In the period of adolescence when youth are
beginning to form their own ideas about family formation and make
decisions about their futures (Markus and Wurf 1987), they may strongly
emphasize their family-oriented values. That is, the influence of develop-

mental processes on youths' family-oriented values may override cultural factors in this developmental period. A strength of our ongoing longitudinal study is that we will have data from younger siblings over time to assess whether the same pattern emerges for them during middle and late adolescence. Comparing siblings when they are the same age using data from different points in time will allow us to assess whether the sibling differences noted here can be attributed to family role (older versus younger) or developmental (early versus middle/late adolescence) status.

We also examined the time that siblings spent with nuclear and extended family members as an indicator of familism behaviors. Siblings reported on their daily activities and companions during seven nightly phone calls. We aggregated the data across these calls (five weekday evenings and two weekend evenings) to investigate the time siblings spent in the company of their family and extended kin. Our findings revealed that older siblings' gender in combination with the family cultural context were linked to the time that both older and younger siblings spent with family.

The pattern for families with older sisters suggested that, regardless of the family cultural context, older sisters and their younger siblings spent similar amounts of time with family (an average of 25 hours over seven days; see figure 5.3). The pattern for families with older brothers, in contrast, revealed that sibling pairs spent more time with family when parents also had strong ties to Mexican culture (i.e., the Mexican-oriented and Mexican/dual-involvement groups) and less time with family when the family cultural context was Anglo-oriented (also in figure 5.3). Older brothers may be granted greater autonomy and be required to spend less time with family members, an opportunity that extends to their younger siblings, when parents have strong ties to majority culture. This is consistent with the notion that Hispanic parents are more likely to socialize their sons, compared to their daughters, to explore their extra-familial environments (Raffaelli and Ontai 2004). For girls, the time with family may be emphasized equally across all family cultural groups and thus the expectations for older sisters to spend time with family extend to their younger siblings as well. The consistency of older sisters' and their younger siblings' time with family across all three family cultural contexts may reflect that daughters are protected more than sons and assume more roles and responsibilities in the family (Azmitia and Brown 2002; Valenzuela 1999).

We also examined the time youth spent in the company of siblings as a reflection of familism behaviors. Differences emerged across the

Figure 5.3. Siblings' Average Time Spent with Nuclear and Extended Family

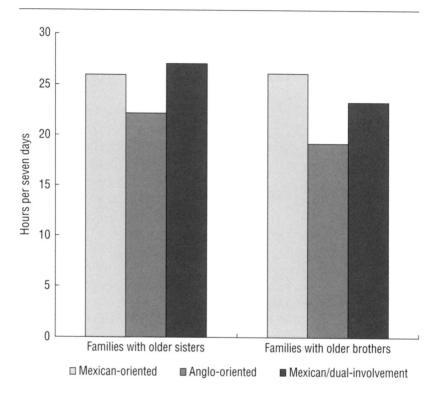

three family cultural contexts; older and younger siblings in the Mexican/ dual-involvement group spent more time in the company of siblings than siblings in the Anglo group, and the pattern was more pronounced for younger than for older siblings (figure 5.4). In the Mexican/dual-involvement group, siblings differed from parents in their involvement in Anglo culture, and older and younger siblings differed from one another in their cultural background characteristics. In this family cultural group, siblings (especially younger siblings) may be particularly important informants and sources of support for experiences outside the family, and their complementary cultural knowledge may serve as a foundation for shared time with siblings. It is also possible that younger siblings' involvement is encouraged by other siblings in the family to help maintain younger siblings' connections to family life.

Figure 5.4. Older and Younger Siblings' Time Spent with Siblings by Family Cultural Group

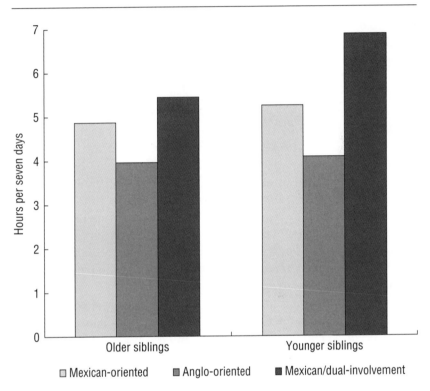

Gender Role Attitudes and Behaviors. Although early characterizations of Mexican American families as rigidly traditional are inaccurate (Madsen 1961, 1964), there is some evidence that mothers assume greater caregiving responsibilities than do fathers and that parents assign more responsibilities to and are more protective of daughters and grant more autonomy and privileges to sons (e.g., Azmitia and Brown 2002; Cauce and Domenech-Rodriguez 2002; McHale et al. 2005; Valenzuela 1999). Evidence suggests that cultural beliefs and values play a role in shaping gender dynamics in Mexican American families but that social and economic conditions also are vital in understanding the gendered division of family roles and responsibilities (Baca Zinn 1980, 1982; Coltrane and Valdez 1993; Williams 1990).

Grounded in ecological and sociocultural models of development (Bronfenbrenner and Crouter 1983; McAdoo 1993; Spencer 1995), we expected that families defined by different patterns of cultural involvement may also differ in parents' gender-typed values and behaviors. Existing evidence led us to expect that families with strong ties to Mexican culture may hold more traditional values and exhibit a more traditional division of labor than families with stronger ties to U.S. mainstream culture (e.g., Leaper and Valin 1996). Connections between the family context and adolescents' gender-typed qualities may be more complex, however (see Crouter et al. 2007). We anticipated that the family cultural context, gender socialization processes, and developmental factors may play a role in adolescents' sex-typed values and behaviors.

Beginning with family members' traditional gender role attitudes, we found that the patterns for parents, older siblings, and younger siblings differed across the three family cultural contexts. Overall, for all four family members, those in the Anglo-oriented group reported less traditional values (reflected by lower scores) than those in the Mexican-oriented and Mexican/dual-involvement groups (figure 5.5). This pattern is consistent with other empirical work highlighting connections between ties to Mexican culture and traditional gender roles (Coltrane and Valdez 1993; Golding 1990; Leaper and Valin 1996). The connections between the Anglo-oriented family cultural context and less traditional gender role values were strongest for parents and least pronounced for younger siblings. That younger siblings were more similar across the three family cultural contexts than were other family members may suggest that developmental processes are working in combination with cultural factors. Younger siblings in this sample are transitioning to adolescence, a developmental period when intensified pressures to behave in gender-typed ways are significant (Hill and Lynch 1983), suggesting that developmental pressures to adopt gender-typed attitudes may be influencing all adolescents and may be slightly stronger for those in family contexts where parents adhere to more traditional values (i.e., Mexican-oriented and Mexican/dual-involvement groups). Longitudinal data to document interactions between developmental and cultural processes over time represent an important direction of study.

Moving beyond family members' gender-typed attitudes, we also examined gender-typed *behaviors*, including parents' division of paid work, housework, and childrearing responsibilities, and siblings' involvement in housework. Maternal employment patterns differed significantly across

Figure 5.5. Family Members' Gender Role Attitudes by Family Cultural Group

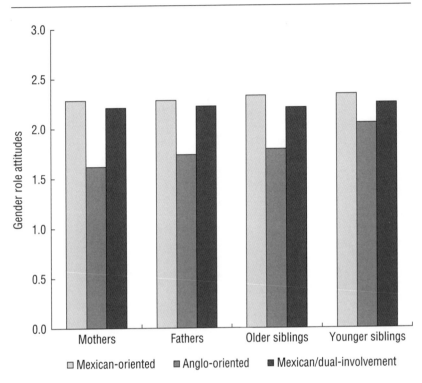

the three groups. Mothers were more likely to be employed (82 percent) than not employed in Anglo-oriented families, equally likely to be employed (49 percent) versus not (51 percent) in Mexican-oriented families, and slightly more likely to be employed (61 percent) than unemployed (39 percent) in Mexican/dual-involvement families. From a feminist perspective, differences between mothers and fathers in their work-related resources are another important indicator of sex-typing in parents' marital roles (Ferree 1990; McHale and Crouter 1992; Updegraff, McHale, and Crouter 1996). Analyses with the 154 dual-earner families revealed that both parents reported more prestigious occupations (based on the National Opinion Research Council; see Nakao and Treas 1994) in the Anglo-oriented group than in the other two groups. In addition, mothers reported more prestigious jobs than did fathers in the Anglo-oriented

Figure 5.6. Mothers' and Fathers' Occupational Prestige in Dual-Earner Families (*n* = 154) by Family Cultural Group

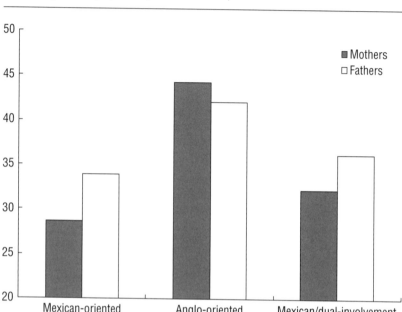

group, with the reverse pattern found in the other two groups (figure 5.6). These findings highlight the significant role of mothers as shared providers in Anglo-oriented families and suggest that gender roles may be negotiated as part of the cultural adaptation process.

Mothers' and fathers' *relative* involvement in housework is represented by a ratio of mothers' involvement divided by mothers' plus fathers' involvement; as such, higher scores indicate that mothers are doing more relative to fathers and lower scores indicate mothers and fathers are relatively more equally involved. We examined parents' relative involvement in all household tasks and in typically feminine household tasks (i.e., tasks completed daily, such as meal preparation, dishes, straightening up, laundry, grocery shopping). We found that parents shared more equally in household tasks in Anglo than in Mexican/dual-involvement families and shared more equally in feminine-typed tasks in Anglo-oriented families than in the other two groups (figure 5.7). The general pattern reveals that the ratio of mothers' and fathers' involvement across the three family cultural context groups ranged from 62 to 71 percent for all house-

Figure 5.7. Ratio of Mother/Father Time Spent in Household Tasks and Feminine Household Tasks by Family Cultural Group

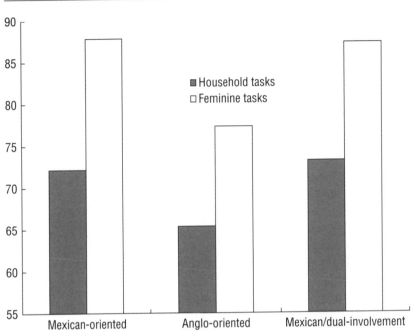

hold tasks and from 75 to 90 percent for traditionally feminine tasks, suggesting that mothers are doing more household tasks and substantially more feminine tasks than fathers in all families.

Another important indicator of parents' gender-typed behavior is their relative involvement with their offspring. Empirical data suggest that mothers in Mexican American families are more involved in child-rearing than are fathers (Azmitia and Brown 2002; Cauce and Domenech-Rodriguez 2002; Valenzuela 1999). We examined the ratio of mothers' and fathers' time spent with adolescent siblings as a function of family cultural group and older and younger sibling gender. Among parents in the Mexican-oriented or Mexican/dual-involvement groups, mothers spent more time with both siblings relative to fathers if the older sibling was a daughter (figure 5.8). A similar pattern was found as a function of younger sibling gender, although only in Mexican-oriented families.

Figure 5.8. Ratio of Mother/Father Time Spent with Target Siblings by Older Sibling Gender and Family Cultural Group

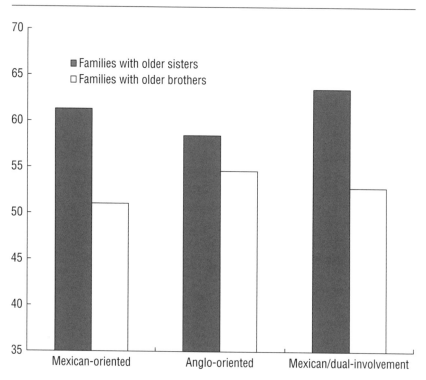

The combination of parents' strong ties to Mexican culture and the presence of a daughter, particularly an older daughter, was linked to mothers' greater involvement relative to fathers' with adolescent siblings.

We also explored the amount of time that older and younger siblings spent doing household tasks overall and feminine-typed tasks as a final indicator of gender-typed behaviors. Because the patterns were similar for involvement in all housework and in feminine-typed tasks and because similar patterns emerged for older and younger siblings' gender as a moderator, we describe only the findings for feminine-typed tasks as a function of older siblings' gender and family cultural group (figure 5.9). When older siblings were girls, they were doing more feminine household tasks in the Mexican-oriented and Mexican/dual-involvement group than in the Anglo group; in addition, younger siblings of older girls also

Figure 5.9. Older and Younger Siblings' Time Spent in Feminine-Typed Household Tasks by Older Sibling Gender and Family Cultural Group

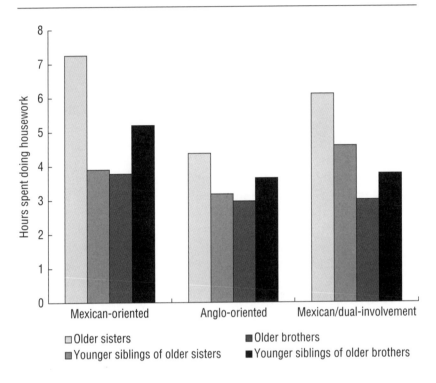

did more feminine household tasks in the Mexican/dual-involvement group than younger siblings in the Anglo-oriented group with older sisters. That is, younger siblings were more involved in housework when they had older sisters and were in a Mexican/dual-involvement family. No differences emerged in younger or older siblings' involvement in household tasks when older siblings were boys in any of the three cultural groups. The consistent pattern that emerged from these findings was that in family cultural contexts where parents had strong ties to Mexican culture and traditional gender roles, being an older sister or the younger sibling of an older sister was associated with more household responsibilities. This pattern of findings is consistent with research in Mexico that also highlights the differential involvement of girls versus boys in housework (Levison, Moe, and Knaul 2001) and in Hispanic immigrant communities in California (Orellana 2001).

Time Spent in Different Ethnic Contexts. In adolescence, youth have more opportunity to explore the world outside the home and have more autonomy in choosing how to spend their time (Brown 1990; Elliott and Feldman 1990). Youths' social networks extend beyond the family to include peers, who are often among the most frequent providers of companionship and support in youths' daily lives (Buhrmester 1992; Larson and Richards 1991). To explore the interconnections between the family cultural context and siblings' involvement in different peer ethnic contexts, we examined older and younger siblings' time spent in three different peer contexts: time spent with Mexican peers, time spent with non-Mexican peers, and time spent in ethnically mixed peer groups (i.e., including both Mexican and non-Mexican peers).

All three family cultural groups differed in the time spent with Mexican peers, with the Mexican-oriented group spending the most time with Mexican peers, the Anglo group spending the least, and the Mexican/ dual-involvement group falling in the middle (figure 5.10). Interestingly, only the Anglo group differed from the other two groups in time spent with non-Mexican peers and in ethnically mixed peer contexts. Thus, Mexican-oriented and Mexican/dual-involvement youth differed from one another in their time spent with Mexican peers but not in their time spent in contexts that provide greater exposure to Anglo culture. With regard to time spent with Mexican peers and child kin, siblings spent more time with Mexican peers when they had older brothers compared with older sisters in the Mexican-oriented group, but no gender differences were found in the other two groups (figure 5.11). In these more traditional families, brothers may be allowed more freedom and time with peers, and this may result in more opportunities for their younger siblings to interact with peers as well (Raffaelli and Ontai 2004).

Connections between Family Cultural Context and Older and Younger Siblings' Adjustment

Our final step was to examine how the family cultural context is linked to youth adjustment. We defined adjustment broadly to include problem behavior (i.e., risky behaviors, depressive symptoms, and sexual intentions) and positive development (e.g., school achievement, educational and occupational aspirations). Further, by focusing on indicators that reflect adaptive as well as problematic adjustment, we move beyond a focus on

Figure 5.10. Siblings' Time in Mexican, Non-Mexican, and Mixed Peer Groups by Family Cultural Group

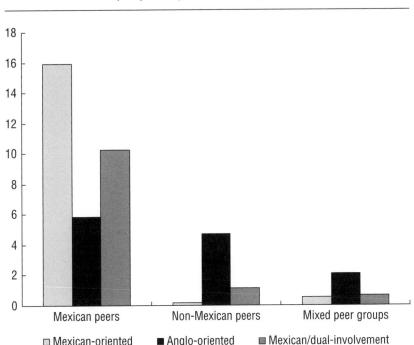

the *negative* implications of cultural adaptation processes to consider "what combination of positive or negative effects will be manifested" (García Coll and Magnuson 1997, 126).

There have been several reviews of research and theory on the links between indices of cultural adaptation and individual adjustment (Gonzales et al. 2002; Hunt et al. 2004; Moyerman and Forman 1992; Rogler et al. 1991), with investigations largely focusing on youths' or parents' cultural adaptation (typically using proxy measures) and rarely examining cultural involvement as a family-level process. Focusing on Hispanic youth, Gonzales and colleagues (2002) conclude that more acculturated Hispanic youth display higher rates of problem behavior, including misconduct and substance use, than their less acculturated peers. Rogler and coauthors (1991) also find positive associations between acculturation and alcohol and substance use and abuse in most studies of Hispanic youth and adults. Associations between cultural-related stressors

Figure 5.11. Siblings' Time with Mexican Peers/Child Kin by Older Sibling Gender and Family Cultural Group

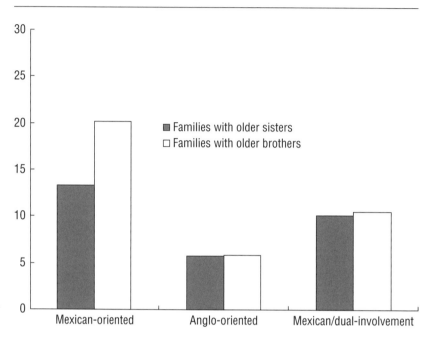

and internalizing symptoms also have been identified (Finch et al. 2001; Romero and Roberts 2003; Szalacha et al. 2003), but links between global indices of cultural adaptation and internalizing symptoms are not consistent (e.g., Gonzales et al. 2002).

We know little about how youths' cultural development may promote positive development (García Coll and Magnuson 1997; Gonzales et al. 2002), although research shows links between culture and educational achievement/attainment in immigrant youth (Fuligni 1997; Fuligni et al. 1999; Gibson and Ogbu 1991; Rumbaut 1997; Suárez-Orozco and Suárez-Orozco 1995). Interest in achievement has risen out of national trends showing, for example, that 61 percent of Mexican immigrants (compared with 31 percent of U.S.-born Mexicans and 11.3 percent of non-Hispanic whites) are high school dropouts (National Center for Educational Statistics 2000). In addition, foreign-born Mexicans are less likely than U.S.-born Mexicans, all other Hispanics, and non-Hispanics to enroll in college or earn associate's or bachelor's degrees. These trends are linked to employment opportunities and earnings: Hispanics are more likely to be in low-skilled employment positions and less likely to hold management and other white-collar positions.[4] Thus, we also consider how the family cultural context is linked to older and younger siblings' school achievement, educational expectations, and occupational aspirations.

Involvement in Risky Behaviors. Cultural group membership combined with older sibling gender was important in siblings' involvement in risky behaviors. In the Mexican/dual-involvement group and at the trend level in the Anglo-oriented group, when older siblings were brothers, *both* siblings were more involved in risky behaviors than when older siblings were sisters (figure 5.12). Examining siblings' affiliations with deviant peers, a construct closely tied to youths' own risky behaviors, we found that both siblings reported spending more time with deviant peers in the Anglo group when older or younger siblings were brothers (see figure 5.13 for older siblings, younger siblings not displayed). These

Figure 5.12. Siblings' Risky Behaviors by Older Sibling Gender and Family Cultural Group

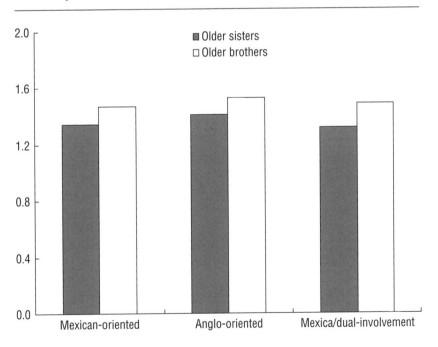

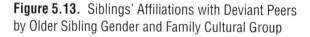

Figure 5.13. Siblings' Affiliations with Deviant Peers by Older Sibling Gender and Family Cultural Group

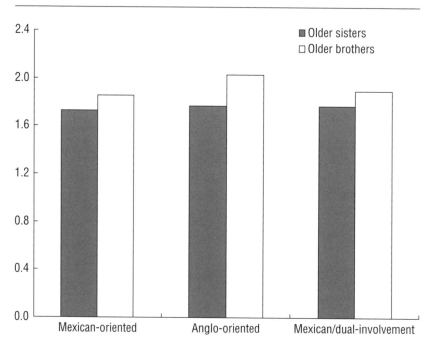

findings highlight how the combination of the family cultural context and having an older brother (who may be a role model or provide opportunities for engagement in risk behaviors) is associated with both siblings' involvement in problem behavior and affiliations with deviant peers. Such patterns are consistent with research documenting the risks for younger siblings of older brothers' involvement in antisocial behaviors (Snyder, Bank, and Burraston 2005) and older siblings as role models and sources of advice regarding peers (Tucker, McHale, and Crouter 2001).

Depressive Symptoms. The connections between youths' cultural background and depressive symptoms have been studied less often than connections between externalizing problems and culture. Again, we found that family cultural context interacted with sibling gender in explaining depressive symptoms. Older sisters in the Mexican-oriented group reported the most depressive symptoms, and older sisters in the Mexican/dual-involvement group reported the least depressive symptoms (figure 5.14);

Figure 5.14. Older Siblings' Depressive Symptoms
by Older Sibling Gender and Family Cultural Group

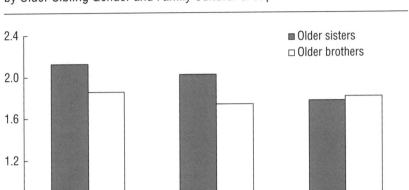

no differences emerged for older boys or for younger siblings as a function
of the family cultural context. Younger siblings, who are just arriving at
the developmental period when depressive symptoms become more
salient (Block and Gjerde 1990; Cicchetti and Toth 1998), may display a
similar pattern over time. The different patterns for older sisters versus
brothers and for older versus younger siblings suggest the possibility of
interactions between culture, gender, and developmental processes.

Sexual Intentions. Hispanic youth are at risk for sexually transmitted
infections and teen pregnancy (Hamilton, Sutton, and Ventura 2003).
Although half of Hispanic high school students reported engaging in sexual intercourse, only 30 percent used a condom during their most recent
sexual activity.[5] A number of studies highlight the role of siblings in youths'
sexual involvement (e.g., East and Jacobson 2001; East and Kiernan 2001;
Rodgers and Rowe 1988; Rucibwa et al. 2003). For example, having an
older sister who is a teen mother is associated with younger sisters' greater
intentions for sex and younger sisters' and brothers' greater likelihood of
engaging in sexual intercourse at an early age (East and Kiernan 2001).

In these analyses, we examined siblings' intentions to engage in sexual activities. A consistent pattern emerged, again with the interaction between family cultural context and sibling gender playing an important role in siblings' sexual intentions. Older brothers in all groups described the highest level of sexual intentions, significantly greater than those of older sisters (figure 5.15). In the Anglo-oriented group, younger siblings of older brothers also reported more sexual intentions than did younger siblings of older sisters, suggesting that the combination of an Anglo-oriented family and an older brother may place younger siblings who are in early adolescence (12 to 13 years old) at greater risk for sexual involvement. Older brothers in Anglo-oriented families may provide opportunities to

Figure 5.15. Older and Younger Siblings' Sexual Intentions by Older Sibling Gender and Family Cultural Group

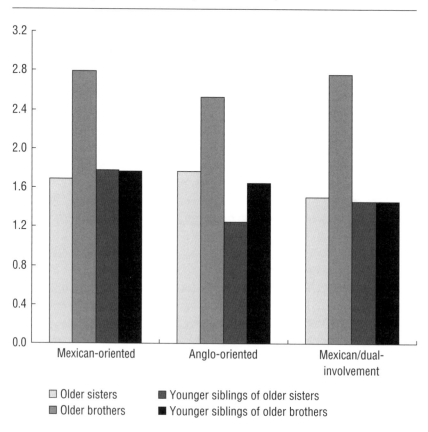

spend time with older peers who are potential partners or serve as role models or sources of encouragement (Snyder et al. 2005).

School Performance, Expectations for Educational Attainment, and Occupational Aspirations. School performance and expectations for attainment in education represent indices of positive development. In the case of siblings' school performance we found that siblings in the Anglo group, on average, reported higher grade point averages (mean = 2.98, standard deviation = .73) than siblings in the Mexican-oriented group (2.32, .80) or the Mexican/dual-involvement group (2.53, .94). Gender of siblings did not play a role in school performance. The advantage that youth have in these Anglo-oriented families, including the English fluency of all four family members and greater educational and economic resources, may place siblings at a distinct advantage in navigating the school environment. This is also consistent with existing work, which suggests that being born in the United States is associated with higher levels of educational attainment among Mexican Americans (Zsembik and Llanes 1996).

Looking at siblings' expectations for their educational attainment, our findings show that older siblings' gender matters for both siblings' expectations for their educational attainment. Siblings in the Anglo group reported high expectations regardless of older siblings' gender, but both siblings in the Mexican/dual-involvement group reported higher expectations when the older sibling was a sister (figure 5.16). A similar but non-significant pattern emerged for Mexican-oriented families. Older sisters may offer a positive role model in their educational expectations, and this may be particularly important in families with strong ties to Mexican culture that also have less socioeconomic resources and knowledge of the U.S. educational system. We did not find that siblings' occupational aspirations differed as a function of the family cultural context.

Conclusions and Future Directions

Understanding the complex role of culture in the lives of immigrant Hispanic children and their families will serve as the foundation for research, intervention, and policy for a substantial and growing proportion of youth in the United States over the next several decades. Although there is strong theoretical consensus among scholars that culture should be viewed as a dynamic and multifaceted construct, and that cultural processes

Figure 5.16. Siblings' Average Expectations for School Attainment by Older Sibling Gender and Family Cultural Group

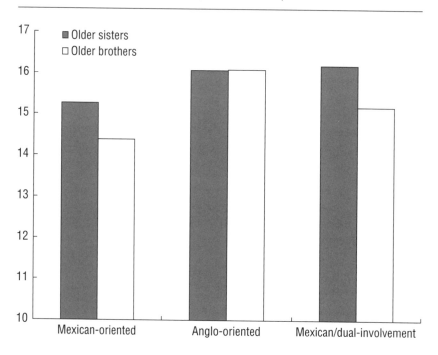

can be best understood in combination with individual, family, and broader contextual factors (García Coll and Magnuson 1997; Gonzales et al. 2002), significant gaps remain between theoretical models and empirical investigations of the role of culture in youth well-being. Addressing one aspect of the complexity in studying culture, we provide examples of how four family members' cultural involvement interact with individual characteristics and family contextual factors in ways that have implications for youth well-being in Mexican-origin families. Using a person-oriented approach (Cairns et al. 1998; Magnusson 1998), we explore *between-* and *within-family* patterns and offer a nuanced picture of how family members' patterns of cultural involvement (as measured by the ARSMA-II; see Cuéllar et al. 1995) are linked to other measures of cultural background and history, culturally linked values and behaviors, and youth well-being.

In this section, we highlight three important themes for future research: family-oriented approaches and patterns of congruence or incongruence; the intersection of gender, culture, and development; and knowledge gained from multiple perspectives on and multiple indicators of culture and youth well-being.

Family-Oriented Approaches: Does Congruence Tell the Whole Story?

The majority of Hispanic youth growing up in the United States reside with their parents, most commonly *both* mothers and fathers, and with their sisters and brothers (Ramirez and de la Cruz 2003).[6] Values attributed to Mexican culture, particularly the strong emphasis on family support, assistance, and obligations, further underscores the central role of family members in this cultural context. A primary contribution of this chapter is the conceptualization of family members' cultural experiences as a *family-level* phenomenon.

Scholars interested in immigrant families have emphasized that a key issue in family-level cultural adaptation is discrepancies between parents and youth (Birman 2006; Portes and Rumbaut 2001; Szapocznik and Kurtines 1980, 1993), particularly when youth acculturate to mainstream society faster than their parents. Discrepancies between mothers and fathers and between siblings also are possible sources of family and individual adjustment problems from a person-environment fit perspective (Eccles et al. 1993; Lerner and Lerner 1983), but these discrepancies have not been a focus of empirical study. Our findings reveal limited support for *incongruence* between parents and youth in their patterns of cultural involvement as conceptualized in this study. In Anglo- and Mexican-oriented family cultural contexts, all four family members reported similar patterns of cultural involvement as measured by the ARSMA-II, nativity, generation status, and language usage.

In Mexican/dual-involvement families, rather than a pattern where parents had strong ties to Mexican culture and youth had strong ties to Anglo culture, we found that parents were involved in Mexican culture and youth were involved in *both* Mexican and Anglo culture. As such, even though these adolescents had high levels of involvement in Anglo culture, it did not come at the expense of their ties to Mexican culture. Such a pattern underscores the value of recognizing that cultural adaptation occurs in reference to both the host and ethnic cultures (Berry 2003; Cabassa 2003; Gonzales et al. 2002).

Potential incongruence in the case of siblings in the Mexican/dual-involvement families was the only evidence of discrepancies among family members in these family cultural contexts. Older and younger siblings in this group were similar in their self-reported involvement in Mexican and Anglo culture (based on the ARSMA-II), but they differed in a number of cultural background indicators. Within-family designs offer an exciting opportunity to explore how differences *within families* in siblings' cultural backgrounds and experiences are linked to different trajectories of cultural adaptation and to investigate the implications for youth well-being and development. Nuanced examinations of discrepancies between family members are essential to provide a more comprehensive understanding of the *family dyads* that may be most likely to experience gaps in cultural adaptation (e.g., mother-adolescent, father-adolescent, adolescent-sibling), the *dimensions* of culture that family members are most likely to diverge on (e.g., behaviors, values, background), the *timing* when discrepancies emerge (e.g., during particular points in the immigration process, during particular developmental periods), and the *contexts* in which discrepancies are most prominent (e.g., when living in particular social contexts, for particular subgroups of Hispanics). Learning about the various conditions under which discrepancies are salient can inform measurement approaches in nationally representative studies. With this type of information, we will be better positioned to understand the implications of congruence and incongruence for youth well-being and family dynamics in Hispanic immigrant families.

The Intersection of Gender, Culture, and Development

Our findings also highlight the significance of *interactions* between individual characteristics, family cultural context, and larger contextual forces in Mexican-origin youths' development and well-being. Some patterns involving older and younger siblings' gender, family cultural context, and developmental status or family role/position are linked to youths' culturally linked values and behaviors and to multiple indices of youth adjustment. Highlighting the possibility of culture by development or family role interactions, we find that the cultural context may play a different role at different points in family members' lives in their culturally linked values. Our cross-sectional snapshot reveals consistent patterns for mothers and fathers with strong ties to Mexican culture and limited socioeconomic resources being associated with traditional gender role attitudes and strong familism values. Families with strong ties to Mexican culture also lived in neighborhoods with profiles similar to immigrant neighborhoods in established areas of migration in the United States as defined by Alba and colleagues (chapter 1, this volume), including a predominant Hispanic population, a substantial percentage of Spanish-speaking families, and limited economic resources compared to nonimmigrant neighborhoods in established areas of migration. Thus, when families have strong ties to Mexican culture and live in neighborhoods that are likely to support their cultural traditions and beliefs, *parents* in middle adulthood describe strong adherence to familism and traditional gender role values.

The pattern for older and younger siblings' gender role attitudes during early and middle/late adolescence suggests that developmental processes in combination with cultural forces are at work. Like parents, older and younger siblings hold less traditional gender role beliefs in Anglo-oriented families versus the other two groups, but findings are less pronounced for older siblings than for parents, and less pronounced still for younger siblings. This pattern may reflect that adolescence, particularly early adolescence, is a period when pressures to adhere to gender-typed ideologies intensify (Hill and Lynch 1983), and thus developmental processes may play a stronger role in early adolescence. Using a within-family design to chart the connections between the development of younger and older siblings' culturally linked values and trajectories of cultural adaptation will offer further insights on the intersection of cultural and developmental processes over time and across different developmental periods.

The role of siblings' gender, particularly *older siblings' gender* for younger siblings, combined with the family cultural context, directs our attention to how siblings may shape family roles and activities as an important direction of future research. When the family cultural context is defined by parents' strong ties to Mexican culture, strong familism values, traditional gender role beliefs, and limited economic and educational resources, older sisters (but not older brothers) *and* their younger siblings are drawn into family life, spending more time with mothers (relative to fathers), completing more daily household chores, and spending less time with peers. Thus, the presence of an older sister in these families has potentially important implications for their own as well as their younger siblings' daily activities and experiences. Understanding the *processes* that explain how older siblings' gender shapes younger siblings' daily activities is an important next step.

The mechanisms underlying the risks associated with the presence of older brothers and the advantages of older sisters for siblings' adjustment is another important future research direction. In family cultural contexts where youth report high levels of involvement in Anglo culture, sibling pairs including older brothers are more involved in risky behaviors. Thus, the combination of families' involvement in U.S. culture and an older brother presents potential risks to both older brothers and their younger siblings. For some indicators of positive development we examined, having an older sister appears advantageous for younger siblings. For siblings in the two groups where parents had strong ties to Mexican culture and more limited economic resources, the presence of an older sister is associated with higher expectations for educational attainment for both siblings than the presence of an older brother. From a social learning perspective, older brothers and sisters may model negative or positive behaviors and encourage their younger siblings. In the case of older brothers, another important mechanism may be providing opportunities for interacting with older (and potentially more deviant) peers and dating partners (Snyder et al. 2005).

Insights from Pattern Analytic Approaches, Multiple Family Members, and Multiple Indicators

Person-oriented approaches offer the opportunity to describe these family cultural contexts by identifying how these different family profiles are linked to other dimensions of family background and culture. We learned the ways that these family cultural contexts are similar versus different in family members' cultural backgrounds and histories, educational and economic resources, cultural values, and culturally linked daily activities and behaviors. By examining the whole pattern we are able to gain a detailed understanding of these family contexts.

Mexican-oriented families can be described as those in which family members have high levels of involvement primarily in Mexican culture, were born in Mexico, have lived in the United States less than 10 years, have limited economic and educational resources, live in neighborhood settings consistent with immigrant neighborhoods in established migration areas (Alba et al., this volume), and have parents who adhere to strong familism values and traditional ideas about gender roles. Knowing about these family cultural contexts in detail can help, for example, interpret the pattern for older sisters in Mexican-oriented families who report high levels of expected educational attainment but also the highest levels of depressive symptoms. The combination of holding high expectations for their future education and being in a family context characterized by traditional gender roles, increased family responsibilities for older sisters, and limited economic and neighborhood resources that can potentially restrict future educational opportunities may, in part, explain the higher levels of depressive symptoms found among older sisters in Mexican-oriented families.

Another strength of a person-oriented approach, in combination with multiple indicators of adjustment, is that we can gain insights about how particular family cultural contexts are linked to a combination of benefits and risks. Youth in the Anglo-oriented group, for example, report the highest levels of school achievement and expectations for their future educational attainment, but older brothers and their younger siblings also are at risk for greater involvement in risky behaviors, sexual activities, and affiliations with deviant peers. Viewing these patterns of adjustment in combination revealed both positive and negative implications—or trade-offs that individuals and families face—in these different family cultural contexts.

Limitations and Future Directions

Four important limitations of this study provide directions for future research. First, our measures of culturally linked values represented those values that are thought to reflect Mexican culture, but we did not have reliable and valid measures of Anglo-oriented values. Developing valid and reliable measures that assess Anglo-oriented cultural values is an important direction for future work. Second, our study was limited in that we used only cross-sectional data. A crucial direction of research on cultural adaptation in immigrant families is longitudinal data from multiple family members to examine interrelations among trajectories of cultural adaptation, and individual and family well-being. Toward this end, we are gathering longitudinal data on these families. Third, our within-family design is naturally confounded in that siblings differ in both their developmental status (early versus middle/late adolescence) and their birth position (older versus younger sibling). Using a cross-sequential design to follow these siblings over time and collecting data when siblings are the same age (at different points in time) will enable us to disentangle potential confounds between development and birth order. Finally, although our sample is not nationally representative, the detailed picture of these families' cultural experiences can provide insights into constructs that are important to measure in large nationally representative studies. Given the findings presented by Alba and colleagues (this volume) demonstrating substantial differences in living conditions and experiences for Latinos living in new destination areas compared with their counterparts living in regions with a long-standing Latino presence, it is important to place the findings of the current study within the context of Latinos living in a large metropolitan area with a long-standing Latino presence. The current findings may differ for Latinos in new destination areas, where common characteristics of the families identified as having a Mexican or Mexican/dual-involvement orientation (e.g., low income status) are not as strongly associated with disadvantage and limited resources as they are in regions with a long-standing Latino presence.

Conclusion

Cultural adaptation occurs within the context of families, which are further embedded in multiple contexts (e.g., work, school, neighborhoods). Although *individuals* go through the process of cultural adaptation, and as social scientists we often study and refer to acculturation and enculturation as processes occurring at an individual level, given the interdependence between family members, each family member's cultural adaptation can be best understood in the context of that of other family members. The current study provides detailed data regarding the intersection of individual, family, and contextual characteristics of Mexican-origin families. This work provides important directions for future research and suggests potential areas for preventive intervention. In particular, findings emphasize the need to consider cultural adaptation as a family-level phenomenon that may be informed not only by cultural adaptation of each individual member, but also work in concert with individual and family characteristics in shaping youth well-being.

NOTES

The authors are grateful to the families and youth who participated in this project, and to the following schools and districts who collaborated: Osborn, Mesa, and Gilbert school districts, Willis Junior High School, Supai and Ingleside middle schools, St. Catherine of Sienna, St. Gregory, St. Francis Xavier, St. Mary-Basha, and St. John Bosco. The authors thank Susan McHale, Ann Crouter, Mark Roosa, Nancy Gonzales, Roger Millsap, Jennifer Kennedy, Melissa Delgado, Sarah Killoren, Shawna Thayer, Lorey Wheeler, Devon Hageman, and Lilly Shanahan for their assistance in conducting this investigation, and Susan McHale for her comments on an earlier draft. They also appreciate the assistance of Lorey Wheeler and Megan Baril in conducting data analyses and the assistance of

Veronica Parra in completing the references for this chapter. Funding was provided by NICHD grant R01HD39666 (Kimberly Updegraff, principal investigator; Ann C. Crouter and Susan M. McHale, co-principal investigators; Mark Roosa, Nancy Gonzales, and Roger Millsap, co-investigators) and the Cowden Fund to the School of Social and Family Dynamics at Arizona State University.

1. U.S. Census Bureau, "Hispanic Heritage Month 2008: Sept. 15–Oct. 15," press release CB08-FF.15, updated September 8, 2008. http://www.census.gov/Press-Release/ www/releases/archives/cb08ff-15.pdf.

2. We also conducted the cluster analyses using mothers' and fathers' Mexican and Anglo orientation scores separately and found that the same groups emerged, with two groups of parents exhibiting strong (and similar) ties to Mexican culture but not Anglo culture and one group of families where parents had strong ties to Anglo culture and not Mexican culture.

3. Family income and older siblings' age (which ranged from 13 to 20) were included as covariates when they predicted the dependent variables. Including these factors as controls did not alter the pattern of findings.

4. U.S. Equal Employment Opportunity Commission, "Table 1. Occupational Employment in Private Industry by Race/Ethnic Group/Sex and by Industry, United States, 1998," *Job Patterns for Minorities and Women in Private Industry,* http://www.eeoc.gov/ stats/jobpat/1998/tables-1.html.

5. National Center for Chronic Disease Prevention and Health Promotion, "Youth Online: Comprehensive Results," http://apps.nccd.cdc.gov/yrbss/CategoryQuestions.asp? Cat=4&desc=Sexual%20Behaviors.

6. See also U.S. Census Bureau, "Hispanic Heritage Month 2008: Sept. 15–Oct. 15."

REFERENCES

Aldenderfer, Mark, and Roger Blashfield. 1984. *Cluster Analysis.* Newbury Park, CA: SAGE Publications.

Azmitia, Margarita, and Jane R. Brown. 2002. "Latino Immigrant Parents' Beliefs about the 'Path of Life' of Their Adolescent Children." In *Latino Children and Families in the United States: Current Research and Future Directions,* edited by Josefina Contreras, Kathryn A. Kerns, and Angela M. Neal-Barnett (77–101). Westport, CT: Praeger.

Baca Zinn, Maxine. 1980. "Employment and Education of Mexican-American Women." *Harvard Educational Review* 50:47–62.

———. 1982. "Chicano Men and Masculinity." *Journal of Ethnic Studies* 10:29–44.

———. 1994. "Adaptation and Continuity in Mexican-Origin Families." In *Minority Families in the United States: A Multicultural Perspective,* edited by Ronald L. Taylor (64–94). Englewood Cliffs, NJ: Prentice Hall.

Bergman, Lars R., and Bassam M. El-Khouri. 2002. Sleipner v2.1. [statistical software] Stockholm University, Stockholm, Sweden.

Bernal, Martha E., and George P. Knight, eds. 1993. *Ethnic Identity: Formation and Transmission among Hispanics and Other Minorities.* Albany: SUNY Press.

Berry, John W. 1980. "Acculturation as Varieties of Adaptation." In *Acculturation: Theory, Models and Some New Findings,* edited by A. M. Padilla (9–25). Boulder, CO: Westview Press.

———. 2003. "Conceptual Approaches to Acculturation." In *Acculturation: Advances in Theory, Measurement, and Applied Research,* edited by Kevin M. Chun, Pamela Balls Organista, and Gerardo Marín (17–37). Washington, DC: American Psychological Association.

Birman, Dina. 2006. "Measurement of the 'Acculturation Gap' in Immigrant Families and Implications for Parent-Child Relationships." In *Acculturation and Parent-Child Relationships: Measurement and Development,* edited by M. Bornstein and L. Cotes (113–34). Hillsdale, NJ: Lawrence Erlbaum Associates.

Block, Jack, and Per F. Gjerde. 1990. "Depressive Symptoms in Late Adolescence: A Longitudinal Perspective on Personality Antecedents." In *Risk and Protective Factors in the Development of Psychopathology,* edited by Jon Rolf, Ann S. Masten, Dante Cicchetti, Keith H. Nuechterlin, and Sheldon Weintraub (334–60). New York: Cambridge University Press.

Bronfenbrenner, Urie. 1979. *The Ecology of Human Development: Experiments by Nature and Design.* Cambridge, MA: Harvard University Press.

Bronfenbrenner, Urie, and Ann C. Crouter. 1983. "The Evolution of Environment Modes in Development Research." In *Handbook of Child Psychology,* vol. 1, edited by Paul Henry Mussen (358–414). New York: John Wiley & Sons.

Brown, B. Bradford. 1990. "Peer Groups and Peer Cultures." In *At the Threshold: The Developing Adolescent,* edited by S. Shirley Feldman and Glen R. Elliot (171–96). Cambridge, MA: Harvard University Press.

Buhrmester, Duane. 1992. "The Developmental Courses of Sibling and Peer Relationships." In *Children's Sibling Relationships: Developmental and Clinical Issues,* edited by Frits Boer and Judy Dunn (19–40). Hillsdale, NJ: Lawrence Erlbaum Associates.

Cabassa, Leopoldo J. 2003. "Measuring Acculturation: Where We Are and Where We Need to Go." *Hispanic Journal of Behavioral Sciences* 25:127–46.

Cairns, Robert B., Lars R. Bergman, and Jerome Kagan, eds. 1998. *Methods and Models for Studying the Individual.* Thousand Oaks, CA: SAGE Publications.

Cauce, Ana Mari, and Melanie Domenech-Rodriguez. 2002. "Latino Families: Myths and Realities." In *Latino Children and Families in the United States,* edited by Josefina Contreras, Kathryn A. Kerns, and Angela M. Neal-Barnett (3–25). Westport, CT: Praeger.

Cicchetti, Dante, and Sheree L. Toth. 1998. "The Development of Depression in Children and Adolescents." *American Psychologist* 53:221–41.

Coatsworth, J. Douglas, Mildred Maldonado-Molina, Hilda Pantin, and Jose Szapocznik. 2005. "A Person-Centered and Ecological Investigation of Acculturation Strategies in Hispanic Immigrant Youth." *Journal of Community Psychology* 33:157–74.

Coltrane, Scott, and Elsa O. Valdez. 1993. "Reluctant Compliance: Work-Family Role Allocation in Dual-Earner Chicano Families." In *Men, Work, and Family,* edited by J. C. Hood (151–75). Newbury Park, CA: SAGE Publications.

Cox, Martha J., and Blair Paley. 2003. "Understanding Families as Systems." *Current Directions in Psychological Science* 12:193–96.

Crouter, Ann C., Beth A. Manke, and Susan M. McHale. 1995. "The Family Context of Gender Intensification in Early Adolescence." *Child Development* 66:317–29.

Crouter, Ann C., Melissa R. Head, Matthew F. Bumpus, and Susan M. McHale. 2001. "Household Chores: Under What Conditions Do Mothers Lean on Daughters?" In *Family Assistance and Obligation during Adolescence, New Directions for Child Development*, edited by Andrew Fuligni (23–41). New Directions in Child Development. San Francisco, CA: Jossey-Bass.

Crouter, Ann C., Shawn D. Whiteman, Susan M. McHale, and D. Wayne Osgood. 2007. "Development of Gender Attitude Traditionality across Middle Childhood and Adolescence." *Child Development* 78:911–26.

Cuéllar, Israel, Bill Arnold, and Genaro González. 1995. "Cognitive Referents of Acculturation: Assessment of Cultural Constructs in Mexican Americans." *Journal of Community Psychology* 23(4): 339–56.

East, Patricia L., and Leanne J. Jacobson. 2001. "The Younger Siblings of Teenage Mothers: A Follow-Up of Their Pregnancy Risk." *Developmental Psychology* 37:254–64.

East, Patricia L., and Elizabeth A. Kiernan. 2001. "Risks among Youths Who Have Multiple Sisters Who Were Adolescent Parents." *Family Planning Perspectives* 33:75–80.

Eccles, Jacquelynne S., Carol Midgley, Allan Wigfield, Christy Miller Buchanan, David Reuman, Constance Flanagan, and Douglas Mac Iver. 1993. "Development during Adolescence: The Impact of Stage-Environment Fit on Young Adolescents' Experiences in Schools and in Families." *American Psychologist* 48:90–101.

Elliot, Glen R., and S. Shirley Feldman. 1990. "Capturing the Adolescent Experience." In *At the Threshold: The Developing Adolescent,* edited by S. Shirley Feldman and Glen R. Elliot (1–13). Cambridge, MA: Harvard University Press.

Erikson, Eric H. 1968. *Identity: Youth and Crisis.* New York: Norton.

Ferree, Myra M. 1990. "Beyond Separate Spheres: Feminism and Family Research." *Journal of Marriage and the Family* 52:866–84.

Finch, Brian K., Robert A. Hummer, Bohdan Kolody, and William A. Vega. 2001. "The Role of Discrimination and Acculturative Stress in the Physical Health of Mexican-Origin Adults." *Hispanic Journal of Behavioral Sciences* 23:399–429.

Fuligni, Andrew J. 1997. "The Academic Achievement of Adolescents from Immigrant Families: The Roles of Family Background, Attitudes, and Behavior." *Child Development* 68:351–63.

———. 2001. "A Comparative Longitudinal Approach to Acculturation among Children from Immigrant Families." *Harvard Educational Review* 71:566–78.

Fuligni, Andrew J., Vivian Tseng, and May Lam. 1999. "Attitudes toward Family Obligations among American Adolescents with Asian, Latin American, and European Backgrounds." *Child Development* 70:1030–44.

García Coll, Cynthia, and Katherine Magnuson. 1997. "The Psychological Experience of Immigration: A Developmental Perspective." In *Immigration and the Family: Research and Policy on U.S. Immigrants,* edited by Alan Booth, Ann C. Crouter, and Nancy Landale (91–131). Mahwah, NJ: Lawrence Erlbaum Associates.

García Coll, Cynthia, Keith Crnic, Gontran Lamberty, Barbara Hanna Waskik, R. Jenkins, H. V. Garcia, and H. P. McAdoo. 1996. "An Integrative Model for the Study of Developmental Competencies in Minority Children." *Child Development* 67:1891–1914.

Gibson, Margaret A., and John U. Ogbu. 1991. *Minority Status and Schooling: A Comparative Study of Immigrant and Involuntary Minorities.* New York: Garland.

Golding, Jacqueline M. 1990. "Division of Household Labor, Strain, and Depressive Symptoms among Mexican Americans and Non-Hispanic Whites." *Psychology of Women Quarterly* 14:103–17.

Gonzales, Nancy A., George P. Knight, Antonio A. Morgan-Lopez, Delia Saenz, and Amalia Sirolli. 2002. "Acculturation and the Mental Health of Latino Youths: An Integration and Critique of the Literature." In *Latino Children and Families in the United States,* edited by Josefina Contreras, Kathryn A. Kerns, and Angela M. Neal-Barnett (45–74). Westport, CT: Praeger.

Hagen, John W., Matthew J. Nelson, and Nick Velissaris. 2004. "Comparison of Research in Two Major Journals on Adolescence." Poster session at the biennial meeting of the Society for Research on Adolescence, Baltimore, March.

Hamilton, Brady E., Paul D. Sutton, and Stephanie J. Ventura. 2003. "Revised Birth and Fertility Rates for the 1990s and New Rates for Hispanic Populations, 2000 and 2001: United States." Updated June 2004. National Vital Statistics Reports Vol. 51, No. 12. Hyattsville, MD: National Center for Health Statistics. http://www.cdc.gov/nchs/data/nvsr/nvsr51/nvsr51_12.pdf.

Hernandez, Donald J., Nancy A. Denton, and Suzanne E. Macartney. 2007. "Family Circumstances of Children in Immigrant Families: Looking to the Future of America." In *Immigrant Families in Contemporary Society,* edited by Jennifer E. Lansford, Kirby Deater-Deckard, and Marc H. Bornstein (9–29). New York: Guilford Press.

Hill, John P., and Mary Ellen Lynch. 1983. "The Intensification of Gender-Related Role Expectations in Early Adolescence." In *Girls at Puberty: Biological and Psychosocial Perspectives,* edited by Jeanne Brooks-Gunn and Anne C. Petersen (201–28). New York: Plenum.

Hirschman, Charles. 1997. "Understanding Family Change across Generations: Problems of Conceptualization and Research Design." In *Immigration and the Family: Research and Policy on U.S. Immigrants,* edited by Alan Booth, Ann C. Crouter, and Nancy Landale (201–04). Mahwah, NJ: Lawrence Erlbaum Associates.

Hunt, Linda M., Suzanne Schneider, and Brendon Comer. 2004. "Should 'Acculturation' Be a Variable in Health Research? A Critical Review of Research on U.S. Hispanics." *Social Science & Medicine* 59:973–86.

Knight, George P., Martha E. Bernal, Camille A. Garza, and Marya K. Cota. 1993. "A Social Cognitive Model of the Development of Ethnic Identity and Ethnic-Based Behaviors." In *Ethnic Identity: Formation and Transmission among Hispanics and Other Minorities,* edited by Martha Bernal and George Knight (213–34). Albany: SUNY Press.

Knight, George P., Nancy A. Gonzales, Delia S. Saenz, Darya D. Bonds, M. Miguelina German, Julieanna Deardorff, Mark W. Roosa, and Kimberly A. Updegraff. Forthcoming. "The Mexican American Cultural Values Scale for Adolescents and Adults." *Journal of Early Adolescence.*

Laosa, Luis M. 1997. "Research Perspectives on Constructs of Change: Intercultural Migration and Developmental Transitions." In *Immigration and the Family: Research and Policy on U.S. Immigrants,* edited by Alan Booth, Ann C. Crouter, and Nancy Landale (133–48). Mahwah, NJ: Lawrence Erlbaum Associates.

Larson, Reed, and Maryse H. Richards. 1991. "Daily Companionship in Late Childhood and Early Adolescence: Changing Developmental Contexts." *Child Development* 62:284–300.

Larson, Reed W., and Suman Verma. 1999. "How Children and Adolescents Spend Time across the World: Work, Play, and Developmental Opportunities." *Psychological Bulletin* 125:701–36.

Leaper, Campbell, and Dena Valin. 1996. "Predictors of Mexican American Mothers' and Fathers' Attitudes toward Gender Equality." *Hispanic Journal of Behavioral Sciences* 18:343–55.

Lerner, Jacqueline V., and Richard M. Lerner. 1983. "Temperament and Adaptation across Life: Theoretical and Empirical Issues." In *Lifespan Development and Behavior,* edited by P. B. Baltes and O. G. Brim, Jr. (197–231). New York: Academic Press.

Levison, Deborah, Karine S. Moe, and Felicia Marie Knaul. 2001. "Youth Education and Work in Mexico." *World Development* 29:167–88.

Madsen, William. 1961. *Society and Health in Lower Rio Grande Valley.* Austin, TX: Hogg Foundation for Mental Health.

———. 1964. "Value Conflicts and Folk Psychiatry in South Texas." In *Magic, Faith, and Healing,* edited by A. Kiev (420–40). New York: Free Press.

Magnusson, David. 1998. "The Logic and Implications of a Person-Oriented Approach." In *Methods and Models for Studying the Individual,* edited by Robert B. Cairns, Lars R. Bergman, and Jerome Kagan (33–64). Thousand Oaks, CA: SAGE Publications.

Marcia, James E. 1994. "The Empirical Study of Ego Identity." In *Identity and Development: An Interdisciplinary Approach,* 4th ed., edited by Harke A. Bosma, Tobi L. Graafsma, Harold D. Grotevant, and David J. De Levita (281–321). Belmont, CA: Wadsworth.

Marín, Gerardo, and Raymond J. Gamba. 2003. "Acculturation and Changes in Cultural Values." In *Acculturation: Advances in Theory, Measurement, and Applied Research,* edited by Kevin M. Chun, Pamela Balls Organista, and Gerardo Marín (83–93). Washington, DC: American Psychological Association.

Marín, Gerardo, and Barbara Vanoss Marín. 1991. *Research with Hispanic Populations.* Newbury Park, CA: SAGE Publications.

Markus, Hazel J., and Elissa Wurf. 1987. "The Dynamic Self-Concept: A Social Psychological Perspective." *Annual Review of Psychology* 38:299–331.

McAdoo, Harriet P. 1993. *Family Diversity: Strength in Diversity.* Newbury Park, CA: SAGE Publications.

McHale, Susan M., and Ann C. Crouter. 1992. "You Can't Always Get What You Want: Incongruence between Sex-Role Attitudes and Family Work Roles and Its Implications for Marriage." *Journal of Marriage and the Family* 54:537–47.

———. 1996. "The Family Contexts of Sibling Relationships. In *Sibling Relationships: Their Causes and Consequences,* edited by Gene Brody (173–96). Norwood, NJ: Ablex.

McHale, Susan M., Ann C. Crouter, and Shawn D. Whiteman. 2003. "The Family Contexts of Gender Development in Childhood and Adolescence." *Social Development* 12: 125–48.

McHale, Susan M., Kimberly A. Updegraff, Lilly K. Shanahan, Ann C. Crouter, and Sarah E. Killoren. 2005. "Siblings' Differential Treatment in Mexican American Families." *Journal of Marriage and the Family* 67:1259–74.

McLoyd, Vonnie C. 1998. "Changing Demographics in the American Population: Implications for Research on Minority Children and Adolescents." In *Studying Minority Adolescents: Conceptual, Methodological, and Theoretical Issues,* edited by Vonnie C. McLoyd and Lawrence Steinberg (3–28). Mahwah, NJ: Lawrence Erlbaum Associates.

Merali, Noorfarah. 2002. "Perceived versus Actual Parent-Adolescent Assimilation Disparity among Hispanic Refugee Families." *International Journal for the Advancement of Counseling* 24:57–68.

Moyerman, David R., and Bruce D. Forman. 1992. "Acculturation and Adjustment: A Meta-Analytic Study." *Hispanic Journal of Behavioral Sciences* 14:163–200.

Nakao, Keiko, and Judith Treas. 1994. "Updating Occupational Prestige and Socioeconomic Scores: How the New Measures Measure Up." *Sociological Methodology* 24:1–72.

National Center for Education Statistics. 2000. "Educational Attainment of Hispanic 25–29-Year-Old High School Graduates, by Citizenship Status." Washington, DC: U.S. Department of Education.

Orellana, Marjorie Faulstich. 2001. "The Work Kids Do: Mexican and Central American Immigrant Children's Contributions to Households and Schools in California." *Harvard Educational Review* 71:366–89.

Phinney, Jean S. 1990. "Ethnic Identity in Adolescents and Adults: Review of Research." *Psychological Bulletin* 108:499–514.

Portes, Alejandro, and Rubén G. Rumbaut. 2001. *The Story of the Immigrant Second Generation: Legacies.* Los Angeles: University of California Press.

Raffaelli, Marcela, and Lenna L. Ontai. 2004. "Gender Socialization in Latino/a Families: Results from Two Retrospective Studies." *Sex Roles* 50:287–99.

Ramirez, Roberto R., and G. Patricia de la Cruz. 2003. "The Hispanic Population in the United States: March 2002." Current Population Report P20-545. Washington, DC: U.S. Census Bureau. http://www.census.gov/prod/2003pubs/p20-545.pdf.

Redfield, Robert, Ralph Linton, and Melville J. Herskovits. 1936. "Memorandum for the Study of Acculturation." *American Anthropologist* 38:149–52.

Rodgers, Joseph L., and David C. Rowe. 1988. "Influence of Siblings on Adolescent Sexual Behavior." *Developmental Psychology* 24:722–28.

Rogler, Lloyd H., Dharma E. Cortes, and R. G. Malgady. 1991. "Acculturation and Mental Health Status among Hispanics." *American Psychologist* 46:585–97.

Romero, Andrea J., and Robert E. Roberts. 2003. "Stress within a Bicultural Context for Adolescents of Mexican Descent." *Cultural Diversity and Ethnic Minority Psychology* 9:171–84.

Roosa, Mark W., Antonio A. Morgan-Lopez, Willa K. Cree, and Michele M. Specter. 2002. "Ethnic Culture, Poverty, and Context: Sources of Influence on Latino Families and Children." In *Latino Children and Families in the United States: Current Research and Future Directions,* edited by Josefina Contreras, Kathryn A. Kerns, and Angela M. Neal-Barnett (27–44). Westport, CT: Praeger.

Rucibwa, Naphtal Kaberege, Naomi Modeste, Susan Montgomery, and Curtis A. Fox. 2003. "Exploring Family Factors and Sexual Behaviors in a Group of Black and Hispanic Adolescent Males." *American Journal of Health Behaviors* 27:63–74.

Rumbaut, Rubén G. 1997. "Assimilation and Its Discontents: Between Rhetoric and Reality." *International Migration Review* 31:923–60.

Sabogal, Fabio, Gerardo Marín, Regina Otero-Sabogal, Barbara Vanoss Marín, and Eliseo J. Perez-Stable. 1987. "Hispanic Familism and Acculturation: What Changes and What Doesn't?" *Hispanic Journal of Behavioral Sciences* 9:397–412.

Silbereisen, Rainer K., Peter Noack, and Klaus Eyferth. 1986. "Place for Development." In *Development as Action in Context: Problem Behavior and Normal Youth Development*, edited by Rainer K. Silbereisen, Klaus Eyferth, and Georg Rudinger (87–107). Heidelberg, NY: Springer.

Snyder, Jim, Lew Bank, and Bert Burraston. 2005. "The Consequences of Antisocial Behavior in Older Male Siblings for Younger Brothers and Sisters." *Journal of Family Psychology* 19:643–53.

Spencer, Margaret B. 1995. "Old Issues and New Theorizing about African American Youth: A Phenomenological Variant of Ecological Systems Theory." In *Black Youth: Perspectives on Their Status in the United States*, edited by Ronald L. Taylor (37–70). Westport, CT: Praeger.

Suárez-Orozco, Carola, and Marcelo M. Suárez-Orozco. 1995. *Transformations: Immigration, Family Life, and Achievement Motivation among Latino Adolescents.* Palo Alto, CA: Stanford University Press.

Szalacha, Laura A., Sumru Erkut, Cynthia García Coll, Odette Alarcón, Jacqueline P. Fields, and Ineke Ceder. 2003. "Discrimination and Puerto Rican Children's and Adolescents' Mental Health." *Cultural Diversity and Ethnic Minority Psychology* 8:141–55.

Szapocznik, Jose, and William Kurtines. 1980. "Acculturation, Biculturalism, and Adjustment among Cuban Americans." In *Acculturation: Theory, Models, and Some New Findings,* edited by A. Padilla (139–59). Boulder, CO: Westview Press.

———. 1993. "Family Psychology and Cultural Diversity: Opportunities of Theory, Research, and Application." *American Psychologist* 48:400–407.

Tucker, Corinna J., Susan M. McHale, and Ann C. Crouter. 2001. "Conditions of Sibling Support in Adolescence." *Journal of Family Psychology* 15:254–71.

Umaña-Taylor, Adriana. 2009. "Research with Latino Early Adolescents: Strengths, Challenges, and Directions for Future Research." *Journal of Early Adolescence* 29:5–15.

Updegraff, Kimberly A., Susan M. McHale, and Ann C. Crouter. 1996. "Gender Roles in Marriage: What Do They Mean for Girls' and Boys' School Achievement?" *Journal of Youth and Adolescence* 25:73–88.

U.S. Census Bureau. Population Division. 2000. "Projections of the Total Resident Population by 5-Year Age Groups, Race, and Hispanic Origin with Special Age Categories: Middle Series, 2001 to 2005." Washington, DC: U.S. Census Bureau. http://www.census.gov/population/projections/nation/summary/np-t4-b.pdf.

Weisner, Thomas S. 1989. "Cultural and Universal Aspects of Social Support for Children: Evidence from the Abaluyia of Kenya." In *Children's Social Networks and Social Supports,* edited by Deborah Belle (70–90). New York: John Wiley & Sons.

Williams, Norma, 1990. *The Mexican American Family: Tradition and Change.* Dix Hills, NY: General Hall.

Valenzuela, Abel, Jr. 1999. "Gender Roles and Settlement Activities among Children and Their Immigrant Families." *American Behavioral Scientist* 42:720–42.

Zsembik, Barbara A., and Daniel Llanes. 1996. "Generational Differences in Educational Attainment among Mexican Americans." *Social Science Quarterly* 77:363–74.

6

Structure and Acculturation

Explaining Outcomes for Children in Mexican American Families

Jennifer Van Hook

I mmigration scholars from different disciplines approach the topic of immigration for different reasons and use different theoretical perspectives, methods, and data, so it is perhaps unsurprising that interdisciplinary research occurs so rarely. In disciplines such as child development, the primary focus is on how the child develops within his or her immediate environment (i.e., the family, schools, peers); accordingly, great efforts are made to measure children's outcomes and the characteristics of these environments in extraordinary detail. Many sociologists (and especially demographers), on the other hand, tend to focus on the broader contexts (neighborhoods, nations and states, racial groups, and time periods) within which groups live; accordingly, great efforts are made to portray the characteristics of various populations and the broader social and economic contexts accurately through randomized sampling methods. Given these relative strengths, I have identified two areas in which fruitful interdisciplinary exchange could occur between sociology and family studies or child development.

The first involves the measurement of key concepts. Here, family studies and child development scholars have made significant strides toward developing good measures of acculturation, and sociologists could benefit from these efforts through collaborative work. Acculturation is a central concept within sociology, dating back to the Chicago school's work on immigrants of the early 20th century. Alba and Nee (2003) conceptualize acculturation as a process involving the decline of ethnic distinctiveness along cultural dimensions—in essence, as the fading or shifting of boundaries that separate "outsiders" from "insiders." Some examples of acculturation would include declines in the importance of ethnicity for the selection of friends or marriage partners, or shifts in values from those that emphasize family obligations to those favoring individual choice. Acculturation as a concept has captured the imagination of the general public as well. It is often viewed favorably (or even as a requirement for successful integration of immigrants) by the general public, perhaps because people tend to feel uneasy with diversity in their communities (Putnam 2007). Yet, sociologists have been slow to incorporate direct measures of acculturation (as opposed to economic or linguistic integration) into their studies.

In-depth studies on acculturation such as those presented by Updegraff and Umaña-Taylor (chapter 5, this volume) push research on immigrants forward through significant innovations in measurement. Directly measuring acculturation through intensive study of multiple family members represents a tremendous improvement over studies that infer acculturation based on such proxies as English language use or the residual effects of nativity and duration of U.S. residence after controlling for other factors. Research that does this reveals complications and nuances in acculturation. For example, John Berry and his colleagues (2006) find that children who maintain social ties and identities with their own ethnic group but also are able to integrate with the host society are better adjusted than those who are integrated within the host society but have not maintained ethnic ties. The major contributions of Updegraff and Umaña-Taylor's work are, first, that levels of acculturation are not uniform within families or among siblings, and second, that acculturation may not have uniform associations with children's outcomes. The findings concerning the positive effects of having an older sister or the negative effects of having an older brother are particularly interesting and provide strong evidence that acculturation needs to be conceptualized as a complex family process. The results presented here ought to be viewed as preliminary because they do not control for possible confounding factors (an issue I will return to shortly) nor do they test for statistical significance. Nevertheless, the data collected by this research project and others like it will help researchers peer within families to develop more nuanced understandings of acculturation and its effects on children.

Demographers and other social scientists who work with population-level data could benefit from these efforts because they help identify fruitful areas for further research and inform how to interpret generational patterns in outcomes among children of immigrants. In addition, these studies help identify the factors most highly correlated with latent constructs such as acculturation. Nationally representative samples almost never include such rich measures of acculturation as were collected in this study—it would be impractical to do so with large samples. But smaller studies such as these could be used to identify a smaller set of items that correlate strongly with acculturation that could then be used in larger surveys. For example, Updegraff and Umaña-Taylor reduce their multiple indicators of acculturation to a single categorical variable that classifies families into one of three groups. Perhaps these families could be similarly classified using common demographic indicators of acculturation such as the ethnic and nativity composition of the parents in the household, nativity, duration of U.S. residence, Spanish language use, English proficiency, naturalization status, and residential segregation.

The second potential area of interdisciplinary exchange involves the wider context. Here, sociological research on the circumstances surrounding immigration and settlement suggests that acculturation or "enculturation" (i.e., maintaining ties with origin culture) is correlated and may even constitute a response to broader structural circumstances of immigrants rather than deriving solely from cultures imported from countries of origin. Family studies and child development scholarship may become enriched by incorporating these ideas into its studies and research designs.

The major idea here is that it is important to consider the sources of cultural differences among groups. Although the origins of cultural differences are left unstated in Updegraff and Umaña-Taylor's chapter, the underlying implication of the acculturation theoretical framework is that cultural differences between immigrants and natives arise from cultural differences between immigrants' source countries—in this case, Mexico—and the United States. Immigrants bring cultural scripts and repertoires with them when they arrive, and these scripts and repertoires in turn influence behaviors and attitudes in the United States. Acculturation occurs when these scripts and repertoires fade and are eventually replaced because of contact with the host society.

There are several limitations to this approach. One is the oft-made assumption that cultural orientations in sending countries are traditional and unchanging, even though many immigrants appear to be American-ized even before migrating. A second is that the intense focus on accul-turation potentially overemphasizes the role of culture and ignores the structural circumstances that shape immigrants' behaviors and attitudes. This is particularly relevant for Updegraff and Umaña-Taylor's study because their results do not control for these structural circumstances. As argued by proponents of segmented assimilation theory, immigrant assimilation pathways depend on the structure of opportunity that immi-grants and their children encounter (Portes and Zhou 1993). Accultur-ation is therefore altered by factors such as racism, anti-immigrant sentiment, residential segregation in impoverished neighborhoods and schools, and a bifurcated labor market.

Of crucial importance for Mexican immigrants are the limitations placed on them because of their undocumented status. Among Mexicans in the country less than five years, an estimated 85 percent are unautho-rized. In addition, nearly one in three children of immigrant parents (and half of all foreign-born children) have at least one unauthorized parent (Passel 2006; Passel, Van Hook, and Bean 2004). Although research on the effects of undocumented status on children of immigrants is cur-rently limited by the lack of appropriate data, it is easy to imagine that the risks and uncertainties associated with living under cover from U.S. officials would impinge on all aspects of life, including employment opportunities, incentives to make long-term plans or investments, inter-actions with public officials and professionals (including teachers and health care workers), and bonds with trusted friends and family members.

Immigrants may thus respond to migration by acting and thinking uniquely, sometimes in ways that suggest strong adherence to family members and the subordination of individual needs. Because undocu-mented status is also correlated with less acculturation, these strong bonds to family may be erroneously attributed to less acculturation (and by implication, to cultural vestiges from immigrants' countries of origin). In other words, the association between acculturation and family-related behaviors and values may be overestimated in analyses that fail to take into account legal status or that fail to make comparisons with nonim-migrants in sending countries.

Research I conducted with Jennifer Glick (Van Hook and Glick 2007) on the living arrangements of Mexican immigrants demonstrates this point. Prior research on Hispanic living arrangements has shown that the tendency to live with other Hispanics is higher for recently arrived immigrants than white natives and declines with longer U.S. residence, even after controlling for socioeconomic status and demographic and health characteristics (Angel and Tienda 1982; Blank 1998; Blank and Torrecilha 1998; Burr and Mutchler 1993; Kamo 2000). Results such as these have been interpreted as evidence of acculturation and a break with the cultural patterns from the country of origin. However, as Blank points out (1998), this line of reasoning assumes that the levels of co-residence among recent immigrants are similar to those from the country of origin, often without direct comparing to these sending countries. Although many immigrants come from less developed countries, these countries are undergoing demographic transitions in mortality, fertility, and family structure. For example, fertility rates in Mexico have been dropping rapidly since the 1970s. Fertility in Mexico is now lower than among Mexican immigrant women living in the United States. It would be hazardous to make assumptions about immigrants' cultural origins given the rapid social changes occurring in their countries of origin.

Further, this focus on adaptation over time in the United States often ignores the possibility that immigrants' family behaviors may be directly affected by the challenges of migration itself. International migration may be associated with extended family coresidence because immigrants encounter additional challenges beyond those faced by nonimmigrants of similar life course stage and socioeconomic status. In the face of these challenges, culturally enforced norms favoring extended family coresidence may become accentuated beyond what is normative in immigrants' country of origin.

To test this idea, Jennifer Glick and I used 2000 Census data from Mexico and the United States to compare the prevalence and age patterns of various types of extended family and nonkin living arrangements among Mexican-origin immigrants and nonimmigrants on both sides of the U.S.-Mexico border. We found that newly arrived immigrants to the United States display unique patterns in the composition and stability of their households relative to nonimmigrants in both Mexico and the United States. For example, Mexican immigrants to the United States are more likely to live in extended family or nonkin households than Mexicans in Mexico, the 1.5 generation (immigrants who arrived when they were younger than 12), and U.S.-born Mexican Americans (figure 6.1). Recently arrived Mexican immigrants with less than five years of experience in the United States are particularly likely to live with extended family, far exceeding levels in Mexico. In multivariate models that controlled

Figure 6.1. Proportion of Mexican-Origin Adults Living in an Extended Family Household in Mexico and the United States by Age, 2000

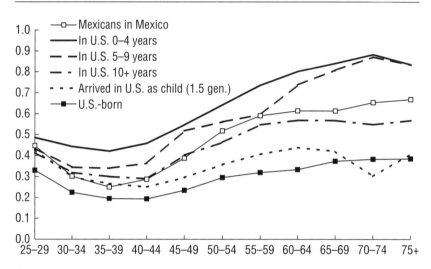

Source: Author's calculations based on 2000 Census data on Mexico and the United States.

for education and demographic factors (age, sex, marital status, presence of children, and urban residence), we found that recently arrived Mexican immigrants were 3.5 times as likely to live with extended kin as U.S.-born Mexican Americans. If we were to focus only on the U.S. side of the border, we might have attributed this to acculturation. However, if we instead compare Mexicans in Mexico with the U.S.-born (and attribute the difference to acculturation), the odds ratio is reduced to 2.5, or about one-third lower than the original estimate of the acculturation effect.

Prior research on marriage and gender roles similarly suggests that "traditional" familial norms are reinforced among newly arrived immigrants, particularly in times of hardship. For example, Bean, Berg, and Van Hook (1996) find that Mexican-origin immigrant women are least likely to divorce at low levels of education. This pattern contrasts with natives of all racial and ethnic groups, among whom divorce is highest at low levels of education. Thus, the combination of being an immigrant and low structural (socioeconomic) incorporation appears to reinforce marital bonds. Parrado and Flippen find similar accentuation of traditional gender roles for migrant Mexican women. They conclude, "it is not that migrant women fail to progress toward more egalitarian norms because of their cultural background or patterns of behavior brought from their communities of origin. Rather, it is their structural position within the United States society including their precarious legal status, unfavorable work conditions, and lack of social support that undermines their well-being and power within relationships" (2005, 628).

It is important to distinguish between cultural and structural explanations of outcomes among immigrants and their children. Cultural arguments have been used in the past to explain the perpetuation of poverty and single parenthood among African Americans, perhaps the most well-known examples being the Moynihan Report (1965) and Oscar Lewis's (1966) culture-of-poverty argument. This use of culture to explain racial and ethnic inequality has been rightly criticized for its tendency to blame the victim. Although the cultural arguments about Mexican immigrants tend to paint a mostly favorable picture of Mexican culture (as opposed to the arguments that were made about African Americans), it would still be a mistake to interpret the associations of indicators of acculturation with children's outcomes as causal if in fact such associations ultimately derived from challenges encountered by Mexican immigrants.

I want to emphasize that I am not arguing that cultural factors are not real or are not important for explaining the behaviors and outcomes of Mexican immigrants and their children. As noted by Skrentny in a recent issue of the *Annals* devoted to the sociology of culture, "Immigrants do not come with a *tabula rasa*. They come with habits, understandings, and perceptions of meaning ingrained over years" (2008, 72). Surely cultural scripts and repertoires continue to influence action following migration. But my point here is that the observed cultural orientations of Mexican immigrants may not originate in Mexico but instead may derive from or become accentuated by the structural challenges encountered by immigrants in the United States. This problem is not solved solely through better measurement of acculturation (although measurement is important). Without making appropriate comparisons with nonimmigrants in sending countries, and without carefully taking into account the structural conditions encountered by new immigrants, we run the risk of overlooking these challenges.

What directions should future research take? First, interdisciplinary collaborations may help sociologists and demographers develop better measures of acculturation that could be added to nationally representative surveys. Such collaborations may also nudge family studies and child development scholars to consider the role of social structure (including unauthorized migration status) in their studies of acculturation. At the very least, statistical analyses that seek to estimate the effects of indicators of acculturation on children's outcomes *must* control for the socioeconomic circumstances of immigrant families and the resources available in their neighborhoods and schools. It would be even better to add controls for migration status if possible (i.e., separating children of undocumented migrants from other children). Second, I would like to encourage all migration researchers regardless of discipline to pursue opportunities to conduct binational research comparing nonmigrants in countries of origin with immigrants in the United States. Binational studies that follow immigrants as they move from one country to another would constitute the gold standard for research on immigrant assimilation; such research designs would help disentangle the effects of cultural origins and acculturation following migration from the effects of migration itself.

REFERENCES

Alba, Richard, and Victor Nee. 2003. *Remaking the American Mainstream: Assimilation and Contemporary Immigration.* Cambridge, MA: Harvard University Press.

Angel, Ronald J., and Marta Tienda. 1982. "Determinants of Extended Household Structure: Cultural Pattern or Economic Need." *American Journal of Sociology* 87:1360–83.

Bean, Frank D., Ruth Berg, and Jennifer Van Hook. 1996. "Socioeconomic and Cultural Incorporation and Marital Disruption among Mexican-Americans." *Social Forces* 75(2): 593–619.

Berry, John W., Jean S. Phinney, David L. Sam, and Paul Vedder. 2006. *Immigrant Youth in Cultural Transition: Acculturation, Identity and Adaptation across National Contexts.* Mahwah, NJ: Lawrence Erlbaum Associates.

Blank, Susan. 1998. "Hearth and Home: The Living Arrangements of Mexican Immigrants and U.S.-Born Mexican Americans." *Sociological Forum* 13(1): 35–59.

Blank, Susan, and Ramon S. Torrecilha. 1998. "Understanding the Living Arrangements of Latino Immigrants: A Life Course Approach." *International Migration Review* 32(1): 3–19.

Burr, Jeffrey A., and Jan E. Mutchler. 1993. "Ethnic Living Arrangements: Cultural Convergence or Cultural Manifestation?" *Social Forces* 72(1): 169–79.

Kamo, Yoshinori. 2000. "Racial and Ethnic Differences in Extended Family Households." *Sociological Perspectives* 43(2): 211–29.

Lewis, Oscar. 1966. "The Culture of Poverty." *Scientific American* 215(4): 19–25.

Moynihan, Daniel Patrick. 1965. *The Negro Family: The Case for National Action.* Washington, DC: U.S. Department of Labor, Office of Policy Planning and Research.

Parrado, Emilio A., and Chenoa A. Flippen. 2005. "Migration and Gender among Mexican Women." *American Sociological Review* 70(4): 606–32.

Passel, Jeffrey S. 2006. *The Size and Characteristics of the Unauthorized Migrant Population in the U.S.* Washington, DC: Pew Hispanic Center.

Passel, Jeffrey S., Jennifer Van Hook, and Frank D. Bean. 2004. *Estimates of the Legal and Unauthorized Foreign-Born Population for the United States and Selected States, Based on Census 2000.* In Sabre Systems White Paper. Washington, DC: U.S. Census Bureau.

Portes, Alejandro, and Min Zhou. 1993. "The New Second Generation: Segmented Assimilation and Its Variants." *The Annals of the American Academy of Political and Social Science* 530:74–96.

Putnam, Robert D. 2007. "E Pluribus Unum: Diversity and Community in the Twenty-First Century, The 2006 Johan Skytte Prize Lecture." *Scandinavian Political Studies* 30(2): 137–74.

Skrentny, John. 2008. "Culture and Race/Ethnicity: Bolder, Deeper, and Broader." *The Annals of the American Academy of Political and Social Science* 619:59–77.

Van Hook, Jennifer, and Jennifer E. Glick. 2007. "Immigration and Living Arrangements: Moving Beyond the 'Instrumental Needs versus Acculturation' Dichotomy." *Demography* 44(2): 225–49.

7

Moving Beyond the Mother-Child Dyad in Prevention Planning for Latino Families

Dads and Siblings Matter, Too!

Rosalie Corona

The chapter by Kimberly Updegraff and Adriana Umaña-Taylor demonstrates the importance of conceptualizing cultural influences on Mexican youths' development from a family perspective. By using reports of acculturation from mothers, fathers, and multiple youth in the household, Updegraff and Umaña-Taylor are able to identify three distinct family patterns of cultural involvement. Their chapter further highlights the importance of considering gender and sibling influences on Mexican youths' adjustment. Each of these contextual factors (family conceptualization of cultural processes, gender, and siblings) is related to positive and negative indices of emotional, behavioral, and physical health in a sample of adolescents of Mexican descent. This family-centered conceptualization is consistent with Latino cultural values emphasizing the interdependence, centrality, and importance of the Latino family. Thus, it is surprising that few researchers have adopted a family-centered orientation when studying youth adjustment in families of Latino descent.

In this chapter, I use this family-centered framework to highlight the important role Latino fathers and siblings play in adolescent sexual health as well as the prevention implications of this family-centered approach for promoting Latino youth sexual health and reducing risk of HIV infection. I end the chapter by discussing the importance of the community context in which a family is embedded when studying family processes and youth adjustment, and in the development and implementation of prevention programs. Although this chapter focuses specifically on adolescent sexuality, many issues are pertinent to prevention programming for other health-related problems (e.g., substance use, obesity) relevant to the Latino community.

A Qualitative Analysis of Parent-Child Communication about Sensitive Issues in Latino Families

Throughout the chapter, I integrate findings from qualitative work with 18 Latino families living in a state with an emerging Latino community. Semi-structured interviews were conducted with 25 Latino youth and their mothers (N = 18) and fathers (N = 11). More than one child was interviewed in 6 of the 18 families. The mean age of youth was 12 years old, with a range from 10 to 15 years. Slightly over half the children were female (56 percent), and 56 percent were immigrants. Of the immigrant children, 10 were from Mexico, 3 from South America (Ecuador, Venezuela, and Colombia) and 1 from the Dominican Republic. The amount of time immigrant children lived in the United States ranged from less than a year to 14 years. Nearly all the children born in the United States (except one child) had at least one immigrant parent. U.S.-born children were of South American (4), Caribbean (6), and Central American (1) descent. Fifty-six percent of children spoke only English during the interview, 40 percent spoke only Spanish, and 4 percent spoke both Spanish and English.

Participants were recruited from the greater Richmond, Virginia, area through flyers posted at local community organizations (e.g., Hispanic Liaison Office, Red Cross), churches, and apartment complexes with high-density Latino populations. Interviews were digitally recorded, transcribed, and checked by bilingual research assistants. Interview transcripts were uploaded into a qualitative data analysis program, which allowed a linking of the themes to the text. Following Bernard's (2002) protocol for content analysis, we created exhaustive and mutually exclusive codes, applied the codes systematically to the narratives, and then tested the consistency between coders. Cohen's Kappa (Cohen 1960), used to check consistency between the two coders, was > 0.84 for all themes (Bakeman and Gottman 1986; Landis and Koch 1977).

Where Are the HIV Prevention Programs for Latino Youth?

Evidence-based prevention programming focused on Latino adolescent sexual health is important given that Latino adolescents are disproportionately affected by negative sexual health outcomes including unplanned pregnancy, dating violence, and HIV infection (Centers for Disease Control and Prevention 2008). Yet, few HIV-prevention programs have been developed for or have included Latino adolescents. In fact, Villarruel, Jemmott, and Jemmott (2006) identify only five adolescent-based intervention studies published between 1994 and 2004 in which Latino adolescents composed at least 25 percent of the study sample and which included sexual behavior outcomes. Latino adolescents were the primary targets in only two studies. In general, the findings from these studies are mixed; different studies find positive effects of the intervention, mixed effects, or no effects.

Although adolescent-focused programs are an important component of health promotion efforts for youth, they may not produce maximum benefits because they do not include parents. Parents play an important role in promoting their children's sexual health because parents can tailor conversations based on their child's current cognitive, social, emotional, and physical development and they can talk to their children about these topics repeatedly as children mature (Kotchick, Shaffer, and Forehand 2001; Martino et al. 2008).

Given the centrality of the family in the Latino culture, parents may play an especially important role in promoting Latino adolescent sexual health. For example, Latino adolescents and parents believe that parents should be involved in the sexual health of their children (Ramirez et al. 2000; Talashek et al. 2004; Villarruel et al. 2003). Moreover, open parent-adolescent communication about sexual topics has been related to decreased risk of pregnancy, increased use of contraception, and less sexual activity among Latino youth (Baumeister, Flores, and Marín 1995; Pick and Palos 1995; Pick de Weiss et al. 1991).

Although open parent-adolescent communication about sexual topics may promote Latino adolescent sexual health, Latino parents may be hesitant to discuss these issues with their children. In fact, Zambrana and colleagues (2004) find that nearly 60 percent of Latino women age 15 through 44 report receiving no sex education from their parents on sexually transmitted diseases, birth control, or how pregnancy occurs.

Other studies have found that Latino adolescents report talking less about sexual topics with their parents than white adolescents (Davis and Harris 1982; DuRant et al. 1990; Raffaelli and Green 2003). Thus, finding ways to increase Latino family communication about HIV prevention is an important priority area for researchers.

Parent-child and parent-only programs have been developed for African American families (e.g., Keepin' It R.E.A.L.! and Parents Matter!; see DiIorio et al. 2006 and Long et al. 2004), but few parent-centered HIV prevention programs have been developed specifically for Latino parents. One notable exception is Familias Unidas (Pantin et al. 2004; Prado et al. 2006). Familias Unidas is based on eco-developmental theory that proposes that "risk and protective processes operating at varying systemic levels compound one another to create an overall profile of risk and protection" (Pantin et al. 2003, 190). Familias Unidas was initially developed to prevent drug use among Latino adolescents by intervening with parents (primarily mothers). Parents in the intervention group reported greater improvements in parental investment and reductions in adolescent problem behaviors (Pantin et al. 2003). The program was later adapted to focus on HIV prevention, and results of the adapted program have been positive; specifically, the adapted program resulted in a decrease of Latino adolescents' unsafe sexual behaviors (Prado et al. 2007). The findings from this culturally based parent-centered prevention program suggest that Latino parents are important primary prevention educators. Moreover, the results suggest that participating in a prevention program can change the way Latino parents and their adolescents communicate about substance use, sex, and HIV, which in turn may affect adolescent attitudes about risk behaviors.

Despite these positive findings, one barrier in prevention programming at the family level is recruiting and retaining parents. Parents encounter numerous environmental barriers (e.g., work conflicts, responsibility for multiple children, transportation) that make it difficult for them to attend parenting programs offered in school and community settings. A potential way to decrease these environmental barriers is to implement parenting programs in worksites (Eastman et al. 2005; Eastman, Corona, and Schuster 2006; Schuster et al. 2001). My colleagues and I developed, implemented, and evaluated (in a randomized-controlled trial) a parenting program (Talking Parents, Healthy Teens) to help parents talk to their children about sex. The eight-session parenting program was offered to groups of about eight to ten parents in the worksite during their lunch hour. After completing a baseline survey, parents were randomly assigned to the parenting group or the control group that did not receive the intervention but completed surveys. Our study showed that intervening at the worksite may reduce some environmental barriers programs encounter when recruiting, engaging, and retaining parents in parent-centered interventions. In fact, our retention rates from baseline to nine months post-intervention ranged from 95 to 97 percent for parents and 94 to 97 percent for their youth, who did not participate in the intervention but did complete surveys (Schuster et al. 2008).

We also found significant differences in parent-child communication between parents who participated in the intervention and control parents. Specifically, parents in the intervention group were more likely than control parents to initiate new sex-related discussions with their adolescents from baseline to nine months post-intervention, and to have more repeated sex-related discussions with their youth (Schuster et al. 2008). This work demonstrates the importance of expanding the focus of worksite health promotion programs to include working parents' children, and the usefulness of worksite-based family health promotion programs in engaging and retaining parents into parent-centered prevention programs.

In summary, prior work has demonstrated that (a) Latino parents are interested in becoming more involved in their adolescents' development, including in areas that are often considered taboo; (b) positive parenting behaviors and open parent-child communication about HIV prevention and sexuality are associated with better sexual health outcomes among Latino youth; (c) few culturally based HIV prevention programs exist for Latino families, but those that do are showing promising effects; and (d) worksite-based health promotion may help diminish some of the environmental barriers parents face when considering participating in prevention programs. In moving forward, researchers need to expand the family-centered conceptualization by better understanding the role of fathers and siblings on Latino youth sexual health.

Moving Beyond the Mother-Child Dyad when Studying and Intervening with Latino Families

Dads Matter, Too!

Much of the literature examining how Latino family relationships affect youth sexual health has emphasized the importance of the mother-child relationship. For example, Romo and colleagues (2001) find that Latino mothers' observed communication of their beliefs and values regarding sexuality is associated with less adolescent sexual behavior about a year later. Moreover, parent-centered HIV prevention programs have typically been implemented with mothers. Although there are important reasons for focusing on Latino mothers, this research provides only a snapshot of how Latino families influence Latino youths' sexual health. Less is known about Latino fathers' roles in promoting adolescent health and reducing risk the of HIV infection.

Based on in-depth interviews with Latino fathers, González-López (2004) finds that Latino fathers are interested in promoting their daughters' sexual health. Specifically, Latino fathers are motivated to protect their daughters from a sexually dangerous society more so than preserving their daughters' virginity. However, in our qualitative study, we found that discussions about drugs were more frequent in father-child discussions than conversations about dating or pregnancy, suggesting that Latino fathers may not feel comfortable or not know how to talk about issues related to HIV prevention and sexual health. Thus, research that identifies the barriers that fathers face in discussing HIV prevention and sexuality with their adolescents is needed so strategies can be developed to engage fathers.

In our study, barriers to father-child communication included (a) children, especially daughters, talking to their mothers; (b) children being too young for the information; (c) perceptions that fathers don't know much about a topic; and (d) discomfort. For example, a 15-year-old adolescent girl said, "I don't really talk to my father about personal things, just 'cause it's a little awkward. I mean I talk to him about school and everything. I really talk to my mom more about boys and stuff." An 11-year-old girl shared that her mother explained things in more detail than her father and that "mi papa no sabe tanto de eso [pregnancy]" ("my father doesn't know much about that [pregnancy]"). These findings suggest that Latino fathers could likely benefit from learning skills to help them start conversations, effectively communicate their values, and overcome adolescents' hesitations to talk to their parents about sensitive issues.

However, in some families we interviewed, father-child conversations about dating or pregnancy occurred within the context of mother-child discussions. When discussing what he talks about in terms of pregnancy with this daughter, a father of a 13-year-old replied, "Yo nada mas escucho lo que mi esposa a veces le dice a ella . . . y hay veces pues que yo me, ahora si que me meto mi platica y ya platicamos entre los tres" ("I only listen to what my wife sometimes tells my daughter . . . and there are times now that I join the conversation and the three of us talk together"). Thus, engaging fathers in mother-father-child discussions may be one way of reducing some of the barriers (e.g., discomfort) fathers face in participating in parent-child discussions about HIV prevention and sexuality.

Before we can teach fathers skills for communicating with their adolescents, we need to better understand the role that cultural factors play in father-adolescent communication and recruit and engage fathers into parent-centered programs. The chapter by Updegraff and Umaña-Taylor highlights that Latino father involvement in their adolescents' lives may depend on the parents' ties to their cultural group and the gender of older siblings in the home. Specifically, Latino mothers are more involved with their adolescents when parents have a stronger tie to their cultural group and when the older sibling in the home is a girl.

With respect to recruiting and engaging fathers into parent-centered programs, intervening at the worksite (as described above) may provide a unique opportunity to engage fathers in youth health promotion and parent-centered programs. More often than not, mothers are the parents participating in parenting programs offered at their children's school or in the community. For example, in the evaluation of the Familias Unidas program, fathers made up 12 percent of the parents in the study (Prado et al. 2007). Although most parents in the evaluation of Talking Parents, Healthy Teens were also mothers, 28 percent of parents in the study were fathers (Schuster et al. 2008). Thus, delivering prevention programs at worksites may provide an avenue for engaging fathers in health promotion activities, which may warrant changes in worksite health-promotion policies. For example, the implementation and evaluation of worksite-based health promotion activities has primarily occurred in relatively large worksites (Linnan et al. 2001). Although there are many reasons for this occurrence, changing policy so all worksites, regardless of size, provide evidence-based health promotion programs for their workers may help promote employee health. Moreover, policies that expand the scope of health promotion activities beyond the employee by focusing on the health of an employee's children and/or other family members are also warranted.

Increasing father attendance and participation in parent-centered programs is only one strategy for engaging fathers. There is also more work prevention researchers can do in engaging fathers when the mother is the primary class participant. For example, parent-centered programs could include homework assignments that include mothers and fathers (even though only one parent is attending the actual sessions) and children. To be successful, however, it is first important for researchers and prevention programmers to determine if mothers who attend parenting sessions share the information they learn with their husbands and reasons for not sharing or reasons fathers may not read the material. Further, identifying the barriers and supports for including fathers in homework activities is needed. Thus, we have to develop a better understanding of why dissemination of HIV prevention information stops in the parenting session.

Siblings Matter, Too

In addition to focusing on the role of mothers and fathers as sexual health educators, it is necessary to identify the prevention messages communicated by other family members. Overlooked family members in risk prevention research are brothers and sisters. Yet, studies have shown that siblings can affect gender role attitudes (Crouter et al. 2007; McHale et al. 2001), which are often associated with sexual behavior, and that siblings are often present during HIV prevention discussions (O'Sullivan et al. 2005). Studies have also found that older siblings can be a more significant influence than parents or peers in determining a younger sibling's sexual behavior (East and Khoo 2005) and substance use risks (Pomery et al. 2005). For example, having a sister who was a teen parent increases the likelihood of a younger sister also becoming a teen parent (East and Jacobson 2001; East, Reyes, and Horn 2007). Moreover, findings by Updegraff and Umaña-Taylor emphasize how culture and sibling gender may interact in affecting younger siblings' sexual intentions. Specifically, Updegraff and Umaña-Taylor find that in Anglo-oriented families, younger siblings in homes with older brothers (as opposed to older sisters) are more likely to report increased sexual intentions.

Few studies have explored sibling communication about sexual topics, risk behaviors, or substance use in Latino families; yet, as one 15-year-old girl in our qualitative study noted, "my sisters get more details" in conversations about dating. Ford and Norris (1991) find that urban African American and Latino adolescents report talking more often with their friends or siblings than with their parents, teachers, and counselors. Together, this work highlights a need for more research on sibling communication including a focus on the content (what they talk about) and process (how they talk about sexual topics) of HIV prevention discussions. Understanding what siblings communicate to each other about HIV prevention has important implications for prevention programming. For example, if siblings are communicating misinformation to younger siblings about HIV prevention, then what youth learn in HIV prevention programs may not be reinforced at home. It will also be important for researchers to identify barriers to sibling communication about HIV prevention and the mechanisms through which siblings affect youth sexual activities. For example, Updegraff and Umaña-Taylor suggest that having an older brother in an Anglo-oriented family may provide younger siblings with more opportunities to spend time with youth engaging in risk behaviors. In sum, there is a great need for research on Latino adolescent sexual health that considers the role that all family members (beyond mothers) play in the sexual health of adolescents and work that identifies strategies that may facilitate family-level involvement in HIV prevention.

Not All Latinos Live in California, Texas, Florida, and New York

Finally, researchers and prevention programmers need to consider the community in which a family is embedded when studying family processes and developing prevention programs. The United States is currently undergoing a geographic shift in the residence patterns of Latino families. Latinos are the largest minority group in the United States, yet their presence in Virginia and some other southern states is a relatively new phenomenon. For example, the Latino population in Virginia tripled between 1990 and 2006 (Cai 2008). Moreover, between 2000 and 2006, two of the top five U.S. counties that experienced significant growth were in Virginia (U.S. Census Bureau 2007).

Although census figures indicate that the majority of Latinos living in the United States are of Mexican descent, some researchers have noted that the population of Central and South American individuals living in the United States may have been underestimated in prior census figures by as much as 47 percent and 41 percent, respectively (Chun 2007; Suro 2002). This increasing diversity of non-Mexican Latinos living in the United States may be likely in newer receiving communities. For example, in prior work my research team and I found that 96 percent of 212 Latino adults (living in the greater Richmond, Virginia, area) had immigrated to the United

States and that 54 percent of the immigrants were from Central America, 28 percent were from Mexico, 11 percent were from South America, and 7 percent were of Caribbean descent (Corona et al. 2009). Despite the significant increase in the Latino population in Virginia, they constitute only 6 percent of Virginians (Cai 2008). As a result, Latinos living in Virginia may not live in ethnically homogenous communities like their counterparts who live in California, Texas, or other states with sizable Latino populations. In fact, most families in our qualitative study reported living in neighborhoods where the Latino population did not exceed 50 percent, and no child reportedly attended a school with predominately Latino students.

These new settlement patterns have important implications for family and youth adjustment since the numbers of ethnic minorities in one's community may affect developmental, cultural, and family processes. For example, exposure to different cultural groups has multiple advantages for youth of all backgrounds. However, as the racial and ethnic composition of neighborhoods change, those positive attributes may not be as readily apparent to community members as the negatives. In fact, we previously found that Latino adults and youth worried about increasing interethnic tensions in their community, primarily between African Americans and Latinos (Corona et al. 2009).

These findings highlight the need for increased attention to the racial and ethnic composition of a school or community when examining the prevalence of bullying and victimization among youth (Peskin, Tortolero, and Markham 2006) and when examining family processes and youth adjustment. Specifically, prevention programmers need to focus on strategies for helping youth negotiate interethnic relationships in these new receiving communities, including ways of encouraging family communication about these experiences. Although 17 of 29 parents in our study said they had spoken with their children about interethnic problems, only seven youth reported talking with their parents about interethnic tensions or problems they had encountered or witnessed.

Conclusions

Updegraff and Umaña-Taylor highlight the importance of considering the influence of multiple family members and the intersection of gender and developmental level when examining Mexican youth adjustment. This chapter furthers that discussion by examining the role of fathers and siblings on Latino adolescent sexual health, and highlighting the need to move beyond youth- and parent-centered interventions to family-centered interventions. Specifically, researchers and prevention programmers need to expand their focus beyond the mother-child dyad and attempt to better understand the role that fathers and siblings play in family processes and youth adjustment. Identifying the environmental barriers and supports for father and sibling participation in HIV-related discussions, and prevention programs are also warranted. Worksite-based health promotion activities may be one avenue for engaging fathers in parent-centered health promotion activities, highlighting a potential area of future study.

REFERENCES

Bakeman, Roger, and John M. Gottman. 1986. *Observing Interaction: An Introduction to Sequential Analysis.* New York: Cambridge University Press.

Baumeister, Lisa M., Elena Flores, and Barbara Vanoss Marín. 1995. "Sex Information Given to Latino Adolescents by Parents." *Health Education Research* 10(2): 233–39.

Bernard, H. Russell. 2002. *Research Methods in Anthropology: Qualitative and Quantitative Approaches.* 3rd ed. Thousand Oaks, CA: SAGE Publications.

Cai, Qian. 2008. "Hispanic Immigrants and Citizens in Virginia." Charlottesville: Weldon Cooper Center, University of Virginia. http://www.coopercenter.org/demographics/sitefiles/documents/pdfs/numberscount/2008hispanics.pdf.

Centers for Disease Control and Prevention. 2008. "Youth Risk Behavior Surveillance—United States 2007." Morbidity and Mortality Weekly Report 57(SS-4). Washington, DC: U.S. Government Printing Office.

Chun, Sung-Chang. 2007. "The 'Other Hispanics'—What Are Their National Origins? Estimating the Latino-Origin Populations in the United States." *Hispanic Journal of Behavioral Sciences* 29:133–55.

Cohen, Jacob. 1960. "A Coefficient of Agreement for Nominal Scales." *Educational and Psychological Measurement* 20:37–46.

Corona, Rosalie, Tanya Gonzalez, Robert Cohen, Charlene Edwards, and Torey Edmonds. 2009. "Richmond Latino Needs Assessment: A Community-University Partnership to Identify Health Concerns and Service Needs for Latino Youth." *Journal of Community Health* 34(3): 195–201.

Crouter, Ann C., Shawn D. Whiteman, Susan M. McHale, and D. Wayne Osgood. 2007. "Development of Gender Attitude Traditionality across Middle Childhood and Adolescence." *Child Development* 78:911–26.

Davis, Sally M., and Mary B. Harris. 1982. "Sexual Knowledge, Sexual Interests, and Sources of Sexual Information of Rural and Urban Adolescents from Three Cultures." *Adolescence* 17:471–92.

DiIorio, Colleen, Ken Resnicow, Frances McCarty, Anindya K. De, William N. Dudley, Dongqing Terry Wang, and Pamela Denzmore. 2006. "Keepin' It R.E.A.L.!: Results of a Mother-Adolescent HIV Prevention Program." *Nursing Research* 55:43–51.

DuRant, Robert H., Carolyn Seymore, Robert Pendergrast, and Rebecca Beckman. 1990. "Contraceptive Behavior among Sexually Active Hispanic Adolescents." *Journal of Adolescent Health Care* 11:490–96.

East, Patricia L., and Leanne J. Jacobson. 2001. "The Younger Siblings of Teenage Mothers: A Follow-Up of Their Pregnancy Risk." *Developmental Psychology* 37:254–64.

East, Patricia L., and Siek Toon Khoo. 2005. "Longitudinal Pathways Linking Family Factors and Sibling Relationship Qualities to Adolescent Substance Use and Sexual Risk Behaviors." *Journal of Family Psychology* 19:571–80.

East, Patricia L., Barbara T. Reyes, and Emily J. Horn. 2007. "Association between Adolescent Pregnancy and a Family History of Teenage Births." *Perspectives on Sexual and Reproductive Health* 39:108–15.

Eastman, Karen L., Rosalie Corona, and Mark A. Schuster. 2006. "Talking Parents, Healthy Teens: A Worksite-Based Program for Parents to Promote Adolescent Sexual Health." *Preventing Chronic Disease* 3(4): A126. http://www.cdc.gov/pcd/issues/2006/oct/06_0012.htm.

Eastman, Karen L., Rosalie Corona, Gery Ryan, Avra Warsofsky, and Mark A. Schuster. 2005. "Worksite-Based Parenting Programs for Parents of Adolescents to Improve Communication and Reduce Sexual Risk—A Qualitative Study." *Perspectives on Sexual and Reproductive Health* 37:62–69.

Ford, Kathleen, and Anne Norris. 1991. "Urban African-American and Hispanic Adolescents and Young Adults: Who Do They Talk to about AIDS and Condoms? What Are They Learning?" *AIDS Education and Prevention* 3:197–206.

González-López, Gloria. 2004. "Fathering Latina Sexualities: Mexican Men and the Virginity of Their Daughters." *Journal of Marriage and the Family* 66:1118–30.

Kotchick, Beth A., Anne Shaffer, and Rex Forehand. 2001. "Adolescent Sexual Risk Behavior: A Multi-System Perspective." *Clinical Psychology Review* 21:493–519.

Landis, J. Richard, and Gary G. Koch. 1977. "Measurement of Observer Agreement for Categorical Data." *Biometrics* 33:159–74.

Linnan, Laura A., Glorian Sorensen, Graham Colditz, Neil Klar, and Karen M. Emmons. 2001. "Using Theory to Understand the Multiple Determinants of Low Participation in Worksite Health Promotion Programs." *Health Education and Behavior* 28:591–607.

Long, Nicholas, Barbara-Jean Austin, Mary M. Gound, Abesie O. Kelly, Adrienne A. Gardner, Rick Dunn, Stacey B. Harris, and Kim S. Miller. 2004. "The Parents Matter! Program Interventions: Content and the Facilitation Process." *Journal of Child and Family Studies* 13:47–65.

Martino, Steven C., Marc N. Elliott, Rosalie Corona, David E. Kanouse, and Mark A. Schuster. 2008. "Beyond the 'Big Talk': The Roles of Breadth and Repetition in Parent-Adolescent Communication about Sexual Topics." *Pediatrics* 121:e612–18.

McHale, Susan M., Kimberly A. Updegraff, Heather Helms-Erikson, and Ann C. Crouter. 2001. "Sibling Influences on Gender Development in Middle Childhood and Early Adolescence: A Longitudinal Study." *Developmental Psychology* 37:115–25.

O'Sullivan, Lucia F., Curtis Dolezal, Elizabeth Brackis-Cott, Lara Traeger, and Claude A. Mellins. 2005. "Communication about HIV and Risk Behaviors among Mothers Living with HIV and Their Early Adolescent Children." *Journal of Early Adolescence* 25:148–67.

Pantin, Hilda, Seth J. Schwartz, Summer Sullivan, Guillermo Prado, and Jose Szapocznik. 2004. "Ecodevelopmental HIV Prevention Programs for Hispanic Adolescents." *American Journal of Orthopsychiatry* 74:545–58.

Pantin, Hilda, Douglas Coatsworth, Daniel J. Feaster, Frederick L. Newman, Ervin Briones, Guillermo Prado, Seth J. Schwartz, and Jose Szapocznik. 2003. "Familias Unidas: The Efficacy of an Intervention to Increase Parental Investment in Hispanic Immigrant Families." *Prevention Science* 4:189–201.

Peskin, Melissa F., Susan R. Tortolero, and Christine M. Markham. 2006. "Bullying and Victimization among Black and Hispanic Adolescents." *Adolescence* 41:467–84.

Pick, Susan, and Patricia A. Palos. 1995. "Impact of the Family on the Sex Lives of Adolescents." *Adolescence* 30:667–75.

Pick de Weiss, Susan, Lucille C. Atkin, James N. Gribble, and Patricia Andrade-Palos. 1991. "Sex, Contraception, and Pregnancy among Adolescents in Mexico City." *Studies in Family Planning* 22:74–82.

Pomery, Elizabeth A., Frederick X. Gibbons, Meg Gerrard, Michael J. Cleveland, Gene H. Brody, and Thomas A. Wills. 2005. "Families and Risk: Prospective Analyses of Familial and Social Influences on Adolescent Substance Use." *Journal of Family Psychology* 19:560–70.

Prado, Guillermo, Hilda Pantin, Seth J. Schwartz, Nichol Lupei, and Jose Szapocznik. 2006. "Predictors of Engagement and Retention into a Parent-Centered Ecodevelopmental HIV Preventive Intervention for Hispanic Adolescents and Their Families." *Journal of Pediatric Psychology* 31:874–90.

Prado, Guillermo, Hilda Pantin, Ervin Briones, Seth J. Schwartz, Daniel Feaster, Shi Huang, Summer Sullivan, Maria I. Tapia, Eduardo Sabillon, Barbara Lopez, and Jose Szapocznik. 2007. "A Randomized Controlled Trial of a Parent-Centered Intervention in Preventing Substance Use and HIV Risk Behaviors in Hispanic Adolescents." *Journal of Consulting and Clinical Psychology* 75:914–26.

Raffaelli, Marcela, and Stephanie Green. 2003. "Parent-Adolescent Communication about Sex: Retrospective Reports by Latino College Students." *Journal of Marriage and the Family* 65:474–81.

Ramirez, Jesus I., Dana R. Gossett, Kenneth R. Ginsburg, S. Lynne Taylor, and Gail B. Slap. 2000. "Preventing HIV Transmission: The Perspective of Inner-City Puerto Rican Adolescents." *Journal of Adolescent Health* 26:258–67.

Romo, Laura F., Eva S. Lefkowitz, Marian Sigman, and Terry K. Au. 2001. "Determinants of Mother-Adolescent Communication about Sex in Latino Families." *Adolescent and Family Health* 2:72–82.

Schuster, Mark A., Rosalie Corona, Marc N. Elliott, David E. Kanouse, Karen L. Eastman, Annie J. Zhou, and David J. Klein. 2008. "Evaluation of Talking Parents, Healthy Teens, a New Worksite-Based Parenting Programme to Promote Parent-Adolescent Communication about Sexual Health: Randomised Controlled Trial." *British Medical Journal* 337:a308.

Schuster, Mark A., Karen L. Eastman, Jonathan E. Fielding, Mary-Jane Rotheram-Borus, Lester Breslow, Lynn L. Franzoi, and David E. Kanouse. 2001. "Promoting Adolescent Health: Worksite-Based Interventions with Parents of Adolescents." *Journal of Public Health Management and Practice* 7:41–52.

Suro, Robert. 2002. "Counting the 'Other Hispanics': How Many Columbians, Dominicans, Ecuadorians, Guatemalans, and Salvadorans Are There in the United States?" Washington, DC: Pew Hispanic Center.

Talashek, Marie L., Nilda Peragallo, Kathleen Norr, and Barbara L. Dancy. 2004. "The Context of Risky Behaviors for Latino Youth." *Journal of Transcultural Nursing* 15:131–38.

U.S. Census Bureau. 2007. "Hispanics in the United States." PowerPoint presentation. Washington, DC: U.S. Census Bureau. http://www.census.gov/population/www/socdemo/hispanic/files/Internet_Hispanic_in_US_2006.pdf.

Villarruel, Antonia M., Esther C. Gallegos, Carol J. Loveland Cherry, and Maria Refugio de Duran. 2003. "La Uniendo de Fronteras: Collaboration to Develop HIV Prevention Strategies for Mexican and Latino Youth." *Journal of Transcultural Nursing* 14:193–206.

Villarruel, Antonia M., John B. Jemmott III, and Loretta S. Jemmott. 2006. "A Randomized Controlled Trial Testing an HIV Prevention Intervention for Latino Youth." *Archives of Pediatrics and Adolescent Medicine* 160(8): 772–77.

Zambrana, Ruth E., Llewllyn J. Cornelius, Stephanie S. Boykin, and Debbie S. Lopez. 2004. "Latinas and HIV/AIDS Risk Factors: Implications for Harm Reduction Strategies." *American Journal of Public Health* 94:1152–58.

8

Mexican-Origin Children in the United States

Language, Family Circumstances, and Public Policy

Donald J. Hernandez, Suzanne Macartney,
Victoria L. Blanchard, and Nancy A. Denton

Children in immigrant families, especially Hispanics (including Mexican-origin children), are important to all Americans for at least five reasons (Hernandez and Charney 1998; Hernandez, Denton, and Macartney 2008, 2009).[1] First, children in immigrant families account for nearly a quarter (23 percent) of all children in the United States. Second, they are the fastest growing population of children. Third, they live in substantial numbers in every state. Fourth, they are leading the racial and ethnic transformation of America. As a result, fifth, when the predominantly white baby boomers reach retirement, they will depend increasingly for their economic support on the productive activities and civic participation, including voting, of younger working-age adults who belong to a wide range of racial and ethnic minorities. Many of these workers will have grown up in immigrant families.

It is especially important to focus on Hispanic children in immigrant families because they account for most (55 percent) of all children in immigrant families. Within the Hispanic immigrant group, children with origins in Mexico account for the vast majority (71 percent). All together, Mexican-origin children in immigrant and native-born families account for one of every seven children (14 percent) age 0 to 17 in the United States.

In this context, the innovative research by Updegraff and Umaña-Taylor takes on special importance because it addresses connections among cultural experiences of mothers, fathers, and siblings in families in the immigrant group that is both the largest and the most geographically dispersed, children in Mexican-origin immigrant families. The focus of the Updegraff and Umaña-Taylor study on how family members are involved in Mexican and Anglo culture as a family constellation, with implications for various child outcomes, is especially welcome, particularly as it connects with the birth order and gender of siblings.

Their pattern cluster analysis identifies three types of family groups, Mexican-oriented families, Mexican/dual-involvement families, and Anglo-oriented families. The data in their table 5.1 indicating the proportions of parents and siblings born in the United States imply the following. In the Anglo-oriented group, the vast majority of sibling pairs, about 80 percent are third or later generation, all born in the United States. At the opposite extreme, a similarly large proportion of sibling pairs in the Mexican-oriented group, about 83 percent, is first-generation immigrants all born in Mexico. In the dual-involvement group, however, there is a mix of first- and second-generation siblings. About 44 percent of the sibling pairs are both first generation, and about 40 percent are both second generation, while about 16 percent are mixed first and second generation.

Comparing the last two groups on language use, among the dual-involvement group, only 10 percent of siblings are Spanish speaking, while about 60 to 64 percent of Mexican-oriented siblings are Spanish speaking. Insofar as these differences in generation and language are rather strongly related to cultural orientation, new results for children distinguished by generation and family language use offer important insights into how the social and economic circumstances of children vary, or are similar, for Mexican-origin children living in families with diverse cultural orientations.

The primary aim of this chapter is to present new results regarding the circumstances of children in immigrant and native-born families with origins in Mexico who are distinguished by parental language use as calculated from the Census Bureau's 2005 and 2006 American Community Survey, and to discuss public policies and programs that can help to assure immigrant children and families successfully integrate into American society.[2]

English Language Use and Fluency among Parents and Children

The term English language learner is most often used in describing the language skills of children, but it also is appropriate for many immigrant parents from countries speaking a language other than English.

Despite the fact that all children in immigrant families have at least one immigrant parent, among Mexican-origin children in immigrant families, only 11 percent live with parents who speak no English at home, while the vast majority (89 percent) speak at least some English at home.

In other words, the vast majority of parents in Mexican-origin immigrant families have learned at least some English, and they no doubt will learn more English the longer they live in the United States. Since only 2 percent of the children in Mexican-origin immigrant families live with parents who speak only English at home, a total of 87 percent live with parents who speak both English and Spanish at home. It also is striking that nearly all (95 percent) of third- and later-generation Mexican-origin children live with at least one English-fluent parent, but that a majority (54 percent) lives with parents who speak both English and Spanish at home. These results indicate that a strong commitment to learning and speaking English fluently by parents in families with Mexican immigrant origins is often combined with continued use of the heritage language, Spanish.

The English language skills of parents have important implications for their children. Children living with parents who are limited English proficient (English language learners) are most likely to have limited English skills themselves, and therefore to be classified by schools as English language learners. On the other hand, children living with parents who speak only English fluently will be least likely to be classified as English language learners. In addition, parents who are English language learners are less likely than English-fluent parents to be able to help their children study for subjects taught in English. Further, insofar as education, health, and social service institutions do not provide outreach in Spanish (or other country-of-origin languages spoken by immigrant parents), these parents and their children may also be cut off from access to important public and private services and benefits.

In view of these important consequences, this chapter distinguishes children by parental English language skill as follows. Parents are classified as English fluent if they speak only English or if they speak English very well, while parents are classified as English language learners if they speak English well, not well, or not at all. This corresponds to the approach used by the Census Bureau to distinguish households that are linguistically isolated from households that are not linguistically isolated.

For the purpose of characterizing the circumstances of children in Mexican-origin immigrant families, this chapter distinguishes three groups of children. First are children with English language–learner parents only. Second are children living with one English language–learner parent and one English-fluent parent. Third are children living with English-fluent parents only.

The vast majority of third- and later-generation Mexican-origin children in native-born families (92 percent) live with English-fluent parents only. Among those in immigrant families, the largest proportion lives with English language–learner parents only (at 63 percent), while 18 to 19 percent live with either English-fluent parents only or mixed-fluency parents.

As suggested above, the English language skills of children are related to the skills of their parents. Among Mexican-origin children in immigrant families with English-fluent parents only, 92 percent of children are English fluent; this proportion declines to 84 percent for children with mixed-fluency parents and to 62 percent for children with English language–learner parents only. Despite these differences, a substantial majority of each group of children, regardless of parental language skills, is English fluent, reflecting substantial integration into English-speaking society.

Deep Roots in America

The deep roots that Mexican-origin children in immigrant families have in America is reflected not only in their own and their parents' English language use and fluency, but also in their own citizenship, their parental length of residence and citizenship in this country, and their family commitment to home ownership.

Parent Born in United States

One-third of Mexican-origin children in the United States are third or later generation, and all these children live with American citizen, U.S.-born parents only. Among children in Mexican-origin immigrant families, all have a foreign-born parent, but many also have a U.S.-born parent who has, therefore, been an American citizen since birth. The proportions with a U.S.-born parent are 48 percent for children in Mexican-origin immigrant families with English-fluent parents only and 40 percent for those with mixed-fluency parents. However, among children with English language–learner parents only, 5 percent have a U.S.-born parent.

Parent a U.S. Citizen

Although all children in Mexican-origin immigrant families have at least one foreign-born parent, many parents become naturalized American citizens.

In fact, a large majority lives with at least one American citizen parent among children with English-fluent parents only (75 percent) and with mixed-fluency parents (70 percent). The proportion is about a third as large for children with English language–learner parents only. But even among this group, a quarter (26 percent) lives with a parent who is an American citizen. These large proportions, even among children with English language–learner parents only, reflect a high level of commitment among these parents to their adopted homeland and to American citizenship.

Additional recent research indicates, in fact, that naturalization rates have increased over the past two decades. Among all legal permanent foreign-born residents between 1990 and 2005, the percentage naturalized nearly doubled from 28 to 52 percent (Passel 2007).

Parent in United States More Than 10 Years

The strong commitment to living in the United States is also indicated by the large number of children in Mexican-origin immigrant families who have at least one parent who has lived in the United States for 10 years or longer; 89 percent for children with English-fluent parents only, 84 percent for children with mixed-fluency parents, and 74 percent for children with English language–learner parents only.

Child Born in United States

Higher still are the proportions of children in immigrant families who are lifelong American citizens because they were born in the United States The proportion born in the United States among children in Mexican-origin immigrant families is 95 percent for children with English-fluent parents only, 92 percent for children with mixed-fluency parents, and 78 percent for children with English language–learner parents.

Thus, the vast majority of these children, regardless of parental language fluency, share with children in native-born families the same rights as American citizens, including eligibility for publicly funded benefits and services.

In fact, although 11 percent of all children in immigrant families are undocumented, even among children with undocumented parents, nearly two-thirds (63 percent) are themselves American citizens because they were born in the United States (Passel 2006).

Family Home Ownership

Many children in Mexican-origin families live in homes owned by their parents or other relatives. Home ownership rates range from 44 percent for children in Mexican-origin immigrant families with English language–learner parents only, to 55 percent for those in native-born families, to 61–62 percent for children in Mexican-origin immigrant families with at least one English-fluent parent.

Clearly, many children in both native-born and immigrant Mexican-origin families live in families who are investing in America and in their adopted cities, towns, and neighborhoods by putting down roots and buying a home.

Nuclear Families with Mixed Citizenship

The 1996 federal welfare reform drew, for the first time, a sharp distinction in program eligibility criteria between noncitizen immigrants and citizens, with noncitizens ineligible for important public benefits and services. As a consequence, many noncitizen parents who are ineligible for specific public programs may be unaware that their citizen children are eligible, or they may be hesitant to contact government authorities to obtain benefits or services for their children because they fear jeopardizing their own future opportunities to become citizens. This "chilling effect" of welfare reform may have serious negative consequences for children who do not obtain needed resources.

Among all children in Mexican-origin immigrant families, more than half who have English-fluent parents only (56 percent) live in mixed-citizenship-status nuclear families with at least one U.S. citizen and one noncitizen in the family. This rises to 71–76 percent for children with at least one English language–learner parent.

Important Strengths of Immigrant Families

The strengths of immigrant families are reflected in the high proportions living in two-parent families, often with other relatives, and with many parents and others in the home working at jobs to the support of the family.

Parents and Other Relatives in the Home

Children living with two parents tend, on average, to be somewhat advantaged in their educational success, compared with children in one-parent families (Cherlin 1999; McLanahan and Sandefur 1994). Most children benefit from the advantages and strengths associated with having two parents in the home. The proportion is very high among children in Mexican-origin immigrant families for all three English language fluency groups, at 75 percent or more. Thus, the vast majority, regardless of parental English fluency, lives with two parents. A somewhat smaller majority (59 percent) of children in Mexican-origin native-born families lives with two parents.

In addition, among Mexican-origin immigrant and native-born families, 9 to 20 percent have at least one grandparent in the home, and 17 to 33 percent have at least one additional adult relative, including older siblings, in the home. Thus, many Mexican-origin children live in families with grandparents and other relatives who can share in providing care for younger children as well as additional economic resources and other forms of assistance.

This familism also is reflected in the number of dependent siblings in the homes of many families. Across generations and parents' English language fluency, between 17 and 22 percent of children in Mexican-origin immigrant families have four or more dependent siblings age 0 through 17 in the home, with a lower range of 16 percent for Mexican-origin children in native-born families.

Family Work Ethic

Most children live in families with strong work ethics. Among children in Mexican-origin immigrant families regardless of parental English fluency, 95 to 96 percent have fathers who are working to support their families, with similar proportions for Mexican-origin children in native-born families (90 to 95 percent). In addition, about half or more children in Mexican-origin families have working mothers. The proportion with working mothers ranges between 49 to 54 percent, for those with English language–learner and mixed-fluency parents, to 69 percent for English-fluent parents, to 66 to 75 percent for those in native-born families.

Reflecting economic contribution of persons in addition to parents, 16 to 26 percent of Mexican-origin children have another adult worker in the home among those in native-born and immigrant families, across various levels of parental English fluency. Thus, the strengths of immigrant and native-born families experienced by Mexican-origin children include a work ethic manifest in the presence of many parents and other workers in their homes providing economic support to the family.

Challenges Confronting Many Immigrant Families

Despite important family strengths, many Mexican-origin children in both immigrant and native families confront major challenges, but especially those with English language–learner parents only, associated with low parental education and high family poverty, which in turn can lead to limited access to early education programs and health insurance coverage.

Father Not a High School Graduate

Children whose parents have completed fewer years of schooling tend, on average, to complete fewer years of schooling and to obtain lower-paying jobs when they reach adulthood (Blau and Duncan 1967; Featherman and Hauser 1978; Sewell and Hauser 1975; Sewell, Hauser, and Wolf 1980). Parents whose education does not extend beyond the elementary level may be especially limited in knowledge and experience needed to help their children succeed in school. Immigrant parents often have high educational aspirations for their children (Hernandez and Charney 1998; Kao 1999; Rumbaut 1999), but they may know little about the U.S. educational system, particularly if they have completed only a few years of school.

Nearly 20 percent of children in native-born Mexican-origin families have fathers who have not graduated from high school. For those in immigrant families, this number jumps to 32 percent for children with English-fluent parents only, 50 percent for those whose parents have mixed language skills, and 69 percent for those with English language–learner parents only. (Results are similar for mothers.)

Some children, in fact, live with fathers who have not entered, let alone completed, high school. The proportion is only 3 percent of Mexican-origin children in native-born families. Among children in immigrant families, however, the proportion rises to 12 percent for those with only English-fluent parents, doubles to 27 percent for those with mixed-fluency parents, and quadruples to 46 percent for children with only English language–learner parents. These immigrant parents are not only unfamiliar with the U.S. education system, they are also unfamiliar with any schools or educational content beyond the elementary level.

Poverty

Children from low-income families tend to experience various negative developmental outcomes, including less success in school, lower educational attainments, and lower incomes during adulthood (Duncan and Brooks-Gunn 1997; McLoyd 1998; Sewell and Hauser 1975). Poverty rates merit considerable attention in part because extensive research documents that poverty has greater negative consequences than either limited mother's education or living in a one-parent family (Duncan and Brooks-Gunn 1997; McLoyd 1998). Children in low-income families also may experience serious deprivation in such basic areas as nutrition, clothing, housing, and health care.

About a fifth (18 to 22 percent) of Mexican-origin children in native-born families and immigrant families with at least one English-fluent parent live below the official poverty threshold. This share jumps to more than one-third (36 percent) for children with only English language–learner parents.

But many scholars, and others, feel that official poverty levels underestimate the amount of real poverty in the United States (Citro and Michael 1995; Hernandez, Denton, and Macartney 2007). In addition, public policy discussions often use a measure focusing on children with family incomes below 200 percent of (or twice) the official poverty threshold (Annie E. Casey Foundation 2006). By this measure, nearly half (47 to 48 percent) of Mexican-origin children are poor if they are third and later generation or live in immigrant families with only English-fluent parents; this share rises to nearly 60 percent for children with mixed-fluency parents and to nearly 80 percent for those with only English language–learner parents.

Moderate or Severe Housing Cost Burden

In view of these high poverty rates, it is not surprising that many children in Mexican-origin families live in households with moderate or severe housing cost burdens—that is, where housing costs amount to 30 percent or more of the household income. The proportion is about 50 percent for children in Mexican-origin native-born families and immigrant families with at least one English-fluent parent; this rises to 61 percent for children with only English language–learner parents.

Early Education: Socioeconomic and Cultural Barriers to Enrollment

Shifting to a focus on children's schooling, high-quality early education programs have been found to promote school readiness and educational success in elementary school and beyond (Gormley 2007; Haskins and Rouse 2005; Heckman and Masterov 2007; Lynch 2004). Children in Mexican-origin families, as well as those in immigrant families from Central America and Indochina, are among those most likely to have low rates of enrollment in pre-kindergarten or nursery school.

One plausible reason sometimes cited, particularly for Hispanic immigrants, is a more familistic cultural orientation. The idea is immigrants from familistic cultures may prefer child care provided at home by parents or other relatives instead of care by nonrelatives in formal settings. Alternative socioeconomic barriers, however, can limit enrollment. Early education programs may cost more than parents can afford to pay, or the number of openings available locally may be too small to meet the demand. Although federal and state governments have policies, including Head Start, that are intended to reduce or eliminate such difficulties for poor families, these policies are underfunded.

Also, available programs may lack home language outreach, or they may lack teachers with a minimal capacity to speak to a child in the home language. In addition, parents with limited educational attainment may not know how to access early education programs or may be unaware that these programs can foster school success for their children.

Explaining Gaps in Pre-K/Nursery School Enrollment

A recent study estimates whether enrollment gaps separating Mexican-origin (and other) children from white children in native-born families can be accounted for by socioeconomic barriers or cultural preferences (Hernandez, Denton, and Macartney forthcoming). All together, for children in immigrant and native-born Mexican-origin families (as well as children in Central American and Indochinese immigrant families), the results indicate that socioeconomic barriers can account for at least half and perhaps all of the enrollment gap separating them from whites in native-born families, while most estimates indicate that cultural influences play a comparatively small role in accounting for the gaps in low pre-K/nursery school enrollment for these groups.

Pre-K Enrollment in Mexico

These results may be surprising. But they are consistent with the strong commitment to early education in contemporary Mexico, where universal enrollment at age 3 is a national requirement as of the 2008–09 school year (Organisation for Economic Co-operation and Development [OECD] 2006). In fact, in 2005, 81 percent of 4-year-olds in Mexico were enrolled in preschool, substantially more than the 71 percent enrolled in preschool at age 4 among whites in native-born families in 2004 (Yoshikawa et al. 2006). (For additional international comparisons and discussion of early education policies and a ranking of various OECD countries, see UNICEF 2008.)

Given that preschool is less costly in Mexico than in the United States, and given that poverty for the Mexican-origin immigrant group in the United States is quite high, it is not surprising that the proportion enrolled in the United States for the immigrant Mexican-origin group at 47 percent is substantially lower than the 81 percent enrolled in Mexico.

In sum, familistic cultural values are sometimes cited to explain lower early education enrollment among immigrants, but this research shows socioeconomic barriers can account for at least 50 percent, and for some groups, perhaps all of the gap. Public policies such as Head Start could be expanded to reduce or eliminate enrollment gaps resulting from to these barriers.

High School Graduation among Young Adults

It is also important to look at the other end of the educational pipeline, high school graduation. Among young Mexican-origin adults, it is necessary to distinguish between first-generation immigrants born abroad and the second generation born in the United States, because many immigrants arrive as adolescents or young adults with very limited education.

Second-generation Mexican-origin youth are about as likely as the third and later generations to graduate from high school, at 77 to 79 percent. But among the first generation, only 40 percent are high school graduates (Hernandez et al. 2008).

Many of these first-generation immigrants should not be viewed as high school dropouts, because many never enter the U.S. education system. Thus, education policy must address two very different populations, children for whom the education system has failed, and adolescents and young adults who have never been touched by the U.S. education system.

Health Insurance Coverage

Good health is important for children to succeed in school and in life. But many children are not covered by health insurance, despite the fact that the State Children's Health Insurance Program was created in 1997. Results are presented from the Census Bureau's Current Population Survey, combining the years 2001–05. (Health insurance data are to be collected in the American Community Survey beginning in 2008.) One in six Mexican-origin children in native-born families (17 percent) are not covered by health insurance. This rises to a third (32 percent) of children in Mexican-origin immigrant groups. Among large immigrant groups in the United States, only children with origins in Central America and Haiti experience this high proportion of people not covered by health insurance (Hernandez et al. 2008).

Resources and Challenges for Children in Mexican-Origin Immigrant Families

To summarize this demographic overview, children in immigrant families often live in strong two-parent families with grandparents or other adults in the home who help provide support and nurturance. These families have strong work ethics and often are home owners who are investing in and committed to their local communities.

But many children confront the challenges of low parental education, high poverty rates, and low rates of pre-K/nursery school enrollment, high school graduation, and health insurance coverage. In addition, many confront the challenges associated with being English language learners. Acting to counterbalance this last point, many children also are poised to become bilingual, and therefore represent a unique resource to the United States in the increasingly globalized economy.

Public Policies Especially Relevant for Children in Immigrant Families

What strategies might federal, state, and local governments (including school districts) pursue to foster the positive development and successful integration of Mexican-origin (and other) children in immigrant families?

First, in the short run, when immigrants first arrive in the United States, many are English language learners with limited English skills. For these children and families, it is important that education, health, social service, and justice system organizations be able to reach out to immigrants in their home language to assure they are successful in reaching all their client population, not just those who speak English fluently. This also involves developing cultural sensitivity and cultural competence in speaking to and working with immigrant families and children.

Second, in the longer run, immigrants and their children learn English. To ensure that this occurs as rapidly and effectively as possible, English language training programs should be expanded, and effective two-generation family literacy programs should be developed to foster not only speaking, but also reading and writing. These programs could help parents in immigrant families improve their capacity to provide economic support for the families, while also fostering children's development. In addition, these programs should foster bilingual fluency in English and the parents' home language to foster optimum development among children of immigrants.

Access to early education programs also is essential to assure that children in immigrant families have the opportunity to develop their potential to become integrated, effective, and productive members of American society. Research indicates that it is not essential for teachers to be fluently bilingual. For example, even when pre-K–3rd grade teachers have no experience with a child's first language, they can introduce English to young English language learners and adopt teaching practices that support home language development. Teachers who encourage the families of children to talk, read, and sing with the child in the parents' home language, and to use the home language in everyday activities, will foster the child's first language development even as the child is learning English (Espinosa 2007, 2008).

In addition, research shows that children who learn English after their home language is established, which is typically around age 3, can add a second language during the pre-K and early school years, and that these bilingual skills leads to long-term cognitive, cultural, and economic advantages. It has also been found that a dual-language approach to teaching is effective for English language learners, while not having negative consequences for other children. In fact, dual-language programs are effective not only for improving the academic achievements of English language–learner students, but also for providing benefits to native English speakers, as reflected in standardized test scores and reports by parents, teachers, and school administrators.

Beyond education policies and programs, children and families require good health to succeed in school and in work. Children in some immigrant groups have low rates of health insurance coverage. It's important that these gaps be eliminated.

Finally, the exclusion of some immigrant parents from eligibility for welfare programs deprives their American citizen children of important public benefits and services (Capps, Kenney, and Fix 2003; Fix and Passel 1999; Fix and Zimmermann 1995; Hernandez and Charney 1998; Zimmermann and Tumlin 1999). The recent eligibility exclusion rules not only jeopardize the health and development of the children who are not receiving needed services, but also affect all Americans who stand to benefit from having a healthy and productive labor force in the future.

Insofar as the exclusion of some immigrant parents from eligibility for health and welfare programs deprives their U.S. citizen children of important public benefits and services, and insofar as most of the children and parents are or will become American citizens, the elimination of these eligibility exclusion rules is in the interest not only of immigrant children and families, but of all Americans, including the baby boomer generation who will benefit from having a healthy and productive labor force to support them during retirement.

NOTES

This chapter draws on a series of related chapters, an article, and a research brief on children in immigrant families by the author and colleagues, but especially on *Social Policy Report*, published by the Society for Research in Child Development (Hernandez et al.

2008). The results presented here are from the 2005–06 American Community Survey, unless otherwise indicated, and additional indicators for children can be retrieved at www.albany.edu/csda/children. For international comparisons see Hernandez, Macartney, and Blanchard (2009). The authors acknowledge and appreciate support from the William and Flora Hewlett Foundation, the Foundation for Child Development, the Annie E. Casey Foundation, the National Institute of Child Health & Human Development (5 R03 HD 043827-02), and the Center for Social and Demographic Analysis at the University at Albany (5 R24—HD 04494301A1). The American Community Survey data file used in this research was prepared by Ruggles et al. (2008).

1. See also U.S. Census Bureau, "U.S. Interim Projections by Age, Sex, Race, and Hispanic Origin: 2000–2050," http://www.census.gov/ipc/www/usinterimproj/.

2. More detailed results for this group and for more than four dozen other immigrant and native-born groups are available at http://www.albany.edu/csda/children.

REFERENCES

Annie E. Casey Foundation. 2006. *2006 KIDS COUNT Data Book*. Baltimore, MD: Annie E. Casey Foundation.

Blau, Peter M., and Otis Dudley Duncan. 1967. *The American Occupational Structure*. New York: John Wiley & Sons.

Capps, Randolph, Genevieve N. Kenney, and Michael E. Fix. 2003. "Health Insurance Coverage of Children in Mixed-Status Immigrant Families." Snapshots of America's Children III, No. 12. Washington, DC: The Urban Institute.

Cherlin, Andrew J. 1999. "Going to Extremes: Family Structure, Children's Well-Being, and Social Sciences." *Demography* 36(4): 421–28.

Citro, Constance. F., and Robert T. Michael, eds. 1995. *Measuring Poverty: A New Approach*. Washington DC: National Academy Press.

Duncan, Greg J., and Jeanne Brooks-Gunn, eds. 1997. *Consequences of Growing Up Poor*. New York: Russell Sage Foundation.

Espinosa, Linda M. 2007. "English-Language Learners as They Enter School." In *School Readiness & the Transition to Kindergarten in the Era of Accountability*, edited by Robert C. Pianta, Martha J. Cox, and Kyle L. Snow. Baltimore, MD: Paul H. Brookes.

———. 2008. "Challenging Common Myths about Young English Language Learners." Advancing PK-3 Policy Brief 8. New York: Foundation for Child Development.

Featherman, David L., and Robert M. Hauser. 1978. *Opportunity and Change*. New York: Academic Press.

Fix, Michael E., and Jeffrey S. Passel. 1999. *Trends in Noncitizens' and Citizens' Use of Public Benefits Following Welfare Reform: 1994–97*. Washington, DC: The Urban Institute.

Fix, Michael E., and Wendy Zimmermann. 1995. "When Should Immigrants Receive Public Benefits?" Washington, DC: The Urban Institute.

Gormley, William T. 2007. "Early Childhood Care and Education: Lessons and Puzzles." *Journal of Policy Analysis and Management* 26(3): 633–71.

Haskins, Ron, and Cecilia Rouse. 2005. "Closing Achievement Gaps." Policy brief. Princeton, NJ: The Future of Children.

Heckman, James J., and Dimitriy V. Masterov. 2007. "The Productivity Argument for Investing in Young Children." T. W. Schultz Award Lecture at the Allied Social Sciences Association annual meeting, Chicago, January 5–7. http://jenni.uchicago.edu/human-inequality/papers/Heckman_final_all_wp_2007-03-22c_jsb.pdf.

Hernandez, Donald J., and Evan Charney, eds. 1998. *From Generation to Generation: The Health and Well-Being of Children in Immigrant Families.* Washington, DC: National Academy Press.

Hernandez, Donald J., Nancy A. Denton, and Suzanne E. Macartney. 2007. "Child Poverty in the U.S.: A New Family Budget Approach with Comparison to European Countries." In *Childhood, Generational Order, and the Welfare State: Exploring Children's Social and Economic Welfare,* Vol. 1 of *COST A19: Children's Welfare,* edited by Helmut Wintersberger, Leena Alanen, Thomas Olk, and Jens Qvortrup. Odense: University Press of Southern Denmark.

———. 2008. "Children in Immigrant Families: Looking to America's Future." *Social Policy Report* 22(3). Ann Arbor, MI: Society for Research in Child Development.

———. 2009. "Children of Immigrants and the Future of America." In *Immigration, Diversity, and Education,* edited by Elena L. Grigorenko and Ruby Takanishi (7–25). London: Routledge/Taylor and Francis Group.

———. Forthcoming. "Early Childhood Education Programs: Accounting for Low Enrollment in Newcomer and Native Families." In *The New Dimensions of Diversity: The Children of Immigrants in North America and Western Europe,* edited by Richard Alba and Mary Waters. New York: NYU Press.

Hernandez, Donald J., Suzanne Macartney, and Victoria L. Blanchard. 2009. *Children in Immigrant Families in Affluent Countries: Their Family, National, and International Context.* Florence, IT: UNICEF Innocenti Research Centre.

Kao, Grace. 1999. "Psychological Well-Being and Educational Achievement among Immigrant Youth." In *Children of Immigrants: Health, Adjustment, and Public Assistance,* edited by Donald J. Hernandez (410–27). Washington, DC: National Academy Press.

Lynch, Robert G. 2004. *Exceptional Returns: Economic, Fiscal, and Social Benefits of Investment in Early Childhood Development.* Washington, DC: Economic Policy Institute.

McLanahan, Sara, and Gary Sandefur. 1994. *Growing Up with a Single Parent: What Hurts, What Helps.* Cambridge, MA: Harvard University Press.

McLoyd, Vonnie. 1998. "Socioeconomic Disadvantage and Child Development." *American Psychologist* 53(2): 185–204.

OECD Directorate of Education. 2006. *Early Childhood Education and Care Policy: Country Note for Mexico.* Paris: Organisation for Economic Co-operation and Development (OECD). http://www.oecd.org/dataoecd/11/39/34429196.pdf.

Passel, Jeffrey S. 2006. "The Size and Characteristics of the Unauthorized Migrant Population in the U.S." Washington, DC: Pew Hispanic Center. http://pewhispanic.org/files/reports/61.pdf.

———. 2007. "Growing Share of Immigrants Choosing Naturalization." Washington, DC: Pew Hispanic Center. http://pewhispanic.org/files/reports/74.pdf.

Ruggles, Steven, Matthew Sobek, Trent Alexander, Catherine A. Fitch, Ronald Goeken, Patricia Kelly Hall, Miriam King, and Chad Ronnander. 2008. *Integrated Public Use Microdata Series: Version 4.0* [Machine-readable database]. Minneapolis: Minnesota Population Center [producer and distributor].

Rumbaut, Rubén G. 1999. "Passages to Adulthood: The Adaptation of Children of Immigrants in Southern California." In *Children of Immigrants: Health, Adjustment, and Public Assistance,* edited by Donald J. Hernandez (478–545). Washington, DC: National Academy Press.

Sewell, William H., and Robert M. Hauser. 1975. *Education, Occupation, and Earnings.* New York: Academic Press.

Sewell, William H., Robert M. Hauser, and Wendy C. Wolf. 1980. "Sex, Schooling, and Occupational Status." *American Journal of Sociology* 83(3): 551–83.

UNICEF. 2008. *The Childcare Transition.* Report Card 8. Florence, IT: UNICEF Innocenti Research Centre.

Yoshikawa, H., K. McCartney, R. Myers, K. Bub, J. Lugo-Gil, M. Ramos, and F. Knaul. 2006. "Educacion preescolar en Mexico." In *Aprender Mas y Mejor: Politicas, Programas y Oportunidades de Aprendizaje en Educacion Basica en Mexico,* edited by F. Reimers. Mexico City: Fonda Cultura y Economica.

Zimmermann, Wendy, and Karen C. Tumlin. 1999. *Patchwork Policies: State Assistance for Immigrants under Welfare Reform. Assessing the New Federalism* Occasional Paper 24. Washington, DC: The Urban Institute.

PART III
Schooling and the Development of Children and Youth in Hispanic Immigrant Families

9

Facing the Challenges of Educating Latino Immigrant-Origin Students

Carola Suárez-Orozco, Francisco X. Gaytán, and Ha Yeon Kim

Latino students are shaping the future of our nation; they now constitute the fastest growing group of students in our elementary and secondary schools. Nationwide, they represent more than 20 percent of all public school students enrolled in kindergarten through 12th grade (Planty et al. 2008); in some states, such as California, Latinos constitute nearly half the student population (Pérez-Huber et al. 2006).

Findings from a number of recent studies suggest that although some Latinos are successfully navigating the American educational system, a majority are struggling academically and leaving schools without acquiring the skills necessary to compete in the knowledge-intensive U.S. economy (Gándara and Contreras 2009; Wirt et al. 2001). Latinos have the highest high school dropout rates and the lowest college attendance rates among all racial and ethnic groups (Pérez-Huber et al. 2006), foreshadowing less-than-optimal outcomes in today's economy. Many face lives at or below the poverty level laboring at the lowest echelons of the service-sector economy. Others may turn to underground economies and may face incarceration in the country that has the largest prison population in the world (Kennedy 2001; Zimbardo and Haney 1998).

In our postindustrial global society, schooling processes and outcomes are powerful barometers of future individual as well as societal well-being (21st Century Workforce Commission 2000; Bloom 2004). Currently Latinos make up 15 percent of our nation's population (46.7 million) and are our most rapidly growing population (estimated to be 30 percent by 2050).[1] Hence, the fact that significant numbers of our Latino youth are failing to meet their academic potential should be a matter of deep national concern (Council of Economic Advisers 2000).

Latinos are extraordinarily diverse, and their experiences resist facile generalizations. Some have ancestors who were established on what is now U.S. territory long before the current borders were set through conquest and land purchases. In recent decades, however, large numbers of Latinos have been immigrating from dozens of countries that fuel this burgeoning population. Today, an estimated *two-thirds* of Latinos are either immigrants or the children of immigrants (M. Suárez-Orozco and Gaytán 2009).[2]

The sending countries, the areas of settlement, the historical timing of the migration, and the economic circumstances vary considerably for Latinos from different backgrounds. The largest Latino subgroups are Mexican origin (constituting 64 percent of all Latinos in the United States), Puerto Rican origin (9 percent), Cuban origin (3.4 percent), and those originating from Central (6 percent) and South America (7 percent) (Gándara and Contreras 2009). Although educational attainment and achievement vary among these Latino populations, the limited data available often lead researchers to treat Latinos as if they were a homogeneous group and report general findings for an aggregated Latino population. When Latino immigrants and native-born Latinos are considered separately, however, findings indicate that both groups are struggling in the educational system.

In this chapter, we present national data that describe the state of Latino education in the United States, examining various indicators of performance across the educational trajectory from preschool to college. In the initial section, we report on the trends of the U.S. Latino population as a whole, including both the U.S.- and foreign-born. We then turn to exploring the dynamics that shape opportunity including family-of-origin resources, socioeconomic status, neighborhood characteristics such as poverty and school segregation, and the schools attended by the majority of Latino students. Because human experience is not solely the product of structural forces, we also consider how academic engagement, language acquisition, and networks of relations mediate academic outcomes. Given the large proportion of *immigrant-origin* Latinos currently in the United States, we particularly consider the challenges of the immigrant experience in this chapter. We conclude with a discussion of research and policy implications for this significant and growing population.

The "Pipeline Problem": Academic Outcomes among Latinos

If we imagine academic trajectories as a pipeline whose flow begins in preschool, prepares students to be carried through successive levels of education, and ultimately results in high school and post-secondary graduation, we would expect that a smooth current of students would arrive at each level, in proportional numbers, regardless of their demographic backgrounds. Unfortunately, this is not the case. At all educational levels, Latino, African American, and Native American students lag behind their white and Asian American counterparts in educational attainment (Gándara and Contreras 2009; Pérez-Huber et al. 2006).

Persistence by Latino students through each stage along the pipeline is hindered by low levels of academic performance and achievement relative to non-Latino peers. National studies have found that this academic achievement gap emerges as early as kindergarten and grows through graduate education (National Task Force on Minority High Achievement 1999; Planty et al. 2008). On average, Latino students achieve below their white and Asian peers upon entering school, and this discrepancy widens over time (Chernoff et al. 2007; Planty et al. 2008).

Although the Latino-white achievement gap (as well as the black-white gap) narrowed during the 1970s and '80s, it stabilized and actually widened during the 1990s (Lee 2002). This gap persists at the beginning of the new millennium: using various outcomes as indicators of performance, Latinos perform poorly throughout their school years and are much underrepresented among students who earn college degrees (Pérez-Huber et al. 2006; Planty et al. 2008). The "educational crisis" for Latinos is thus not merely at its endpoint; rather, systematic leaks from the earliest stages onward contribute to poor educational outcomes for Latino students (Gándara and Contreras 2009).

Preschool Enrollment

Research findings suggest that Latino children are at a disadvantage from the very beginning of their academic careers. Latino children have the lowest preschool attendance rates of any minority group (Planty et al. 2007). In 2005, while 59 percent of white children between the ages of

3 and 5 were in preschool programs, only 43 percent of Latinos attended such programs. Preschool attendance by African Americans (66 percent) is also higher than the rate for Latinos, as programs such as Head Start have particularly targeted them. The gap in enrollment between whites and Latinos has remained steady through the 1990s and into the new millennium; from 1991 to 2005, the percentage of white children attending preschool increased 5 percent (from 54 to 59 percent), while the preschool attendance rate of Latino children rose 4 percent (from 39 to 43 percent) (Planty et al. 2007).

Prohibitive costs of early childhood education make participating in preschool impossible for most Latino families (National Task Force on Early Childhood Education for Hispanics 2007). Further, lower enrollment rates are partly a result of cultural models that shape narratives around the primacy of the family in the "educacíon" of their young children as well as the importance of sharing language and ethnic background with caretakers (Fuller et al. 1994). This lower participation in preschool contributes to lower English vocabulary acquisition as well as other markers of reading and schooling readiness as young Latino immigrant-origin students enter kindergarten (Chernoff et al. 2007; Crosnoe 2006).

Kindergarten

Kindergarten is a critical period in children's early school careers, as it sets students on a path that influences their future learning and achievement. Disturbing gaps in achievement among different racial/ethnic and socioeconomic groups exist as children enter kindergarten and are widened by the end of 1st grade (Wirt et al. 2001). Research has demonstrated several family risk factors are associated with poor performance in school-age children. The Early Childhood Longitudinal Study program identified four main risk factors: low maternal education, welfare dependency, single-parent household status, and parents whose primary language is not English. Children who entered kindergarten with at least one risk factor demonstrated lower proficiency in early reading and mathematics skills as well as in general funds of knowledge. In 2000, 33 percent of Latino children who entered kindergarten had two or more of these risk factors, compared with 27 percent of African Americans and 6 percent of whites (West, Denton, and Germino-Hauksen 2000).

National Test Scores through Elementary and Middle School

Throughout elementary and middle school, Latinos students demonstrate lower grades and test scores than their white and Asian peers. In grades 3 and 7, Latinos score one to two grade levels below national norms on reading, math, science, social science, and writing tests (García 2001). Further, analysis of the National Assessment of Educational Progress (NAEP) testing, conducted most recently in 2007, shows Latinos averaging much lower scores in writing, reading, and mathematics than whites and Asian/Pacific Islander students (Planty et al. 2008). For example, 4th-grade Latino students receive scaled scores on the mathematics composite test that are on average 20 points below those of their white peers. This gap is even greater (26 points) on the 4th-grade reading composite test. Similar patterns exist for 8th graders; Latinos lag behind their white peers by 26 points on the mathematics composite test and by 25 points on the reading test.

Some of this gap may be attributable to a variation in skills, but some variation is no doubt attributable to second language acquisition assessment-related issues (Solano-Flores 2008; Valdés and Figueroa 1994). Performance on standardized tests is often compromised for English language learners by lack of familiarity with vocabulary and lack of exposure to concepts, test formats, and the like. Indeed, "the development, adaptation, administration, and scoring of tests" (and often the lack thereof) renders many educational assessments, including the NAEP, far from valid assessments of English language learners' actual skills or knowledge (Solano-Flores 2008).

High School Dropout and Graduation Rates

The achievement gap carries into high school years, resulting in poor performance as well as in eventual high dropout rates. By 12th grade, Latino students average only an 8th grade reading level and are more likely to drop out of high school than all other groups (Fry 2003; García 2001). The National Center for Education Statistics reports that, in October 2006, 22.1 percent of 16- to 24-year-old Latinos were high school dropouts, compared with 5.8 percent of whites and 10.7 percent of African Americans (Planty et al. 2008). School dropout rates and high school completion rates are correlated. In 2006, only 63.2 percent of Latinos between the ages of 25 and 29 had completed high school, compared with 93.4 percent of whites and 86.3 percent of blacks. Further, 23.9 percent of Latinos had less than a 9th-grade education compared with only 3.5 percent of whites.[3]

The Bureau of Census data show that Latino immigrants (which include those who arrive in their late teens and adulthood) have lower high school graduation rates than U.S.-born Latinos. For example, in 2000, 14 percent of 16- to 19-year-old Latinos born in the United States had dropped out of high school, compared with 33.7 percent of Latino immigrants (Fry 2003). It should be noted, however, that Latino immigrants inflate the dropout rates in part because many arrive in mid- to late adolescence with the intention of working and therefore never enroll in school; thus, they technically never "drop-in" to school. Estimates suggest that 90 percent of immigrant Latinos between the ages of 16 and 19 who were educated abroad (as opposed to those educated only in the United States) are classified as dropouts.

The federal testing and accountability standards implemented by the No Child Left Behind Act also have particular implications for the secondary education of Latino students. The introduction of statewide tests in Texas in the late 1980s was accompanied by a sharp increase in dropout rates for black and Latino students, and these rates have not returned to previous levels since (Bracey 2000). In 1997, the Mexican American Legal Defense and Educational Fund filed a suit against the Texas Education Agency in a federal district court, pointing out that "over half of Texas' minority students in the sophomore year do not pass one or more parts of the TAAS test, and approximately 85 percent of the students who do not pass the TAAS in May before graduation are Mexican American or African American" (as cited in Natriello and Pallas 1999).

When Massachusetts joined Texas in the growing number of states requiring test scores for high school graduation, students showed striking ethnic/racial disparities in failure rates. For example, in 2001, while 12 percent of white 10th grade students failed the English language arts component of the exam, 48 percent of Latino students did so. And for the mathematics component, 18 percent of white students failed, compared with 58 percent of Latino students. For limited English proficient (LEP) students, the disparities are even more striking: 84 percent did not pass the English language arts test, and 74 percent did not pass the mathematics test. Overall, 77 percent of white students earned a "competency determination," while only 29 percent of Latino students did so.

Latino students are significantly underrepresented in higher-level math and science courses that would prepare them for the MCAS exam, thus barring them from the knowledge and skills necessary for high school graduation in Massachusetts (Gastón Institute for Latino Community Development and Public Policy 2001).

Data suggest that Latino immigrant youth who arrive during adolescence and enter secondary schools are at a particular disadvantage in their education (Ruiz-de-Velasco and Fix 2000; C. Suárez-Orozco, Suárez-Orozco, and Todorova 2008). Frequently, they are not awarded credits for previous course work completed in their countries of origin. Older immigrant youth who have had longer gaps in their previous schooling and enter schools far behind their age levels are particularly at risk; they enter an educational climate where academic success depends upon high-stakes tests that have not been designed with second language learners in mind. As a result, English language learners tend to do particularly poorly on standardized tests (Butler and Castellon-Wellington 2000; MacSwan and Rolstad 2003; Menken 2008), which have serious consequences for their future. Consequently, dropout rates among older Latino immigrant youth are reaching disconcertingly high levels (Amrein and Berliner 2002; Capps et al. 2005).

Even U.S.-born Latinos whose parents were also born in the United States (third generation and beyond) have dropout rates twice that of whites: 12 percent versus 6 percent (Planty et al. 2008). Further, research shows that Latinos born in the United States are more likely than any other native-born racial/ethnic group to drop out of school (Wirt et al. 2001; Kaufman, Alt, and Chapman 2001) with Latino boys at a particular risk by demonstrating the highest dropout rates of all groups (U.S. Department of Education 1995).

This disparity between native-born and immigrant Latinos also interacts with gender. Latino males have particularly low average scores on NAEP reading tests (National Task Force on Minority High Achievement 1999). They are placed at higher rates in special-needs programs than their female counterparts (Connell 2000). In 2000, there was a roughly even split between U.S.-born Latino male dropouts and Latina female dropouts. However, among immigrant Latinos, males constituted 57.7 percent of the dropouts (Fry 2003), a pattern which is consistent with other groups (Connell 2000; M. Suárez-Orozco and Qin-Hilliard 2004).

College Preparation and Application

Among Latinos who complete high school, many graduate without the necessary credentials to be accepted into college. Latino high school graduates are less likely than their white counterparts to take advanced science and mathematics courses (Gándara and Contreras 2009). Latino students are also less likely to take the SAT or to receive high scores (Chapa 2002; Gándara and Contreras 2009). Even among those who perform well academically, fewer Latinos are likely to apply or be accepted to college (Gándara and Contreras 2009; Solorzano, Villalpando, and Oseguera 2005).

Even when Latinos have the necessary academic credentials to enter college, many encounter strong socioeconomic and structural barriers that jeopardize their college attendance. Thus, the typical Latino college student is more likely to attend a community college than a four-year college (Fry 2002). While community colleges offer much promise as an avenue for academic second chances, they are most often a missed opportunity (Solorzano et al. 2005). While most Latino students who enter community colleges enroll with the intent of transferring to four-year institutions, the majority never do so (Fry 2002; Solorzano et al. 2005).

College Persistence

All too many Latinos enter college but leave without completing their degrees (Fry 2002). Based on 2000 U.S. Census data, of 100 Latino students who enter elementary school, 46 graduate from high school, and 26 go onto college, of which 9 enroll in four-year colleges and 17 enroll in community colleges. Of the 17 community college enrollees, only 1 transfers to a four-year college; notably, of the 26 who enroll in college, only 8 complete their four-year degrees, and 2 earn graduate or professional degrees (Yosso and Solorzano 2006). The proportion of Latinos with college degrees is much lower than the same age cohort of whites; only 10.6 percent of Latino males and 12.8 percent of females between age 26 and 35 have college degrees, compared with 22.8 percent of whites males and 25 percent of females (Alba 2009).

The challenges to college persistence are many. Latinos are awarded the lowest average amount of financial aid by type and source of aid among all racial/ethnic groups (Gándara and Contreras 2009). Latino students are also much more likely than their white or Asian peers to study part time while working rather than relying largely on parental financial aid, loans, or scholarships (King 1999). These financial obstacles limit their ability to earn bachelor's degrees.

The barriers to college persistence, however, are not only economic. Many Latino students face the challenges associated with being the first in their families to attend college (Tinto 1993); many have no one to guide them through the process, suffer from "imposter syndrome," and feel distanced from their family during return visits. Many do not find a community of peers at college with whom they feel comfortable, who they can identify with, and who support them. They often report difficulty finding faculty members on campus and mentors who have common interests or who are willing to engage them. Undocumented immigrant students face all these barriers in addition to those associated with their resident status, such as not being eligible for federal financial aid and living in fear of immigration authorities.

On a more encouraging note, Latinos have increased their enrollment in graduate education in the past quarter-century. In 1990, Latinos represented only 3 percent of graduate students; by 2000, their enrollment had grown to 5.2 percent. Despite this positive trend, however, Latinos are still less represented in graduate school than all other racial/ethnic groups (Chapa and De La Rosa 2004). Nationwide, Latinos enroll in law school at higher rates than other minority groups (11 percent), although whites still represent 75 percent of the enrollment in law programs (U.S. Department of Education 1995). Unfortunately, enrollment in law and medical schools in California declined considerably from 1994 to 1999, after Proposition 209 denied affirmative action as a basis for admissions (Gándara and Chávez 2001).

Latinos face particular academic hardship as they pursue graduate training; Latinos studying for master's degrees receive less financial aid and work more than either white or black students. In the 2003–04 academic year, for example, Latino students received proportionally about the same number of grants as white students (63.2 percent versus 61.3 percent) and fewer grants than black students (75.7 percent); however, among those who were granted financial aid, Latinos received the least amount of aid of all racial/ethnic groups (Santiago and Cunningham 2005). Among full-time master's students, Latinos received significantly less financial aid than other groups. Only 65 percent of Latinos received any aid, compared with 76 percent of whites and 90 percent of blacks.

The status of educational attainment for Latinos in the United States should be reason for concern. Using a variety of indicators across the developmental trajectory, we witness that Latino origin youth are at a significant educational disadvantage from the time they enter kindergarten. Presently, the educational gap persists during all school years through college. Future projections foreshadow continued or worsening trends unless significant interventions are made (Gándara and Contreras 2009). In order to develop meaningful interventions, we need to understand what factors serve as impediments to opportunity.

Structuring Opportunity

Whether or not Latino students will be successful in school is determined by a convergence of factors: *family capital* (including poverty, parental education, and whether they are authorized migrants); the kinds of *schools* that Latino immigrant students encounter (school segregation, the language instruction they are provided, how well prepared their teachers are to provide services to the them); *student resources* (their socioemotional challenges, their facility in acquiring a second language, and academic engagement); and their *networks of relational supports*. This complex constellation of variables serves to undermine or, conversely, bolster academic integration and adaptation.

Latino immigrant families arrive to their new land with distinct social and cultural resources (Perreira, Harris, and Lee 2006). Their high aspirations (Fuligni 2001; Portes and Rumbaut 2001), dual frame of reference (C. Suárez-Orozco and Suárez-Orozco 1995), optimism (Kao and Tienda 1995), dedicated hard work, positive attitudes toward school (C. Suárez-Orozco and Suárez-Orozco 1995), and ethic of family support for advanced learning (Li 2004) contribute to the fact that some immigrant youth educationally outperform their native-born peers (Perreira et al. 2006). On the other hand, many immigrant youth encounter such a myriad of challenges—xenophobia, economic obstacles, language difficulties, family separations, under-resourced neighborhoods and schools, and the like—that they struggle to gain their bearings in an educational system that often puts them on a downward trajectory (Huynh and Fuligni 2008; Pong and Hao 2007; Portes and Zhou 1993).

Latino immigrant youth arrive from multiple points of origin. Some are the children of educated professional parents, while others have illiterate parents. Some receive excellent schooling in their countries of origin, while others leave educational systems that are in shambles. Some escape political strife. Others are motivated by the promise of better jobs, while still others frame their migrations as opportunities to provide better education for their children (Hagelskamp, Suárez-Orozco, and Hughes forthcoming). Some are documented migrants, while millions are unauthorized (see Bean and Lowell 2007). Some join well-established communities with robust social supports, while others move from one migrant setting to another (Ream 2005). The educational outcomes of immigrant youth will vary considerably depending on their network of resources (Portes and Rumbaut 2001).

Likewise, as we have seen, native-born Latinos also struggle academically. Below, we review key factors shared by many Latino-origin youth and distinguish those factors that are particular salient for those of immigrant origin.

Family-of-Origin Capital

Poverty. Poverty has long been recognized as a significant risk factor for poor educational outcomes (Luthar 1999; Weissbourd 1996). Children raised in socioeconomic deprivation are vulnerable to an array of distresses including difficulties concentrating and sleeping, anxiety and depression, and a heightened propensity for delinquency and violence. Those living in poverty often experience the stress of major life events as well as the stress of daily hassles that significantly impede academic performance. Poverty frequently coexists with other factors that augment risks, such as single parenthood; residence in neighborhoods plagued with violence, gang activity, and drug trade; and school environments that are segregated, overcrowded, and poorly funded. High poverty is also associated with high rates of housing mobility and concurrent school transitions, which are highly disruptive to educational performance (Gándara and Contreras 2009).

Although some Latino students come from privileged backgrounds, large numbers suffer from the challenges associated with poverty. In 1999, 22.8 percent of Latinos were living in poverty, compared with 7.7 percent of whites (Ramirez and Therrien 2000). In 2006, the poverty rate for Latino students (28 percent) was nearly double that of white children (16 percent) (Fry and Gonzales 2008). For immigrant Latino families, poverty reaches much higher rates: 35 percent of foreign-born

Latino students live in poverty, compared with 27 percent of their native-born counterparts. Immigrant children are more than four times as likely as native-born children to live in crowded housing conditions, and 37 percent of Latino immigrant families report difficulties affording food (Capps 2001). A large proportion of these children is raised in families where parents are working, but many are employed in very low paying professions with erratic working conditions. Further, while the majority of the children are citizens, approximately a quarter have parents who are unauthorized migrants who thus do not access social services that could mitigate the harshest conditions of their poverty.

Such impoverished family conditions may lead Latino students to shoulder financial responsibility for the family; many Latino students contribute to their family income by working after school. According to a recent survey in 2007, 17 percent of Latino students between the ages of 16 and 18 held jobs (Morisi 2008). Working long hours can distract from concentration on school work and is related to lower grades (Warren, LePore, and Mare 2000). After-school work is also associated with lower achievement on math and science scores of the National Educational Longitudinal Study data, and it has a particularly negative effect on boys (Post and Pong 2000).

Unauthorized Status. An estimated 11.1 million immigrants live in the United States without authorization; of that population, 78 percent are from Mexico and Latin America (Bean and Lowell 2007). Among the undocumented population in the United States, 1.8 million are children or adolescents (Passel 2006). These undocumented youth often arrive after multiple family separations and traumatic border crossings (C. Suárez-Orozco, Todorova, and Louie 2002). In addition, an estimated 3.1 million U.S.-citizen children live in households headed by at least one undocumented immigrant (Passel 2006).

Unauthorized children and youth in households with unauthorized members often experience fear and anxiety around being separated from family members if they or someone they love are apprehended or deported (Capps et al. 2007); such psychological and emotional duress can take a heavy toll on the academic experiences of children growing up in these homes. Further, while unauthorized youth legally have equal access to K–12 education, they do not have equal access to either health, or social services, or jobs (Gándara and Contreras 2009). In addition, undocumented students with dreams of graduating from high school and going on to college will find that their legal status stands in the way of their access to postsecondary educational opportunities (Gándara and Contreras 2009; C. Suárez-Orozco et al. 2008). Thus, immigrant Latinos who are unauthorized or who come from unauthorized families suffer from a particular burden of unequal access.

Seasonal Migrant Status. Being a Latino child whose parents do seasonal migrant work presents additional challenges; multiple moves, frequent interruptions in schooling, deep poverty, and harsh working and living conditions are realities in their lives. In a representative national survey, Latinos composed 83 percent of the migrant farm workers interviewed, with 75 percent born in Mexico (Carroll et al. 2005). Many families lived in conditions of poverty with household incomes that averaged between $15,000 and $17,499 per year. It is estimated that over 750,000 children travel with their migrant parents in the United States each year (DiCerbo 2001). The lack of continuity in their schooling trajectories (because of interruptions during the school year, the difficulty of transferring school records, health problems, and lack of English language skills) contributes to an acute risk of low attendance and high dropout rates (Ream 2005).

Family Educational Background. Parental education matters. Highly literate parents are better equipped to guide their children in studying, accessing, and making meaning of educational information. Children with more educated parents are exposed to more academically oriented vocabulary and interactions at home, and they tend to be read to more often from books that are valued at school (Goldenberg, Rueda, and August 2006). More educated parents understand the value of and have the resources to provide additional books, a home computer, and Internet access. They are also more likely to seek information about how to navigate the educational system in their new land.

Unfortunately, however, many Latino parents have limited schooling. The number of Latino students who have no parent with a high school diploma will grow from 37 percent to 59 percent by 2015 (National Task Force on Minority High Achievement 1999). Moreover, low parental education is compounded by parents' limited English language skills, which may index the support children receive for learning English at home (Carhill, Suárez-Orozco, and Páez 2008; Portes and Hao 1998).

Such disadvantaged backgrounds have implications for the educational transition: unsurprisingly, youth arriving from families with lower levels of education tend to struggle academically, while those who come from more literate families and with strong skills often flourish (Kasinitz et al. 2008; Portes and Rumbaut 2001).

Immigrant Latino parents, however, often do not possess the kind of cultural capital that serves middle-class mainstream students well (Perreira et al. 2006); not knowing the dominant cultural values of the new society limits immigrant Latino parents' ability to provide an upward academic path for their children. Parental involvement is neither a cultural practice in their countries of origin nor a luxury that their financial situation in this country typically allows. They come from cultural traditions where parents are expected to respect teachers' recommendations rather than to advocate for their children (Delgado Gaitan 2004). Not speaking English and having limited education may make them feel inadequate. Lack of documentation may make them worry about exposure to immigration raids (Capps et al. 2007). Low-wage low-skill jobs with off-hour shifts typically do not provide much flexibility to attend parent-teacher conferences and access child care. The impediments to coming to school are multiple and are frequently interpreted by teachers and principals as "not valuing" their children's education.

Ironically, however, Latino immigrant parents often frame the family narrative of migration around providing better educational opportunities to their children (C. Suárez-Orozco et al. 2008). While they may care deeply about their children's education and may often urge their students to work hard in school so they do not have to do hard physical labor as their parents do, Latino immigrant parents frequently do not have first-hand experience in the American school system or in their native system (López 2001). They also have very limited social networks that could provide the educational resources to help them navigate the complicated college pathway system in the United States (Auerbach 2004). Thus, they often have limited capacities to help their children successfully "play the educational game" in their new land.

School Resources

School Contexts. Segregation in neighborhoods and schools has negative consequences on academic success for minority students (Massey and Denton 1993; Orfield and Lee 2006; Orfield and Yun 1999). In all but a few "exceptional cases under extraordinary circumstances, schools that are separate are still unquestionably unequal" (Orfield and Lee 2006, 4). Nationally, Latinos tend to settle in highly segregated and deeply impoverished urban settings and attend the most segregated schools of any group in the United States: in 1996, only 25 percent of Latino students attended majority-white schools. The degree of segregation results in a series of consequences. In general, Latinos who settle in predominantly minority neighborhoods have virtually no direct, systematic, or intimate contact with middle-class white Americans. This in turn affects the quality of schools they attend and the networks that are useful to access desirable colleges and jobs (Orfield 1995; Portes 1996).

Segregation for Latino-origin immigrant students often involves isolation at the levels of race and ethnicity, poverty, and language—aptly named "triple segregation" (Orfield and Lee 2006). These three dimensions of segregation have been associated with reduced school resources with various negative educational outcomes, including low expectations, difficulties learning English, lower achievement, greater school violence, and higher dropout rates (Gándara and Contreras 2009). Such school contexts typically undermine students' capacity to concentrate, their sense of security, and hence their ability to learn.

The Longitudinal Immigrant Student Adaptation (LISA) was a mixed-methods, five-year longitudinal study using data collected from student, parent, and teacher perspectives to document the factors associated with the cultural and academic adaptation of immigrant youth (C. Suárez-Orozco et al. 2008). In terms of triple segregation, all the Latino groups in the study (Mexican, Central American, and Dominican) were most likely to attend highly segregated schools. Numerous negative qualities were associated with this level of segregation. For example, when asked to relate their perceptions of school in the new country, many students spoke of crime, violence, gang activity, weapons, drug dealing, and racial conflicts. Students who attended highly segregated schools with high levels of perceived school violence were more likely to demonstrate patterns of academic disengagement and grade decline over time. Indicators of school inequality—including percentages of inexperienced teachers as well as out-of-subject certification rate, greater-than-average school size, dropout rate, daily attendance, higher-than-average suspension and expulsion rates, percentage of students performing below proficiency on the state-administered English language arts and math standardized tests, and a significant achievement gap on the standardized exam between one or more ethnic groups that attend the school—were linked to these highly segregated schools and, consequently, lower student performance.

Indicators of school segregation and violence were consistent with poor performance schoolwide on standardized tests across the Latino groups. The LISA study found that only 20 percent of Dominican and Central American students, and 16 percent of Mexican students, in low-quality schools reached proficiency level or higher on the federally mandated, statewide English language arts exam. There was also a significant relationship between segregated schools and individual achievement outcomes including both grades and students' standardized achievement test scores (C. Suárez-Orozco et al. 2008).

Segregation places students at a significant disadvantage as they strive to learn a new language, master the necessary skills to pass high-stakes tests, accrue graduation credits, get into college, and attain the skills needed to compete in workplaces increasingly shaped by the demands of the new global economy. Unfortunately, all too many schools that serve the children of immigrants, like schools that serve other disadvantaged students, are those that seem designated to teach "other people's children" (Delpit 1995). Such segregated, suboptimal schools offer the very least to those who need the very most, structuring and reinforcing inequality (Oakes 1985).

Second-Language Instruction. Seventy percent of English language learners (ELL) in grades 6–12 are Latinos; as such, second language instruction is a critical component to ensuring their academic success (Batalova, Fix, and Murray 2007). Frequently, Latino ELL students are placed in some kind of second-language instructional setting (pull-out programs, sheltered instruction, English as a second language [ESL], and dual-language instruction) as they enter their new school (Gándara and Contreras 2009). Students are then moved out of these settings in various schools, districts, and states with very little rhyme or reason for the transition (C. Suárez-Orozco et al. 2008; Thomas and Collier 2002).

Research considering the efficacy of second language instruction and bilingual programs reveals contradictory results. This should not be surprising, given that there are nearly as many models of bilingual and language assistance programs of a wide array of practices and programs as well as philosophical approaches (Thomas and Collier 2002) as there are school districts. ESL programs often consist of limited pull-out instruction and academic support with the rest of the day spent immersed in regular classes; ESL classrooms most often have learners from many different countries speaking many different languages. Transitional bilingual programs focus on providing academic support while students transition out of their language of origin into English. In one-way developmental bilingual programs, students of one language group are schooled in two languages (for example, English and Spanish) so they can keep up with academic material in their native language as they learn English. In structured immersion programs, the curriculum is simplified and is taught more slowly, and with a great deal of repetition, in English. And in sheltered English programs, all lessons in every subject are at least in part a second-language lesson; thus a science class is also an opportunity to learn new vocabulary. Dual-language immersion classes, the state-of-the-art of bilingual education, involve students' learning half the time in English and half in their native Spanish, with half of the class native speakers of English and the other half native speakers of Spanish. This kind of program offers greater opportunity for students to truly become bilingual—they develop their second language while maintaining their first. They also develop and expand their academic skills by drawing on both languages.

Studies of the relative merits of such programs have established that dual-language programs most consistently produce the best results. Excellent results as measured by high performance of students are also found in one-way developmental programs offered in high-achieving districts (Thomas and Collier 2002). Well designed and implemented programs offer good educational results and buffer at-risk students from dropping out by easing transitions, providing academic scaffolding, and providing a sense of community (Padilla et al. 1991).

There is, however a huge disparity in quality of instruction between settings. While it has been well demonstrated that high-quality programs produce excellent results, those plagued with problems, not surprisingly, produce less-than-optimal results (August and Hakuta 1997; Thomas and Collier 2002). Many bilingual programs, unfortunately, face real challenges in their implementation—inadequate resources, uncertified personnel, and poor administrative support. Perhaps the most common problem in the day-to-day running of bilingual programs is the dearth of fully certified bilingual teachers who are trained in second-language acquisition and who can serve as proper language models to their students (Gruber et al. 2002). Because many bilingual programs are ambivalently supported throughout the nation, they simply do not offer the breadth and depth of courses immigrant students need to get into a meaningful college track. Hence, there is an ever-present danger that once a student enters the ESL or bilingual track, she will have difficulty switching to the college-bound track. The mission of the schools is often not focused on meeting the needs of newcomer students; at best, they tend to be ignored, and at worst, they are viewed as a problem contributing to low performance on state-mandated high-stakes tests (C. Suárez-Orozco et al. 2008).

Teacher Preparation and Teacher Expectations. Teacher shortages are a chronic problem for U.S. schools. Every year, the number of teachers leaving their classrooms for reasons such as retirement and career changes exceeds the number of new teachers attracted to a low-paying, low-status, and increasingly highly stressful profession, with student enrollments increasing all the while (Ingersoll 2003; Planty et al. 2008). This phenomenon of high teacher turnover rate is especially true in schools in impoverished urban settings with racial and linguistic segregation (ibid.), which Latino students typically attend (C. Suárez-Orozco et al. 2008).

Such teacher shortfalls often result in lower teacher quality (National Commission on Teaching and America's Future 1997). For example, these schools are more likely to hire teachers with three or fewer years of teaching experience (Planty et al. 2008). In addition, attrition rates are particularly high among beginning teachers: 40 to 50 percent of all beginning teachers leave their profession in five years (Ingersoll and Smith 2003). Further, most teachers across the United States have had very limited training to work with English language learners: 87.5 percent have received less than 8 hours of instruction to teach students with limited English proficiency, although they are increasingly likely to encounter such students in their classrooms (Gruber et al. 2002). Consequently, Latino students, who are often ELLs and attend such segregated urban schools, tend to be taught by inexperienced teachers who have not received enough training to serve this population. This also precludes the possibility of achieving a critical mass of experienced and caring teachers at some of the most under-resourced schools.

Unfortunately, in schools that serve Latino immigrant students, we commonly find cultures of low teacher expectations where what is sought and valued by teachers is student compliance rather than curiosity or student cognitive engagement (Bang et al. 2009; Conchas 2001). Low teacher expectations fundamentally shape the educational experience and outcomes of their students beyond simply exposing them to low educational standards (Weinstein 2002). Classrooms and schools typically sort students into those who are thought to be talented versus those who are thought to be less so. These expectations may be made based on impressions of individual capabilities, but they are often founded upon stereotyped beliefs about their racial, ethnic, and socioeconomic backgrounds as well (e.g., "Asian students are smart and hard-working" while "Latino students are not"). Students are very aware of the perceptions that teachers have of them: well-regarded students receive ample positive social mirroring (or reflections and feedback) about their capacity to learn and thus are more likely to redouble their efforts (C. Suárez-Orozco 2000). Students who are found wanting on any combination of these characteristics, however, tend to either become invisible in the classroom or are actively disparaged. Under these circumstances, only the most resilient of students tend to remain engaged. Latino students from immigrant families who do not always share the culture of the teachers who teach them are particularly susceptible to such negative social mirroring (C. Súarez-Orozco and Súarez-Orozco 2001).

Individual Child Resources and Challenges

Socioemotional Challenges. For many Latino students, their educational journey begins with their migration to the United States. Migration is a transformative process with profound implications for the family as well as the potential for lasting impact on socioemotional development (García Coll and Magnuson 1997; C. Suárez-Orozco and Suárez-Orozco 2001). By any measure, immigration is one of the most stressful events a family can undergo (Falicov 1998; C. Suárez-Orozco 2001): it removes family members from predictable contexts—community ties, jobs, and customs—and strips them of significant social ties—extended family members, best friends, and neighbors. New arrivals who experienced trauma (either before migrating or as secondary to the "crossing") may remain preoccupied with the violence and may also feel guilty about having escaped when loved ones remained behind (Lustig et al. 2004).[4] Undocumented new arrivals face the growing realities of workplace raids that can lead to traumatic and sudden separations (Capps et al. 2007).

For some Latino immigrants, the dissonance in cultural expectations, the cumulative stressors, and the loss of social supports lead to affective and somatic symptoms (Alegría et al. 2007; Mendoza, Javier, and Burgos 2007). Some Latino parents are relatively unavailable psy-chologically owing to their own struggles in adapting to a new country, thus posing a developmental challenge to their children (C. Suárez-Orozco and Suárez-Orozco 2001). The immigrant parents of Latino youth, whether their children are first or second generation, often turn to them in navigating the new society. Children of immigrants are asked to take on "parentified" roles, including translation (Faulstich-Orellana 2001). Such tasks often fall more on the shoulders of daughters, leading to positive and negative consequences for their development (C. Suárez-Orozco et al. 2005).

Latino children and youth also face the challenges of forging an identity and sense of belonging to a country that may reflect an unfamiliar culture while honoring the values and traditions of their parents (Berry et al. 2006; C. Suárez-Orozco 2004). Acculturative stress has been linked to high levels of intergenerational conflict as well as psychological and academic problems (Gibbs 2003; C. Suárez-Orozco 2000). Children and youth are often asked to take on responsibilities beyond their years including sibling care, translation, and advocacy (Faulstich-Orellana 2001), which at times undermine parental authority. These often highly gendered roles may have both positive and negative consequences for development (Smith 2002; M. Suárez-Orozco and Qin-Hilliard 2004).

First-generation Latino youth face their parents' challenges of adjusting to a new context. They also, often, immigrate not simply to new homes but to new family structures as many are separated for long periods from their parents during migration (C. Suárez-Orozco et al. 2002). Further, the first generation must learn a new language, going through a difficult transition when they are unable to communicate their thoughts with ease; while some acquire competency over time, most are marked by accents, and others never gain proficiency (Mendoza et al. 2007). The significant time it takes to acquire academic English presents significant educational as well as social challenges for immigrant students (Cummins 1991; C. Suárez-Orozco et al. 2008).

The second generation (Latinos born in the United States to immi-grant parents) often has limited facility in their parents' native language (Portes and Hao 1998), which presents other challenges in maintain-ing communication at home (C. Suárez-Orozco et al. 2008). While American-born Latinos and their first-generation parents may share a lack of access to those who can guide them through the institutions of the unfamiliar dominant society, they are spared the challenges of premigratory trauma, status-related stress, and family separations. On the other hand, children often face the stressors of poverty, typically in urban contexts (Noguera 2006), without the protection of immigrant optimism (Kao and Tienda 1995) and a dual frame of reference (C. Suárez-Orozco and Suárez-Orozco 1995). The burden of forging a transcultural identity where they can navigate both their parents' culture and the dominant culture also falls more to them (C. Suárez-Orozco 2004).

Data examining the well-being of immigrant origin populations in general and Latinos in particular across generations and ages reveal mixed results according to country of origin, developmental group, cohort, and age of arrival as well as developmental outcome (Rumbaut 2004; Takeuchi et al. 2007). While there is a fairly consistent "immigrant paradox" showing a decline across generations with greater length of residency for *physical health* outcomes and engagement in *risk behaviors,* the results are inconsistent regarding the risk to *psychological health.* Further, the body of evidence on the immigrant health has focused on adults and families rather than on adolescents (Lansford, Deater-Deckard, and Bornstein 2007; Taningco 2007). Immigrant youth of refugee origin appear to be at greatest risk for affective disorders (Lustig et al. 2004). Latino and immigrant adolescents show patterns of progressive risk-taking behaviors the longer they are exposed to U.S. culture (Vega et al. 1998). This is also the case for academic engagement—an increasingly important indicator of well-being in the knowledge-intensive economy; it decreases across time across generation and with increasing time in the United States, particularly for Latinos (Fuligni 1997; Portes and Rumbaut 2001; Sirin 2005). Given the limited and mixed evidence on the developmental trajectories of this growing population of urban-residing Latino adolescents, more research on indicators of their well-being is needed using both qualitative and quantitative lenses.

Challenges of Language Acquisition.   Many Latino children experience difficulties with English in school. In 2000, about three-quarters (71 percent) of all children who spoke English less than very well were Latinos in pre-kindergarten to 5th grade (Capps et al. 2005). A more recent survey in 2006 revealed that 18.4 percent of all Latino school-age children (5–17) spoke English with difficulty (Planty et al. 2008). The struggle to speak English among Latino students is not just a challenge for immigrant children. Among pre-kindergarten–to-5th-grade Latino children in the United States, 62 percent of foreign-born children spoke English less than very well, as well as 43 percent of U.S.-born children of immigrants and 12 percent of children of U.S.-born Latinos (Capps et al. 2005).

Learning a second language often takes a long time, and being a competent language user at an academic level takes even more. The complexity of oral and written academic English skills generally requires between four and seven years of optimal academic instruction to develop academic second language skills comparative to native English speakers (Collier 1987, 1995; Cummins 1991, 2000). Struggles in language are well presented in LISA data; only 7 percent of the sample had developed academic English skills comparable to those of their native-born English-speaking peers after seven years on average in the United States (Carhill et al. 2008). Yet, Latino ELLs do not typically encounter robust second-language-acquisition educational programs, as noted earlier, and often face individual disadvantages and structural linguistic isolations that may hinder their adequate academic English development.

Many Latino immigrant students from strife-ridden or poverty-stricken countries enter U.S. schools with little or no schooling, and they often may not read or write well in Spanish (Páez 2001). Moreover, growing numbers of Latino immigrants are indigenous speakers who do not speak Spanish as their first language. For these children, English is their third language, doubling the effort to master academic proficiency in English. Research in second-language acquisition suggests that when students are well grounded in their native language and have developed reading and writing skills in that language, they appear able to efficiently apply that knowledge to the new language when provided appropriate instructional supports (August and Shanahan 2006; Butler and Hakata 2005). Unfortunately, however, many Latino students do not enter schools with this advantage. In addition, many Latino ELL students cannot receive support for learning English from their parents at home. Latino parents often have limited education (National Task Force on Minority High Achievement 1999) and limited English skills and may thus be unable to provide rich English learning contexts for their children. Indeed, nearly a quarter of Latino students are linguistically isolated (Capps et al. 2005), living in households where all members over age 14 are limited English proficient.

This linguistic isolation is a reality in the social contexts of many Latino students in segregated neighborhoods. Many Latinos live in predominantly minority neighborhoods that do not promise much direct contact with well-educated native English speakers. At school, ELL students in general and Latino students in particular are often segregated from their native-English-speaking peers, relegated to the basement or a wing of the school (Olsen 1997). In many cases, children have almost no meaningful contact with English-speaking peers (Carhill et al. 2008). Indeed, more than a third of immigrant students in the LISA study reported that they had little opportunity to interact with peers who were not from their country of origin, which no doubt contributed to their linguistically isolated state (C. Suárez-Orozco et al. 2008). This isolation is clearly disadvantageous to Latino ELL students by minimizing exposure to the English they need to learn. Research suggests that sustained interactions with educated native speakers, particularly in informal situations (such as at work, with friends, in the cafeterias and hallways of school, and in neighborhood contexts) in peer and community contexts, predicts stronger academic English proficiency outcomes (Carhill et al. 2008; Jia and Aaronson 2003). Without such contact, an important source of language modeling is missed.

Less-developed academic English proficiency often masks actual skills and knowledge of Latino English learners. Even when English learners are able to participate and compete in mainstream classrooms, they often read more slowly than native speakers, may not understand double entendres, and simply may not be exposed to the same words and cultural information of native-born middle-class peers. Their academic language skills may also not allow them to be easily engaged in academic contexts and to perform well on "objective" assessments designed for native English speakers. Taken together, then, it is not surprising that limited English proficiency is often associated with lower grade point averages, repeating grades, poor performance on standardized tests, and low graduation rates (DeVoe et al. 2004; Ruiz-de-Velasco and Fix 2000).

Student Engagement.   In recent years, a corpus of literature has pointed to individual factors examining the role of academic engagement in academic adaptation. Engagement is how strongly students are connecting to what they are learning, how they are learning it, and who they are learning it with (Fredricks, Blumenfeld, and Paris 2004). Highly engaged students are actively involved in their education, completing and internalizing the tasks required to perform well in school. Somewhat engaged students may be doing "good enough" work but not reaching their full potential. In cases of more extreme academic disengagement, a student's disinterest, erratic attendance, and missed or incomplete assignments can lead to failure in multiple courses, an outcome that often foreshadows dropping out of school (Rumberger 2004). Academic disengagement may not be immediate, but it may occur over time in response to long-term difficulties in community, school, and family circumstances.

Engagement is a broad dimension that has been used in the social sciences in various ways. Cognitive engagement is how engrossed and intellectually involved students are in what they are learning (C. Suárez-Orozco et al. 2008). Cognitive engagement is the antithesis of "being bored" in school, and data show that attitudes toward school and academic self-efficacy are important in fostering student academic involvement (Schunk 1991). LISA data reveal that cognitive engagement is a significant predictor of whether students put effort into their studies (C. Suárez-Orozco et al. 2008).

Relational engagement is how strongly students feel connected to their teachers, peers, and others in schools. Such relationships are important for the academic adaptation of students (Levitt, Guacci-Franco, and Levitt 1994). Social relations can provide a sense of belonging, emotional support, tangible assistance, guidance, role modeling, and positive feedback (Wills 1985). Latino students who are most likely to adapt successfully to school are able to forge meaningful, positive relationships at school. Relationships in school can play an important role in promoting socially competent behavior in the classroom and in fostering academic engagement and achievement. LISA data reveal that students who report better school-based relations are more behaviorally engaged in their studies (C. Suárez-Orozco et al. 2008). Relational engagement also bolsters cognitive engagement. Students with better relationships in school find their academic work more interesting and engaging. Academic self-efficacy— a feeling of mastery over learning—is also highly related to greater relational engagement in the LISA study. The more meaningful, nurturing relationships a student has with teachers and peers at school, the more she feels able to tackle learning.

Behavioral engagement (often referred to as academic engagement) reflects students' participation and efforts to perform academic tasks (Fredricks et al. 2004). When students do their best on class work and homework, turn in assignments on time, pay attention, behave appropriately in class, and maintain good attendance, they are behaviorally engaged. Using data from the LISA study, we assessed whether the students completed the tasks necessary to be successful in school, including attending class, participating in discussions and classroom activities, and completing homework and course assignments (C. Suárez-Orozco et al. 2008). Behavioral engagement is highly correlated with grades. Longitudinally, we found a pattern of accelerating behavioral disengagement for the sample as a whole and particularly for Latinos. There was little difference in the amount of effort boys and girls expended in their studies initially. Over time, however, girls maintained their levels of behavioral engagement while boys were more likely to disengage. High-achieving students were significantly more behaviorally engaged in school than were the low or precipitously declining performers.

As expected, school problems interfered with behavioral engagement: the greater the student's perceptions of school problems, the less engaged they were in their studies. Further, cognitive engagement contributed to behavioral engagement: when students were curious and interested in their schoolwork, they were more likely to try harder. In addition, students with supportive school-based relationships were more likely to expend greater effort on their schoolwork.

Networks of Relationships

From the time of arrival in a new country, social supports and networks of relations provide families with tangible aid, guidance, and advice as well as emotional sustenance. These supports are critical for newcomers who can find their new environment disorienting. Positive relationships maintain and enhance self-esteem, while providing acceptance, approval, and a sense of belonging. During migration, extended family members—godparents, aunts, uncles, older cousins, and the like—are often important sources of tangible support. Family cohesion and the maintenance of a well-functioning system of supervision, authority, and mutuality can shape the well-being and social outcomes of children.

No family is an island, so wellness is enhanced when it is part of a larger community offering what Felton Earls termed "community agency" (Earls 1997). For immigrant youth, community agency can inoculate against the toxic elements in their new settings (De Vos 1992). In immigrant communities, these organizations are often associated with churches or religious organizations. Sociologist Min Zhou reports that community-based organizations serving Latino youth in the United States often focus on problem behaviors such as gang interventions or pregnancy prevention. In contrast, however, community-based organizations serving Asian youth tend to emphasize proactive activities such as SAT preparation, math, and English tutoring (Zhou and Li 2004).

Peers can serve as both positive and negative social capital (Portes 1998). Peers can encourage maladaptive behavior, promote drug use, and discourage competent academic engagement. In this case, peers distract their classmates from performing optimally in school (Gibson, Gándara, and Koyama 2004). Peers may contribute to unsafe school and community environments, which can undermine students' ability to concentrate, their sense of security, and their ability to experience trusting relationships in school. On the positive side, peer relationships can prove powerful role models as they provide a sense of belonging and tangible help (Gibson et al. 2004; Stanton-Salazar 2004). For new Latino immigrant students, the companionship of co-nationals is an important source of information on school culture (C. Suárez-Orozco, Pimentel, and Martin 2009). Peers can act as "vital conduits" (Stanton-Salazar 2004) of information to disoriented newcomers. Peers not only buffer the loneliness new arrivals often experience but also can enhance self-confidence and self-efficacy, providing the sustenance that nourishes the development of new psychosocial competencies (C. Suárez-Orozco et al. 2009).

Mentoring relationships are often important in the lives of immigrant youth (Crul 2007; Rhodes 2002). In stressed families with limited social resources, mentors support healthier relationships by alleviating pressure on the family (Roffman, Suárez-Orozco, and Rhodes 2003). Bicultural mentors can serve to bridge the old and new cultures (Crul 2007). Bicultural mentors act as fonts of information about the new cultural rules of engagement. Mentors can heal ruptures in relationships that result from long immigrant separations and complicated reunifications. Because Latino immigrant parents are often not available given their work schedules, the guidance and affection from a mentor fills the void in the life of a youngster. Mentoring relationships have been shown to reduce substance abuse, aggressive behavior, and delinquency (Rhodes 2002). Research suggests that college educated co-ethnic mentors particularly can help their protégés perform better in school by helping them with homework, by providing informed advice about educational access, and through positive role modeling (Crul 2007; C. Suárez-Orozco et al. 2008).

Research and Policy Implications

Taking in the panorama of the current immigrant Latino crisis is a daunting enterprise. As we have considered, a plethora of structural, familial, school, and student-level factors interacts to impede educational opportunity. Given economic and demographic realities, the future does not appear much more promising if we stand by and do nothing. To develop meaningful interventions and tackle these large-scale issues we need to strengthen our research and evidence. In tandem, we need to implement promising models that address the many leaks in the educational pipeline. There is reason for hope; we already have ample evidence that can make a difference in the educational trajectories of Latino immigrant origin youth. Below we make recommendations for research, policy, and practice.

Research Recommendations

Specifying and Defining Populations. As noted earlier, the term Latino (or Hispanic) encompasses a wide range of individuals from different generational statuses, linguistic and racial backgrounds, and countries of origin. Defining the population under consideration is therefore essential. Researchers need to be specific whenever they include first, second, or third generations in their sample. They should specify country of origin whenever that is available or known (e.g., Mexican for the first generation or Mexican American for the second generation and beyond). Further, it is important to distinguish between children of immigrants and limited English proficient children (defined by the U.S. Census as speaking a language other than English at home and speaking English less than very well). Other terms that are sometimes used and which should be carefully defined include English language learners, newcomers, and Latin American immigrants. Further, whenever possible it is important to include comparison groups (C. Suárez-Orozco and Suárez-Orozco 1995). These comparison groups can include a range of immigrant origin populations as well as others from nonimmigrant populations who encounter similar contexts. These comparison groups provide valuable contextualization of findings.

Mixed-Method Approaches. Cross-cultural research with diverse populations compels us to reexamine many traditional social science assumptions around validity and reliability and requires new approaches (McLoyd and Steinberg 1998; C. Suárez-Orozco and Suárez-Orozco 1995). Mixed-method designs, linking "outsider" (etic) and "insider" (emic) perspectives, triangulated data, and embedding findings into an ecological framework are essential to the endeavor (Bronfenbrenner 1988; Hughes and Seidman 1993; C. Suárez-Orozco et al. 2008). We have much to learn from our colleagues in economics, sociology, anthropology, public health, and linguistics. Interdisciplinary teams whose members are "bilingual" (or "multilingual")—that, is well versed in one another's methodologies—lead to more robust research contributions. Just as is the case with language abilities, it is rare that complete mastery (with equal ease in reading, writing, and oral fluency) is achieved in both languages/methodologies. Thus, it is important to have multidisciplinary teams where at least one member is dominant in one language/discipline but also "fluent" in the other language/discipline.

Bilingual and Bicultural Researchers.   Combining outsider and insider approaches to diverse populations is important in both data collection and analysis (Cooper et al. 1998). Bicultural and bilingual researchers are better able to establish rapport and trust within the communities and gain entry into Latino immigrant populations that might otherwise be difficult to access (see Moll et al. 1992 and González, Moll, and Amanti 2005). Further, insiders are essential for appropriate linguistic and cultural translations of protocols. Their perspective is also essential to accurate and culturally relevant interpretations. If members of the immigrant community do not conduct the research, it is essential that cultural experts be consulted in the both in the development of instruments as well as the interpretation of findings. Outsiders provide a fresh interpretive perspective and may lend specific disciplinary expertise. Interpretive communities of insiders and outsiders as well as individuals representing a range of disciplinary expertise are highly recommended.

Linguistically Appropriate Tools.   Questions and prompts that are valid for one group may not be valid for another. It is a challenge to develop single instruments or approaches that capture the experiences of individuals from diverse backgrounds. Of course, research protocols should always be provided in the language of dominance of the informant. Measures developed with mainstream English-speaking populations (as are many standardized instruments) are often culturally and linguistically biased (Doucette-Gates, Brooks-Gunn, and Chase-Lansdale 1998). New tools, either adapted from preexisting instruments or developed entirely anew, are often a necessity for accurate research with immigrants. The process of development should be dynamic and inductive, involving theoretically based formulations along with themes emerging from the field. As culturally informed questionnaires are developed they must be careful translated and piloted.

Triangulated Data. Using triangulated data, from various perspectives and using various strategies, is crucial when faced with the challenges of validity in conducting research with groups of diverse backgrounds. Such an approach allows more confidence that data is accurately capturing the phenomenon under consideration. By sifting through a variety of perspectives—self-reports, parent reports, teacher reports (in the case of youth) or other community members (in the case of adults) as well as researcher observations—concurrence and disconnections can be established between what informants say they do, what others say they do, and what the researcher sees them do. Researchers should consider various levels of analysis in their research including the individual, interpersonal relations (peers, family), context-specific social groups (work, schools, neighborhood, church), and cultural dimensions. Focusing on the numerous and interrelated developmental contexts that Latino immigrant youth grow up in is crucial to successfully conducting research with this or any population (Bronfenbrenner 1977).

It is also essential that we systematically recognize the sources of bias in assessment, particularly with second-language learners. In a nutshell the sources of bias include "Who is given tests in what language by whom, when, and where?" (Solano-Flores 2008). When students do poorly on tests, it cannot simply be assumed that they lack the skills (though in some cases that is a partial explanation). Sometimes students have not been exposed to culturally biased materials or do not have the vocabulary in English. Sometimes this issue is one of retrieval time; second-language learners may simply need more time to process two languages. Double negatives are an issue for second-language learners. Unfamiliar test formats place newcomer immigrants at a disadvantage. Issues of cultural and linguistic fairness in assessment are a critical area of research importance (Valdés and Figueroa 1994).

Longitudinal Research. Though time-consuming and expensive, longitudinal research has much to offer and should be pursued when possible (Fuligni 2001; C. Suárez-Orozco 2001). Cross-sectional data and data collected only once limit our ability to detect changes over time. Identifying such changes are essential to understanding the dynamic nature of educational progress and the efficacy of interventions.

Gendered Experiences. Gendered migratory experiences are another domain of significant neglect within the Latino immigration research community (Donato et al. 2006). Scholars all too often fail to consider whether females are motivated by the same forces as males as well as how their respective experiences within the new context may or may not differ. Ample evidence suggests that there are many dimensions of experience, which indeed differ by gender (Hongdagneu-Sotelo 1999; Mahler 1999). Girls and young women demonstrate more favorable academic trajectories than do young men (C. Suárez-Orozco et al. 2008) who often must contend with more unforgiving, hostile receptions within the new country (López 2001; C. Suárez-Orozco and Qin 2006). On the other hand, assuming that gender will always lead to different experiences is a mistake. Although there are certainly differences between immigrant males and females, there are also many similarities (Connell 2000; M. Suárez-Orozco and Qin-Hilliard 2004). Future research should consider *how, when,* and *why* it makes a difference to be an immigrant or to be from a particular country or to be female rather than male (Eckes and Trautner 2000; C. Suárez-Orozco and Qin 2006).

Racialized Experiences. Overlooking the racialized experiences of Latinos is another serious oversight in much research. Latinos encounter very different receptions depending on whether they are "racially marked" by phenotype (Bailey 2001; López 2001). Latinos embody the spectrum of ethnic and racial diversity. Latinos are phenotypically black, white, indigenous, and every *mestizaje* thereof. Within the same family there are often wide variations in skin, hair, and eye color, along with the consequential differences in how society or even parents react to those differences (C. Suárez-Orozco 2001). Such differences elicit not only overt discrimination, but also everyday racial micro-aggressions, which despite their seeming insignificance can have lasting negative effects (Sue et al. 2007). Given the color spectrum represented by Latinos, keeping this perspective in mind is essential while researching the adaptation of new Latino immigrants in a racially conscious society.

Documentation Status. Considering documentation status is another important, though extremely challenging, research issue. We currently have the largest undocumented population in history. Whether students or their parents are documented is likely to have numerous implications for well-being (Kalil and Chen 2008; Yoshikawa, Godfrey, and Rivera 2008), as well as educational trajectories (see earlier discussion). There are, of course numerous limitations in regards to the ethics as well the reliability of gathering this kind of data; however, creative, sensitive, and ethical approaches must be developed to understand this important issue in the lives of many Latinos.

Sending Origins. Learning as much as possible about sending origins is essential when working with first-generation Latino populations (Rumbaut and Cornelius 1995). The sending context, including historical, political, and economic conditions at the time of the migration, can have fundamental importance. Some Latino-origin families come to the United States for largely economic reasons, but others are forced out because of extreme political repression; still others come for a combination of reasons. The sending frame of migration has implications for the notion of whether the family may return, how much of the family resources are remitted back to the country of origin, and the significance education may play in the equation of success (Hagelskamp et al. forthcoming).

Resiliencies and Strengths. Despite the myriad of challenges facing Latino students and families, it is imperative to not lose sight of the strengths that these families have. Investigating resilience and "funds of knowledge" of the Latino community rather than focusing solely on deficits can improve the educational outlooks of its children and youth. Research consistently shows that Latino parents and children care deeply about education (Gándara 1995; C. Suárez-Orozco and Suárez-Orozco 1995). Taking this starting point along with drawing on the close caring nature of many Latino families can aid in the development of educational interventions that are truly "additive," incorporating the strengths of both American and Latino culture to achieve their educational success (Valenzuela 1999).

Policy and Practice Implications

There are no facile solutions to the complex problems facing Latino immigrant students. To ameliorate this pressing issue, we must face head on a challenge that has been created by a combination of structural barriers, cultural and linguistic challenges, and schoolwide problems.

Sink-or-Swim Integration Policies. As a nation, we have no systematic strategy to ease the transition of newcomer immigrant-origin youth into secondary schools, college, or the labor market. Instead, we seem to rely on an unreasonable faith that once young immigrants cross the border, the logic of the market will magically transform them into productive citizens. Or perhaps if we ignore them, they will simply fade away (C. Suárez-Orozco et al. 2008). We generally do the same with our most at-risk students. This current "non-policy" fails our neediest students; it also robs the United States economy of many promising future contributors. We should look to our neighbors in Canada for a more systematic integration policy that serves to bridge those in most need.

The DREAM Act. An in-depth examination and critique of immigration policy is beyond the scope of this chapter, though regularizing the status the 12 million individuals who are de facto if not de jure members of our society must be a national priority. By not providing a means for mobility for this population, we are creating a permanent underclass of low-educated and low-skilled labor that may ultimately have negative effects for all Americans (Ruge and Iza 2004). At the very least, we recommend passage of federal legislation that makes higher education more accessible for undocumented students in the United States. The Development, Relief, and Education for Alien Minors Act (DREAM Act) is a federal bill that takes important strides toward improving the educational prospects of undocumented immigrants, including Latinos. The main provisions of the act are eligibility for in-state tuition benefits and state and federal financial aid and a path to citizenship. These benefits would generally be available to undocumented individuals who were brought to the United States as minors, have continuously lived in the United States for five years, attended and graduated from a U.S. high school, and have no criminal record along with demonstrated good moral character (Ruge and Iza 2004). The benefits of such legislation, apart from college access, include the increased likelihood of financial productivity with a college degree and improved job prospects.

Increased Preschool Opportunities. There is ample evidence that many Latino students begin school behind their peers as they enter kindergarten (Chernoff et al. 2007; Crosnoe 2006). As many live in linguistically isolated neighborhoods and have parents with limited educations, Latino children often do not have the schooling readiness skills that place their middle-class English-dominant peers at an advantage—and this achievement gap simply increases exponentially over time. We need to work to make preschool academic enrichment programs financially accessible to Latino families. Further, as placing young children in preschool is not a familiar cultural practice for many Latino parents (Fuller et al. 1994), we need to strive to make these programs culturally responsive and help educate parents to the significant opportunities they will provide their children in the long run.

Rigorous 21st Century Education. Education for our global era requires higher-order skills than ever before to ensure cognitive, behavioral, and ethical engagement with the world (M. Suárez-Orozco and Qin-Hilliard 2004). For youth to develop the ethics, skills, sensibilities, and competencies needed to identify, analyze, and solve problems from multiple perspectives, schools must nurture students who are curious and cognitively flexible, who can tolerate ambiguity, and who can synthesize knowledge within and across disciplines (Gardner 2004; Schleicher and Tremley 2006; M. Suárez-Orozco and Sattin 2007; Wagner 2006). Unfortunately, all too many schools serving Latino immigrant youth, like schools that serve other disadvantaged students in our nation, are those relegated to teaching "other people's children" (Delpit 1995). Such segregated, suboptimal schools typically offer the very least to those who need the very most. Schools can no longer continue to provide Latino immigrant students curricula designed for the last century if they are to be prepared to enter the realities of the global economy. Indeed, their schools must offer them the new essential three Rs that all our children need—rigor, relevance, and relationships.[5] In addition, these schools must provide supplemental resources to educationally at-risk Latino students to ease their educational transition and ameliorate their outcomes in the American educational system.

Teacher Education. Schools of education and school districts need to provide better opportunities for quality training to prepare teachers to work with Latino immigrant students and English language learners. Teachers often hold many misperceptions about language acquisition (Reeves 2006) and cultural practices in Latino families (Moll and Ruiz 2002). Training topics should include language acquisition, classroom modifications, homework modification, and cultural training and exchange programs that provide exposure to and appreciation of the contexts from where Latino immigrant students come. Training and exposure to promising innovative practice models that have a track record of success like the International Schools Network in New York would serve administrators, teachers, and students well (Fine, Stoudt, and Futch 2005).

Second-Language Education. While not all Latino students are second-language learners, two-thirds come from homes where their parents speak Spanish. It must be recognized that learning academic English at a competent level takes considerable time (Cummins 1991, 2000; Hakuta, Butler, and Witt 2000). Students with limited literacy in their native language will need further time to solidify their academic skills in a new language. Thus, Latino immigrant students entering U.S. secondary schools with little background of English require systematic and effective long-term curriculum plans for language education. Schools in the United States, unlike schools in other countries of immigration like Canada and Sweden, do not have systematic or consistent bilingual or second-language-acquisition policies and practices, placing their ELL students at a disadvantage.

English language learners should be placed into a progressive and systematic program of instruction that first identifies the student's incoming literacy and academic skills (Christensen and Stanat 2007) according to the district population and resources. It is essential to provide consistency of instruction for students as frequent transitions place them at considerable disadvantage (Gándara and Contreras 2009). High-quality English instruction must be provided with continued transitional academic supports—like tutoring, ongoing second-language instruction, homework help, and writing assistance—as the language learners integrate into mainstream programs (Christensen and Stanat 2007). Teachers also should understand and comply with the model thoroughly to "ensure articulation between grades and continuity, allowing for development of skills."[6] Assessment of skills growth should be done annually using portfolio assessment and testing to measure progress and adjust intervention (Christensen and Stanat 2007). Further, we recommend schools implement dual-language programs in both English and Spanish; these programs consistently produce excellent results for students' academic and language development and prepare competent bilingual/biliterate speakers required in a global era.

Reconsidering High-Stakes Testing. Research reveals that high-stakes testing accountability systems create unintended consequences for ELLs that appear to outweigh what few benefits standardized tests may have (Amrein and Berliner 2002; Menken 2008). The No Child Left Behind Act's strong emphasis on high-stakes tests is making Latino English language learners' educational context extremely challenging. To meet the required adequate yearly progress, ELLs' curricula and daily instructions have become increasingly focused on English language skills rather than academic content knowledge for the high-stakes test, and many are tested well before their skills are adequately developed (Menken 2008). In this sense, high-stakes tests in states across the country are a "de facto language policy" (Menken 2008, 4), having implications for dropout rates as well as college access of Latino students (Amrein and Berliner 2002; Gándara and Contreras 2009).

For a valid and just assessment for these students, we urge educational policymakers to reconsider accountability systems with over-reliance on standardized tests. Students should be assessed by their yearly progress (against their own baselines) rather than an national outcomes standard, particularly on English exams (Menken 2008) as well as math tests that rely on word problems. Tests should provide linguistic accommodation, such as well-translated version of the tests in minority languages. Flexible time frames for ELL students should be provided. Alternative measures of students' achievement such as portfolio of student work, grades, classroom performance, and teacher recommendations also should be taken into account on higher-stakes decisions (Menken 2008). At the school level, we recommend designing curricula for ELLs to promote their language and academic skills development rather than focus entirely on test-focused curriculum. Although the curriculum needs to address exam skills to help ELL students pass high-stakes test, a test-focused one is pedagogically unsound (Menken 2008) and does not provide the knowledge and skills required for students' future in the knowledge-intensive U.S. economy. Additionally, students should receive instructions in language that matches the language of required tests to help them become familiar with the terms they need to know at test time and yield valid scores.

After-School Programs. Many Latino students from low-income families do not have the supports at home that middle-class students have readily at hand: educated parents who can help them organize essays and proofread them, a computer with Internet access, a tutor who can help them master trigonometry or chemistry problems, or a quiet place to work. Not recognizing such educational impediments contributes to augmenting the already-considerable achievement gap. To better serve Latino students, we recommend principals and community leaders collaborate to organize and systematize after-school programs or community education centers where immigrant students can receive benefit from supervision and mentoring (Perkins and Borden 2003). It is particularly important that these after-school programs provide tangible academic supports, homework help, and meaningful, high-standards future-focused academic information and project a "yes you can!" narrative about academic potential and pathways (Zhou and Li 2003). After-school programs with a focus on positive Latino cultural identity as well as sports, dance, and other extracurricular activities can also serve a role in positive youth development, but they are not enough to make an academic difference.

Mentorships. Mentoring relationships often evolve organically in after-school and community organizations and make a tremendous difference in adolescents' lives (Rhodes 2002; C. Suárez-Orozco et al. 2008). For youth in stressed families with limited social resources, mentors can support healthier family and peer relationships by alleviating pressure on the family (Roffman et al. 2003). Mentoring relationships could particularly be useful in serving newly arrived immigrant youth, as a bicultural mentor can bridge the old and new cultures; an acculturated mentor can act as font of information about the new cultural rules of engagement. Mentoring relationships can also heal ruptures in relationships that have resulted from long separations and complicated reunifications (C. Suárez-Orozco et al. 2002). Since immigrant adolescents' parents may not be available given their work schedules, the guidance and affection from a mentor can fill the void. Further, mentoring relationships have been shown to reduce substance abuse, aggressive behavior, and incidences of delinquency (Rhodes 2002), a path which boys are a greater risk to engage in (Vigil 2002). In addition, college-educated mentors can help their protégés perform better in school by helping them not only with homework but also by providing them with informed advice about their own path to college.

Systematic College Pathway Instruction. How to access the mysterious path to college seems nearly impenetrable to many first-generation Latino immigrant students (Bohon, Macpherson, and Atiles 2005). They are not able to turn to their parents or neighbors, who have often not gone to college themselves or, if they have, went to a system in a country entirely different than the one in the United States. High school counselors often have low expectations or are overburdened and too often overlook students who are not highly motivated from early on in their high school careers. Explicit information must be provided to students and their families systematically. Schools are of course a place to start, but partnerships with community organizations is fundamental to increase access. Interactive web sites like KnowHow2Go.org are another promising avenue.

Building on the Strengths of Latino Families. While immigrant-origin Latino families clearly face a number of academic challenges, they also embody a number of admirable cultural traits and resources that have been associated with positive academic outcomes (Perreira et al. 2006), including school attachment (Johnson, Crosnoe, and Elder 2001), parental closeness (Fuligni 2001; White and Glick 2000), parental monitoring (Anguiano 2004), immigrant optimism (Kao and Tienda 1995), and recognition of the value of hard work (C. Suárez-Orozco and Suárez-Orozco 1995). Together, these "family-mediated outlooks and values" (Perreira et al. 2006) explain why first-generation immigrant students who enter school intent on pursuing an education (rather than entering the workforce) do relatively well compared with later-born generations who begin to succumb to the frustrations, discouragement, and anomie that plague disenfranchised minority youth (Perreira et al. 2006; Rumbaut 1997).

The maintenance of these native linguistic and cultural resources is important to positive identity development, higher self-esteem, and, ultimately, academic achievement of Latino and immigrant youth (Tse 2001; Valenzuela 1999). A bicultural balance allowing flexible movement between the language and values of two cultural groups while maintaining positive attitudes toward both can help an individual in the cultural minority develop a healthy sense of self (LaFromboise, Coleman, and Gerton 1993). There is evidence to support that for Latinos, maintaining a bicultural balance between the native culture and the new culture may protect against negative educational outcomes. For example, research shows that Mexican youth who speak both Spanish and English fluently and whose household members do the same are the least likely to drop out of school (Feliciano 2001). Rodriguez and colleagues (1995) describe the maintenance of native language as beneficial as it allows a child to access social support from both family and the larger community, particularly when the family and community are non-English speaking.

Further, a Latino child who experiences his or her home language and culture in an institution such as school will likely feel more valued in that setting and in larger society, making the possibility of his or her academic success seem more likely. Moll and coauthors (1992) present an example of how teachers, researchers, and parents can collaborate to create such a curriculum that respects the home culture of students and their families while preparing them for success in larger society and the dominant culture. Moll and his colleagues had the explicit goal of developing a curriculum for the largely Mexican-descent community that they were working in. Researchers and teachers collaborated in collecting qualitative data to "develop innovations in teaching that draw upon the knowledge and skills found in local households," (1992, 132) which they termed the "funds of knowledge." The researchers adhered to the Latino value of "confianza"— literally translated, trust; the researchers and teachers extended this concept to include the notion of mutual respect for the knowledge that both the researchers/teachers and the families brought to the table. In so doing, teachers were able to bridge the gap between the students' home world and their classroom experience, culminating in a learning module created in collaboration with students, families, researchers, and teachers (Moll et al. 1992).

Schoolwide efforts should be made to reach out to parents by using Spanish-speaking community liaisons. Flyers in Spanish are not enough: a personal invitation is often much more effective. Calling under positive circumstances instead of simply waiting for a crisis is another important strategy. Providing English as a second language courses on campus for parents also can bring them to the school. Accommodating schedules as much as is possible will allow greater participation as well. Such promising practices can serve to welcome, engage, and incorporate Latino families into the fabric of the schools.

Conclusion

Latinos are now the nation's largest minority group in American schools. The majority are immigrants or the children of immigrants. Latinos, especially those of immigrant origin, share optimism and hope in the future that must be cultivated and treasured: they see schooling as the key to a better tomorrow. Tragically, over time, Latino youth, especially those enrolled in highly impoverished and deeply segregated schools, face negative odds and uncertain prospects. Too many Latino youngsters are leaving our schools without developing and mastering the kinds of higher-order skills needed in today's global economy and society. The future of our country will in no small measure be tied to the fortunes of all young Americans. As Latinos, immigrant and U.S.-born, are an increasing part of the American future, harnessing their energy, optimism, and faith in the future is in everyone's interest. Doing so is arguably one of the most important challenges to our country's democratic promise.

NOTES

1. U.S. Census Bureau, "State and County Quickfacts. Data Derived from Population Estimates, 2000," http://quickfacts.census.gov/qfd/states/00000.html.

2. U.S. Census Bureau, "State and County Quickfacts," http://quickfacts.census. gov/qfd/index.html.

3. U.S. Census Bureau, "American Community Survey. Table B15002i. Sex by Educational Attainment for the Population 25 Years and Over (Hispanic or Latino)," http://factfinder.census.gov/servlet/DTTable?_bm=y&-state=dt&-ds_name= ACS_2006_EST_G00_&-CONTEXT=dt&-mt_name=ACS_2006_EST_G2000_ B15002I&-redoLog=true&-_caller=geoselect&-geo_id=01000US&geo_id=

NBSP&-format=&-_lang=en; and U.S. Census Bureau, "American Community Survey. Table B15002h. Sex by Educational Attainment for the Population 25 Years and Over (White Alone, Not Hispanic or Latino)," http://factfinder.census.gov/servlet/DTTable?_ bm=y&-state=dt&-ds_name=ACS_2006_EST_G00_&-CONTEXT=dt&-mt_ name=ACS_2006_EST_G2000_B15002H&-redoLog=true&-_caller=geoselect&geo_id= 01000US&-geo_id=NBSP&-format=&-_lang=en.

4. See also Amnesty International, "From San Diego to Brownsville: Human Rights Violations on the USA-Mexico Border," press release, May 20, 1998, http://www. amnesty.org/en/library/asset/AMR51/033/1998/en/0cb50f5d-daae-11dd-80bc-797022e51902/amr510331998en.html.

5. Bill and Melinda Gates Foundation, "The 3Rs Solution," http://www.gates-foundation.org/Education/RelatedInfo/3Rs_Solution.htm (accessed August 1, 2006).

6. From Julie Sugarman and Elizabeth R. Howard, "Development and Maintenance of Two-Way Immersion Programs: Advice from Practitioners," March 2001, http://www.cal.org/resources/digest/PracBrief2.html.

REFERENCES

21st Century Workforce Commission. 2000. *A Nation of Opportunity: Building America's 21st Century Workforce.* Washington, DC: 21st Century Workforce Commission. http://digitalcommons.ilr.cornell.edu/cgi/viewcontent.cgi?article=1003&context= key_workplace.

Alba, Richard. 2009. *Blurring the Color Line: The New Chance for a More Integrated America.* Cambridge, MA: Harvard University Press.

Alegría, Margarita, William Siboney, Meghan Woo, Maria Torres, and Peter Guarnaccia. 2007. "Looking Beyond Nativity: The Relation of Age of Immigration, Length of Residence, and Birth Cohorts to the Risk of Onset of Psychiatric Disorders for Latinos." *Research in Human Development* 4(1/2): 19–47.

Amrein, Audrey L., and David C. Berliner. 2002. *An Analysis of Some Unintended and Negative Consequences of High-Stakes Testing.* Tempe: Education Policy Research Unit, Arizona University.

Anguiano, Ruben P. V. 2004. "Families and Schools: The Effects of Parental Involvement on High School Completion." *Journal of Family Issues* 25:61–85.

Auerbach, Susan. 2004. "Engaging Latino Parents in Supporting College Pathways: Lessons from a College Access Program." *Journal of Hispanic Higher Education* 3(2): 125–45.

August, Diane, and Kenji Hakuta, eds. 1997. *Improving Schooling for Language-Minority Children: A Research Agenda.* Washington, DC: National Academy Press.

August, Diane, and Timothy Shanahan, eds. 2006. *Developing Literacy in Second-Language Learners: Report of the National Literacy Panel on Language-Minority Children and Youth.* Mahwah, NJ: Routledge.

Bailey, Benjamin H. 2001. "Dominican-American Ethnic/Racial Identities and United States Social Categories." *International Migration Review* 35(3): 677–708.

Bang, Hee Jin, Carola Suárez-Orozco, Juliana Pakes, and Erin O'Connor. 2009. "The Importance of Homework in Determining Newcomer Immigrant Students' Grades." *Educational Research* 51(1): 1–25.

Batalova, Jean, Michael Fix, and Julie Murray. 2007. *Measures of Change: The Demography and Literacy of Adolescent English Learners.* Washington, DC: Migration Policy Institute.

Bean, Frank D., and Lindsay B. Lowell. 2007. "Unauthorized Migration." In *The New Americans: A Guide to Immigration since 1965,* edited by Mary C. Waters, Reed Ueda, and Helen B. Marrow (70–82). Cambridge, MA: Harvard University Press.

Berry, John W., Jean S. Phinney, David L. Sam, and Paul Vedder, eds. 2006. *Immigrant Youth in Cultural Transition: Acculturation, Identity, and Adaptation across National Contexts.* Mahwah, NJ: Lawrence Erlbaum Associates.

Bloom, David E. 2004. "Globalization and Education: An Economic Perspective." In *Globalization: Culture and Education in the New Millennium,* edited by Marcelo Suárez-Orozco and Desirée Qin-Hilliard (56–77). Berkeley: University of California Press.

Bohon, Stephanie A., Heather Macpherson, and Jorge H. Atiles. 2005. "Education Barriers for New Latinos in Georgia." *Journal of Latinos and Education* 4(1): 43–58.

Bracey, Gerald. 2000. "High Stakes Testing." Milwaukee: Center for Education Research, Analysis, and Innovation, University of Wisconsin–Milwaukee.

Bronfenbrenner, Urie. 1977. "Toward an Experimental Ecology of Human Development." *American Psychologist* 32(7): 513–31.

———. 1988. "Foreword." In *Ecological Research with Children and Families: Concepts to Methodology,* edited by Alan R. Pence (ix–xix). New York: Teachers College Press.

Butler, Frances A., and Martha Castellon-Wellington. 2000. *Students' Concurrent Performance on Tests of English Language Proficiency and Academic Achievement. The Validity of Administering Large-Scale Content Assessments to English Language Learners: An Investigation from Three Perspectives.* Los Angeles: National Center for Research on Evaluation, Standards, and Student Testing, University of California, Los Angeles.

Butler, Yuko G., and Kenji Hakuta. 2005. "Bilingualism and Second Language Acquisition." In *The Handbook of Bilingualism,* edited by T. K. Bhatia and W. C. Ritchie (114–44). London: Blackwell.

Capps, Randy. 2001. "Hardship among Children of Immigrants: Findings from the 1999 National Survey of America's Families." *Assessing the New Federalism* Policy Brief B-29. Washington, DC: The Urban Institute.

Capps, Randy, Rosa Maria Castañeda, Ajay Chaudry, and Robert Santos. 2007. *Paying the Price: The Impact of Immigration Raids on America's Children.* Washington, DC: The Urban Institute.

Capps, Randy, Michael Fix, Julie Murray, Jason Ost, Jeffrey S. Passel, and Shinta Herwantoro. 2005. *The New Demography of America's Schools: Immigration and the No Child Left Behind Act.* Washington, DC: The Urban Institute.

Carhill, Avary, Carola Suárez-Orozco, and Mariela Páez. 2008. "Explaining English Language Proficiency among Adolescent Immigrant Students." *American Educational Research Journal* 45(4): 1155–79.

Carroll, Daniel, Ruth M. Samardick, Scott Bernard, Susan Gabbard, and Trish Hernandez. 2005. *Findings from the National Agricultural Workers Survey (NAWS) 2001–2002: A Demographic and Employment Profile of United States Farm Workers.*

Washington, DC: U.S. Department of Labor, Office of the Assistant Secretary for Policy.

Chapa, Jorge. 2002. "Affirmative Action, X Percent Plans, and Latino Access to Higher Education in the Twenty-First Century." In *Latinos: Remaking America*, edited by Marcelo Suárez-Orozco and Carola Suárez-Orozco (375–88). Berkeley: University of California Press.

Chapa, Jorge, and Belinda De La Rosa. 2004. "Latino Population Growth, Socioeconomic and Demographic Characteristics, and Implications for Educational Attainment." *Education and Urban Society* 36(2): 130–49.

Chernoff, Jodi J., Kristin D. Flanagan, Cameron McPhee, and Jennifer Park. 2007. *Preschool: First Findings from the Preschool Follow-up of the Early Childhood Longitudinal Study, Birth Cohort (ECLS-B)*. NCES 2008-025. Washington, DC: U.S. Department of Education, Institute of Education Sciences, National Center for Education Statistics.

Christensen, Gayle, and Petra Stanat. 2007. "Language Policies and Practices for Helping Immigrants and Second-Generation Students Succeed." Washington, DC: Migration Policy Institute and Bertelsmann Stiftung.

Collier, Virginia P. 1987. "Age and Rate of Acquisition of Second Language for Academic Purposes." *TESOL Quarterly* 21(4): 617–41.

———. 1995. "Acquiring a Second Language for School." *Directions in Language and Education* 1(4).

Conchas, Gilberto Q. 2001. "Structuring Failure and Success: Understanding the Variability in Latino School Engagement." *Harvard Educational Review* 71(3): 475–504.

Connell, R. W. 2000. *The Men and the Boys*. Berkeley: University of California Press.

Cooper, Catherine R., Jacquelyne F. Jackson, Margarita Azmitia, and Edward M. Lopez. 1998. "Multiple Selves, Multiple Worlds: Three Useful Strategies for Research with Ethnic Minority Youth on Identity, Relationship, and Opportunity Structures." In *Studying Minority Adolescents: Conceptual, Methodological, and Theoretical Issues*, edited by Vonnie C. McLoyd and Laurence Steinberg (111–25). Mahwah, NJ: Lawrence Erlbaum Associates.

Council of Economic Advisers, The. 2000. *Educational Attainment and Success in the New Economy: Analysis of Challenges for Improving Hispanic Students' Achievement*. Washington, DC: The Council of Economic Advisers.

Crosnoe, Robert. 2006. *Mexican Roots, American Schools: Helping Mexican Immigrant Children Succeed*. Palo Alto, CA: Stanford University Press.

Crul, Maurice. 2007. "The Integration of Immigrant Youth." In *Learning in the Global Era: International Perspectives on Globalization and Education*, edited by Marcelo M. Suárez-Orozco (213–31). Berkeley: University of California Press.

Cummins, John. 1991. "Language Development and Academic Learning." In *Language, Culture, & Cognition*, edited by Lilliam M. Malavé and Georges Duquette (161–75). Clevedon, England: Multilingual Matters.

———. 2000. *Language, Power, & Pedagogy*. Clevedon, England: Multilingual Matters.

Delgado Gaitan, Concha. 2004. *Involving Latino Families in Schools: Raising Student Achievement through Home-School Partnerships*. Thousand Oaks, CA: Corwin Press.

Delpit, Lisa. 1995. *Other People's Children: Cultural Conflict in the Classroom.* New York: The New Press.

DeVoe, Jill F., Katharin Peter, Phillip Kaufman, Amanda Miller, Margaret Noonan, Thomas D. Snyder, and Katrina Baum. 2004. *Indicators of School Crime and Safety: 2004.* NCES 2005-002. Washington, DC: U.S. Department of Education, Institute of Education Sciences, National Center for Education Statistics.

De Vos, George. 1992. "The Passing of Passing." In *Social Cohesion and Alienation: Minorities in the United States and Japan,* edited by George De Vos (266–99). Boulder, CO: Westview Press.

DiCerbo, Patricia Anne. 2001. "Why Migrant Education Matters." Issue brief. Washington, DC: National Clearinghouse for Bilingual Education.

Donato, Katharine M., Donna Garbaccia, Jennifer Holdaway, Martin Manalansan IV, and Patricia R. Pessar. 2006. "A Glass Half Full? Gender in Migration Studies." *International Migration Review* 40(1): 3–26.

Doucette-Gates, Ann, Jeanne Brooks-Gunn, and Lindsay P. Chase-Lansdale. 1998. "The Role of Bias and Equivalence in the Study of Race, Class, and Ethnicity." In *Studying Minority Adolescents: Conceptual, Methodological, and Theoretical Issues,* edited by Vonnie C. McLoyd and Laurence Steinberg (211–36). Mahwah, NJ: Lawrence Erlbaum Associates.

Earls, Felton. 1997. "Tighter, Safer, Neighborhoods." *Harvard Magazine* (November–December): 14–15.

Eckes, Thomas, and Hanns M. Trautner. 2000. "Developmental Social Psychology of Gender: An Integrative Approach." In *The Developmental Social Psychology of Gender,* edited by Thomas B. Eckes and Hanns M. Trautner (3–32). Mahwah, NJ: Lawrence Erlbaum Associates.

Falicov, Celia Jaes. 1998. *Latino Families in Therapy: A Guide to Multicultural Practice.* New York: Guilford Press.

Faulstich-Orellana, Marjorie. 2001. "The Work Kids Do: Mexican and Central American Immigrant Children's Contribution to Households and Schools in California." *Harvard Educational Review* 71(3): 366–89.

Feliciano, Cynthia. 2001. "The Benefits of Biculturalism: Exposure to Immigrant Culture and Dropping Out of School among Asian and Latino Youths." *Social Science Quarterly* 82:865–80.

Fine, Michelle, Brett Stoudt, and Valerie Futch. 2005. *The International Network for Public Schools: A Quantitative & Qualitative Cohort Analysis of Graduation & Dropout Rates: Teaching and Learning in a Transcultural Academic Environment.* New York: The Graduate Center, City University of New York.

Fredricks, Jennifer A., Phyllis C. Blumenfeld, and Alison H. Paris. 2004. "School Engagement: Potential of the Concept, State of the Evidence." *Review of Educational Research* 74(1): 54–109.

Fry, Richard. 2002. *Latinos in Higher Education: Many Enroll, Too Few Graduate.* Washington, DC: Pew Hispanic Center.

———. 2003. *Hispanic Youth Dropping Out of U.S. Schools: Measuring the Challenge.* Washington, DC: Pew Hispanic Center.

Fry, Richard, and Felisa Gonzales. 2008. *One-in-Five and Growing Fast: A Profile of Hispanic Public School Students.* Washington, DC: Pew Hispanic Center.

Fuligni, Andrew J. 1997. "The Academic Achievement of Adolescents from Immigrant Families: The Roles of Family Background, Attitudes, and Behavior." *Child Development* 69(2): 351–63.

————. 2001. "Family Obligation and the Achievement Motivation of Adolescents from Asian, Latin American, and European Backgrounds." In *Family Obligation and Assistance during Adolescence: Contextual Variations and Developmental Implications (New Directions in Child and Adolescent Development),* edited by Andrew J. Fuligni (61–76). San Francisco, CA: Jossey-Bass.

Fuller, Bruce, Constanza Eggers-Pierola, Susan D. Holloway, Xiaoyan Liang, and Marylee F. Rambaud. 1994. "Rich Culture, Poor Markets: Why Do Latino Parents Choose to Forgo Preschooling?" *Teachers College Record* 97(3): 400–18.

Gándara, Patricia. 1995. *Over the Ivy Walls: The Educational Mobility of Low-Income Chicanos.* Albany, NY: SUNY Press.

Gándara, Patricia, and Lisa Chávez. 2001. *Putting the Cart before the Horse: Latinos and Higher Education.* Berkeley: University of California.

Gándara, Patricia, and Frances Contreras. 2009. *The Latino Education Crisis: The Consequences of Failed School Policies.* Cambridge, MA: Harvard University Press.

García, Eugene E. 2001. *Hispanic Education in the United States: Raíces Y Alas.* New York: Rowman and Littlefield.

García Coll, Cynthia T., and Katherine A. Magnuson. 1997. "The Psychological Experience of Immigration: A Developmental Perspective." In *Immigration and the Family,* edited by Alan Booth, Ann C. Crouter and Nancy Landale (91–132). Mahwah, NJ: Lawrence Erlbaum Associates.

Gardner, Howard. 2004. "How Education Changes: Considerations of History, Science, and Values." In *Globalization: Culture and Education in the New Millennium,* edited by Marcelo M. Suárez-Orozco and Desirée B. Qin-Hilliard (235–58). Berkeley: University of California Press.

Gastón Institute for Latino Community Development and Public Policy. 2001. "New Study Finds Few Latinos Prepared for MCAS." *The Newsletter of the Mauricio Gastón Institute for Latino Community Development and Public Policy.*

Gibbs, Jewelle T. 2003. "Biracial and Bicultural Children and Adolescents." In *Children of Color: Psychological Interventions with Culturally Diverse Youth,* edited by Jewelle T. Gibbs and Larke N. Huang (145–82). San Francisco, CA: Jossey-Bass.

Gibson, Margaret, Patricia Gándara, and Jill P. Koyama, eds. 2004. *School Connections: U.S. Mexican Youth, Peers, and School Adjustment.* New York: Teachers College Press.

Goldenberg, Claude, Robert S. Rueda, and Diane August. 2006. "Synthesis: Sociocultural Contexts and Literacy Development." In *Report of the National Literacy Panel on Language Minority Youth and Children,* edited by Diane August and Timothy Shanahan. Mahwah, NJ: Lawrence Erlbaum Associates.

González, Norma, Luis Moll, and Cathy Amanti. 2005. *Funds of Knowledge: Theorizing Practices in Households, Communities, and Classrooms.* Mahwah, NJ: Lawrence Erlbaum Associates.

Gruber, Kerry J., Susan D. Wiley, Stephen P. Broughman, Gregory A. Strizek, and Marisa Burian-Fitzgerald. 2002. *Schools and Staffing Survey, 1999–2000: Overview of the Data for Public, Private, Public Charter, and Bureau of Indian Affairs Elementary and Secondary Schools.* NCES 2002-313. Washington, DC: U.S. Department of Education, Office of Educational Research and Improvement, National Center for Education Statistics.

Hagelskamp, Caroline, Carola Suárez-Orozco, and Diane Hughes. Forthcoming. "Migrating to Opportunities: How Family Migration Motivations Shape Academic Trajectories among Newcomer Immigrant Youth." *Journal of Social Intervention.*

Hakuta, Kenji, Yuko Goto Butler, and Daria Witt. 2000. "How Long Does It Take English Learners to Attain Proficiency?" Policy Report 2000-1. Santa Barbara: University of California Linguistic Minority Research Institute.

Hondagneu-Sotelo, Pierrette. 1999. "Gender and Contemporary U.S. Immigration." *American Behavioral Scientist* 42:565–76.

Hughes, Diane, and Edward Seidman. 1993. "Cultural Phenomena and the Research Enterprise: Toward a Culturally Anchored Methodology." *American Journal of Community Psychology* 21(6): 687–704.

Huynh, Virginia W., and Andrew J. Fuligni. 2008. "Ethnic Socialization and the Academic Adjustment of Adolescents from Mexican, Chinese, and European Backgrounds." *Developmental Psychology* 44(4): 1202.

Ingersoll, Richard M. 2003. "The Teacher Shortage: Myth or Reality." *Educational Horizons* 81(3): 146–52.

Ingersoll, Richard M., and Thomas M. Smith. 2003. "The Wrong Solution to the Teacher Shortage." *Keeping Good Teachers* 60(8): 30–33.

Jia, Gisela, and Doris Aaronson. 2003. "A Longitudinal Study of Chinese Children and Adolescents Learning English in the United States." *Applied Psycholinguistics* 24:131–61.

Johnson, Monica K., Robert Crosnoe, and Glen H. Elder Jr. 2001. "Students' Attachment and Academic Engagement: The Role of Race and Ethnicity." *Sociology of Education* 74(4): 318–40.

Kalil, Ariel, and Jen-Hao Chen. 2008. "Mothers' Citizenship Status and Household Food Insecurity among Low-Income Children of Immigrants." *New Directions for Child and Adolescent Development* 2008(121): 43–62.

Kao, Grace, and Marta Tienda. 1995. "Optimism and Achievement: The Educational Performance of Immigrant Youth." *Social Science Quarterly* 76(1): 1–19.

Kasinitz, Phillip, John H. Mollenkopf, Mary C. Waters, and Jennifer Holdaway. 2008. *Inheriting the City: The Children of Immigrants Come of Age.* Cambridge, MA, and New York: Harvard University Press and Russell Sage Foundation.

Kaufman, Phillip, Martha Naomi Alt, and Christopher Chapman. 2001. *Dropout Rates in the United States: 2000.* NCES 2002-114. Washington, DC: U.S. Department of Education, Office of Educational Research and Improvement, National Center for Education Statistics.

Kennedy, Randall. 2001. "Racial Trends in the Administration of Criminal Justice." In *America Becoming: Racial Trends and Their Consequences, Vol. 2,* edited by Neil J. Smelser, William J. Wilson, and Faith Mitchell (1–20). Washington, DC: National Academy Press.

King, Jacqueline. 1999. *Money Matters*. Washington, DC: American Council on Education.

LaFromboise, Teresa, Hardin L. K. Coleman, and Jennifer Gerton. 1993. "Psychological Impact of Biculturalism: Evidence and Theory." *Psychological Bulletin* 114:395–412.

Lansford, Jennifer E., Kirby Deater-Deckard, and Marc H. Bornstein, eds. 2007. *Immigrant Families in Contemporary Society*. New York: Guilford Press.

Lee, Jaekyung. 2002. "Racial and Ethnic Achievement Gap Trends: Reversing the Progress toward Equity?" *Educational Researcher* 31(1): 3–12.

Levitt, Mary J., Nathalie Guacci-Franco, and Jerome L. Levitt. 1994. "Social Support and Achievement in Childhood and Early Adolescence: A Multicultural Study." *Journal of Applied Developmental Psychology* 15(2): 207–22.

Li, Jin. 2004. " 'I Learn and I Grow Big': Chinese Preschoolers' Purpose for Learning." *International Journal of Behavioral Development* 28(2): 116–28.

López, Gerardo R. 2001. "The Value of Hard Work: Lessons on Parent Involvement from an (Im)migrant Household." *Harvard Educational Review* 71(3): 416–37.

Lustig, Stuart L., Maryam Kia-Keating, Wanda G. Knight, Paul Geltman, Heidi Ellis, David J. Kinzie, Terence Keane, and Glenn Saxe. 2004. "Review of Child and Adolescent Refugee Mental Health." *Journal of the American Academy of Child & Adolescent Psychiatry* 43(1): 24–36.

Luthar, Suniya S. 1999. *Poverty and Children's Adjustment*. Thousand Oaks, CA: SAGE Publications.

MacSwan, Jeff, and Kellie Rolstad. 2003. "Linguistic Diversity, Schooling, and Social Class: Rethinking Our Conception of Language Proficiency in Language Minority Education." In *Sociolinguistics: The Essential Readings,* edited by Christina B. Paulston and G. Richard Tucker (329–40). Oxford: Blackwell.

Mahler, Sarah J. 1999. "Engendering Transnational Migration: A Case Study of Salvadorans." *American Behavioral Scientist* 42(4).

Massey, Douglas, and Nancy Denton. 1993. *American Apartheid*. Cambridge, MA: Harvard University Press.

McLoyd, Vonnie C., and Laurence Steinberg, eds. 1998. *Studying Minority Adolescents: Conceptual, Methodological, and Theoretical Issues*. Mahwah, NJ: Lawrence Erlbaum Associates.

Mendoza, Fernando S., Joyce R. Javier, and Anthony E. Burgos. 2007. "Health of Children in Immigrant Families." In *Immigrant Families in Contemporary Society*, edited by Jennifer E. Lansford, Kirby Deater-Deckard, and Marc H. Bornstein (30–50). New York: Guilford Press.

Menken, Kate. 2008. *English Language Learners Left Behind: Standardized Testing as Language Policy*. Clevedon, England: Multilingual Matters.

Moll, Luis C., and Richard Ruiz. 2002. "The Schooling of Latino Children." In *Latinos: Remaking America*, edited by Marcelo M. Suárez-Orozco and Mariela Páez (362–74). Berkeley: University of California Press.

Moll, Luis C., Cathy Amanti, Deborah Neff, and Norma González. 1992. "Funds of Knowledge for Teaching: Using a Qualitative Approach to Connect Homes and Classrooms." *Theory into Practice* 31(2): 132–41.

Morisi, Teresa L. 2008. "Youth Enrollment and Employment during the School Year." *Monthly Labor Review* 131(2): 51–63.

National Commission on Teaching and America's Future. 1997. *Doing What Matters Most: Investing in Quality Teaching.* New York: National Commission on Teaching and America's Future.

National Task Force on Early Childhood Education for Hispanics. 2007. *Para Nuestros Niños: Expanding and Improving Early Education for Hispanics, Main Report.* Tempe: Arizona State University.

National Task Force on Minority High Achievement, The. 1999. *Reaching the Top.* New York: The College Board.

Natriello, Gary, and Anthony M. Pallas. 1999. "The Development and Impact of High-Stakes Testing." Paper presented at the High Stakes K–12 Testing Conference, New York.

Noguera, Pedro A. 2006. "Latino Youth: Immigration, Education, and the Future." *Latino Studies* 4:313–20.

Oakes, Jeannie. 1985. *Keeping Track: How Schools Restructure Inequality.* Hartford, CT: Yale University Press.

Olsen, Laurie. 1997. *Made in America: Immigrant Students in Our Public Schools.* New York: The New Press.

Orfield, Gary. 1995. *Latinos in Education: Recent Trends.* Cambridge, MA: Harvard Graduate School of Education.

Orfield, Gary, and Chungmei Lee. 2006. *Racial Transformation and the Changing Nature of Segregation.* Cambridge, MA: The Civil Rights Project, Harvard University.

Orfield, Gary, and John T. Yun. 1999. *Resegregation in American Schools.* Cambridge, MA: The Civil Rights Project, Harvard University.

Padilla, Amado, Kathryn Lindholm, Andrew Chen, Richard Duran, Kenji Kahuta, Walace Lambert, and Richard Tucker. 1991. "The English-Only Movement: Myth, Reality, and Implications for Psychology." *American Psychologist* 46(2): 120–30.

Páez, Mariela. 2001. "Language and the Immigrant Child: Predicting English Language Proficiency for Chinese, Dominican, and Haitian Students." Cambridge, MA: Harvard Graduate School of Education.

Passel, Jeffrey S. 2006. "The Size and Characteristics of the Unauthorized Migrant Population in the U.S." Washington, DC: Pew Hispanic Center.

Pérez-Huber, Lindsay, Ofelia Huidor, María C. Malagón, Gloria Sánchez, and Daniel G. Solorzano. 2006. "Falling through the Cracks: Critical Transitions in the Latina/o Educational Pipeline: 2006 Education Summit Report." Los Angeles: UCLA Chicano Studies Research Center.

Perkins, Daniel F., and Lynne M. Borden. 2003. "Key Elements of Community Youth Development Programs." In *Community Youth Development: Programs, Policy, and Practices,* edited by Francisco A. Villarruel, Daniel F. Perkins, Lynne M. Borden, and Joanne G. Keith (90–117). Thousand Oaks, CA: SAGE Publications.

Perreira, Krista M., Kathleen M. Harris, and Dohoon Lee. 2006. "Making It in America: High School Completion by Immigrant and Native Youth." *Demography* 43(3): 1–26.

Planty, Micheal, William Hussar, Thomas Snyder, Stephen Provasnik, Grace Kena, Rachel Dinkes, Angie Kewal Ramani, and Jana Kemp. 2008. *The Condition of Edu-*

cation 2008. NCES 2008-031. Washington, DC: U.S. Department of Education, Institute of Education Sciences, National Center for Education Statistics.

Planty, Michael, Stephen Provasnik, William Hussar, Thomas Snyder, Grace Kena, Gillian Hampden-Thompson, Rachel Dinkes, and Susan Choy. 2007. *The Condition of Education 2007*. NCES 2007-064. Washington, DC: U.S. Department of Education, Institute of Education Sciences, National Center for Education Statistics.

Pong, Suet-ling, and Lingxin Hao. 2007. "Neighborhood and School Factors in the School Performance of Immigrants' Children." *International Migration Review* 41(1): 206–41.

Portes, Alejandro. 1996. "Children of Immigrants: Segmented Assimilation and Its Determinants." In *The Economic Sociology of Immigration: Essays on Networks, Ethnicity, and Entrepreneurship,* edited by Alejandro Portes (248–80). New York: Russell Sage Foundation.

———. 1998. "Social Capital: Its Origins and Applications in Modern Sociology." *Annual Review of Sociology* 22:1–24.

Portes, Alejandro, and Lingxin Hao. 1998. "E Pluribus Unum: Bilingualism and Loss of Language in the Second Generation." *Sociology of Education* 71:269–94.

Portes, Alejandro, and Rubén Rumbaut. 2001. *Legacies: The Story of the Second Generation.* Berkeley: University of California Press.

Portes, Alejandro, and Min Zhou. 1993. "The New Second Generation: Segmented Assimilation and Its Variants." *Annals of the American Academy of Political & Social Science* 530:74–96.

Post, David, and Suet-ling Pong. 2000. "Employment during Middle School: The Effects on Academic Achievement in the U.S. and Abroad." *Educational Evaluation and Policy Analysis* 22:273–98.

Ramirez, Roberto, and Melissa Therrien. 2000. "The Hispanic Population in the United States: March 2000." Current Population Report P20-535. Washington, DC: U.S. Census Bureau.

Ream, Robert K. 2005. *Uprooting Children: Mobility, Social Capital, and Mexican American Underachievement.* New York: LFB Scholarly Publishing LLC.

Reeves, Jenelle R. 2006. "Secondary Teacher Attitudes toward Including English-Language Learners in Mainstream Classrooms." *Journal of Educational Research* 99(3): 131–42.

Rhodes, Jean E. 2002. *Stand by Me: The Risks and Rewards of Youth Mentoring Relationships.* Cambridge, MA: Harvard University Press.

Rodriguez, James L., Rafael M. Diaz, David Duran, and Linda Espinosa. 1995. "The Impact of Bilingual Preschool Education on the Language Development of Spanish-Speaking Children." *Early Childhood Research Quarterly* 10:475–90.

Roffman, Jennifer G., Carola Suárez-Orozco, and Jean E. Rhodes. 2003. "Facilitating Positive Development in Immigrant Youth: The Role of Mentors and Community Organizations." In *Community Youth Development: Programs, Policy, and Practices,* edited by Francisco A. Villaruel, Daniel F. Perkins, Lynne M. Borden, and Joanne G. Keith (90–117). Thousand Oak, CA: SAGE Publications.

Ruge, Thomas R., and Angela D. Iza. 2004. "Higher Education for Undocumented Students: The Case for Open Admission and In-State Tuition Rates for Students without Lawful Immigration Status." *Indiana International and Comparative Law Review* 15:257–78.

Ruiz-de-Velasco, Jorge, and Michael Fix, with Beatriz Chu Clewell. 2000. *Overlooked and Underserved: Immigrant Students in U.S. Secondary Schools.* Washington, DC: The Urban Institute.

Rumbaut, Rubén G. 1997. *Passages to Adulthood: The Adaptation of Children of Immigrants in Southern California.* New York: Russell Sage Foundation.

———. 2004. "Ages, Life Stages, and Generational Cohorts: Decomposing the Immigrant First and Second Generations in the United States." *International Migration Review* 38:1160–1206.

Rumbaut, Rubén G., and Wayne Cornelius. 1995. "California's Immigrant Children: Theory, Research, and Implications for Policy." La Jolla, CA: Center for U.S.-Mexican Studies.

Rumberger, Russell. 2004. "Why Students Drop Out of School." In *Dropouts in America: Confronting the Graduation Rate Crisis,* edited by Gary Orfield (131–55). Cambridge, MA: Harvard Education Press.

Santiago, Deborah, and Alisa Cunningham. 2005. *How Latinos Pay for College: Patterns of Financial Aid in 2003–2004.* Washington, DC: Excelencia in Education and the Institute for Higher Education Policy.

Schleicher, Andreas, and Karine Tremley. 2006. "Education and the Knowledge Economy in Europe and Asia." *Challenge Europe* 15:24–36.

Schunk, Dale H. 1991. "Self-Efficacy and Academic Motivation." *Educational Psychologist* 26:207–31.

Sirin, Selcuk. 2005. "Socioeconomic Status and Academic Achievement: A Meta-Analytic Review of Research." *Review of Educational Research* 75(3): 417–53.

Smith, Robert C. 2002. "Gender, Ethnicity, and Race in School and Work Outcomes of Second-Generation Mexican Americans." In *Latinos: Remaking America,* edited by Marcelo M. Suárez-Orozco and Mariela Páez (110–25). Berkeley: University of California Press.

Solano-Flores, Guillermo. 2008. "Who Is Given Tests in What Language by Whom, When and Where? The Need for Probabilistic Views of Language in the Testing of English Language Learners." *Guillermo English Education Researcher* 37(4): 189–99.

Solorzano, Daniel, Octavio Villalpando, and Leticia Oseguera. 2005. "Educational Inequities and Latina/o Undergraduate Students in the United States." *Journal of Hispanic Higher Education* 4(3): 272–94.

Stanton-Salazar, Ricardo D. 2004. "Social Capital among Working-Class Minority Students." In *School Connections: U.S. Mexican Youth, Peer, & School Achievement,* edited by Margaret A. Gibson, Patricia Gándara, and Jill P. Koyma (18–38). New York: Teachers College Press.

Suárez-Orozco, Carola. 2000. "Identities under Siege: Immigration Stress and Social Mirroring among the Children of Immigrants." In *Cultures under Siege: Social Violence & Trauma,* edited by Antonius C. G. M. Robben and Marcelo M. Suárez-Orozco (194–226). Cambridge: Cambridge University Press.

———. 2001. "Psychosocial Factors in the Adaptation of Immigrant Youth: Gendered Responses." In *Women & Human Rights: A Global Perspective,* edited by Marjorie Agostin (170–88). Piscataway, NJ: Rutgers University Press.

———. 2004. "Formulating Identity in a Globalized World." In *Globalization: Culture and Education in the New Millennium,* edited by Marcelo M. Suárez-Orozco and Desirée B. Qin-Hilliard (173–202). Berkeley: University of California Press.

Suárez-Orozco, Carola, and Desirée B. Qin. 2006. "Gendered Perspectives in Psychology: Immigrant Origin Youth." *International Migration Review* 40(1): 165–98.

Suárez-Orozco, Carola, and Marcelo M. Suárez-Orozco. 1995. *Transformations: Immigration, Family Life, and Achievement Motivation among Latino Adolescents.* Palo Alto, CA: Stanford University Press.

———. 2001. *Children of Immigration.* The Developing Child Series. Cambridge, MA: Harvard University Press.

Suárez-Orozco, Carola, Allyson Pimentel, and Margary Martin. 2009. "The Significance of Relationships: Academic Engagement and Achievement among Newcomer Immigrant Youth." *Teachers College Record* 111(3): 712–49.

Suárez-Orozco, Carola, Marcelo M. Suárez-Orozco, and Irina Todorova. 2005. "Wandering Souls: The Interpersonal Concerns of Adolescent Immigrants." In *Narrative Themes in Comparative Context,* vol. 2 of *Cross-Cultural Dimensions in Conscious Thought,* edited by George De Vos and Eric S. De Vos. Boulder, CO: Rowman and Littlefield.

———. 2008. *Learning a New Land: Immigrant Students in American Society.* Cambridge, MA: Harvard University Press.

Suárez-Orozco, Carola, Irina Todorova, and Josephine Louie. 2002. " 'Making Up for Lost Time': The Experience of Separation and Reunification among Immigrant Families." *Family Process* 41(4): 625–43.

Suárez-Orozco, Marcelo M., and Francisco X. Gaytán. 2009. "Preface." In *Latinos: Remaking America,* 2nd ed., edited by Marcelo M. Suárez-Orozco and Mariela M. Paez (xi–xiii). Berkeley: University of California Press.

Suárez-Orozco, Marcelo M., and Desirée B. Qin-Hilliard. 2004. *Globalization: Culture and Education in the New Millennium.* Berkeley: University of California Press.

Suárez-Orozco, Marcelo M., and Carolyn Sattin. 2007. "Introduction: Learning in the Global Era." In *Learning in the Global Era: International Perspectives on Globalization and Education,* edited by Marcelo M. Suárez-Orozco (1–43). Berkeley: University of California Press.

Sue, Derald, Christina M. Capodilupo, Gina C. Torino, Jennifer M. Bucceri, Aisha M. B. Holder, Kevin L. Nadal, and Marta Esquilin. 2007. "Racial Microaggressions in Everyday Life: Implications for Clinical Practice." *American Psychologist* 62(4): 271–86.

Takeuchi, David T., Seunghye Hong, Krista Gile, and Margarita Alegría. 2007. "Developmental Contexts and Mental Disorders among Asian Americans." *Research in Human Development* 4(1/2): 49–69.

Taningco, Maria T. 2007. "Revisiting the Latino Health Paradox." Policy brief. Boston, MA: Tomás Rivera Policy Institute.

Thomas, Wayne P., and Virginia P. Collier. 2002. *A National Study of School Effectiveness for Language Minority Students' Long-Term Academic Achievement.* Berkeley: Center for Research on Education, Diversity & Excellence, University of California, Berkeley.

Tinto, Vincent. 1993. *Leaving College: Rethinking the Causes and Cures of Student Attrition.* 2nd ed. Chicago: University of Chicago Press.

Tse, Lucy. 2001. "Resisting and Reversing Language Shift: Heritage-Language Resilience among U.S. Native Biliterates." *Harvard Educational Review* 71:676–708.

U.S. Department of Education. 1995. *Findings from the Condition of Education 1995: The Educational Progress of Hispanic Students.* NCES 95-767. Washington, DC: U.S.

Department of Education, Office of Educational Research and Improvement, National Center for Education Statistics.

Valdés, Guadalupe, and Richard A. Figueroa. 1994. *Bilingualism and Testing: A Special Case of Bias.* Norwood, NJ: Ablex.

Valenzuela, Angela. 1999. *Subtractive Schooling: U.S.-Mexican Youth and the Politics of Caring.* Albany, NY: SUNY Press.

Vega, William A., Ethel Alderete, Bohdan Kolody, and Sergio Aguilar-Gaxiola. 1998. "Illicit Drug Use among Mexicans and Mexican Americans in California: The Effects of Gender and Acculturation." *Addiction* 93(12): 1839–50.

Vigil, Diego. 2002. *A Rainbow of Gangs: Street Cultures in the Mega-City.* Austin: University of Texas.

Wagner, Alan. 2006. *Measuring up Internationally: Developing Skills and Knowledge for the Global Economy.* San Jose, CA: The National Center for Public Policy and Higher Education.

Warren, John R., Paul C. LePore, and Robert D. Mare. 2000. "Employment during High School: Consequences for Students' Grades in Academic Courses." *American Educational Research Journal* 37(4): 943–69.

Weinstein, Rhona S. 2002. *Reaching Higher: The Power of Expectations in Schooling.* Cambridge, MA: Harvard University Press.

Weissbourd, Richard. 1996. *The Vulnerable Child.* Reading, MA: Perseus Books.

West, Jerry, Kristin Denton, and Elvie Germino-Hausken. 2000. *America's Kindergartners.* NCES 2000-070. Washington, DC: U.S. Department of Education, Office of Educational Research and Improvement, National Center for Educational Statistics.

White, Michael J., and Jennifer Glick. 2000. "Generation Status, Social Capital, and the Routes out of High School." *Sociological Forum* 15:671–91.

Wills, Thomas Ashby. 1985. "Supportive Functions of Interpersonal Relationships." In *Social Support and Health,* edited by Sheldon Cohen and S. Leonard Syme (61–82). Orlando, FL: Academic Press.

Wirt, John, Susan Choy, Debra Gerald, Stephen Provasnik, Patrick Rooney, Satoshi Watanabe, Richard Tobin, and Mark Glander. 2001. *The Condition of Education 2001.* NCES 2001-072. Washington, DC: U.S. Department of Education, Office of Educational Research and Improvement, National Center for Education Statistics.

Yoshikawa, Hirokazu, Erin B. Godfrey, and Ann C. Rivera. 2008. "Access to Institutional Resources as a Measure of Social Exclusion: Relations with Family Process and Cognitive Development in the Context of Immigration." *New Directions for Child and Adolescent Development* 2008(121): 63–86.

Yosso, Tara, and Daniel G. Solorzano. 2006. "Leaks in the Chicana and Chicano Educational Pipeline." Latino Policy & Issues Brief 13. Los Angeles: UCLA Chicano Studies Research Center.

Zhou, Min, and Xi-Yuan Li. 2004. "Ethnic Language Schools and the Development of Supplementary Education in the Immigrant Chinese Community in the United States." In *Understanding the Social Worlds of Immigrant Youth: New Directions for Youth Development,* edited by Carola Suárez-Orozco and Irina Todorova (57–73). New York: Jossey-Bass.

Zimbardo, Philip, and Craig Haney. 1998. "The Past and Future of U.S. Prison Policy: Twenty-Five Years after the Stanford Prison Experiment." *American Psychologist* 53(7): 709–27.

10

The Challenges of Educating Latino Students

Engaging Parents as Partners

Katharine M. Donato and Melissa Marschall

I n their extensive analysis of the challenges faced by Latino children in the U.S. educational system, Suárez-Orozco and her colleagues clearly describe how Latino children, whether immigrants or U.S.-born, struggle in schools. No matter how one approaches this issue, the current state of Latino education in the United States is dismal.

Beginning with preschool and moving upward through college, Latino children consistently perform at lower levels than non-Latinos (see chapter 9, this volume). The gap begins when children enter kindergarten and grows through college and beyond. Further, although studies suggest it narrowed in the 1980s, the gap widened in the 1990s and now persists into the 21st century. Not surprisingly, Latinos are more likely to exhibit risk factors associated with poor performance in school, they have lower grades and test scores than their white and Asian peers, and they are more likely to drop out of high school than other groups. The latter difference is quite dramatic. In 2006, 22 percent of 16–24-year-old Latinos were high school dropouts compared with 5.8 percent of whites and 10.7 percent of African Americans. Among Latinos, the gap between immigrant and nonimmigrant children is also very large: 14 percent of U.S.-born Latino teens between the ages of 16 and 19 dropped out of high school, compared with 33.7 percent of comparably aged foreign-born Latinos. This situation subsequently worsens at the college level and beyond, where Latinos are substantially underrepresented among students who graduate.

Understanding the factors that underlie this lack of opportunity must therefore become a national mandate if we are serious about solving this problem and creating positive and successful academic trajectories for Latino children. Suárez-Orozco and her colleagues discuss several converging factors that limit educational opportunities for Latino students. These include family capital, such as poverty, parental education, and whether students are authorized to be in the United States; school characteristics, such as levels of segregation, provision of language instruction, and teacher preparation; student resources, such as academic engagement, competency in acquiring a second language, and socioemotional challenges; and students' networks of relational support. For example, 28 percent of Latino students live in poverty compared with 16 percent of whites; among foreign-born Latino students, 35 percent live in poverty compared with 27 percent of their U.S.-born counterparts. As a result, many Latino students have jobs and need to contribute to the family's income while attending secondary or postsecondary schooling.

A related problem is unauthorized status. Although we are not sure exactly how many Latino immigrant children are unauthorized, among the 12 million undocumented migrants, 1.8 million are children or adolescents and at least 3 million are U.S.-citizen children living in a household headed by at least one undocumented parent (Passel 2006). The fear and instability that undocumented status brings to families is likely to affect Latino children's educational attainment, even though all have equal access to K–12 education.

After graduating from high school, unauthorized students increasingly have fewer options to continue their education. Interestingly, prior studies show that the challenge to staying in college is not only economic. Because many Latinos are the first in their families to attend college, they often do not have anyone to guide them through the process. They are also less likely to be eligible for federal financial aid but more likely to be affected by national and state policies that affect Latino student's access to higher education (Flores and Chapa forthcoming). At the same time, they are more likely to live fearful of immigration authorities.

Therefore, there is no doubt that, as Suárez-Orozco and her colleagues state, Latino students and families face enormous educational challenges. Yet Latino communities in the United States have an attribute that is often overlooked or less emphasized in prior studies: these families care about education (Gándara 1995; Suárez-Orozco and Suárez-Orozco 1995). This is, we argue, an important starting point given studies that suggest parental interest in children's education is a critical determinant of their involvement and students' subsequent, positive educational experience (Muller 1998).

If Latino parents care about their children's education, then are they involved in their children's schools? Do their participation rates differ from non-Latino parents, and what explains these differences? And how does this type of participation link to the larger citizenship process in which most Latino families are engaged? These questions are posed by the Immigrants-in-Schools Project (IISP) which is designed to understand and explain variation in parental involvement in schools (Donato and Marschall 2006; Marschall, Shah, and Donato forthcoming). Latino families, many of which are headed by at least one foreign-born parent, face numerous obstacles to being involved in their children's schooling. Suárez-Orozco and colleagues note, as do Perreira, Harris, and Lee (2006), that Latino immigrant parents may not have the cultural capital that serves students well. They also may not understand the practice of parent involvement and how to advocate for their children in schools. As Delgado Gaitan (2004) suggests, many immigrants originate from places where parents respect teachers' recommendations about children rather than advocate on their behalf. This is in part because many Latino students have parents who did not complete high school (Planty et al. 2008). Together with higher poverty, limited English proficiency, unauthorized status, low-skilled jobs that offer little schedule flexibility, and difficulties in finding child care and transportation to go to their children's school, Latino immigrant parents face many obstacles. In addition to lacking first-hand experience at being involved (López 2001), immigrant parents often lack access to networks that may offer the resources and information to help them navigate schools and the personal sense of efficacy or feeling that their involvement can matter (Schunk 1991; Suárez-Orozco, Suárez-Orozco, and Todorova 2008).

Yet despite such obstacles, Latino parents are motivated and care about their children's schooling. IISP argues that what really fosters opportunity for Latino children in schools is how parental interest and involvement in children's education interacts with the attributes of schools and school districts. Its focus is to understand whether and how parents of immigrant children engage in schools, and differences in the form and frequency across immigrant/ethnic groups situated in different structural circumstances and local school contexts. The project relies on two forms of data: the Schools and Staffing Surveys (SASS) from the National Center for Educational Statistics, and microdata from Latino parents in six neighborhoods across three cities. The latter dataset targets hard-to-reach immigrant/ethnic parents who are often not well represented in district-, city- or statewide surveys of parents. These microdata are collected from parents in different immigrant neighborhoods across three cities: Chicago, New York, and Nashville.[1] The focus is on predominantly immigrant communities that represent distinct ethnic groups: Chinese and Puerto Ricans in both cities, Mexicans in Chicago and Nashville, and Dominicans in New York. In contrast, the SASS data offer information about school practices and procedures that influence parental involvement. Together, the two datasets permit us to explicitly examine how school and teacher practices influence the pattern and form of involvement among immigrant parents, whether and how parents respond to these practices, and how school involvement links to other forms of civic and political participation.

Given that parental involvement improves educational outcomes, in the analysis below we ask a simple question. To what extent do schools offer programming for parents, and does this programming vary by type and region? Answering this question is the first step toward understanding Latino parent involvement in schools. For the analysis we use 2003–04 SASS data from more than 3,000 schools and examine how school practices and programs vary across different types of immigrant gateways. Using Singer's (2004) classification, we define three types of gateways: continuous, post-World War II, and new destinations.[2] To these three, we add another category (border destinations) that represents counties located along the U.S.-Mexican border.

To investigate nationwide school practices and policies, we begin by defining several different dimensions of parent involvement. The first, parental outreach, captures schools' parental involvement outreach efforts, and the second, institutionalization, measures how firmly parental involvement policies have become institutionalized at schools. These two indexes include the following survey items:

Parental outreach: (1) Does the school have a requirement that information be sent home to parents? (2) Does the school have a requirement that teachers send home suggestions for parent-child activities? (3) Does the school have a requirement that teachers explain homework assignments to parents? (alpha = .6846)

Institutionalization: (1) Does the school have a written contract for parent involvement? (2) Does the school have a staff member assigned to parental involvement? (3) Does the school keep a log of parental involvement kept by a staff member? (4) Does the school provide regular opportunities for parental involvement? (5) Does the school offer parental involvement workshops or courses? (6) Does the school have a reliable system of communication with parents? (alpha = .5767)

As the indicators suggest, parental outreach measures whether schools have required modes of engaging parents. These types of policies are the minimum that we would expect all districts to engage in. The second measure, institutionalization, also captures traditional parent involvement activities but in ways that schools formally recognize the role of parents. We expect schools that do not serve immigrant populations to score highest on these measures because U.S.-born parents are presumably more likely than immigrant parents to have role expectations that more closely approximate those of the school. At the same time, schools in border destinations may also offer more of these policies and programs because they have served Latino children for years and therefore have experience bridging cultural differences between schools and immigrant parents. However, because schools, districts, and state and federal policies mandate some parental outreach practices, it is also possible that schools will vary little in the programs they offer.

Although both measures are targeted at all parents, we also investigate whether schools implement policies and programs aimed to engage limited English proficient (LEP) parents. Therefore, we construct a third index called LEP policies, which captures school programs designed to reach out to LEP parents. The LEP policies index includes three survey items:

LEP policies: Schools provide (or not) the following services for parents with limited English proficiency skills: (1) interpreters for meetings or parent-teacher conferences; (2) translations of printed materials such as newsletters, school notices, or school signs; and (3) outreach or referral services (alpha = 0.754).

Our expectations regarding differences across immigrant gateways are more straightforward for these three types of school-initiated practices because they are designed to respond to the particular needs of many immigrant parents. Thus, we expect these policies to be more prevalent in places where there are more immigrants and more parents who do not speak English. In particular, we expect schools in border destinations to score highest on these measures, followed by schools in continuous gateways. We expect that schools in new destinations will score lowest because they are neither accustomed to nor familiar with the needs of immigrant parents. Finally, we include two additional measures of parental involvement. If schools have a parent lounge, they are coded as 1 and 0 otherwise. If schools have other services to support parent involvement, they are coded as 1 and 0 otherwise.

Table 10.1 presents summary statistics for the five types of parent involvement. For the indexes, we present means (representing the number of policies schools reported having), scaled between 0 (no policies) and 1 (all policies) to facilitate comparisons. For the two remaining indicators, the numbers correspond to the proportion of schools reporting these policies.

We focus first on parental outreach and find relatively low scores for schools across all contexts. This finding is surprising given that these policies constitute the minimum that most schools employ and the growing

Table 10.1. Parent Involvement Programs and Policies by Type of Immigrant Gateway

	Continuous	Post-WWII	New-destination	Border	Nonborder/nongateway
Traditional policies/practices					
Parental outreach	.339	.468	.383	.440	.356
	(.367)	(.395)	(.358)	(.371)	(.357)
Institutionalization	.677	.795	.709	.797	.671
	(.228)	(.208)	(.226)	(.219)	(.251)
Nontraditional policies/practices					
Limited English proficiency	.690	.864	.730	.888	.538
	(.369)	(.239)	(.345)	(.246)	(.402)
Parent lounge	.302	.421	.327	.410	.196
	(.460)	(.495)	(.469)	(.496)	(.397)
Parental support	.182	.364	.208	.303	.284
	(.387)	(.482)	(.406)	(.463)	(.451)
Number of schools	208	173	685	56	2,309

Source: Immigrants-in-Schools Project, 2009.

Notes: Table entries for the indexes (the first three indicators) are means; for the parent lounge and parental support measures, they are proportions. Standard deviations are in parentheses.

emphasis that education reform initiatives have placed on parent involvement.[3] The means range from .339 (for continuous gateways) to .468 (post-WWII gateways), which roughly correspond to schools offering between 1 and 1½ policies out of 3. Moreover, although there is little variation across contexts, schools in post-WWII gateways offer significantly more parental outreach than those in nongateway locations.

In contrast, scores for institutionalized parent involvement policies are much higher, with means ranging from .671 (in nonborder/nongateway) to .797 (in border gateways). These figures correspond to schools offering approximately 4–4½ policies out of 6. Interestingly, schools in nonborder/nongateways are comparable to those in continuous gateways. Given that schools in these districts have had the longest relationships with immigrant and minority parents, it is not surprising that they most resemble nonborder schools that largely serve the U.S. born. We speculate that in these locations, parents and schools have similar expectations of how schools should accommodate involvement. In contrast, however, schools in border, post-WWII, and new-destination gateways offer significantly more of these policies.

Results for policies targeting LEP immigrant parents are more telling of how the context of reception matters in determining school policies. Here the means range from .538 for nongateways to .888 for border gateways, and all gateway contexts significantly differ from nonborder/ nongateways. The large difference in LEP policies between border and nonborder schools suggest that the former offer these policies to respond to the need and demand of immigrant, and largely Latino, populations. Moreover, the difference between schools in post-WWII and those in new-destination gateways lies in the histories of immigration in these places. Schools in new destinations lag behind schools in other immigrant gateways in their ability to address the special needs of immigrants. However, that they attempt to bring parents into schools and support their involvement at all suggests that they have begun to develop an institutional response toward engaging parents. In other words, schools in areas with large concentrations of immigrants from the same linguistic or national-origin group may face lower costs when reaching out to parents.

In sum, these descriptive findings suggest two key findings. First, school-initiated parental involvement practices are not universal. Although few schools require that information be sent home to parents, or that teachers send home suggestions for parent-child activities and explained homework assignments to parents, schools report more institutionalized

forms of parent involvement such as assigning a staff member to super-
vise such programs and having a reliable communication system with
parents. Moreover, for schools in gateways where substantial numbers
of immigrants live, the most common type of school-initiated parental
involvement is LEP programs. The second key finding is that the school
involvement policies and programs vary significantly by type of immigrant gateway. The biggest difference is between schools in areas that have
large numbers of immigrant parents and those that do not. These results
suggest that the policies schools develop and implement are largely determined by where schools are located and the immigrant populations that
they serve.

Although noteworthy nationally, these findings do not describe the
actual involvement of immigrant parents. In the future, analysis of the IISP
microdata from parents of Latino children in Chicago, New York, and
Nashville neighborhoods will offer additional insight into parent involvement. Moreover, the new data will permit comparison of Mexicans in
Chicago (Lower West Side) to those in Nashville, to Dominicans in New
York (Washington Heights/Inwood), and to two Puerto Rican communities in Chicago and New York (West Town and University Heights).
Together they will help us assess how citizenship status influences participatory patterns among immigrants and U.S.-born residents.[4] We will
examine whether they are participating and to what extent, compare their
involvement with that of other groups that have low rates of naturalized
citizens, and then compare their involvement to the practices reported by
schools in these neighborhoods.

To sum, although Latino children face bleak educational prospects,
improving outreach to parents of Latino children in schools is one solution likely to make a difference. This is a straightforward policy response
that is relatively low cost and mandated by No Child Left Behind. Yet, in
many schools, parent involvement either does not exist or exists in forms
that are less accessible to immigrant parents.

Grassroots efforts in cities around the nation have begun to change this
situation. For example, in Nashville, a city whose public school enrollment has increased from approximately 3,400 students in 2001 to slightly
more than 10,000 in 2007, a nonprofit organization that serves the immigrant community has partnered with Metro Schools to fund a Parents as
Partners program. Modeled after the National Council of La Raza, and
with support from Conexion America's Hispanic Advisory Council,
the program trains parents to teach other parents about how to interact

with their children's teachers and schools. After its first two months, the peer-to-peer program had trained more than 150 Latino high school parents. This is one of many examples of local organizations seizing the opportunity to engage Latino parents and improve their children's long-term educational prospects.

NOTES

1. We chose the first two cities because they have attracted immigrants for more than 100 years, but they differed in the extent parents were empowered to participate civically. In Chicago, for example, noncitizens have been eligible to run for office and vote in elections for local school council members. In contrast, New York revoked this privilege when it eliminated its elected school boards, and despite efforts by city officials to involve immigrant parents in schools, studies suggest limited success. The last city—Nashville—represents a new gateway for immigrants since the late 1980s.

2. Singer defines gateways as cities with metropolitan populations greater than 1 million, foreign-born populations greater than 200,000, and foreign-born shares greater than the national average in 2000 (11%) or foreign-born growth rates greater than the national average in 2000 (57%), or both. We differ from Singer by having a new destinations category that combines three of Singer's (2004) categories: emerging, reemerging and preemerging gateways. In addition, we do not distinguish former gateways from nongateways.

3. Indeed, the reauthorized Elementary and Secondary Education Act (ESEA) of 2002, also known as the No Child Left Behind Act, requires schools to involve parents in programs by mandating every district and school receiving federal Title I funds to develop a written policy jointly with parents of children participating in Title I programs.

4. Puerto Ricans offer the project a comparative advantage; as U.S. citizens, they have full rights to vote and participate in schools and communities.

REFERENCES

Delgado Gaitan, Concha. 2004. *Involving Latino Families in Schools: Raising Student Achievement through Home-School Partnerships.* Thousand Oaks, CA: Corwin Press.

Donato, Katharine M., and Melissa Marschall. 2006. "Immigrant Parent Involvement in Schools, Communities and Politics." Proposal funded by the National Science Foundation.

Gándara, Patricia. 1995. *Over the Ivy Walls: The Educational Mobility of Low-Income Chicanos.* Albany, NY: SUNY Press.

Flores, Stella M., and Jorge Chapa. Forthcoming. "Public Policy Geography and Immigrant Students in Higher Education." *Journal of Latinos in Higher Education.*

López, Gerardo R. 2001. "The Value of Hard Work: Lessons on Parent Involvement from an (Im)migrant Household." *Harvard Educational Review* 71(3): 416–37.

Marschall, Melissa, Paru Shah, and Katharine M. Donato. Forthcoming. "Parent Involvement in Schools: A Macro-Level Analysis of Immigrant Gateway Districts." *Social Forces.*

Muller, Chandra. 1998. "Gender Differences in Parental Involvement and Adolescents' Mathematics Achievement." *Sociology of Education* 71(4): 336–56.

Passel, Jeffrey S. 2006. "The Size and Characteristics of the Unauthorized Migrant Population in the U.S." Washington, DC: Pew Hispanic Center.

Perreira, Krista M., Kathleen M. Harris, and Dohoon Lee. 2006. "Making It in America: High School Completion by Immigrant and Native Youth." *Demography* 43(3): 1–26.

Planty, Michael, William Hussar, Thomas Snyder, Stephen Provasnik, Grace Kena, Rachel Dinkes, Angie Kewal Ramani, and Jana Kemp. 2008. *The Condition of Education 2008*. NCES 2008-031. Washington, DC: U.S. Department of Education, Institute of Education Sciences, National Center for Education Statistics.

Schunk, Dale H. 1991. "Self-Efficacy and Academic Motivation." *Educational Psychologist* 26:207–31.

Singer, Audrey. 2004. "The Rise of New Immigrant Gateways." Washington, DC: The Brookings Institution.

Suárez-Orozco, Carola, and Marcelo M. Suárez-Orozco. 1995. *Transformations: Immigration, Family Life, and Achievement Motivation among Latino Adolescents*. Palo Alto, CA: Stanford University Press.

Suárez-Orozco, Carola, Marcelo M. Suárez-Orozco, and Irina Todorova. 2008. *Learning a New Land: Immigrant Students in American Society*. Cambridge, MA: Harvard University Press.

11

Latino Academic Achievement and Dropping Out of School

Suet-ling Pong

C hapter 9 by Suárez-Orozco and colleagues is a much-needed review of the status of Latino students' education. Until recently, we have known little about Latinos' education (Tienda and Mitchell 2006). Suárez-Orozco and colleagues have filled the vacuum by addressing three "W" questions regarding the status, mechanisms, and policies of Latino students' schooling: What is the current status of Latino education in the United States? Why is Latino education the way it is? And, what can we do about it? Their review in each of these areas is thorough and valuable.

Given the importance of education for an individual's future well-being, the future of Latino students is disconcerting. Latino students are failing in large numbers at virtually every level, from preschool to college. As Suárez-Orozco and colleagues observe, at each stage along the educational pipeline, Latino students are hindered by low levels of academic performance and achievement relative to non-Latino whites. A large Latino-white achievement gap exists even before Latino children enter kindergarten. A large proportion of Latino students does not make it through middle and high school to graduation. Even though Latino parents have high expectations and deeply care about their children's education, the American dream of Latino immigrants' children is largely unfulfilled.

Is there any light at the end of this tunnel? Or is the situation of Latino students hopeless? The evidence I present suggests reasons to be cautiously optimistic. In this chapter, I review some of the positive aspects of Latino's K–12 schooling. I fill in missing information about trends of the Latino-white achievement gap and extend discussions on Latino students' achievement and school dropout. And, I raise questions about the role of the school in the transmission or the transformation of disadvantage among Latinos.

Trends of Latino-White Achievement Gap

The achievement gap has been seen as an indicator for the inequality of educational opportunity. This gap between Latino and white students is large for various school subjects, it is true. But, to see the brighter side of the Latino school experience, we must look beyond the current status to the over-time trends. Widely considered the nation's report card, the National Assessment of Educational Progress (NAEP) is the most valued source for trends of achievement gap. According to NAEP, the Latino-white gaps were smaller in 2004 than in the 1970s by 11 points in reading and 9 points in math on a 0–500 scale. From 1999 to 2004, the Latino-white math gap narrowed from 26 to 18 points (U.S. Department of Education 2005).

However, one needs to be cautious about inferring long-term trends from cross-sectional data. Dropout rates of Latino youth are large, and they vary from year to year. To examine the school progress of Latino students, longitudinal data that track the same individual students over time are superior to cross-sectional data.

The use of longitudinal data to track the Latino-white achievement gap in math is well under way. Based on young children in kindergarten and elementary school, four recent studies show a narrowing Latino-white gap (Clotfelter, Ladd, and Vigdor 2006; Fryer and Levitt 2006; Reardon and Galindo 2007, 2009). Although not the focus here, these studies show increasing black-white differentials. By contrast, the Latino-white gaps in math and reading have shrunk by roughly a third in the first two years of schooling, and the greatest achievement gains go to first- and second-generation Mexican and Central American students, as well as to students who have limited English proficiency when they begin school (Reardon and Galindo 2009). Among at-risk kindergartners, defined as kindergartners in the lowest two socioeconomic quintiles and possessing at least three risk factors (e.g., poverty, welfare, teen mother, parental health problems), the black-white math gap in kindergarten is enlarged by 5th grade, after the school's sector, socioeconomic status, and minority context are controlled. The contrast with Latino progress is clear. Even though at-risk Latino kindergartners start out significantly behind their at-risk white counterparts in math, they gain enough to outperform their at-risk white counterparts by 5th grade (Farkas and Bodovski forthcoming).

The Role of the School

What is the power source of the light at the end of the tunnel? Suárez-Orozco and colleagues have suggested various factors, including immigrants' high aspirations, dual frame of reference, optimism, dedicated hard work, positive attitudes toward school, and ethic of family support. They did not consider the school itself among this list of positive factors. For example, is school as important as the family in shaping Latino children's education?

Sociologists of education came up with an innovative way to address this question, and that is to compare achievement growth in the summer, when school is out, with achievement growth during the school year. Barbara Heyns (1978) was the first sociologist who showed that students' summer learning is unequally distributed by social class. Entwisle, Alexander, and Olson (1997) propose the "faucet" theory that characterizes the equalizing role of the school in their Baltimore school data. When the school is in session, the faucet is on, and resources flow more equally to disadvantaged children. When the school is out, the faucet is off, and few resources are available to disadvantaged children, who are eventually left behind. Using this same analytic strategy and a nationally representative sample, Downey, von Hippel, and Broh (2004) find an equalizing role of kindergarten and 1st grade, because the achievement gaps by socioeconomic status increase in the summer before 1st grade but decrease when kindergarten or 1st grade is in session. Further, when socioeconomic status is controlled, no clear pattern shows that Latino children benefit more in school than out of school (summer), compared with white children. However, because Latino children tend to come from lower socioeconomic backgrounds, the implications of Downey and colleagues' findings is that the school is an equalizer to Latino children as a whole.

It seems paradoxical that school can be equalizing to Latino children, given that they are overrepresented in schools with a wide variety of undesirable factors. Children are unlikely to perform well in resource-poor learning environments. However, Latino children who are placed in problematic schools are also likely to live in poverty-stricken families and in difficult neighborhoods. When out-of-school learning approaches zero, schools may be the only safe haven for disadvantaged Latino children's educational progress.

Suárez-Orozco and colleagues suggest school segregation harms Latino children through cutting contact with middle-class white Americans, and through isolation at the levels of poverty and language. Surely, segregated schools have a lot of problems, such as large class sizes, lower teacher qualifications, and poor disciplinary climates. The worse cases involve violence and gang activities. However, segregated schools may have some advantages to Latino immigrant children that are not evident to other minority children. Segregated schools with high percentages of Latino students are also schools predominated by students who have limited English proficiency. A recent study by the Urban Institute finds that nearly 70 percent of English language learners (ELL) enroll in only 10 percent of elementary schools nationally (Cosentino de Cohen, Deterding, and Clewell 2005). This study also finds several positive characteristics of these high-concentration ELL schools. Compared with other schools, high-ELL schools are more likely to provide support and programs (pre-kindergarten, enrichment, after-school, and summer school); are more likely to be involved in parental outreach and support activities; and have more external, standardized procedures to identify ELL students, rather than teacher's subjective judgments. In addition, these high-ELL schools are more likely to offer native language instruction to meet the needs of ELL students. Other techniques such as structured immersion, bilingual education, and English as a second language (ESL) are also more likely to be available in these high-ELL schools.

Fifty-four years ago, the Supreme Court ruled that segregated schools are inherently unequal. Unfortunately, segregated schools still exist, and Latino students have a higher chance of attending them than do any other ethnic group. Paradoxically, when there is a large share of ELL students in school, it becomes politically more feasible for the school to justify funds for programs meeting ELL students' needs. Suárez-Orozco and colleagues report that dual-language programs consistently produce the best results. Note that dual-language classes require a critical mass of ELL students to make them work. Segregated ELL schools may not shortchange Latino children as much as one would typically assume.

Today, seven years after the No Child Left Behind legislation, few educators believe schools alone can close the racial/ethnic achievement gap. Any effort to promote student's learning needs to combine policies intended to improve K–12 schools with policies designed to transform the out-of-school contexts in which children and youth develop. We must remember that the Latino-white achievement gap is significantly large when children enter kindergarten. This achievement gap reflects more factors that are out of U.S. schools' control than the performance of U.S. schools.

Policies that include early childhood education, summer school, or after-school programs could help put Latino children on a more equal footing before kindergarten. Latino children's enrollment in Head Start, a federally funded program that has a small positive effect on Latino children's cognitive development (Currie and Thomas 1996), has shown a positive trend. Latino children's participation increased from 26.4 percent in 1998 to 30.6 percent in 2003, whereas African American children's participation dropped from 35.8 to 31.5 percent during the same period (Schneider, Martinez, and Owens 2006). This increasing participation in Head Start does not reflect increasing poverty rates among Latinos because, according to the U.S. Census Bureau, household income increased faster for Latinos than for African Americans from the late 1990s to the early 2000s.

Dropping Out of School

An important indicator used to evaluate how well schools perform is the dropout rate. This rate usually measures the proportion of a population within an age bracket that is not enrolled in school. But, for Latino youth, there are two problems with the interpretation of this rate. First, the dropout rate includes nonenrollment of children of labor migrants, who come to the United States to work and never intend to set foot in school. In 2000, about 27 percent of foreign-born Mexican youth age 16–17 were not in school. Half these teens had never entered school. By contrast, the nonenrollment figure for native-born non-Latino white youth is only 4 percent (Oropesa and Landale 2009). The reasons for Latino nonenrollment are thus related to the nature of child migration, so dropout rates cannot always be considered a school effect.

Second, the dropout rate changes for different age brackets. The National Center for Education Statistics calculates the rates for 16–24-year-olds. Dropout rates calculated from different age brackets differ substantially. For example, in 2000, Latino students' dropout rate was 21 percent based on the age group of 16–19 (Fry 2003), but it was 6.8 percentage points higher when the calculation was based on the age group of 16–24 (Kaufman, Alt, and Chapman 2001). Fry argues that ages 20–24 should not be included in the calculation of dropout rates because a large number of Latinos immigrating to the United States between the ages of 20 and 24 are unlikely to attend secondary school. When Fry (2003) limits his analysis to high school students' ages of 16–19, he finds a slight decrease in Latinos' dropout rates from 21.6 percent in 1990 to 21.0 percent in 2000. This is the bright side of the picture.

Of course, the gloomier side is that these dropout rates for 16–19-year-olds are still much higher than the dropout rates of either non-Hispanic whites (8 percent in 2000) or non-Hispanic blacks (12 percent in 2000), even though we know that the 21 percent Latino dropout rate is an overestimate because some 16–19-year-old Latino immigrant youth never attended U.S. schools. A more accurate comparison requires us to consider longitudinal surveys tracking school children over time.

Using data from the Education Longitudinal Study of 2002 (ELS), I analyzed youths' high school dropout rates from 10th to 12th grade. The sample is restricted to third-plus generations of non-Hispanic black ("black" hereafter) and non-Hispanic white ("white" hereafter) youth, as well as all Latino youth, regardless of their generational status. Figure 11.1 shows that, without any adjustment, Latino youths' odds of dropping out are more than twice as high as the odds for white youth but do not differ from the odds for black youth ($t = .71$). There are no generational differences in the odds in dropping out among Latino students. Accounting for prior math test scores in 10th grade alone washes out all racial/ethnic differences in the odds of dropping out. Nor are there generational differences among Latinos. These results confirm previous research on the strong relationship between academic performance and dropouts (Driscoll 1999; Rumberger 1995). It is impressive that in the ELS, academic achievement explains all the racial/ethnic differentials in dropping out of senior high school.

These results bring us directly back to academic achievement. Figure 11.2 shows racial/ethnic differences in 12th grade math test scores. Consistent with past research, white youth score significantly higher than do Latino youth, and Latino youth score significantly higher than do black youth ($t = 3.98$). Among Latino youth, the first generation has the lowest math scores. After accounting for prior math scores in 10th grade, we see no

Figure 11.1. Odds Ratios of Dropping Out from 10th to 12th Grade, by Race/Ethnicity and Generation

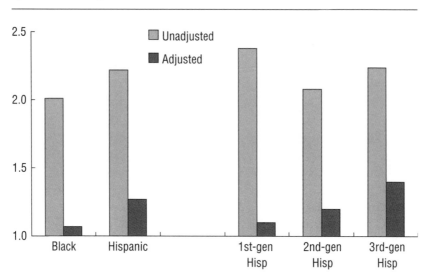

Notes: Results from logistic regression models of dropout on race/ethnicity and immigrant generation, first without (unadjusted) and then with (adjusted) the control of 10th grade math test scores. The reference group is non-Hispanic white students. All unadjusted odds ratios are significant at the $p < .01$ level. All adjusted odds ratios are statistically insignificant.

significant differences between white youth and second- and third-generation Latino youth. In other words, when initial achievement is controlled, the achievement gap between native white and U.S.-born Latino youth does not grow between 10th and 12th grade. That is, the gap already exists at senior high school entry. The years in senior high school do not exacerbate this gap. In contrast, the achievement gap between first-generation Latino adolescents and native white students grows during senior high school years.

School Transition

The problem of first-generation Latino students' low academic achievement is another point of concern. To further investigate the role of the school, I divided first-generation Latino students into those who received all their education in the United States and those who attended school outside the United States. Consistent with one previous study (Fry 2003), table 11.1 shows that Latino students who studied abroad and had to make

Figure 11.2. Twelfth-Grade Math Test Scores, by Race/Ethnicity and Generation

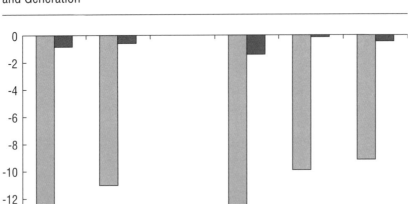

Notes: Results from OLS regression of math scores on race/ethnicity and immigrant generation, first without (unadjusted) and then with (adjusted) the control of 10th grade math test scores. The reference group is non-Hispanic white students. All unadjusted coefficients are significant at the $p < .05$ level. All adjusted coefficients are statistically insignificant.

a school transition tend to have lower math test scores in 10th grade and higher odds of dropping out than did Latino students who only attended United States schools and made no school transition.

Are different types of school transition related to different school outcomes? At the moment, we have little information about how Latino immigrant children make their transition to U.S. schools. Suárez-Orozco and colleagues rightfully describe the policy of integrating newcomer immigrant-origin youth into secondary school as "sink or swim integration policies." Fortunately, the ELS contains detailed information about the grades immigrant students studied abroad and the grade they started in U.S. schools. Restricting the sample to Latino students, I constructed a variable that indicates four types of school transitions: U.S. educated and never made a transition, skipped a grade, promoted to the next grade, and

Table 11.1. Tenth-Grade Math Achievement and Dropping Out between 10th and 12th Grade among Hispanic Students, by Type of School Transition

	Math score (1)	Math score (2)	Dropout (3)	Dropout (4)
No transition (U.S.-educated)	3.655**		0.655*	
	(5.24)		(2.30)	
Skipped a grade		−5.719**		1.042
		(4.10)		(0.07)
Promoted to next grade		−3.732**		1.330
		(4.51)		(1.24)
Repeated a grade		−2.674*		2.180**
		(2.36)		(2.93)
Missing transition	1.910+	−1.746+	0.557+	0.849
	(1.86)	(1.91)	(1.74)	(0.53)
Male	1.213*	1.192*	1.331+	1.327+
	(2.55)	(2.49)	(1.88)	(1.85)
Parental education	1.519**	1.516**	0.819**	0.819**
	(11.31)	(11.28)	(5.25)	(5.24)
Constant	23.482**	27.159**		
	(32.15)	(50.38)		
R-squared	0.10	0.11		

Source: Author's calculations based on the Education Longitudinal Study of 2002 and 2004 data.

Notes: Robust *t* statistics are in parentheses. Results shown here are ordinary least square regression coefficients for models 1 and 2, and odds ratios for models 3 and 4. Sample size is 1,924.

+Significant at the $p < .10$ level.

*Significant at the $p < .05$ level.

**Significant at the $p < .01$ level.

repeated a grade. Among the 301 students who studied abroad, 59 percent were promoted to the next grade when they started school in the United States, 12 percent skipped a grade, and 29 percent repeated a grade. To keep things in perspective, this group of overseas-educated is the minority. Most (83 percent) Latino students have all their education in the United States, including the 12 percent of first-generation Latinos.

Descriptive statistics show that U.S.-educated Latinos who make no school transitions have the highest achievement and the lowest dropout probability. In a multiple regression analysis that controls for students' gender and parental education, I find that each school transition is significantly associated with Latino students' lower achievement scores (table 11.1). However, logistic regression analysis reveals that repeating a grade during school transition significantly increases the risk of dropping out from senior high school. Other types of school transitions do not differ from the U.S.-educated group in the association with dropping out.

These analyses are useful for identifying Latino dropouts as those who have studied abroad and repeat a grade when they start school in the United States. Latino repeaters are not only low achievers, relative to Latino students educated in the United States, but they are also old for their grade. These repeaters are a small group, making up only about 6 percent of the Latino student population in the ELS. Identifying this group of repeaters is important because education policies that target specific groups for dropout prevention would be more successful than policies implemented across the board.

Premigratory Factors

The last issue remaining in these analyses is why Latino students who have studied abroad tend to have lower test scores. Most likely this results from the quality of education in immigrant children's home countries. Cross-national comparisons in Trends in International Math and Science Study (TIMSS) and the Programme for International Student Assessment (PISA) have shown large variations of math and science achievement across more than 50 countries. Mexico consistently ranks far below the U.S. averages in these tests, even though the U.S. averages are not high internationally (Lemke et al. 2004). It is likely that Mexican children learned less in school than did U.S. students. Also, parents of Mexican immigrant children are less selected in their pre-migratory educational attainment than immigrant parents from most other countries (Feliciano 2006). This double jeopardy may produce less academically prepared Mexican adolescents as they enter U.S. schools. Achievement scores lower than the U.S. averages have also been shown for eight other Latin American countries that participated in the international studies: El Salvador, Honduras, and Colombia in the TIMSS; and Chile, Argentina, Brazil, Peru, and Uruguay in the PISA (Baldi et al. 2007; Gonzales et al. 2000; Lemke et al. 2004). Thus, newly arrived students from these Latino countries tend to have academic difficulty in the U.S. school system.

Policy Implications and Concluding Remarks

Some policy implications can be derived from these analyses. First, immigrant students who make a transition to U.S. schools should be targeted for remedial instructions after school so they can catch up with the subject matters they did not learn. Second, immigrant parents should be discouraged from pushing their children to skip a grade when they enter U.S. schools, because skipping a grade is associated with lower test scores. Third, immigrant parents should also be discouraged from allowing their children to repeat a grade when they arrive in U.S. schools. The slightly higher test scores of this group of immigrant students hardly compensate for their high risk of dropping out from senior high school. Overage can be an issue in American society. Older students may feel that they do not belong in school.

In sum, I question whether the problem of Latino children's educational disadvantage originates in school. By contrast, schools appear to be acting in ways that prevent Latino children from further falling behind non-Hispanic whites. However, schools must not stop there. My analysis of ELS suggests that resources can be put to good use to improve achievement and prevent dropouts by identifying immigrant students who have to make transitions from abroad to U.S. schools. But again, to solve this and many other school problems facing Latino students, schools cannot do it alone, and neither can families or communities. We need social policies that unite efforts from various social institutions to work together toward education progress for all Latino-origin children.

NOTE

The author is grateful for the research assistance provided by Vivien Chen.

REFERENCES

Baldi, Stéphane, Ying Jin, Melanie Skemer, Patricia J. Green, and Deborah Herget. 2007. *Highlights from PISA 2006: Performance of U.S. 15-Year-Old Students in Science and Mathematics Literacy in an International Context.* NCES 2008-016. Washington, DC: U.S. Department of Education, Institute of Education Sciences, National Center for Education Statistics.

Clotfelter, Charles T., Helen F. Ladd, and Jacob L. Vigdor. 2006. "The Academic Achievement Gap in Grades Three to Eight." Working Paper 12207. Cambridge, MA: National Bureau of Economic Research.

Cosentino de Cohen, Clemencia, Nicole Deterding, and Beatriz Chu Clewell. 2005. *Who's Left Behind? Immigrant Children in High- and Low-LEP Schools.* Washington, DC: The Urban Institute.

Currie, Janet, and Duncan Thomas. 1996. "Does Head Start Help Hispanic Children?" Working Paper No. 5805. Cambridge, MA: National Bureau of Economic Research.

Downey, Douglas B., P. T. von Hippel, and B. A. Broh. 2004. "Are Schools the Great Equalizer? Cognitive Inequality during the Summer Months and the School Year." *American Sociological Review* 69(5): 613–35.

Driscoll, Anne K. 1999. "Risk of High School Dropout among Immigrant and Native Hispanic Youth." *International Migration Review* 33(128): 857–75.

Entwisle, Doris R., Karl L. Alexander, and Linda S. Olson. 1997. *Children, Schools, and Inequality.* Boulder, CO: Westview Press.

Farkas, George, and Katerina Bodovski. Forthcoming. *Early Inequality.* New York: Russell Sage Foundation.

Feliciano, Cynthia. 2006. "Beyond the Family: The Influence of Premigration Group Status on the Educational Expectations of Immigrants' Children." *Sociology of Education* 79(4): 281–303.

Fry, Richard. 2003. *Hispanic Youth Dropping Out of U.S. Schools: Measuring the Challenge.* Washington, DC: Pew Hispanic Center.

Fryer, Roland G., and Stephen D. Levitt. 2006. "The Black-White Test Score Gap through Third Grade." *American Law and Economics Review* 8:249–81.

Gonzales, Patrick, Christopher Calsyn, Leslie Jocelyn, Kitty Mak, David Kastberg, Sousan Arafeh, Trevor Williams, and Winnie Tsen. 2000. *Pursuing Excellence: Comparisons of International Eighth-Grade Mathematics and Science Achievement from a U.S. Perspective, 1995 and 1999.* NCES 2001-028. Washington, DC: U.S. Department of Education, Office of Educational Research and Improvement, National Center for Education Statistics.

Heyns, Barbara. 1978. *Summer Learning and the Effects of Schooling.* New York: Academic Press.

Kaufman, Phillip, Martha Naomi Alt, and Christopher Chapman. 2001. *Dropout Rates in the United States: 2000.* NCES 2002-114. Washington, DC: U.S. Department of Education, Office of Educational Research and Improvement, National Center for Education Statistics.

Lemke, Mariann, Anindita Sen, Erin Pahlke, Lisette Partelow, David Miller, Trevor Williams, David Kastberg, and Leslie Jocelyn. 2004. *International Outcomes of Learning in Mathematics Literacy and Problem Solving: PISA 2003 Results from the U.S. Perspective.* NCES 2005-003. Washington, DC: U.S. Department of Education, Institute of Education Science, National Center for Education Statistics.

Oropesa, R. S., and Nancy S. Landale. 2009. "Why Do Immigrant Youths Who Never Enroll in U.S. Schools Matter? School Enrollment among Mexican Americans and Non-Hispanic Whites." *Sociology of Education* 82(3): 240–66.

Reardon, Sean F., and Claudia Galindo. 2007. "Patterns of Latino Students' Math Skill Proficiency in the Early Elementary Grades." *Journal of Latinos and Education* 6(3): 229–51.

————. 2009. "The Hispanic-White Achievement Gap in Math and Reading in the Elementary Grades." *American Educational Research Journal* 46(3): 853–91.

Rumberger, Russell W. 1995. "Dropping Out of Middle School: A Multilevel Analysis of Students and Schools." *American Educational Research Journal* 32(3): 583–625.

Schneider, Barbara, Sylvia Martinez, and Ann Owens. 2006. "Barriers to Educational Opportunities for Hispanics in the United States." In *Hispanics and the Future of America,* edited by Marta Tienda and Faith Mitchell (179–227). Washington DC: National Academies Press.

Tienda, Marta, and Faith Mitchell, eds. 2006. *Hispanics and the Future of America.* Washington DC: National Academies Press.

U.S. Department of Education. 2005. *NAEP 2004 Trends in Academic Progress: Three Decades of Student Performance in Reading and Mathematics.* NCES 2005-463. Washington, DC: U.S. Department of Education, Institute of Education Sciences, National Center for Education Statistics.

12

The Academic Desire of Students from Latin American Backgrounds

Andrew J. Fuligni

I t is difficult to believe that there will be any changes in the educational progress of Latinos in the United States without large-scale and dramatic efforts to address the shocking inequities in the resources and opportunities that exist for this rapidly increasing segment of the American population. Suárez-Orozco and colleagues effectively lay out the laundry list of challenges faced by this population. Students from Latin American backgrounds attend schools that are segregated by ethnicity, poverty, and language. When in school, they encounter inexperienced teachers with limited training to work with English language learners and who must manage overcrowded classrooms in extremely large schools. Not surprisingly, these schools do not have climates conducive to learning. The schools have high dropout, suspension, and expulsion rates, and the Latin American students who attend them are more likely to report fears of being attacked or harmed in their school, avoiding certain places in their school, and the presence of gangs in their schools (Fuligni and Hardway 2004).

Any parent and student facing these difficulties would be intimidated. But these difficulties are especially detrimental for families from Latin American backgrounds because of their limited socioeconomic resources. As Suárez-Orozco and colleagues describe, many parents from Latin America receive little schooling before they come to this country, often not completing a high school degree. As a result, they find themselves limited to the low-wage labor market that offers little stability, benefits, or opportunities for advancement. Because such a large segment of the population faces these challenges, it is likely more difficult for families to obtain the kind of informal information and advice about schooling options, course requirements, and college application procedures that is available in other communities (Zhou and Kim 2006).

From a policy standpoint, the typical arguments made for breaking down the resource and opportunity barriers facing students from Latin America are because such structural factors make a difference in school success and because such inequities violate principles of equality in public education. Such points were the key arguments made in a long-standing class-action lawsuit in California *(Williams v. State of California)* filed on behalf of students in poorer, underresourced school districts, most of whom were from Latin American backgrounds, that was settled in 2004.

Yet another argument can be made for why addressing the structural barriers faced by Latino students should be addressed, one that was touched upon in chapter 9 but is not emphasized often in policy discussions. The argument is that this group is *primed* to take advantage of educational opportunity. Students and parents from Latin American backgrounds already have high educational aspirations, strongly believe in the importance of education for their future economic success, and show levels of motivation that are often greater than their peers from European backgrounds. There is no need to change the "hearts and minds" of this population, which most interventionists will tell you is one of the most difficult things to do. Latinos already value education at high rates and have a strong desire to get good grades, finish high school, and complete college. They just don't have the resources, opportunities, and knowledge to do these things successfully.

Although this point is simple to make, it is worth making it frequently and forcefully because most people don't believe it despite the strength of the evidence. My colleagues and I have spent a lot of time in the past few years examining the educational aspirations and motivations of this population, and we have strong support for the contention that adolescents from Latin American backgrounds have a strong belief in the importance of education and would very much like to take advantage of what it can offer to their future lives as adults. The results are taken from two longitudinal studies of adolescents from Latin American, Asian, and European backgrounds that took place in the San Francisco and Los Angeles metropolitan areas. The total sample sizes ranged from 750 to over 1,000 students. Participants completed questionnaires that assessed various educational attitudes, and indicators of the students' academic performance were obtained from their official school records.

Figure 12.1 shows ethnic differences in adolescents' belief in the utility of education from the San Francisco study (Fuligni 2001). The data are from two cohorts of 10th and 12th grade students combined. Using a scale that ranged from 1 "not at all true of me" to 5 "very true of me," students responded to such items as "Going to college is necessary for what I want to do in the future," "I need to get good grades in school to get a good job as an adult," and "Doing well in school is the best way for me to succeed as an adult." Although most adolescents believe in the future utility of education, those from Latin American backgrounds more strongly endorse the idea than their peers from European backgrounds.

We see this pattern in many different aspects of motivation. Students from Mexican and other Latin American backgrounds generally report levels of motivation that are either equal to or greater than those of their peers from European backgrounds. Figure 12.2 shows similar results that we obtained using the same measure among 9th grade students who participated in the study in the Los Angeles area (Fuligni, Witkow, and Garcia 2005). Finally, figure 12.3 shows that the students from Mexican backgrounds also identify with school at the same level as do their peers from Asian and European backgrounds. These results are based upon a measure in which students used a scale from 1 "strongly disagree" to

Figure 12.1. Ethnic Differences in Adolescents' Belief in the Utility of Education, San Francisco

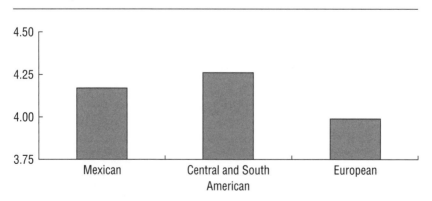

Source: Based on results presented in Fuligni (2001).

Figure 12.2. Ethnic Differences in Adolescents' Belief in the Utility of Education, Los Angeles

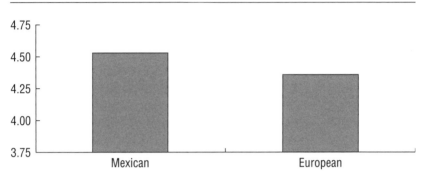

Source: Based on results presented in Fuligni (2001).

5 "strongly agree" to respond to such items as "I feel close to people at my school," "I feel like I am a part of my school," and "I am happy to be at my school."

Among the students from Latin American backgrounds, those from the first and sometimes second generations (i.e., those with immigrant parents) tend to have higher levels of academic motivation than those from the third generation (Fuligni 1997). Yet it is important to note that despite the slight generational decline, even third-generation students

Figure 12.3. Ethnic Differences in Adolescents' Identification with School, Los Angeles

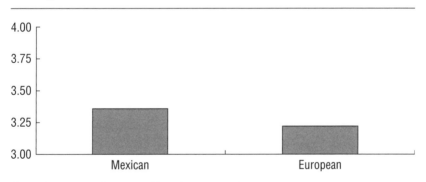

Source: Based on results presented in Fuligni et al. (2005).

from Latin American backgrounds report a value of education that is at least equal to that of their peers from European backgrounds.

The relatively high level of motivation and school identification among students from Latin American backgrounds exists during high school despite the fact that they receive significantly lower grades than their peers. What this discordance in the ethnic differences in motivation and achievement suggests is that it takes more motivation for students from Latin American backgrounds to attain the same level of success in school as their peers from European backgrounds. This is indicated by figure 12.4, in which students' grade point averages (GPAs) are plotted against their belief in the utility of education separately for students from Latin American and European backgrounds. As you can see by the relatively parallel lines, the importance of the belief for actual achievement is similar across the two groups. This indicates that the greater level of motivation among students from Latin American backgrounds is not because their beliefs and values are more abstract or disconnected from their actual achievement in school. Rather, their motivation is just as important for their school success. It just takes more motivation to reach the same GPA as their peers from European backgrounds, as suggested by the horizontal gap between the lines.

This gap raises some important questions about the educational performance of students from Latin American backgrounds. First, why does it

Figure 12.4. The Association between Belief in the Utility of Education and Grade Point Average, According to Ethnicity

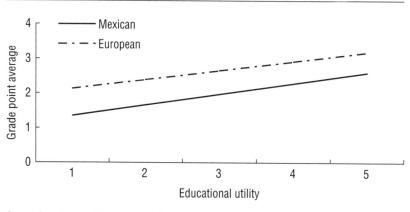

Source: Based on results presented in Fuligni et al. (2005).

take more motivation for students from Latin American backgrounds to achieve the same GPA as their peers from European backgrounds? That is an easy question to answer if we go back to long list of economic, social, and structural challenges faced by the students and their families. Their parents often have lower levels of education, unstable jobs in lower-wage occupations, and little experience with the American educational system. Add to that the low-quality instruction and diminished expectations children encounter in school, and it should not be a surprise that a student with a Latin American background should have to be more motivated to reach the same level of academic success as his or her peers who encounter fewer hurdles in their education.

Second, where does that additional motivation come from? In our research, we have found ample evidence that adolescents' sense of obligation to their family and identification with their cultural background serve as important sources of their aspirations and desire. As Suárez-Orozco found in her earlier work (Suárez-Orozco and Suárez-Orozco 1995), we have observed a strong sense of obligation to support, assist, and respect the family among adolescents from Latin American backgrounds. Although this sense of obligation may change somewhat across generations, it still remains stronger than that of adolescents from European backgrounds among adolescents from the third and later generations (Fuligni, Tseng, and Lam 1999). Adolescents from Latin American backgrounds, like many children from ethnic minority families in the United States, also have a strong sense of identification with their ethnic and cultural background (Fuligni et al. 2005). These identifications with family and culture likely remain strong in part because their parents spend more time teaching them about their cultural background than do parents with European backgrounds (Huynh and Fuligni 2008).

These factors all play roles in the academic motivation of adolescents from Latin American backgrounds. Table 12.1 shows an example of some associations of a belief in the utility of education with measures of a sense of family obligation, strength of ethnic identity, and frequency of cultural socialization that we observed in our studies. Adolescents who report higher levels of all these factors also place significantly more importance on the value of education. Mediation analyses we have conducted indicate that a significant portion of the higher motivation levels of adolescents from Latin American backgrounds compared with their equally achieving peers from European backgrounds is accounted for by the ethnic differences in family obligation, ethnic identity, and

Table 12.1. Associations of the Belief in Educational Utility
with Family Obligation, Ethnic Identity, and Cultural Socialization

	Family obligation r	Ethnic identity r	Cultural socialization B
Educational utility	.22–.33**	.12–.21**	.18**

Sources: Correlations for family obligation and ethnic identity taken from Fuligni (2001) and Fuligni, Witkow, and Garcia (2005). The association for cultural socialization is a beta coefficient taken from Huynh and Fuligni (2008) with a slightly different measure of the utility of education that focused on the usefulness of what is learned in school for the future.

**p < .01

cultural socialization (Fuligni 2001; Fuligni et al. 2005; Huynh and Fuligni 2008).

These results naturally lead to a third question. Is enhancing the belief in the utility of education the magic bullet for interventions with Latin American students? The answer to that is clearly no. In the first place, their endorsement of the value of education is already high. It is important to maintain, as suggested by the fact that it is indeed as significant for the academic performance of these students as it is for other students. But, as shown in figure 12.4, it is not more significant than it is for students from European backgrounds. If it was, you would see converging lines, and the ethnic difference in achievement would attenuate at higher levels of motivation. Instead, as one follows the line for the Latin American students in figure 12.4, even the highest level of motivation does not get the students to a "B" (i.e., 3.0) grade point average. Motivation and desire can get you only so far, particularly when you consider the enormous obstacles facing students from Latin American backgrounds. This figure is one of the strongest arguments for focusing on truly providing these students and families with the resources and opportunities that they need.

The final question that this figure and the rest of the information that I have presented raises is perhaps the most important one. How long can they keep it up? How long can students from Latin American backgrounds keep up their belief in the importance of education and their desire to do well in school in the face of such seeming societal indifference and neglect? I do not have an answer to this question, but I fear that we have a very narrow window within which to work. Students from Latin American backgrounds and their families are primed to take advantage of educational opportunities that they do not have. If we do not give them those opportunities soon, I am concerned that we may be missing a golden opportunity that could soon disappear.

REFERENCES

Fuligni, Andrew J. 1997. "The Academic Achievement of Adolescents from Immigrant Families: The Roles of Family Background, Attitudes, and Behavior." *Child Development* 68(2): 351–63.

———. 2001. "Family Obligation and the Academic Motivation of Adolescents from Asian, Latin American, and European Backgrounds." In *Family Obligation and Assistance during Adolescence: Contextual Variations and Developmental Implications (New Directions in Child and Adolescent Development)*, edited by Andrew J. Fuligni (61–76). San Francisco, CA: Jossey-Bass.

Fuligni, Andrew J., and Christina Hardway. 2004. "Preparing Diverse Adolescents for the Transition to Adulthood." *The Future of Children* 14(2): 99–119.

Fuligni, Andrew J., Vivian Tseng, and May Lam. 1999. "Attitudes toward Family Obligations among American Adolescents with Asian, Latin American, and European Backgrounds." *Child Development* 70(4): 1030–44.

Fuligni, Andrew J., Melissa Witkow, and Carla Garcia. 2005. "Ethnic Identity and the Academic Adjustment of Adolescents from Mexican, Chinese, and European Backgrounds." *Developmental Psychology* 41(5): 799–811.

Huynh, Virginia, and Andrew J. Fuligni. 2008. "Ethnic Socialization and the Academic Adjustment of Adolescents from Mexican, Chinese, and European Backgrounds." *Developmental Psychology* 44(4): 1202–08.

Suárez-Orozco, Carola, and Marcelo M. Suárez-Orozco. 1995. *Transformations: Immigration, Family Life, and Achievement Motivation among Latino Adolescents.* Palo Alto, CA: Stanford University Press.

Zhou, Min, and Jung Ha Kim. 2006. "Community Forces, Social Capital, and Educational Achievement: The Case of Supplementary Education in the Chinese and Korean Immigrant Communities." *Harvard Educational Review* 76:1–29.

PART IV
Access to Health Care and Well-Being of Children and Youth from Hispanic Immigrant Families

13

A Sociocultural Framework for Understanding the Mechanisms behind Behavioral Health and Educational Service Disparities in Immigrant Hispanic Children

Margarita Alegría, Norah Mulvaney-Day,
Nicholas J. Carson, and Meghan Woo

In the past 15 years, the number of children in immigrant families has grown at a rate seven times that of native-born families (Hernandez 2004). In 2000, one in five children living in the United States was either an immigrant or a child of immigrants. Most children living in immigrant families (84 percent) were from Latin America or Asia; 39 percent of all immigrant children (about 5.2 million) were from Mexico. The remaining families were tremendously diverse. The increase in immigrant children has affected virtually all states, not just those that historically have had large immigrant populations, such as California, New York, and Texas.

Over the past 35 years, the large and rapidly increasing number of immigrant children in the United States has had and will continue to have a profound impact on schools. The number of school-age children in the United States who do not speak English well or are from families with adults who lack English proficiency has vastly increased. According to the 2000 Census, about 3.5 million children age 5–17 reported not speaking English "very well," and 2.7 million children lived in linguistically isolated households in which all household members over age 14 had limited English proficiency.[1]

In light of these population changes, schools, for one, face many opportunities as well as challenges in providing the support needed by immigrant students to learn and achieve their academic goals. In educational systems, ethnic and racial minority youth often are viewed as less appealing to schools if they seem disproportionately at risk for academic failure and require more intensive academic or ancillary services. For example, the Public Advocate for the City of New York and Advocates for Children of New York (2002) examined student discharge rates published by the New York City Department of Education. Unusually high discharge numbers for racial and ethnic minorities (over 160,000 high school students) were found during the 2000–01, 1998–99, and 1997–98 school years.

Mental health services are one example of ancillary services provided by school systems. According to Wood and colleagues (2005), approximately 80 percent of all children who receive mental health services are seen by providers within the school system. One challenge for schools has been linking Hispanic immigrant children to appropriate and effective school-based mental health services (with mental health defined in this context as diagnosed conditions that include attention deficit hyperactivity disorder [ADHD], depression, other psychiatric disorders, and learning disabilities that require enrollment in remedial or special education classes).

In this chapter, we present a framework of mechanisms linked to behavioral health service disparities for immigrant youth, focusing on school-based behavioral/mental health services. Our three main questions are as follows: What do we know about disparities in behavioral health services for immigrant youth, particularly Hispanic immigrant youth, in school-based contexts? What do these disparities mean for Hispanic immigrant youths' academic achievement and mental health problems? Finally, which mechanisms could reduce and eliminate these service disparities, particularly for Hispanic immigrant youth? In the remainder of this chapter we discuss these questions using examples from the literature and from our community-based participatory research work in schools with immigrant children to inform our framework. We close with a discussion of how these mechanisms are likely to operate for immigrant Hispanic children in the United States and with recommendations for the future.

Behavioral Health Services
for Minority Immigrant Youth

In almost every area of health services examined in the Institute of Medicine report (Smedley, Stith, and Nelson 2002), minority youth were more likely to receive inferior mental health care services than their non-Hispanic white counterparts, a finding confirmed by other research (Beal 2004). Immigrant children, particularly Hispanic youth, suffer from significant unmet need for mental health services. Despite this, Hispanic youth exhibit lower rates of mental health service than non-Hispanic whites (Kataoka, Zhang, and Wells 2002; Yeh et al. 2003; Zahner and Daskalakis 1997).

Only two psychiatric epidemiological studies have compared mental health prevalence rates for Mexican American and white adolescents from representative samples of schools and households (Roberts, Roberts, and Chen 1997; Roberts, Roberts, and Xing 2007a, 2007b). In the first study, Mexican American youth consistently report higher levels of depression symptoms than do white youth. The results of the second study demonstrate that after adjusting for impairment, Mexican American youth have higher rates of anxiety disorders but not of major depressive disorders than whites. National surveys also reveal that Hispanic adolescents present with higher suicidal ideation and behavior rates relative to their African American and white counterparts (Kann 2001). In a school-based study of 163 Mexican American families, Polo and López (2009) show that as many as 40 percent of Mexican American youth exhibit significant levels of social anxiety and depression, with immigrant Mexican American youth displaying higher levels of social anxiety and loneliness than their U.S.-born Mexican American counterparts. Acculturation stressors such as discrimination and cultural conflicts, parental psychological control and acceptance, and peer victimization are identified as potential key contributors to children's psychosocial maladjustment.

How closely acculturation and immigration may relate to the potential for psychopathology among Hispanic children has seldom been assessed (Canino and Alegría 2009). A study by Duarte and colleagues (2008) shows that youths' acculturation level (as measured by the Cultural Life Style Inventory; see Magafia et al. 1996) is not related to antisocial behavior problems or internalizing symptoms. However, parents' level of acculturation is significantly linked to youths' antisocial behavior across the three waves of the study. Youths' acculturative stress, rather than level of acculturation as measured by the Hispanic stress inventory (Cervantes, Padilla, and Salgado de Snyder 1990), is positively correlated with internalizing symptoms one year after baseline. Parental acculturative stress is associated with the child's psychopathology over time. The findings indicate that integration, not acculturation, is most stressful for both parents and youth and may be the reason for youths' psychopathology.

Portes and Rumbaut (1990) also find an impact of exit and reception on immigrants' mental health. The following circumstances in the context of exit play a significant role in immigrants' predisposition toward mental illness: exposure to war or social unrest, personal or family violence, and imprisonment or other separation from family members. Positive mental health also appears linked to characteristics of the receiving contexts or communities into which immigrant youth must integrate, such as the availability of an established like-ethnic community and of a healthy functioning family network. In addition, a Suárez-Orozco, Todorova, and Louie study (2002) of 385 youth who immigrated to the United States shows that the quality of parenting and the ability to forge a new relationship after separation are the most important factors in ascertaining whether separation will have negative mental health consequences for immigrant youth.

Given the substantial risk of psychopathology and maladjustment in Hispanic youth and the potential link to acculturative stress, access to quality behavioral health services appears critical. Yet linguistic minorities report worse care than racial and ethnic minorities (Weech-Maldonado et al. 2003). At the same time, the scarcity of empirical research makes it difficult for mental health service providers to ascertain which issues to target in mental health interventions for immigrant Hispanic youth and how to devise effective treatments for them. A number of barriers, including language, cultural attitudes toward help-seeking, and stigmas attached to mental health problems, contribute to Hispanic immigrant children's poor access to care (Alegría 2004). Further, parents' inability to recognize their child's mental health problems is an important factor in explaining the underutilization of mental health services for minority and immigrant children (Roberts et al. 2005). Several studies suggest that minority parents are less likely than white parents to recognize and/or label their children's behavior a mental health problem requiring intervention (Gleser et al. 1980; Roberts et al. 2005; Wachtel et al. 1994; Walton, Johnson, and Algina 1999).

Although higher uninsurance rates are often thought to explain disparities in access to mental health services among racial and ethnic minority groups, disparities remain even among those enrolled in the Medicaid system. For example, Hispanic children receive on average half as many counseling sessions (Pumariega et al. 1998) and significantly fewer specialty mental health services and at later ages (Hough et al. 2002) than whites. Minority youth, including Hispanic children, are also less likely to receive multimodal treatment for ADHD (Bussing, Schoenberg, and Perwien 1998). Striking racial/ethnic disparities also exist among youth suffering from severe mental illness, such as those reporting recent suicidal ideation. In one study of adolescents who reported recent suicidal thoughts, Hispanic adolescents were 55 percent as likely as white adolescents to report service use, even after controlling for relevant demographic factors (Freedenthal 2007).

Yet, regional studies of health and substance abuse service disparities among immigrant minority youth report inconsistent findings, with some revealing underuse of behavioral services, others finding no difference, and still others reporting overuse of services by ethnic and racial minorities (Bui and Takeuchi 1992; Cuffe et al. 1995; McCabe et al. 1999; Snowden and Cheung 1990; Sue et al. 1991; Wu et al. 1999; Yeh et al. 2003; Zahner and Daskalakis 1997). It is difficult to draw conclusions from these studies because of regional differences in the samples and in methods and sample composition. The vast majority fail to disaggregate the data by nativity, hindering conclusions about immigrant Hispanic children.

The few *population-based national studies* of behavioral service disparities among different ethnic and racial youth groups also report mixed findings. For example, Kodjo and Auinger (2003) analyzed the National Longitudinal Study of Adolescent Health and find in the second wave of that study that Hispanic youth are as likely as non-Hispanic white youth to have received psychological counseling, but again, data here were not disaggregated by nativity. In contrast, based on analysis of three nationally representative household surveys, Kataoka and colleagues (2002) find that both African American and Hispanic youth have lower rates of mental health service use than their non-Hispanic white counterparts. In part, the mixed results appear related to how these studies defined need for services based on psychiatric symptoms or screening scales rather than on psychiatric disorders ascertained by structured diagnostic interviews.

Although data on mental health service disparities among Hispanic immigrant youth are limited, study findings on access to mental health treatment by English language proficiency suggest an area of particular vulnerability. Hispanics in general are significantly less likely to seek care than whites (Alegría et al. 2008; Vega and Alegría 2001). However, in one study, access patterns between English-speaking Hispanics and whites are similar, while Spanish-speaking Hispanics are considerably less likely to receive services (Fiscella et al. 2002). These findings are further supported by results from a more recent study in California that finds that Hispanic and Asian/Pacific Islander respondents who do not speak English are 70 percent less likely to receive needed mental health services than those who only speak English, controlling other factors (Sentell, Shumway, and Snowden 2007).

Other issues include insurance, or the lack thereof, and the impacts of state and federal regulations. Employer insurance coverage of both children and adults has weakened over time,[2] eroding coverage of the near poor, who are less likely to qualify for public insurance. These coverage gaps can contribute to disparities in health service delivery for minority youth since minorities are overrepresented among the under- and uninsured (Bodenheimer 2005; Rylko-Bauer and Farmer 2002). Minority populations may also face new challenges as a result of state and federal regulations aimed toward cost control, such as decreasing income thresholds for working parents' eligibility for the State Children's Health Insurance Program (SCHIP—a program that provides health insurance to low-income uninsured children who do not qualify for Medicaid). In addition, Medicaid eligibility has been strongly associated with use of mental health services among adolescents. In one study, Medicaid-eligible youth are nearly five times as likely as non-Medicaid-eligible youth to use mental health services within a given year (Deck and Levy 2006). However, owing to policy restrictions and an over-burdened system, Medicaid eligibility, positive mental health outcomes, and baseline characteristics are unevenly distributed across racial and ethnic groups. For example, one study on SCHIP enrollment finds that enrolled minority children are poorer, in worse health, and less likely to have had a usual source of care or private insurance before enrolling in SCHIP (Brach et al. 2003).

Reducing and Eliminating Potential Service Disparities

Minority children, particularly immigrant youth, face a number of barriers to effective mental health care that result in mental health service disparities. These include *sociodemographic* barriers, such as socioeconomic disadvantage, stigma, poor health education, and lack of activism; *provider factors,* including deficits in culturally competent care, youth-orientation, and youth/provider interaction; and *systemic factors,* such as location of services, availability of linguistic-appropriate services, and policy restrictions that reduce access to services (Pumariega, Rogers, and Rothe 2005). Drawing from these barriers, we posit six main mechanisms tied to these service disparities:

1. failure of health care markets, institutional bias, and limited financing leading to decreased access to and use of behavioral health care services;
2. differential pathways into behavioral health care and educational services leading to differential experiences of service, no services, or inadequate services;
3. poor youth-teacher interaction leading to miscommunication, disproportional in-school referrals for behavioral problems, low school retention, elevated rates of suspensions, and expulsions;
4. mismatches between behavioral health and educational service offerings, minorities' services needs, and their living circumstances leading to low or no service use;
5. lack of community trust and erroneous expectations of services leading to disengagement and poor collaboration in the educational and behavioral service systems; and
6. limited workforce availability and training of service providers to treat ethnic and racial minority youth, especially immigrant youth who are non-English speakers, leading to reliance on informal or poorly trained service providers.

Factors in Decreased Access to and Use of Behavioral Health Care Services

Certain federal laws, specifically the Individuals with Disabilities Education Act (IDEA), the Americans with Disabilities Act and Section 504 of the Rehabilitation Act of 1973, Medicaid, and SCHIP, have as a primary purpose the provision of services and supports that enable children to thrive and successfully integrate into their communities. Because education and health care for children are primarily state responsibilities, these federal laws provide states with considerable latitude regarding implementation on such key matters as eligibility standards; amount and range of services made available; timing, location, and manner of such services; and how well such services are fully integrated in ways that maximize their effectiveness, quality, and utility. The design choices made by states can vary considerably and are of central importance in determining their ultimate effectiveness in ensuring available and appropriate services.

For example, substantial variation has been observed across states in minority children's enrollment patterns in SCHIP and in subsequent disparities in health care (Shone et al. 2003). Programmatic factors such as differences in outreach efforts and other state-specific policies may account for much of this variation, although variation also likely stems from differences in population characteristics such as primary language and level of acculturation, and differences in health status and experiences with the health system before eligibility for SCHIP enrollment. In a survey of community leaders from four East Coast cities about the needs of Hispanic youth, the leaders consistently asserted that these youth experience substantial stress in the United States and endure severe difficulties in accessing appropriate behavioral health services and resources, which were limited in number and lacking in cultural sensitivity (Acosta et al. 2004). States' ability to tailor their programs to fit the needs of immigrant children may vary depending on fiscal and sociodemographic factors that influence the supply of providers who speak Spanish and are culturally matched to patients.

Effects of Differential Pathways into Behavioral Health Care Services on Services

Academic failure is sometimes related to deficiencies in the teaching and learning environment and to difficulties due to linguistic, cultural, or social-class differences (Ortiz and Yates 2001). Students with inadequate English proficiency may wrestle with school because they do not have access to effective instruction in English as a second language (ESL) or special educators who are trained to simultaneously address their language-

and education-related needs (Lozano-Rodriguez and Castellano 1999). When immigrant and linguistic minority children face enormous academic lags, disruptive behaviors may be one way to cope and maintain status in an environment that values academic success. Yet, academic failure is rarely addressed as a lack of social competence (defined as the effectiveness of one's behaviors in enabling appropriate interactions and participation as well as the appropriateness of the behavior to that setting; see Odom, McConnell, and McEvoy 1992) or understood by the teacher as the only available behavioral option to allow these failing immigrant and linguistic minority children to maintain face and continue their social interactions. This may be students' only option in a setting that lacks personnel trained to conduct linguistically and culturally relevant instruction and remediation.

In this real-world intersection, educators, researchers, parents, and mental health providers must collaborate to develop service delivery models that ideally help improve academic and mental health outcomes for Hispanic immigrant children. If these difficulties become more serious because teaching does not address the students' specific needs, these children begin to struggle and exhibit emotional and behavioral problems (Rappaport 2004).

There is strong evidence of the relationship between school performance and emotional problems (Rousseau, Drapeau, and Corin 1996). Yet when immigrant children experience social and academic difficulties, the problems are more likely to be addressed from the youth's individual learning circumstances than from a cultural or environmental perspective. Findings by Eccles and Midgley (1988) suggest that students appear to demonstrate behavioral and conduct problems when the school climate is not beneficial to learning. When teachers lack information on how school systems may precipitate or exacerbate immigrant youth's emotional problems, they may view a child's problems as individual learning or academic deficits, rather than indicating problems at the systems level. Under such circumstances, offering only minimum remediation may be merely palliative without altering the educational system's limitation that feed the students' behavioral problems. Lack of mental health services, when the problems are framed as learning problems, may limit Hispanic immigrant youths' ability to successfully transition and integrate into the school system. The consequence could be even more negative in the form of dropout or expulsion linked to disruptive behaviors.

A recent study of adolescent mental health service use by Stiffman and colleagues (2001) finds that gateway teachers' perceptions play a pivotal role in the access, content, and use of mental health services by adolescents. When teachers and health care providers cannot identify themselves and the school system as part of the problem, children may be referred to services ill suited to fulfilling their needs.

Poor Youth-Teacher/Parent-Provider Interaction and Subsequent Negative Outcomes

Immigrant Hispanic parents' attempts to interact with monolingual English-speaking school staff may affect the level of disclosure, trust, and impressions relevant for intervention. As a result, when less acculturated immigrant families with limited English proficiency need school-based mental health services or referrals from schools to community mental health services for their children's care, they may face linguistic and cultural distances due to a shortage of bilingual school staff.

The problem of language incompatibility is compounded by cultural variation in views about health care (Blendon et al. 1995; Carrasquillo et al. 1999) and the threshold for what is considered dysfunctional or impaired behavior (Achenbach et al. 1990; Crijnen, Achenbach, and Verhulst 1999; Weisz et al. 1993, 1988). Even after adjusting for the child's clinical need profile and level of impairment and the parents' sociodemographic characteristics, Hispanic parents (mainly Mexican American) rate their adolescents' mental health and life satisfaction as better than that of their non-Hispanic white counterparts with the same level of problems, and perceive fewer emotional or behavioral problems in their children (Roberts et al. 2005). Apparently, parents' cultural background influences their interpretation of and response to their children's mental health problems.

Clearly, these variations will affect service use since the child's impairment is one of the most important factors in determining whether parents will take their children to services (Alegría 2004; Canino 2004) and believe that referral or treatment is necessary to resolve the problem (Florsheim, Tolan, and Gorman-Smith 1996; Mann et al. 1992). To explain this phenomenon, Weisz and colleagues (1988) propose that culture may influence the labeling of mental health problems by affecting parental evaluations of and responses to problems manifested by children. If parents in certain cultures have elevated thresholds concerning mental health problems, then they will report lower prevalence rates of such disorders. The threshold model suggests that not only parents but also teachers coming from differing cultures might use different thresholds as they label or endorse mental health or behavioral problems in youth. Lower thresholds might lead to overreporting of behavior problems and augmented referrals for disruptive behavior problems, while lower thresholds might lead to under-detection and missed opportunities for treatment.

Skiba and colleagues (2002) confirm previous work showing an over-representation of minority students in school suspensions. They attribute this to differences in the rates of teacher referrals for behavioral infractions, since these disparities cannot be explained by higher levels of misbehaviors by minority youth than by non-Hispanic white youth. In educational services, cultural misinterpretation between teachers and minority students may lead to miscommunication, confrontation, negative outcomes for minority students (Townsend 2000), and higher dropout rates (Felice 1981).

Mismatches between Services and Needs Leading to Low or No Service Use

There is also evidence that students with limited English proficiency fail in part because they do not have access to effective bilingual or ESL instruction or to special educators who are trained to address their language- and disability-related needs (Lozano-Rodriguez and Castellano 1999). Hispanic youth, particularly those with limited English proficiency, have the highest school dropout rate in the country, which consequently leads to a less-skilled workforce, increased unemployment, and greater demands on social services (Flores 2000). The empirical knowledge generated about school context seems essential to understanding school system and provider variables that are often ignored in mental health treatment and service interventions (Hoagwood and Johnson 2003), but this knowledge appears crucial in achieving and sustaining change. The utility of school-based mental health services has been emphasized as vital in addressing the unmet mental health needs of immigrant populations (Garrison, Roy, and Azar 1999). At the same time, schools may facilitate increased health literacy for immigrant and linguistic minority parents who may benefit from health promotion and prevention activities about mental health and education but may have the least access to such information.

Hispanic youth in public schools who are at risk for mental health problems access school mental health services less and at later ages than do non-Hispanic white youth (Wood et al. 2005). This correlates with Hispanic youths' later entry into outpatient specialty mental health services. There is a small but growing literature on school mental health treatments on Hispanic youth, ranging from validation of mental health screening measures (described below) to comprehensive school-based treatment programs, such as the AMIGO program in Maryland (Garrison et al. 1999).

Several screening tools, some used in intervention studies, have been applied with immigrant Hispanic populations (Birman et al. 2008). These include the strengths and difficulties questionnaire (Rousseau et al. 2007), child behavioral checklist (Achenbach 1991), behavioral assessment system for children (Flanagan et al. 1996), life events scale (Stein et al. 2003), and UCLA PTSD reaction index (Saltzman et al. 2001). The PTSD checklist–terror was used to diagnose posttraumatic anxiety among Hispanic school youth after the 9/11 terrorist attack (Calderoni et al. 2006).

School-based interventions for anxiety include Stein's study (2003) of the cognitive behavioral intervention for trauma in schools, which used rigorous methods to demonstrate a decrease in posttraumatic stress, depression, and psychosocial dysfunction at three months among a group of predominantly immigrant Latino youth. The intervention did not affect classroom acting-out, shyness, or learning.

School-based interpersonal psychotherapy has been shown to improve depressive symptoms and psychosocial functioning in a random sample of predominantly female Hispanic high school students (71 percent) with a range of depressive disorders.

For disruptive behavior disorders, the Schools and Homes in Partnership (SHIP) intervention has been studied with a randomized, predominantly Mexican American sample of early elementary students with aggressive behavior or reading difficulties (Barrera et al. 2002). The SHIP program delivered school-based social behavior therapy and reading instruction, and parent training. Hispanic participants showed improvements after one year in negative behavior and reading although, unlike a white comparison group, they did not improve significantly on internalizing symptoms.

Drama- and narrative-based interventions have also been studied with Hispanic youth. Rousseau's pilot study (Rousseau et al. 2007) used a drama-based intervention to help South American immigrant youth improve their social adjustment and math performance. *Cuento* (folktale) therapies have also been conducted. In the first study, a series of *cuentos* were adapted to represent adaptive social functioning and then read to a group of Hispanic students in grades K–3 in 20 sessions of 90 minutes each (Malgady, Constantino, and Rogler 1986). Both adapted and traditional *cuentos* groups were rated as less anxious by their mothers after one year, compared with the art therapy group and no-intervention groups. A "hero/heroine intervention" later tested among at-risk Puerto Rican students in grades 8–9 contained stories of Puerto Rican historical figures whose lives exemplified overcoming adversity (Malgady, Rogler, and Constantino 1990). Recipients reported positive impacts on self-concept, ethnic identity, and anxiety compared with a control group that had less contact with the research team.

In addition, the prevalence of trauma experiences among young Hispanic children and adolescents may have a significant impact on school completion and subsequent academic achievement (Dyregrov 2004; Rousseau, Drapeau, and Platt 1999; Thompson and Massat 2005). Only recently have educational systems begun to direct attention to psychological support and intervention services. Teacher preparation at pre- and in-service professional development is limited in providing any training in mental health (Koller et al. 2004). Psychiatric conditions may be interpreted by educators with limited knowledge of mental health as simple lack of interest in school or as disruptions that should be dealt with punitively rather than therapeutically; this may be exacerbated for minority youth.

Lack of Community Trust and Erroneous Expectations of Services Leading to Disengagement and Poor Collaboration in Service Systems

Local perceptions of behavioral health services and educational services may depend on prior experience with service provision and the efforts made by the local service system to understand and adapt to the cultural needs and demands of Hispanic immigrants. For example, students in immigrant families are more likely than those in native-born families to face stressors related to the immigration experience, including long-term separation from parents or grandparents, severe trauma, and abuse. The former also share many of the same problems in accessing and using services faced by low-socioeconomic-status children in native-born families, in addition to issues specific to the immigration experience, such as language barriers, discrimination/racism, acculturation, and lack of access to public assistance programs due to status (Alegría et al. 2004). However, very little attention has been paid to these problems in traditional educational and behavioral services.

A report from The Equity Monitoring Project for Immigrant and Refugee Education (2007) indicated that limited English proficient parents in New York City were not receiving the translation and interpretation services needed to engage in their children's education from schools. Insufficient use of services often stems from and increases as a result of repeated negative contacts with the health and educational system (Burnette 1998). While school-based services may be a promising strategy for addressing the mental health needs of immigrants and linguistic minorities, few schools have developed and sustained systems that help multicultural families access linguistically and culturally appropriate services. In collaborative research over three years with elementary schools, we found that even in a relatively well-funded school system, significant coordination and communication difficulties prevented immigrant children from accessing needed services (Mulvaney-Day et al. 2006).

Limited Workforce Availability and Training of Service Providers to Treat Ethnic and Racial Minority Youth Leading to Reliance on Informal or Poorly Trained Providers

The disproportionately low geographic supply of providers, particularly multilingual service providers, in communities with ethnic and racial minorities compared with nonminority communities (Derose and Baker 2000) could influence the availability of providers and consequently affect service disparities. Provider biases may interfere with both diagnosis and intervention when linguistic and cultural distance leads to misinterpretation of verbal and nonverbal responses to the assessment inquiry (Malgady and Zayas 2001).

Research and Policy Implications

Expanded school-based mental health systems that combine resources and perspectives from school, community, and mental health agencies are a potentially effective and increasingly used way to link underserved children to services (U.S. Surgeon General 2001; Weist and Schlitt 1998).

However, developing such a system in schools for underserved Hispanic immigrant children poses challenges. Collaboration between school communities and mental health providers is necessary for understanding immigrant Hispanic children's and families' perspectives and identifying what may be important for schools to know in helping children learn and thrive. The findings presented in this chapter present a stark picture of mental health services for Hispanic immigrant youth. Hispanic families in particular underuse mental health services for their children because of language and cultural barriers as well as fear of stigma (Pumariega et al. 2005). Hispanic youth are also far less likely to receive school-based mental health services and begin service use at a later age than non-Hispanic white children (Wood et al. 2005). This finding is particularly problematic given that, as noted earlier, approximately 80 percent of all children who receive mental health services are seen by providers within the school system. Further, the age at which children first receive mental health care may be particularly critical to their long-term health and functioning, with studies showing that children with unmet mental health needs are at higher risk for academic underachievement (Patterson, Reid, and Dishion 1992; Wood et al. 2005). Based on the above findings, several recommendations are offered as strategies to reduce mental health problems and increase access to mental health services among Hispanic immigrant children in the United States.

Research Recommendations

1. When examined as a group, Hispanics report lower rates of service usage and educational achievement than their non-Hispanic white counterparts (Alegría, Mulvaney-Day, et al. 2007). Still, mental health service use varies greatly across subgroups of the Hispanic population. For example, study findings indicate that the odds of dropping out of school are significantly higher for individuals who immigrated to the United States between the ages of 13 and 17 than for those who immigrated before age 13 (Finkelhor, Ormrod, and Turner 2007; Giaconia et al. 1995). Service use outcomes also vary across Hispanic subethnic groups, with Mexicans reporting the lowest rates of past-year service use and Puerto Ricans reporting some of the highest (Alegría, Mulvaney-Day, et al. 2007). These findings point to the importance of designing research studies that allow for subgroup comparisons within the Hispanic youth population,

including nativity, language proficiency, and ethnic subgroups. These studies will enable identification of particularly vulnerable subgroups within the Hispanic population and set the groundwork for targeted interventions.

2. Recent epidemiological findings emphasize the need to understand the role of context in the risk for mental health disorders, particularly risk for substance use disorders and access to services for immigrant youth (Alegría, Shrout, et al. 2007). However, additional research is needed to further disentangle these effects as well as develop interventions to prevent negative consequences of exposure to these environments when immigrants integrate into U.S. neighborhoods. Further, mental health interventions should focus on decreasing neighborhood violence and on increasing neighborhood safety and guardianship behaviors that might help avoid integrating in risky peer networks.

3. Mental health disparities research has largely ignored the many aspects of Hispanic culture that may protect against mental illness or facilitate better treatment outcomes. These aspects include social networks and family support. In particular, our work suggests two areas that appear related to increased resilience in Hispanic immigrant youth. Foreign-born Hispanic parents may increase a child's opportunity to retain a strong attitudinal and normative anchor in a simpler life that reduces distress. Further, foreign Hispanic parental nativity may inhibit internalization of U.S.-society lifestyles, including expectations incongruous with one's perceived social status, diminishing the risk for anxiety disorders in immigrant Hispanic youth. More research is needed to better understand the effect of these cultural factors on mental health outcomes for use in future intervention work. It is our belief that effective strategies for improving the mental health of Hispanic youth should involve bolstering social support systems and social networks as well as resolving family conflict. Research studies that examine the effectiveness of such interventions on improving mental health outcomes among Hispanic youth should be conducted.

4. Finally, appropriate health and mental health treatment services for immigrant youth require comprehensive and ongoing collaborative efforts. Such collaborations must address the emergence of childhood problems and responses to them as navigated through a culture's values, expectancies, and child-rearing practices (Weisz et al.

1988) and how immigrant youth prioritize, respond to, and adhere to school expectations. This approach is particularly critical when addressing the needs of immigrant children and their caregivers.

Policy and Practice Recommendations

1. Adjusting to a new school system and potentially growing up in a disenfranchised community pose potential risks for dropping out of school (Velez and Ungemack 1989) and increased hazard for mental health problems (Cardemil, Reivich, and Seligman 2002). Therefore, special considerations are necessary to tailor school-based mental health programs to the demographic, cultural, linguistic, and family structure characteristics of immigrant and linguistic minority families so psychotherapeutic modalities can facilitate their social adjustment and adaptation in a culturally responsive manner. Some psychological interventions for depression, including cognitive behavioral therapy and interpersonal therapy, are feasible to administer and are effective with school-age Hispanic youth (Cardemil et al. 2002; Roselló and Bernal 1996). Yet, much more work is needed to help identify their needs, since the intervention and prevention literature on the mental health of ethnic minorities and immigrant youth is scarce (Iwamasa, Sorocco, and Koonce 2002; López and Guarnaccia 2000), particularly treatment outcome studies (Miranda, Nakamura, and Bernal 2003). We therefore recommend changes at the intervention level to make treatments receptive and effective for immigrant and linguistic minority youth and their families.

2. Another layer of complexity in offering school-based mental health services to immigrant and linguistic minority children is that recent public policies force schools to operate in an increasingly performance-driven and financially constrained environment. The President's Commission on Mental Health calls for improved access to quality care and services for all Americans with mental illness without recommending an increase in public expenditures (New Freedom Commission on Mental Health 2003). Similarly, the federal special education law, the Individuals with Disabilities Education Act reauthorized in 2004, emphasized the importance of providing appropriate educational services to students with disabilities, without additional funding. Along with these

explicit pressures to improve cost-effectiveness, school-based services are now often asked to support other areas of social services
that contribute to the underlying problem (e.g., family domestic
violence, gangs, and family instability). It is therefore imperative
to ensure that school-based mental health services are appropriately funded and incentivized.

3. As discussed throughout this chapter, there are many flaws in the
Hispanic youth–health care provider or teacher relationship. We
therefore recommend client, provider, and school system changes
to augment access and retention in mental health treatment. At the
client level (immigrant and linguistic minority youth), nonrecog-
nition of mental health problems and health literacy, stigma and
shame in receiving mental health care, cultural meanings and interpretations of mental health symptoms for immigrant parents, and
life circumstances that make mental health a low priority for Hispanic immigrant youth are of primary importance. Interventions
should focus on improving the health literacy of Hispanic youth
and their families in an effort to facilitate successful navigation and
functioning within the U.S. health care and educational system.
Conversely, it is also necessary to ensure that all forms, medical
documentation, and even verbal instructions from clinicians are
presented at an appropriate literacy level for patients. Moreover,
interpreter services must be expanded so they are readily available
to all Spanish-speaking caregivers who require them.

Adoption of interventions to improve entry into services should
be prioritized for Hispanics who do not recognize and attend to their
own or their child's psychiatric illness but need preventive treatment before they become disabled or impaired. Public symptom-
recognition campaigns may be useful as well as anti-stigma social
marketing campaigns. These strategies may require innovative
modalities, such as social marketing, to engage immigrant and linguistic minority youth and their families in mental health care.

When targeting *provider-level factors*, we recommend implementing cultural awareness training programs that examine issues
such as provider attitudes and misconceptions of immigrant
youth and their families (such as, immigrant families are too busy
working to be concerned about their children's academic problems); the importance for providers to build relationships with
their patients and connect with immigrant families under non-

crisis situations; and the need to recognize the day-to-day struggles that may hinder treatment-seeking and adherence. Further, there is great need to recruit and train bicultural and bilingual providers who are better able to access Hispanic immigrant communities and build trusting relationships with community members as well as deliver more culturally appropriate services in a patient's preferred language.

4. To change *school-level factors,* we recommend targeting linguistic barriers that influence immigrant youths' assessment, referral, and treatment availability. Changes at the intervention level should range from increased provider competency with evidence-based behavioral health care to adaptations and modifications of educational models to better fit resource-poor school systems that have a significant population of immigrant youth. They may also include increasing access to mental health specialists, including child psychiatrists who are often separated from the children who need them by distance, time, or socioeconomic factors. In the case of immigrant children and families, there is also a shortage of providers who are skilled in integrating culture, psychosocial, academic, and emotional needs in treatment planning and in engaging multicultural families. To address these treatments and service gaps for immigrant and linguistic minority youth and families, we propose developing telemedicine consultation and education programs focused on addressing the specific needs of this population. Telemedicine (the use of teleconferencing technology, including videoconferencing cameras and images, for virtual face-to-face communication, meetings, and medical assessments) has become an increasingly popular and helpful means of providing health education and medical consultation for underserved populations (Boydell, Greenberg, and Volpe 2004; Pesamaa et al. 2004).

5. We also recommend adding components to enroll immigrant and minority families in insurance or state plans, or linking them to community services for undocumented immigrant families. Policymakers should explore interventions targeting poverty reduction and augmentation of educational achievement among Hispanic youth and their families as a way to reduce mental health problems, eliminate disparities in access to care, and acknowledge the increasing political power of immigrant Hispanics. Examples of potential policy interventions are the expansion of Title I programs in schools

in which poor Hispanic youth are overrepresented as well as the earned income tax credit for poor families.

6. Finally, sustainability improvement in educational and mental health service disparities cannot occur without substantial changes in federal, state, and local organization and financing of behavioral health care so immigrant and linguistic minority youth can obtain adequate delivery of mental health services. When we concentrate on changes in the organization and financing of care, we recommend collecting cost data to better inform decision-making on what works and how much it costs versus other options, as well as creatively looking for ways to finance services through state- or county-level sources.

Conclusion

Recommendations for tackling these behavioral health service disparities include more integrated behavioral and special education services through a universal intervention approach offered in regular education classrooms (Donovan and Cross 2002). School-based services are judged to be perfect settings to bring in changes that can help immigrant Hispanic youth attain academic competence and lessen emotional distress (Rones and Hoagwood 2000). Previous literature has stressed the importance of schools for dealing with prevention of minority children's emotional problems (Sameroff, Peck, and Eccles 2004; Stein et al. 2002). We believe that the best approach is to identify through a community participatory research project (CBPR, comprising parents, teachers, and researchers) what works in the real-world setting, where schools face multiple practical challenges in addressing the needs of immigrant and linguistic minority students. Ideally, the CBPR team can gain insight from schools regarding whether the proposed recommendations can close the gap between the services needed and those that can be practically offered, accessed, and sustained in the school setting. Our collaboration with schools demonstrated that building communication infrastructure may be particularly important in the provision of mental health services for children of immigrant families who may face language barriers, variations in family systems (including role reversals between parents and children), and effects of subtle and overt racism (Kirmayer et al. 2003). Misunderstanding resulting from a cultural mismatch can lead to erroneous assumptions about parental engagement and interest, and lost opportunities for schools to better serve Hispanic immigrant and linguistic minority children and their families.

As a whole, these linguistic, cultural, and diversity issues highlight the need to approach the assessment, design, and delivery of services from a consumer perspective, which is the central tenet of social marketing strategy (Kotler, Roberto, and Lee 2002). Additionally, a social marketing approach will lead to the optimal positioning and branding (Engelberg and Kirby 2001) of school-based mental health programs, based on an understanding of how mental health issues are perceived by the targeted Hispanic immigrant families, as well as by service providers. The notion of one size fits all is the antithesis of a social marketing approach, which employs principles of audience analysis and segmentation, narrowcasting, and message tailoring to match the product or program to the needs and desires of the target audience (Kotler et al. 2002). This is particularly important when communicating with marginalized populations (Ford, Goodman, and Meltzer 2003) about health issues that run the risk of stigmatization and deterioration of trust.

Translation of evidence-based care to school settings depends on the communication and relational infrastructure that links teachers, parents, counselors, and students (Jensen, Hoagwood, and Trickett 1999). Schools that serve multiethnic populations with few mental health resources and personnel require creative and flexible mechanisms to understand immigrant and limited English proficient students' needs, to link these students with appropriate resources, and to ensure sustainability (Massey et al. 2005). Mental health researchers who work in schools must continue to emphasize the need for community participatory methods in order to ensure effective implementation and sustainability of promising initiatives (Atkins et al. 2003).

NOTES

1. U.S. Census Bureau, Table QT-P17, "Ability to Speak English: 2000," http://factfinder.census.gov/servlet/QTTable?_bm=y&-geo_id=01000US&-qr_name=DEC_2000_SF3_U_QTP17&-ds_name=DEC_2000_SF3_U&-redoLog=false.

2. Kaiser Family Foundation, "About the Healthcare Marketplace Project," http://www.kff.org/about/marketplace.cfm.

REFERENCES

Achenbach, Thomas M. 1991. "Integrative Guide to the 1991 CBCL/4-18, YSR, and TRF Profiles." Burlington: University of Vermont, Department of Psychology.

Achenbach, Thomas M., Hector R. Bird, Glorisa Canino, Vicky Phares, Madelyn S. Gould, and Mercedes Rubio-Stipec. 1990. "Epidemiological Comparisons of Puerto Rican U.S. Mainland Children: Parent, Teacher, and Self Reports." *Journal of the American Academy of Child & Adolescent Psychiatry* 29(1): 84–93.

Acosta, Olga, M., Mark D. Weist, Fernando A. Lopez, Michael E. Shafer, and L. Josefina Pizarro. 2004. "Assessing the Psychosocial and Academic Needs of Latino Youth to Inform the Development of School-Cased Programs." *Behavior Modification* 28(4): 579–95.

Alegría, Margarita. 2004. "Outreach to Youth Living in Underserved Communities: Challenges and Recommendations." *NAMI Beginnings* 4:3–6.

Alegría, Margarita, Norah Mulvaney-Day, Maria Torres, Antonio Polo, Zhun Cao, and Glorisa Canino. 2007. "Prevalence of Psychiatric Disorders across Latino Subgroups in the United States." *American Journal of Public Health* 97:68–75.

Alegría, Margarita, Pinka Chatterji, Kenneth Wells, Zhun Cao, Chih-nan Chen, David Takeuchi, James Jackson, and Xiao-Li Meng. 2008. "Disparity in Depression Treatment among Racial and Ethnic Minority Populations in the U.S." *Psychiatric Services* 59(11): 1264–72.

Alegría, Margarita, Patrick Shrout, Meghan Woo, Peter Guarnaccia, William Sribney, Doriliz Vila, Antonio Polo, et al. 2007. "Understanding Differences in Past Year Psychiatric Disorders for Latinos Living in the U.S." *Social Science & Medicine* 65(2): 214–30.

Alegría, Margarita, David Takeuchi, Glorisa Canino, Naihua Duan, Patrick Shrout, Xiao-Li Meng, William Vega, et al. 2004. "Considering Context, Place and Culture: The National Latino and Asian American Study." *International Journal of Methods in Psychiatric Research* 13(4): 208–20.

Atkins, Marc S., Patricia A. Graczyk, Stacy L. Frazier, and Jaleel Abdul-Adil. 2003. "Toward a New Model for Promoting Urban Children's Mental Health: Accessible, Effective, and Sustainable School-Based Mental Health Services." *School Psychology Review* 32(4): 503–14.

Barrera, Manuel, Anthony Biglan, Ted K. Taylor, Barbara K. Gunn, Keith Smolkowski, Carol Black, Dennis V. Ary, and Rollen C. Fowler. 2002. "Early Elementary School Intervention to Reduce Conduct Problems: A Randomized Trial with Hispanic and Non-Hispanic Children." *Prevention Science* 3(2): 83–94.

Beal, Anne C. 2004. "Policies to Reduce Racial and Ethnic Disparities in Child Health and Healthcare." *Health Affairs* 23:171–79.

Birman, Dina, Sarah Beehler, Emily M. Harris, Mary Lynn Everson, Karen Batia, Joan Liautaud, Stacy Frazier, et al. 2008. "International Family, Adult, and Child Enhancement Services (FACES): A Community-Based Comprehensive Services Model for Refugee Children in Resettlement." *American Journal of Orthopsychiatry* 78(1): 121.

Blendon, Robert, A. Scheck, K. Donelan, C. Hill, M. Smith, D. Beatrice, and D. Altman. 1995. "How White and African Americans View Their Health and Social Problems: Different Experiences, Different Expectations." *Journal of the American Medical Association* 273(4): 341–46.

Bodenheimer, Thomas. 2005. "High and Rising Healthcare Costs, Part 1: Seeking an Explanation." *Annals of Internal Medicine* 142(10): 847–54.

Boydell, Katherine M., Natasha Greenberg, and Tiziana Volpe. 2004. "Designing a Framework for the Evaluation of Paediatric Telepsychiatry: A Participatory Approach." *Journal of Telemedicine and Telecare* 10:165–69.

Brach, Cindy, Eugene M. Lewit, Karen VanLandeghem, Janet Bronstein, Andrew W. Dick, Kim S. Kimminau, Barbara LaClair, et al. 2003. "Who's Enrolled in the State Children's Health Insurance Program (SCHIP)? An Overview of Findings from the Child Health Insurance Research Initiative (CHIRI)." *Pediatrics* 112(6): e499.

Bui, K. V., and David T. Takeuchi. 1992. "Ethnic Minority Adolescents and the Use of Community Mental Healthcare Services." *American Journal of Community Psychology* 20(4): 403–17.

Burnette, Jane. 1998. "Reducing the Disproportionate Representation of Minority Students in Special Education." ED417501. Reston, VA: ERIC Clearinghouse on Disabilities and Gifted Education.

Bussing, Regina, Nancy E. Schoenberg, and Amy R. Perwien. 1998. "Knowledge and Information about ADHD: Evidence of Cultural Differences among African-American and White Parents." *Social Science & Medicine* 46(7): 919–28.

Calderoni, Michelle E., Elizabeth M. Alderman, Ellen J. Silver, and Laurie J. Bauman. 2006. "The Mental Health Impact of 9/11 on Inner-City High School Students 20 Miles North of Ground Zero." *Journal of Adolescent Health* 39(1): 57–65.

Canino, Glorisa. 2004. "Are Somatic Symptoms and Related Distress More Prevalent in Hispanic/Latino Youth? Some Methodological Considerations." *Journal of Clinical Child and Adolescent Psychology* 33(2): 272–75.

Canino, Glorisa, and Margarita Alegría. 2009. "Understanding Psychopathology among the Adult and Child Latino Population: An Epidemiologic Perspective." In *Handbook of U.S. Latino Psychology: Developmental and Community-Based Perspectives,* edited by Francisco A. Villarruel, Gustavo Carlo, Josefina M. Grau, Margarita Azmitia, Natasha Cabrera, and T. Jaime Chahin (31–44). Thousand Oaks, CA: SAGE Publications.

Cardemil, Esteban V., Karen J. Reivich, and Martin E. Seligman. 2002. "The Prevention of Depressive Symptoms in Low-Income Minority Middle-School Students." *Prevention and Treatment* 5.

Carrasquillo, Olveen, E. John Ovar, Troyen A. Brennan, and Helen R. Burstin. 1999. "Impact of Language Barriers on Patient Satisfaction in an Emergency Department." *Journal of General Internal Medicine* 14(2): 82–87.

Cervantes, Richard C., Amado M. Padilla, and Nelly Salgado de Snyder. 1990. "Reliability and Validity of the Hispanic Stress Inventory." *Hispanic Journal of Behavioral Sciences* 12:76–82.

Crijnen, Alfons A., Thomas M. Achenbach, and Frank C. Verhulst. 1999. "Problems Reported by Parents of Children in Multiple Cultures: The Child Behavior Checklist Syndrome Constructs." *American Journal of Psychiatry* 156(4): 569–74.

Cuffe, Steven, Jennifer L. Waller, Michael L. Cuccaro, Andres J. Pumariega, and Carol Z. Garrison. 1995. "Race and Gender Differences in the Treatment of Psychiatric Disorders in Young Adolescents." *Journal of the American Academy of Child & Adolescent Psychiatry* 34(11): 1536–43.

Deck, Dennis, and Kelly V. Levy. 2006. "Medicaid Eligibility and Access to Mental Health Services among Adolescents in Substance Abuse Treatment." *Psychiatric Services* 57(2): 263–65.

Derose, Kathryn P., and David W. Baker. 2000. "Limited English Proficiency and Latinos' Use of Physician Services." *Medical Care Research and Review* 57(1): 76–91.

Donovan, M. Suzanne, and Christopher T. Cross, eds. 2002. *Minority Students in Special and Gifted Education.* Committee on Minority Representation in Special Education. Washington, DC: Division of Behavioral and Social Science and Education, National Research Council.

Duarte, Cristiane S., Hector R. Bird, Patrick E. Shrout, Ping Wu, Roberto Lewis-Fernandez, Sa Shen, and Glorisa Canino. 2008. "Culture and Psychiatric Symptoms in Puerto Rican Children: Longitudinal Results from One Ethnic Group in Two Contexts." *Journal of Child Psychology and Psychiatry* 49(5): 563–72.

Dyregrov, Atle. 2004. "Educational Consequences of Loss and Trauma." *Educational and Child Psychology* 21(3): 77–84.

Eccles, Jacquelynne S., and Carol Midgley. 1988. "Stage/Environment Fit: Developmentally Appropriate Classrooms for Early Adolescents." In *Research on Motivation in Education: Student Motivation,* edited by Russell E. Ames and Carole Ames. New York: Academic Press.

Engelberg, Moshe, and Susan D. Kirby. 2001. "Identity Building in Social Marketing." *Social Marketing Quarterly* 7(2): 8–15.

Equity Monitoring Project for Immigrant and Refugee Education, The. 2007. "School Year Filled with Missed Communication: Despite Chancellor's Regulation, Immigrant Parents Still Face Language Barriers." New York: New York Immigrant Coalition.

Felice, Lawrence G. 1981. "Black Student Dropout Behavior: Disengagement from School Rejection and Racial Discrimination." *Journal of Negro Education* 50(4): 415–24.

Finkelhor, David, Richard K. Ormrod, and Heather A. Turner. 2007. "Polyvictimization and Trauma in a National Longitudinal Cohort." *Development and Psychopathology* 19(1): 149–66.

Fiscella, Kevin, Peter Franks, Mark P. Doescher, and Barry G. Saver. 2002. "Disparities in Healthcare by Race, Ethnicity, and Language among the Insured: Findings from a National Sample." *Medical Care* 40(1): 52–59.

Flanagan, Dawn P., Vincent C. Alfonso, Louis H. Primavera, Laura Povall, and Deirdre Higgins. 1996. "Convergent Validity of the BASC and SSRS: Implications for Social Skills Assessment." *Psychology in the Schools* 33(1): 13–23.

Flores, Glenn. 2000. "Culture and the Patient-Physician Relationship: Achieving Cultural Competency in Healthcare." *Journal of Pediatrics* 136(1): 14–23.

Florsheim, Paul, Patrick H. Tolan, and Deborah Gorman-Smith. 1996. "Family Processes and Risk for Externalizing Behavior Problems among African American and Hispanic Boys." *Journal of Consulting and Clinical Psychiatry* 64(6): 1222–30.

Ford, Tasmin, Robert Goodman, and Howard Meltzer. 2003. "The British Child and Adolescent Mental Health Survey 1999: The Prevalence of DSM-IV Disorders." *Journal of the American Academy of Child & Adolescent Psychiatry* 42(10): 1203–11.

Freedenthal, Stacey. 2007. "Racial Disparities in Mental Health Service Use by Adolescents Who Thought about or Attempted Suicide." *Suicide and Life-Threatening Behavior* 37(1): 22–34.

Garrison, Ellen Greenberg, Ila S. Roy, and Viviana Azar. 1999. "Responding to the Mental Health Needs of Latino Children and Families through School-Based Services." *Clinical Psychology Review* 19(2): 199–219.

Giaconia, Rose M., Helen Z. Reinherz, Amy B. Silverman, Bilge Pakiz, Abbie K. Frost, and Elaine Cohen. 1995. "Traumas and Posttraumatic Stress Disorder in a Community Population of Older Adolescents." *Journal of the American Academy of Child & Adolescent Psychiatry* 34(10): 1369–80.

Gleser, Goldine C., Roslyn Seligman, Carolyn Winget, and Joseph L. Rauh. 1980. "Parents View Their Adolescents' Mental Health." *Journal of Adolescent Healthcare* 1(1): 30–36.

Hernandez, Donald J. 2004. "Demographic Change and the Life Circumstances of Immigrant Families." *The Future of Children* 14(2): 17–47.

Hoagwood, Kimberly, and Jacqueline Johnson. 2003. "School Psychology: A Public Health Framework: I. From Evidence-Based Practices to Evidence-Based Policies." *Journal of School Psychology* 41(1): 3–21.

Hough, Richard L., Andrea L. Hazen, Fernando I. Soriano, Patricia Wood, Kristen McCabe, and May Yeh. 2002. "Mental Health Services for Latino Adolescents with Psychiatric Disorders." *Psychiatric Services* 53(12): 1556–62.

Iwamasa, Gayle Y., Kristen H. Sorocco, and Daniel A. Koonce. 2002. "Ethnicity and Clinical Psychology: A Content Analysis of the Literature." *Clinical Psychology Review* 22(6): 931–44.

Jensen, Peter S., Kimberly Hoagwood, and Edison J. Trickett. 1999. "Ivory Towers or Earthen Trenches? Community Collaborations to Foster Real-World Research." *Applied Developmental Science* 3(4): 206–12.

Kann, Laura. 2001. "The Youth Risk Behavior Surveillance System: Measuring Health-Risk Behaviors." *American Journal of Health Behavior* 25(3): 272–77.

Kataoka, Sheryl H., Lily Zhang, and Kenneth B. Wells. 2002. "Unmet Need for Mental Healthcare among U.S. Children: Variation by Ethnicity and Insurance Status." *American Journal of Psychiatry* 159(9): 1548–55.

Kirmayer, Laurence J., Danielle Groleau, Jaswant Guzder, Caminee Blake, and Eric Jarvis. 2003. "Cultural Consultation: A Model of Mental Health Service for Multicultural Societies." *Canadian Journal of Psychiatry* 48(3): 145–53.

Kodjo, Cheryl M., and Peggy Auinger. 2003. "Racial/Ethnic Differences in Emotionally Distressed Adolescents Receiving Mental Healthcare." *Journal of Adolescent Health* 32(2): 132–33.

Koller, James R., Steven J. Osterlind, Kami Paris, and Karen J. Weston. 2004. "Differences between Novice and Expert Teachers' Undergraduate Preparation and Ratings of Importance in the Area of Children's Mental Health." *International Journal of Mental Health Promotion* 6(2): 40–45.

Kotler, Philip, Ned Roberto, and Nancy Lee. 2002. *Social Marketing: Improving the Quality of Life.* Thousands Oaks, CA: SAGE Publications.

López, Steven Regeser, and Peter Guarnaccia. 2000. "Cultural Psychopathology: Uncovering the Social World of Mental Illness." *Annual Review of Psychology* 51:571–98.

Lozano-Rodriguez, Jose R., and Jaime A. Castellano. 1999. "Assessing LEP Migrant Students for Special Education Services." ED425892. Charleston, WV: ERIC Clearinghouse on Rural Education and Small Schools.

Magafia, Raul J., Olivia de la Rocha, Jaime Amsel, Holly A. Magafia, Isabel M. Fernandez, and Sarah Rulnick. 1996. "Revisiting the Dimensions of Acculturation: Cultural Theory and Psychometric Practice." *Hispanic Journal of Behavioral Sciences* 18(4): 444–68.

Malgady, Robert G., and Luis H. Zayas. 2001. "Cultural and Linguistic Considerations in Psychodiagnosis with Hispanics: The Need for an Empirically Informed Process Model." *Social Work* 46(1): 39–49.

Malgady, Robert G., Giuseppe Constantino, and Lloyd H. Rogler. 1986. "Cuentos Therapy: A Culturally Sensitive Modality for Puerto Rican Children." *Journal of Consulting and Clinical Psychology* 54:639–45.

Malgady, Robert G., Lloyd H. Rogler, and Giuseppe Constantino. 1990. "Hero/Heroine Modeling for Puerto Rican Adolescents: A Preventive Mental Health Intervention." *Journal of Consulting and Clinical Psychology* 58(6): 469–74.

Mann, E. M., Y. Ikeda, C. W. Mueller, A. Takahashi, K. T. Tao, E. Humris, B. L. Li, and D. Chin. 1992. "Cross-Cultural Differences in Rating Hyperactive-Disruptive Behaviors in Children." *American Journal of Psychiatry* 149(11): 1539–42.

Massey, Oliver T., Kathleen Armstrong, Michael Boroughs, Kelli Henson, and Linda McCash. 2005. "Mental Health Services in Schools: A Qualitative Analysis of Challenges to Implementation, Operation, and Sustainability." *Psychology in the Schools* 42(4): 361–72.

McCabe, Kristen, May Yeh, Richard L. Hough, John Landsverk, Michael S. Hurlburt, Shirley Wells Culver, and Beth Reynolds. 1999. "Racial/Ethnic Representation across Five Public Sectors of Care for Youth." *Journal of Emotional and Behavioral Disorders* 7(2): 72–82.

Miranda, Jeanne, Richard Nakamura, and Guillermo Bernal. 2003. "Including Ethnic Minorities in Mental Health Intervention Research: A Rational Approach to a Long-Standing Problem." *Culture, Medicine & Psychiatry* 27:467–86.

Mulvaney-Day, Norah, Nancy Rappaport, Margarita Alegría, and Leslie Codianne. 2006. "Developing Systems Interventions in a School Setting: An Application of Community-Based Participatory Research for Mental Health." *Ethnicity and Disease* 16(1): 107–17.

New Freedom Commission on Mental Health. 2003. *Achieving the Promise: Transforming Mental Health Care in America.* DHHS Pub. No. SMA-03-3832. Rockville, MD: New Freedom Commission on Mental Health.

Odom, Samuel L., Scott R. McConnell, and Mary A. McEvoy. 1992. *Social Competence of Young Children with Disabilities: Issues and Strategies for Intervention.* Baltimore, MD: Paul H. Brookes Publishing Company.

Ortiz, Alba A., and James R. Yates. 2001. "A Framework for Serving English Language Learners with Disabilities." *Journal of Special Education Leadership* 14(2): 72–80.

Patterson, Gerald R., John B. Reid, and Thomas J. Dishion. 1992. *A Social Interactional Approach: Antisocial Boys.* Eugene, OR: Castalia Publishing Company.

Pesamaa, Lilli, Hanna Ebeling, Marja-Leena Kuusimaki, Ilkka Winblad, Matti Isohanni, and Irma Moilanen. 2004. "Videoconferencing in Child and Adolescent Telepsychiatry: A Systematic Review of the Literature." *Journal of Telemedicine and Telecare* 10:187–92.

Polo, Antonio, and Steven López. 2009. "Culture, Context, and the Internalizing Distress of Mexican American Youth." *Journal of Clinical Child and Adolescent Psychology* 38(2): 273–85.

Portes, Alejandro, and Rubén G. Rumbaut. 1990. *Immigrant America: A Portrait.* Berkeley: University of California Press.

Public Advocate for the City of New York, The, and Advocates for Children of New York, Inc. 2002. *Pushing Out At-Risk Students: An Analysis of High School Discharge Figures.* New York: Advocates for Children of New York, Inc.

Pumariega, Andres J., Kenneth Rogers, and Eugenio Rothe. 2005. "Culturally Competent Systems of Care for Children's Mental Health: Advances and Challenges." *Community Mental Health Journal* 41(5): 539–55.

Pumariega, Andres, Saundra Glover, Charles Holzer, and Huang Nguyen. 1998. "Administrative Update: Utilization of Services. II. Utilization of Mental Health Services in a Tri-Ethnic Sample of Adolescents." *Community Mental Health Journal* 34(2): 145–56.

Rappaport, Nancy. 2005. "Survival 101: Assessing Children's and Adolescents' Dangerousness in School Settings." *Adolescent Psychiatry: Developmental and Clinical Studies* 28:157–81.

Roberts, Robert E., Catherine Ramsay Roberts, and Y. Richard Chen. 1997. "Ethnocultural Differences in Prevalence of Adolescent Depression." *American Journal of Community Psychology* 25(1): 95–110.

Roberts, Robert E., Catherine Ramsay Roberts, and Yun Xing. 2007a. "Are Mexican American Adolescents at Greater Risk of Suicidal Behaviors?" *Suicide and Life-Threatening Behavior* 37(1): 10–21.

———. 2007b. "Rates of DSM-IV Psychiatric Disorders among Adolescents in a Large Metropolitan Area." *Journal of Psychiatric Research* 41(11): 959–67.

Roberts, Robert E., Margarita Alegría, Catherine Ramsay Roberts, and Irene Ger Chen. 2005. "Mental Health Problems of Adolescents as Reported by Their Caregivers: A Comparison of European, African, and Latino Americans." *Journal of Behavioral Health Services & Research* 32(1): 1.

Rones, Michelle, and Kimberly Hoagwood. 2000. "School-Based Mental Health Services: A Research Review." *Clinical Child and Family Psychology Review* 3(4): 223–41.

Roselló, Jeannette, and Guillermo Bernal. 1996. "Adapting Cognitive-Behavioral and Interpersonal Treatments for Depressed Puerto Rican Adolescents." In *Psychosocial Treatments for Child and Adolescent Disorders,* edited by Euthymia D. Hibbs and Peter Jensen (157–86). Washington, DC: American Psychological Association.

Rousseau, Cecile, Aline Drapeau, and Ellen Corin. 1996. "School Performance and Emotional Problems in Refugee Children." *American Journal of Orthopsychiatry* 66(2): 239–51.

Rousseau, Cecile, Aline Drapeau, and Robert Platt. 1999. "Family Trauma and Its Association with Emotional and Behavioral Problems and Social Adjustment in Adolescent Cambodian Refugees." *Child Abuse & Neglect* 23(12): 1263–73.

Rousseau, Cecile, Maryse Benoit, Marie-France Gauthier, Louise Lacroix, Neomee Alain, Musuk Viger Rojas, Alejandro Moran, and Dominique Bourassa. 2007. "Classroom Drama Therapy Program for Immigrant and Refugee Adolescents: A Pilot Study." *Clinical Child Psychology and Psychiatry* 12(3): 451.

Rylko-Bauer, Barbara, and Paul Farmer. 2002. "Managed Care or Managed Inequality? A Call for Critiques of Market-Based Medicine." *Medical Anthropology Quarterly* 16(4): 476–502.

Saltzman, William R., Alan M. Steinberg, Christopher M. Layne, Eugene Aisenberg, and Robert S. Pynoos. 2001. "A Developmental Approach to School-Based Treatment of Adolescents Exposed to Trauma and Traumatic Loss." *Journal of Child and Adolescent Group Therapy* 11(2): 43–56.

Sameroff, Arnold J., Stephen C. Peck, and Jacquelynne S. Eccles. 2004. "Changing Ecological Determinants of Conduct Problems from Early Adolescence to Early Adulthood." *Development & Psychopathology* 16:873–96.

Sentell, Tetine, Martha Shumway, and Lonnie Snowden. 2007. "Access to Mental Health Treatment by English Language Proficiency and Race/Ethnicity." *Journal of General Internal Medicine* 22:289–93.

Shone, Laura P., Andrew W. Dick, Cindy Brach, Kim S. Kimminau, Barbara J. LaClair, Elizabeth A. Shenkman, Jana F. Col, Virginia A. Schaffer, Frank Mulvihill, and Peter G. Szilagyi. 2003. "The Role of Race and Ethnicity in the State Children's Health Insurance Program (SCHIP) in Four States: Are There Baseline Disparities, and What Do They Mean for SCHIP?" *Pediatrics* 112(6): e521.

Skiba, Russell J., Robert S. Michael, Abra Carroll Nardo, and Reece L. Peterson. 2002. "The Color of Discipline: Sources of Racial and Gender Disproportionality in School Punishment." *The Urban Review* 34(4).

Smedley, Brian D., Adrienne Y. Stith, and Alan R. Nelson, eds. 2002. *Unequal Treatment: Confronting Racial and Ethnic Disparities in Health Care.* Institute of Medicine. Washington, DC: National Academies Press.

Snowden, Lonnie R., and Freda K. Cheung. 1990. "Use of Inpatient Mental Health Services by Members of Ethnic Minority Groups." *American Psychologist* 45(3): 347–55.

Stein, Bradley D., Lisa H. Jaycox, Sheryl H. Kataoka, Marleen Wong, Wenli Tu, Marc N. Elliott, and Arlene Fink. 2003. "A Mental Health Intervention for Schoolchildren Exposed to Violence: A Randomized Controlled Trial." *Journal of the American Medical Association* 290(5): 603–11.

Stein, Bradley D., Sheryl Kataoka, Lisa H. Jaycox, Marleen Wong, Arlene Fink, Pia Escudero, and Catalina Zaragoza. 2002. "Theoretical Basis and Program Design of a School-Based Mental Health Intervention for Traumatized Immigrant Children: A Collaborative Research Partnership." *Journal of Behavioral Health Services & Research* 29(3): 318–26.

Stiffman, Arlene, Catherine Striley, Violet Horvath, Eric Hadley-Ives, Michael Polgar, Diane Elze, and Richard Pescarino. 2001. "Organizational Context and Provider Perception as Determinants of Mental Health Service Use." *Journal of Behavioral Health Services & Research* 28(2): 188–204.

Suárez-Orozco, Carola, Irina Todorova, and Josephine Louie. 2002. "'Making Up for Lost Time': The Experience of Separation and Reunification among Immigrant Families." *Family Process* 41(4): 625–43.

Sue, S., D. C. Fujino, L. Hu, D. Takeuchi, and N. Zane. 1991. "Community Mental Health Services for Ethnic Minority Groups: A Test of the Cultural Responsiveness Hypothesis." *Journal of Consulting and Clinical Psychology* 59(4): 533–40.

Thompson, Theodore, and Carol Ripley Massat. 2005. "Experiences of Violence, Post-Traumatic Stress, Academic Achievement, and Behavior Problems of Urban

African-American Children." *Child and Adolescent Social Work Journal* 22(5): 367–93.

Townsend, B. L. 2000. "The Disproportionate Discipline of African American Learners: Reducing School Suspensions and Expulsions." *Exceptional Children* 66(3): 381–91.

U.S. Surgeon General. 2001. *Mental Health: Culture, Race, and Ethnicity. A Supplement to Mental Health: A Report of the Surgeon General.* Washington, DC: U.S. Department of Health and Human Services.

Vega, William A., and Margarita Alegría. 2001. "Latino Mental Health and Treatment in the United States." In *Health Issues in the Latino Community,* edited by Marilyn Aguirre-Molina, Carlos W. Molina, and Ruth Enid Zambrana (179–209). San Francisco, CA: Jossey-Bass.

Velez, Carmeni Noemi, and Jane A. Ungemack. 1989. "Drug Use among Puerto Rican Youth: An Exploration of Generational Status Differences." *Social Science & Medicine* 29(6): 779–89.

Wachtel, Janice, James R. Rodrigue, Gary Geffken, John Graham-Pole, and Clara Turner. 1994. "Children Awaiting Invasive Medical Procedures: Do Children and Their Mothers Agree on Child's Level of Anxiety?" *Journal of Pediatric Psychology* 19(6): 723–35.

Walton, Janice Wachtel, Suzanne Bennett Johnson, and James Algina. 1999. "Mother and Child Perceptions of Child Anxiety: Effects of Race, Health Status, and Stress." *Journal of Pediatric Psychology* 24(1): 29–39.

Weech-Maldonado, Robert, Leo S. Morales, Marc Elliott, Karen Spritzer, Grant Marshall, and Ron D. Hays. 2003. "Race/Ethnicity, Language, and Patients' Assessments of Care in Medicaid Managed Care." *Health Services Research* 38(3): 789–808.

Weist, Mark D., and John Schlitt. 1998. "Alliances and School-Based Healthcare." *Journal of School Health* 68:401–404.

Weisz, John R., Marian Sigman, Bahr Weiss, and Julie Mosk. 1993. "Parent Reports of Behavioral and Emotional Problems among Children in Kenya, Thailand, and the United States." *Child Development* 64:98–109.

Weisz, John R., Somsong Suwanlert, Wanchai Chaiyasit, Bahr Weiss, Bernadette R. Walter, and Wanni Wibulswadi Anderson. 1988. "Thai and American Perspectives on Over- and Undercontrolled Child Behavior Problems: Exploring the Threshold and Model among Parents, Teachers, and Psychologists." *Journal of Consulting and Clinical Psychology* 56(4): 601–609.

Wood, Patricia A., May Yeh, David Pan, Katina M. Lambros, Kristen M. McCabe, and Richard L. Hough. 2005. "Exploring the Relationship between Race/Ethnicity, Age of First School-Based Services Utilization, and Age of First Specialty Mental Healthcare for At-Risk Youth." *Mental Health Services Research* 7(3): 185–96.

Wu, Ping, Christina Hoven, Hector Bird, Robert Moore, Patricia Cohen, Margarita Alegría, Mina Dulcan, et al. 1999. "Depressive and Disruptive Disorders and Mental Health Service Utilization in Children and Adolescents." *Journal of the American Academy of Child & Adolescent Psychiatry* 38(9): 1081–90.

Yeh, May, Kristen McCabe, Richard L. Hough, Deborah Dupuis, and Andrea Hazen. 2003. "Racial/Ethnic Differences in Parental Endorsement of Barriers to Mental Health Services for Youth." *Mental Health Services Research* 5(2): 65–77.

Zahner, Gwendolyn E. P., and Constantine Daskalakis. 1997. "Factors Associated with Mental Health, General Health, and School-Based Service Use for Child Psychopathology." *American Journal of Public Health* 87(9): 1440–48.

14

Where Policy Intervenes

An Application of Alegría's Sociocultural Framework for Understanding Health and Service Disparities of Immigrant Hispanic Children

Deborah Roempke Graefe

In the previous chapter, Dr. Alegría and her colleagues provide us with a lot of food for thought. They have taken on that question raised by many about where we need to start to develop a theoretical framework for the study of Hispanic immigrant child developmental disparities. While their focus is on mental and behavioral health, they have brought together the many factors found in prior research to influence immigrant child well-being as an overarching and complex conceptual model applicable to understanding a wide range of health, schooling, and transition-to-adulthood outcomes of immigrant children. This framework sets the stage for what I take away as one of their main messages—that policies are needed to reduce immigrant child health and health service disparities, and that these policies need to be sensitive to the challenges facing immigrant families.

That said, the sheer complexity of this model complicates the statistical modeling of immigrant child outcomes, and adequate tests of efforts to eliminate disparities between immigrant and native children will require an information-rich, prospective longitudinal dataset including larger subsamples of Hispanic immigrant children from sending countries other than Mexico than are currently available.

Understanding What the Framework Tells Us

Even presenting this conceptual framework on a single graph is challenging. So it is useful to consider parts of the framework by the outcome variables of interest: mental health, access to and use of health services, and school outcomes. Alegría and her colleagues tell us that immigrant child mental health problems are greater for children in families experiencing acculturative stresses—where there are mismatches between the acculturation of parents and that of their children—and that these stresses decline over time in the United States (figure 14.1). So, for instance, we might expect children in Updegraff and Umaña-Taylor's (chapter 5) study families, where parents had a Mexican orientation but children had an Anglo orientation, would experience greater acculturative stress.

Alegría and colleagues also tell us that English proficiency reduces immigrant child mental health problems. Of course, we might also draw an arrow between English proficiency and acculturative stress. Parent English proficiency may increase with more time in the United States, giving us an assimilation/acculturation measure. But as we see in chapter 8, better-educated immigrant parents are more likely than less-well-educated immigrant parents to be English proficient; understanding the assimilation/acculturation and acculturative stresses for these families thus requires more information than we typically have in large datasets. In particular,

Figure 14.1. Framework for Understanding Behavioral Health Disparities of Hispanic Immigrant Children

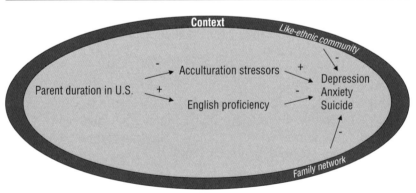

Source: Synthesis of literature in chapter 13.

this speaks to Van Hook's point in chapter 6 that knowing something about culture of origin and U.S. cultural differences is needed. Importantly, though, we cannot presume that cultural orientations in countries of origin do not vary by socioeconomic or racial/ethnic status; that is, that immigrant-sending nations do not exhibit within-country cultural heterogeneity that may influence the acculturation experiences of immigrant families.

Alegría and colleagues also point out that contexts of supportive family networks and like-ethnic communities (ethnic enclaves) are supportive of good mental health for immigrants. From Van Hook's discussion in chapter 6, we know that family networks as measured by extended kin living arrangements are yet another potential indicator of time lived in the United States, rather than acculturation, potentially representing structural opportunities that increase with time in the United States.

As shown in figure 14.2, Alegría and her colleagues also tell us that Hispanic immigrants are less likely to use child behavioral health services when English proficiency is poor, when the parents stigmatize mental health problems and do not seek help for their children, and when parents do not recognize that the child has a problem—all factors that are most likely for less acculturated/assimilated immigrant parents.

The lack of health insurance coverage is another important factor influencing service use, although here federal and state public policies can, and

Figure 14.2. Framework for Understanding Behavioral Health Service Access and Use of Hispanic Immigrant Children

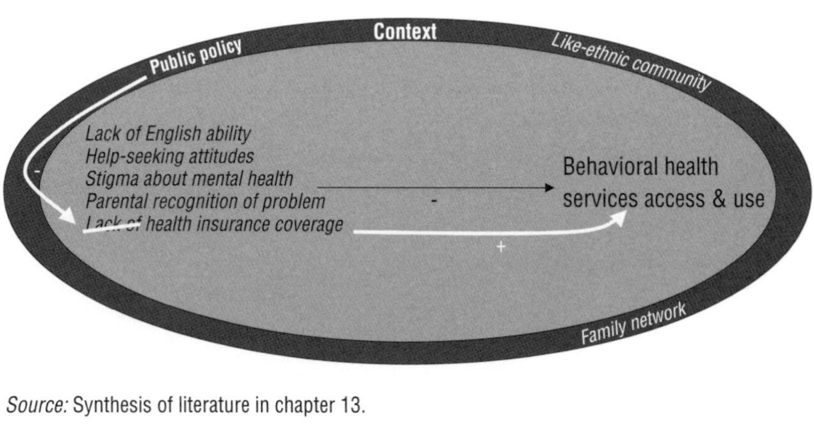

Source: Synthesis of literature in chapter 13.

have, reduced the lack of coverage for immigrant children, particularly those born in the United States. We expect that policies to increase coverage will increase access to and use of behavioral health services.

Alegría and colleagues also bring school outcomes into the model, pointing out that school failure should be considered here as a factor promoting poor mental and behavioral health (figure 14.3). It is here that they bring in the negative impact of residential mobility on school outcomes by increasing family stresses. Of course, change in residence itself may be the result of a stressful event that may also be partly to blame for poor school outcomes. Nevertheless, Alegría and colleagues say, public policy could improve school settings to overcome family socioeconomic disadvantages and stressors in order to achieve better school outcomes for immigrant children.

When they consolidate these conceptual models, in simplest terms, they have a framework that looks something like figure 14.4. As we saw in the first three figures, they note that public policy can affect the school context in ways that influence school outcomes, which in turn influence mental health. For example, not only can policy be changed to eliminate the unintended negative impacts of the No Child Left Behind policy on school completion, but opportunities exist to reduce the cultural/linguistic mismatch between school personnel and immigrant families to improve school completion rates. Further, schools can be first points

Figure 14.3. Framework for Understanding School Outcomes of Hispanic Immigrant Children

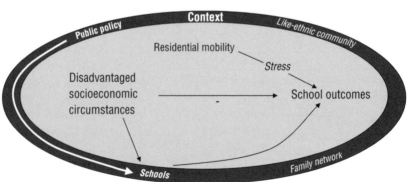

Source: Synthesis of literature in chapter 13.

Figure 14.4. Framework for Understanding Behavioral Health Disparities and School Outcomes of Hispanic Immigrant Children

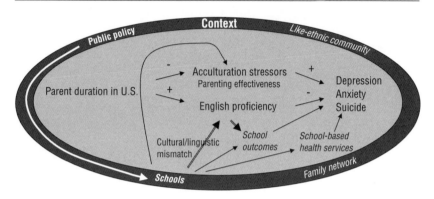

Source: Synthesis of literature in chapter 13.

of contact with health services to reduce mental health problems when they occur.

To address acculturation stressors and parenting effectiveness, schools also provide contexts where parents can be brought into the picture, by educating parents about the factors affecting healthy child development and how to recognize behavioral health problems, involving parents as advocates for their children, and increasing parent-child communication. An example would be the Talking Parents, Healthy Teens parent-centered HIV-prevention program discussed by Corona in chapter 7. Alegría's framework considers schools as places for a more holistic development of children, but it does not consider the role of health insurance coverage, an aspect we can examine with existing data.

Testing the Framework

To consider the effectiveness of school-based health service access, we can first look at a simpler model (shown in figure 14.5) to see whether having access to health care, as measured by health coverage, intervenes in the effects of factors expected to decrease the mental and behavioral health of immigrant children. Keep in mind that health problems potentially increase the likelihood of health coverage. We need longitudinal data to

Figure 14.5. The Role of Health Coverage in Hispanic Immigrant Child Mental and Behavioral Health Using the Chapter 13 Framework

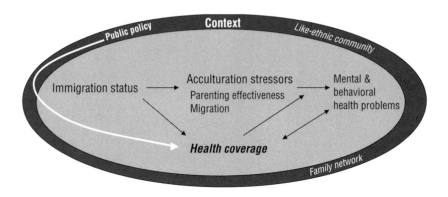

appropriately time independent variables before the mental/behavioral health outcome, as well as a measure of prior mental/behavioral health to eliminate the confusion resulting from reciprocal influences of health problems on having health coverage. I will come back to this in a moment.

Of course, immigration status also influences access to health insurance coverage. Using National Center for Health Statistics data for 1997 through 2001, Escarce and Kapur (2006) show that Hispanic American children are much more likely to be without health coverage than non-Hispanic white children (figure 14.6). Among Hispanics, Mexican-origin children are the most likely to be without coverage, and Puerto Ricans and Cubans are the least likely.

Dramatic variations in the source of coverage by Hispanic origin are also clear (figure 14.7), with Hispanic children much more likely to receive coverage through public programs. And among Hispanic children, the source of coverage varies considerably by national-origin identification. Here you see that Puerto Rican children—the least likely to be without coverage—are the most likely to be covered by public health insurance. Cuban children are not very different from Puerto Ricans when it comes to a lack of coverage, but they are most likely to be covered through employer-sponsored insurance. We can understand that most likely these differences result from socioeconomic differences between Puerto Ricans and Cubans, and that the differences between Puerto

Figure 14.6. Percentage of Children without Health Insurance, by Ethnic Group

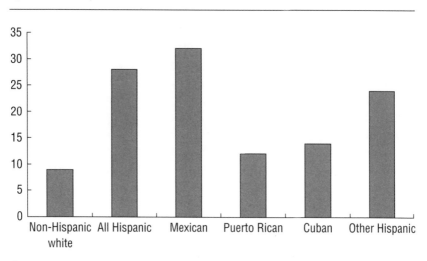

Source: Escarce and Kapur (2006), based on 1997–2001 National Center for Health Statistics data.

Figure 14.7. Source of Health Coverage, by Ethnic Group

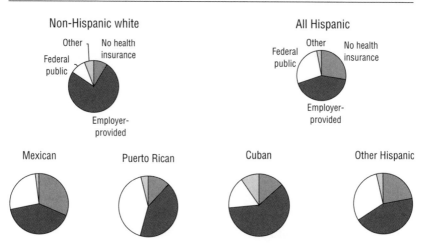

Source: Escarce and Kapur (2006), based on 1997–2001 National Center for Health Statistics data.

Ricans and other Hispanic groups most likely result from differences in citizenship status.

Length of residence in the United States—a good proxy for citizenship status for all groups except Puerto Ricans—also matters. Among Hispanics, just under 30 percent of U.S.-born adults are without coverage, compared with almost 50 percent of foreign-born adults (figure 14.8). When we look at percentages without coverage for Hispanics who have lived in the United States for less than five years, we find more dramatic disparities compared with U.S.-born Hispanics.

Escarce and Kapur (2006) do not provide similar statistics for children, but they do show that Hispanic children—who are more likely to be without coverage—are less likely than non-Hispanic white children to see medical professionals (figure 14.9). This is particularly the case for Mexican-origin children, a group most likely not to have medical insurance.

Figure 14.8. Hispanic Adults without Health Coverage, by Nativity and Length of U.S. Residence

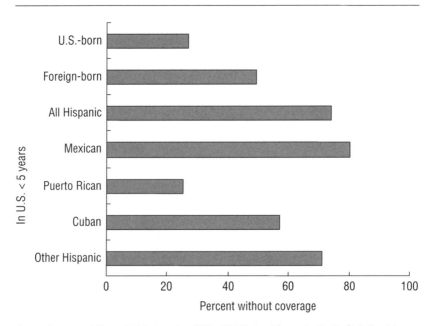

Source: Escarce and Kapur (2006), based on 1997–2001 National Center for Health Statistics data.

Figure 14.9. Health Care Use among Hispanic Children, by Ethnic Group

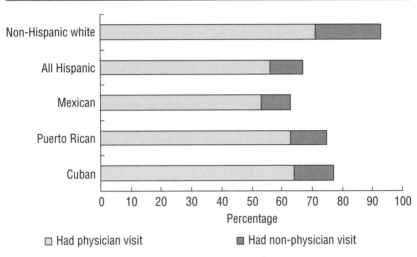

Source: Escarce and Kapur (2006), based on 1996–2000 Medical Expenditure Panel Survey data.

My own work on health care access has relied primarily on the Survey of Income and Program Participation (SIPP). My next comments are based on the 2004 panel of the SIPP, which provides nationally representative data of U.S. households for 2004–06. SIPP data are collected by the Bureau of the Census. The survey provides a wealth of information on the demographic and socioeconomic characteristics of all household members, as well as insurance coverage and migration information, for each month a participant is in the survey. Special topic-specific modules are collected at different interview waves. Health-related measures in the currently released files are observed in the 20th month of the survey. Immigration histories for household members age 15 and older are obtained at the second wave (the eighth month) of data collection.

Using monthly indicators of an individual's citizenship status together with parents' immigration history information, I have identified that among the more that 28,000 children for whom SIPP provides information during the first 20 months of the survey, almost 1,800 are of Mexican heritage, over 1,600 of whom are U.S.-born with at least one foreign-born parent and 81 of whom were born in Mexico. The sample includes 102 black Hispanics, only a handful of whom are immigrants. Over 2,600 children in the sample are nonblack, non-Mexican Hispanics, 187 of whom are second-generation immigrants and 97 of whom are first-generation immigrant children.

Using monthly information on the type of coverage and lack of coverage, for each child I can identify the type of coverage he or she has most often during the first 20 months of the survey. Each bar in figure 14.10 shows the percentage of children who were covered mostly by Medicaid, mostly by the State Children's Health Insurance Program (SCHIP), mostly by privately purchased insurance, and mostly by employer-provided coverage, along with who were mostly without health insurance coverage.

As expected, native-born children tend to have some type of coverage most of the time. Hispanic children are more likely to be covered most of the time by Medicaid, although these percentages are lower for first-generation immigrant children, who also are least likely to be covered primarily by employer-sponsored insurance. The bottom line here is that first-generation immigrant children appear to face a structural disadvantage when it comes to health insurance coverage.

Since immigrant relocation is a potential source of stress for immigrant children, it is also interesting to compare these groups on the basis

Figure 14.10. Share of Children Covered Mostly by Medicaid, SCHIP, Private, and Employer-Provided Health Insurance, by Ethnic Group

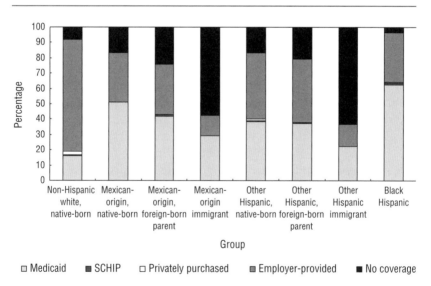

Source: Author's calculations based on 2004 Survey of Income and Program Participation data.

of whether they had ever moved during the 19 months before the health outcome measures were collected. As indicated in figure 14.11, within-U.S. migration is not negatively associated with health coverage for U.S.-born Hispanic children, but it clearly increases the likelihood of having been mostly without coverage among immigrant Hispanic children.

Figure 14.12 shows the share of children for whom a mental or behavioral health problem was reported in month 20 of the survey. The darker bars show the percentage with such impairment and the lighter bars show the percentage with such impairment who also were without coverage for most of the 20 months. There are two points here. First, mental and behavioral health problems are most likely to be reported for first-generation immigrant Hispanics. Second, except for non-Mexican immigrant children, children with mental or behavioral health problems are likely to have been covered by health insurance most of the 20 months. This suggests that having access to health coverage may not intervene to

Figure 14.11. Share of Hispanic Children without Health Coverage Most of the Time, by Race and Nativity

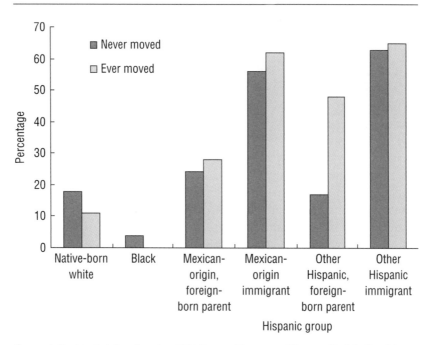

Source: Author's calculations based on 2004 Survey of Income and Program Participation data.

Figure 14.12. Share of Children Having a Mental or Behavioral Health Problem, by Race/Ethnic/Nativity Group

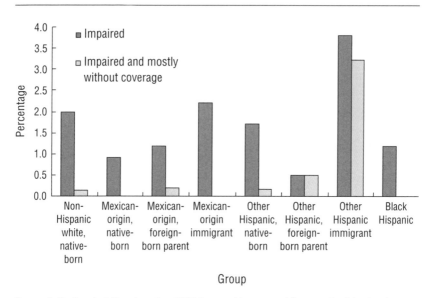

Source: Author's calculations based on 2004 Survey of Income and Program Participation data.

reduce these problems, although it certainly is likely to be needed in order to obtain treatment for these problems.

Interestingly, figure 14.13 shows that children whose families moved during these 20 months were slightly more likely to have a mental or behavioral health problem than children whose families did not move. Further, non-Mexican Hispanic first-generation immigrant children were a great deal more likely to have a problem.

Now if you recall that small portion of the framework on which I wanted to focus, shown in figure 14.5, in a multivariate model we would want to see if having health coverage moderates the negative impact of immigration status and acculturation stresses on mental and behavioral health problems. To evaluate this, I regress mental or behavioral health problem on country of origin and immigrant generation status among school-age Hispanic immigrants, shown by model 1 in table 14.1. Model 2 adds indicators of family stress, including acculturation stresses— whether the family moved in the months leading up to the health outcome, whether the household is linguistically isolated, and whether the parent

Figure 14.13. Share of Children Having a Mental or Behavioral Health Problem, by Race/Ethnic/Nativity Group

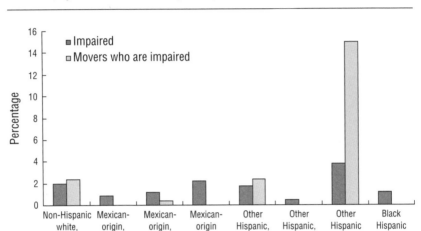

Source: Author's calculations based on 2004 Survey of Income and Program Participation data.

reports having trouble coping with daily stresses—to evaluate whether these indicators explain immigrant generation. Model 3 adds an indicator that the child had health coverage for most of the time, and model 4 adds an interaction term to evaluate whether having had coverage reduces the likelihood of a problem for first-generation immigrants.

What stands out here is the variation in having a mental or behavioral health problem by country of origin; that first-generation immigrants are more likely than second-generation immigrants (U.S.-born children with foreign-born parents) to have a problems; and that family stresses do not explain this difference, and neither does having had health coverage. Although not statistically significant, the negative effect of having coverage does imply that for Hispanic immigrant children, having access to health care may play a role in helping keep them mentally healthy. The factor having greatest impact is the indicator of family stress—that at least one parent reports having trouble coping with daily stresses.

There are some problems with this analysis, however, that point to the importance of having longitudinal data for both independent and dependent variables. The parent stress indicator is observed in the same

Table 14.1. Logistic Regression Predicting a Mental or Behavioral Health Problem among Hispanic Immigrant Children ($n = 1,698$)

Variables	Model 1	Model 2	Model 3	Model 4
Country/region of origin				
Mexico	Ref	Ref	Ref	Ref
South America	1.03 (2.8)	**1.59 (4.9)**	**1.59 (4.9)**	1.60 (4.95)
Central America	−16.4	−15.8	−15.7	**−15.7 (.06)**
Caribbean	−.40	−.93	−.95	−.96
Other	−1.5 (.22)	−2.1 (.13)	−2.04 (.13)	−2.06 (.13)
1st-generation immigrant	**1.89 (6.6)**	**2.6 (13)**	**2.5 (12)**	2.41
Ever moved		−1.28 (.28)	−1.33 (.27)	−1.33 (.27)
Household is linguistically isolated		−1.5 (.22)	**−1.54 (.22)**	**−1.54 (.22)**
Parent has trouble coping		**3.0 (20)**	**3.1 (21)**	**3.1 (21)**
Has coverage most of time			−.25	−.29
Interaction				
1st-generation X covered				.20

Source: Author's calculations based on 2004 Survey of Income and Program Participation data.

Notes: Models control for age of child, household poverty, and multiple children in household.

Odds ratio are shown in parenthesis for coefficients that are statistically significant at the $p \le .10$ level; bolded coefficients are statistically significant at the $p \le .01$ level.

month as the child's mental/behavioral health and could result from that child's problem. Further, a failure to control for prior mental/behavioral health problems that could influence whether the child has been covered by health insurance means that any potential relationship between coverage and health outcomes may be confounded. There is no clear and certain evidence that health coverage intervenes to reduce mental health problems here.

Another, better test of the role of having health coverage, though, would be to include in the model a control for mental or behavioral health problems at an earlier time. To determine whether access to health care, as provided by health coverage, improves mental/behavioral problems would require us to limit the sample to children who had problems at time 1 and to regress problems at time 2 on coverage between times 1 and 2. SIPP's nationally representative data include too few Hispanic immigrant children for whom such a problem was reported, however, for conducting that analysis.

Nevertheless, what we gain from the analysis shown is that high-quality school-based programs must do more than make health services available; they must actively engage parents and children in understanding the sources, the symptoms, and the availability of treatments for mental and behavioral health issues. Implementing such programs will require committed public policies, just as Alegría and her colleagues tell us, as well as robust evaluations of these programs to determine what works and what does not.

To conclude, if we believe that Hispanic immigrant children are important to the future of our nation—and demographic trends tell us that they are—we will need more longitudinal information that can be used to tease out the reciprocal relationships between outcomes of interest and the factors we expect to affect them. We will need larger study samples from the different countries of origin. Alegría and her colleagues have presented us with an expanded opportunity for increasing our understanding of the development of healthy Hispanic immigrant children, and they also have presented us with a challenge in doing so.

REFERENCE

Escarce, José J., and Kanika Kapur. 2006. "Access and Quality of Health Care." In *Hispanics and the Future of America*, edited by Marta Tienda and Faith Mitchell (411–46). Washington, DC: National Academies Press.

15

Observations on the Mental Health of Mexican American Youth

Robert E. Roberts and Catherine R. Roberts

Alegría and colleagues do an excellent job reviewing the literature related to the mental health of immigrant Latino children. Based on their review, they make three recommendations related to future research and seven related to policy and practice.

We limit our discussion to issues relating to future research. Discussion of policy and practice we leave to others whose expertise lies in those domains.

First, the recommendation that research is needed permitting analyses that disaggregate Latino children into meaningful ethnic/nativity groups is well taken. Latinos are diverse, and diverse in many ways. No study done to date permits examination of the roles of such factors as age, nativity, ethnic status, length of time in the United States, age at immigration, level of acculturation, acculturative stress, ethnic identity, perceived and experienced discrimination, rural-urban residence, neighborhood context, and family socioeconomic status. Beyond this, we do not have for even the largest Latino subgroups such as Mexicans, Cubans, and Puerto Ricans nationally representative data on the population-based estimates of prevalence of DSM-IV psychiatric disorders for children and adolescents. The samples to date are local and have insufficient power for the fine-grained analyses we need, and none include the array of measures needed (Roberts and Roberts 2007).

Regarding the second recommendation concerning the role of contextual factors in promoting or impairing the mental health of Latino children, again Alegría and colleagues have identified an important domain for inquiry. However, whereas there are substantial data on the importance of neighborhood context for mental health functioning in general, there are no data from studies that use multilevel research strategies to examine the impact of neighborhood on risk for psychiatric disorders for diverse groups of Latino children and whether different neighborhood contexts operate differently across Latino groups versus European, African, or Asian American subgroups.

The third recommendation by Alegría and colleagues stems from the fact that research on ethnic disparities in mental health has largely ignored factors that promote or protect the mental health of Latino children. In particular they note the potential roles of social networks and social support, especially the family context. Again, this is an excellent suggestion. The literature on this subject is essentially silent in relation to psychiatric disorders and their manifestation across Latino subgroups and in comparison to children and adolescents from non-Latino groups. There is, of course, an enormous literature on social networks and social support in general, but little of it informs us about the nature of ethnic differentials and implications for risk of psychiatric disorders and subsequent help-seeking for such mental health problems.

Having made these observations on chapter 13, we would now like to make some observations based on our own research, and other published data where appropriate, related to the mental health of Latino youth, in particular Mexican Americans.

As Alegría and colleagues note, there have been few studies of Mexican American children and adolescents, citing our studies as examples. We would like to summarize some of our results to date and what we think our data suggest. A major caveat is that we do not have data on immigrant youth, since there were too few in our sample to sustain group comparisons.

Teen Health 2000

Our data are taken from Teen Health 2000, a multiwave study contrasting the mental health of European (EA), African (AA), and Mexican American (MA) adolescents. The methods and detailed results can be found in published articles (Roberts and Roberts 2007; Roberts, Roberts, and Chan

2006; Roberts, Roberts, and Xing 2006, 2007). Outcomes examined have been DSM-IV psychiatric disorders, suicidal behaviors, and insomnia.

Psychiatric Disorders

In Teen Health 2000, data from the first wave ($n = 4,175$ teens age 12–17) indicated very few differences in the one-year prevalence of DSM-IV disorders among the three ethnic groups (Roberts, Roberts, and Xing 2006). EA youth were at lower risk of anxiety disorders and greater risk of mood and substance abuse disorders than were AA youth, and there were essentially no differences between EA and MA youth in prevalence of DSM-IV disorders.

Suicidality

When we explored ethnic differences in risk of suicidal behaviors, we also found no differences overall in past-year or lifetime attempts, past-year thoughts, or past-year plans (Roberts et al. 2007). When we focused on attempts, adjusting for a range of potential confounders, there were no differences between MA and EA youth in lifetime or past-year attempts. AA youth were at lower risk of past-year attempts in terms of crude prevalence, but not after adjustment for covariates.

Insomnia

When we turned our focus to poor sleep as a manifestation of emotional and behavioral dysfunction (Roberts, Roberts, and Chan 2006), again we found few ethnic differences. While crude prevalences of certain symptoms of sleep disturbance differed (3 of 15 ethnic contrasts), when we examined insomnia using diagnostic criteria there were no ethnic differences in either crude rates or rates adjusted for an array of potential confounders.

Ethnic Specific Patterns

As we have noted elsewhere, rates of psychiatric disorders may be similar or different across ethnocultural groups (Roberts and Roberts 2007). In the latter case, such differentials may result from (1) different (unique) risk and protective factors in the groups or ethnic-specific factors, (2) the same (generic) risk and protective factors operating differently across groups, or (3) the effects of both generic and unique factors across groups (Roberts 2000). Lincoln, Chatters, and Taylor (2003) note that there is little information about the role of generic risk and protective factors in the mental health of minorities. Wu and colleagues (2003) point out that factors may operate differently within specific subgroups. Further, there is some evidence that general stress-diathesis models do not predict mental health outcomes as well among AAs, for example, as among EAs (Lincoln et al. 2003). To what extent these observations reflect the effects of generic and ethnic-specific factors has not been demonstrated.

How might ethnicity affect risk for psychiatric disorders (if, indeed, it does)? Studies of the relationship between ethnicity and psychological distress or psychiatric disorder implicitly examine two competing hypotheses, one of which argues that observed ethnic differences primarily result from disadvantaged social status (particularly social class) and the other that there are ethnic effects (both positive and negative) on mental health over and above social status effects (Roberts 2000). Mirowsky and Ross (1980) label these two arguments, respectively, the minority status perspective and the ethnic culture perspective. The former argument asserts that to the extent an ethnic group is both a minority group and disadvantaged, there are chronic social stressors associated with disadvantaged position that produce greater distress. The latter argument assumes that psychological well-being varies with different cultural patterns in terms of beliefs, values, and lifestyles. Thus, disadvantaged social class does not necessarily place a member of an ethnicity collectively at greater risk for disorder.

A number of authors have addressed the role of risk and protective factors in the epidemiology of psychiatric disorders among children and adolescents. Space limitations preclude detailed presentation of those discussions here.[1] The theme emerging from this body of literature is that risk and protective factors can be subsumed under four broad domains: family history of disorder, status attributes, personal and social resources, and stressors.

What is ethnicity's role in this conceptual framework? By extension, given a particular family history constellation and given a particular combination of status factors such as age, gender, and ethnic status, to the extent ethnic experience reduces stressors and enhances resources, its impact on mental health should be positive. To the extent ethnicity increases stressors and decreases resources, its impact should be negative.

To provide more data on the prevalence of DSM-IV psychiatric disorders among adolescents, and to ascertain whether differentials attributable to ethnic culture or ethnic status exist, we contrasted prevalences among three different ethnic groups. We employed a multipronged analytic strategy. First, we compared crude prevalence rates among adolescents from different ethnocultural groups. Second, we made the same comparisons, adjusting for differences in generic risk and protective factors. Third, we introduced controls for factors that may reflect youth experiences emanating specifically from ethnic experience. In our first attempt using this strategy, we examined four dimensions of ethnic experience: acculturative or ethnic stress, ethnic identity, salience of ethnicity, and perceived discrimination (Roberts and Roberts 2007).

The results mirrored our earlier findings. That is, there were few differences between ethnic groups in risk of DSM-IV psychiatric disorders. No evidence was found that AA and MA youth, disadvantaged by lower socioeconomic status, were systematically at increased risk of psychiatric disorders. Crude prevalences for the three ethnic groups revealed few differences. Multivariate analyses adjusting for status factors, resources, and stressors had little impact. Only 2 of 18 odds ratios (substance use disorders and comorbid disorders) remained significant, and AA youth were at lower risk for both.

The role of factors hypothesized to reflect ethnic experience had little impact and, in fact, explained very little ethnic differences net of status, resources, and stress factors. Only 4 of 72 contrasts were significant for AA youth, and only 10 of 72 were significant for MA youth. For the latter, acculturative stress increased risk for anxiety, mood, any disorder, and comorbid disorders. Prejudice increased risk for substance use and any disorder. Salience decreased risk for substance use.

However, all things considered, the overriding conclusion is that there were few differences between groups observed initially and fewer still when an array of putative risk and protective factors were controlled. From the perspective of psychiatric epidemiology, this suggests there was little unique risk associated with ethnic background for the groups examined. The differences observed were few in number and small in effect size. Does this mean that there is no action, epidemiologically, for risk of psychiatric disorders among ethnic groups? Not really. We did not observe numerous or large differentials in prevalences of DSM-IV disorders between EA, AA, and MA youth. We did observe pronounced and systematic differences in patterns of risk and protective factors within ethnic groups.

Two general patterns are worth noting. First, among generic indicators of status factors, personal and social resources, and stressors, many more indicators were significantly associated with prevalence of DSM-IV disorders for EA youth than for either AA or MA youth. In fact, what is striking is that the role of risk and protective factors extant in the literature were indeed associated with risk of disorder among EA youth but not AA and MA youth. Perhaps this should come as no surprise because most research presented in the literature has been based on samples of EA youth or samples for which data for different ethnic groups have not been disaggregated.

When data are disaggregated, as we did, markedly fewer of these generic factors were related to prevalence of psychiatric disorders among AA or MA youth. In fact, on average, only a third to half as many associations were significant. The good news is that, for those that were significant, the associations were in the same direction as for EA youth. So, there was some evidence for the role of generic factors.

The most surprising finding, in some respects, was the lack of association between indicators of ethnic experience. There was essentially none after controls for generic risk and protective factors (Roberts and Roberts 2007). We should note that others have reported little explanatory power is observed for ethnic-specific risk and protective factors in adolescent mental health. For example, LaFromboise and colleagues (2007) report multivariate analyses indicated no significant effects of cultural factors on risk of suicidal ideation among adolescents from Northern plains tribes.

How do these results compare with other studies? Costello and others (1997) find no overall difference between EA and Native American youth. Angold and colleagues (2002) find no overall difference between EA and AA youth. Turner and Gil (2002) find AA youth have lower rates of any disorder (overall prevalence). More recently, Simpson and coauthors (2005) report Hispanic or Latino youth have lower prevalence of emotional or behavioral problems than either blacks or whites. Chen, Killeya-Jones, and Vega (2005) find that using the DISC Predictive scales in a national sample of 12- to 17-year-olds, AAs reported more symptom clusters than EAs or Latino Americans.

Looking at specific disorders, Costello and colleagues (1997) report higher rates of substance use disorders among Native American youth, whereas Angold and others (2002) report lower rates of depressive disorders among AAs. Turner and Gil (2002) find AA participants have lower rates of affective disorders and substance use disorders than other groups. Chen and coauthors (2005) find AAs report more anxiety cluster symptoms but fewer affective and substance abuse cluster symptoms than their EA or Latino American counterparts.

The results reported here, and those from other studies cited, albeit limited in number and scope, clearly suggest that the developmental epidemiology of psychiatric disorders may differ across ethnic groups, as the literature from developmental psychopathology suggests (Cicchetti and Cohen 1995; Costello and Angold 1995; Rutter and Sroufe 2000; Sroufe and Rutter 1984). That is, ethnicity appears to influence differences in symptom presentation as well as the association of risk and protective factors with symptom manifestation and disorder (Boyce et al. 1998; Cicchetti and Toth 1998; Costello, Foley, and Angold 2006).

Immigration, Acculturation, and Mental Health

As noted initially, there were too few immigrant MA youth in our sample to permit comparisons of foreign-born and U.S. youth. But, in this regard, why would we expect immigrant youth to manifest greater risk for mental health problems? Data for adults suggest that the prevalence of psychiatric disorders is generally lower for the foreign born, and the longer the immigrants have been in the United States the greater the risk for developing psychiatric disorders (Burnam et al. 1987; Grant et al. 2004; Ortega et al. 2000; Vega, Gil, and Wagner 1998). However, Alegría and coauthors (2007) report that foreign nativity is protective only for some Latino groups (e.g., Mexicans) but not others (e.g., Puerto Ricans) and that protection varies by disorder. Alegría and her colleagues then demonstrate that it is not immigrant status per se that protects from psychiatric disorder, but rather family, contextual, and social status factors associated with nativity and age of arrival in the United States. The literature on Latino children is very limited, and the results for the role of immigration and acculturation is not very informative (see Duarte et al. 2008; Portes and Rumbaut 1990; and Suárez-Orozco, Todorova, and Louie 2002). The samples are small, the array of factors examined is limited, different ethnic/nativity groups are not compared, and the focus typically is not on a full array of psychiatric disorders using diagnostic criteria.

One theme that emerges from these few studies is the importance of family context, in particular parenting behavior. We also found in Teen Health 2000 that family context, in particular family stress, increased risk across all groups (Roberts and Roberts 2007). We found that ethnic stress increased risk for anxiety, mood, and any disorder among MA youth but only disruptive disorders among AA youth. School and neighborhood stress also increased risk for most disorders in all three groups. Thus, our results clearly confirm the results of Alegría and colleagues (2007) for adults, albeit not for the role of immigrant status since we could not examine this.

Role of Parents

As we have noted above, the role of parents in understanding the etiology of mental health problems among children and adolescents is important. This goes beyond the obvious role of family history and genetics, reflecting the role of social and cultural factors. However, it also applies to our conceptual frameworks, which attempt to better understand help-seeking and use of mental health services.

As pointed out in chapter 13, help-seeking reflects in large part parental definitions of need for services. In Teen Health 2000, EA caregivers were more likely than the two groups of minority parents to rate the mental health of their adolescents as worse; rate their life satisfaction as worse; and report they thought their adolescents had an emotional, behavioral, drug, or alcohol problem in the past year. These differences were large, with the prevalences reported by EA caregivers about twice those of the two minority groups. Introduction of statistical controls for age and gender of youth, education of caregiver, youth-reported DISC-IV disorders, ratings of youth functional impairment, and parent mental health did not alter this pattern appreciably. And, as is clear from our results presented above, there are essentially no differences in mental health problems reported by youth (Roberts et al. 2005a, b).

More recently, Duarte and colleagues (2008) find that more acculturated Puerto Rican parents report more mental health problems in their children than less acculturated parents. The concept of different thresholds for symptom recognition across cultural groups has been well documented by Weisz and colleagues (Weisz and McCarty 1999; Weisz et al. 1988, 1993).

Understanding factors affecting decisions to seek help for child mental health problems is important. It is generally parents who refer children for help. It appears that psychological factors (attitudes, beliefs, intentions) are relatively more important than practical considerations (financial costs, availability, time) when deciding to seek care.

Cultural influences appear to affect recognition of mental health problems among minority youth. The results of our study strongly suggest that different threshold effects are one such factor. Minority parents appear to have higher thresholds for problem recognition. Logically, and empirically, one would predict such a threshold effect to influence use of mental health services. There is evidence indicating this is so.

The literature documents that African and Latino American youth are less likely to use specialty mental health services than other groups. Unpublished data from our study also document such ethnic differentials. For specialty mental health services, there is a strong tendency for EA youth to receive such services, contrasted with AA and MA youth. For example, EA youth are twice as likely to use any outpatient services, 2.5 times more likely to see a mental health professional, twice as likely to see a primary care physician for mental health problems, and 1.5 times more likely to use school-based mental health counseling or therapy than are AA or MA youth. Thus, in Teen Health 2000, ethnic differentials in parent reports of mental health functioning of their children parallel differences in use of specialty mental health services by their children.

These data, along with data from other studies, suggest strong ethnocultural differences in factors promoting or inhibiting help-seeking for child emotional or behavioral problems. As noted above, barriers to services use may be both psychosocial and practical. At this point, neither clinicians nor researchers fully understand how these factors play out in parental decisions to seek, and receive, services from the specialty mental health sector.

Given the available evidence, the question arises that if prevalence rates are similar between ethnic groups of adolescents (and that appears to be the case) but the risk factor profiles may differ considerably, then what forces might be involved in the etiology of the disorder? The answer to this question, we submit, will require more extensive and systematic examination of the role of risk and protective factors within different ethnic groups. In particular, studies need to include many of the measures that have been suggested in recent articles on correlates of mental health in minority populations (Brown 2003; Lincoln et al. 2003; Ryff, Keyes, and Hughes 2003; Wu et al. 2003). Brown (2003) suggests that we examine outcomes such as nihilism, suppressed anger, delusional denial, and racial paranoia. Others argue that constructs such as hedonic and eudaimonic well-being should be examined in regard to ethnicity and mental health (Ryan and Deci 2001; Ryff et al. 2003). Researchers have little examined the role of personality traits, although some authors have suggested this may account for substantial variance in risk across adolescent ethnic groups (e.g., Blumentritt, Angle, and Brown 2004). Lincoln and colleagues (2003) find negative interaction operates differently across ethnic groups in risk for psychological distress. Beyond generic coping skills, there may be ethnic-specific coping strategies in response to stress related to ethnic experiences (Noh et al. 1999; Williams, Takeuchi, and Adair 1992). Alegría and coauthors (2007) suggest further that concepts drawn from acculturation and acculturative stress, nativity/generational status, social networks and social support, family context, and neighborhood context also be included, a theme echoed by Duarte and colleagues (2008).

However, as Boyce and Fuligni (2007) note, there is little agreement on what cultural processes are most salient for mental health across different life stages. Not surprisingly, studies of the epidemiology of psychiatric disorders reflect different conceptual frameworks and measurement strategies. As a result, analytic models have been severely underspecified. For example, in its 2001 report, the National Advisory Mental Health Council Workgroup on Child and Adolescent Mental Health Intervention Development and Deployment stated that most research studies on child and adolescent interventions have not attended to relevant issues of race, ethnicity, and culture. Little has changed since because the epidemiologic research has not provided the necessary evidence base.

Beyond these considerations, Boyce and Fuligni (2007) have suggested guidelines that could help remedy the paucity of data on culture and mental health more generally:

1. Integrate social and cultural influences into multidimensional approaches for human development including basic biological and behavioral levels.
2. Include descriptions of participants that include characteristics of culture, race, and ethnicity that respect heterogeneity of diverse subgroups.
3. Operationalize constructs relevant to social and cultural processes and mental health with increased specificity to increase the knowledge base.
4. Further develop and disseminate methodologies that disentangle developmental issues, psychiatric diagnoses, and mechanisms related to mental health disparities.
5. Consider the social and cultural environment in gene and environment interactions that occur across the life span and may affect mental health.

Until our explanatory models more fully reflect the cultural context of groups and our designs permit analyses of the role of putative etiologic factors within and between ethnic and nativity groups, our understanding of the etiology of psychiatric disorders among ethnic minority children and adolescents will remain limited.

NOTE

This research was supported in part by grants MH49764 and MH65606 (R. Roberts) and PO1-1MH59876 (M. Alegría).

1. See American Psychiatric Association (2000); Birmaher, Ryan, and Williamson (1996); Gore, Aseltine, and Colton (1992); Graham, Turk, and Verhulst (1999); Hops et al. (1990); Lewinsohn et al. (1993); Roberts (2000); Roberts and Roberts (2007); and Rutter (2000).

REFERENCES

Alegría, Margarita, Norah Mulvaney-Day, Maria Torres, Antonio Polo, Zhum Cao, and Glorisa Canino. 2007. "Prevalence of Psychiatric Disorders across Latino Subgroups in the United States." *American Journal of Public Health* 97:68–75.

American Psychiatric Association. 2000. *Diagnostic and Statistical Manual of Mental Disorders: DSM-IV.* 4th ed. Text Revision. Washington, DC: American Psychiatric Association.

Angold, Adrian, Alaattin Erkanli, Elizabeth M. Farmer, John A. Fairbank, Barbara J. Burns, Gordon Keeler, and E. Jane Costello. 2002. "Psychiatric Disorder, Impairment, and Service Use in Rural African American and White Youth." *Archives of General Psychiatry* 59:893–901.

Birmaher, Boris, Neal D. Ryan, and Douglas E. Williamson. 1996. "Childhood Adolescent Depression: A Review of the Past Ten Years—Part I." *Journal of the American Academy of Child & Adolescent Psychiatry* 35:1427–39.

Blumentritt, Tracie L., Rebecca L. Angle, and Jeffrey M. Brown. 2004. "MACI Personality Patterns and DSM-IV Symptomology in a Sample of Troubled Mexican-American Adolescents." *Journal of Child and Family Studies* 13:163–78.

Boyce, Cheryl A., and Andrew J. Fuligni. 2007. "Issues for Developmental Research among Racial/Ethnic Minority and Immigrant Families." *Research in Human Development* 4(1/2): 1–17.

Boyce, W. Thomas, Ellen Frank, Peter S. Jensen, Ronald C. Kessler, Charles A. Nelson, and Lawrence Steinberg. 1998. "MacArthur Foundation Research Network on Psychopathology and Development, Social Context in Developmental Psychopathology: Recommendations for Future Research from the MacArthur Network on Psychopathology and Development." *Development & Psychopathology* 10:143–64.

Brown, Tony. 2003. "Critical Race Theory Speaks to the Sociology of Mental Health: Mental Health Problems Produced by Racial Stratification." *Journal of Health and Social Behavior* 44:292–301.

Burnam, M. Audrey, Richard L. Hough, Javier I. Escobar, Marvin Karno, Diane M. Timbers, Cynthia A. Telles, and Ben Z. Locke. 1987. "Six-Month Prevalence of Specific Psychiatric Disorders among Mexican Americans and Non-Hispanic Whites in Los Angeles." *Archives of General Psychiatry* 44(8): 687–94.

Chen, Kevin W., Ley A. Killeya-Jones, and William A. Vega. 2005. "Prevalence and Co-occurrence of Psychiatric Symptoms Clusters in the U.S. Adolescent Population Using DISC Predictive Scales." *Clinical Practice and Epidemiology in Mental Health* 1:22.

Cicchetti, Dante, and Donald J. Cohen. 1995. "Perspectives on Developmental Psychopathology." In *Developmental Psychopathology. Vol. 1: Theory and Methods,* edited by Dante Cicchetti and Donald J. Cohen (3–22). New York: John Wiley & Sons.

Cicchetti, Dante, and Sheree Toth. 1998. "The Development of Depression in Children and Adolescents." *American Psychologist* 53:221–41.

Costello, E. Jane, and Adrian Angold. 1995. "Developmental Epidemiology." In *Developmental Psychopathology. Vol. 1: Theory and Methods,* edited by Dante Cicchetti and Donald J. Cohen (23–56). New York: John Wiley & Sons.

Costello, E. Jane, Debra L. Foley, and Adrian Angold. 2006. "10-Year Research Update Review: The Epidemiology of Child and Adolescent Psychiatric Disorders: II. Developmental Epidemiology." *Journal of the American Academy of Child & Adolescent Psychiatry* 45:8–25.

Costello, E. Jane, Elizabeth M. Farmer, Adrian Angold, Barbara J. Burns, and Alaattin Erkanli. 1997. "Psychiatric Disorders among American Indian and White Youth in Appalachia: The Great Smoky Mountains Study." *American Journal of Public Health* 87:827–32.

Duarte, Cristiane, Hector Bird, Patrick Shrout, Ping Wu, Roberto Lewis-Fernandez, Sa Shen, and Glorisa Canino. 2008. "Culture and Psychiatric Symptoms in Puerto Rican Children: Longitudinal Results from One Ethnic Group in Two Contexts." *Journal of Child Psychology and Psychiatry* 49(5): 563–72.

Gore, Susan, Robert H. Aseltine, and Mary E. Colton. 1992. "Social Structure, Life Stress, and Depressive Symptoms in a High School Aged Population." *Journal of Health and Social Behavior* 33:97–113.

Graham, Philip, Jeremy Turk, and Frank C. Verhulst. 1999. *Child Psychiatry: A Developmental Approach.* Oxford: Oxford University Press.

Grant, Bridget F., Frederick S. Stinson, Deborah S. Hasin, Deborah A. Dawson, S. Patricia Chou, and Karyn Anderson. 2004. "Immigration and Lifetime Prevalence of DSM-IV Psychiatric Disorders among Mexican Americans and Non-Hispanic Whites in the United States: Results from the National Epidemiologic Survey on Alcohol and Related Conditions." *Archives of General Psychiatry* 61:1226–33.

Hops, Hyman, Peter M. Lewinsohn, Judy A. Andrews, and Robert E. Roberts. 1990. "Psychological Correlates of Depressive Symptomatology among High School Students." *Journal of Clinical Psychology* 19:210–19.

LaFromboise, Teresa D., Lisa Medoff, Caroline C. Lee, and Alex Harris. 2007. "Psychosocial and Cultural Correlates of Suicidal Ideation among American Indian Early Adolescents on a Northern Plains Reservation." *Research in Human Development* 4(1/2): 119–43.

Lewinsohn, Peter M., Hyman Hops, Robert E. Roberts, John R. Seeley, and Judy A. Andrews. 1993. "Adolescent Psychopathology: I. Prevalence and Incidence of

Depression and Other DSM-III-R Disorders in High School Students." *Journal of Abnormal Psychology* 102:133–44.

Lincoln, Karen D., Linda M. Chatters, and Robert J. Taylor. 2003. "Psychological Distress among Black and White Americans: Differential Effects of Social Support, Negative Interaction, and Personal Control." *Journal of Health and Social Behavior* 44:390–407.

Mirowsky, John, and Catherine E. Ross. 1980. "Minority Status, Ethnic Culture, and Distress: A Comparison of Blacks, Whites, Mexicans, and Mexican Americans." *American Journal of Sociology* 86:479–95.

Noh, Samuel, Morton Beiser, Violet Kasper, Feng Hou, and J. Rummens. 1999. "Perceived Racial Discrimination, Depression, and Coping: A Study of Southeast Asian Refugees in Canada." *Journal of Health and Social Behavior* 40:193–207.

Ortega, Alexander, Robert Rosenheck, Margarita Alegría, and Rani Desai. 2000. "Acculturation and the Lifetime Risk of Psychiatric and Substance Use Disorders among Hispanics." *Journal of Nervous and Mental Disease* 188:725–35.

Portes, Alejandro, and Rubén Rumbaut. 1990. *Immigrant America: A Portrait.* Berkeley: University of California Press.

Roberts, Robert E. 2000. "Depression and Suicidal Behaviors among Adolescents: The Role of Ethnicity." In *Handbook of Multi-Cultural Mental Health,* edited by I. Cuellar and F. H. Paniagua (360–80). San Diego, CA: Academic Press.

Roberts, Robert E., and Catherine R. Roberts. 2007. "Ethnicity and Risk of Psychiatric Disorder among Adolescents." *Research in Human Development* 40(1-2): 89–118.

Roberts, Robert E., Catherine R. Roberts, and Wenyaw Chan. 2006. "Ethnic Differences in Symptoms of Insomnia among Adolescents." *Sleep* 29:359–65.

Roberts, Robert E., Catherine R. Roberts, and Yun Xing. 2006. "Prevalence of Youth-Reported DSM-IV Psychiatric Disorders among African American, European, and Mexican American Adolescents." *Journal of the American Academy of Child & Adolescent Psychiatry* 45(11): 1329–37.

———. 2007. "Are Mexican American Adolescents at Greater Risk of Suicidal Behaviors?" *Suicide and Life-Threatening Behavior* 37(1): 10–21.

Roberts, Robert E., Margarita Alegría, Catherine R. Roberts, and Irene G. Chen. 2005a. "Concordance of Reports of Mental Health Functioning by Adolescents and Their Caregivers: A Comparison of European, African, and Latino Americans." *Journal of Nervous and Mental Disease* 193(8): 1–7.

———. 2005b. "Mental Health Problems of Adolescents as Reported by Their Caregivers: A Comparison of European, African, and Latino Americans." *Journal of Behavioral Health Services Research* 32(1): 1–13.

Rutter, Michael. 2000. "Psychosocial Influences: Critiques, Findings, and Research Needs." *Development and Psychopathology* 12:375–405.

Rutter, Michael, and L. Alan Sroufe. 2000. "Developmental Psychopathology: Concepts and Challenges." *Development and Psychopathology* 12:265–96.

Ryan, Richard M., and Edward L. Deci. 2001. "On Happiness and Human Potentials: A Review of Research on Hedonic and Eudaimonic Well-Being." *Annual Review of Psychology* 52:141–66.

Ryff, Carol, Corey Keyes, and Diane Hughes. 2003. "Status Inequalities, Perceived Discrimination, and Eudaimonic Well-Being: Do the Challenges of Minority Life Hone Purpose and Growth?" *Journal of Health and Social Behavior* 44:275–91.

Simpson, G. A., B. Bloom, R. A. Cohen, S. Blumberg, and K. H. Bourdon. 2005. "U.S. Children with Emotional and Behavioral Difficulties: Data from the 2001, 2002, and 2003 National Health Interview Surveys." *Advance Data* (360):1–13.

Sroufe, L. Alan, and Michael Rutter. 1984. "The Domain of Developmental Psychopathology." *Child Development* 55:17–29.

Suárez-Orozco, Carola, Irina Todorova, and Josephine Louie. 2002. " 'Making Up for Lost Time': The Experience of Separation and Reunification among Immigrant Families." *Family Process* 41(4): 625–43.

Turner, R. Jay, and Andres G. Gil. 2002. "Psychiatric and Substance Use Disorders in South Florida: Racial/Ethnic and Gender Contrasts in a Young Adult Cohort." *Archives of General Psychiatry* 59:43–50.

Vega, William A., Andres G. Gil, and Eric Wagner. 1998. "Cultural Adjustment and Hispanic Adolescent Drug Use." In *Drug Use and Ethnicity in Early Adolescence,* edited by William A. Vega and Andres G. Gil (125–48). New York: Plenum Press.

Weisz, John R., and Carolyn A. McCarty. 1999. "Can We Trust Parent Reports in Research on Cultural and Ethnic Differences in Child Psychopathology? Using the Bicultural Family Design to Test Parental Culture Effects." *Journal of Abnormal Psychology* 108(4): 598–605.

Weisz, John R., Marian Sigman, Bahr Weiss, and Julie Mosk. 1993. "Parent Reports of Behavioral and Emotional Problems among Children in Kenya, Thailand, and the United States." *Child Development* 64:98–109.

Weisz, John R., Somsong Suwanlert, Wanchai Chaiyasit, Bahr Weiss, Bernadette R. Walter, and Wanni Wibulswadi Anderson. 1988. "Thai and American Perspectives on Over- and Undercontrolled Child Behavior Problems: Exploring the Threshold and Model among Parents, Teachers, and Psychologists." *Journal of Consulting and Clinical Psychology* 56(4): 601–609.

Williams, David R., David T. Takeuchi, and Russell K. Adair. 1992. "Socioeconomic Status and Psychiatric Disorder among Blacks and Whites." *Social Forces* 71:179–94.

Wu, Zheng, Samuel Noh, Violet Kaspar, and Christoph M. Schimmele. 2003. "Race, Ethnicity, and Depression in Canadian Society." *Journal of Health and Social Behavior* 44:426–41.

16

Reducing the Unequal Burden of Mental Health for Hispanic Children in Immigrant Families

Cheryl Anne Boyce

The increasing diversity of the United States brings exciting challenges and prospects for the mental health of children and their families. By 2050, the share of minority children in the United States is projected to rise to 62 percent, with a significant increase in Hispanic children. By mid-century, 39 percent of the child population is projected to be Hispanic, while the share of single-race, non-Hispanic white children is projected to trend downward to 38 percent.[1]

An Unequal Burden

Over the past two decades, the general health of the nation has improved. Yet disparities continue in the burden of illness and death experienced by African Americans, Hispanics, Native Americans, Alaska Natives, Asians, and Pacific Islanders. The most striking disparities include shorter life expectancy as well as higher rates of cardiovascular disease, cancer, infant mortality, birth defects, asthma, diabetes, stroke, sexually transmitted diseases, and mental illness among minority populations (National Institutes of Health [NIH] 2002).

Health disparities are associated with both racial/ethnicity and socioeconomic status (Adler and Rehkopf 2008), further complicating understanding of Hispanic children in immigrant families. The growing economic inequality among Hispanic populations suggests that a large number of Hispanic immigrant children may live in poverty, thereby increasing the risk and burden of serious mental health problems as these children age. Given the predicted large increase of immigrant populations, specifically Hispanic children living in immigrant families, it remains unknown what the actual impact of health disparities will mean for mental health and educational service systems. Most people with a history of mental disorder have first onsets in childhood or adolescence (Kessler and Wang 2008). Immigrant children may be at heightened risk for depression, anxiety disorders, substance abuse, and other mental health problems (Lamberg 2008). The growing number of Hispanic children in immigrant families suggests that identifying and preventing mental disorders for these children and adolescents may be a key emerging issue for the long-term public health of our nation.

The U.S. Surgeon General charged the nation to consider culture, race, and ethnicity in an effort to eliminate mental health disparities (U.S. Department of Health and Human Services [HHS] 2001) and to address the specific mental health needs of children, including service disparities of access and quality (U.S. Public Health Service [PHS] 2000). Key findings were that racial and ethnic minorities were less likely to have access to available mental health services, were less likely to receive needed mental health care, often received poorer quality mental health care, and were significantly underrepresented in mental health research (HHS 2001). Therefore, disease burden and suffering associated with mental disorders falls disproportionately on ethnic minority populations (NIH 2002). Hispanic immigrant children will make up the majority of the U.S. ethnic minority population and may shoulder an unequal majority of the burden of mental health disparities.

Several reports have attempted to disentangle the factors that contribute to health disparities. In 2002, the Institute of Medicine published *Unequal Treatment: Confronting Racial and Ethnic Disparities in Health Care.* This landmark report concluded that racial and ethnic minorities tend to receive lower-quality health care than nonminorities, even when such access-related factors as health insurance and economic status are controlled (Smedley, Stith, and Nelson 2003). The report further suggested that the reasons for the differences included patient stereotyping, misallocation of resources, culturally related communication barriers, provider biases, and uncertainty regarding appropriate treatment. The lack of culturally appropriate education programs to improve patient knowledge regarding access to care and clinical decisionmaking increased the health care disparity (Smedley et al. 2003). Similar factors were identified in the 2001 Surgeon General's report on mental health and care considerations for mental health service, access, and use by Hispanic immigrant families.

Notably, the President's New Freedom Commission on Mental Health (HHS 2003) was the first comprehensive study of the nation's public and private mental health service delivery systems in nearly 25 years. The commission examined the U.S. mental health system, including both private- and public-sector providers, and found disproportionate disparities in service delivery. Among other related service systems, the lack of a culturally responsive mental health system contributed to inappropriately placing minorities in the criminal and juvenile justice systems. In response to their findings, the commission called for transformation in mental health services to eliminate disparities through improved access to quality care that is culturally competent and in rural and remote geographical areas (HHS 2003). While there are promising changes in culturally and linguistically competent values, attitudes, policy, structures and practices, and/or evidence-based treatments for children's mental health care,[2] a transformation has yet to be fully realized for Hispanic children of immigrant families.

An Unequal Debt

Without a transformation in our nation's approach to the mental health needs of Hispanic immigrant children, the gap in their psychological functioning and well-being will continue to exist and may widen. A challenge remains concerning how to best quantify pervasive disparities among racial/ethnic minority populations and the cost of these disparities. Educators have proposed that focusing on an achievement gap is actually "misplaced" and have called for a focus on the "educational debt" that has accumulated over time (Landson-Billings 2006). This concept is analogous to the idea of a "mental health debt" due to the continuing gap or disparity in mental health care. Specifically, the burden of mental health disparities among Hispanic children in immigrant families can have immeasurable economic and personal costs. Calculating the unequal debt from the unequal burden of mental health disparities requires examination of historical factors, sociopolitical histories, and even moral considerations.

Economic costs include mental health service costs and educational services costs. Children may not function at their highest potential when suffering from emotional and behavioral problems. Those children who manifest serious emotional disturbance often require additional special education services and may enter juvenile justice systems. As children transition to adulthood, mental health problems can also lead to lost productivity. On the more severe spectrum of mental disorder, the costs of mental health disorders can include reduced years of life and mortality. Perhaps most profound, the human costs are innumerable from suffering and disability from mental illness. There is also the potential for intergenerational effects and cumulative costs if disparities are not reduced within a future generation.

The unequal debt of mental health disparities for Hispanic immigrant children also includes underlying historical, economic, sociopolitical, and moral components (e.g., Landson-Billings 2006). The historical debt includes long-term disparities in education and income for Hispanic families. Factors such as legal status influence education, income, and the availability and use of mental health services. In addition, a lack of culturally appropriate mental health services has remained a long-standing problem, despite promising efforts in enhancing cultural competence among providers. The sociopolitical debt includes a social and political history of Hispanic immigrant populations and their migration to the United States. Geographically, the Hispanic population originates from locations throughout the world with different sociopolitical histories (i.e., variability in political environments, education systems, civic engagement processes, and economic circumstances). The heterogeneity of Hispanic immigrants also includes variability in reason for migration, socioeconomic status at time of migration, and family composition. Despite the multiple underlying factors, a disparity in the provision of evidence-based and optimal services for Hispanic children of immigrant families means that the nation is not providing for a significant population of its children. These racial/ethnic disparities in the systems that serve children are deemed by some as immoral,[3] therefore contributing to a moral debt.

Reducing Disparity and Debt through Research and Dissemination

Regrettably, there has been limited inclusion of Hispanic immigrant children and their families in research and community-based participatory research, services, and interventions among Hispanic populations to inform culturally responsive mental health and educational systems. Federal agencies such as the National Institutes of Health require including children and racial/ethnic minorities in research where possible.[4] However, a recent review of National Institute of Mental Health–funded clinical trials published between 1995 and 2004 in five major mental health journals found that most studies reported gender information and gender representation, but less than half provided complete racial and ethnic information (Mak et al. 2007).

Increased participation in clinical research by diverse populations is necessary but insufficient (Boyce and Fuligni 2007). Attention to acculturative processes and the depth of the immigrant experience are fundamental constructs for participants with diverse backgrounds. While some research studies may exclude Hispanic immigrant children and their families as participants because of the complexities of their experience, other researchers have recently advanced relevant research constructs of the immigrant experience. For example, research suggests a complex relationship between nativity and the risk for psychiatric illness including the age of arrival and the developmental stage of the immigrant when moving to the United States (Alegría et al. 2007). While some research findings suggest that Latino immigrants benefit from a protective context in their country of origin (e.g., protection from substance disorders), particularly if they immigrated to the United States as adults (Alegría et al. 2008), other data suggest that this is not always the case. For example, in the case of Mexican Americans, ethnic experiences may not be protective (Roberts and Roberts 2007). Differences between immigrants versus nonimmigrant U.S. Latinos also complicate methodologies. There is limited evidence on developmental risk patterns for mental health and substance use disorders affected by specifics of the immigration experience of Hispanic youth.

Culturally informed and anchored methodologies (Hughes and Seidman 2002; Quintana et al. 2006) can enhance inclusive research and clarify the impact of the immigrant experience. Research studies may address cultural context through variables that examine the individual's experience, family, community, chronology of movement and place, and language use and proficiency (Boyce and Fuligni 2007). Parents of Latino children give key messages about race and discrimination through racial socialization, which has been linked to emotional and behavioral functioning (Hughes 2003). Yet traditional psychological and educational histories and measurement batteries do not ask for information about these immigrant experiences.

Paradigms of geography and place matter for understanding the lives of Hispanic immigrant children. Recently, an Institute of Medicine Study examined economic indicators, geographical differences, and residential patterns for health disparities among the 100 largest metropolitan areas (Institute of Medicine 2008, 32). The best neighborhood environments for Hispanic children were Ann Arbor, Michigan; Cincinnati, Ohio; and Washington, D.C., while Bakersfield, California; Providence, Rhode Island; and Springfield, Massachusetts, were found among the worst neighborhood environments for Hispanic children. Language factors are also significant for Hispanic immigrant children. Non-English-speaking participants, including parents of immigrant children and other familial data informants, may need additional considerations to enhance the cultural congruence of measurement. Translation of measures into native languages is not enough; the underlying constructs must be understood by the respondents. Nonetheless, linguistic factors and cultural congruence of measures are not routinely considered to build culturally informed research.

Addressing the research challenges and complexities of Hispanic children in immigrant families will increase our knowledge about emotional and behavioral functioning and risk for all children. As advances are made, we will need to translate our knowledge quickly into empirically validated practice and policy for mental health as well as education and juvenile justice. Given the projections for mid-century estimates, we have time to prepare for the existing Hispanic immigrant children and future migrations to reduce disparities and reduce the debt. However, unless we act quickly, the burden may increase and the debt and future costs may increase with negative trajectories for emotional, behavioral, and educational outcomes.

Service systems for mental and physical health, behavior, education, and justice may suffer if needs of Hispanic immigrant children are not considered. The infrastructure of these service systems must be prepared for the needs of an increasing Hispanic immigrant child population. Moreover, empirically validated treatments for dissemination within mental health service systems and educational systems need to have validity for the diverse needs and experiences of Hispanic immigrant children.

In chapter 13, Alegría and colleagues identify potential mechanisms for service disparities for Hispanic immigrant children, including the failure of health care markets and behavioral and educational settings. The role of youth and teacher communication, mismatch of appropriate services, community trust issues, and limited workforce availability are also considered as factors contributing to health service disparities. Several strategies have shown promise to reduce these service disparities.

Placing mental health services within other key systems such as education can improve access (PHS 2003). Schools can serve as familiar bases for service and supports for Hispanic immigrant children and families. School mental health has already proven a promising system structure for improving mental health among children (American Academy of Pediatrics Committee on School Health 2004; Hoagwood and Erwin 1997; Nabors and Reynolds 2000). Specifically, services provided through school mental programs can overcome various barriers to care, such as limited finances, lack of health insurance, and language differences, faced by many Latino children (Garrison, Roy, and Azar 1999). Culturally informed teacher training for new and existing education personnel may also influence behavioral and educational disparities.

Disparate, differential pathways and service use by Hispanic immigrant children and families could be reduced through quality improvement in school and other community-based services. Addressing historical traumas from various immigrant experiences, cultural mistrust, and discrimination can build community trust in behavioral health and educational systems that serve the needs of Hispanic families. Offering incentives for culturally informed training and bilingual language fluency for providers could increase the workforce of service providers.

Despite adversity experienced in the country of origin and/or in the United States, some immigrant Hispanic children fare better than others. A differential outcome or resilience in the face of adversity is a highly complex construct (Luthar and Brown 2007; Luthar, Cicchetti, and Becker 2000). As we continue to disentangle gene and environment relationships for risk or resilience for mental disorder, the case of immigrant Hispanic children becomes an interesting example of environmental influences for risk and resilience. Variable immigrant experiences and environments may place Hispanic children at risk or contribute toward resiliency for mental health problems. Sensitive, critical periods of development may be more stressful and affect outcomes for emotional and behavioral functioning, while other developmental periods may be protective. Immigration by Hispanic populations may be more protective or risky at various developmental time points. Much can be learned from positive trajectories or resilience of Hispanic immigrant children and their families to benefit all children. It is hoped that through research, dissemination, and rapid translation into services and policy, the unequal burden of mental health for Hispanic children in immigrant families may be eliminated and the unequal debt will be reduced.

NOTES

The views expressed are those of the author and do not necessarily represent the views or policy of the U.S. Department of Health and Human Services.

1. See U.S. Census Bureau, "An Older and More Diverse Nation by Midcentury," press release CB08-123, August 14, 2008, http://www.census.gov/Press-Release/www/releases/archives/population/012496.html.

2. See National Center for Cultural Competence, 2008, "Promising Practices," http://www11.georgetown.edu/research/gucchd/nccc/resources/practices.html.

3. See Marian Wright Edelman, February 9, 2009, "The Cradle to Prison Pipeline: America's New Apartheid," http://www.huffingtonpost.com/marian-wright-edelman/the-cradle-to-prison-pipe_b_165163.html.

4. See "NIH Policy and Guidelines on the Inclusion of Children as Participants in Research Involving Human Subjects," http://grants.nih.gov/grants/guide/notice-files/not98-024.html, and "NIH Policy and Guidelines on the Inclusion of Women and Minorities as Subjects in Clinical Research—Amended, October 2001," http://grants.nih.gov/grants/funding/women_min/guidelines_amended_10_2001.htm.

REFERENCES

Adler, Nancy F., and David H. Rehkopf. 2008. "U.S. Disparities in Health: Descriptions, Causes, and Mechanisms." *Annual Review of Public Health* 29:235–52.

Alegría, Margarita, William Scribney, Meghan Woo, Maria Torres, and Peter Guarnaccia. 2007. "Looking Beyond Nativity: The Relation of Age of Immigration, Length of Residence, and Birth Cohorts to the Risk of Onset of Psychiatric Disorders for Latinos." *Research in Human Development* 4(1/2): 19–47.

Alegría, Margarita, Glorisa Canino, Patrick E. Shrout, Meghan Woo, Naihua Duan, Doryliz Vila, Maria Torres, Chih-nan Chen, and Xiao-Li Meng. 2008. "Prevalence of Mental Illness in Immigrant and Non-Immigrant U.S. Latino Groups." *American Journal of Psychiatry* 165(3): 359–69.

American Academy of Pediatrics Committee on School Health. 2004. "Policy Statement: School-Based Mental Health Services." *Pediatrics* 113(6): 1839–45.

Boyce, Cheryl A., and Andrew J. Fuligni. 2007. "Issues for Developmental Research among Racial/Ethnic Minority and Immigrant Families." *Research in Human Development* 4(1/2): 1–17.

Garrison, Ellen Greenberg, Ila S. Roy, and Viviana Azar. 1999. "Responding to the Mental Health Needs of Latino Children and Families through School-Based Services." *Clinical Psychology Review* 19(2): 199–219.

HHS. See U.S. Department of Health and Human Services.

Hoagwood, Kimberly, and Holly D. Erwin. 1997. "Effectiveness of School-Based Mental Health Services for Children: A Ten-Year Research Review." *Journal of Child and Family Studies* 6(4): 435–51.

Hughes, Diane. 2003. "Correlates of African American and Latino Parents' Messages to Children about Ethnicity and Race: A Comparative Study of Racial Socialization." *American Journal of Community Psychology* 31(1/2): 15–33.

Hughes, Diane, and Edward Seidman. 2002. "In Pursuit of a Culturally Anchored Methodology." In *Ecological Research to Promote Social Change: Methodological Advances from Community Psychology,* edited by Tracey A. Revenson, Anthony R. D'Augelli, Sabine E. French, Diane L. Hughes, David Livert, Edward Seidman, Marybeth Shinn, and Hirokazu Yoshikawa (243–55). New York: Kluwer Academic/ Plenum Publishers.

Institute of Medicine. 2008. *Challenges and Successes in Reducing Health Disparities: Workshop Summary.* Washington, DC: National Academies Press.

Kessler, Ronald C., and Philip S. Wang. 2008. "The Descriptive Epidemiology of Commonly Occurring Mental Disorders in the United States." *Annual Review of Public Health* 29:115–29.

Lamberg, Lynne. 2008. "Children of Immigrants May Face Stresses, Challenges That Affect Mental Health." *Journal of the American Medical Association* 300(7): 780–81.

Landson-Billings, Gloria. 2006. "From the Achievement Gap to the Education Debt: Understanding Achievement in U.S. Schools." *Educational Researcher* 35(7): 3–12.

Luthar, Suniya S., and Pamela J. Brown. 2007. "Maximizing Resilience through Diverse Levels of Inquiry: Prevailing Paradigms, Possibilities, and Priorities for the Future." *Development & Psychopathology* 19:931–55.

Luthar, Suniya S., Dante Cicchetti, and Bronwyn Becker. 2000. "The Construct of Resilience: A Critical Evaluation and Guidelines for Future Work." *Child Development* 71(3): 543–62.

Mak, Winnie W. S., Rita W. Law, Jennifer Alvidrez, and Eliseo J. Pérez-Stable. 2007. "Gender and Ethnic Diversity in NIMH-Funded Clinical Trials: Review of a Decade of Published Research." *Administration and Policy in Mental Health and Mental Health Services Research* 34(6): 295–310.

Nabors, Laura A., and Matthew W. Reynolds. 2000. "Program Evaluation Activities: Outcomes Related to Treatment for Adolescents Receiving School-Based Mental Health Services." *Children's Services: Social Policy, Research, and Practice* 3(3): 175–89.

National Institutes of Health. 2002. *Strategic Research Plan and Budget to Reduce and Ultimately Eliminate Health Disparities Volume I.* Bethesda, MD: National Institutes of Health. http://ncmhd.nih.gov/our_programs/strategic/pubs/VolumeI_031003EDrev.pdf.

NIH. See National Institutes of Health.

PHS. See U.S. Public Health Service.

Quintana, Stephen M., Frances E. Aboud, Ruth K. Chao, Josefina Contreras-Grau, William E. Cross, Jr., Cynthia Hudley, Diane Hughes, Lynn S. Liben, Sharon Nelson-Le Gall, and Deborah L. Vietze. 2006. "Race, Ethnicity, and Culture in

Child Development: Contemporary Research and Future Directions." *Child Development* 77(5): 1129–41.

Roberts, Robert E., and Catherine R. Roberts. 2007. "Ethnicity and Risk of Psychiatric Disorder among Adolescents." *Research in Human Development* 4(1/2): 89–117.

Smedley, Brian D., Adrienne Y. Stith, and Alan R. Nelson. 2003. *Unequal Treatment: Confronting Racial and Ethnic Disparities in Health Care.* Washington, DC: National Academies Press.

U.S. Department of Health and Human Services. 2001. *Mental Health: Culture, Race, and Ethnicity—A Supplement to Mental Health: A Report of the Surgeon General.* Rockville, MD: U.S. Department of Health and Human Services, Substance Abuse and Mental Health Services Administration, Center for Mental Health Services.

———. 2003. *New Freedom Commission on Mental Health. Achieving the Promise: Transforming Mental Health Care in America.* Rockville, MD: U.S. Department of Health and Human Services.

U.S. Public Health Service. 2000. *Report of the Surgeon General's Conference on Children's Mental Health: A National Action Agenda.* Washington, DC: Department of Health and Human Services.

17

The Bumpy Road Ahead for Hispanic Families

Matthew Hall and Anna R. Soli

Over the past four decades, the United States has undergone rapid ethnic change. Consider that in 1970, 1 in 20 Americans were of Hispanic ethnicity; by 2010, nearly 1 in 6 will be. Over the past six years, Hispanics have accounted for half of the nation's population growth; if the future is anything like the past, their young ages, elevated fertility rates, and consistently high levels of Latin American immigration ensure that the Hispanic contribution to population change will be substantial. As baby boomers age into retirement, the fuel for the nation's economic engine is also increasingly being provided by the Hispanic population. In 2007–08, Hispanics accounted for two-fifths of the growth in the labor force and had higher labor force participation rates than any other racial or ethnic group. While all signs point to an American future chartered by Hispanics, the road for them is anything but smooth. On multiple levels, the Hispanic experience is unique. And, even in comparison to earlier arrivals to the United States, Hispanics' contexts of departure, reception, and migration are distinct.

If a clear message is to be drawn from the chapters in this book, it is that the current state of affairs for the Hispanic community is bleak: accessibility and use of social and health services are limited, Hispanic neighborhoods are segregated and of low quality, Hispanic children exhibit many risk factors associated with poor school performance, and complex family arrangements potentially hinder sociocultural incorporation. While there are reasons to believe the future will be brighter than the past, ensuring so requires a bold policy agenda that recognizes the challenges faced by Hispanic families. The call for action is urgent, not only because of the moral imperative it presents, but also because the country simply cannot afford the human and economic costs of inaction.

In this final chapter, we have three main goals. First, we provide an overview of the state of the Hispanic family based on the insights garnered from the chapters in this volume. Second, we discuss both the limitations of prior research and the avenues future research will need to explore. Finally, we highlight the policy implications of the research presented in this volume.

The Challenges and Prospects for Hispanic Families

The authors of this volume have identified several troubling signs for the prospects of Hispanic families. In considering these challenges, we focus on four domains that have important implications for Hispanic adaptation: political and legal structures, residential contexts, the education system, and sociocultural incorporation.

Political and Legal Structures

Political support mechanisms and institutional contexts play integral parts in Hispanic incorporation (Alba and Nee 2003). Equal opportunity employment and housing laws, for example, create a supportive environment for new arrivals searching for work and shelter. But, in other institutional capacities, recent immigrants are severely handicapped. Eligibility for public support programs is one area in which immigrants are placed at a systematic disadvantage. This is particularly true in the context of welfare reform, where immigrant restrictions on federal programs were expected to amount to nearly half of the total savings generated from reform (Congressional Budget Office 1995). Federal guidelines deem recent immigrants ineligible for cash-assistance welfare programs (e.g., TANF) and several in-kind programs (e.g., Food Stamps). And, although some states have crafted their own programs to aid this vulnerable population (Graefe et al. 2008), the institutional context for new immigrants in need of support remains unwelcoming.

Undoubtedly, the foremost institutional challenge for many Hispanic families is their legal status. Estimates pin the unauthorized migrant population at around 12 million—about 30 percent of all immigrants—and a large majority of them hail from Latin American countries (Passel and Cohn 2008). Nearly 7 million families in the United States have an unauthorized household head or spouse, and nearly 5 million children are unauthorized themselves or are the offspring of unauthorized parents. Unauthorized migrants are restricted by the type and quality of work available and by housing policies that prohibit them from receiving loans and, in some municipalities, renting property. These factors alone have implications for the children of undocumented migrants, yet they are further institutionally disadvantaged by a lack of educational opportunities (see chapters 9 and 10, this volume).

As Graefe describes in chapter 14, access to and use of health insurance among Hispanic children is also poor. In fact, their rates of uninsurance are more than three times those of non-Hispanic white children. Even among the insured, Hispanic children are substantially more likely to be covered by second-rate public health providers. The challenges do not end with insurance, however. As Alegría and colleagues maintain in chapter 13, Hispanic children receive inferior health treatment compared with non-Latino white children. Discriminatory practices may play a role in sustaining these health service disparities. More likely, health officials may lack cultural competence or, at least, face challenges in delivering health services because of language barriers. In light of these institutional constraints, the Hispanic "health paradox" becomes even more perplexing (see Markides and Coreil 1986).

Despite proudly proclaiming to be a nation of immigrants, the United States exhibits widespread hostility toward and discrimination against immigrants, particularly those of Hispanic origin (see Pager and Shepherd 2008). Policy decisions are partially a reflection of this animosity toward new arrivals, and state legislatures have responded by proposing bills to essentially bar the undocumented and their foreign-born children from receiving public services. In 2007, for example, Arizona offered legislation mandating that undocumented migrants and their children "not be eligible to receive any public benefit provided by this state or any political subdivision of this state."[1] These institutional constraints not only have tangible effects for Latinos, they also send a frosty welcome message.

Residential Contexts

Neighborhood conditions affect individuals' and families' lives in important ways. Racial and ethnic disparities in neighborhood conditions are thus a powerful form of social inequality, and a group's ability to close these gaps is a means for assessing social status. Traditionally, these inequalities have been gauged by evaluating the spatial distance between minority and majority groups. Despite the fact that black-white segregation has declined steadily over the past few decades, the segregation of Hispanics from non-Hispanic whites has changed little (Logan, Stults, and Farley 2004), or by some measures actually increased (Iceland, Weinberg, and Steinmetz 2002). As Alba and colleagues show in chapter 1, the typical Hispanic child lives in a neighborhood in which half of his or her neighbors are also Hispanic.

Underlying segregation research is the assumption that the separation of social groups results in unequal opportunities and differential exposure to social pathologies. But, this assumption is based largely on involuntary processes that have isolated African Americans in inner-city ghettos. One major contribution of Alba and colleagues is their finding that, like black children, the segregation of Hispanic children from white children corresponds with inequalities in neighborhood quality. The typical Hispanic child in the United States is raised in a neighborhood where most adults have no more than a high school education, where one-fifth of households are in poverty, and where half of households do not own their homes. In these neighborhoods, recent arrivals to the United States, those not fluent in English, and overcrowded households are overrepresented because of the large presence of immigrants in the Hispanic population. For Hispanic children living in "immigrant rich" communities, residential environments are markedly worse, even more so than those of black youth. On a more optimistic note and consistent with the spatial assimilation model, Alba and colleagues find that neighborhood conditions do improve as Hispanic families' incomes rise; but they never (even at high income levels) attain the conditions of white families.

The redistribution of Hispanic families away from traditional immigrant gateways and into new destinations across the American landscape has both positive and negative ramifications. On the positive side, as Alba and colleagues show, the residential circumstances of Hispanics in new destinations areas are significantly better than those in more traditional destinations. This is largely a reflection of the fact that there are too few immigrants in new destinations to form the most disadvantaged "immigrant rich" neighborhoods. In addition, migrants who move to new destination areas tend to have lived in the United States longer and have more education (Stamps and Bohon 2006). Capps, Koball, and Kandel also find in chapter 2 that Hispanics in new rural destinations fare well economically. On the negative side, however, because institutional supports are weak, services delivered poorly, and immigrant receptivity often less welcoming, neighborhood conditions in new destinations may deteriorate as these areas lose their "new" status. Thus, Hispanic success in these areas may be short lived.

But, the rise in new destinations begs the question: What will happen to Hispanic neighborhoods in traditional gateways? Drawing parallels with the plight of inner-city black neighborhoods resulting from middle-class black flight (see Wilson 1996), there are worries about the formation of permanent Hispanic ghettos in large immigrant hubs as more established and better-resourced members depart. The finding in chapter 1 that there is a high presence of "idle youth" (i.e., unemployed, high school dropouts) in immigrant-rich neighborhoods is a troubling sign of what may come. A driving force in the development of these durable Hispanic ghettos is the concentration of unauthorized Hispanic immigrants, a segregating process that results from limited job and housing opportunities and fears of being identified as undocumented. The increased crackdown on undocumented immigration in rural areas, via industrial raids and restrictions on public services, may force unauthorized immigrants to concentrate in fewer areas. Clearly then, residential integration is a mixed blessing, facilitating incorporation and leading to greater tolerance while at the same time further isolating those left behind in Hispanic barrios.

Education System

Measures of academic performance and educational attainment provide perhaps the most dismal picture of Hispanic progress. Hispanic immigrant students have lower grades and test scores and are more likely to drop out of high school and college than both non-immigrant Hispanics and non-Hispanic whites. Suárez-Orozco and colleagues (chapter 9) chronicle the inequalities in academic outcomes at each point in the educational pipeline and suggest that these disparities widen as children age. As Pong points out in chapter 11, however, it is important to consider long-term trends, as well as how immigration processes affect academic outcomes (see also Oropesa and Landale 2009). In particular, she suggests that the Hispanic high school dropout rate may be inflated because many adolescent immigrants never intended to enroll in school after their arrival to the United States. In addition, the age at which immigrant children enter the U.S. education system and the number of school transitions they make have important implications for their achievement.

One of the most daunting challenges faced by Hispanic immigrant students and the schools that serve them is the language barrier. Many children begin school with few or no English skills and lack familiarity with basic vocabulary. The rate of preschool enrollment among Hispanics is low (chapters 8 and 9, this volume), creating a large gap between native and immigrant children in cognitive and academic skill when they enter kindergarten. Throughout the school years, the quality, implementation, and consistency of English as a second language programs vary widely, and many students fail to develop the academic English skills necessary for higher education (chapter 9, this volume). In addition, few classroom teachers are trained to address language difficulties, and some may have misperceptions about language acquisition. The language issue is compounded in schools experiencing "triple segregation"—a combination of high poverty levels, a concentration of minority students, and linguistic isolation. These schools are greatly lacking in resources, experience elevated levels of violence, and struggle to provide an environment conducive to learning.

A second educational challenge is the need for meaningful ties between schools and parents. This is a paradoxical problem because, despite many obstacles, Hispanic students and their parents care deeply about education (chapter 12, this volume). In fact, many immigrant parents cite better educational opportunities for their children as a central reason for migration. Many schools, however, do not have policies that require parental outreach (chapter 10, this volume); this problem is further complicated by the fact that many immigrant parents do not speak English. In addition, immigrant parents may not have access to informal advice networks where parents share important information about such topics as school policies and practices or higher education (chapter 12).

Beyond poor ESL services and parental outreach, many schools fail to address needs specific to Hispanic students. Social and cultural adaptation can be daunting for children, and when schools are ill equipped to aid in the process, unique problems may arise. Quintana's (chapter 4) qualitative work with a bilingual school in Madison, Wisconsin, suggests just this: schools undergoing ethnic turnover may be unable to handle the complex issues of ethnic conflict and discrimination that result from school diversification. By ignoring cultural distinctions, the "color-blind" approach frequently adopted by schools may actually be counter-productive for promoting racial and ethnic integration. The legal status of students and their parents is also a major concern. Unauthorized parents may be reluctant to enroll their children in special programs (e.g., Title I) out of fear of dealing with school officials. Students interested in attending college face an uncertain future if they or their parents are unauthorized because of barriers to financial aid and college admission (chapter 9). In sum, the authors in this volume point to the many ways in which the U.S. education system is not currently prepared to tackle the complex challenges faced by Latino immigrant students.

Sociocultural Incorporation

The family is an important context for development, and it plays a central role in Hispanic culture (Marín and Marín 1991). The immigration process has major implications for family structure and relationships. In some cases, family members are separated during the early phases of migration. As Van Hook (chapter 6, this volume) points out, children may experience disruptive residential transitions, and the co-residence of family and friends among new immigrants can create complex home arrangements. Family members' legal status presents a particularly difficult challenge. Although some children may be U.S. citizens by virtue of their birthplace, their parents, older siblings, or other household members may face the uncertainty of being unauthorized, so family members live in fear of being separated.

In addition to these structurally grounded challenges, immigrants must confront the difficult task of adapting to a new society, and the family is one context in which acculturation issues may be particularly salient. Updegraff and Umaña-Taylor (chapter 5, this volume) highlight the variability of acculturation within families and show that family members may experience U.S. culture in very different ways. Their findings emphasize the interdependence among Latino family members and suggest that how individual family members negotiate dual cultural frames has implications for the family as a whole. Cultural adaptation may also create tensions between family members. For example, Alegría and colleagues suggest that when parents experience acculturative stressors, it diminishes their children's well-being. Children who are expected to take on the role of interpreter for their parents may feel overly burdened and unprepared for such responsibility.

Parents and siblings are important sources of support and strength for Hispanic children, but they may also play a part in some of the problems faced by immigrant youth. Corona (chapter 7, this volume) reports that Hispanics are at high risk for negative sexual outcomes and that parent-adolescent communication about sexual health may be particularly effective in reducing their risk of teenage pregnancy and sexually transmitted infections. However, Corona notes that even when Hispanic teenagers express the desire to communicate openly about sexual topics, many parents are reluctant to engage in such conversations. Work by Updegraff and Umaña-Taylor (chapter 5) demonstrates that siblings also influence one another both positively and negatively. For example, older siblings with high academic aspirations may enhance those of their younger siblings. Under some circumstances, however, older siblings may introduce their younger siblings to deviant peers and encourage participation in risky behavior. Hispanic parents are significantly less likely to recognize and to seek professional help for their children's emotional and behavioral problems than white parents, perhaps because of language issues or cultural stigma against mental health services. Because of these low levels of service use, a disproportionate number of immigrant children may suffer from untreated mental health problems (chapters 13 and 15, this volume). Thus, although Hispanic families provide many important resources for children, they also face numerous challenges in adapting to life in the United States.

Limitations and Future Directions for Research with Hispanic Populations

Although the body of literature devoted to studying Hispanic immigrants has grown in the past two decades, our knowledge is still limited in several ways. Perhaps the most obvious limitation is the lack of research on the consequences of undocumented status. Legal status is often the elephant in the room in studies on Hispanic populations. Because of sensitivity concerns, legal status is rarely included as a direct question in surveys or interviews; in fact, the government places several restrictions on federally funded researchers' ability to inquire about immigrants' legality.

There are also problems related to mismeasurement, as unauthorized migrants may be reluctant to identify their legal status, and coverage, if the undocumented are less likely to participate in surveys or interviews. This is unfortunate because some preliminary evidence suggests that unauthorized status has implications for neighborhood quality (chapter 1), access to health and educational services (chapter 9), family relationships (chapter 6), and individual adjustment (chapter 13). Although there is no clear solution to this limitation, the effects of legal status must be considered and addressed as thoroughly as possible in all research on Hispanic immigrant populations. In addition to the major limitation presented by undocumented status, more work is needed in several different areas including a more refined approach to Hispanic diversity, greater consideration in measuring cultural processes, and research designs that recognize the multigenerational nature of incorporation.

Hispanic Diversity

The population in question in this volume is considerably more diverse than the umbrella terms Hispanic or Latino suggest. Dozens of Latin American countries send immigrants to the United States each year; these countries and the immigrants making the journey differ greatly economically, politically, socially, and culturally. Compare, for example, Cuban and Mexican immigrants. The former are largely drawn from the upper echelons of the socioeconomic structure, tend to be lighter skinned, can more easily find work in professional jobs, and acquire legal status as political refugees. For these reasons, Cuban immigrants tend to settle in the United States permanently. The latter tend to be rural migrants lacking professional skills. Because of their often-undocumented status, Mexican immigrants are frequently employed in the periphery of the labor market. Thus, two "Hispanic" immigrants may face very different challenges in the United States.

The distinction between origin groups is still less than ideal, as even Hispanic subpopulations are considerably diverse. For example, not all Mexican immigrants hail from rural areas; nor do they all cross the border illegally. Thus, researchers need to consider differences both within and between countries of origin. It is also imperative for future studies to distinguish between U.S.-born and foreign-born Hispanics. Immigrants and natives differ in important ways, whether it is access to public services (chapter 14), neighborhood quality (chapter 1), educational outcomes (chapter 11), or family structure and cultural orientations (chapters 5 and 6).

Hispanics also differ in terms of race. "Hispanicity" is an ethnic term that, while arguably becoming racialized, is independent of skin tone. White and black Hispanics experience their new country in very different ways (see Waters 1994). For example, black Hispanics, while having more years of schooling, have lower wages, higher rates of unemployment and poverty, and live in neighborhoods with more non-Hispanic blacks than white Hispanics (Logan 2003). For many Hispanic immigrants, race in their home country has both class and skin color undertones, and many new arrivals are surprised to find out that they are not considered "white" or, for many West Indians, are seen as "black" by the native masses.

This inattention to the diversity of the Hispanic population is not a new concern, and researchers have made great strides in documenting the unique experiences of Hispanic subgroups. The emergence of large-sample datasets that capture the heterogeneity among Hispanics (e.g., the American Community Survey) and targeted data projects that seek to better understand the progress of Latinos (e.g., Latin American Migration Project, Latino National Political Survey) is promising. Equally important are ethnographies and case studies that are able to paint a more nuanced picture of Hispanic groups' experiences not typically captured by quantitative analyses (e.g., chapter 7, this volume; Menjívar 2006).

Measuring Cultural Processes

A common theme in this volume is the need for direct, comprehensive measures of cultural processes. Assimilation is a social construct measured in various ways. English language use and the number of years in the United States are often used as proxies for acculturation, but as Updegraff and Umaña-Taylor argue in chapter 5, it is necessary to develop multidimensional measures to capture the complexity of this process. They cite the importance of examining intra-culture variation in acculturation processes and recognizing that individuals from the same ethnic group, and even from the same family, experience incorporation differently.

Van Hook seconds this call in chapter 6 but warns that researchers must be careful in evoking culture as an explanation, since migration and adaptation often necessitate household strategies and coping mechanisms that are unique from the majority population but that do not necessarily reflect cultural proclivities. It is thus imperative to develop cross-national comparative studies that consider cultural practices in both host and origin countries to better understand what constitutes culture. Nonetheless, even when interethnic discrepancies are observed under this study design strategy, researchers must be cautious in assuming that the differences are due to Hispanics holding more traditional cultural orientations than the host population.

Another concern is that ethnicity and socioeconomic status are often confounded (chapters 5 and 13, this volume). An important goal for future research is to separate the effects of low socioeconomic status, minority status, and cultural processes. The problem is both conceptual and statistical. Conceptually, because the Hispanic population is economically disadvantaged, research quickly becomes detached from reality when relying too heavily on *ceteris paribus* arguments. At the same time, ethnic-based forces (e.g., racism, culture) can be wrongly attributed when socioeconomic status is ignored. Technically, because Hispanic and non-Hispanic distributions on socioeconomic characteristics are rarely equivalent, statistical assumptions can easily be violated and bias may be introduced. One way that future researchers can address this issue is to recruit samples with a broad range of socioeconomic statuses to capture middle- and upper-class Hispanics as well as the more commonly studied working-class populations.

Failing to consider findings within a broader historical context is an additional limitation of current scholarship. There are historical precedents for major immigrant waves into the United States, and there is much to be learned from those past examples. The future has the potential for large-scale changes for ethnic minorities, as suggested by Alba and colleagues' and Capps and colleagues' analyses of new Hispanic destinations (chapters 1 and 2). Careful comparative work needs to be undertaken before we can know whether Hispanics will catch up with the majority population in the same way that European immigrants did in the previous century.

Incorporation Is Multigenerational

In order to make these comparisons and assess the future for Hispanics, research needs to better recognize that incorporation into the mainstream does not happen overnight. Rather, it is a multigenerational process. This was certainly true for earlier immigrants to the United States, such as Italians and Jews, who were initially considered racial minorities by native whites (Foner 2000). The assimilation trajectory of these earlier immigrants was also much bumpier than popularly believed (Gans 1992). At this early stage in Hispanic assimilation, with large first- and second-generation cohorts, but much smaller older ones, it would be hasty to claim that all is lost. As Trejo (chapter 3, this volume) and Alba and Nee (2003) make clear, evidence of contemporary assimilation among the new Hispanic immigrants actually is apparent.

The problem researchers face when gauging Hispanic progress is not only one of temporal prematurity, but also one of data and measurement. The decennial census no longer includes questions regarding parents' places of birth, and few large-scale surveys link respondents across generations, making the identification of second and higher generation Hispanics challenging. Trejo warns in chapter 3 that even when data on later Hispanic generations are available, the selectivity of Hispanic identification can lead to inaccurate assessments of the progress of these groups. Crucial in this process is the intermarriage (and subsequent childbearing) of Hispanics and non-Hispanics. Compared with other racial and ethnic groups, Hispanic intermarriage is relatively high (Lichter and Qian 2004). This is problematic for Hispanic studies because the children of these families are less likely to self-identify as Hispanic than are the children of endogamously married Hispanics. And, because those who intermarry tend to be better educated and more highly paid, estimates of the success of later-generation Hispanics will be biased downward.

A related issue is the need for longitudinal research strategies, not only to examine Hispanic outcomes over time and across generations, but also to accurately specify analytic models. Graefe (chapter 14) and Trejo (chapter 3) show the importance of using lagged models when evaluating Latino progress, both to identify causal relations correctly and as a tool to account for unobserved heterogeneity. For example, Graefe demonstrates that because of the endogeneity between mental/behavioral health and health care coverage, properly modeling the argument that limited health coverage leads to poorer health outcomes requires measures of both variables at multiple time points.

Where to Go: Policy Implications

This volume documents the dire position of Hispanics in the United States and echoes the resounding call for policy changes that will improve the lives of Hispanic children and their families. To effect positive change, it is necessary to implement a comprehensive program that uses multiple entry points and addresses the spectrum of immigrant challenges, from political and structural barriers to individual and sociocultural difficulties. Fuligni (chapter 12) stresses that time is of the essence; there is a very narrow window of opportunity within which to act. According to Boyce (chapter 16, this volume), the key is to be able to translate our knowledge quickly into empirically validated practices and policies. This is a daunting task, but the contributors to this volume have taken a major step toward articulating an agenda for policy change that can reduce disparities between Hispanic children and the majority population.

Of foremost political importance for Hispanic families is addressing immigrants' legal status. This issue affects not only the undocumented, but also authorized Hispanic immigrants and their native compatriots who are often falsely assumed to be in the country illegally. Most relevant to the chapters in this volume is the negative impact of Hispanic parents' legal status on their children, regardless of the children's legal status. In particular, policies should ensure that citizen children of undocumented migrants receive access to the benefits and services for which they are eligible, notwithstanding their parents' legal status. Policymakers need to recognize that the children of the unauthorized are here to stay, and the current sink-or-swim immigration policy that ignores the challenges children and families face is both fiscally and socially costly (chapter 9). This issue should not, as it often is, be conflated with U.S. immigration policy, but rather needs to be considered separately and pragmatically.

Gaining political support for such initiatives is integral to their ultimate success, but recent legislative attempts have shown that public support of immigrant policy reform is equally important. A majority of Americans believe that undocumented migrants should be required to return home and that immigrants are more a burden than an asset to the country (Pew Research Center 2006). These attitudes are particularly prevalent in many new destination areas to which Latinos are flocking. While some of these sentiments are undoubtedly race-based, many are founded on views of immigrants as economic threats and misunderstandings about immigrants' use of public services. Targeted public awareness campaigns that address misperceptions about these issues may improve natives' attitudes toward immigrants and better the receptivity climate in new destinations. Community organizations that seek not only to cater directly to the needs of Hispanic families (e.g., assist in language acquisition or the search for work), but that bring Hispanics and non-Hispanics together to work on common goals may likewise be a valuable means for improving interethnic relations (chapter 4).

But the political response cannot stop there. In addition to bold structural reforms, policies aimed directly at addressing the challenges elucidated in this volume will be needed. Reform in the education system may be one of the most efficient ways to reach a large number of Latino immigrant children. Early childhood education and school readiness are potential targets for reform: a body of research points to the benefits of intervening as early as possible. Hernandez and colleagues (chapter 8) and Suárez-Orozco and colleagues (chapter 9) cite the prohibitive cost of early childhood education as a major barrier to preschool enrollment among Latinos, a problem that can in part be addressed with federally funded child development programs such as those proposed by Duncan, Ludwig, and Magnuson (2007). In addition to financial support, many preschools as well as elementary and secondary schools would benefit from culturally and linguistically appropriate resources to create a more welcoming atmosphere for Latino students and their parents. Along the same lines, efforts to address teachers' misconceptions about Hispanic culture and reduce the possibility of discrimination against Hispanic students could help improve the educational outcomes of immigrant children.

There is also room for improvement in how schools address the challenges faced by students with limited English proficiency. For example, ESL programming could be made more effective by ensuring consistency across grade levels and through explicit classroom teacher training on how to handle language difficulties (chapter 9). In addition, research by Pong (chapter 11) suggests that it may be beneficial to target immigrant children who transition into the U.S. education system after having some years of education abroad for remedial classes to bring them up to speed with their classmates. Another important step may be to rethink the high-stakes testing environment imposed by the No Child Left Behind Act and consider a model that does not require high levels of English proficiency. Under current educational policy regimes, federal school funding is largely determined by students' test scores. Resources in schools with many English-language-learner students are thereby systematically limited. Poor performance on these tests negatively influences students not only via its role on school funding, but also through students' lowered educational aspirations and expectations.

Schools can also implement policies designed to involve parents in their children's education. As Donato and Marschall (chapter 10) suggest, parental interest in education is linked to students' subsequent achievement. Strategies to involve Hispanic parents must consider parents' language capabilities and legal status, as well as their expectations and beliefs about the role of teachers and schools in their children's education. Schools must also be sensitive to parents' work schedules and financial resources and develop flexible strategies to accommodate them as best as possible.

Any policy change concerning immigrant children should capitalize on the many strengths of the Latino family, such as their strong beliefs in the value of education, motivations to achieve (chapter 12), and commitments to family and community (chapters 5, 7, and 8). For example, Corona's work with the Talking Parents, Healthy Teens program suggests that a promising avenue for promoting healthy sexual practices and reducing sexually transmitted infections among Hispanic adolescents is to incorporate multiple family members (i.e., mothers, fathers, and siblings) into discussions about sexual behavior. She demonstrates that creative strategies for getting parents involved, such as delivering the program in the parents' workplace, can have important implications for parental participation. Parents can also play a major role in improving the mental health outcomes of Hispanic children. Efforts to inform Hispanic parents about how to identify risk factors for behavioral, emotional, and substance use problems in their children may be an important step toward reducing disparities between Hispanic and white children in the use of mental health services (chapters 13 and 15).

Concluding Remarks

The resounding theme from the chapters in this volume is that the current state of affairs for the Hispanic family is poor. These families face serious challenges in gaining political and legal support, their residential environments are spatially segregated and lacking in resources, Hispanic children suffer from low academic achievement and struggle with a language barrier, and the stress of adjusting to a new country can create sociocultural challenges for families and individuals. Yet, while these problem areas represent bumps in the road ahead for Hispanics, they should not be considered insurmountable. Hispanic families have many strengths to draw on, and a bold policy agenda that works with these strengths can redress many of these challenges. This volume represents an important step toward illuminating how the lives of Hispanic immigrant families can be improved, and it points to the possibility of a smoother road ahead.

NOTES

The authors are grateful to Alan Booth, Nancy Landale, Susan McHale, Katherine Stamps, Carolyn Scott, and Nate Walters for their useful suggestions in improving this chapter.

    1. Migration Policy Institute and NYU School of Law, "State Responses to Immigration: A Database of All State Legislation," http://www.migrationinformation.org/datahub/statelaws.cfm.

REFERENCES

Alba, Richard D., and Victor Nee. 2003. *Remaking the American Mainstream: Assimilation and Contemporary Immigration.* Cambridge, MA: Harvard University Press.

Congressional Budget Office. 1995. "Immigration and Welfare Reform." Paper 36. Washington, DC: Congressional Budget Office.

Duncan, Greg J., Jens Ludwig, and Katherine A. Magnuson. 2007. "Reducing Poverty through Preschool Interventions." *The Future of Children* 17:143–60.

Foner, Nancy. 2000. *From Ellis Island to JFK: New York's Two Great Waves of Immigration.* New Haven, CT: Yale University.

Gans, Herbert. 1992. "Comment: Ethnic Invention and Acculturation, A Bumpy-Line Approach." *Journal of American Ethnic History* 12:42–52.

Graefe, Deborah Roempke, Gordon F. De Jong, Matthew Hall, Samuel W. Sturgeon, and Julie Van Eerden. 2008. "Immigrants' TANF Eligibility, 1996–2003: What Explains the New across-State Inequalities?" *International Migration Review* 42:89–133.

Iceland, John, Daniel H. Weinberg, and Erika Steinmetz. 2002. *Racial and Ethnic Residential Segregation in the United States, 1980–2000.* Special Report Series, CENSR # 3. Washington, DC: U.S. Census Bureau.

Lichter, Daniel T., and Zhenchao Qian. 2004. *Marriage and Family in a Multiracial Society.* New York and Washington, DC: Russell Sage Foundation and Population Reference Bureau.

Logan, John R. 2003. *How Race Counts for Hispanic Americans.* Albany, NY: Lewis Mumford Center.

Logan, John R., Brian J. Stults, and Reynolds Farley. 2004. "Segregation of Minorities in the Metropolis: Two Decades of Change." *Demography* 41:1–22.

Marín, Gerardo, and Barbara V. Marín. 1991. *Research with Hispanic Populations.* Newbury Park, CA: SAGE Publications.

Markides, Kyriakos S., and Jeannine Coreil. 1986. "The Health of Hispanics in the Southwestern United States: An Epidemiological Paradox." *Public Health Reports* 101: 253–65.

Menjívar, Cecilia. 2006. "Liminal Legality: Salvadoran and Guatemalan Immigrants' Lives in the United States." *American Journal of Sociology* 111:999–1037.

Oropesa, R. S., and Nancy S. Landale. 2009. "Why Do Immigrant Youth Who Never Enroll in U.S. Schools Matter? An Examination of School Enrollment among Mexicans and Non-Hispanic Whites." *Sociology of Education* 82(3): 240–66.

Pager, Devah, and Hana Shepherd. 2008. "The Sociology of Discrimination: Racial Discrimination in Employment, Housing, Credit, and Consumer Markets." *Annual Review of Sociology* 34:181–209.

Passel, Jeffrey S., and D'Vera Cohn. 2008. *Trends in Unauthorized Immigration.* Washington, DC: Pew Hispanic Center.

Pew Research Center. 2006. *America's Immigration Quandary: No Consensus on Immigration Problems or Proposed Fixes.* Washington, DC: Pew Research Center.

Stamps, Katherine, and Stephanie Bohon. 2006. "Educational Attainment in New and Establishing Latino Metropolitan Destinations." *Social Science Quarterly* 87:1225–40.

Waters, Mary C. 1994. "Ethnic and Racial Identities of Second-Generation Black Immigrants in New York City." *International Migration Review* 28:795–820.

Wilson, William Julius. 1996. *When Work Disappears: The World of the New Urban Poor.* New York: Alfred A. Knopf.

About the Editors

Nancy S. Landale is professor of sociology and demography and director of the Population Research Institute at The Pennsylvania State University. Dr. Landale's areas of interest include family demography, immigration and immigrant incorporation, the Hispanic population, and children's health. She is widely known for her research on the implications of migration to the U.S. mainland for family processes and maternal/infant health among Puerto Ricans. Her current work focuses on the educational and health outcomes of Mexican children of immigrants. A major issue addressed in this work is how migration and assimilation affect key aspects of the family environment (socioeconomic status, family relationships, and health practices), thereby influencing children's outcomes. Dr. Landale is also currently conducting a study of academic achievement among children of legal immigrants. Dr. Landale served as a member of two panels of the National Research Council that are relevant to the present volume: "The Health and Adjustment of Immigrant Families and Children" (1996–98) and "Transforming Our Common Destiny: Hispanics in the U.S." (2003–05).

Susan McHale is director of the Social Science Research Institute and The Children, Youth, and Family Consortium and professor of human development at The Pennsylvania State University. Her research focuses on children's and adolescents' family roles, relationships, and daily experiences and how these family dynamics are linked to youth development and adjustment. She is particularly interested in gender dynamics in families. Dr. McHale has studied how differential family roles and experiences of sisters and brothers are linked to the choices they make in education, work, and family formation. Dr. McHale's research also investigates the cultural contexts of family dynamics including how parents' and youths' sociocultural values, practices, and daily experiences have implications for family life and youth adjustment in African American and Mexican American families. Most recently, she has extended her research to examine the role of family dynamics, particularly family stressors, in youths' physical health.

Alan Booth is Distinguished Professor of Sociology, Demography, and Human Development & Family Studies at The Pennsylvania State University. He has been a senior scientist in Penn State's Population Research Institute since 1991. Dr. Booth has co-organized the university's National Symposium of Family Issues since its inception in 1993. He is the author of more than 100 scholarly articles and 4 books, and editor of 16 volumes. He was editor of *Journal of Marriage and the Family* from 1985 to 1991. Dr. Booth directed a 20-year study of marital instability in a national sample of 2,000 married people. The project has been the basis for many studies on the causes of divorce; the effects of divorce on children's well-being; remarriage and step families; and the effects of having a nonresident parent on psychological distress, educational achievement, romantic relationships, and family formation. A major focus of Booth's research is on hormones (e.g., testosterone and cortisol) and family relationships (i.e., parent-child relationship quality, peer relationships, and marital happiness).

About the Contributors

Richard Alba is a distinguished professor of sociology at the Graduate Center, City University of New York. His teaching and research focus on race/ethnicity and international migration, in the United States and in Europe. His research has been supported by the Guggenheim Foundation, the German Marshall Fund, the National Science Foundation, the National Institutes of Health, and the Russell Sage Foundation. Dr. Alba's most recent book is *Blurring the Color Line: The New Chance for a More Integrated America* (2009).

Margarita Alegría is the director of the Center for Multicultural Mental Health Research at the Cambridge Health Alliance. She is a professor in the department of psychiatry at Harvard Medical School and currently serves as the principal investigator of three National Institutes of Health–funded research studies. Dr. Alegría's published work focuses on the improvement of health care services delivery for diverse racial and ethnic populations, conceptual and methodological issues with multicultural populations, and ways to bring the community's perspective into the design and implementation of health services. Dr. Alegría also conducts research to help understand the factors influencing service disparities, and to test interventions aimed at reducing disparities for ethnic and racial minority groups. Her other work has highlighted the importance of contextual, social, and individual factors that intersect with nativity and are associated with the risk for psychiatric disorders.

Victoria L. Blanchard is a doctoral student in sociology at the University at Albany, State University of New York. Her broad interests include family studies and demography. She is particularly interested in fertility and child well-being. Among other research projects, she has contributed to a meta-analytic study examining the effectiveness of marriage education.

Cheryl Anne Boyce is the chief of the behavioral and brain development branch and associate director for child and adolescent research within the Division of Clinical Neuroscience and Behavioral Research at the National Institute on Drug Abuse, National Institutes of Health, Department of Health and Human Services. In this role, she provides guidance on scientific research programs and consults with federal agencies, those in clinical practice, and the nation's public regarding clinical and translational research, developmental psychopathology, substance use, child abuse and neglect, early childhood, traumatic stress, health disparities, and social and cultural issues.

Randy Capps is a demographer and senior policy analyst at the Migration Policy Institute. Dr. Capps has published national-level reports on trends in the U.S. immigrant labor force, health care coverage of immigrants, health and well-being of young children of immigrants, characteristics of immigrants' children in public schools, and integration of immigrants in rural areas. He recently participated in studies of employment services in the federal refugee resettlement program and the impact of immigration enforcement operations on children of unauthorized immigrants. He is currently investigating workforce preparation programs for immigrant youth and the implementation of agreements that allow state and local police to enforce U.S. immigration laws.

Nicholas J. Carson is a research associate with the Center for Multicultural Mental Health Research at the Cambridge Health Alliance and an instructor in psychiatry at Harvard Medical School. His research focuses on improving the quality of mental health services for culturally and ethnically diverse communities. He has studied mental health service use among Haitian youth as well as culturally sensitive patient activation interventions for adults receiving mental health treatment.

Rosalie Corona is an assistant professor of psychology at Virginia Commonwealth University and the founding director of the VCU Latino

Mental Health Clinic. Dr. Corona's research focuses on health promotion and risk reduction, primarily among African American and Latino youth and youth whose parents are infected with HIV. She conducts qualitative and quantitative community-based studies and has been involved in the development and evaluation of prevention programs aimed at increasing family communication about youth risk behaviors and family health history. Dr. Corona's publications reflect her interdisciplinary work and include manuscripts published in psychology, public health, and medical journals.

Nancy A. Denton is a professor of sociology at the University at Albany, State University of New York, where she is also director of the Lewis Mumford Center for Urban and Regional Research and associate director of the Center for Social and Demographic Analysis. Her research interests include race, residential segregation, urban sociology, demography, and housing. Currently she is working on projects on the neighborhood contexts of children in immigrant families, home ownership, and immigration to upstate New York.

Katharine M. Donato is professor and chair of sociology at Vanderbilt University. Her broad interests focus on social stratification and demography, especially international migration between Mexico and the United States. Dr. Donato's research has addressed questions related to the impact of immigration policy on the economic incorporation of U.S. migrants, the relationship between gender and migration over time and across space, social network and migration effects on the health of Mexican families, and immigrant incorporation in new U.S. destinations. She is currently writing about immigrant parent school involvement in three U.S. cities, a project funded by the National Science Foundation and Russell Sage Foundation. Dr. Donato is also editor of the *American Sociological Review.*

Ilir Disha is a doctoral student in sociology at the University at Albany, State University of New York. His broad research interests focus on the relations between race/ethnicity and crime. His master's thesis focused on anti-Arab/Muslim hate crimes in the immediate aftermath of the events of September 11. He is currently working on his dissertation, which explores the links between immigration and crime. More specifically, the dissertation incorporates measures of segregation and examines the effects of immigrant segregation on urban crime rates.

368 About the Contributors

Andrew J. Fuligni is a professor in the department of psychiatry and biobehavioral sciences and the department of psychology at University of California, Los Angeles. Dr. Fuligni's research focuses on adolescent development among culturally and ethnically diverse populations, with particular attention to teenagers from immigrant Asian and Latin American backgrounds. He is a recipient of the American Psychological Association's Boyd McCandless Award for Early Career Contribution to Developmental Psychology and is a fellow in the American Psychological Association and the Association for Psychological Science. Dr. Fuligni currently is an associate editor of the journal *Child Development.*

Francisco X. Gaytán is an assistant professor of social work at Northeastern Illinois University in Chicago. His research focuses on the socioemotional and academic development of first- and second-generation immigrant youth in the United States. More specifically, he has examined the role of social support and social capital on the cultural, academic, and psychological adaptation of the growing Mexican immigrant student population in New York City.

Deborah Roempke Graefe is a research associate with Penn State's Population Research Institute. Her research uses population-focused approaches to study public policy and family behavior and well-being, including family formation, health, and migration behaviors, particularly regarding immigrant families. Her study of gaps in health insurance coverage, with Pamela Farley Short, demonstrated coverage instability as a widespread problem demanding public policies to improve continuity. Her current health disparities research addresses the importance of residential context, including availability of medical facilities and the immigrant receptivity climate, for health care among children of Mexican immigrants and for immigrants' health-related outcomes.

Matthew Hall is a doctoral candidate in sociology and demography at Penn State with interests in urban sociology, migration and immigration, social demography, and labor markets. His current research activities examine the residential segregation and attainment of new immigrant groups, the impact of immigration on native residential mobility, and the effect of legal status on Mexican immigrants' economic and educational progress.

Donald J. Hernandez is a professor of sociology at Hunter College and The Graduate Center, City University of New York. He recently completed research on 140 indicators of child well-being for race-ethnic/immigrant groups by country of origin for the United States and a study assessing the extent to which socioeconomic disparities versus cultural differences can account for low enrollment in early education programs among Hispanic children. Dr. Hernandez also recently led a UNICEF project to develop internationally comparable indicators for children in immigrant and native-born families in eight affluent countries, and is using the Foundation for Child Development's Index of Child Well-Being to explore race-ethnic, immigrant, and socioeconomic disparities.

William Kandel is an immigration specialist with the Domestic Social Policy Division of the Congressional Research Service, where he specializes in legal immigration policy. Before his current position, he was a sociologist with the Economic Research Service of the U.S. Department of Agriculture where he conducted research on new geographic destinations of rural immigrants, immigrant integration, public policy impacts of rural Hispanic population growth, farm labor, and the role of industrial restructuring in demographic change. Before moving to Washington D.C., he conducted postdoctoral research in international demography and income inequality at Penn State's Population Research Institute. His book, *Population Change and Rural Society,* edited with David Brown of Cornell University, was published by Springer in 2006.

Ha Yeon Kim is a doctoral student of developmental psychology at the Steinhardt School of Culture, Education, and Human Development at New York University. Her broad research interests include immigrant children's academic and psychological adaptation in U.S. schools, focusing on how their English proficiency affects their classroom interaction, relationships, academic beliefs, and performance.

Heather Koball is a senior researcher at Mathematica Policy Research in Princeton, New Jersey. Her training is in demography and statistics. Dr. Koball's main research interest is evaluating the effectiveness of government programs and policies, particularly those that relate to the support of families and the welfare of more vulnerable populations. Her most recent work has focused on the integration of immigrants into new destinations, rural communities; the effectiveness of home visiting programs to reduce child maltreatment; and the relationship between marriage and health in the African American community.

Suzanne Macartney is pursuing her doctoral degree at the University at Albany, State University of New York, where she examines children in immigrant families and their neighborhoods. She is also a poverty analyst for the U.S. Census Bureau in Washington, D.C., where she is researching alternative poverty measures. Her research interests include poverty and social and economic policy.

Melissa Marschall is an associate professor of political science at Rice University and, in 2009–10, a visiting scholar at the Russell Sage Foundation in New York. Marschall's research focuses on local politics, educational policy, participation, and issues of race and ethnicity. Her book, *Choosing Schools: Consumer Choice and the Quality of American Schools* (Princeton University Press, written with Mark Schneider and Paul Teske) received the Policy Studies Association Aaron Wildavsky Award for the Best Policy Book in 2000–01. She is currently writing two books: one examining immigrant parent involvement in schools, communities, and politics; and the other analyzing minority incorporation in local politics.

Brian McKenzie is an analyst for the Journey to Work and Migration Statistics branch of the U.S. Census Bureau and a doctoral candidate at the University at Albany, State University of New York. His academic research explores neighborhood-level variation in spatial mobility and access to opportunity across metropolitan landscapes. McKenzie's most recent work explores access to full-service supermarkets across neighborhoods in the Portland, Oregon, region. The GIS-based project sheds light on the role of public transportation in improving access to community amenities for residents of low-income neighborhoods.

Norah Mulvaney-Day is a research associate at the Center for Multicultural Mental Health Research, Cambridge Health Alliance, and an instructor in psychiatry at Harvard Medical School. Her broad interests focus on the mechanisms that may contribute to the persistence of mental health service disparities across the life span. Much of her research examines reasons for differential access to care at multiple levels of the mental health care system, from individual patient preferences, to community-level factors, to policies that have disproportionate effects on the delivery of care to certain groups. Recent interests include the role of social network factors in health behavior change, and how these factors may facilitate the dissemination of interventions and policies at the community level.

Jeffrey Napierala is a doctoral student in the sociology department at the University at Albany, State University of New York. His general interests are social demography and quantitative research methodology. Much of his research has focused on U.S. immigration, specifically its impacts on incarceration rates of the native born, the incorporation and assimilation of Middle Eastern immigrants, and patterns of Mexican immigration and settlement.

Suet-ling Pong is professor of education, demography, and sociology at Penn State. Dr. Pong's research focuses on children's academic performance and educational attainment, and how they relate to family, parental practices and involvement, teen employment, education policies, family policies, race/ethnicity, gender, and immigrant status. With support from a Fulbright scholarship, Dr. Pong has been studying the integration of immigrant children from mainland China to Hong Kong. More recently, Dr. Pong has been examining how the cognitive performance of immigrants' children is influenced by parents' migration experiences and pre-migration characteristics.

Stephen M. Quintana holds a joint appointment with the University of Wisconsin departments of counseling psychology and educational psychology. His current research involves developing and evaluating a model of children's understanding of social status, which includes ethnicity, race, gender, and social class. Dr. Quintana's multicultural research has focused on students' adjustment to higher education, children's understanding of ethnic prejudice, and multicultural training in professional organizations. He has been associate editor for the *Journal of Counseling Psychology* and editor for *Handbook of Race, Racism, and the Developing Child* as well as the special issue *Race, Ethnicity, and Culture in Child Development*.

Catherine R. Roberts is assistant professor of community psychology at the University of Texas Medical School, Department of Psychiatry and Behavioral Sciences. She has a long-time interest in the effects of social stress on mental health outcomes such as psychiatric disorders, sleep disorders, and suicidal behaviors. Dr. Roberts has conducted research on a specific form of stress, peer victimization and bullying, among adolescents. In her research, Dr. Roberts has focused on developing measures of victimization that better capture gender differences and differences among ethnocultural groups. She has been working on long-term effects of social stress on youth functioning using data from a large, three-wave prospective study of youth (Teen Health 2000) followed from age 12 to age 24.

Robert E. Roberts is professor of behavioral sciences, Division of Health Promotion and Behavioral Sciences, at the School of Public Health, University of Texas Health Science Center at Houston. His research focuses on the role of culture in relation to the etiology and natural history of mental health problems. He has conducted research comparing ethnocultural groups within the United States and cross-national research, examining the cross-cultural reliability and validity of measures. More recently, he has been working on obesity as a risk factor for psychological distress among adolescents and adults. He has published widely on depression, suicidal behaviors, and insomnia comparing European, African, and Latino American youth.

Anna R. Soli is a doctoral candidate in the department of human development and family studies at Penn State. Her broad interests are in family dynamics, sibling relationships, and family-based prevention/intervention programming. Her research focuses on family relationships and how they function as risk and protective factors in shaping youths' individual development and the practical application of this research to family-based prevention/intervention programs. She is also interested in cultural values and practices and their impact on such family dynamics as parenting, co-parenting, and sibling influence processes.

Carola Suárez-Orozco is a professor of applied psychology at NYU Steinhardt School of Culture, Education, & Human Development as well as codirector of Immigration Studies at NYU. She publishes widely in the areas of immigrant families and youth, immigrant identity formation, immigrant family separations, and gendered experiences of immigrant youth. Her books include *Children of Immigration; Learning a New Land: Immigrant Students in American Society; Transformations: Migration,*

Family Life, and Achievement Motivation among Latino Adolescents; and *The New Immigration: An Interdisciplinary Reader.* Professor Suárez-Orozco is a member of the Institute for Advanced Study in Princeton and has received an American Psychological Association Presidential Citation for her contribution to the field.

Stephen J. Trejo is an associate professor of economics at the University of Texas at Austin. His research focuses on public policy issues involving labor markets, including overtime pay regulation, the experiences of immigrants, and obstacles to the economic progress of minority groups. Dr. Trejo's recent work analyzes patterns of intergenerational improvement among Mexican Americans and how selective intermarriage and ethnic identification might bias standard measures of socioeconomic progress for the U.S.-born descendants of Mexican immigrants.

Adriana J. Umaña-Taylor is an associate professor of family and human development at Arizona State University in the School of Social and Family Dynamics. Although her research has included adolescents from various ethnic groups in the United States, the majority of her work has focused on Latino adolescents and their families. She is currently conducting research on adolescents and families of Mexican origin, with one study focusing specifically on Mexican-origin teen mothers, their mother figures, and their infants. Dr. Umaña-Taylor's research interests focus broadly on Latino youth and families and, more specifically, on ethnic identity formation, familial socialization processes, culturally informed risk and protective factors, and psychosocial functioning among Latino adolescents.

Kimberly A. Updegraff is a Cowden Distinguished Professor in the School of Social and Family Dynamics at Arizona State University. Her research focuses on the role of family and peer relationships in youth well-being, with a particular interest in understanding culture and gender dynamics. Her current work involves a longitudinal study of Mexican American families funded by the National Institute of Child Health and Human Development, beginning with youth in early adolescence and following them into young adulthood. The goal is to understand how cultural adaptation processes unfold over time and are linked to youth and parent well-being.

Jennifer Van Hook is an associate professor of sociology at Penn State whose research focuses on the relationships among sending country characteristics, the social and policy contexts of reception in the United States, and the health and well-being of the children of immigrants, including outcomes related to household/family structure, child poverty, welfare receipt, and food security. Her most recent work compares the levels of obesity of Mexican-origin children who live in Mexico with those living in the United States. Dr. Van Hook has also evaluated and revised methods for estimating the size, growth, and characteristics of the unauthorized migrant population living in the United States.

Meghan Woo is a doctoral student at the Harvard School of Public Health and a research consultant for the Center for Multicultural Mental Health Research at the Cambridge Health Alliance. Her doctoral work concentrates on the impact of racial identity, acculturation, and immigration on racial/ethnic mental health disparities with a focus on multiracial populations.

Index

premigratory factors, 260
preschool enrollment. *See* Early education programs
repeating grade, 259–60, 261
research recommendations, 215–20
school resources, 202–7
school transition, 257–60
seasonal migrant status, 201
second language instruction, 204–6
segregation, consequences of, 202–4, 254, 265
skipping grade, 259, 261
structuring opportunity, 198–214
teachers. *See* Teacher education and experience
Elementary and Secondary Education Act (ESEA). *See* No Child Left Behind Act
Elementary education. *See* Education and educational attainment
ELL. *See* English language learners
Employment. *See* Full-time employment in rural areas
Enculturation, defined, 99
English language learners (ELL), 204–6
    advantages of high-concentration ELL schools, 254
    biased assessment of, 217
    children living with parents who speak only Spanish, 171
    high-stakes testing and, 195
    indigenous speakers as, 210
    instruction and programs for, 69–70, 181, 210
    in Mexican-origin families, 171, 173
    policy and practice implications, 181, 222–23, 358
    teacher education and experience with, 206–7, 350
English language proficiency
    acculturation and parent-child gap linked to, 170–72
    challenges to school children, 209–11, 350
    child acting as parent's interpreter, 352

economic integration and, 66–67
in Latino neighborhoods, 16, 30
limited English proficient (LEP) parents, policies to engage in children's education, 245–49
linked with poverty, 52
neighbors of Latinos and blacks and, 22–23, 30
in new vs. traditional destinations of Latinos, 40–41
parental educational background and, 201–2
preschool enrollment and, 192
as research issue, 340
segregation consequences due to, 203
statewide high school tests and Latino pass rates, 194
as variable in analysis, 56
Entwhisle, Doris, 253
The Equity Monitoring Project for Immigrant and Refugee Education, 288
Escarce, José, 310, 312
Ethnic comparative research, 98
Ethnic segregation. *See* Racial/ethnic segregation
Ethno-racial composition of immigrant vs. nonimmigrant neighborhoods, 30
European Americans. *See also* Whites
    mental health study on, 322–27, 328
    parental involvement based on gender of children, 102
Extended family living arrangements, 149–50, 175, 307, 351

Familias Unidas (HIV prevention program), 158, 161
Families. *See also* Mexican-origin families; Neighborhoods; Parents; Rural destinations
    sociocultural incorporation and, 351–52. *See also* Acculturation
    strengths of Latino families, 175–76, 219–20, 225–27, 242, 270
Familism, importance to Mexican Americans, 110–22, 148, 175, 178

SARAH BEARD

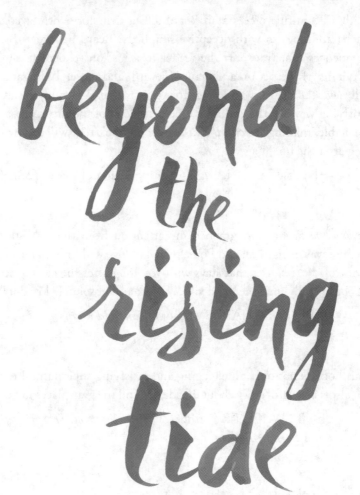

beyond
the
rising
tide

SARAH BEARD

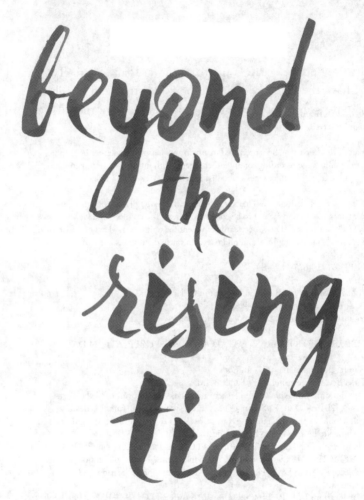

beyond the rising tide

SWEETWATER BOOKS
AN IMPRINT OF CEDAR FORT, INC.
SPRINGVILLE, UTAH

This is a work of fiction. The characters, names, incidents, places, and dialogue are products of the author's imagination and are not to be construed as real. The opinions and views expressed herein belong solely to the author and do not necessarily represent the opinions or views of Cedar Fort, Inc. Permission for the use of sources, graphics, and photos is also solely the responsibility of the author.

ISBN 13: 978-1-4621-1874-8

Published by Sweetwater Books, an imprint of Cedar Fort, Inc.
2373 W. 700 S., Springville, UT 84663
Distributed by Cedar Fort, Inc., www.cedarfort.com

LIBRARY OF CONGRESS CATALOGING-IN-PUBLICATION DATA

Names: Beard, Sarah, 1977- author.
Title: Beyond the rising tide / Sarah Beard.
Description: Springville, Utah : Sweetwater Books, an Imprint of Cedar Fort, Inc., [2016] | ©2016 | Summary: Seventeen-year-old Kai Turner is dead, so he should be the one haunting, but instead it is Avery Ambrose, the girl whose life he saved, who haunts him.
Identifiers: LCCN 2016003638 (print) | LCCN 2016010823 (ebook) | ISBN 9781462118748 (perfect bound : alk. paper) | ISBN 9781462126668
Subjects: | CYAC: Love--Fiction. | Dead--Fiction. | Ghosts--Fiction. | LCGFT: Fiction.
Classification: LCC PZ7.B380234 Be 2016 (print) | LCC PZ7.B380234 (ebook) | DDC [Fic]--dc23
LC record available at http://lccn.loc.gov/2016003638

Cover design by Michelle May Ledezma
Cover design © 2016 Cedar Fort, Inc.
Edited and typeset by Melissa J. Caldwell

Printed in the United States of America

10 9 8 7 6 5 4 3 2 1

Printed on acid-free paper

*To Diane and Mel,
for always letting me know you're there,
even when I can't see you.*

ALSO BY SARAH BEARD

Porcelain Keys

1

KAI

I don't know how it's decided, who lives and who dies. Why some are granted more time among the living, and others are snatched away into the land of the dead. All I know is that tonight, a decision has been made. And of the two critically injured people sprawled on the highway, I've been assigned to save only one.

Raindrops pound against the asphalt, and ambulance lights wash the scene in bursts of red like an outdoor rave. Only, there's no one dancing here. Just a heap of metal that was once a car, an obliterated highway divider, and a handful of paramedics giving new meaning to the term *graveyard shift*. They don't know I'm here, but without my help, the boy I've been assigned to won't be leaving here alive.

My feet don't disturb the water as I stride through a puddle, as though it's a mirage in a desert. In truth, I'm the mirage. The thing with no real substance. The paramedics don't acknowledge me as I kneel beside the boy. Not because they're busy cinching a tourniquet around his leg or searching for a heartbeat, but because I'm invisible to them.

I've grown accustomed to the invisibility, but after being a healer for six months, I still can't handle the sight of blood. The boy's jeans are soaked with it, and the rain thins it out as it spills onto the asphalt like a polluted stream. So I look at his face instead. His eyes are closed, his mouth open as raindrops fall between his lips. Something about him startles me. Like I've unexpectedly looked into a mirror. His wild tawny hair. His brokenness. Or maybe it's just his age. Late teens—the same age I was when I died. Lucky for him, I'm here to make sure he doesn't share my fate.

As the paramedics begin CPR, I rest my hand on the boy's shoulder. My fingers sink into him a bit, and I grimace as I feel the wreckage of his body. His ribs are broken, his pelvis shattered, his aorta ruptured. The paramedic doing chest compressions is thick and heavy-handed, tearing the boy's heart more with each pump.

Wasting no more time, I summon the power of my healing wristband. The metal begins to burn on my wrist, and the inlaid stone brightens like smoldering embers. Inside of me, the power whirls and swells like a firestorm until it's too much to contain. Then it leaves me and moves through the boy, sewing up his ruptured heart as if it were torn fabric. It doesn't heal his other injuries, only what medicine and his own body can't heal quickly enough.

A moment later, a female paramedic declares that they have a pulse. The heavy man rocks back on his heels in relief, and the boy is lifted onto a backboard and carried to the ambulance.

My work here is done, but I can't bring myself to leave. My eyes travel over the wet road until I find the other victim. A woman, probably the boy's mother. She's been extracted from the car and lies on the road, and beneath all the scarlet, the original color of her dress is uncertain. Her feet are bare, and I'm grateful I can't see around the paramedics to glimpse her face. Two of them are kneeling over her, doing their best to keep her alive. And Grim stands at her head, ready to seal her death.

His real name is Jerick, but in my head, he's almost always Grim. Not only because of his job, but because I've never seen the man crack a smile. I guess if I were the one always taking people from their loved ones, I wouldn't feel much like smiling either.

I take a couple of steps toward the woman. I don't see her spirit anywhere, so she must still be in her body. It's not too late. That boy back there doesn't have to go through the pain of losing his mother. Not when I possess the power to save her. I take another step toward her.

"Don't come any closer, Kai," Grim warns with weariness, like a teacher who's told his student one too many times to keep their hands in the confines of their own workspace.

"Why?" I ask, and my voice is tired too. Tired of asking why any of us have to be torn from the people we love. Tired of never getting an answer.

He raises his scepter, reminding me that he has a job to do. The diamond-shaped tip of the scepter burns orange like a flame, a sign that he's only moments away from sealing her death. "If you want to help people, then help only the ones you've been assigned to. You wouldn't want to lose that privilege again, would you?"

My gaze returns to the woman, a heaviness settling over me. The boy's life may have been spared, but if Grim takes his mother, he'll be left with wounds that will never fully heal. Wounds like mine.

Grim is right, though. I know the consequence of working outside of my jurisdiction, and if I want to keep helping people at all, I can't cross that line again.

Despite the paramedics' efforts, the woman's soul rises and leaves her body like cotton pulled from a withered boll. When Jerick hovers the glowing specter over her lifeless body, I have to turn away. And when I hear her voice asking why she has to leave her son, I can't stay any longer. I quicken away to the only place where I can put this tragedy out of my mind.

It's raining where I stand in front of Avery's house, but my clothes and hair are dry. If I could feel the air, it would be heavy and humid. If I could inhale, I would smell soil and damp foliage, like the vineyard in Marquette when the black earth soaked up the rain and the leaves were beaded with dew. Summer scents I always took for granted when I was alive.

I shouldn't enter her house. There are all kinds of rules and boundaries when it comes to people's sanctuaries. But tonight, the need to be near her is stronger than ever. I've been in the rain far too long, and she's my only pavilion. If I can glimpse her face, maybe I can forget about the woman who died tonight. My hands are heavy with unused power, and my heart is a dead weight in my chest.

I don't bother with the front door. Doors are for people who can open them, for hands that have substance and can grasp a doorknob. So I walk through the wall next to the front door. It pulls on me a bit, like walking through a turnstile in a subway station. And then I'm in her living room.

The house is dark save for one rectangle of light falling from a doorway in the hall. I drift down the hallway, passing an empty bedroom and then an office lit by the glow of a computer monitor. Her mom is asleep in front of the computer, half sitting, half sprawled across the desk.

At the end of the hall, I find Avery's room. Strewn on her floor are her Converse All-Stars, clothes, and a marine science book, open with the spine up. Her laptop balances precariously on the edge of the bed, ready to be accidentally kicked off.

Her blankets are in disarray, a sea of restless waves. She's curled beneath them like a crumpled paper boat, all folds and sharp edges. Her hair is splayed around her head, pale gold in the night-light blooming behind her bed.

Even without crossing the threshold, the heaviness inside me lifts a bit. I don't know why, but when Avery's near, I'm more at ease. Maybe because she's the last person I came in contact with before my death. Maybe because I know she thinks about me when few others in this world do. She cares about me, and she doesn't even know my name.

Her alarm clock reads two thirty in the morning, so I flinch when she sits up and flings a spiral notebook at the wall. She heaves a discouraged sigh, then falls back into bed, curling on her side. I hesitate for a minute in her doorway, wondering what's up. Wishing I could just ask. Maybe her ex-boyfriend is being a jerk again. Or maybe she's upset about her parents' split, or her mom's ups and downs.

She starts crying, so I toss the rules aside and come in, circling her bed so I can see her face. Her eyes are shining with tears, and she's got one hand wrapped around her forearm, her nails digging into her skin. It drives me crazy when she does that. I want to wrench her hand away and smooth out the moon-shaped marks her nails have made. I try. But she sifts through my hand like fine sand.

As I pass my hand through her arm, I taste her pain. Not the reasons behind it, just the feeling. Like sinking. Drowning. A feeling I'm all too familiar with. It makes me want to go to her ex-boyfriend's house and yank him out of bed and slam him against the wall for breaking her heart. But I've already tried that a few times since he broke up with her, and a punch isn't very satisfying when it doesn't connect with anything.

"Breathe," I whisper, even though she can't hear me. "Breathe, Avery." After a long minute, she draws in a shuddery breath. But then she digs her nails deeper as more tears spill from under her wet lashes.

If I weren't already dead, the sight of her crying like this would kill me. So I look away, to the notebook she tossed on the floor. It has her curvy handwriting on it:

Him

1. Scar on back.

2.

Below that, a mass of scribbles. Not doodle-scribbles. Frustrated, ripping-the-paper-with-your-pen scribbles.

The list is about *me*. It's all she remembers about me. My scar. And then it dawns on me that tonight, she's crying over me. Hurting because of *me*. Digging her nails into her arm because of her grief over me.

The weight of her sorrow presses me down, down, until I'm kneeling beside her. I have the ability to save lives. But in this moment, I feel utterly powerless.

If I could only talk to her. If I just had the power to show myself like some others do, I could convince her that she doesn't need to grieve over me. That I don't regret saving her life, even though it meant sacrificing my own.

As I listen to her cry herself to sleep, an idea surfaces in my mind. The same one that's been bobbing up and down for the past several weeks. I don't have to feel so helpless. I learned as a kid that the only way to escape helplessness was to take things into my own hands. If I want Avery to be happy again, maybe it's time for me to take her healing into my own hands. I don't have to remain unseen to her. Not when there's a way to gain a temporary body. It's risky, and it would involve dishonesty and thievery. It would require me to be the despicable person I left behind a long time ago. I'm not even sure I could pull it off. But I've been watching Avery's life unravel since I saved it last winter, and it's only a matter of time before the threads holding her together fray and snap completely.

*Y*ou need to chill out," Paige says. She has her bare feet up on the dashboard of my '96 Cherokee, and she's brushing on some last-minute toenail polish on our way to the beach. It's dark out, so she has the vanity mirror open and the dim light makes her plum polish look black.

"You know the sand is just going to stick to that, right?"

She twists the cap back on the bottle of Berry Naughty and cranks on the floor heater, sticking her toes beneath the vent. "Don't change the subject. I mean, I know you're still like, shaken up or whatever from what happened. I would be too. But you can do this. For Tyler. You can show him you're still the same girl he fell in love with."

My hands tighten on the steering wheel. "I *am* the same girl."

"You know what I mean. You're the same, but you're not. You're like, Boring Avery. Not Fun, Live-by-the-Seat-of-Your-Pants Avery. That's why he broke up with you, right? Because he doesn't like Boring Avery."

Right. He doesn't like Boring Avery. Crying-Under-a-Blanket-in-Your-Room Avery. Grieving Avery *weighs him down* too much. The words sting just as much when I think them as when he said them to my face. But I don't want to talk about it, so I smile and say, "There's more than one definition of *fun*."

"So your new definition is working sixty hours a week and holing up at your mom's on the weekends?"

"I don't work sixty hours."

She rolls her eyes. "You're at the chocolate shop when I come in for my shift. You're there when I leave. You're there when I come in later for free chocolate. You're there—"

"Okay, fine. I work a lot. But what do you expect when my dad owns the business?"

"I expect your dad to comply with child labor laws so his workaholic daughter will get out and enjoy her summer break. I mean, I could understand if you lived in Barstow. But, *hello*, you live in the sweetest little beach town in California."

Beads of sweat are gathering on my forehead, so I reach over and shut off the heater, then roll down the window. The briny Pacific air rushes in, and I sense a charge in the atmosphere—most likely an impending sequel to last night's rainstorm. The June Gloom has been extra gloomy this year, and I wish it would pass already. "He doesn't force me to work."

She levels a look at me that punctuates my own words. "My point exactly. So tonight, you're going to have fun. You're going to chill out and dance around the bonfire like the kickin' teenage girl that you are. And you're going to get in the water."

I feel the blood drain from my hands. "I'm going to the beach. That's a big enough step for tonight. Tyler will see that I'm making an effort."

"At least get your feet wet. Come on," she begs in her whiniest voice. It's the same voice that convinced me to come tonight, and the same voice that persuaded me to dye my hair pink when we were thirteen.

We're nearing the beach at Port San Luis, so I shift into a lower gear. "I'm not making any promises."

"I'll be there with you. I won't leave your side, okay?" She wrangles her long dark hair into a ponytail. "Actually . . . that depends on Dillan. He's been doing the hot-cold thing again lately. If he's cold tonight, I won't leave your side. But if he's hot . . ."

"I don't need a babysitter," I snap. The nearness of the ocean has my nerves on end like porcupine quills, and my words come out sharper than I intend.

"Well, if you decide you need one," she says, a glint of humor in her brown eyes, "I charge only ten dollars per hour. Twelve if you want me to put you to bed."

This pulls a smile from me, but as we approach the beach and I see the bonfire blazing, my stomach clenches again. We bounce into a bumpy parking lot across the street, and I look in the rear-view mirror for one last appraisal. After work I stopped at home to change into a tank top and shorts, but with Paige texting me every five seconds to urge me out the door, I didn't bother much with my hair. It's still in a long braid down my back, so I undo it and shake it out with my fingers.

"You look great!" Paige says impatiently, already halfway out of the Cherokee. "Let's go!"

I can't pick out Tyler from the crowd surrounding the fire, but I know he's down there. According to Paige, he's the one who planned this whole thing. I wasn't going to come, but Paige spent all day convincing me that if I did, it would put me on the path to winning Tyler back.

The night is warm, and the ocean breeze feels good on my skin. We follow a sandy trail down to the beach, and the anticipation of talking to Tyler sends my stomach all aflutter. I see him almost daily since he works at the surf shop down the street from Dad's chocolate shop, but it's been weeks since we've had a real conversation.

Dillan comes up and plants a kiss behind Paige's ear, and she gives me a secret smile and mouths, "Hot," as she slips her hand into his. I scan the crowd for Tyler but don't see him.

"He went for a night swim," Dillan says, looking at me as Paige twirls one of his dreads around her finger.

I search the dark waves for Tyler, and finally my eyes fall on a figure standing waist-deep in the water—along with a second, more petite figure. I recognize her instantly as the tourist Tyler gave surfing lessons to earlier today. At least she's wised up and put on a wetsuit. I wrap my arms around my waist, trying to squeeze out the jealousy.

Paige nudges me. "Go out there! If you want him, fight for him!"

"But I—"

Paige grabs my elbow and looks me in the face, her big brown eyes offering the steadiness I lack. "You can do it. Just . . . focus on him, not the water. And besides, the surf is totally mild tonight. Nothing is going to happen."

Everyone thinks it's fear that keeps me from the water. But that's not it at all. I've never been afraid of the water, and I'm not now. My reasons for avoiding the ocean don't make sense to anyone but me, so I don't even attempt an explanation. I swallow and give Paige a weak nod, trying to muster up courage.

Fight for him, I repeat her words in my mind. *Fight.*

Dillan leads Paige to the fire, and I kick off my Converse and approach the water as a whirlpool of apprehension churns in my belly. The surf reaches for me and laps at my toes, and I jump back as the chill of the water sends my heart racing and floods my mind with unwanted memories. It takes all my strength to force them out.

Tyler's back is turned so he doesn't see me. It's Tourist Girl who alerts him to my presence, tugging his arm and pointing me out. He twists around, and when he sees me, his mouth falls open. It's hard to tell with the fire casting sporadic shadows across his face, but I swear he looks guilty. The girl grabs his arm and pulls him into an oncoming wave. As the wave slams into them, he laughs and she squeals.

All I can think is how *I* should be the one with him in the water. I should be the one in his arms. After spending countless days last summer in the ocean together, surfing and swimming and free-diving, how can he so easily forget that *I'm* the one who belongs there with him?

The remnants of the wave wash up to shore and stretch toward me. Instead of stepping back, I hold my breath, clench my fists, and step forward.

Fight.

I have to show Tyler that I'm brave enough to do this—for him. I let the wave wash over my feet, and it swells until my calves are underwater. As the water recedes, sand loosens under my feet as it's swept back to sea.

And that's when the panic seizes me.

Every muscle in my body freezes—except my heart, which is hammering so brutally against my chest it might crack a rib. My lungs refuse to expand, and my nails dig into my arm so deeply I'm sure they're drawing blood. Because to me, the white caps of the waves look like ghosts, the inky shadows beneath the water like silhouetted bodies. The ocean is haunted now, and the salt-water stings my raw guilt like an open wound.

I want to retreat, but my legs won't move.

Tyler's lips form my name as he sloshes through the water toward me, his face etched with concern. He comes over and curls a wet hand around my arm, tugging me to dry sand. Turning me toward him, he braces his cold hands on my arms. "Are you okay? Geez, Avery. You're shaking." Orange firelight illuminates one side of his face, flickering in the water droplets on his skin.

He's right. I'm shivering as if it's twenty degrees outside. I cross my arms and try to still myself. *Get a grip, Avery. Get a grip.*

He leans down so his face is closer to mine. Too close. "Take a deep breath. Breathe in—" He demonstrates by inhaling deeply through his nose. I follow his example; then he exhales slowly, and I do the same. "There. That's it. One more time. In. That's right. Now out."

I feel my body calming, but now I feel a different kind of unease. I glance at the people by the bonfire, and everyone is looking our way. Some of them are whispering to each other.

"You came," Tyler says softly, and when I look back at him, his lips are slanted into a sad half-smile. "That's a big step. But you don't have to get in the water, okay? Not if you're not ready."

He doesn't understand. I *want* to go in the water. I want to join my friends, to be myself again. But there's a deep ravine between them and me now, and I don't know how to cross it. I don't know where the bridge is. And I don't know how to ask for directions.

Tyler glances back at Tourist Girl with a tinge of regret. She's gotten out of the water and is heading toward the bonfire.

"I didn't mean to interrupt your swim," I say, gauging his loyalty.

"It's okay. I think Gem was getting cold anyway."

"Gem?" The name is so unexpected, it takes me a second to attach it to Tourist Girl. "Are her parents jewelers or something?"

He gives a one-syllable courtesy laugh, then looks toward Tourist Girl, who's peeling away her wetsuit like a corn husk to reveal her bikini top. She eases up to the fire and glances our way, giving me the stink eye like I'm a stray dog digging up her new flower bed.

"Is she paying you to be her tour guide?" I ask. "Or are you showing her the ropes out of the kindness of your heart?"

He gives me a chiding look. "It's not like that. She's here for a couple weeks on vacation, and her parents are out doing something tonight, so I invited her to hang out."

A breeze pushes a lock of hair into my face, and I brush it away, tucking it behind my ear. "How nice of you." I try for sincerity, but my voice hitches on the last word, betraying my hurt.

"Avery," he says, his brow puckering, "we're friends now, right?"

Friends. Is it even possible for two people to be friends after ten months of dating? Ten months memorizing the lines of each other's faces? Ten months stripping away barriers, sharing adventures and passions and pineapple milkshakes? All of those kisses and *I love you's* made invalid with six little words: *It's just too much for me.*

"Of course," I say quietly, pushing sand around with my toes. Because at least with friendship, there's a ray of hope that things will return to how they once were. That someday he'll see me not as a weight, but as the buoy I'd once been to him.

"Good." He leans down and plants a kiss on my forehead. It's excruciating, a sting that spreads hot venom through my entire body. "I still care about you, Avery. I hope you know that." He gazes at me for a moment, his jade eyes striking me again, deep inside, a wound I know will take days to heal. "Are you going to be okay?"

I divert my eyes to the fire so he doesn't see the pain there. Everyone is still casting curious glances our way, and I realize they've been watching us this whole time. I want to leave so I don't have to see them look at me like I'm weird, don't have to hear them whispering about last winter, about the boy who drowned saving me. About how they never found his body, and how I've changed since.

"I'm fine," I lie through a tight throat as I slide on a mask of serenity. I've gotten so good at it that it takes almost no effort.

"Come on. I'll introduce you to Gem. She's really cool."

Lightning flashes on the horizon, and I take it as my cue to leave. "That's okay. I think I'm just going to head home."

His shoulders slump. "But you made such an effort to come. Don't leave now."

I want to laugh. Who's he to tell me not to retreat when things get tough? "I'm really tired," I say with honesty. "Long day at work. Can you tell Paige to get a ride home with Dillan?"

He purses his lips and stares at me for a long moment. "Sure. I'm really glad you came. I'm proud of you."

I nod, feeling like a child, and then watch him go back to the bonfire and to Gem. She brightens as he sidles up to her and says something I can't hear.

I grab my shoes and walk away, the crowd's laughter and chatter fading with each step. When I reach the road, I climb on a boulder to sit and watch the dark ocean from afar. Rows of foamy waves billow and roll in like storm clouds fallen to earth, their rhythmic sound lulling me back to the memories I just ran from. A familiar emptiness spreads through me, a sort of hunger that can't be satiated with food. I hug my knees to my chest and bury my head in my arms, wishing I could go back to last winter, wishing I hadn't been so careless, wishing that boy hadn't jumped in the ocean to save me. Not that I wish I'd died, but if I had, maybe he would still be alive.

If only I knew his name. Or at the very least, remembered what he looked like. If there's one thing I can do to pay respect to the boy who saved my life, it's to remember his face. But I can't even recall the color of his hair.

A light wind ruffles my hair, tickles my arms and neck. It carries with it a soft sound. Not one I hear with my ears, but one that touches me somewhere deeper. Like a breath, or a whisper.

It's the sound of my name.

"Avery."

3

KAI

I know what a person looks like when they're broken. Their eyes are vacant, the way my mom's were after being married to my dad for thirteen years. They look fragile, like a thin and hollow reed that will blow over in the slightest breeze. The way my two little sisters looked after living under my dad's unpredictable hand their whole lives.

The way Avery Ambrose looks now, curled up on a boulder and staring at the black sea. She's not the same girl I first saw in the ocean the day I drowned. That girl had her feet planted firmly on her surfboard as she fearlessly sliced up monster waves. She held the reins, and the ocean was her domain.

I may have saved her life that day, but I also stole it and replaced it with a counterfeit. The life she has now is broken. Because I wasn't strong enough to swim back to shore.

Over the past few months, I've watched in frustration as others have tried to help her. All in their own way, with an array of tactics. And I'm not even sure that mine would produce a different result. What I do know is that Avery's happiness has become more important to me than anything else. Because you can't spend six months as someone's silent companion without growing to care for them. And I care for Avery. So much that I would pay any price to repair what my death has broken.

I close my eyes and picture my mentor, Charles, and then quicken away to find him. Seconds later, I open my eyes to someplace new—somewhere dark with branches and leaves overhead.

"Haven't seen you in a while."

I whip around at the sound of Charles's voice, and then see him behind me sitting on a log. He's wearing mortal clothes—overalls and a flannel shirt that remind me of how he used to dress when we were both alive and working together in his vineyard. Beneath his baseball cap, his hair is white instead of his usual gray, which is how I can tell he's materialized. The ring on his right hand confirms it.

"On assignment?" I ask, forcing my eyes away from the ring. I peer into the darkened mountainside to guess who he might be helping. It's raining again, and other than leaves shuddering under falling raindrops, I see no other sign of life.

"Waiting for a couple of straggling hikers to point them in the right direction."

"Why? The trail is pretty clear."

"Look behind you."

I twist around to see that the rain has washed a section of the trail away, leaving a forty-foot drop to jagged rocks. If I weren't already dead, I'd be scrambling from the edge. I turn back to the trail, squinting through the rain. "What are they doing hiking in the rain, in the dark?"

"They must have lost track of time. They should be here any minute now."

I'm restless, and I try not to fidget. I haven't felt this nervous since I stole a package of chicken from the Food Mart when I was ten. I recall how cold it felt against my stomach when I slipped it under my Pistons sweatshirt, how the juices ran down my leg as I ducked out of the store and booked it all the way home.

My eyes flick to Charles's ring again. I didn't expect him to be wearing it. He only takes it out of his pocket every couple months when an assignment makes it necessary to be seen by mortals. But I've waited this long for the chance to help Avery; I can wait a little longer.

I sit beside him. He's got his hand open, palm up on his knee, and the rain is falling into it, gathering into a little pool. I want to ask him how it feels. Not just the rain, but what it's like to put on the ring and have your body become solid again. Whether being materialized feels like being alive, or different somehow. But I don't want him to know how interested I am in his ring at the moment, because he might guard it more vigilantly if he does.

"Is something troubling you?" he asks.

I stretch out my legs in an attempt to appear relaxed. "No. Why?"

He gives me a paternal pat on the shoulder. "You usually only visit me when you need advice."

He's right, and his words cause a twinge of guilt. "I'm sorry. I just . . . don't like being in Demoror. I like hanging out here on Earth. It makes me feel almost alive."

Okay, it never makes me feel anywhere close to being alive. But it's more interesting than hanging out on the sterile shores of Demoror, where people go first when they die. It's like a scenic waiting room, smack dab in the middle of the afterlife. It's pretty, I guess. But it's about as exciting as . . . well, a waiting room.

Through the trees, I hear voices, and I rise. Charles stands too and steps onto the trail. He adjusts his baseball cap, then starts whistling the melody to "Blackbird." My fingers twitch as they recall how to play the chords on the guitar. I can almost feel the strings under my fingers as they slide up and down the fretboard. With an ache in my chest, I think of my neglected guitar, stashed at the back of a shed, untouched since my death.

As the sound of the hikers' footsteps gets closer, their voices grow quieter. Maybe because Charles's whistling makes them curious. I realize that that's probably the reason he's whistling—so they're not startled when they come around the bend and see a strange old man standing on the trail. Their flashlight beam shows up before they do, and when the young couple sees him, they skid to a stop. The girl shines the flashlight in Charles's face. He shields his eyes, and she lowers the beam to the bib of his overalls.

"I heard you coming," Charles says. "And I wanted to make sure you saw this drop-off here."

The flashlight beam moves right through me to where the trail has been washed away, and the girl gasps.

"Whoa," the boy says, taking the girl by the arm as though he doesn't trust her to keep a safe distance from the edge. "Thanks for the warning."

Charles nods, and the two hikers step through some undergrowth to where the trail picks up again. The girl pauses and gives Charles a curious look. "Are you up here alone? Do you want to walk down with us?"

"Thanks for the offer," he says. "But go ahead. I have friends nearby."

She gives a satisfied nod, and she and the boy continue, disappearing into the trees.

Just like that, Charles's assignment is complete. He waits until the hikers' voices fade, then he slips off the ring. I've seen him dematerialize before, but still find it fascinating. His hair darkens to its natural gray, and even though I can still see him, he disappears to mortal eyes. His clothes have changed to his slightly luminous shirt and pants, and his mortal clothes now lie in a heap on the ground. I wonder now if the stray hunting garb I sometimes found in the woods as a kid were left there by people like him.

I look away as he slips the ring into his left pocket. Nothing raises a red flag like staring at the object you're about to steal. I step toward him, a plan solidifying in my mind. I've had lots of practice at this kind of stuff, so it comes easy. Distraction and a sleight of hand—that's all it takes.

"Charles," I say. "You haven't heard anything about my mom, have you?" The question sounds completely sincere, because it is. The mystery of my mom's whereabouts is something that torments me almost constantly.

Charles shakes his head, his features softening into commiseration. "Why don't you come back to Demoror with me, and we'll see if anyone else has."

I nod, stepping closer and casually positioning my hand near his left pocket. "I think I will."

As we quicken back to Demoror, the movement of my hand is so swift he doesn't even notice it dipping in and out of his pocket.

I am not a thief.

I repeat the words in my mind before saying them out loud. "I am not a thief. I'm only borrowing Charles's ring." There's no one around to hear it but me, yet I don't even manage to convince myself.

Beneath the pier at Avila Beach, an unending procession of waves explodes against the posts. It's still raining, the tide high and the water rough. I don't know what time it is, but the sky is black and the streets and shops above the beach are vacant.

I unfurl my fingers to reveal Charles's ring. It looks similar to my wristband—silverish metal with a stone inlay—yet serves an entirely different purpose. And even though it's smaller than my wristband, it feels heavier. Maybe it's the weight of guilt, of something stolen.

Only, it's *not* stolen. It's *borrowed*. I'm not a thief.

I'll have it back to Charles before he even notices it's gone. I hope, anyway. If I'm going to help Avery, I'll need at least a couple weeks. Charles shouldn't need his ring before then, but I hope that if he notices it missing, he'll forgive me. That he'll understand.

Brushing aside the guilt, I hold the ring over the tip of my finger and hesitate only a second before sliding it on.

For a long moment, I wait to feel something or see a change, but nothing happens. Maybe it's that easy. Maybe I materialized without realizing it. To test, I reach for a wooden post.

My hand sweeps right through it.

A wave of disappointment washes over me as I consider that maybe the ring only works for Charles.

I'm about to take the ring off when a light mist begins to rise from the sand at my feet. I watch with wide eyes as it thickens into a cloud of dust, like dry dirt in a gust of wind. It swirls around me and starts clinging to me. I hold perfectly still, partly because I'm a bit terrified at what's happening, and partly because, if this is how a materialized body is formed, I don't want to mess it up.

I feel something moving inside of me, rapid bursts of energy darting from the center of my chest to my limbs. Like a rush of adrenaline, only more electric, and it cycles through me over and over. I'm on the verge of crying out in pain when it abruptly stops.

I look around, and the mist is gone. With apprehension I hold up my hand, and it looks the same as it did before. But then I notice something else.

I can smell the rain. And the ocean. The wet sand and salt, ancient things that have been turned over in the surf again and again. I'm still under the pier, so I step over to where the rain is falling. Slowly, I stretch out my open hand, terrified that I'm not really solid.

And then I feel the rain. Not falling through my hand, but hitting it. Gathering in my palm. It's cold and wet and tangible. I step out into the open and raise my face to the sky, letting the rain sprinkle my face. For just a minute I'm a kid again, carefree in a summer rainstorm, wet sneakers splashing through puddles and leaves racing down overfilled gutters. And then for the first time in months, I shiver from being cold.

In this moment, I know two things. One, I need to see Avery. And two—which maybe should have been number one—I need to find some different clothes. If I'd planned this out a little better,

I would have materialized in Macy's or the Goodwill or something. My pants and shirt are the shade and brilliance of the moon and cut like a karate gi. Standard apparel in the afterlife, but here I look like some sort of extraterrestrial white ninja screaming for attention.

I try to quicken to the shops lining the beachfront. But that doesn't work with this body, so I start treading through the sand. After months of quickening, walking feels tedious. So I run instead. The sand feels gritty on the soles of my feet, and the night air is cool as it fills my lungs. The muscles in my thighs and calves contract and expand with each stride. It may not be as fast as quickening, but it feels amazing.

The shops are dark and empty. Preferable, seeing how I'm about to commit burglary. I wish crime didn't have to be my first act as a materialized being, but my options are pretty limited. I don't have any money, and even if I did, strolling through a store when I'm dressed like a radioactive Luke Skywalker would attract way too much attention.

I can always find a way to pay for the damages later.

If I have a later.

It doesn't take long to scope out the shops and decide on one bordering an alleyway. I slip down the alley as stealthily as my luminous clothes allow, then peer through the windowed side door, scanning the walls and ceiling to make sure they're free of security cameras. To cushion my fist, I pull off my shirt and wrap it around my hand.

As I turn back to the glass door, I'm met with my own reflection. I barely recognize myself. My hair has always been sandy blond, but now it's *really* blond. Like, white blond. Charles's hair is always white when he materializes, but I thought that was just because he's old. My eyebrows are still dark, but my skin looks smoother, the edges of my face more defined. And my eyes are less shadowed, like someone with a clean conscience.

Not for long.

I make a fist beneath my shirt, cock my hand back, and then slam it into the glass. The glass cracks, and something cracks inside of me too. The recently acquired conviction that I'm a good person.

It's for Avery, I tell myself, but it doesn't lessen the sting or tremors that are starting to rock this new body. I reach through the jagged break, unlocking the door and pushing it open. As I pull my hand back, I feel a sharp burn on my forearm. I've cut myself, but don't have time to worry about that now.

I hurtle into the shop and grab a Rip Curl tee. Cargo shorts. Canvas flip-flops. As I'm about to exit, I see a display of pocket-knives. I slide to a stop and grab one. You never know when you'll need a sharp blade. Then I book it out of there.

I guess I'm a thief after all.

I sprint up the street and into the posh neighborhood perched on a hill above the beach. Avery's neighborhood. At least during the weekdays when she stays with her dad. But it's the weekend, so she's probably at her mom's.

Behind a big flowering bush on the side of someone's yard, I strip off the rest of the Skywalker clothes. As soon as they hit the ground, they lose their luminosity like an unplugged lamp, as though I was the power source making them glow. I dress in the new clothes and slide on the flip-flops. The knife goes in my front pocket, my afterlife clothes get tossed in a trash bin, and then I continue up the road, slowing my pace to a casual stroll. An innocent stroll. From the corner of my eye, I see the flashing of blue and red lights down by the beach. I turn and watch for a measured minute, because if there's one way to label yourself guilty, it's to look away from the crime.

When I'm confident I won't be pegged as a suspect, I turn and follow the street's incline, passing colorful stucco houses with flowering vines and clay tile roofs. The sky is still blotchy with rain clouds, but the rain is tapering off. I close my eyes and inhale deeply, savoring the earthy scents I've been deprived of for so long.

The air is cool and damp, and all of the hair on my body stands on end as though the atmosphere is charged with electricity.

The sting on my forearm returns, and I look to see where the glass cut it, expecting to see blood. But it's clean. I look closer. There's an opening in my skin, a long, jagged gash, but no blood. Just a bit of shimmery clear liquid oozing out. I shudder and thrust my hand in my pocket so I don't have to look at it.

As I suspected, Avery's car isn't in her dad's driveway. And I realize now that since I've never been to her mom's without quickening there, I'm not sure how to get there by walking.

No matter, because as I think about Avery, I feel a tug inside my chest, the same magnetism that brings me to people when I quicken without a body. So I follow the pull. It leads me out of the neighborhood and onto a highway. I focus on her face, on the desire to go where she is, and surrender to the current leading to her.

4

avery

*t*he rain is coming at me in two directions. Pelting down from
the sky, and then splashing up as it hits the surface of the ocean.
Between the water in the air and the salt in my eyes, the beach
has all but vanished. But even though I'm out here in the waves with
nothing but a surfboard keeping me from the bottom of the ocean,
and even though a current is tugging me farther and farther from
land, I feel strangely serene. Because the boy sharing my surfboard just
saved me from drowning, and fate wouldn't be so cruel as to deal me
a death sentence right after delivering me from one.

He's on the opposite side of my board, half-turned toward shore,
one arm stroking wide circles in the water, the other stretched across
my board. His skin is warm against my arm, his muscles taut with the
effort of holding on. On his back, a long, white scar stretches across his
shoulder blade, like someone once laid a curling iron on him.

He shouts a question, but the wind tears his words away. He
turns to me for an answer, and I think, Finally. I can see his face.
But then I can't see at all. The sea and sky are conspiring, hurling so
much water in my eyes that I'm blinded.

I'm shivering when I awake from the dream, curled with my knees pulled to my chest. My blankets are everywhere but on me, and the smell of rain and the morning light seep through my open window. In the distance, I hear the sound of the waves on the beach, like the static of mom's broken car radio.

Somewhere out there, far from Avila Beach, the boy who drowned probably has a family. A mother and father, maybe brothers and sisters and grandparents. They must not have known he was at the beach that day, or even in the area, because no one came forward to help us connect the drowned boy to a missing person. Which means they don't know he's dead. They must wonder where he is, must have sleepless nights and nightmares like I do. Maybe they scour the Internet regularly for his where-abouts or have even hired a private detective to find him. But until I remember what he looked like, until I can find out his name, they'll never know what became of him. Because it's impossible to identify someone when their body is still missing.

I sit up and reach for my cell on the nightstand, and I realize I'm still wearing my clothes from the night before. There's sand in my bed, and my ankles are raw from grating against it. I lean back on the headboard and pull up a browser, going directly to the tab for the missing persons database that the sheriff's detective referred me to. He thinks that maybe if I see a picture of the boy, it will jog my memory and I'll be able to identify him.

I type in the information I do know, which isn't much.

Age: 17–22
Race: Caucasian
Last seen: December of last year
Hometown: Unknown

We ruled out the possibility that he was a local, because no locals went missing that day. And he must have been at the beach alone, because no one reported a missing member of their party. The other information—height, weight, and eye color—I don't have either. So I leave those fields blank and hit search.

A few dozen profiles pop up, and I scroll through them, squinting at each photo, trying to project the face onto the boy who briefly shared my surfboard that stormy afternoon. But none of them seem to fit. And in truth, all of them seem to fit. I simply don't remember.

A text from Paige pops up. One simple line:

Thanks for ditching me.

I don't blame her for being mad. I haven't exactly been the ideal friend lately. But I don't have the energy to try to mend things at the moment, so I don't text her back.

I check the time—just past ten—and then shut off my phone and set it back on the nightstand. It's then that I realize how quiet Mom's condo is. Usually I can hear her scuttling around dusting imaginary things, or typing furiously on her keyboard, or talking to herself.

"Mom?" I call.

No answer.

I get out of bed and shuffle into the hall, glancing into her bedroom. Her bed is unmade, but she's not in it. So I go to her office, and she's not there either. Her desk is a disaster of open books and coffee-stained, scribbled-on scraps of paper. An over-sized whiteboard on the wall is congested with notes and scene outlines, and the dry-erase marker extends onto the wall in a few places where she ran out of room. Multiple pairs of mismatched socks are strewn on the floor by her chair, peeled off absentmindedly during brainstorming sessions. Mom is a screenwriter who specializes in romantic period dramas. But from the look of her house, you'd think she wrote slasher films.

She's not in the kitchen or living room either, and I don't find a note. Though it could easily be hiding under all the clutter on her kitchen counters. I call her cell from the landline and then follow a distinct buzzing to her phone, buried under a pile of mail on the dining table. Maybe she ran to the store and couldn't find her phone. But when I check the garage, her vintage Impala is snug in its tight spot, still sleeping in. And the cruiser bicycle Dad got her for one Christmas hangs above it, collecting dust.

Assuming she went for a morning walk, I eat breakfast and straighten up the kitchen, then go to the bathroom where I splash some water on my face. My eyelids are swollen from all my crying the night before, and my smeared mascara makes me look like *I'm* the one who should be penning slasher films.

After rummaging through my bag and realizing I must have left my makeup remover at Dad's, I open Mom's medicine cabinet to find some. But all I see are shelves lined with prescription bottles. She can't be on this many meds. I turn the bottles to read the labels, and sure enough, most of them are empty or expired, remnants of failed trial runs. I do her a favor and dump the empty and expired containers in the trash, then hop in the shower.

As I'm getting dressed, I notice another prescription container on the counter—this one open and empty. When I turn it to read the label, my hands go cold. It's the same sleep aid she took too much of last winter before sleepwalking down to the beach. We found her the next morning, curled up in a rocky alcove, her temperature dropping and the tide rising.

I'm out the door in five seconds, hair still damp and sneakers untied. Mom's condo sits on a bluff overlooking the ocean, and I head for the stairway that leads down to the beach. Dread rises inside me as I get closer, as though the stairs are imaginary and I'm about to take a fifty-foot plunge. I can hear the ocean slamming against rocks below. Shattering. Breaking. Like a china cabinet plummeting from a three-story building and hitting the pavement.

Although the stairway is solid beneath my feet, my stomach thinks I'm falling toward the rocky beach. My feet trill down the steps, and my heart beats even faster. *Please let her be okay. Let her be conscious and beachcombing, or swimming, or chatting the ears off of strangers.* I can't even think the alternative.

When my feet hit the sand, I scan the beach to my left and right for a woman with wild curls. It's a Sunday morning, and the tide is low. The sand gives way to rock slabs that resemble petrified tree bark, and the shoreline is speckled with people exploring the tide pools. If Mom is in trouble, no doubt someone would have already seen her. Unless she was swept away in the middle of the night.

Shaking the image from my mind, I force my feet to move south toward the place we found her last time. My eyes search figures in the distance and faces as I pass them, but there's no sign of Mom's red scarf or her bright-green shawl or the polka dot pajamas she wore to bed last night. My hands are cold and clammy, and my breakfast is not feeling too welcome in my stomach. The water is a good thirty feet away, but I feel trapped between it and the cliffs, like it's a bully pushing me against the wall. I hug the cliffs as I move along, bending and peering into every alcove and crevice. They're full of shadows, decorated by algae and clumps of mussels, but void of human life. My steps are careful, as though I'm passing through a minefield. Because, at any moment, my worst fears might detonate.

Something stings my forearm, and I glance down to see my fingernails digging into my skin. I loosen my grip.

Down the shoreline, something catches my eye: a thin woman kneeling on a stretch of black rock, her curly auburn hair blowing in the breeze and a bright-green shawl around her shoulders.

"Mom!" My voice sounds strangled because my throat is so tight. Her head snaps up to look at me, and I exhale a sigh of relief as I jog over. I kneel beside her and drop an arm across her back, pulling her close. "Are you okay?"

"The sun is finally out," she says brightly, oblivious to my distress. "I'm only a tick away from happiness." She's crouched over a tide pool, holding a scrap of fishing net. "Now if I can only get this little guy free, this could be the perfect day."

Finally I see what she's fussing over. There's a crab the size of her hand tangled in the net. Its legs are moving, like it's trying to break free.

"I was worried about you." I'm panting, but not from my jog. "You didn't leave a note."

"I left at sunrise, and you were dead asleep. I didn't think I'd be gone for long. I just needed to clear my head, and . . ." She shrugs. "I lost track of time. And then I found Sebastian here. I've gotten most of his legs untangled, but there are a couple tight spots I can't get to."

I put a hand on hers. "Mom, it's almost lunch. Let's go back to the condo."

She shakes her head. "Not until I free this little guy. Would you want someone to leave you tangled in a net?"

I exhale quietly, reminding myself to be patient with her. She needs to eat. When she doesn't, things get bad. "Why don't you go back up to the house and get something to eat, and I'll take over?"

She lowers the crab and leans back, considering. "Good idea. And if you're not back by the time I'm done eating, I'll bring down some pliers and scissors." She gathers her feet under her and stands, then adds, "Promise me you won't just toss him back in the water still tangled in the net."

I give her a you-know-me-better-than-that look. "You have my word."

My word must be good, because she nods and turns to leave.

"Okay, Sebastian," I say to the crab, "let's get you free so you can grow up and become a seagull's lunch." I'm in a sundress, so it's not easy getting comfortable on the rock. I end up sitting on one hip with my legs folded to one side. The netting is wound tightly around the crab's pincers and legs, and after a few minutes of trying to unravel it, I haven't gotten anywhere. The surf seems to be growing louder, hissing in my ear.

I do my best to shut it out and focus on the thin green net. The things I do for my mom. My fingers aren't quite small enough to reach into the tiny space near the crab's legs. I tug at the knots, but they remain stubbornly in place.

The morning sun beats down on me, yet it feels like someone's holding an ice pack to the back of my neck. My arms and legs have more bumps than the sea cucumber in the tide pool beside me.

Hiiissss, the ocean whispers to me as it spills water and words onto the rocks. *In the folds of my waves he lies, forever to stay. Hiiisssss. I captured him, but you're the one who lured him in.*

My eyes are drawn to the shadowed spaces in the cliff wall. And now I'm not looking for Mom, but for *him.* It's like an ever-present instinct, even after all this time. As though I expect to see his bones washed up by the tide and caught in a hollow of the rock. My chest feels tight as I think about how it will always be this way now. The ocean I once loved is now my tormentor. My playground and refuge have become a desolate graveyard, my joy and peace buried beneath a vast and sandy headstone.

5
KAI

I'm not sure if I have a heart, but something in my rib cage swells at the sight of Avery. Her hair shimmers like spun gold in the sunlight, falling over her shoulder and hiding her face. She's sitting on a sheet of black rock, head bent, and the flowery skirt of her sundress ripples in the breeze.

If she turns around, she'll see me. If I speak, she'll hear my voice. I open my mouth to do that, but it's parched, hit with an unexpected drought of words.

I've been walking for hours, and I still don't have a solid plan. I have an end goal, but it's like looking up at the peak of a mountain when I'm still in the valley. I want Avery to find happiness again, but I have no idea how to get her there.

One thing is sure—she can't know I'm dead. Not only would it freak her out, but if I don't want to be banned from Earth, that's one rule I can't break.

Maybe I can tell her I'm the guy who saved her life, but convince her that I made it back to shore alive. Only, she *watched* me die. Saw my drowned body ten feet underwater, half a mile from shore. She may not remember what I look like, but she *knows* the guy who saved her is dead.

So I guess my plan is this: Don't let her know I'm dead. And don't let her know I'm the guy who saved her life.

It's not much of a plan at all, but luckily, improvising is what I'm best at. Writing songs on the fly, talking myself out of trouble, and ad-libbing life in general. When I had a life, I was dropped into a new environment every few months with no time for planning. Survival depended on my ability to improvise, because it was the only way to keep my head above water.

As I inch toward Avery, I turn phrases over in my mind, trying to choose the best way to introduce myself. I hate to think how she'll react if she recognizes me, but I doubt she will. I saw her run across my picture on a missing persons report once, and she scanned right past it. Besides, I saw my reflection in the shop window this morning, and although my face is the same, I don't exactly look like myself with my new Jack Frost hair.

Over her shoulder, I see she's holding a fishing net in her lap. Her fingers are working with it like she's trying to free something. A crab. Her hands tremble as she tries to unravel it, so she's not really getting anywhere.

Without thinking, I fish the pocketknife from my shorts, unfold the blade, and lower it in front of her in offering. She flinches and whips around to look at me, eyes wide.

So much for improvising.

I nod toward the tangled mess in her lap. "For the crab." Yes. Those are the words I've waited six months to speak to her. If Charles comes in the next moment to take back his ring, at least I can live in eternal peace knowing I was able to utter those three words.

Her brows pinch together, then she shakes her head and turns back to the crab. "I'm trying to free him, not eat him."

For a few breaths, I'm speechless. In awe that she just talked to me. She can see me. And hear me. If I reach out and touch her shoulder, she'll feel my fingertips on her skin. I don't, of course. I've scared her enough for one day.

"I know," I say, trying to keep my voice soft and non-threatening. I crouch down and offer the knife again, this time handle first. "It's for the net."

Her hands go still, and then she smiles sheepishly. "Oh. Right." She takes the knife and goes to work, biting her lower lip as she concentrates on plucking away strands of netting. I wonder why she's going to so much trouble to free a half-dead crab, but I say nothing because for some reason it seems really important to her.

The knife makes her task easier, but when the crab is free, she frowns at the water, swallowing hard. Seeing the reluctance in her face, I stand and open my hand. "Here. I'll throw it in."

She deposits the crab in my palm, and I carry the newly liberated creature to where the waves are pitching against the rock. I toss it back home, and it disappears beneath the marbled surface.

When I turn back, Avery is standing with her arms twined around her waist. As I stroll toward her, the wind kicks up and sends golden strands of hair flying around her. With the way she's standing there on the rocks, she looks like some kind of mythical siren. I feel just as scared as if she were one, just as bewitched. The haunting song in her eyes lures me in until I'm standing right in front of her. She gazes up at me a long moment, searching my face as if she's hunting for familiarity. For a minute I worry she recognizes me. But then she folds the knife and hands it back.

"Thanks," she says. "Do you always carry a pocketknife?"

I take the knife and pocket it, recalling the last time I used a pocketknife to save her life, right before I died. "Yeah. You never know when you'll need a sharp blade."

A subtle pensiveness slides over her features, and I wonder if her thoughts went to the same place. I hold out a hand, partly in greeting, but mostly from the urge to steady her. "I'm Kai."

As though I'm still invisible to her, she stares through my outstretched hand. But then she blinks, and her eyes find mine.

"Avery." She puts her hand in mine, and as our skin meets, it feels like a long-sought-after prize has fallen into my hand. I close my fingers around her cold palm and savor the warmth that spreads through my body at her touch. The handshake lasts only a second, but it's enough to make all my trouble worth it.

There are so many things I want to say, but they're all mixed up with the things I can't say, and just as I'm starting to sort them out, a woman's voice calls Avery's name.

I turn to see her mom approaching, out of breath and waving scissors and pliers over her head. I feel thwarted, as though I've been skipped in a game of Uno and now I have to wait another turn before making my play. Her mom comes up, her eyes darting around on the ground. "Where is it?"

"It's free," Avery says, and I realize her mom is inquiring after the crab. Now I get why Avery was so determined to free it.

"Oh!" her mom exclaims, scissors and pliers flying up in triumph. From her wild hair, mismatched clothes, and childlike expression, she looks like she's teetering on the edge of her rocker. "How did you do it?"

Avery motions to me. "Kai here lent me his pocketknife."

Something lifts in my chest at the sound of Avery saying my name. Her mom gives me an appreciative look, and when she reaches for my hand, I meet her halfway.

"I'm Beth," she says. "And that was so nice of you." She gives my hand a good shake for emphasis, and her shoulders visibly relax as she looks at Avery. "I feel so much better. Don't you feel better?"

"Did you eat lunch, Mom? You got back pretty quick."

She releases my hand and waves off Avery. "Not yet. I was too anxious over Sebastian."

"Mom—"

"Don't start. I'm a big girl, Avery. With ample energy storage." She pats a miniscule pad of belly fat. "And now that our crisis is over, I can eat." She divides a look between me and Avery, and her mouth curves conspiratorially as her gaze settles on me. "Are you hungry? I feel like I should feed you something for helping us."

"Uh . . ." Is she offering me lunch? I wasn't expecting this and don't know what to say. Not wanting to make Avery feel uncomfortable, I look to her, wordlessly seeking permission.

She smiles at me, and it's like watching the sun rise. "He does look pretty hungry."

"I agree," Beth concurs. "You can tell by the way he's grimacing."

I'm not sure if I'm grimacing or not, but if lunch means more time with Avery, then I'm in. "You're right. I'm starving."

Beth claps and bounces on the balls of her feet, and Avery smooths her skirt and bites her lip into a half-smile that makes my insides feel all funny.

"Boys are always hungry," Beth says to Avery like she's instructing her in the proper care of an exotic pet. I half expect her to add, "But don't put your finger in their mouths, because they bite." Instead, she just waves for me to follow and says, "This way. We live up on the bluff."

Beth leads the way, and I slow my pace to match Avery's so I can walk beside her. Beth is going on about how nice it was for me to help free the crab, and how most people would have just joked about taking it home for lunch, and something about the world's chivalry deficit. The wind is blowing half of her words away, and she's talking so fast I'm only catching a portion of the rest. Her hands are fluttering like the words that can't fit through her mouth are fidgeting anxiously at the tips of her fingers.

Avery's not really paying attention; she's just staring at the sea as we walk. Her arms are folded and her shoulders are all tensed up like she's leaning against an imaginary wind. There's something in her eyes, a sort of longing as she follows the movement of the waves.

What are you thinking? I want to ask her. *Why haven't you gone back in the water when you used to love it? Are you afraid? Or is it something else?* But I can't ask her, because that would be weird. She thinks I don't even know her. So what do I say? How is it that as soon as she can hear my voice, I'm at a loss for words? I let out a sigh, and it must be louder than I think because she turns to look at me.

"You must actually be hungry," she says after a couple steps. "You really are grimacing now."

I compose my face into a less tormented state. "I am. I haven't eaten in months."

She must think I'm joking because she doesn't even lift a brow. "So, do you do this often?"

I hop over a tide pool to keep from stepping in it. "Do what?"

"You know—help out random people on the beach in the hope that they'll bring you home and feed you?" The corner of her mouth quirks up in a teasing smile.

"Usually I get at least a seafood dinner for my heroics. I'm feeling a little cheated, actually."

"Well, maybe if you'd freed the crab yourself." She unfolds her arms, and they fall to her sides. "But I did all the work. All you did was hand me your knife."

"Who returned the crab to its home, though?" I say. "That was me."

"Not very gently, I have to point out."

"Next time, you'll have to instruct me in the art of habitat reintroduction."

Beth, who's been talking to herself this whole time, turns around and walks backward. "Whatever you want to know about sea life," she announces, "Avery can tell you. She's a walking marine biology textbook."

I assumed as much from all the books on Avery's bookshelf. But since Avery doesn't know I've seen her bookshelf, I nod in interest. This is one more reason she needs to overcome whatever is keeping her from the water. It's pretty hard to study sea life when you won't go near the sea.

36

"Mom—watch out for that tide pool."

Beth spins around to walk forward again and starts ticking off a list of all of Avery's hobbies while Avery groans and begs her to stop. Rock climbing. Hiking. Fishing. Sailing. Longboarding. Volleyball. I'm thinking, *Is there* anything *this girl can't do?* But the thing is, I haven't seen her do any of these things. And I'm further convinced that Avery isn't living the life she was before I came into it.

"Mom—please," Avery says firmly. "You're boring Kai."

There's that lift in my chest again. "No, she's not," I argue as my eyes find Avery's. "I want to hear more."

Beth smiles at us over her shoulder. "Kai, may I bring you as a specimen to my next writing lecture? Most women these days wouldn't know how to spot a gentleman if they saw one."

"Mom—" Avery's voice is a warning, probably because this isn't the first time her mom has mounted this soapbox.

Beth ignores the warning and goes on about how her purpose in writing screenplays about decent men is to remind women not to accept anything less and to not allow men to treat them any less decently than the men in her stories treat their ladies.

By the time we reach the stairway, Avery's cheeks are bright pink, and Beth has barely paused for breath.

"She gets extra chatty when she's hungry," Avery explains as we climb the steps, and she slows her pace to put more space between us and her mom.

"Hey," I say with a shrug, "chatty is better than grouchy. I know people who turn into orcs when they're hungry."

As we enter her condo, Beth is giving us a detailed history of the demise of dating etiquette, claiming it all started with the feminist movement. I'm feeling too tense to sit, so when Beth drops into a stool and pulls one out for me, I just stand behind it and grip the curved iron back for support.

Avery is on the other side of the bar pulling things out of the fridge. A smile plays on her mouth as she removes tinfoil from a large bowl. "Do you like crab salad?" she asks me.

I smile at the irony of eating crab after just rescuing one, and then nod in the affirmative because there's no room for a yes in Beth's diatribe against feminism.

"It's not men's fault they don't know how to treat ladies anymore," she's saying. "Some women don't want to be treated like ladies and it ruins it for the rest of us."

"Mom," Avery says sharply as she slides a French bread loaf from a paper sleeve and points it at her, "I don't think you understand what feminism is. It's not about rejecting chivalry; it's about mutual respect between men and women and—"

Beth cuts her off with a passionate and long-winded rebuttal about how it doesn't matter what true feminism is; it only matters what men perceive it to be and how they see it as a threat. I can't see most of Avery's face as she slices the French bread, but the tips of her ears are red. Her knife is moving at jigsaw speed, and something tells me she's as eager as I am to get something into her mom's mouth. So I go over to help her. She seems reluctant to hand over the knife, and instead points me to a large spoon anchored in the crab salad. I pick it up and start spreading crab salad on the bread.

"Kai," Beth says, and I stiffen at her tone because it's like a fired-up teacher about to call on a slacking student. "Help me out here. As a man, do you feel threatened by feminism? I mean, what goes through your mind when you see women picketing and shouting at the top of their lungs, 'Down with men'?"

Avery rolls her eyes. "Mom—that's such a stereotypical—"

"Just—let him answer."

How did I go from happily making crab salad sandwiches to standing on a stage under a burning spotlight? I feel beads of sweat surfacing on my forehead. I try to think of something clever to say, but all I come up with is honesty.

"I don't know." I turn around to face Beth and lean against the counter, holding the big spoon in my hand. "I guess I feel . . . bad. I feel their pain. I think anyone who stands up to demand respect or rights does it only because they've been deprived of those things."

I think about my mom, how I used to wish she had the courage to demand more respect from my dad. But maybe it wasn't courage she needed. Maybe she just needed someone to tell her she deserved better.

"People need to know they're worth something," I say. "And if feminism teaches women that they have the right to be treated as human beings, then that shouldn't threaten men; it should motivate them to be better."

I glance at Avery, and the way she's looking at me makes me think I just earned some points on her trustworthiness scorecard.

Avery's mom slides her stool back abruptly and stands. Her eyes are wide and transfixed on some imaginary thing, as if she's staring out a window at a UFO. Only she's not facing a window.

Without warning, she circles the counter, takes my face in her hands, and plants a kiss on my cheek. "Thank you. That's the line I've been looking for!" Then she rushes down the hall and disappears into her office.

I stand there baffled for a moment, and then look to Avery. "What was that all about?"

Avery smiles and goes back to washing blueberries in a strainer under the tap. "I think your words are about to be immortalized in my mom's latest screenplay."

"Seriously?" I think back on what I said, trying to figure out what was so profound about it.

"Next thing you know, Jude Law will be repeating your words. You have to be careful with what you say around my mom." She sets the washed blueberries on the counter and dries her hands on a dish towel. "Have you ever seen *The Velvet Sparrow*?"

I give her a blank look.

"It's a historical film my mom penned. There's this scene where the main character dramatically cries, 'If this is love, then

I hate love. And I'd rather tear my heart out with a fishhook than feel love again.'"

"Is that something you said?" I ask, intrigued and amused.

She drops a handful of blueberries on one of the plates. "When I was ten, when my cat died."

"You must have really loved your cat."

She shrugs. "It was my first real-life experience with death. I didn't take it very well."

The sandwiches are done, so I set the spoon back in the bowl and replace the tinfoil. "I don't think anyone should have to take death well. I mean, it's probably the worst thing that can happen to anyone, losing someone they care about." I should know. Over the last six months working with Grim, I've seen more than my fair share of the effects of death. "Believe me. No one takes it well."

"You sound like you know from experience."

I move my plate to the bar and sit on a stool. "Death is part of the human experience. And I'm human." Or was, anyway.

She sets her plate beside mine, but before sitting down she grabs her mom's plate. "I'm going to take this into her office." She starts walking away, then twists and adds, "If she's too immersed in her story, I may have to prod her to eat. So . . . sit tight for a minute."

She disappears down the hall, and I look at my sandwich, realizing that I don't even know if this body is capable of digesting food. I've never seen Charles eat while materialized. But that doesn't mean it's not possible or even necessary. In fact, now that I think about it, the beginning of hunger pains are pinching my insides. Or maybe it's nerves.

Avery returns and sits beside me, plucking a blueberry off her plate and putting it in her mouth. I pick up my sandwich. Just to be safe, I start small, tearing off a bit of bread with my teeth. It tastes great, chewy and soft, like French bread should be. I take the next step and swallow, waiting for something to happen—I don't know what—maybe vomiting or asphyxiation or spontaneous combustion. But nothing happens. So I take another bite, bigger this time. And it goes down as easily as the first.

Now that I'm confident eating won't turn me into a gremlin, I return my attention to Avery. I can't believe I'm sitting beside her, eating a sandwich we made together. She's close enough that I can feel warmth radiating from her skin. And she smells amazing, like coconut and some other fruity scent.

All the death talk should make an easy transition into the things I really want to talk to her about. But I can't exactly turn to her and say, "You don't need to take my death so hard. My life wasn't really worth living anyway." Not only would it sound totally creepy, but she can't know who I am. No, I'm going to have to be creative about this. Deliver my message in a roundabout way.

I look around her mom's condo. I've seen the decor before. Sailboat paintings and knickknacks, and a wooden yacht club plaque. I study it now with feigned interest, as though I've never seen it before. "Do you love sailing as much as your mom?"

She finishes chewing, then says, "It's her passion, not mine. I think she gets a lot of writing inspiration on the waves. But we usually take a family trip to the Channel Islands at the end of the summer before school starts."

"Are you going this year?" With her aversion to the ocean, I don't see why she would. But if I can get her to explain why, it will steer our conversation in the direction I want.

"I'm not sure." She rolls a blueberry between her thumb and index finger. "A lot of things have changed since last year."

Now we're getting somewhere. "Like what?"

Her fingers go still, and she gazes down at her blueberry as though it's a crystal ball showing her the answer to my question. Whatever she sees darkens her expression into something pained. Her lips part, and just when I think she's going to voice her thoughts, she slides on a cheerful façade. It may fool other people, but through the tiny cracks, I can still see her pain.

She smiles in the way she usually does right before making a joke. "My sister dyed her hair black, and I don't think my mom will let her on the boat when she no longer looks like a California girl."

I give her a courtesy smile, then gaze at her and wait for a real answer. She doesn't give it to me, though. She eats her blueberry and says, "What about you? Do you sail? Wait—let me guess. You surf."

I try to tell myself that it's okay she's not ready to open up yet, that I can be patient. I shake my head. "I've never tried it."

Her eyebrows lift in surprise. "Why not?"

"Just haven't had the chance." I saw the ocean only once when I was alive, on the same day I drowned in it.

Her brows come back down and pinch together. "Don't you live around here?"

I've never had a conversation like this, where I've had to construct my answers so that they're both truthful and vague. "No—I'm only here for a little while."

She picks up her sandwich, but doesn't take a bite. "Well, you can't visit SLO county without giving surfing a shot. If you catch even one wave, you'll be hooked for life." Her expression sobers, and I glimpse that pain in her eyes again before she blinks it away. "I know someone who could give you lessons. His name is Tyler, and he works at the surf shop at Avila Beach. Just go in and tell him I sent you."

"I might just do that." Or not. I should probably avoid Tyler so I don't end up accidentally throwing my fist in his face.

A cell phone on the counter starts vibrating, and Avery reaches for it and looks at the screen. "Sorry, I have to take this." She takes the phone into the living room. I try not to listen but can't really help it when there's nothing else to listen to. It sounds like someone is asking her for a favor, because Avery is saying, "Yeah. I probably could."

Beth returns to the kitchen and pulls a glass from the cupboard. The beach's humidity has done a number on her curls, and they're springing out of her scalp like a jester's hat. She looks at me. "Did you know Avery makes the most amazing chocolates?"

"Does she?" Of course I already know she works in a chocolate shop. I even sampled the chocolate once before I died.

"If you go to the surf shop like Avery suggested," Beth says, apparently having eavesdropped on our conversation, "you should stop by her father's chocolate shop, the Chocolate Couture. Avery works there. She'll give you some free samples."

Avery comes back into the kitchen, moves her plate to the sink, and then looks at her mom regretfully. "Dad needs me at work."

"Avery," Beth chides. "It's your day off."

"I know, but . . . he needs me. They're slammed today, and he had to fire one of the new summer employees for giving out a bunch of free chocolate to his friends."

Beth huffs. "So much for the perfect day."

Avery turns to me and smiles a little. "You've probably been itching for an escape anyway. Do you want a bag for the rest of your sandwich? You didn't eat very much."

I look down at my food, which is almost untouched. I guess I was too focused on Avery to eat. "Sure," I say, standing.

As she bags my sandwich, I stand there hoping I'll have more time with her. Maybe I'll visit her at the chocolate shop tomorrow like her mom suggested. Or maybe I'll visit her later today, in case I don't have a tomorrow.

She walks me to the door and hands me the paper bag. "Thanks again for helping save the crab."

I nod as I walk through the doorway and turn back to her. "Thanks for the crab sandwich."

She smiles, and it actually touches her eyes. "Maybe I'll see you around."

"Maybe." There has to be something else to say, something meaningful in case this is the last time she sees me. I open my mouth, willing the perfect words to come out. "Well . . . it's been real."

She nods, waves, and then shuts the door.

I stand there a moment, like I'm waiting for her to open it back up, even though I know she won't.

It's been real? That's what I went to all this trouble to tell her? It's been real. Brilliant. I sigh and look down at Charles's ring. It could be minutes before he notices it missing, or weeks. There's no way of knowing. So I need to make the most of my time here. Avery's going to be heading to work soon, so I turn and start walking in that direction, intending to take her mom's suggestion to get some chocolate samples.

6

avery

he air is extra clear after last night's rainstorm, and from where I'm driving, I can see the ocean below, rippling shades of blue and fringes of white foam. My chest aches at the sight of it, so I move my sun visor over the side window and focus on the road instead.

Up ahead, a boy is walking on the shoulder of the highway. He's tall, and his platinum-blond hair glows like a beacon in the sunlight.

I know that hair. I just said good-bye to it on Mom's doorstep fifteen minutes ago. I slow down and pull up behind him, lowering my window and leaning out. "Car trouble?"

When he turns and sees me, his eyebrows rise, and the corner of his mouth follows. "You could say that."

"Can I give you a ride somewhere?"

He comes to my window and lays his hand on the door. "Hasn't anyone ever told you not to pick up strangers?"

More than once, Dad has told me not to pick up strangers.

Probably because when I first got my drivers license, I did it all the time. A lot of people don't like to pay for parking near the beach, so when I'd see them struggling with their surfboard and beach bags, I'd pick them up if I was already on my way there.

Kai is less of a stranger than all the others I've picked up. However, thanks to our crab rescue, I do know for a fact that he's carrying something sharp.

I stick my hand out the window and open my palm. My forearm touches his hand where it rests on my door, and I feel a little zing. "Hand over your pocketknife, and I'll give you a lift."

He grins and produces his pocketknife, dropping it in my palm. I curl my fingers around it and tuck it in the side pocket of my door.

"Hop in."

He circles the car and gets in. His legs are so long he has to slide the seat back a foot, and even then, his knees almost touch the glove compartment. The last person to sit there was Paige, and she's half an inch over five feet. And very proud of that half inch.

"Where to?" I ask as I get back on the road.

He hesitates, as if he's not really sure. "Just stay on the highway. I'll tell you when to turn."

"So," I say, cringing a bit, "I'm sorry about my mom. She gets a little carried away sometimes."

"I think she's nice. Passionate, but nice." He's looking down, to where the sun is glinting off his ring. He's wearing a wristband that matches the ring—silver with a stone-like vein. I wonder where he got them, and if they mean anything special, but it feels like such a nosy question to ask.

"This probably isn't exactly an ideal vacation day for you," I say instead. "First, getting harangued by an overzealous screenwriter, and now car trouble."

"Actually, it's been a great day. And anyway, I'm not on vacation." He glances at me, then back to his ring. "I came here to work. For a little while."

"For the summer?"

He purses his lips. "I hope so."

Even though I only just met him, I hope so too. He seems like someone I'd like to get to know better. "Where are you working?"

"I . . . I'm not sure yet."

"So you're still looking for a job?" I almost tell him to apply at the Chocolate Couture to replace the guy Dad fired yesterday, but I would never hear the end of my sister Sophie's teasing if I brought in a cute guy for Dad to hire. "What kind of work are you looking for? Maybe I know someone who's hiring."

The lines of concentration deepen between his brows as if he's making a mental inventory of his skills. "I'm good with my hands. Fixing things. And I spent last summer working in a vineyard."

"Well, you've come to the right place, then." I make a sweeping motion with my hand, as though I'm Vanna White presenting a grand prize of vineyard-wrapped hills.

He nods in agreement. "I'm sure I'll find something." My window is still down, and he lowers his too. The humid air rushes in, swirling around us, pulling pieces of hair free from my messy bun. He gazes out the window at a passing orchard, watching rows of apple trees fly by. Then he sticks his hand out the window and spreads his fingers to catch the wind. He closes his eyes, like he's savoring the sensation. And I find my own hand slipping out the window to do the same.

After a minute, he opens his eyes and looks at me. "I wouldn't have guessed white."

"White what?"

He tugs gently on my sleeve. "For a chocolate shop uniform."

My heart gives a little lurch at his touch. "My black apron is on the back seat." I slide a hand over my stomach, like I'm touching an imaginary apron. "My dad's shop is like a fine restaurant. Black and white uniforms, stuffy decor, and gourmet chocolates you can't find anywhere else. And at least with white, stains can be bleached."

He goes back to catching the wind, appearing to contemplate this. "Wouldn't it be nice if people could be bleached too?"

I give a breathy laugh. "You mean like your hair?" I can't quite get over how white his hair is, and how it makes a stark contrast with his dark lashes and eyebrows.

His hand goes to his hair, and he meets my smile. "I didn't do this. It just . . . happened." And then his expression stills, grows serious. "What I mean is," he says slowly, "what if whenever we were stained, or hurt, scarred, there was some magical liquid that would just . . . wash it all away?" He says this like he knows there are things I wish I could wash away. Of course he knows, because what person hasn't done things they regret, or have wounds that never seem to heal? I wonder which of his stains he wishes could be washed away.

"Some people like their stains," I say. "They wear them like a badge. Proof that they've lived and survived. I think some would choose not to use this magical liquid, even if it were available."

"Would you?" he asks.

I consider his question. What would it mean to have all my pain washed away? If the hurt from my parents' separation was gone, would it bring them back together? No—it would only change me so I wouldn't be bothered by it anymore. And what about my grief over the death of the boy who saved my life? It would be a relief to not feel it anymore. But would I keep searching for his identity if it didn't hurt so much? Probably not. And his family would never know what became of him. But maybe they wouldn't care, because they would use the magical liquid too. Our entire society would be full of apathetic, uncaring people. Because it's what hurts us that makes us human. It's the pain that makes us compassionate.

"No," I say after careful deliberation. "The price would be too steep."

"What if it were free?"

"Nothing is really free."

He seems to ponder my words for a long moment, then frowns and nods in agreement. At least I think he's agreeing, until he says, "Maybe things are just harder to see when they don't have a price tag." His words swirl around with the air in the car until I see my exit approaching.

"How much farther am I taking you?" I ask. "My exit's coming up."

He scratches the back of his head like he's really not sure where he's going. "Go ahead and take it."

I take the exit and head down the ramp. "Where am I taking you anyway? Home?"

He shakes his head. "I'm still working on that too. I only got here this morning."

"So you don't have a place to stay?" At the bottom of the ramp I turn right and pull over.

My concern seems to amuse him, because there's a glint of humor in his eyes when he says, "I have a place. I just haven't found it yet." He pulls the handle and swings the door open. "Thanks for the ride. I can get out here."

"But there's nothing around here." The shops on the beachfront are still a mile away, and in the opposite direction, waves of orchards and vineyards stretch endlessly. "At least let me take you to the beachfront."

He gets out and looks around, like someone at a fork in the road, debating whether to go left or right. "I think I'll visit some of the vineyards, see if they need help." He shuts the door, and I feel panicky, like it will be the worst thing in the world if he walks away and I never see him again. But he doesn't walk away. He gazes at me through the open window for one, two, three breaths. There's a strange charge in the air, like a thunderstorm is hovering overhead, but the clouds above us are white and wispy. He rests his arm on the passenger door and leans toward me. "Can I come see you later? At the chocolate shop?"

I nod, trying to pace the up-and-down bobbing of my head so I don't appear too eager.

"Maybe we can get some dinner when you get off work. That is, if I find a job before then, and get paid. I'm sort of short on cash." He shuts his eyes and grimaces, like he regrets this admission.

"It's okay," I say, biting my lip to keep my smile in check. "I could pay or—"

He shakes his head. "I'm not going to be one of those guys your mom was complaining about. If I can help it, I'm keeping chivalry alive and well."

"I'm a twenty-first century kind of girl. And I have a healthy savings account."

"And I'm a twenty-first century kind of guy with a healthy ego."

So much for keeping my smile in check. I feel it spreading across my face with abandonment. "Dutch?"

"American. I'm buying."

I slide my gearshift into drive and stifle a laugh. "Come by later. We'll figure something out."

His gaze lingers on my face for a moment longer, and then he nods and straightens, waving before he turns and walks away.

The Chocolate Couture is packed when I walk in, tourists come to top off their lunch with something indulgent. As I step into the bustle, a familiar peace washes over me. Cold air falls from the vent above the entrance, but inside the shop it always feels warm to me. Maybe it's the walls that are painted the color of melted caramel and cherry ganache, or the sweet air, as though the dust motes are coated in sugar.

Paige wonders why I spend so much time here. It's because the only time I feel truly calm is when I'm immersed in busy work. Work is where I can forget about heroes who can't be identified, parents who can't be reconciled, and a longing for an ex-boyfriend that can't be satisfied. I can get lost in the flurry of tasks, in tastes and aromas, in customers' euphoric expressions when they taste something I've created. But today, something is on my mind that I don't want to leave behind. Kai. His great smile, and his empty pockets, and our penciled-in plans for tonight.

Dad is at the register ringing someone up. He's wearing his usual white dress shirt, black tie, and black apron, and a sheen of sweat shines beneath his thinning blond hair. There's no one else behind the glass counters to attend the swarm of customers, and as I'm wondering where Paige and my sister Sophie are, I see them near the display window, bickering about something.

"Your dad said to work the counter," Paige is insisting, hand on hip.

Sophie ignores her and continues with her meticulous arranging of gift boxes on a display shelf. A silky sheet of cropped black hair hides her face. Her natural color is showing at the roots, golden blonde like mine.

"Just because he's your dad," Paige says, "doesn't mean you don't have to—"

"Don't you have something else to do?" Sophie says without looking at her. "You're cramping my artistic process."

"This isn't art!" Paige grabs the boxes from Sophie's arms and shoves them on the shelf in two untidy stacks. "Now come help me!"

Sophie is unfazed. "I think the Sundries Shack is hiring down the street. Why don't you go work there, and you can pile things into baskets all day." She rearranges the boxes, taking her sweet time, while Paige groans in exasperation. Sophie is only fifteen, but somehow manages to rule the place.

"I'll help you, Paige," I call out.

She looks at me, noticing me for the first time since I walked in, and releases a sigh of relief. "Finally. Someone who actually knows how to work."

I follow Paige around the glass display case and greet Dad with a smile as I pass.

"Hey, Avery," he says, "thanks for coming in on such short notice."

"No problem." I consider telling him about Mom's manic behavior, but I don't want to worry him. The lows always follow the highs, and it's almost time for her to crash.

I tie on my black apron and get to work. The rest of the afternoon is filled with hazelnut truffles and mint squares and "Does that have nuts in it?" and "I'll take three of those" and "Can I sample the bacon chocolate bars?" and "Wow, who knew curry and chocolate made such a great combination!"

Things finally slow down as the late afternoon sun breaks through the storefront windows. Dad takes the opportunity to fix a wonky hinge on the front door. Sophie goes to the kitchen to make a batch of caramel, and Paige and I take care of the last customers of post-lunch rush.

As I'm ringing someone up, the door chimes. I glance up to see Tyler, the sunlight behind him making his edges all soft. My knees go soft too, and I brace my hands on the counter to steady myself. He hasn't been in here since we broke up, and I wonder what he's doing here now. He lingers at the front of the shop, studying a display of chocolate-covered mangos, but from the way he keeps casting glances my way, I know he's here to see me.

The lady I'm ringing up is asking something, but I don't know what, because all I can think is that maybe my appearance at the beach last night had a bigger effect on Tyler than I thought, and he's here to reconcile.

"Miss?" the lady asks.

"Sorry, what?"

"What time do you close? I'd like to bring my granddaughter back tomorrow night."

"Oh. We close at seven."

She nods and takes her box of assorted chocolates out the door, stepping carefully around Dad, who's still kneeling on the floor tinkering with the hinge. Now that I'm free, Tyler approaches me with slow, measured steps as if he's deciding what to say on his way. I grip the edge of the counter for added support, like a feeble old lady leaning on a walker.

He comes up and spreads his hands on the counter. He's wearing a black wetsuit, and his dark hair is still damp, like he just waded out of the sea. His jade-green eyes look right into mine, and I think my heart might beat right out of my chest.

"Hey," he says in a gentle voice that makes me feel even weaker. "How you doing?"

"Fine."

He tilts his head and knits his brows, like he's eager to know what I'm thinking. But it's more than an expression. It's a hundred memories. A hundred times I've seen that exact look, when he's broken down my walls and gotten me to confide in him. He leans closer. "You know what I mean. I want to make sure you're okay . . . after last night."

The truth is I'm feeling rather discarded. Like a broken toy tossed in the recycle bin. But I don't want to get into that, so I slide my hands up on the counter and say, "Really. I'm fine."

He looks down at our fingers, at the small space between them. Maybe he's wishing he could touch my hand the way he used to. Or maybe he's thinking I need to scrub out the cocoa under my nails. "So we're back to barriers, huh?"

"You're the one who put them back up, remember?"

He lets out a long sigh, and his cool breath touches my cheeks. It smells like peppermint bark. "Avery," he says, his tapping index finger betraying how bothered he is. "There's something I need to say."

For a second, I think he's going to lean closer and tell me, "I'm sorry. I was wrong. I regret ending things between us. I want to be here for you while you're going through all this, and I love you for so many more reasons than just your mad surfing skills." That's all it would take for me to throw myself into his arms and tell him all was forgiven. But the words I want him to say don't come.

Instead, he says, "You don't have to prove anything to me. If you don't feel comfortable going in the water, then don't. I want you to take as much time as you need to get better." His hands slide toward mine until our fingertips touch. "I meant what I said last night. I care about you. I still have feelings for you, and they're not going away anytime soon. So do what you need to heal completely, and when you're okay, I'll be here waiting."

"What if I'm never okay?" I whisper.

He shakes his head. "I know you. You're fearless and strong. You'll be okay."

I almost ask why he can't be with me now, the way I am. Why I have to be fixed before we can get back together. But I already know the answer. He told me himself the day we broke up. It was too hard for him. Too emotionally exhausting to deal with a grieving girlfriend. I didn't blame him then, and I don't blame him now. I saw the effort he made when we were still together. Coming to my house when I didn't want to go out, trying to comfort me when I couldn't be comforted. He tried to get me to open up about my feelings, but he couldn't pry them out no matter how hard he tried.

It's not his fault my heart has been doubly broken. It's mine.

I look at his long, tan fingers spread on the counter, and wish I could press them to my cheek and promise him things will be different. That I am better. Fearless and strong, like he believes I am. But it would be a lie, so I say nothing, just nod and clench my teeth, biting back the tears I feel coming.

There's a high-pitched cough at the shop entrance, and I look up to see Tourist Girl—Gem—standing there, arms folded over her bare midriff and sandaled foot tapping impatiently.

"I'm giving her another lesson today," Tyler explains, but it does nothing to assuage the jealousy rearing inside me.

"I have to get back to work," I manage, and then turn and go to the kitchen before he can see the stupid tears welling in my eyes.

On the counter in the kitchen lies a sheet of nougat, ready to be cut into squares. It's exactly what I need. I grab a butcher knife and slice into it, cutting off a long strip.

My sister Sophie comes up behind me, a small, understanding smile on her cherry-red lips. "Harder." She grabs another knife and plunges it into the sheet, tip first. "Like that. If you're going to pretend you're killing someone, don't slice. Stab."

I raise the knife and bring it back down, stabbing the nougat right in the middle. It feels pretty good.

"You need more force," Sophie says. "Try raising it high above your head before coming down."

I do, and when I bring the knife down, the nougat breaks into two jagged halves.

"What are you doing?" I turn to see Paige in the doorway, hands on hips, mouth wide open. "Stop it or we're going to have to make a whole new batch!"

"Better the nougat than Tyler's spleen," Sophie says.

Paige takes the knife and points it at me, huffing out a sigh. "Why don't you see? It's a no-brainer! He wants you, Avery. You can see it in his eyes. All you have to do is be yourself. Is that so hard? I mean, look at that girl he's hanging out with. She's like how you used to be. Fun. Spontaneous. Carefree. Just be the same, and he's yours!"

I've lost count of the times people have said things like that to me recently. *If you want Tyler back, then go after him. Fight for him. Be happy. Be yourself.* But I'm stuck somewhere inside this body. I don't even know who I am anymore, or what will make me happy. And I'm tired of people making it sound like it should be so easy.

Sophie takes another swipe at the nougat. "I'm never falling in love. It sounds worse than having my toenails ripped off."

Paige makes a disgusted face. "Ew. And it's only torture when the person you love doesn't love you back. Or when they do love you, but they don't know it. Or they know it, but they don't know how to show you or tell you. Or when—"

Dad pokes his head into the kitchen. "Girls, there are customers."

"I'll take care of the nougat," Sophie whispers, standing in front of it so Dad doesn't see the mess. Paige and I go up front to tend to the customers, and something white catches my eye through the window.

This afternoon may not turn out so bad, because pacing slowly outside the shop window is my new friend, Kai.

7

KAI

I have a twenty-dollar bill in my front pocket. It took me four hours of hard labor to earn, give or take thirty minutes to convince a vineyard manager to let me work one afternoon for cash, without identification. And now I'm loitering beneath the striped awning of the Chocolate Couture, trying to get up the nerve to go in and see Avery again. I've been here at least ten minutes, long enough to see Tyler talking with her, and long enough to see him leave with the same petite blonde he was with at the beach last night.

I don't know what Tyler and Avery were talking about, but hopefully he didn't say anything to make things worse for her. He has a habit of doing that, and I wish he would just stay away and let her move on and heal.

Through the glass, I see Avery come out of the back of the shop to greet a customer. Something lifts inside me at the sight of her, the way cliff jumping makes your stomach rise to your throat. And when she meets my gaze through the window, the submersion is complete.

"Hey." The voice comes from behind me and makes me jump. At first I think it's Charles or someone from the other side, come to reclaim the stolen ring. But it's just Tyler. He knuckles me in the shoulder. "You waiting for someone?" By someone, he means Avery, because he glances through the window at her. "Don't bother, man. She's my girl."

I glare at him, annoyed at his interference. "Oh yeah? That's not what she said." So the statement is a little deceptive, but not entirely untrue. She hasn't said anything about Tyler today.

"It's complicated."

Something about his words awakens a viper inside of me. I feel it snake through me, tightening my muscles as it goes. I think about all the times I've swung at him in the last couple months. The times my fist has gone straight through him, leaving him untouched and me frustrated. I think of all the thoughtless words he's said to her, the tears she's cried over him, her agony he could have softened, but instead magnified.

My eyes slide to the blonde girl who's still waiting for him at the top of the steps. Her eyes are playing connect-the-dots around Tyler and me, trying and failing not to look at us, her face irritated and impatient. "So," I say, "*complicated* means you're free to hang out with other girls, but Avery isn't allowed to be looked at by other guys?"

Tyler glances at Gem and then back at me. "It's not like that, dude. She's a customer."

My stomach twists as my anger rises. I always feel sick when I get angry, because it makes me feel like my dad. I spent my childhood trying to be everything he wasn't. I brought home dinner for my sisters, even if it meant stealing it. I told them they were smart and pretty and strong, instead of tearing them down. I refused to use the vile language my dad did, and tried so hard to not let my temper rage. But the anger always came, grew on my bones like muscle and sinew, begging to be used. And when kids at school picked on me or my sisters, they didn't stand a chance against the power that was released in my first hit. I hated myself for it, for being just like my dad. I'd always felt powerless, like I'd been cut from the same fabric and pattern as him, and there was no altering it. That was until I met Charles Kelsey, who showed me a better way. But he's dead now, like me. And at the moment, I can't seem to remember anything he taught me.

In my already-clenched fists, I feel all those unconnected punches from the past few months, all my anger for Tyler still lingering, building. I try to rein it in, tie it up. I shrug. "I'm a customer too. I'm just here to get something sweet." I turn away before my fist ends up in his face, but before I make it past the threshold, Tyler grabs my arm. And although it's probably not meant to instigate anything, his touch is like a razor, slicing through the restraints holding my hand at my side. Before I can stop myself, I swing around, my fist landing squarely on his mouth. He stumbles back, clutching his mouth in his hand.

"What was that for?" he shouts when he finds his balance. His face is screwed up into a mixture of shock and outrage.

"What's going on?" Avery charges out of the shop, eyes and mouth wide open. There's a big white smudge across her black apron, and stupidly, all I can think is how maybe black can be stained too.

I'm still looking at Avery when Tyler plows into me, and the impact sends us both to the ground. Tyler straddles me and swings at my face, but I block him easily enough, and I wonder if he took sparring lessons from a sloth or if this body's reflexes are faster than a mortal's.

"Tyler!" Avery screams as she yanks on the back of his shirt. "Get off him!"

Tyler glances back at Avery, then jumps to his feet and backs away, chest so inflated I half expect him to pound it gorilla-style.

"What are you guys doing?" Avery demands.

I stand and dust myself off, too ashamed to meet her eyes. I don't know what part of me thought that hitting Tyler would make Avery trust me more, but I mentally send that part of me to the doghouse.

Blood is oozing from Tyler's split lip, and he dabs it with the back of his hand. "He was watching you," he growls to Avery. "I saw him."

"So?" she says. "I know him!" Tyler's face goes slack, and I fight back a smug smile.

Someone clears their throat behind me, and I turn to see Tyler's petite blonde standing there, arms folded, looking the way my little sister used to when she was carefully considering a tantrum. She's left her big surfboard at the top of the steps, and a family is trying to navigate around it. "Should we reschedule my surfing lesson?" she asks. Her voice reminds me of Betty Boop, and I wonder if she's forcing it on purpose to sound cutesy or something.

Tyler looks at Avery, and his lip isn't the only thing on his face that looks wounded. "No," he says to Betty Boop. "Let's go." He picks up a surfboard from a nearby bench and follows his "customer" down to the beach.

Which leaves me alone with Avery and her fiery gaze. I duck away from the intensity of it and sit on a concrete bench in front of the shop to collect and reorganize my thoughts. She comes and sits beside me, propping one knee up and hugging it against the smudge on her apron. "You okay?"

I shrug. "I've had tickle fights more brutal than that." I glance at her, hoping to see a smile, but her lips are razor straight.

"Why did you hit him?"

"I . . ." My hands fall open and I offer a repentant look. "I'm sorry. I shouldn't have done that. He didn't want me to come in, and then—"

"So when people get in your way, you just knock 'em down?"

In her eyes, I see her second-guessing our dinner plans. I need to fix this—fast. "No," I say, scrambling for a way to explain myself. "It was more than that."

"Then what?"

I can't exactly tell her the truth, that I've been hanging around for six months, catching bits of her conversations with people. That I've heard Tyler say hurtful things to her face and behind her back. I can't tell her I've seen him flirt with countless girls on the beach while she sat at home and cried over his absence. That I've watched him keep his distance while she suffered, like she was a leper and he was afraid of being contaminated with her grief.

I can't say any of this, so I say, "He hurt someone I care about."

Her lips part in surprise. "Oh." Then her brows crash together, as though she's perplexed and even hurt by my words. "So . . . you know him?"

I shrug. "Not really. I mostly know *of* him through a mutual acquaintance. And he was already on my bad side when he grabbed my arm, so . . ." I sigh. Charles always says that excuses only take away our power to set things right, so I stop. "It doesn't matter. I shouldn't have hit him."

She starts playing absentmindedly with a button at the top of her white blouse and gazes toward the beach where Tyler and Betty Boop went. She's probably wondering who Tyler hurt, and what exactly he's been doing since they broke up. Or maybe she's trying to think of a way to get out of dinner.

"I've blown it, haven't I?" I ask.

She tilts her head one direction and her mouth the other, and looks at me like I'm some sculpture in a museum and she's trying to decide if I'm art or trash. "I don't know. I'm debating whether it's smart to go to dinner with someone when all I know about him is that he carries a pocketknife and has a lethal left hook."

"You have my pocketknife," I remind her. "And I really am sorry about the left hook. If it makes any difference, that's the first time I've used it in over two years."

The corners of her mouth are subtly indented, so I know she's softening. "It looked well-practiced. You must have used it a lot at some point."

"I used to get into fights at school," I admit. "But I've never hit a girl, if that makes you feel any better."

She stands up. "It does. Sort of." Her hand is on her stomach, and she absentmindedly runs her thumb along the apron tie at her waist. "I guess this would be the perfect application for your magical human bleach?"

"Yeah." I sigh and make a penitent face. "No more picking fights. I promise. And you can keep my pocketknife."

She bites her lip, considering. Finally she says, "I have some work to finish up. But I'll meet you back here in an hour."

She leads me to a little outdoor café down the street where wind chimes dangle from a trellised dining area. It's her favorite place, she tells me, but she hasn't been here in months. Maybe because it overlooks the ocean, or because she hasn't had anyone to come here with. There's a mermaid mural on the exterior, and we step up to an outdoor counter that's framed with bamboo. I order clam chowder since I've never had clam chowder that didn't come from a can, and because it's five bucks and I only have twenty. She orders the pesto shrimp linguine for twelve dollars and a Sprite, and as the girl at the register adds up our orders, I pray that I'll have enough.

"Nineteen seventy-one," the girl says. Avery reaches into her purse, but I slide my twenty across the counter before she can produce any currency.

"I got it," I say.

She smiles at me. "So you found a job?"

The girl at the register gives us a funny look, like she's not sure if she should take money from someone who was recently unemployed. I nod at the twenty and give her an encouraging smile, and she takes it and returns a quarter and four pennies. I drop them into my pocket, feeling like I just hit the jackpot.

"Never underestimate the power of determination," I say to Avery.

We take our food to a little round table at the edge of the veranda. The tabletop is a colorful seascape mosaic, and a stained-glass wind chime clinks softly overhead. Avery sits across from me and pulls the pins from her hair and shakes it out. Golden waves spill over her shoulders, and with the evening sun pouring into the veranda, she looks like she's the one who should be running around on an angel's errand, not me.

"So," she says after taking a bite of her linguine, "have you found a place to stay?"

"Not yet," I admit. "But I know some people around here, so if all else fails, I'll drop in on them." My sisters live nearby with my aunt and uncle, but dropping in on them isn't really a possibility, so I'll have to make sure that not all else fails.

"Where are you from, anyway?"

Not for the first time, it occurs to me that I need to be careful with what information I divulge. If I give away too many clues, it could lead her to my identity. I don't want to lie, though, so I'll just keep things vague. "Michigan."

She looks surprised by this. "You don't look Michiganese."

I laugh, and the rumbling feeling catches me off guard because I haven't felt it in so long. "Michiganese?"

"Yeah. Michiganian. Or Michiganerd, or whatever. You look straight-up Californian. Or Australian." She points to the top of her head and says, "It's the hair."

I eat a spoonful of chowder. It's creamy and savory, with an entirely different flavor than the canned stuff. "What exactly do you think Michiganiots look like?"

Now she's the one laughing. It's a great laugh. Musical and subtle, like the wind chime above us. "Okay, what's the correct term for a person who lives in Michigan?"

"I like Michiganese. It makes me sound exotic."

"Okay then. What brought a Michiganese boy like you all the way to the west coast?"

Now we're getting into trickier waters. "It's a long story."

"I don't have anywhere to be." She takes a bite and watches me expectantly as she chews.

"I already told you. I'm here to work."

"But why not get a summer job in Michigan? There must be another reason you came here."

Down the street, I see Tyler and blonde Betty Boop come up the stairs from the beach. He's carrying both of their surfboards under one arm, and she's carrying a beach bag in one hand and talking with the other.

Avery twists to see what I'm looking at, and her whole body tenses. When she turns back, she sets down her fork and leans away from her food, like she's suddenly lost her appetite.

I don't know what Tyler is thinking, going around with another girl when it's clear that he and Avery both still have feelings for each other. What keeps two people apart when they'd both be happier together?

An idea comes to me. I hold it in my palm, weighing it. If Avery is in love with Tyler, he must have *some* redeeming qualities. There must be another side of him that I've never seen. The side capable of winning Avery's heart. So even though a wave of nausea rolls my stomach at the notion, maybe Tyler needs to be part of this plan. Maybe I need to get them back together to make her happiness and healing complete.

"Tyler said you were his girl," I say, swallowing the bitter taste in my mouth. "Is that true?"

Her eyes flash to mine, and there's a mixture of pain and anger in them. Then she quickly looks away, and I see her trying to compose herself. She puts on the smile she uses to cover up what she's really feeling. "If it were true, would I be here with you?"

I don't answer, just keep my eyes on her, hoping she'll feel the need to fill the silence. It works, because after stacking half a dozen grilled shrimp on her fork, she sets it down and gives a surrendering sigh. She answers quietly, like she's afraid he'll hear. "We were together, but not anymore."

"Do you still love him?" The words just come out, because I really want to know. If I'm going to try to get them back together, I need to make sure it's what will truly make her happy.

Her eyebrows go up. "Is this a date? Because if so, exes are a taboo topic."

I lean back. "What would you rather talk about?"

"Tell me about Michigan."

I slowly stir my chowder, watching steam rise from the creamy surface. I decide to humor her, but fully intend on circling our conversation back to Tyler. "Where I lived last, it's green. And there's a really big lake."

She stares at me, waiting for more. I eat a spoonful of soup to let her know I'm out of descriptive words. "Wow," she says. "With descriptions like that, you should host a travel show or something."

I work on my soup for a minute, then say, "Can you do better? Tell me, how would you describe Avila Beach?"

She pulls in a deep breath and looks around. From where we sit, we have a sweeping view of the ocean in the west and green rolling hills in the east. "Green," she says. She's not smiling, but her eyes are sparkling. "There's a really big ocean."

It's official. She's adorable. I could sit here all night with her, discussing green hills and large bodies of water, and it would still be the best night I've ever had. "I'm humbled by your eloquence," I tease.

"I know," she says proudly. "In fact, I think I'll petition the city to use it as their new slogan."

"Tourists would flock, I'm sure." I glance down the road to see Tyler and Betty Boop walking our way, minus the surfboards. They must have dropped them off at the surf shop. Avery glances back in time to see them settle on a platform bench overlooking the ocean. They're sitting cross-legged, facing each other, and close enough to us that I can see Tyler's swollen lip where I hit him. As if feeling our eyes on him, he turns and looks at us. He does a slight double take, and after a moment of bewilderment, his expression turns angry.

Some human instinct inside of me wants to turn up the charm and tell Avery to forget about him. But I remind myself, as I have countless other times, that long-distance relationships don't work when two people live on opposite sides of a country, let alone opposite spiritual realms. I want Avery to be happy. It just can't be with me.

As much as I would like to sit here all night bantering with her, I need to use my time more wisely. Under the table, I bump my foot softly against hers to get her attention. She turns back to me, her smile gone and a restless storm brewing in her eyes. I set down my spoon and lean forward, letting her know that what I'm about to say is serious business. "Avery," I say softly, "I don't think most people realize how short life is. If there's something out there that makes you happy . . ." I glance at Tyler, and at the vast, shimmering ocean behind him. "Then you should go after it."

The storm in her eyes slowly dies, leaving behind a wake of sadness. Her arms fold around her waist, and she shakes her head. "Everyone makes it sound so easy," she whispers so quietly that I wonder if she meant for me to hear. She sits there, perfectly still, like she's disappeared somewhere inside herself. I've said something wrong. But before I can backpedal, she looks at me and says, "Is that why you're here? Because you're chasing what will make you happy?"

I wouldn't know the first place to look for happiness. "No. I'm just here to help someone I care about."

A white SUV pulls up beside Tyler and the blonde. She stands and shoulders her beach bag, then raises her arms like she's going to hug him. But at the last second, Tyler steps back and holds up his hands as if to say, "Whoa, there." Lowering one hand, he offers a cordial handshake. She doesn't take it, just quirks her mouth awkwardly at the rejection, and then gets in the SUV.

Huh. Maybe I've misunderstood Tyler. Maybe all those girls

I saw him flirt with on the beach were just customers, and being friendly is part of his job. And the truth is, I wasn't there to hear most of his conversations with Avery after my death—I only caught bits and pieces. So maybe I don't fully understand his reasoning for breaking things off. Maybe he's capable of being good to Avery, but she pushed him away somehow.

Tyler watches the SUV drive off and round a corner, then turns and stares me down. I hold his glare, challenging him to come and take back what was once his. But after a minute, he dips his head and stalks off. I rake a hand through my hair and lean even closer to Avery.

"He obviously still has feelings for you," I whisper. "And you for him. So . . . what's in the way?"

The wind chimes stir in the breeze, casting colorful triangles across her face. She gives me a labored smile. "Sorry, but I make a point not to pour my heart out to people I just met."

I happen to know that she makes a point not to pour out her heart to anyone.

"You don't have to pour it out," I say. "It's written all over your face."

Her smile vanishes, then reappears in a weaker version. She's barely hanging on to it. "Well, I keep some things inside, and that's where they're going to stay."

I sink back in my chair, studying her. In the last few months, I've thought a million times, *If I could talk to her, I could find out what she's thinking. I could help her work through it all. I could comfort her.* Well, here I am now, her ears within the reach of my voice, and I feel just as powerless and voiceless as when I was invisible to her. Because she won't open up to me the way I thought she would.

But what did I expect? I know her, but she doesn't know me. I know she eats oatmeal with mangos for breakfast. I know she stays at her dad's during the week, and her mom's on the weekends, and that her little sister never goes to their mom's. I know she walks to work from her dad's house every morning, and even though there's a dazzling view of the ocean on the way, she keeps her head down and her eyes on the sidewalk. I know she has half a dozen surfboards in her garage that she sometimes looks at longingly but hasn't touched since my death. I know all this, and yet I'm a stranger to her. Of course she's not going to open up to me. And it occurs to me that, if my plan is going to work at all, I'll need a lot of time to break down her barriers.

Only, I think I have that wrong too. Here I've been thinking that I'd be able to come and sledgehammer through her walls. But now I see that it's not a wall I have to break through. Her barrier is thin, like a veil, and a sledgehammer won't break it; it will only bend the veil and break her.

If I want her to talk tonight, it needs to be about whatever she wants to talk about. "We're called Yoopers," I say. And when she gives me a funny look, I explain, "That's what people who live on Michigan's Upper Peninsula are called."

She mulls this over a moment, and then picks up her shrimp-heavy fork. "You said you worked in a vineyard last summer. Was that here, or there?"

"There."

"I didn't know there were vineyards that far north."

So I tell her about the vineyard in Marquette at the edge of Lake Superior. I tell her about the harsh winters and thick forests. I tell her nothing about me, only about the place I left behind. And soon she starts telling me things she feels safe sharing. She tells me about the sea lions at Port San Luis, and how she once had a crazy goal to hold her breath as long as they could. She talks about the marine science club at school and which classes she'll be taking her senior year. Since I'll never finish my senior year, I tell her I'm going to be an EMT. Which I already am, I just don't use the same life-saving techniques mortals do.

The sun sets slowly over the ocean, and when the horizon disappears into a wash of indigo, she stands and stretches.

"I'd better get home," she says. "I have to work again tomorrow."

"Avery," I say, hoping I can leave her with something more substantial than "it's been real." "You're amazing. I hope you know that."

She looks down at her sneakers and bites her lip, as though she's deciding whether to swallow my compliment or spit it back out. A breeze flicks her hair and ripples her blouse like a white flag. "Thank you," she says simply.

"No regrets, okay?"

I can see her gears turning, trying to find context for my words. I'm not sure if she succeeds or not, but she nods. And I think, if this evening with her is all I get, it was worth taking the ring for. And maybe it's enough.

But as I walk her to her car, I can't bring myself to say goodbye. One day isn't enough. I want more. More time in this body, more time with her. I ante up another day, hoping I don't lose the gamble, and say, "Can I come see you tomorrow?"

She nods again. "I can give you my number."

"I don't have a phone."

"Then come see me." She smiles. Then her expression turns concerned. "Can I give you a ride somewhere?"

There's nowhere for her to take me, so I say, "I think I'll stick around and enjoy the scenery."

She nods and waves good night as she gets in her car, and then I watch her brake lights disappear around a corner.

8

avery

When I was ten, I qualified for a local juniors surfing competition. They even wrote about me in the local paper, calling me "fearless" and a "strategic executioner." Mom had spent the evening calling our relatives to brag and shopping online for surfing gear that I didn't need. I'd spent the evening sitting in a happy trance on the couch, dreaming of all the possibilities.

I feel the same way now. I got home from dinner with Kai an hour ago, and I'm still sitting in my driveway, staring at the watermarks on my windshield and holding Kai's pocketknife in my hand. There's something steadying about it, like I've just found a handrail after balancing for months on a rickety bridge.

I unfold the different tools of the knife, as though his secrets are hidden among them. There's a file and a tiny pair of scissors, a screwdriver and the sharp blade I used earlier to free the crab. I study each one, as if they'll reveal something about him. But they're shiny, clean, and unscratched, like they've never been used.

My phone chirps on the passenger seat, and I look down to see a text.

From Tyler.

You up?

It's been weeks since he texted me. And something tells me it's no coincidence that his first text came on the day I went out with another guy.

No regrets, Kai said before I left him tonight. I don't know why he said it. Maybe it was some Michiganese way of saying goodbye. But the words struck me somewhere deep inside. Because I've spent the last six months doing nothing but regretting. Looking back and wishing I could undo the choices I made, and the consequences of those choices.

Maybe Kai is what I need right now. I've been hanging around the same group of friends for years. If I switch things up, maybe I can get out of this rut I'm in. When I was at dinner with Kai, I felt something shift inside of me. Like I'd stumbled onto a new path that I never realized was there. After floundering along the same path for six months, maybe it's time to explore a new one.

I reach over and turn off my phone.

9

KAI

From where I sit huddled in an alcove on the beach, I can see the clock tower on the pier. The minute hand looks like a dagger, and it's killing time painfully slowly. Morning will bring another chance to see Avery, and it can't come soon enough.

It's past midnight, and the beach is empty. I've been sitting in the same spot for two hours, breathing in the salty air and running my fingers through the gritty sand. Partly because it makes me feel alive, and partly because I don't have anywhere else to go.

The vineyard I worked at today had trailers for the workers, but the manager told me not to come back until I had my ID. And since my wallet is lost at the bottom of the ocean, that's not an option.

I look out at the vast body of water before me, a dark abyss peppered with moonlight. Somewhere out there, along with my drivers license, is my mortal body. Or whatever is left of it. The elements are probably scattered across miles of craggy ocean floor. The thought makes me sad. But also more grateful for this temporary body.

I run a hand over the smooth skin on my forearm. This body feels different than my mortal one, and yet the same. My arm is already healed where I cut it on the broken store window last night. And even though there's no blood in this body, I've been able to eat. So there must be some kind of digestive and circulatory system. I press my fingers to my wrist to feel for a pulse, but there's nothing. I try my neck, just under my jaw, and there—I feel something. A low humming, more of a current than a pulse. It sort of creeps me out, so I pull my fingers away and return them to the wet sand.

I feel weighed down and exhausted, and I realize that this body needs rest. I've been awake since the middle of last night, and my legs ache from walking miles to find Avery. I haven't felt this tired since the night I left Michigan and walked fifteen miles in the snow before a trucker picked me up. I need a place to rest before I see her again tomorrow. Unless . . .

I look down at Charles's ring. Moonlight glints off the metal, and the stone inlay catches the light, turning slightly luminous. I could take it off for a while and go back to Demoror, and I'd probably feel rested when I returned. But if I do, I'll receive an assignment. And I can't take another assignment until I'm finished with the one I've given myself. Besides, it was unexpectedly painful to materialize, and if I take the ring off, I'll have to put it on again and re-materialize. And anyway, I like having this body, even when it's worn out.

So I stand and head back the way I came, past the shops and inns, to the mouth of the small canyon where Avery dropped me off earlier. I follow the canyon road toward the vineyard where I worked earlier, determined to find a place to sleep for the night even if it's behind an old barn. It won't be the first time I've had to sleep outside.

No street lamps light my way, only moonlight sifting through a tunnel of arching trees. As I wander down the dark path, I have a sense of déjà vu. Not that I've been here before, but that I've felt this way before. Uncertain. Like I don't know where I'll be when tomorrow comes, or if my plans will work out. I used to come up with one half-baked plan after another. When I was a kid, my plan was to run away with my little sisters and live in the woods. I even tried it once, but when it got dark and the wolves started howling, my sisters cried so hard I finally brought them back home. It wasn't much safer there, but at least we wouldn't be eaten alive.

My sisters are safe now, but I'm still full of half-baked plans. What makes me think they'll work out now?

I'm half a mile past the vineyard now, and there's nothing but a steep hill on one side of the road and a thick grove of trees on the other. I step off the road and into the trees, thinking it's as good a place as any to sleep. The long grass feels soft and cushiony, and as I weave through the trees, I hear something. A woman's voice, calling for someone. Curious, I follow the sound through the trees until I stumble onto a dirt driveway.

"Dacio!" the woman is calling. Her voice is strained, worried. I jog down her driveway, stopping at the edge of her yard when I see her. She's an elderly woman, standing on her porch in a long night-gown and slippers. Then I hear the unmistakable sniffing sound of a dog behind me, and before I can turn around, I feel its wet nose and tongue on my hand. I look down to see a golden retriever nuzzling my hand. "Hey there," I say quietly, rubbing his head.

"Dacio!" the woman calls again. "*¿Dónde estás, muchacho?*"

Assuming the dog is Dacio, I say, "Come on, boy," and lead him across the yard to the woman. When I near the porch, I use my gentlest voice so I don't startle her. "Are you looking for him?"

She turns in my direction, and even in the dim light of the porch I can see that her eyes are glazed white. Yet, she looks directly at me, into my eyes, as though she can see beyond whatever disease or condition has made her blind.

"Are you here for me?" she asks, her Rs rolling with a Span-ish accent.

"No. I was out on the road and heard you calling out. I came to see if you needed help."

She takes a step toward me, holding onto the porch post for balance. "What's someone like you doing walking around in the middle of the night?"

I'm not sure what she means by "someone like me," but I decide to go for honesty. "I'm looking for a place to sleep."

Cautiously, she hobbles down the steps and stands right in front of me. Her black and silver hair is long and stringy, draped over her frail-looking body like a tattered cloak. "Have you seen my son Miguel?" She squints at me, deepening the leathery wrinkles around her eyes.

Apparently she's lost more than just her dog. Her son, and possibly her mind. I shake my head and then realize she probably can't see the movement. "No. What does he look like?"

"Black hair, big brown eyes. Tall, but not like you. He died two years ago, when he was only forty-five, bless his soul." She makes the sign of the cross.

Dacio puts his head under my hand again. I rub it, because I don't know what else to do or say. Somehow, this woman knows what I am. And she's asking if I've seen her dead son. For a second I worry what consequence I'll have to pay for her knowing. But then I realize I didn't actually *tell* her I'm dead, so surely I won't be banned from Earth.

She must sense my astonishment, because her hand comes to rest reassuringly on my arm. Wonder flickers across her face when she touches me, and she squeezes my wrist. Then she hesitantly lifts her withered hand and runs it over the lines of my face. I hold perfectly still, letting her.

"These eyes may be blind," she finally says, "but they can see."

"How?" I'm suddenly wondering if there are others who know what I am too.

She shakes her head slowly. "That's simply how it is. I see others like you. Sometimes I talk to them." Finally she lowers her hands, but clings to my forearms as though she'll fall over if she lets go. "But I've never touched one of you until now. I didn't expect you to be . . . solid."

"I'm not. I mean, not usually. I'm on a special . . . errand."

She holds onto me, staring up at me with frosted eyes, thin lips and chin quivering. "And you need a place to stay. Are you hungry? I can make you *chupe de camarones*. It is my specialty."

I've never had *chupe de camarones*, but it doesn't exactly sound like throwing tacos together. "It's the middle of the night," I say, and my voice sounds tired. "I just need a place to sleep."

"I can give you a place to stay. And you tell me about Miguel."

"But—" There's nothing to tell. I don't know her son. I open my mouth to tell her this, but before I can say anything, she stops me.

"Tonight, you rest. Tomorrow, we talk. Wait here." She turns and shuffles back up the stairs and into the house. Dacio stays at my side, wagging his tail and tilting his head like he's waiting for me to start speaking canine or something. A minute later, she comes back out and hands me a key attached to a little crocheted doll. "Tell me, what is your name?"

"Kai."

She puts a hand to her chest. "Isadora. And I have always given refuge to those in need. But it has been many years since I have taken someone in. And never someone like you. Usually, people like you are the ones who help me. So this is a great honor." She points away from the house. "Go through the vineyard. There's an empty cottage, behind the lavender field. It's not much. A bed, running water. It was for the workers, but they're all gone now. You stay there tonight. Tomorrow, we talk." She reaches up and pats my cheek affectionately, like I'm her own son.

"Thank you," I say, swallowing back an unexpected wave of emotion at the kindness I didn't see coming. And I can't help thinking that for whatever reason, maybe this is exactly where I'm supposed to be.

That night, I dream for the first time since my death. Of my childhood, of broken glass on a filthy kitchen floor, of trying to pick up the shards before my baby sisters put them in their mouths. I dream of weed stashed in an empty bread basket, of flashing police car lights, and the *clack, clack, clack* of a social worker's high heels in a sterile hospital hallway. I dream of unfamiliar bedrooms and faces, of a well-worn Hefty bag that holds all my earthly possessions. I dream of callused fingertips on guitar strings, of my vocal cords vibrating with gritty lyrics. Of semitrucks eating up white dashes on the highway, and street corners in Omaha, coins dropping into my open guitar case.

And then I dream of Avery. Of a fearless girl on a surfboard in a stormy sea. I feel the air rush over me as I drop twenty feet from the pier, feel the sting of the Pacific in December. I dream of a blade slicing through a surfboard leash, of Avery's lips drawing breath, of her in my arms, warm and alive. And I think, *It was all for this*. My life, everything leading up to this moment, was all for her, so that she could live. And if given the chance, I would do it all over again.

I open my eyes to an unfamiliar room. Morning sunlight pours through a window onto faded blue walls, and a wooden cross hangs over my head. My bed isn't the only one in the room, but the other two are empty, their blankets tucked neatly in place. As my eyes sweep the rest of the room, they find an oval picture frame on the wall, and an old Hispanic woman standing in the doorway. *Isadora*.

She hobbles over, her golden retriever following close behind, and pulls up a twig chair. She sits and smooths out her long, striped skirt. "You sleep. Now you tell me about Miguel."

I sit up slowly and drop my feet to the floor, the remnants of my dream fading with the shadows in the room. This woman has done me a great kindness by letting me sleep here, and now I can't give her what she wants in return. I look at her wrinkled face, at the hope held there, and my heart breaks a little. "I'm sorry," I say. "I don't know your son. You have to understand, thousands of people die every day, and . . ."

She closes her eyes. Her withered hand reaches for mine, and a tear seeps from beneath her eyelid and travels down a crevice in her skin.

I blanket my hand over hers, doing my best to comfort her. But clearly time hasn't dulled the pain of losing her son. "I can tell you what happened to me when I died," I offer. "Maybe that'll help you know what happened to him."

She opens her mother-of-pearl eyes. "Yes," she whispers. "Please. Tell me."

I let my mind wander back to that fateful day. I skip over the part where I died, because it's not important to her, and because the details aren't something I enjoy reliving. "I found myself in a beautiful place," I say, "and then someone came to greet me."

"Who?"

"Someone I knew on Earth, who died before me." I asked Charles once why he'd been the one to greet me and not my mom, but he couldn't give me an answer. Knowing Isadora can't see well, I take her hand and place it over my wristband. "He gave me this."

Her fingers run over the smooth metal and stone. "What is it for?"

"It gives me the power to heal people. That's my job."

Her hand leaves my wrist and goes to Dacio's head, where she strokes his fur. Her knuckles are swollen, and the skin on her hand is spotted with years of working in the sun. "If some have the power to heal, why was no one sent to heal Miguel when he was dying?"

It's the same universal question I've asked countless times but have never found the answer to. "I wish I could tell you," I say. "All I know is that some mortals' time comes earlier than others. I was only seventeen when I died."

She keeps her hand on Dacio as she absorbs my inadequate answer, and then says, "So Miguel is working."

"If he chooses to, yes. No one is forced."

"He was a hard worker when he was here. I'm sure he is still working hard." She lays her other hand on my wrist and leans forward, clinging to me. "I just want to know if he's happy. Is he happy?"

Another question I can't answer. There are places on the other side, like Elysium, where everyone is happy and at peace. And then there's the Briar, where confusion and pain and anger reign. In between those is Demoror, where we wait and work and change for the better or worse, until we feel at home in either Elysium or the Briar. People have ups and downs, just like on Earth. I don't know her son, so I don't know where he ended up. "Was he happy here?"

"Always."

"Then he's happy there." Based on my experience of seeing hundreds of people cross over to the other side, it's my best guess.

She closes her eyes and nods as her hand curls around mine. When her thumb touches Charles's ring, she stops to feel it. "What is this for?"

"It's what makes me . . . solid." I don't tell her it's not mine, that I'm breaking the rules by wearing it. "I don't usually wear it, but like I said last night, I'm on a special errand."

"Are you here to heal someone?"

"You could say that."

"Who?"

I take a deep breath as my thoughts turn to Avery. I picture her face, hear her soft, musical laughter, feel the warmth that radiates from her. "A girl. She lives down by the beach."

"Well, if you have someone to heal, what are you doing here?"

"I only have the power to heal physical ailments. She needs a different kind of healing, one that will take more time."

"And so you need a place to stay. You are welcome here for as long as you need. Is there anything else I can do for you?"

I look down at myself. I'm wearing the same stolen clothes from the day before, and I realize I might want to find a way to expand my wardrobe. If I had more cash, I could make a run to a thrift store for some extra clothes, and maybe pick up some soap and toothpaste. I also need to repay the store owner for the things I took, and for the broken window.

"I need a job," I say. "Work that I can do for pay."

"There's always work to do. Come with me."

10
avery

*f*ive minutes to closing, Tyler walks into the chocolate shop with Gem on his heels. I'm on the phone taking a custom order, and my pencil lead snaps off. Gem is wearing daisy dukes and sandals with straps laced halfway up her calves like ballet slippers. Not exactly appropriate attire for a surfing lesson.

"Miss?" comes a woman's voice from the phone receiver. "Are you writing this down?"

"Yes." I tear my eyes from Gem and scramble for a new pencil or pen, anything to write with. I finally find a sharpie in my apron pocket. "Sixty boxes of assorted chocolate-covered fruit. Got it."

"No apricots."

"Right. No apricots." I make a note on the form.

Tyler and Gem come up to the display case, and he points out his favorite chocolates to her. I already know what they are. Salted caramels and ginger-wasabi truffles. From the look of Gem, she's probably a sugar-free peppermint kind of girl.

"And you're sure they can be ready by tomorrow morning?" the woman on the phone asks.

"Yes. It's no problem."

Sophie clomps out of the kitchen in her combat boots with a tray of samples for Tyler and Gem, and I finish gathering the woman's information while trying to figure out why, of all places, Tyler would bring Gem here. Either he's trying to make me jealous, or he likes this girl so much that he's willing to hurt me in order to get her some good chocolate.

Only after I hang up do I realize that Dad may not be able to help me fill the order because he's helping Mom with some things today. If he doesn't show up, I'll have to stay late to finish it. And if Kai stops by like he said he would, I'll only be able to hang out with him for a few minutes.

I take the order to the back where I tack it to a bulletin board, and when I come back up front, Gem is saying to Sophie, "I want to try something that I can't get anywhere else."

And I think maybe that's what Tyler is to her. She's probably from someplace where surfer boys are a novelty, and she's sampling them while she's here.

Sophie's black hair is knotted into a dozen little buns all over her head, and I see her cheek rise with a smile. "I have just the thing in the back," she says. "I've been working on a new recipe. Wait here."

Gem smiles at Tyler, her doe eyes practically sparkling with anticipation, and Sophie walks past me with her brows arched in a mischievous way that makes me nervous.

To avoid having to converse with Tyler, I grab a notepad and begin listing our existing fruit inventory so I'll know how much we still need to make for the big order. When I duck behind the case to count the chocolate-covered grapes, Gem starts briefing Tyler on some chemtrails seminar her parents attended the night before. I can tell he's tuning her out because when I glance over the case at him, he's wearing the same face that he wears during algebra and English lit. And world history, and economics. And pretty much any topic he doesn't find fascinating. The only science Tyler is interested in is how waves are formed. If she really wants his attention, she should talk low-pressure systems and swell obstacles and wave energy.

Just as Gem is getting into some really good conspiracy theory, Sophie comes out of the kitchen with two perfectly domed truffles on a silver plate. She holds it out over the display case, waiting for Gem and Tyler to take one.

"What's in it?" Gem asks, and from the plastic smile on Sophie's face, I have a feeling it's not something we would give our typical customers.

"Yeah, Sophie," I say with a hint of warning. "What's in it?"

"See if you can guess," Sophie says, keeping her eyes on Gem. When Gem hesitates, Sophie adds, "I wouldn't offer this to just anyone. But you seem like the adventurous type."

I know I should say something. I should warn Gem or go snatch the chocolates and dump them in the trash before she has the chance to taste whatever wild concoction Sophie has come up with. But I want to see how adventurous Gem is. And I want Tyler to see too.

Gem is still glowing from Sophie's flattery when she takes the truffle. I think she's going to take a nibble, but instead, she pops the entire thing in her mouth and gives Tyler a triumphant look. It only takes a couple seconds for the enjoyment on her face to slip into disgust, and then panic. Gooey chocolate spews from her mouth, and on the way to the floor, it gets all over her white tube-top.

"Ugh!" she screeches. "What's in those things?"

"Just a little something I like to call, *creme de habanero*." Sophie's voice is all saccharine. "What? You don't like it?"

"They're disgusting!" Gem's eyes are watering, and she starts coughing. "And . . ." *Cough.* "Hot!" *Cough, cough, cough.* One hand comes to her throat as the other frantically fans her face.

"My bad," Sophie says, sounding genuinely remorseful. "I thought Tyler only liked adventurous girls."

Gem wipes some brown spit from the side of her mouth and glowers at Sophie, then looks to Tyler for help. Tyler is fighting a smile, but he straightens it out and gives Sophie a chiding look. "Sophie, why don't you go back in the kitchen and play with your Easy Bake Oven?"

Sophie smirks. As she walks past me to the kitchen, I mumble, "Way to drum up business."

I take a steadying breath and then fill up a cup of water and bring it to Gem, feeling guilty because I could have prevented her pain. "I'm really sorry. She wasn't trying to be mean or anything. She just likes people to try out her new recipes. I'm sorry you didn't like it."

She takes the water and gulps it down while Tyler takes the remaining *creme de habanero* truffle and pops it in his mouth. He chews for a minute, and even though his eyes start watering, he says, "Hmm. Pretty spicy, but I like it."

"Do you have a bathroom in here?" Gem asks, grabbing a handful of napkins and scrubbing her tongue with them.

I point outside. "There's some right out there, by the pier."

She gives me a rotten look, then turns and walks out of the shop. I expect Tyler to follow, but he watches her leave and then turns back to me.

"Sorry about that," I say.

His lips are straight, but his green eyes are alight with amusement. They're made even brighter by the green Cannibal Surfboard T-shirt he's wearing—the one I got him for Christmas last year. He probably forgot I gave it to him. Otherwise, why would he wear it here, on a date with Gem? Unless he's playing some stupid game with me.

"That's okay," he says. "I know Sophie well enough to not take it personally." His smile fades and a crease appears between his brows. "So you're hanging out with the guy who gave me a fat lip?"

It takes me a moment to realize he's referring to my dinner with Kai. "Yeah," I say. "I guess I am. He's really nice."

"Oh, yeah. It's real nice to punch someone in the face." He points to his lip, which is still swollen.

I can't look at his lips without thinking of all the kisses we've shared. Even after all this time, I can still feel them tingling on my lips. I force myself to look into his eyes instead. "You grabbed him first. I saw you. And he said something about you hurting someone he knows. What's that all about?"

Tyler's head rocks back. "What?"

I shrug. "That's what he said."

Tyler's jaw tenses and he looks away, confirmation enough for me. So it's true. I wonder who she was. I haven't seen him with anyone besides Gem since we broke up, but then, I haven't exactly been an active participant in the social scene. He finally looks back to me and huffs out a breath. "Whatever. Are you going to see him again?"

The edge in his voice makes me feel defensive, and I fold my arms across my chest. "What does it matter to you?"

"I . . ." He shuts his mouth, then opens it again, but no more words come out to complete his sentence.

"You and I are friends now," I say, "and that's it. That's what you wanted, right?"

He takes my words square in the chin, and then looks at me miserably. "It's not that simple, Avery. You know that."

I, of all people, know that love is not simple. I witness the complexity of it on a daily basis, watching Mom and Dad. "It should be simple," I say firmly. "I mean, heaven forbid a girl and a boy just love each other and stick by each other no matter what." I lock eyes with him, challenging him to prove his love for me. But he refuses the challenge.

He falls back a step and lets out a long sigh. "Just be careful, okay?"

"You know me. If I'm anything, it's careful."

Anger flits across his face, and he comes back and slams his palm on the counter. "No," he grinds the word out between his teeth. "That's not the Avery I know. The Avery I know tames ten-foot waves, and dives off cliffs, and climbs vertical mountains with no harness. You're everything *but* careful."

"Well," I say calmly, even though there is nothing calm inside of me, "that's not who I am now."

He shakes his head dubiously, fire in his eyes. "I don't believe that."

A wayward lock of dark hair has fallen into his eye, and I have the urge to reach out and push it back like I have so many times before. But I don't. Because breaking up means unlearning old habits, living by new rules. He's staring at me, as though searching for remnants of the girl he once loved. He must find a shred of her, because when he speaks again, his voice is tender, almost a murmur. "I know you're in there somewhere, Avery. Come back."

"I'm. Right. Here," I say with quiet force, enunciating each word to be sure he understands. "I'm dealing with some tough things right now. Tougher than any wave or mountain. I don't expect you to understand. But trust me when I say I'm still *me*." My voice breaks on the last word, and I turn away so he can't see the tears pooling in my eyes. I step over to the back counter and stare down at the pad of blank order forms while I get my emotions in check.

Tyler is perfectly quiet. When I turn around to see if he's still there, he's standing right behind me. "There's a party tonight at Dillan's. Will you come?"

"I don't know." My voice is nonchalant, but my throat is still burning with unshed tears. "Are you bringing Gem?"

He hesitates, and then shakes his head decisively. "I'm not planning on it." His hand slides up my arm and comes to rest on my shoulder. "Avery, she's a customer."

"I've never seen you so cozy with a customer."

"I like her. As a friend. She's fun to be around. And her

parents are here for some tree-hugger convention with meetings and dinners and stuff, so she doesn't have anyone to hang out with." When I say nothing, he adds, "She's leaving in two days, back to Connecticut or Rhode Island or one of those tiny eastern states." He raises an eyebrow. "See? I can't like her that much if I don't even remember where she's from."

"Geography was never your star subject," I say, smiling despite myself. The door chimes, and when I look over Tyler's shoulder to see who it is, my breath catches in my throat. Kai stands in the shop entrance, the evening sun catching in his hair and lighting it up like a crown of white fire. He glances my way, and then wanders over to the dark chocolate section like he's waiting for me to finish my conversation with Tyler.

"Come tonight," Tyler says softly, not noticing Kai. "I really want you to."

I glance at the clock on the wall. We're officially closed, but my work is far from over. "I have seven hundred and twenty pieces of chocolate to make by morning."

"Can't your dad help?"

"He's . . . helping my mom." I give him a look, and he understands exactly what I mean. I miss that about him. Never having to explain, because he already knows about Mom and Dad. "She called at four this morning crying because she broke a light bulb while trying to change it, and it was stuck in the socket."

"What's she doing changing a light bulb at four in the morning?"

I shrug. "Her muse keeps wacky hours. So my dad went to help her because she was plunging into crazy mode, and he's still not back."

"What about Sophie?"

"She'll help with the order, but even then, it'll take us half the night."

"Well, you know Dillan's parties. We'll be there until sunrise."

I glance again at Kai, catching his eyes. He greets me with

a little smile. This time Tyler notices, because he twists to see what I'm looking at. When he turns back to me, he looks stung. "So that's the real reason you won't come. You already have plans."

"No—I don't. I really am making chocolates all night."

"What's he doing here then?" he whispers.

The door chimes again and Gem reappears, beckoning Tyler with a pathetic pout. Her tube top is all wet, and there's a vague stain where she didn't manage to get the chocolate out. Tyler glances at her and then back at me. His thumb trails along my collarbone, and I notice how his touch feels different than it used to. Less electric. Heavier. "Come," he says earnestly. "Come late if you need to. But come."

"I'll do my best."

11

avery

After Tyler leaves with Gem, I lock Kai inside with me and turn over the *Closed* sign. "Hey," I say. He's standing so close that I have to tip my head back to look at his face. It's kind of like looking into sunshine, especially after Tyler's dreary expressions.

"Sorry," he says, "I didn't mean to interrupt." He glances out the window at Tyler's retreating figure.

"It's okay. There wasn't much to interrupt."

He gives me a skeptical look, but before he can say anything else, I turn and head back behind the counter, saying over my shoulder, "So—did you find somewhere to crash last night?"

He strolls over with his hands in his front pockets. He's wearing the same board shorts as yesterday and a faded cobalt blue T-shirt with a white phoenix on the front. "You sound concerned."

I open the cash register and start sorting and counting the contents. "Last night as I was falling asleep, I pictured you curled beneath a eucalyptus tree in the woods. It was a very sad image."

He doesn't say anything, and when I glance at him, one corner of his mouth is tipped up, like he's amused that I was thinking of him before falling asleep. "I did find a place," he says. "A little vineyard where I'll be working for a while. It's up Sienna Canyon Road."

I stop counting. "Isadora's place?"

His dark brows lift in surprise. "Yeah, actually."

I finish counting the tens and twenties and write down the total. "My dad used to buy grapes from her. But she stopped selling a couple years ago, when her son died. There's still a sign on her driveway that says, 'Temporarily Closed.'"

"Yeah, the vineyard looks like it's been neglected for a while. But I did some major pruning today, so hopefully she'll get a yield from it."

"Well," I say, emptying the quarter compartment, "let me know when you're harvesting and I'll come buy some from you."

He looks down at his feet, like he's not sure if he'll still be around during harvest. His flip-flops, which looked new yesterday, appear more than broken in. They're the shoes of someone who doesn't stay in one place for very long. And I get the feeling that when he told me he was from Michigan, he left out a lot of stops between here and there.

While I finish recording the day's earnings, Kai falls back a step and surveys the display case. "You have quite a selection here."

"Do you want to try something? On the house."

He runs a hand through his hair, leaving it like a white sea anemone. "What would you suggest?"

I shrug. "Depends on your taste. We have plain, dark, salty, spicy . . ." I think about Sophie's stunt minutes earlier. "*Really* spicy, fruity, savory, flowery . . . you get the idea."

He peruses the glass shelves, seeming overwhelmed by the abundance of choices. "What's your favorite?"

I look at the different chocolates Dad has created over the years, some of them old recipes, some new. Products of countless trials and errors of different flavors and combinations until he reached perfection. But I can't answer Kai's question honestly. Because there's something I've never told anyone, especially Dad: I hate chocolate. I didn't always hate it, but after spending years as a guinea pig for new recipes, I can't taste chocolate without grouping it with that weird asparagus experiment, or the seaweed-noni mishap, or worst of all, the *Crab Cacao* that surprisingly, food critics raved about.

"I'm still deciding," I finally say.

He tilts his head curiously, then points to something on the wall behind me. "You grew up in a chocolate shop and you're still deciding?"

I twist to see what he's looking at. It's a photo of our family posing in front of the shop on the day it opened a decade earlier. Sophie and I are in matching yellow eyelet dresses, our hair in curly pigtails and our expressions like sunshine. Mom's smile is wide and genuine. Beautiful. And Dad had a lot more hair back then. I avoid looking at the picture if I can help it because it hurts to remember how good things were when Mom and Dad were happy together. I turn back to Kai. "How can I decide when we're always coming up with new recipes? I can't keep up."

"Okay, then. Why don't you just give me something you think I'll like?"

"I've only known you for a day. I don't have much to go on."

He shrugs. "Do your best."

I study him a moment, from his snowy, unruly hair to his exposed toes. He's a complete mystery to me. But when I think of him—which I do more than I should for someone I hardly know—I think of stillness and of soothing warmth. I reach into the display case and select a chocolate cube with a red swirl on top. I hand it to him, and when my fingertips brush his open palm, I swear the nerve endings in my fingers have suddenly multiplied.

"What's this?" he asks, looking at the chocolate in his palm.

"Molten chocolate. Don't chew. Just let it sit on your tongue."

He puts it in his mouth, and his jaw remains stationary as I instructed. I watch his face, expecting to see pleasure or surprise, expressions I always see on our customers when they sample something new. But Kai's face is serious and thoughtful, his eyes far away as though he's savoring a beautiful sunset while contemplating the meaning of his life. And then his eyes turn wistful, like the colors of the sky have melted with his chocolate, and he'll never taste chocolate or see the sun rise again.

"What's wrong?" I ask.

He looks at me. "Nothing. It's just . . . been a long time since I've had something so good." His voice is soft and forlorn, reflecting his eyes. "Thank you." He leans his elbows on top of the display case so that we're eye-level. "So, are you and Tyler working things out?"

The question catches me off guard, and I don't know what to say.

"I'm asking," he says, "because if you are, I don't want to get in the way."

"You're not," I say automatically. But the truth is, I don't really know what's happening between Tyler and me.

"Is that why he was here? To make up?"

"No. He brought in his 'customer,'" I say with air quotes, "for some chocolate. She got some stuff on her shirt, and"—I skip over the details of the *creme de habanero* incident—"she went to clean up. Then he invited me to a party tonight."

"So you're going?" he says with an unexpected amount of encouragement.

"I can't. I'll be working on a big order all night."

"But do you want to go?"

I hear Sophie's voice back in the kitchen. "*Willst du mich küssen?*"

"Is that . . . German?" Kai asks, looking confused.

"That's my sister, Sophie. She's been listening to German lessons on her iPhone."

"Does she have travel plans?"

92

I shake my head. "She wishes. Her favorite band is from there, and she's kind of obsessed with them. They're like Radiohead meets a German Everly Brothers."

"The Astromotts?"

"Oh—you know them? They seem so obscure."

"I used to listen to them, before I . . ." He purses his lips, as though he almost said something he shouldn't. "Before I got tired of them. They've got some killer guitar riffs."

"*Du hast eine schöne Stimme!*" I don't know what Sophie is saying, but her voice is all sultry. For someone who insists she'll never fall in love, she sure is crazy for German boys.

"Anyway, I would love to get out of here," I say. "It's been a long day. But when your dad's a small-business owner, duty calls."

"Let me help you."

"Are you asking for a job?"

"No—I already have one, remember? I'm asking if you want some free help."

I give him an incredulous look. "Let me get this straight. You're going to help me make chocolates so I can go to a party with my ex-boyfriend?"

He considers for half a second. "Yeah."

"Why would you do that?"

"Because I—" His gaze rises to meet mine, and I glimpse something like tenderness before a wave of neutrality sweeps it away. "I like you, Avery. I want to be your friend. And if going to a party with Tyler will make you happy, then I want to help."

I stare at him for a long moment, waiting in vain for that tenderness to resurface in his eyes, and it slowly and sadly occurs to me that he sees me only as a friend. It's probably why he wants me to get back together with Tyler, so I won't get the wrong idea.

"Well," I say, flustered by a surge of disappointment, "if you want to volunteer here, I need to know your last name." When he hesitates, I add, "It's policy." More of a personal one, seeing how we don't have a volunteer policy, but I don't tell him that.

He shifts his feet and then clears his throat. "Lennon."

"Okay, Kai Lennon." I grab a black apron from a hook on the wall and hand it to him over the display case. "You'll want to put this on."

He follows me into the kitchen, and we find Sophie dipping pieces of dried mango into a vat of tempered chocolate, earbuds in ears and yelling, "*Ich liebe dich*!" There is zero embarrassment in her face when she sees us, and after laying the drowned mango on a sheet of wax paper, she eyes Kai up and down critically. "Who's he?" she yells as if we have on headphones too.

"This is Kai," I yell back. "Can I use those mangos for a big order?"

She yanks the earbuds from her ears and unties her apron. "Sure, take 'em. I'm leaving."

"You can't. You have to help me."

"I'll help you tomorrow."

"The order has to be ready by morning."

She gives me a withering look. "What happened to our forty-eight hour notice policy?"

"The woman begged."

She lets out a loud sigh. "It's not my fault you're softer than ganache. You took the order, so do it yourself."

"It's sixty dozen pieces! That'll take me all night!"

Kai nudges me. "I'm helping, remember?"

Sophie divides a weird look between Kai and me. "Who's this again? And where did he come from?"

"Michigan," Kai says, though we all know that's not the answer she's looking for.

"Whatever," Sophie says, taking off her apron. "I have plans tonight, so if Michigan Boy is helping, I'm out. *Auf Wiedersehen*."

She tosses her apron on the granite countertop and escapes out the back entrance before I can object. I stare after her a moment, then turn to Kai. "Sisters," I mutter.

Kai smiles, but it's half-hearted and short-lived, and leaves a strange nostalgic shadow.

"Do you have sisters?" I ask, hunting for an explanation for the longing in his face.

He looks away at the sheet of chocolate-covered mangos Sophie just finished up. "So—are you going to show me how it's done?"

"Are you just going to dodge my question?"

He drops the apron over his head, ties it around his lean waist, and then looks at me. "When questions are like daggers, I dodge."

I regard him for a long moment, wondering what he's been through, and why a simple question about family feels like a dagger to him. But no matter how robust my curiosity gets, I won't push him to tell me. Because I understand what it's like to have secrets buried so deep that extracting them would shred everything on the way out. I nod. "Okay, then. Let's wash our hands and get to work."

I show him how to dip each type of fruit, how to enrobe the grapes and raspberries, how to avoid the chocolate "foot," and how to drizzle colored cocoa butter for the finishing touch. We stand side by side in front of the chocolate tempering machine and work through one type of fruit at a time. Dried kiwis and oranges, pineapple and coconut, fresh strawberries and grapes, apples and pears. No apricots. The air is rich with nectar and chocolate, and every time Kai's arm brushes mine, my intake of the decadent air surges.

He's quiet as we work, and I find myself talking about chocolate, imparting all my confectioner's knowledge as though he's an eager apprentice. He humors me, nodding in all the appropriate places and asking questions when he senses a lull in my rambling.

"So what happens if the beta-prime crystals aren't melted?" he asks after I explain the science of chocolate tempering.

"Then you get chocolate bloom."

"And bloom is bad."

"Yes—unless you like white blotchy film on your chocolate."

We fill up sheet after sheet of chocolate-covered fruit, stacking them in bakery racks. When we finish the last batch, our aprons and hands are splattered with chocolate, and we move to the sink to wash up before packaging the chocolates.

As Kai runs his hands under the tap, I notice a big glob of chocolate on his ring. "Here," I say, reaching for it. "Take that off. I have something that gets the oil off better than soap."

But before I can touch it, he jerks away. "It's okay. Soap will work fine." He lathers up his hands and rinses them under the running water.

I've never seen anything like his matching ring and wristband, and I want a closer look. So when he turns off the water and dries his hands, I ask, "Can I see that?"

When he sees me eyeing his wristband, his expression turns wary.

"I'm not going to steal it," I assure him, though that can't possibly be what he's worried about.

He seems to be weighing something, and finally, he steps toward me and holds out his wrist. I curl my fingers around his forearm. His skin is warm and smooth, and touching him makes something bloom just behind my sternum. I gently tug him closer so I can get a better look at the wristband.

It's beautiful. The metal has an unusual satin sheen, and the stone inlay is so brilliant, it's almost luminous.

"What is this stone? Opal?"

"Um . . . I don't know."

"Where did you get it? And the ring?"

I feel the muscles in his arm tense, like he's been caught in the act of a crime and is preparing to flee. I look into his eyes expecting to see guilt, but the face I see isn't that of a thief. It's of someone who's had something precious stolen from him.

"I got them from a friend," he says simply, his voice low.

"Sounds like there's a story behind them." Maybe he shared

the wristband or ring with a girlfriend, like those "best friend" hearts that are split in two. And maybe they broke up, and he wears them both now because he can't let go.

He smiles slightly. "Everything has a story."

"So let's hear it."

He glances at the clock. "It's a quarter past eleven. If you want to make it to that party, we should focus on getting all this fruit boxed up."

I release his wrist. "Did you take a course in the art of evasion, or are you a natural?"

"I'm not evading. I just don't want to waste your time with a boring story when you have a party to go to."

"Maybe I don't want to go to the party." I turn away and grab an empty gift box, mentally adding his wristband and ring to my growing Mysteries of Kai Lennon list.

He steps beside me and grabs a box too, and we start clothing the fruit in foil candy cups and filling the boxes with a dozen pieces each. After filling a few in silence, Kai pauses and turns to me with an earnest expression. "Were you happy with him? With Tyler?"

So it *is* about a girl, and now he wants to swap breakup stories. "Yeah. I guess I was."

"You guess?" He raises a dark eyebrow at me, then goes back to boxing fruit. "Romeo and Juliet, eat your heart out."

I knock him with my elbow. "Well, first of all, define *happy*."

"That kind of sounds like a blind person asking someone to define *yellow*." He slides a lid on. "Happiness is subjective. I can only define it for myself."

"So what's happiness to you?"

He gives me a sidelong glance. "Who's doing the evading now?"

I sigh. "Fine. I was happier with him."

"Happier? Happier than what? A rock? A sunflower? Ronald McDonald?"

I laugh, and then search deeper for a more complete answer. "Happier with him than without him." I move an empty tray to the sink and grab a new one that's filled with chocolate-covered grapes from the baker's rack. I set it on the counter next to all the other trays we have laid out. "He was the only one with the guts to join me on my most extreme adventures. He made me feel . . . less lonely. And when I was with him, the things that weighed me down seemed easier to carry."

"Like what?"

I shrug. "My parents' marriage falling apart, my mom's ups and downs, my sister's anger, which was caused by my mom but directed at me because I was an easier target . . . you know—those kinds of things."

He nods slowly, like he does know.

"Anyway, he and I would go surfing or free-diving, and hang out on the beach all day. If I wanted to talk, he'd listen. If I didn't, he was cool with that. He was always sweet and adorable and . . ." I look up at Kai, and he's watching me like he's hanging on my every word. "I was happy with him. Does that answer your question?"

Something flickers in the depths of his eyes, the way a candle quivers in a gust of wind right before it's extinguished. "So, if you were happy with him, what's keeping you apart?"

When I don't respond, he slowly gets back to work. Then he says softly, "You can tell me, Avery."

The way he says my name is caressing and warm, the way you say something that means a lot to you. The way Dad says *Guittard*, or the way Sophie says *German boys*, or the way Tyler says *Billabong*. It makes me feel exposed, vulnerable. Because it makes me want to open up to him. But with that vulnerability comes a weight. The heaviness of everything I'm carrying inside that's aching to be freed. It's too much to bear when I'm as tired as I am, so I turn around and slide down the cabinet until I'm sitting on the floor. "My feet are tired."

Kai sits beside me, resting his forearms on his knees and turning to look at me. "So what exactly happened with you two?"

My mind retraces the past few months, all the conversations Tyler and I have had, the words we've said and haven't said, all stemming from one incident, one day. And then I'm thrown back to that afternoon, back into the ocean and the cold, roiling waves. I feel them around me, tossing me this way and that, pounding over my head like a stampede of wild horses. I feel the salt stinging my eyes and see the abyss below me in the moment I dove under to find the boy. I saw him there, motionless and suspended in the deep, just out of reach.

Just out of reach.

My face feels hot, and I can't breathe. But I keep my panic cloaked beneath my skin. A violent earthquake rattles my insides, but I tense my muscles, holding it in, restraining it, refusing to let it show. I dig my nails into my arm, anchoring them there, anchoring me into stillness, and I focus all my attention on the present physical pain in my arm.

Kai's hand reaches for mine. His touch stills my insides, draws out the tremors as though they're water and he's a sponge.

"Why do you do that?" he asks gently as he removes my hand from where my fingernails have left crescent indents in my skin.

My lungs expand, filling with air. "You say that like I do it all the time." I force a smile, trying to make light of it.

He rubs a thumb over the indents on my arm and then looks at me, his brow creased with worry. "You did it at dinner last night too."

I shrug. "I guess it's a bad habit I picked up a few months back."

"But why?"

With a weary sigh and a small voice, I say, "I guess it distracts me from the things I don't want to feel."

Kai looks heartsick, and he turns his face away, as though it hurts too much to look at me.

"I used to do other things to distract me," I say. "I'd go out and do something crazy, like rock climbing without a harness, or free-diving alone at night, or surfing big waves. It made it easy to shut out the things I didn't want to think about because I had to focus on surviving. But . . . I can't bring myself to do those things anymore."

"Maybe your newfound caution isn't such a bad thing," he says without looking at me. "Though, you seem to have gone to the opposite end of the spectrum." He pauses. "Why the change?"

Maybe I should just let it out. Say the words, release the pressure that swells and rattles my insides anytime my memories are stirred. If I let them out, maybe I can be free of them, of the torment they cause.

"Last winter," I say quietly, "something happened." I want to tell him everything, to heave these memories out of me. But they won't come, because I can't seem to translate them into words. So I settle for the vague. "Something that was very traumatic, and it threw me into a sort of depression. And then . . . it was like all the fears and hurt I'd repressed for years came crushing down on me. I didn't have the strength to push back anymore. It paralyzed me to the point that I didn't even want to leave my house. And I guess Tyler got tired of dealing with me. He says he still loves me and wants to be with me, just not when I'm like this. He wants me to be the girl I was, but every time I try, I fail." I release a shaky breath. "It's hopeless."

The air conditioner turns on overhead, blowing cool air down on us. It feels good on my skin and carries an airy fusion of fruit and chocolate.

He finally turns to look at me, his eyes holding the same tenderness I glimpsed earlier. But this time, it stays. "Nothing is hopeless." He holds my gaze, cradles it, lulls it into a serene place I never want to leave. "I can help you get him back."

Looking into Kai's eyes, I'm not sure I even want Tyler back. But then Kai blinks and refocuses on the cabinet doors in front of us, and I remember that he sees me only as a friend. "How?" I ask.

Kai slides his feet out, straightening his legs, and picks at a fleck of chocolate on his apron. "Let me hang around. He'll get a taste of what it would be like to really lose you."

I have to admit that Tyler has been acting differently since Kai showed up, but I'm not sure I like what Kai is suggesting. "I don't know. I don't like playing games."

He meets my eyes again. "This isn't a game. It's serious business. And your happiness depends on it."

Kai is right. It's what I've wanted ever since Tyler broke up with me, for him to realize that I'm much more to him than a partner in adventure. "You'd do that for me?"

He gives me a look that says, *Of course, dummy*. "Let's wrap things up here and go to that party. I'll make sure that tonight, he feels the loss of you."

12

KAI

I t's closing in on midnight as we drive along a winding road toward Dillan's house, the headlights of Avery's car illuminating the endless tunnel of trees ahead of us. She's at the wheel, her eyes focused on the road, so I'm free to sit in the shadow of the passenger seat and observe her. She's brushed blue with the light of the dashboard, and her hair is a wavy curtain draped over her shoulder, hiding most of her face. The way she's sitting—her back ramrod straight and her hands gripping eleven and one—reminds me of the way my mom used to drive in snowstorms. Tense and fearful, just waiting for the bald tires to let go of the road. But the roads tonight are dry, and I'm sure Avery's anxiety has nothing to do with the weather.

She opened up to me tonight, not as much as I would have liked, but more than I expected. Enough to confirm my suspicion that it's me, and my death, that's keeping her apart from the boy she loves. I'm convinced more than ever that I can fix this. That I can restore the life she had before.

Her phone chirps. She grabs it from the console and glances at the screen. "Crap. I forgot to text my dad." She hands me her phone. "Would you text him back? Just say I'm going to a party with Paige and I'll be home by two."

I do as she instructs and then return her phone to the console. "Don't you have a curfew?"

She shrugs. "I used to, before my parents separated. But now . . . I don't know. My dad has never really laid down an official curfew. He's fine as long as he knows where Sophie and I are."

"And your mom?"

Avery tucks her hair behind her ear, pulling back the curtain to reveal the rest of her profile. "She's just glad to have one daughter speaking to her. She'd probably let me hitchhike across the country as long as I called her twice a week." Her hands slide down the steering wheel to a more relaxed position, and her back curves, settling into her seat. "What about you? What do your parents think about you spending the summer across the country?"

Why does it always have to come back to me? Of course I can't keep her in the dark about everything—if I want her to open up to me, I need to open up a bit to her. But how can I tell her the truth? Do I really want her to know that the last time I talked to my dad it was through a glass partition and he was wearing an orange jumpsuit? And that the last time I saw my mom she was wearing her only Sunday dress and lying in an open coffin? I'm trying to buoy Avery up, not weigh her down with all my baggage, so I simply say, "They give me a lot of space."

My thoughts drift to my mom, and I wonder for the millionth time why I haven't seen her on the other side. After I died, I looked for her. I called to her, but she never came. I asked about her, but no one could tell me where she was. I hope that she's in Elysium, happy and at peace. I can't think of the alternative, of her being in the Briar. Though with the memories I have of her, of her threadbare clothes, her callused hands, and the fear that was constantly in her eyes, it's easier to picture her in the Briar than the pillowy heavens of Elysium. I've never seen Elysium, but I've watched spirits walk through the entrance—a shimmering, vibrant waterfall that's probably only a hint of the beauty that lies beyond.

Avery takes a right turn into a beachside neighborhood situated on a bluff. It's similar to her Dad's—Spanish-style homes with manicured yards and big windows. Beyond the edge of the bluff, the black ocean stretches out, endless and foreboding.

We pull up to a unique two-story house that's practically made of glass, and with all the lights on, it glows like a beacon on the otherwise dark and sleeping street. There's no parking, so Avery drives down the street until we find an open spot on the curb. She parks and kills the engine, then looks in the rearview mirror and rakes a hand through her hair.

"You look great," I assure her.

She lifts a piece of her hair to her nose, inhales, and tosses it aside. "I smell like work."

I reach over and nab a lock of her hair. It's soft and satiny, like morning glory petals. I put it under my nose and slowly inhale. She smells like cotton candy. I lower her hair but keep it between my fingertips. "At least you don't work in a seafood cannery."

"Good point." She smiles, then takes a deep breath and yanks the keys out of the ignition. "Okay—let's go." She glances at my hand, which is still holding a lock of her hair. I reluctantly release it.

We walk up the street to the beacon house, and on the front door there's a "Come In!!!" sign scrawled with red marker on a pizza box lid. I hear the thump of music and the fluctuating hum of conversation on the other side of the door, plus what sounds like someone massacring a Weezer song with a microphone. Just as I reach for the doorknob, the door opens and a handful of girls spill onto the porch between Avery and me. One of the girls is Paige, Avery's best friend. When she sees Avery, she squeals and pulls her into a hug. "You're here!"

"Are you leaving?" Avery asks.

"No—but Mattie and Fiona are." She waves to the departing girls. "See ya tomorrow!" They wave back, and when they see me, their smiling faces turn curious. Paige finally notices me too and raises a questioning eyebrow at Avery.

We're introduced, though after haunting Avery for the last six months, I don't really need introductions to her friends.

Paige gives Avery a look that says, *We need to talk*, and Avery mouths the word "Later."

"Tyler's still here," Paige says in a hushed tone, grabbing Avery's wrist. "But before you come in . . . I'm warning you . . ."

"Gem's here, isn't she?" Avery asks.

Paige answers with an apologetic look, and Avery's shoulders sink a notch. "I don't think he was expecting you to come. None of us were. Anyway, it doesn't matter. Come on." Paige tugs on Avery's wrist, but Avery digs in her heels.

"Just . . . give me a minute," Avery says, her voice tired.

Paige looks at her for a long moment, and I can tell she's hurting for her friend. "Okay," she says, letting go of Avery's wrist. "I'll be inside." She goes back in, leaving the door cracked open.

Avery looks up at me with eyes that are desperate for reassurance. "Remind me what I'm doing here—especially when Gem is already in there with Tyler."

"Hey, don't worry about Gem. I saw her try to hug Tyler last night, and he totally shot her down."

Her eyes brighten. "Really?"

I nod. "Whatever's going on between them, it's not what you think. So forget about her. You're here for Tyler. You want him back, right?"

She seems to think hard for a few seconds, then nods. "And how exactly am I getting him back again?"

I have the urge to reach over and rub out the little crease between her brows. Instead I say, "Just be yourself."

"I told you. I—"

"No—I'm not talking about the person you used to be. Or the

person you want to be, or the person Tyler wants you to be. Just be you. Who you are today, right now. It's enough." I find her hand and give it a gentle squeeze. "And leave the rest to me."

She considers a moment, and then nods. I loop her arm through mine and lead her into the house. She doesn't resist, just clings to my arm and follows my lead.

We step into an enormous room clearly built for entertaining. Vaulted ceilings rise to the second floor, circled with a balcony. A staircase spirals up one corner of the house, and an over-sized C-shaped sectional is parked on Spanish tile in front of a huge flat screen. Three guitars—a bass, an electric, and an acoustic—rest on stands next to a karaoke machine, and some guy with an overgrown mullet stands there with a microphone, belting out the last lines of "Say It Ain't So." He finishes with a few fist pumps, and clapping and whistling ensue.

The sectional is crowded, and Tyler is lounging in the middle with Gem wedged between him and another guy. I know the exact moment Avery sees them, because her grip on my arm tightens. I look down at her, and her face has lost all color.

"Remember," I say, dipping my head closer to hers. "It's nothing. Once he sees you're here, he'll forget all about her."

We find a tight open spot on the couch and sit down, and I have to put my arm around Avery for us to fit. It takes Tyler until halfway through the next karaoke number to notice we're here, and when he does, he shifts uncomfortably on the couch, putting a bit of space between him and Gem. He spends the remainder of the song throwing troubled glances our way, and as soon as the song ends, he gets up. He goes to the karaoke machine, where he sifts through the CDs. Gem heads for the kitchen, giving Avery a crusty look on her way.

Avery's face is unreadable as she sits quietly beside me, watching Tyler.

"You okay?" I ask her. She's so close my mouth is an inch from her ear, but I have the urge to draw her even closer.

She nods. "I'm good. I'm glad I came."

Tyler drops in a CD and hits some buttons, and the opening guitar riff of "I Won't Give Up" sounds through the speakers. He looks right at Avery, lifts the microphone to his mouth, and starts singing to her. Avery lowers her eyes, color slowly returning to her cheeks. Tyler's voice is off key by half a step, but from the way he's looking at Avery, it seems like he means every word. I should feel happy that my plan is working so well, but instead I feel sick, like I've just opened my wallet to discover I've been robbed.

And then Gem walks in front of us on her way back to the couch, holding a cup of something and swaying her hips in her tight capris. Tyler's gaze shifts to her, and follows her, staying with her even after she sits down. Gem's not even looking at him. She's talking with some guy in Ray-Bans, and Tyler is now singing at her, as though trying to get her attention. Avery watches the whole thing, her face appalled. A surge of anger rushes through me, and all the muscles in my arms tighten. What is he thinking? No—what was I thinking, coming here and trying to get her back together with this idiot? She may love him, but she deserves so much better than this. Her happiness should not be in his hands. In fact, now that I really think about it, maybe her happiness shouldn't be in anyone's hands but her own.

Avery turns toward me, her face a breath away, and says, "I want to leave."

I'm about to get up and usher her out of the house, but as my eyes fall on the acoustic guitar near the karaoke machine, it calls out to me, suggesting an idea. I drop my hand on Avery's wrist. "Wait. Just . . . ten more minutes."

She doesn't say anything, but she doesn't try to get up either. She wraps her arms tightly around her waist and bites her lower lip, as though trying to keep it from trembling.

In this moment, I want nothing more than for the world to

stop and look at Avery, to see everything beautiful about her. Not to make her look desirable for Tyler, but for Avery to remember her own worth so that she can take it and find her own happiness. And I can think of only one way to accomplish this.

When Tyler finishes serenading Gem, I turn to Avery. "Don't go anywhere." I get up and cross the room to the guitar.

"What do you wanna sing, man?" The kid at the karaoke machine offers me the microphone, but I wave it off and point to the Martin guitar. "Can I provide my own music?"

"It's not mine. Hey, Dillan! Can this dude play your guitar?"

Dillan is over by the kitchen chatting with some guys, his arm dangling over Paige's shoulder. "You break it, you buy it, man," he calls over his shoulder, not even looking at me.

I pull a stool over from the kitchen bar and sit, propping the guitar in my lap. It's a nice guitar, and when I run my fingers over the strings, feeling their texture and vibrations, something electric courses through me. It's something I haven't felt in so long, and I'm taken back to six months earlier. Playing my guitar on a street corner in Denver, suspended halfway between the life I left behind and the life I hoped to live, the music coming out of me like a fiery anthem.

And then I'm gazing out the window of a box truck, watching rows of orange trees fly by, my stomach hollow and aching. Alone at a rest stop, afraid and uncertain, like I've tripped into an open pit and I'm falling, falling, falling, with nothing to grab and no light to see when or where I'll land. And I remember now what Charles taught me to do with all those feelings. All the anger, the fear, the loneliness, the sorrow.

I tweak the tuning pegs, bringing a string down a half-note and another up until they hum just right, and then spread my fingers across the fretboard to make a G. And then I start strumming.

The chords vibrate through me, filling the empty spaces, the loneliness, the missing pieces, the chasm between peace and torment, between life and death. Music is my servant, the one thing I can control. I can bend and shape it to be whatever I want it to be. But this song is for Avery, not me, so I surrender to the music, letting it take its own shape.

avery

quiet settles over the room as all eyes turn to Kai. There's nothing self-conscious about his playing. His long fingers move along the guitar's neck with surety and deftness, like he's been playing all his life. He's strumming a gorgeous chord progression, his body moving with the rhythm, like the guitar is an extension of him.

I glance around the room to see people raising their eyebrows and nodding approvingly at each other, clearly as impressed as I am. I don't think it's possible for the room to grow any quieter, but when Kai starts singing, it does. As soulful tones sail through his lips, people gather around like he's the Pied Piper. His music commands the room, demands to be heard.

"I see her face through silver glass . . . She's woven of rain and stardust . . ."

His words reach deep inside me like soft fingers, wrapping around the core of my soul. His eyes are closed, his expression intense, as though he's feeling every word, reliving every moment that inspired them. He's obviously singing about a girl he loves, and I'm surprised at the pang of jealousy that hits me.

"With numbered sunsets and bated breath . . . I'll swallow her tears; mend the unjust . . ." Kai opens his eyes and looks at me through his dark lashes, and his gaze is so piercing that it startles me. My mouth is open, and I shut it. But I can't pull my eyes away from his. They've captured me, wrapped me up like an embrace.

I have to remind myself that he isn't really singing to me. He's singing *at* me to make Tyler jealous—for my sake. But the way he's singing, the angst and yearning in his voice, the longing in his eyes, makes me feel like every word is meant for me.

"She's jasmine and lilies; a restless reprise . . . with slumbering wings on white waves . . ."

People are glancing at me, like they believe he's really singing to me. Either Kai is a talented actor, or he truly feels something for me. But how can that be when we just met yesterday? Only, as I meet his eyes again, still gazing at me with raw, uncloaked tenderness, I feel something flicker inside me, a recognition of truth, sincerity.

As he sings the last words, he shuts his eyes and grimaces, like he's uttering a last plea for a death pardon. "A sojourn in silence; a borrowed reprieve . . . I'll take her sorrow to my grave . . ."

For a couple of heartbeats, awed silence fills the room. Then it erupts in applause and whistles. When Kai stands, he's swarmed by people. They're asking for more songs and where he learned to play like that and if he wrote that song. Dillan takes the guitar from Kai, staring at it like he didn't even know it was capable of making those sounds.

Tyler appears in front of me, blocking my view of Kai. He looks frustrated, and he tips his head toward the French doors that lead to the back deck. "We need to talk."

This is the last thing I expected, especially after his performance to Gem, so I sit there a minute waiting for him to say, "Just kidding." But he doesn't. He bends down and hooks my arm, tugging me off the couch; then he leads me by the elbow out of the loud room to a deck overlooking the bluff.

He shuts the door behind us, blocking out the noise of the room, but my ears are still humming with Kai's beautiful music.

Tyler turns to me, a wild mix of jealousy and incredulity in his eyes. "So—are you, like, *with* him now?"

I fold my arms. "What does it matter to you? You're in there singing your heart out to Gem."

He shuts his eyes and winces, then turns from me and moves to the railing. He spreads his hands wide on it and dips his head low, as though he's contemplating jumping over. I can hear the sound of water crashing into the rocks below, like something shattering. "I'm an idiot," he mutters.

I can't disagree with him, but the despondent way he's standing pricks my compassion. I approach him hesitantly. "Tyler, what's going on?"

He shakes his head and turns to face me, leaning his back against the railing. "I sang to her . . . to make you jealous. Okay? You were sitting there with that guy—"

"Kai. His name's Kai."

"Whatever." He comes closer until there's only a foot between us, and my heart does a little flip. "Look—I'm sorry. That song was meant for you, and you alone." Now my heart does a big flip. His face is in shadow, but the deck light reflecting off the house is enough to see the pain in his eyes.

"You don't need to make me jealous," I say. "And you don't need to play games to get my attention. You already have it."

"I just thought . . ." He lets out a loud sigh, and his peppermint breath brushes my face. "Avery . . . am I too late?"

I stand there for a minute in shock, unable to believe that Kai's plan worked so well. But it did work, and now I don't know what to say. Because at the thought of having Tyler back, I feel empty and unsatisfied, like someone has poured a teaspoon of lemonade into my empty cup. And suddenly I'm not sure if this is even what I want anymore.

Tyler's hand comes slowly to my face. His fingertips brush my cheek, along my jaw, across my lips. It reminds me of the first time he kissed me, and I find myself leaning into him. He slides his hand to the back of my neck, and I don't have time to think whether or not I want him to kiss me before he leans in and presses his lips to mine. At first it feels nice because it's familiar. Something I've longed for since the last time he kissed me. I try to surrender to it, to savor it. But after a few seconds, it starts to feel strange. Like an intrusion of my personal space. I open my eyes, and I don't even recognize the face that's an inch from mine. He's been away for so long, he's become someone different to me.

Right as I'm about to pull away, he releases my lips. He leans away to look in my eyes and slides his hands from my neck down to my shoulders. "I can't lose you. We can work this out, I know we can. I haven't been patient enough with you and I'm sorry. I know you'll be okay, that you'll be back to yourself someday. It'll just take some more time, right? My cousin was saying how she went through something kind of like this, and after she got some counseling, and started on some meds—"

I pull out of his arms and glare up at him, feeling the hurt on my face. "Tyler—what is it exactly about me that you love?"

"What? What does that have to do with—"

"I mean, is there anything about *me*"—I point to my chest, trying to make him understand that I'm talking about my character, not my hobbies—"that you love? That would make you want to be with me even if I never surfed again? Like kindness, or devotion, or intelligence, or . . . anything?"

He stares at me for a minute. "Avery, don't do this."

"I'm just trying to understand—"

"You're acting like your mom. Overthinking. Overprocessing. Why don't you get it? I just want *you* back. So come back. Get on some meds and get off the train to crazytown."

"What?" I fall back a step, like I've been struck. He knows my sensitivity about mental illness, my fear that I'll inherit my mom's struggles someday. I shake my head. "I can't believe you'd say that. You think meds are going to fix our broken relationship? Well, unless there's a pill that makes you stop being a jerk, meds aren't going to solve our problems. What I need from you is patience. And unconditional love."

He sighs loudly. "I'm just trying to help. You've got to snap out of this. Don't get all offended just because I think you could use some help."

"What's wrong with me the way I am now?" I shout. "Why am I worthless to you just because I can't get on a surfboard?" I glare at him, at his stunned face, and all I can think about are Kai's words earlier.

Just be yourself. It's enough.

But just being me will never be enough for Tyler. There's only one version of myself that's enough for him, a version that's impossible to maintain one hundred percent of the time. "I have to go." I take another step back.

"Avery—don't." He reaches out like he's going to try and stop me, so I spin on my heel and go back inside, scanning the room for Kai. I have to leave *now*. But I don't see Kai anywhere.

I search the kitchen and hallways. I make my way up the stairs, and it's even more crowded on the balcony. I'm drowning in a sea of people, tossed by the waves of their movements, their chatter, their stares. I can see it in their eyes. I'm the messed-up girl with the messed-up mom. I can't breathe, and I search in vain for a lifebuoy to cling to, for Kai. But he's nowhere to be found, so I start asking around to see if anyone has seen him. A redhead hanging on some guy by the front door says she saw him leave.

"When?" I ask.

She gives a lazy shrug. "A few minutes ago."

I hurry through the front door, hoping that Kai is waiting by my car. But when I get there, he's nowhere in sight.

14

avery

i'm in the ocean, hanging onto my surfboard. A storm rages
around me, but at least I'm not alone. A boy clings to the opposite
side of my surfboard. The boy who just saved my life.

I feel the remains of my surfboard leash snaking around my legs.
The boy's shoulder dips beneath the surface as he fishes it out of the
water; then he grabs my wrist and cinches the leash around it with a
messy knot. "You don't want to lose this," he shouts over the roaring
waves.

I'm shaking, but not only because I'm cold. For the first time in
my life, I'm truly afraid. He must see the fear in my eyes, because he
reaches across the surfboard and captures my hand. We've got our
thumbs interlocked like arm wrestlers, but my hand is on top, like I
just won. I want to see his face, but with the rain pelting me I can't
keep my eyes open. So I look at his hand, at his long fingers curled
around mine. The waves move us up and down, up and down. But
with my hand in his, I feel steady. And just as I start to believe that
we'll make it back to shore safely, his hand is ripped from mine.

My eyes open to a dark room, and the image of the boy's hand is still branded in my mind. My heart is racing, and I find my own hand clutching my blanket, like I'm still trying to hold on to him. I try to calm my breaths and force my fingers to unfurl.

There are some details of that fateful afternoon that I keep to myself. Like him tying the leash around my wrist. And him holding my hand. Because they're sacred to me. And I don't think I can share them without betraying a truth that I keep hidden deep inside.

That I love him.

I can't tell anyone that, because they'll think it's ridiculous. They'll say I can't love someone I don't even know, someone I've only spent twenty minutes of my life with. But what nobody realizes is that I do know him. I learned everything there was to know in the short minutes we spent together on my surfboard. He was selfless and brave, caring and strong. The best qualities a person can possess. And the bond we forged in that small space of time was stronger than any other bond I've made. Because no one else has ever sacrificed so much for me.

A subtle light pours into my room from the hallway, and soon I feel the give of my bed. I turn to see Dad sitting on the edge, the remnants of his blond hair sticking up in all directions. "Bad dream?" he whispers.

It's then I realize I'm crying, and although I wasn't making much sound, it was enough to alert him. It takes me a minute to find my voice, and when I do, it comes out with a pathetic vibrato. "I should have wrapped the leash around his wrist."

"Avery—"

"No—he wouldn't have died if I had. I wasn't thinking. At least not about anything but myself. There was plenty of leash. I could have—"

"Stop." His voice is gentle, but there's enough authority in it to quiet me. "What you're doing right now is unproductive. It won't change anything. All you're doing is punishing yourself."

When someone causes the death of another human being, they're punished. They go to jail, sometimes are even executed. Why shouldn't I be punished too? I don't say this to Dad, I just lay there quietly for a few heartbeats, grappling for the remains of my memories of the boy. But I may as well be trying to hold on to wisps of smoke. An angry tear escapes from the corner of my eye. "I need to find out who he was, Dad."

"You've explored every avenue." He takes my hand and gives it a gentle squeeze. "You're going to drive yourself nuts looking for something you'll never find."

"No—there has to be something I'm missing. Some little detail I'm forgetting that will help me figure out who he was."

Dad is quiet for a long moment, then says, "Avery, I know we've talked about this before, but—"

"I'm not going to see a counselor."

He releases my hand and folds his hands in his lap. "I think someone would be able to help you."

I shake my head. "The only thing that will help me is remembering what that boy looked like. Figuring out who he is. Letting his family know what happened to him. A counselor can't help me with that."

Dad sighs. "Maybe they can. And . . . it seems like you have a lot of emotions to work through. I wish you would talk to someone about what you're feeling."

"Well, a complete stranger is the last person I want to open up to."

"Sometimes a stranger is the best person to open up to. There's no risk, no judgment."

I slowly sit up and look into Dad's eyes. "I'm too afraid," I whisper.

He knows exactly what I'm talking about, because he says, "If you see a counselor, it doesn't mean you're going to end up like your mom. It doesn't mean you have mental illness. It just means there are some knots in here"—he taps his temple—"that you can't quite untangle." He smooths out a wrinkle in my blanket. "But you know what? Even if you were like your mom, there'd be nothing wrong with that. I love your mom. She's funny and full of life. She has so much love in her heart. And when she shares it with you, there's no better feeling in the world."

His voice reflects his pain, and I reach out to touch his arm. "What happened yesterday? Did you two talk?"

"We didn't really have a chance. She had me fixing things all day. First it was the broken light bulb, then a leaky pipe in her bathroom. Then it was a squeaky door hinge and a sticky kitchen drawer. She made me lunch and ordered pizza for dinner and kept me working all day. Every time I would go to leave, she'd think of something else for me to do."

I lay back down. "Sounds like she misses you."

"She's just lonely." He sighs. "But I miss her. I wish she would come home." He looks at me for a long moment, and then reaches for my hand again. "I love you. You know I'd do anything to help you, right?"

I nod. "I love you too, Dad."

He sits there quietly on the edge of my bed holding my hand, the dim light of the hall illuminating the lines of his face. Neither of us says anything else, and I can tell from the sad crease at the side of his mouth that he's still feeling Mom's absence. I give his hand a little squeeze, and he squeezes back. The small gesture connects us, allows us to share our sorrows without words. For the moment, my hand is his anchor, and his is mine, and the comfort it gives calms me enough that I fall back asleep.

When I wake up again, there's a different boy in my mind. A boy who stays up late to help a friend make chocolates, who wields a guitar like a knight wields a sword, who sings haunting and lovely lyrics that echo in my ears long after the song is over.

He's probably working right now, and I have to work today too. But I have an overwhelming desire to see him, to find out what happened to him last night. Maybe he saw me with Tyler and assumed we were working things out, so he didn't feel the need to stick around. I just hope he didn't end up walking all the way home, that he caught a ride with someone.

If I go see him now, he'll probably ask about things I don't want to talk about, like what happened with Tyler. I don't want Kai to know that everything fell apart, especially after he went to so much trouble. But the thought of not seeing Kai this morning feels unbearable. So I get up and shower, throw on a blue sundress and Converse, then get in my car. I stop at the chocolate shop to pick up a gift for Kai and tell Paige I'll be in later, and then I head to Isadora's vineyard.

KAI

My chest feels heavy when I come out of the cottage in the morning, though I can't pinpoint exactly why. Maybe it's the mounting guilt of breaking rules and of taking something that doesn't belong to me. Maybe it's my looming departure from the living world, the knowledge that the sounds of the tide and the scents of the earth will soon be barred to me again. But I think it has more to do with Avery, because it's her that I can't get out of my mind. It was her face I saw before I fell asleep last night. It was she who inhabited my dreams. And it was the desire to see her again that woke me up with the sun. My time with her will be over soon, and the weight of her coming absence is already threatening to crush me.

I'm dead, so I should be the one haunting. Instead, Avery haunts me. I smell her scent even when she's not beside me. I hear her voice echoing inside my head long after she's gone. And when I'm not looking, she moves things around inside the chambers of my still heart.

It was too much to see her with Tyler last night out on the deck, and as much as I wanted to wait for her, I couldn't stay to hear her say the words: that she and Tyler were back together. I guess it's what I want for her because it's what she wants. But that doesn't make it any easier to take.

The air is warm and humid, and I follow a path through the fragrant lavender field where bees are busily gathering nectar, moving from one flower sprig to the next. I pass through a wooden swinging gate into the vineyard, and the land slopes downward into green rolling hills folding into one another. Beyond the hills, a sparkling ocean stretches to the horizon. The vines are as tall as I am, clad in wide leaves and green clusters of budding fruit. Morning dew clings to the leaves and grass at my feet, making the vineyard smell like fresh rain and earth. It makes me think of the vineyard in Marquette, and how I would give almost anything to reclaim the life I had there. Only, it was a life without Avery. And even though I know I can't be with her, I wouldn't give up knowing her for anything.

I see Isadora at the end of the row, her golden retriever, Dacio, trailing her. She's in a colorful muumuu and bare feet, and she's ambling down the row, her hands exploring the newly pruned vines. I meet her halfway, and she looks up at me with milky eyes.

"You did good," she says with a smile. "Now if I only had a crew to follow through until harvest."

"Why don't you hire help?"

She shakes her head. "No one can take care of the vineyard like Miguel. And it's hard to trust new people when you can't see their faces." Her hand finds my face and pats my cheek. "I can see you, though. And you are someone to trust."

"I wish I could stay longer," I say, and I mean those words more than she can possibly comprehend.

"That is okay. When I leave here, and go to Miguel, my vineyard will go to someone else. And they can do what they want with it." She waves dismissively and continues down the row, touching the leaves and humming to herself. Dacio licks my hand and then trots after her.

I go to the shed for some wire, then return and start repairing places where the support wire has broken or become loose. As I'm working, a light breeze rustles my hair, and the sun on my back suddenly burns warmer. I feel a presence behind me, and I know who it is even before I turn around.

"Kai." Charles's voice behind me is gentle, but it pierces me to the bone, because I know now with certainty that my time here is over.

Avery will never see me again. I only hope I've done enough to help her. I inhale deeply, smelling the damp earth and reveling in the breeze on my face one last time.

"What are you doing?" I can hear sorrow in Charles's voice, confirmation that I've let him down. I never cared what anybody thought of me until I met him. Because I knew that he truly cared about me, and still does. So it's torture to turn and face him.

He's outlined by a white aura, because it's his soul I'm seeing, uncovered by flesh and bone. His blue eyes are as soulful as ever, the wrinkles around them heavy with sadness. He walks over to me and lays a gentle hand on my shoulder, looking me in the eye, directly into my soul. "Why?" he asks simply.

I lower my eyes to escape the intensity of his gaze. "I'm sorry. I needed to help Avery. It just . . . it hurt so much to see her like that. And I felt responsible. I had to do something."

Charles drops his hand and looks around, as if he's only now noticing where we are. "And what are you doing in a vineyard?"

I tell him how I needed a place to stay, and about Isadora's generosity. Then I say, "So, what happens now?"

"If you give me back the ring and come with me now, nothing. No one on the other side has to know."

I consider, but I can't come back now, not yet. Avery still needs my help. "And if I don't?"

"Kai, please. You're placing me in a very difficult position. You've taken my ability to fulfill certain assignments. And now that I know you have the ring, I'm breaking a rule by allowing you to use it."

I let out a long sigh, realizing for the first time that my choice has affected more than me. "I'm sorry. You're right." I know I should take off the ring and hand it back to Charles. But then I think of Avery, of the torment on her face when she opened up to me in the chocolate shop, and I know there's more to heal than just her relationship with Tyler. "I need a little more time."

"Sometimes when we think we're helping people, we're really hindering them. Avery is stronger than you give her credit for."

"I know she's strong. But she doesn't seem to know." I shove my hands in my pockets and give a weary sigh. "It's my job to heal people, isn't it?"

"It's your job to heal physical ailments and injuries. But emotional healing isn't that simple. It takes time, willingness, and work on the part of the person being healed, and a greater power than you possess."

I look down and kick the soil with my flip-flop. I know from experience that he's right. Even now, after my death, there are emotional wounds I'm still healing from.

"Your intentions are noble. But this is dangerous. If she finds out who you are—"

"I know the consequence. And I've been careful. She won't find out." I press a hand to my forehead to ease the pressure building there.

"If she does, not only will you lose your healing power and be banned from Earth, but it may only deepen her wounds—not to mention cause irreparable emotional and psychological damage."

"That won't happen," I say again, enunciating each word slowly. "I'm not here to hurt her. I'm here to help her. And I've already seen a difference. A new light in her eyes."

My words appear to worry him more than reassure. "Have you even considered what the punishment might be if you're caught wearing a ring that isn't yours?"

I have wondered, but figured asking would give away my plan. "What is the punishment?"

"I don't know. But I'm sure it's steep."

I picture Avery, the carefree way she smiled at me in the chocolate shop yesterday, and measure the worth of her happiness. "Whatever it is, she's worth it. I died for her, and if given the chance, I would die for her again. I know I can help her. And if I have to pay another price for it, so be it."

Charles's face turns firm. He steps toward me and holds out his hand. "Kai, I'm not giving you a choice. There's too much risk for too many people. Hand over the ring, and come with me now." He stares at me for a long moment, waiting. And then his eyes shift to something over my shoulder, his face slackening.

I twist around, and there's Avery standing at the end of the row, framed softly by vines and the morning sun.

She's far enough away that I don't think she heard me talking, but I can't be sure. Time seems to slow as she moves toward me down the alley of vines, the way it does when you're intensely studying something and trying to commit it to memory. She's wearing a sky-blue sundress, and the fabric at her knees flutters with each step. Her wavy hair hangs over one shoulder in a loose ponytail, and her hands grip a little white box. When she's at arm's length, she stops and greets me with a shy smile.

"You found me," I say. Then remembering Charles, I twist around to introduce him. But he's gone. And I realize that even if he were still there, she wouldn't be able to see him. I don't know where Charles went, but I have the feeling he's still watching me.

She offers me the box, the same type we filled with chocolate-covered fruit the night before. "This is for you," she says. "For helping me last night."

I accept it soberly, because it feels like a going away present, one I can't even take with me. "Thank you."

"Don't eat it all in one sitting. Especially if you're lactose intolerant. But if you're not, then well . . . just pace yourself." Her lips quirk into an adorable smile, and she looks up at me, waiting for me to smile in return. But I can't. Not when I feel like I'm sinking with a boulder chained to my ankle. She bites her lip and shifts her feet, like my graveness is making her nervous. "So . . . what happened to you last night?"

What happened? I fell entirely and completely in love with a girl I can't have. I watched her kiss a boy who doesn't deserve her. I hitched a ride home with a stranger and lay in an empty room, trying to remember how to breathe. But I don't say any of this. I just give her the clipped version. "I left."

She takes a deep breath, and it seems to calm her a bit, because her feet stop doing the two-step. "How did you get home?"

"I caught a ride with some guy . . . Jason, I think. He said it wasn't out of his way, so . . ."

"Why didn't you wait for me?"

Because to watch you with Tyler would have been like drowning all over again. "Well, from the look of things, I thought you'd want to stay with Tyler for longer, and I was pretty tired."

"You could've at least told me you were leaving." From the agitated way she's looking at me, she's clearly upset.

"I'm sorry. I didn't want to interrupt. How did it go, anyway?"

She takes a handful of her skirt and fidgets with it. "What can I say? Your plan worked."

"So . . . you're back together?"

She shrugs, then gets a faraway look on her face, as though she's replaying the night before. "He kissed me," she says absently.

"Yeah—I saw that."

She sighs, and her face clears. "And then his mouth got in the way."

I don't know if she means that he's a messy kisser, or if he said something dumb. Knowing his history, it was probably the latter. "What do you mean?"

She opens her mouth to answer, then closes it. She shakes her head. "Nothing. To be honest, I'd rather talk about you." The line between her brows deepens. "That song you sang last night . . . it was beautiful. Did you write it?"

It takes a minute to purge the image of her and Tyler kissing from my head before I can answer. "Yeah. Kind of in the moment, actually. I mean, the lyrics have been sort of rolling around in my head for a few months, but last night was the first time I put them to music."

She gapes at me. "What are you doing working in a vineyard? Shouldn't you be off in New York or LA or wherever, signing a music contract and recording an album?"

I shrug. "That was the plan."

"Was? What happened?"

"Got derailed."

"By what?"

"Life." Or the loss of it, more accurately. A bug buzzes near my ear, and I sweep it away.

She's looking at me expectantly, as though waiting for me to say more. But there's nothing more to say. At least nothing that won't make her question my sanity. "There's this thing called communication," she says. "Do you want me to explain how it works?"

I feel a smile spread over my lips. "I don't know. You seem like a novice yourself."

She slugs me in the arm. "At least I'm trying." I hear the buzzing again, but this time I see the source. A bee hovers around Avery's neck, and it lands right below her ear. I reach out to swipe it away, but I'm not quick enough.

"Ow!" she cries, wincing and grabbing her neck.

"Here—let me see." I move her hand away and examine her neck. There's the beginning of a welt with a stinger poking out of it. I pull the stinger out. "That's what happens when you smell like sugar."

"Very funny," she says, grimacing.

"Come here—I have something that will help." I curl my fingers around the bare flesh of her wrist, which feels sort of like holding a live wire, and lead her through another wooden gate to a small herb garden behind Isadora's house. I bend down and pluck some leaves from a couple random herbs. I've no idea what they are, but it doesn't matter. They're nothing more than a disguise for the remedy I'll really be using. I put the leaves in my palm with a couple drops of water from the dripping garden hose and mash them into a pulp. It smells like mint, and maybe basil.

When I step over to her, she gives me a wary look, and I smile encouragingly. "Just . . . trust me." I reach out to apply the concoction to her neck, but when I touch the welt, she flinches backward in pain.

"It stings," she complains.

"Which is why it's not called a bee hug. Here—" I step closer so I'm only inches away, then slide my free hand around the back of her neck to hold her still. As I apply a bit of herb goop to the sting, I gently press my finger against it. The wound is small, so it doesn't take long to heal. But I leave my hand there a little longer than necessary, because I'm pretty sure this is the last time I'll touch her, the last time I'll feel the warmth of her skin. I look down into her face, letting my eyes slowly wander over it, and try to memorize every line and curve, every shade of pink, every location of every freckle. I meander from her blue eyes down to her full lips. They're parted slightly, and I can hear her breaths growing shallow, feel their warmth on my face. The pulse in her neck is racing, and she's looking up into my eyes, seeming to search for something there. I'm not sure what she's looking for, or whether she finds it. All I know is that things are getting fuzzy.

I was so sure she loved Tyler, so invested in the idea of getting them back together, it never crossed my mind that she might fall for me. But from the way she's looking at me now, I can see it's possible. And it kills me. It's one thing to break my own heart trying to help her. But to break hers too . . .

She can't fall for me. Not now, not ever. Because it will only hurt her more when I have to leave. "Avery," I say softly. I don't know how to tell her. But I have to. "I don't think I'm going to be here as long as I thought. Definitely not for the whole summer."

"You're leaving?" She blinks. "When?"

"I don't know, exactly. But soon." Her neck is healed, so I lower my hand and take a step away, creating a small distance between us. It hurts, like I've been stung too. Only, my sting won't heal as easily as hers.

She absorbs my words for a minute, and I see the light slowly disappear from her face like a setting sun.

"I'm sorry," I say, "it's just that I . . . I have some other obligations and—"

"It's okay. You don't have to explain." She takes a deep breath and bites her lower lip. "Well, it's been nice knowing you while you were here. Really nice." She looks disappointed, and her feet start doing the shuffle thing again. "And you probably have a lot to get done, and I have to get to work, so . . ." She takes a step back as though she's going to leave.

"Wait." This can't be how we say good-bye. I have to use this last opportunity to finish what I started, to fulfill the reason I came to be with her. I step closer, undoing the gap she created. "Listen, Avery. Whatever happened that's causing you pain and keeping you from living your life . . ." I think for a long moment, searching for the right words. "You need to let it go. Life is too short to stay down when we fall. Get up. Get up and keep going."

For one second, something cold and angry hardens her face. Maybe I've said the wrong thing. But when I blink, it softens into something else I can't define. "Is this the last time I'll see you, then?" Her jaw is set firm, like she's trying not to cry.

"I don't know. Things are really unpredictable right now. If I can, I'll come see you later."

"Okay." Her voice is small, like she's not counting on it. "I'll be at the shop, as usual."

She gives a wave and a half-hearted smile, then turns and walks away. I take a couple steps after her, not wanting to let her go. But I have no choice. I have to let her go, no matter how much it hurts.

16

avery

*t*he sun is spilling a trail of gold across the rippling sea when I lock up the chocolate shop. The sight leaves me empty, because so much more than the day has ended. Kai never came to see me. And after our conversation this morning, I'm pretty sure I'll never see him again.

I walk away from the shop, trying to figure out why it hurts so much to lose someone I only met two days ago. Maybe because in that time, he effortlessly unmasked me as though he were my oldest friend. And even though I still don't know much about his personal life, I feel like I know who he is. He's kind and giving, willing to do anything for a friend. He's a great listener and an amazing musician. And there are things in his past that cause him pain. I wish he would've trusted me enough to share them. But now I'll never know what they are. And something tells me that the mysteries of Kai Lennon will haunt me for the rest of my life.

The waves are flat tonight, the surf a mere curtain of foam that pulls back and forth from the beach. A group of sandpipers chases the receding water, poking the sand with their long beaks in search of dinner. Some people are packing up their beach bags, others still strolling along the wet sand or down the pier.

My phone chirps in my purse, and I pull it out to see a text from Mom.

Can you spend the night here tonight?

I stop walking and text back.

Why? What's up?

It takes a good minute to get her response.

Please.

Maybe she's having a bad night. Or maybe she's been skipping her meds again and is plummeting into the valley of her bipolar coaster. I start walking again, figuring I better go check on her.

OK, I text. **Stopping at Dad's first to get some things.**

But as I pass the pier, something at the end catches my eye and makes me stop mid-stride. At first I can't tell whether it's someone's white hat or a head of platinum hair. With my heart and feet tripping all over themselves, I jog to the mouth of the pier and squint, putting a hand to my forehead to block the sun.

And then my heart rises to my throat. Because Kai is still here.

On their own accord, my feet move toward him. But when a wave washes beneath the pier, I stop. There's no way I'm going out there. Not when he's standing in the exact spot where the boy jumped from last winter to rescue me.

I look down the pier at Kai again, hoping he'll see me and come to me. But his back is turned, his face toward the sun. He's too far to hear my voice if I call to him, so I'll just have to wait.

I pace for a minute, but he doesn't budge, just keeps watching the shrinking space between horizon and sun. Mom needs me, but I can't go to her now. Because there's an unseen current traveling from me to Kai, so overpowering that there's no getting out of it. So I surrender, shutting out everything around me—the pier at my feet, the people around me, the breeze, the surf crawling and crashing below. I focus on Kai instead, on this unexplainable need to be where he is. My feet move almost of their own will, taking slow and steady steps toward him.

The waves are far below me under the pier. But they may as well be crashing into my spine for how they make me feel. They toss me back to last winter, and I feel them sloshing around me, pounding over me, ripping from my hands the boy who saved my life. I keep my eyes on Kai, on the soft light tracing his broad shoulders, on his white hair stirring in the breeze. I hear his words in my mind. *Get up. Keep going.*

My mouth is a desert, and my lungs are so constricted there's barely enough room to hold a mouthful of air. But I inch closer and closer, down the long pier until I finally reach him.

He's leaning on the rail, eyes still on the sunset. I step to his side and grasp the rail as though it's the only thing keeping me from a thousand-foot drop. As my arm brushes his, he turns to look at me. The golden sun catches in his sea-blue eyes, turning them a soft green. There's no surprise in his face, as though he's been expecting me.

"You're still here," I say, but my lungs are working overtime, and the words come out breathy.

His mouth pulls into a thin, slightly somber smile. Then he turns back toward the sunset. "It's mesmerizing, isn't it? The way the light moves across the water."

I gaze at the water to see ripples catching and moving orange sunlight across the sea. It is mesmerizing, and beautiful. And painful. I shut my eyes and force in a few shallow breaths, trying to make myself relax. Then I look back at him. "You wanna walk back to shore with me?"

His brow wrinkles with concern. "You okay? You're paler than a ghost."

"I just . . . don't like being out here. I'm gonna head back, but I'll wait for you on the beach." I try to move my feet, but they won't obey. Maybe because they worked so hard to get me out here to Kai, and now they don't want to leave him.

He tilts his head slightly as though puzzled by something. "What are you afraid of?" He says it like it's something he's wanted to ask for a long time, and only now found the right moment.

My eyes fall to his shirt, because it seems like the only safe place to look at the moment. Only it's not safe, because it's his Rip Curl T-shirt with a menacing wave on the front.

"What's keeping you out of the water," he asks, "when you used to love it so much?"

I move my gaze to a more comfortable spot, the crook of his elbow. The skin there is smooth and strangely unmarked by veins. "What makes you think I used to love the water?"

"You said at your mom's that if I tried surfing, I'd be hooked for life. I'm assuming you know from experience. And you told me that you once had a goal to hold your breath as long as a sea lion. Only someone who loves being underwater would have a goal like that." He turns fully toward me and cinches the already narrow space between us, then presses the pad of his thumb between my eyes. "But mostly, because of this little furrow you get in your brow every time you look at the sea." He gently rubs it out, and then in the softest voice says, "So tell me, Avery Ambrose. What's keeping you from what you love?"

He pins me with his soul-piercing gaze, and I've never felt so vulnerable. Because there's something so sincere in his eyes, so desperate for my answer, that I know I can't keep my secrets from him anymore. They're crowding at the surface, rallying to be heard, spilling onto my tongue and prodding my lips to part.

"Someone drowned out there," I say quietly, "because of me."

I look away, down to the water, because I don't want to see his reaction. I don't want to see the confusion, or shock, or pity my confession has provoked. The sea is calmer out here, away from the break, and it's a long way down. I imagine what it must have been like for the boy to jump from this high into a storming sea, like dropping into the open jaws of a frothing monster. And I wonder if, in the moment he leapt over the railing, he knew he had just exchanged his life for mine. Maybe he didn't think at all, just saw me drowning and reacted. And maybe when he hit the water, that's when he wondered what he'd gotten himself into.

"This is where he jumped from," I whisper, almost to myself.

When Kai doesn't say anything, I look at him. The wind is blowing his hair this way and that, and his eyes are full of answers, not questions, as though he already knows the story and just wants to hear it in my words. So I tell him.

"I was out here one day, surfing. I got rolled by a set of huge waves, and my leash got tangled around my neck." My hand moves to my throat, because I'm having trouble breathing, as though the leash is still there. "I've never felt so helpless. Even when I managed to get my face above the surface, I couldn't get any air. Just when everything started to go black, I felt a hand on my arm. And something sharp slipped under the leash around my neck. It hurt. But then, I was free. His hands were around my waist, lifting me onto my board."

Kai's wristband is glinting in the sun, and his large, strong hands grip the railing so tight his knuckles are white. The boy's hands were strong too. But not strong enough to resist the wave that swept him from my board.

I don't want to continue, because the hardest part comes next. The part where I dove underwater to find him and saw him beneath me, face down. If he had been conscious, he could have reached out and grabbed my hand. If my leash hadn't been half its original length, I could have swum down farther. But he was just out of reach, and when I came up for breath and went back down, he was gone.

It torments me to know what he probably went through. I learned that day what it feels like to almost drown, and it's not quick and painless. He must have felt the claustrophobia, the fire in his lungs, and the moment when he gave in to his lungs' demands to inhale, and instead of air, they were flooded with liquid. And then he must have just *known*. Maybe in the same moment that he regretted jumping in to save me, he knew that his life was over. That all the things he hoped for and worked for would never happen. That all the people he loved would soon be weeping over his grave. Only, they can't grieve for him, because whoever they are, they don't even know he's dead.

I scan the shoreline, from the mouth of the pier all the way to Port San Luis, miles of sand and rock, searching for him even now. "They never found his body," I say. "Or even his identity." I rest my elbows on the railing and drop my head into my hands. "The worst part is, I don't even remember what he looked like. It was raining, and I only got a couple brief glimpses of his face. But even then, you'd think I'd remember the face of the person I owe my life to. I've spent hours combing through missing persons databases, hoping I'll recognize him. But it's no use. And every time I go near the water, it's excruciating to be reminded that because of me, someone so brave and noble . . . is gone." My stomach hurts, and my throat feels like it's being flooded with saltwater all over again.

"Brave and noble," Kai echoes thoughtfully, and when I look at him, there's a trace of wonder in his expression before it turns consoling. "But it's not your fault—"

"I shouldn't have been in the water that day. I was being even more reckless than usual. It was storming, and I knew it was dangerous, but I didn't care."

"What were you doing out there in a storm?"

"That was the day my mom packed her bags. It hurt *so* much. And the ocean was the only place I could put it out of my mind."

"And you're afraid of the water now?"

I consider his question for a moment, then shake my head slowly. "It's not the water I'm afraid of. It's . . ." It's something so complex I'm not sure I can put it into words. I try anyway. "The fear of loss. Of guilt and shame. Of what's at risk. When that boy drowned, I realized the danger in living life to its fullest. You can get hurt. And worse, you can hurt other people." I look down at the railing, running my finger along the grain of the wood, and then say quietly, "And then there's simple reverence. The ocean is where he died, and surfing and having fun in it feels like dancing on his grave. Not only that, but I took his life to preserve my own. How is it fair for me to live my life to its fullest, when he can't even have a portion of his?"

His face clears, like I've just solved a riddle that's been perplexing him. And then it falls into agony. "Avery." His voice catches on my name. He clears his throat and then tries again, his tone warm, almost affectionate. "You didn't take his life. He *gave* it." He reaches out and tucks a stray lock of hair behind my ear, sending warm tingles down my arm. His hand comes to rest on my shoulder, his thumb molding perfectly into the indent above my collarbone. "And have you ever thought that maybe he doesn't regret what he did? That saving you was the crowning moment of his life?" He releases a sad sigh. "Avery, look at me." I try, but he's all blurry now. I feel the backs of his fingers sweeping over my wet cheek, feel more tears pouring over the place he just dried. "And did you ever think of how it would make him feel to know that after giving so much for you, you're throwing his sacrifice away?"

I shake my head. "I'm not. I—"

"He gave his life so you could live. But you're not living." He lays both hands on my shoulders and leans down to eye level. His hands steady me, calm me, and the last of the sunlight is lighting the tips of his hair like a halo. "So *live.*"

Behind him, the sun is disappearing beneath the liquid horizon. For a moment, everything goes silent. All movement stops on the pier and the beach, everyone pausing to witness a miracle, as though the sun sets only once in a lifetime instead of thousands. And I think how maybe I've just witnessed my own miracle. Because after six months of being held under the waters of guilt and grief, I can breathe again.

Maybe Dad was right. Maybe sometimes the best person to talk to is a stranger.

After the sun disappears, we stay there for a long time, wordlessly watching the horizon fade. Finally, Kai says, "Come on, I'll walk back to shore with you."

We start walking, and maybe it's because Kai is beside me, but I feel steadier now than I did when I first walked onto the pier. "I thought you left," I say.

He doesn't respond right away. We pass a couple sitting on a bench, engaged in conversation and hands intertwined. What would it feel like to have Kai's fingers laced between mine like that? Probably like having my hand out the window of a moving car, the wind sliding through my fingers. Amazing, but impossible to hold.

"I'm going to be around for a bit longer than I thought," he says.

I nod slowly, and I can't seem to restrain the smile that spreads over my lips. "Good. Then it's your turn."

He raises an eyebrow.

"Come on," I say, nudging him with my elbow. "I just poured my heart out to you *again*. And what have you shared with me? Next to nothing. So it's your turn. Tell me something about yourself. Something I don't already know. And something that matters. No favorite foods or zodiac signs."

He smiles. "Scorpios are known to be mysterious."

"Kai—"

"They sting too. So before you bare your soul next time, make a bargain. Sometimes it's the only way to get what you want." He says this last part darkly, as though he himself recently made a heavy bargain.

I grab his arm and stop him from walking. "Wait a minute— that's not fair. I've told you about Tyler and about—"

"How is Tyler, anyway? Have you talked to him since last night? And what exactly happened anyway?"

"Nothing happened."

"But you kissed."

I shake my head. "You can't keep doing this. Every time I try to get you to talk about yourself, you spin it back to me."

My phone chirps, and I remember Mom. I pull out my phone, and sure enough, it's another text from her. A long one. I skim through it—a poem with plenty of dark imagery, probably one she just wrote. She's spiraling downward faster than usual. I shoot her a quick text to let her know I'll be there soon, then release a long sigh. "You're off the hook. I have to go."

"Where?"

I start walking again. "My mom needs me tonight. But . . . what are you doing tomorrow?"

He catches up and walks beside me. "My day's open."

"Don't you have to work?"

"I could probably get some time off. Why? What do you have in mind?"

I shrug. "I don't know. Is there anything you've been wanting to do while you're here in Avila Beach?"

He thinks. "Actually, there's one thing."

"What's that?"

"I'd really like to take your suggestion to try surfing."

An incredulous sound comes out of my mouth. "Like I told you, there's a great surf school right over there. Tyler works there. Maybe he could teach you."

Kai turns around and walks backward, smiling at me with the left side of his mouth. "I was actually hoping you could give me some tips."

I open my mouth to say no, but he holds up his hands to silence me. "Hear me out. You don't have to get in the water. Just come to the beach with me and give me some tips from the shore."

I recall his words from a moment earlier. *Make a bargain first. Sometimes it's the only way to get what you want.*

"I'll tell you what. I'll *think* about it, but only if you tell me something about yourself first."

"What do you want to know?"

I want to know everything. I want to open him up like a book and read every page. I want to know what inspires him and what haunts him. What comforts him, and what keeps him up at night. I want to know his brand of toothpaste and his favorite song. But since I have to start somewhere, I say the first thing that comes to mind. "Why can't you stay for the whole summer?"

His hand moves to his stomach, where he absentmindedly gathers a handful of T-shirt in his fist. "When I came here, I left my old job without much notice. They really need my help, and they're begging me to come back."

"Why did you come here to begin with?"

He purses his lips and tilts his head as though carefully weighing something. "If I tell you, will you come to the beach with me tomorrow?"

"I will very heavily lean toward yes."

A family walks past us on the sidewalk, the two kids chasing circles around their parents. Kai's face softens as he watches them pass, and when they're out of earshot, he says, "My little sisters live here with my aunt and uncle. I came to see if I could live with them. But it didn't work out."

"Oh," is all I can think to say. Because his answer is miles from what I was expecting. I don't know what I was expecting exactly, but not that. Suddenly a million new questions are spinning in my head like the *Price Is Right* wheel, and I'm not quite sure yet which one the needle's going to land on.

My phone chirps yet again, but this time I don't bother looking because I know it's Mom. Kai glances at my phone, then gives an understanding nod. "Tomorrow?"

"The jury's still out on the surfing tips. But either way, I'll pick you up in the morning."

17

avery

i find Mom in her darkened bedroom under a pile of blankets, and I go sit on the edge of her bed. From the hallway light, I can see she's clutching a tattered tissue and wearing her polka-dot pajamas.

"Mom," I say gently, brushing messy curls from her forehead, "what's going on?"

She reaches for my hand as if it's a piece of bread and she's starving. "Just stay with me," she says shakily.

We've been here many times before, so even though I'm worried, I know she'll get through this. She only needs time, and someone to paddle through the doldrums with her. I slide under the covers and drape my arm over her, cradling her against me.

"I'm a terrible mom," she sobs.

"No—you're not."

"Then why won't Sophie talk to me? I've been calling her all week, and she won't pick up."

I stroke her hair. "She just doesn't understand why you left." I don't either. Every time I try to talk to Mom about it, her explanations are more complicated than wave physics. "She'll come around. She's only mad because she loves you and wants you to come home. I think she's using herself as bait."

For a couple minutes, there's no sound in the room except the ticking clock and an occasional sniffle from Mom. Then she says quietly, "I thought I would be happier."

"What do you mean?"

Her tissue is soaked, so she tosses it on the floor and pulls her pajama sleeve over her wrist, wiping her eyes. "I thought . . . if I could be by myself for a while, and focus on only me, I could get myself together, you know? I could come back and be a better mom, and a better wife. But I feel even more scattered and lost now than when I left."

It's true that she's put us through a lot of ups and downs over the years. But the ups have made the downs bearable, because those are the times I see who she really is—a fun, creative, loving and generous person—and that's the mom I try to remember when she's wading through the valleys of depression.

"We don't want a better mom," I say. "We just want *you*."

She sniffles. "When was the last time I washed your clothes?"

"Who cares? You've never missed one of my surfing competitions."

"But I've missed all your parent-teacher conferences."

"That's what Dad is for. You've never missed the important stuff. You've never failed to help Sophie and me get ready for a dance, or redecorate our rooms on a whim, or take us to the best—and worst—chick flicks."

Her feet find mine under the blankets, and her fuzzy socks rub against my ankles.

"You're the one who taught us how to sail," I continue, "and I'll never forget your lesson on the perils of face glitter."

She draws in a deep, stuttering breath, but doesn't say anything else. We lie there, listening to the ticking clock and the muffled sound of the surf through the window.

"You can always come back," I say faintly after a long moment. I don't even know if she hears me, because soon I feel her body relax and her breathing deepen. I stay beside her for a few minutes until I'm sure she's asleep, then I slip out of her bed and go across the hall to the bathroom. I open the medicine cabinet and pull out Mom's current prescriptions to make sure she's not out. The lithium bottle is empty, so I text Dad to see if he can get it refilled tomorrow.

When I close the cabinet, I'm startled by my own reflection in the mirror because for a split second I don't recognize myself. My eyes are tired and troubled, my face timid and full of fear. This is who I've become. And it's not who I want to be.

Kai said I didn't need to be someone else, I just needed to be me. But I don't even know who *me* is. I stare deep into my own eyes, searching for myself, for someone I recognize as Avery Ambrose. Someone with courage and determination, with hope and optimism, who's not afraid to chase what she loves. Just like my mom's fears keep her from the people she loves, my own fears have been keeping me from the life I want to live.

But I don't want to live in fear anymore. I don't want to be controlled by it the way my mom is. Because it's the moments I've feared most that have come right before my greatest experiences. Like taking on a huge wave and coming out of the tube standing, or diving into the black ocean at night to see the underwater world lit up in neon blue by phytoplankton. Or walking out onto the pier tonight and sharing my burdens with an amazing boy.

I want to be someone who experiences great things. Someone who dares to live and fail and succeed and love.

I lean forward and search the depths of my own eyes. And finally, beyond the blue irises in my reflection, I catch a glimpse of her. Of the girl who, despite being afraid to stand up and move forward, has the courage to rise and take the first step.

18

KAI

The cab of Isadora's truck sounds like a rolling snare drum and smells like diesel exhaust. She warned me it hadn't been used in years and needed an oil change, but neglected to tell me I'd need a gas mask to drive it. I roll down the windows and let the clean night air rush in, and hope this ancient thing can at least make it ten miles to my aunt and uncle's house. Because I don't have time to make this trip twice.

Three days. That's all Charles gave me to wrap things up. In exchange, I promised that when the three days were over, I would let go of Avery. Move on and never visit her again. It was the hardest bargain I've ever made, but the only way to get the time I still need to help her.

It feels like a bomb is ticking inside of me now, set to detonate in exactly sixty-seven hours. Every second counts, so I need to make the most of each one.

I've been to my aunt and uncle's house only once before—not counting the times I dropped in on my sisters after my death—so it takes me a bit of wandering to find their neighborhood. It's after midnight when I turn onto their street, and most of the one-story bungalows are dark. They all look the same—little clapboard boxes with double gables—so I look for the one with the big ash tree in front.

I slow down when I see it, making sure their lights are out before I get close. The windows are dark except a dim light in the kitchen window, probably a night-light. I park a couple houses down and get out, hoping no one is looking out their window. A teenage boy creeping behind someone's house in the middle of the night is the very definition of suspicious, and the last thing I need is a patrol car showing up.

Their lawn is freshly cut and damp from sprinklers. As I sneak along the side of the house and through a creaky gate into the backyard, I can't help thinking how this could have been my home too had my aunt and uncle taken me in seven years ago along with my sisters. I try not to be bitter about it, but even after all this time, the rejection stings.

At the back of the house, Helen and Jane's bedroom window is dark. My chest aches at the thought of them being so near. Seven years have passed since my aunt and uncle brought them here from Michigan. Seven years without a hug or a face-to-face conversation.

I have the impulse to tap on their window so I can see them. So they can see *me*, and know I'm okay. At least, *believe* I'm okay. I'm sure they've been worried about me since my disappearance. But what good will it do for them to see me now? It will only give them false hope, delay and prolong their grieving process. So with a heavy heart, I pass their window and return to my original errand.

I edge along the wooden fence toward the shed, trying to stay in the shadows of the trees. When I get there, I'm relieved to see the shed's metal door cracked open. It whines a bit as I swing it open, and I peer inside, waiting for my eyes to adjust to the darkness. In the very back corner, behind bikes and camping gear, I can barely make out the tip of my guitar case. Exactly where I stashed it six months ago.

It took me a whole summer to save for my Gibson guitar. And since I can't take it with me, I may as well do something useful with it. Like pawn it so I can repay the shop owner for the broken window and stolen items. Isadora has given me some money for the work I've done in her vineyard, but not enough to cover the damage. And no way am I asking for more after she's sheltered and fed me.

I dig out my guitar case as quietly as I can. It feels lighter than it used to, so to make sure the guitar is still inside, I lay it on the shed's concrete floor and open it. My guitar lies inside like a corpse in a coffin waiting to be resurrected. I run my hand over the smooth rosewood and deeply inhale the scent that brings back so many memories. I open the compartment under the neck of the guitar and find my picks and extra strings, and the pocket notebook with my lyrics scribbled inside.

Maybe I don't need to be so hasty about pawning it. Maybe I'll keep it for one more day so I can play it. I close the lid and secure the latches, then grip the handle to leave. But before I can lift it off the ground, I hear the scuff of a foot behind me.

I whip around to see a woman standing in the shed's doorway, long dark hair silhouetted by the patio light. For a split second I think it's my mom, and with a lurch in my chest, I think, *Finally. I've found her.* But then I notice the way she's standing. I could never mistake my sister's slouchy posture. I set down my guitar case and straighten.

"Helen."

Her hand comes to her mouth, muffling her voice as she says my name and, "I knew it was you." She closes the distance between us, hauling me into a hug. The top of her head comes to my chin, and her messy hair tickles my neck. It's the best feeling in the world, and I let my arms fall around her skinny shoulders.

I suddenly wish we could go back seven years and do things differently. I wish I would have been a better kid so my aunt and uncle would have taken me in too, so my sisters and I could have grown up together. My childhood was stolen from me because I couldn't share it with the people I love. But as I hold Helen now, it's returned to me for a brief moment.

"I thought you were dead." Her voice hitches on the last word, and I have to clench my jaw to endure the sting. The pain in her voice convinces me that it's better for her not to know the truth. That it will be better to let her believe I'm alive and living abroad, and too busy to keep in touch.

She finally releases me and takes a small step back, though she still has part of my shirt clutched in her hand. "Where have you been?" she whispers.

For a second, I want to tell her the truth. I want to say, "Helen, I went to the ocean last winter, and I drowned. I received the power to save lives, but I still haven't figured out how to salvage my own." I imagine what her reaction would be if I said these things, and it isn't pretty. So instead I say, "I've been all over the place, working here and there."

She lets out a shaky breath, and her eyes shine with tears. "Were things that bad in Michigan?"

She'll never know what I went through in my seven years in foster care. And I don't want her to know. I don't want her to hurt because of what I had to endure. Because I'm sure she has plenty of things she's still hurting over.

"It was all right," I lie. "But I felt like a prisoner. So I set myself free."

Her hand comes up to wipe her cheek. "Jane and I have been counting down the months until you turn eighteen, hoping you'd come live nearby when you were finally free to."

Her words strangle me, because as much as I want to be a part of my sisters' lives, it is an absolute impossibility. "Helen," I say in a choked whisper, "would you go wake up Jane? I want to see her too."

She hesitates a second, and then nods. "Don't go anywhere." She disappears into the house and then comes out a few minutes later with Jane in tow. Jane is fourteen now, but almost as tall as Helen. Her hair is dark blonde like mine used to be, and it's cropped to her chin. When she sees me, she races across the wet grass and throws herself into my arms. She asks all the same questions Helen did, and then with hope brimming in her eyes, she says, "So are you going to come and live nearby?"

"I'd love to," I say, trying to keep my voice steady, "but I have other plans. You know how I've always wanted to backpack across Europe?"

They both look at me, and behind the pain in their eyes, there's understanding that I need freedom. Helen smiles. "I wish we could come with you."

I shake my head. "No, you don't. You guys have a good life here."

Helen's smile fades. "I'm so sorry, Kai." She shakes her head regretfully. "We tried so hard to convince Laurel and Gerald to take you in too. We begged and cried until they threatened to put us back in foster care." She tears up again, and so does Jane.

"Hey," I say, pulling them both into my arms. "No regrets. I'm glad you two get to be together, in a safe place." For a few minutes, we say nothing else. Then I say, "Listen. I don't want anyone to know where I am, okay? So don't tell anyone you saw me tonight."

"Why?" Helen leans back to look at me. "Are you in trouble?"

"No—not like criminal or anything. It'll just . . . make things a lot harder if you tell anyone you saw me."

"You know you're a missing person, right?" Jane says.

"Sure, but you two are the only ones who really care. And now you know where I am. Besides, I turn eighteen in a few months. So what difference does it make? I'll be on my own anyway."

They both nod, wordlessly agreeing to say nothing about my visit. Helen notices the guitar at my feet and her brows pinch together. "Has that been here all this time?"

"Yeah. I came here last December, but no one was home. It was raining, so I stashed it here in the shed."

She tips her head. "Why didn't you wait for us to get home?"

"I did. For a couple days." I point to the covered back patio with cushiony patio furniture. "I slept there." And then I went to the ocean, where I drowned.

She releases a sad sigh. "It must have been when we went on the cruise. Prices are cheaper in December, so . . ." She waves it off. "Where are you staying now?"

"Around."

Jane grabs my hand and holds it the way she used to when she was scared, when she was four and I was eight. "Kai—are you homeless?"

"No. I live at the place I work. And I'm getting fed and everything, okay?"

"Well," Helen says, "I'm glad you're being taken care of . . . or taking care of yourself. You always were good at that. And . . . always good at taking care of us." Her chin quivers. "Thanks for that."

I pull them both into a hug again, mostly so they can't see the tears welling in my eyes. "I love you guys. Never forget it."

"When will we see you again?" Jane asks.

I don't reply for a long time, because I don't have a clue of how to answer. There is no good answer. No answer that won't leave them with false hope or no hope at all. "I don't know," I say. "But I will see you again." They just won't be able to see me.

19

avery

t he next morning, I pass row after row of vines at Isadora's vineyard, peering down the alley between each one in search of Kai. The sun is peeking over the rolling horizon, and the tops of the vines are gilded with light. The air is crisp and clean, full of the possibilities of a new day.

I woke this morning with a surge of newfound courage to take back the life I discarded six months ago. Mom was still sleeping, so I left her a note, and then went to Dad's where I put on a surf tee and board shorts, packed a beach bag, and strapped two surfboards to the top of my Cherokee. I'm not sure how this day is going to go, but I'm optimistically prepared.

Down at the end of one of the rows, I glimpse a wooden gate with a lavender field and a little cottage behind it. I pause, wondering if that's where Kai is staying. And then I hear something. Faint music, coming from the direction of the cottage. I follow the sound down the row of vines, and it gets more distinct the closer I get to the cottage. Guitar strings, being plucked in a downpour of melancholy notes, and I don't have to see Kai now to know exactly where he is.

The gate squeaks loudly as I pass through, but Kai must not hear because there's no pause in his music. I approach the front of the cottage slowly, wanting to listen without him knowing I'm here. When I reach the bottom of the porch steps, I see him through the screen door. He's sitting on the cottage floor, bent dejectedly over the guitar in his lap. His voice joins the guitar, the sounds entwining in a divine duet, and I hold my breath because the only thing I want to hear is him.

"Weak heart and untimely fate . . . await me at this broken gate."

His tones travel the distance between us and spill into my chest, as though through his voice, I feel what he's feeling. His eyes are shut tight as he sings, his brow a series of ripples that reminds me of a restless sea right before a storm.

"Forbid heaven to alter; For her, I would die but not falter."

I rest my head against the porch post and watch him through the screen, thinking how I could stand here and listen to him all day. And then I wonder who he's singing about, what memories are inspiring such deep emotion. Maybe it's for a girl he loves. Or something to do with what he told me yesterday, about not having a place to call home. I find myself moving slowly toward him, questioning myself with each step. I feel like I'm intruding, because I've never seen him quite so vulnerable, so unmasked.

A wooden board creaks under my step, and the music stops. His head snaps up, and I glimpse the pain in his eyes before he quickly composes his expression into pleasant surprise.

He leans his guitar against the wall and rises, then comes to the screen door, pausing a heartbeat before pushing it open and joining me on the porch. He smells like lavender and mint, and the sad tones of his song are still resounding in my ears.

"Hey," I say.

One corner of his mouth turns up. "I didn't expect you so soon."

"I got today off." It took some finagling with Sophie, but I was finally able to convince her to swap days with me in exchange for the newest Astromotts album.

I want to ask Kai what he was singing about. From the way his smile faded just now, I can tell he's still in whatever dark place inspired that song. His lips are moving, like he's fighting with them, trying to produce another smile.

"What's wrong?" I ask.

It takes him a minute to find his voice. "That's a very glass-half-empty question to ask." His smile returns. "Why don't you ask me what's *right*?"

If it'll get him to talk about himself, I'll play along. "Okay— what's right?"

He takes a half step toward me, and with his head dipped and his eyes on my purple toenail polish, he says, "This moment, right here."

My heart does a weird triple beat, because I think he might lean down and kiss me. Just like I thought he was going to kiss me yesterday when we were in the herb garden.

He closes his eyes, but instead of moving in for a kiss, he leans away and says, "The humid, eighty-degree breeze on my arms. It's just right." He inhales deeply. "The scent of lavender in the air. That's just right." He opens his eyes and looks down at my board shorts and surf tee, and a smile spreads across his lips, so wide it makes a little crease in his cheek. "And a friend, here on my porch, come to take me surfing. It's perfect."

"I'm not making any promises," I say. "But I *am* taking you to the beach."

"How much farther?" Kai asks from the passenger seat.

I glance at the clock on the dashboard. We've been driving for about thirty minutes now. "Patience."

"Where are we going, exactly?"

150

I don't answer, just look over at him and smile. The wind is blowing through the windows, flipping his hair in his eyes and making little ripples in his shirt. My hair is everywhere—in my face, on my arms, halfway out the window. Kai reaches over and gathers it up, securing it at the nape of my neck. His hand on the back of my neck makes me feel warm. I keep my face forward and try to concentrate on the road, hoping he won't notice the burn in my cheeks.

The turnoff to the beach comes sooner than I expect, and I almost miss it. I slam on the brakes and make a sharp turn onto a faint sandy road. Our seats bounce beneath us as we wind through dried grass and sand down to a secluded beach not visible from the road.

"There's no one here," Kai says.

"You're not the only one with fiercely guarded secrets." I open my door and step into the warm sand, leaving my flip-flops under the gas pedal.

Rocky cliffs contain the crescent-shaped beach on either side, and the morning sun cuts directly through them, lighting up the water like sapphires. A salty breeze brushes my cheeks and pushes my hair off my shoulders. *A southerly*, I think as I close my eyes. *Perfect.*

I listen to the waves crashing on the shore, and for the first time in months, instead of tormenting me, they beckon to me. For a moment, I imagine them beneath me, lifting me, pushing me forward like wind behind a sail.

"If it's a secret," Kai says, his voice close to me, "how did you find it?"

I open my eyes. He's standing right beside me, my beach bag slung over his shoulder, one of my neglected surfboards tucked under his arm.

"My dad," I say. "He used to come here with his buddies before the chocolate shop took over his life. This is where he taught me to surf." I point to the cliffs. "The shape of the cove and the contours of the ocean floor create the perfect surf. At high tide, the waves are usually mild and spilling—perfect for beginners." I give him a pointed look. "And then when the tide drops, the shallow reef makes the waves steep and fast. With an onshore wind, you get crystal clear tubes. It's pretty much surfer heaven." I shoot Kai a warning look. "Only a handful of locals know about it."

A faint, secretive smile softens his lips. "Don't worry. I'll take it to my grave."

I look at the surfboard under his arm. He has my five-foot short board. "You can't start with that. Try the long board first, to get a feel for the waves. Once you master that, you can try the short board."

He looks like he's about to object, but instead says, "Teacher knows best." He hands me the short board and slides the long board off the car rack. We take a short walk through parched grass and sand, then set our things down out of the water's reach. Kai peels off his T-shirt so he's wearing only board shorts, and it takes conscious effort not to gawk.

I spread out a towel and sit down, gazing at the sea for a long time and taking slow, deep breaths, trying to re-acclimate to a place I haven't been to in so long. I feel a little jittery, but as I run my hand through the warm sand and focus on the feeling, it calms me a bit.

"So," Kai says, laying the surfboard on the sand near me, "you gonna show me how it's done?"

I pull sunglasses from my beach bag and slide them on, thinking about what Kai said the day before about bargains. "I'll tell you what. For every question you answer, I'll give you a surfing tip."

He stares down at me, and I see his gears turning, considering. Finally he crouches beside me and says, "I have a better idea."

"You always do," I say, digging a paperback from my bag.

"Let's play a game."

"Aren't we already?"

He ignores my attempt at banter. "It's called Truth and Dare."

I set my book down. "You mean Truth *or* Dare?"

"No—I mean Truth *and* Dare."

I raise an eyebrow, intrigued.

"If you dare to come in the water with me, I'll tell you the truth about anything you want to know."

Warily, I look at the water and debate whether or not it's a good trade-off. On one side of the cove, the waves are curling into perfect cylinders. I picture myself gliding through them on my surfboard, and for a split second, I want to abandon our pending deal and paddle out to sea. But then I think of the last time I was on my surfboard, and my skin turns cold. "I like my offer better."

"It's a lopsided bargain," he argues, "so it's no good. I want more than surfing tips for my secrets."

I stare at him, seriously considering, and my heart is suddenly throbbing in my throat. In his eyes, I see the same message he gave me yesterday in the vineyard. *Get up. Life is too short to stay down when we fall. Get up.*

"Just . . . get your feet wet," he says.

My mouth is parched, and I have to swallow before I can speak again. "Are you saying if I get my feet wet, you'll tell me anything I want to know?" I mentally recall my Mysteries of Kai Lennon list, preparing to ask him about every item.

He holds out his hands. When I don't move, he reaches down and takes my wrists, pulling me to my feet. He removes my sunglasses and tosses them on my towel. Then he backs up a few paces until he steps into the sizzling foam of a wave. "Ask me something," he says.

"Hasn't anyone ever told you not to turn your back on the ocean?"

"Is that really the question you want me to answer?" When I say nothing, he says, "Come on. Ask me something."

Where is that brave girl I saw in the mirror last night? My pulse is racing, and even though the weather is perfect, the back of my neck is suddenly on fire. There is so much I want to know about Kai. But are his answers worth the guilt and panic and pain I'll feel the moment my toes touch the water?

Searching for strength, I look into his face and find something unexpected. My fear and pain seem to be reflected in his eyes. And I realize I'm not alone. That maybe, in some small way, he understands. He has wounds to heal from and demons to battle like I do. And here he is, offering to share them with me.

I take a step toward him, then another, and another, until I'm standing right in front of him on the wet sand. My question comes out breathy. "What were you singing about this morning?" My lips are dry, and I moisten them with the tip of my tongue.

"I was singing about things I've lost. Things I worked hard for, that were taken from me."

"Like what?"

He takes three steps back at the same time a flood of water rushes up behind him, past him, and reaches for me. I brace myself, clenching my fists and keeping my eyes on Kai as cold water rises to my ankles and then gradually recedes. He raises his hand and summons me closer.

I'm trembling at the core, and I fold my arms tightly to still myself, making a conscious effort to distance my nails from my skin. I can do this. I can face my fears for a moment so I can hear Kai's answer. Just this one, then I can go back to dry sand. I come to him and lift an eyebrow, waiting for his answer.

"Like home. And dreams. And family. Things I love, that are just out of reach."

Another wave rushes over my feet, rising to my calves. I have the impulse to run for dry sand, get in my car, and drive to the middle of the Mojave Desert. But my desire to uncover Kai's secrets is even stronger. "What happened to your family? Why are your sisters living with your aunt and uncle? Where are your parents?"

"That's three questions."

"So pick one and answer."

He backs up again. This time, the waves crest at his thighs, and a surge of panic is cresting in my throat. Curse him. Why won't he just tell me? Why is it such a big deal to him that I go in the water? The half-smile on his lips asks what I'm waiting for. Then he says something so quietly I can't hear it.

"What?" I yell over the waves.

He motions for me to come closer. I take a few deep breaths, and then clenching my fists so tight that my nails dig into my palms, I come.

"My mom died when I was eight," he says. "A couple years later my dad went to prison. My aunt and uncle adopted my sisters, and I grew up in foster care." His calm expression doesn't match his words. He should be grimacing or getting teary-eyed or something. But maybe he's already cried all his tears. And for a moment, instead of seeing him as a platinum blond hunk, I picture him as a young boy, crying in the back of a social worker's car as he's torn from the only family he knows.

"Why didn't they adopt you too?"

He takes five big steps back until he's waist-deep. He drops his hands, letting them float on the top of the water. I step closer. With each stride, my feet sink deeper into the soggy ocean floor. It's like walking into quicksand, knowing that I'll soon be pulled under to suffocate. My breaths are coming fast now, as though they're the last ones I'll take. But I keep my eyes on Kai, and somehow, I push through the fear and make it to him. He gives me a little smile that says, *I'm proud of you.*

"So?" I coax breathlessly for an answer.

He looks down thoughtfully. The sun reflects off the water and catches in his sea-blue eyes, making them almost luminous. "Because I was trouble, and they were afraid of me." He glances up at me as though looking for my reaction. I have no idea what my face looks like, but whatever he sees makes him divulge a little more. "I had a rap sheet. Which made me a major liability."

I want to ask what kind of rap sheet a ten-year-old could possibly have, but it doesn't matter. I know Kai. I know he's good, and if his aunt and uncle really knew him, they'd have taken him no matter what he'd done. And then I remember what he said last night on the pier, about how he came to Avila Beach to see if he could stay with them. "So you're grown up now, and this . . . amazing person, and they still won't let you live with them?"

He shrugs. "It doesn't matter. I'm on my own now."

His words make me think of the boy who saved my life. Because I've always sensed that he was on his own too. No one at the beach could tell us who he was. No one in the area came forward to report a missing person. Maybe the boy was as alone as Kai is now.

The waves roll in, one after another, and the water rises to my hips and then drops to my calves. A bass drum pounds in my chest. *Thump. Thump. Thump.* The waves crash into us, pushing us toward shore, then pulling us farther out to sea.

Rise, drop. Rise, drop. Push, pull. Push, pull.

This is where the boy died. Not in this spot, or on this beach. But the ocean is one, big connected mass. This is still his grave.

Thump. Thump. Thump. Thump.

The water is frigid, cutting to my bones. But my body is on fire, every cell burning with guilt.

I shut my eyes, trying to push the thoughts aside. I feel Kai's fingers, warm and steady, wrap around my hands.

"Look at me," he says, and when I open my eyes, his clear, aquamarine gaze holds me in place. He's standing in front of me, a barrier between me and the sea, and I feel safe here in his harbor. "Ask me another question."

"Why are you doing this?" Of all the things I want to know, this has suddenly become the most important.

He studies me for a long moment, then says, "Because I can see how much you want it." A breeze pushes my hair into my face, and Kai reaches up and brushes it back. "It's time to stop

156

punishing yourself, Avery. It's what he would want. It's what *you* want. Let yourself *live*."

He's right. It *is* what I want. To live again. To embrace life, even when it's scary. To chase the things I love, even when they seem unobtainable. I can do this. For me. For Kai. And most of all, for the boy who saved my life.

The waves are rolling around my waist now, and I feel a different kind of tug. A tugging in my heart, the ocean tugging me toward it like it used to. Instead of wanting to flee, I feel the desire to go deeper.

"Want to go back?" he asks softly.

"No," I say with a slight shake of my head.

One corner of his mouth tips up. "You sure?"

"I'm sure."

The other corner of his mouth rises, completing his smile. He pulls me into a hug, and now my heart is pounding for an entirely different reason. He dips his head and murmurs in my ear, "You did it."

"No." I shake my head, my cheek rubbing against his bare chest. "*We* did."

20

avery

"I grew up on a skateboard," Kai says tiredly after I make him show me a good surfing stance for the eighth or so time. He's standing on my surfboard in the dry sand, feet shoulder-width apart, knees slightly bent. One arm is extended toward the nose of the board, the other bent at his shoulder like he's a ninja preparing to fight. "Surfing can't be that different."

"First of all," I say, hands on hips, "steering a surfboard is nothing like steering a skateboard. It's all about how you throw your shoulders and waist. And look at how big of a surface you're standing on compared to a skateboard. So many more places to put your feet. How do you know your feet are even in the right spot?"

"Because . . . this is where you told me to put them."

I look down at his feet, and they've migrated since I told him where to stand. I give him a good shove in the chest, and he staggers backward onto the sand to catch his balance. "If you'd been standing where I told you to," I say with a smile, "you would've stayed on your board. And bend your knees more next time."

His eyes dance with amusement. "I'm a kinesthetic learner, okay? Let's stop talking and start doing." He scoops up the board and starts toward the water, looking over his shoulder at me in a beckoning way.

"Okay," I say. "Just remember—"

"I got it." He turns and walks backward toward the water. "Duck dive under the breakers to get out. Head to the peak of the swell. When I see a wave and feel it start to lift, turn and paddle like crazy and pop up. Piece of cake." His tone is bored, as if he's already done this a thousand times.

"Yeah—and all the other stuff I just told you. And one more thing—you're surfing over shallow reef. The tide is heading out, so don't fall head first."

"Who says I'm going to fall?" He bites his lower lip and gives me a crooked grin that sort of makes me want to go over and kiss it off his face. Instead, I look at his feet, because at least I can do that without wanting to kiss him.

Something is dragging in the sand near his feet—his leash, which isn't strapped to his ankle. "Wait!" A jolt of terror rushes through me, and I go to him and crouch down to strap it on for him. "Don't be reckless," I say soberly.

His smile fades. "Hey . . . don't worry, okay? I'm a good swimmer."

So am I, but that didn't stop me from getting into trouble. And the boy who jumped off the pier must have been a strong swimmer to get through the waves to me, but that didn't stop him from drowning.

Kai must guess my thoughts, because he says, "I'll be careful, okay?" The sun is right behind his head, making the tips of his hair glow. "Go get your board. Come in with me."

I stand up, hesitating. An hour ago after I got in the water with him, I felt so brave and determined. But as soon as we got out, all my courage fled. I'm trying to summon it back now, but it's still cowering somewhere behind my left rib cage. "You go out first," I say. "I'll watch from here to make sure you're doing it right."

His smile returns. "Way to lay on the pressure."

I give him a shove toward the water. "Just go."

"Okay then," he says, laughing. "I'll see you in a bit."

He paddles out, diving under the breakers like I instructed him, though he gets caught and rolls a couple times when he doesn't go deep enough. When he finally gets past the break, he sits up and looks back at me, chest heaving and hair dripping wet. I feel that pull again, and it occurs to me that maybe it's not a pull toward the ocean. Maybe it's a pull toward Kai. I want to be where he is, and I'm willing to cross any obstacle to get there. I back up to my board, keeping my eyes on Kai, and pick it up.

There's a lull before the next set. Then, when he sees it coming, he lies down on his board and turns the nose toward shore. When the first mound of water swells up behind him, he's ready.

"Go! Go! Go!" I shout, cupping a hand to my mouth. He paddles hard shoreward, then springs to his feet. He's a bit too late though, and the wave passes under him. He drops off the board into the water and then climbs back on, ready for the next one.

The next time, he paddles sooner and faster, pops up at the right moment, and sails down the face of the wave on his board. Just before the tip of his surfboard hits the trough, he throws a hard left turn and glides horizontally along the swell, pumping the tip of his board to pick up speed. My jaw drops, and all I can think is that either he's done this before, or skateboarding must have more in common with surfing than I realized. He veers upward and launches off the lip, going airborne for a second before disappearing behind the crest.

I hold my breath, waiting for him to resurface. But after a few seconds, I don't see him. I crane my neck, trying to see over the peaks. There's no sign of him. With a spasm of panic, I rush for the water with my surfboard and dive in, paddling hard toward the spot I last saw him. I dive and pull under the breaking waves, a heaviness in my belly that has nothing to do with water pressure. Every time I resurface, I scan the water, searching for a sign of Kai. But I can't see over the peaks when I'm in the valleys. So when the next wave comes, instead of diving under, I paddle to the peak. And finally, I see him. Just beyond the next crest, halfway out of the water, arms spread across his board.

I exhale in relief, catching his eye before dropping into the next trough. I dive under the coming wave and kick hard, and when I resurface, Kai is a few feet away. He slides his board under him and sits up, shaking the water out of his hair. The way he's sitting, surrounded by rolling hills of water and speckled with reflected sunlight, makes him look like some sort of sea god.

"You scared me," I say, out of breath. "Slow down. No more aerials until I teach you how to do them safely."

He gives me an apologetic look. "I don't have time to slow down. If I'm going to surf, I'm going to *surf.*"

I swat the surface with my palm, sending a big splash his way. "If you don't want me to have a heart attack, slow down."

His eyes soften, and after a long moment, he nods in concession.

I glance back at shore, realizing how far away it is, and then it hits me, really *hits me*, that I'm out here, in the ocean, on my surfboard. A tingling sensation makes its way from my stomach to the tips of my fingers and toes, and I feel a surge of energy inside of me, an ache on the threshold of fulfillment.

Another set is approaching, and I study the shape of the incoming swell, looking for the peak. I lie on my board and paddle north, positioning myself where the wave will be fullest.

The first one feels too weak, so I let it pass under. There's a humming under my skin, as though I'm plugged into some great source of power. As the next wave approaches, it grows louder, more powerful. I feel it in my muscles, in my bones. I turn the tip of my board toward shore. When the water starts to swell, and I feel its energy surging inside of me, I know this is the one. It's moving fast, so I paddle hard, then spring to my feet in one swift movement. My arms spread out like wings, and then I'm flying. The waves are the wind, and I'm a bird, soaring over the face of the sea. I sail toward the crest, throw a hard turn, then speed back down a clear wall of water. I feel alive and free. I reach out and drag my fingers through the water, proving to myself that it's real. That *I'm* real. That I'm really doing this.

The wave curls over me, and I crouch down, barreling through a crystal blue cylinder. I come through and launch over the crest, then plunge into the foaming water. When I resurface, I'm breathing hard. I climb back on my board and straddle it, sitting up. My eyes roam the water for Kai, and I find him back where I left him. He's watching me, his gaze piercing mine even through the distance. For a long moment he doesn't smile, but when he does, it's a broad grin that reaches into me, and even though I didn't think it was possible, I feel even more alive now than a moment ago.

I watch him catch another small but smooth wave, and this time he doesn't try anything fancy. He rides the wave's energy toward me, making gentle turns here and there before losing momentum and letting the wave roll under him. He paddles over to me and sits up.

"You're amazing," he says breathlessly, his expression completely serious. I want to say the same, but I can't seem to get any words out. My whole body is humming, my chest full to bursting, and it's all I can do to get air in and out of my lungs.

I dip my hand in the ocean, letting the crisp water run through my fingers. I feel the pulse of the sea beneath me, a repetitious, soothing rhythm. Lifting me, dropping me. Up and down, sliding over hills into valleys and back again. This is home to me. The one place I belong. The place where I can be *me*.

I'm shivering, but not from the cold. I look over at Kai, who's still watching me, and I whisper, "Thank you." Only, the words aren't just for him, but also for the boy who saved my life. Because without him, I wouldn't be here in this perfect moment, on this perfect swell, with this perfect boy. And it occurs to me that the best way to honor him isn't to stay out of the water, but to immerse myself in it; accept his gift and live my life to its fullest.

Lying on my towel, my hair is half-dry, coiled up like dreadlocks and sticking to my arms and back. The late afternoon sun warms my skin, and my muscles feel shaky from surfing all day. Kai lies beside me on his stomach, head resting on folded arms and turned toward me. His shoulder hides his nose and mouth, so all I can see are his eyes, but they hint at a smile. A tattered sheet of clouds moves across the sky, and his face alternates from shadow to light, and light to shadow.

"Thanks again," I say softly, "for today."

He doesn't say anything, just keeps looking at me in a way that says, *My pleasure.* I think about what he did this morning, using his secrets as bait to lure me into the water, and all the things he told me are only now sinking in. His mom dying when he was eight. His dad in prison. Being separated from his sisters and growing up in foster care. I'm beginning to understand why he's always hesitant to talk about himself. And then I think of something else he said, about how he's on his own now.

"Kai—how old are you?"

Another shadow moves across his face, and a damp onshore breeze ruffles his hair. "Seventeen."

"So . . . aren't you still supposed to be in foster care?"

He props himself on his elbows and gazes at the ocean. The tide is low now, and the waves are steep and fast, curling into tubes at the break. Here and there, the sun breaks through the clouds and scatters patches of sparkling light across the distant sea. "The last foster parent I had died unexpectedly of a heart attack. He was this old guy, Charles." Kai's fingers are drawing circular patterns in the sand, going around and around and around. "I couldn't bear the thought of going to another home. Another strange place with strange people who pretend to care about me, but don't really know anything about me." He sweeps away the pattern, making a clean sandy slate. "So I ran. I hitchhiked across the country, hoping that if I could talk to my aunt and uncle face-to-face, I could convince them that I wouldn't be any trouble."

"What did they say?"

"I never got the—" He pauses, then shakes his head and releases a long breath. "It didn't work out."

I find myself studying his profile—his strong brow and straight nose, his sharp jaw and generous lips. Something about his face feels so familiar, as though I've seen it somewhere, even before this week. His picture is probably posted on one of the missing person reports I've scoured. "So you're a runaway."

He gives me a sidelong glance and a slight, guilty smile. "Just give me a head start before you call the authorities."

I tap his wrist lightly. "I won't be calling anyone."

He goes back to gazing at the sea, whispering, "Thanks."

I roll onto my back and watch the frayed edges of a rain cloud inch across the sky in our direction. "What about your sisters?" I ask. "Do you ever get to see them?"

"Yeah—sometimes." His voice is sad. "I like to make sure they're being taken care of."

With everything he's done for me the last few days, this doesn't surprise me. He must have been a great big brother, and it makes me sad to think that for the last few years they didn't have him around to look out for them. Something occurs to me, and I sit up, twisting my hair over one shoulder. "Kai—when you fought with Tyler the other day, you said he hurt someone you cared about. Were you talking about one of your sisters?"

He sits up and dusts sand off his elbows, then says quietly, "No."

"Then who was it?"

His eyes move slowly over my face, his lips twitching restlessly like he can't decide whether or not to answer. The restlessness spreads to his limbs, and he stands up and wanders to a boulder nearby. He paces in front of it a few times, then hoists himself onto it and dangles his bare feet, brushing the sand with his toes.

When he finally gives me an answer, it comes out so quietly that I barely hear it. "It doesn't matter anymore."

His heartbroken tone tells me it clearly does matter. And even if it doesn't matter to him, it matters to me. "Was it . . . a girl? Someone you . . . love?"

His feet go still. *Bingo*. And then the rest of him goes rigid, as though he's tensing every muscle, trying to keep the truth captive, or maybe trying to hold himself together. His lips are pressed into a tight line, the muscles in his jaw bulging, and his hands are squeezing the edge of the rock so tightly he just might break a piece off.

"You can tell me, you know," I say softly. Even though it will hurt to hear him say he loves someone else, I want him to confide in me. He has spent the last few days drawing out my secrets, my burdens, and they're lighter now because of it. I want to do the same for him, even if his secrets crush me. I stand up and brush the sand off my board shorts, and then cautiously go to him. "Who is she?" I ask gently.

His stillness shifts into unease, and his eyes dart around, looking for someplace safe to land. They settle on my hand, which is nervously clutching the hem of my shorts.

The line between his brows deepens, and he gets a faraway look in his eyes, as though he's picturing her, or maybe recalling a specific memory. "She's the reason I came here," he says faintly.

"But . . . I thought you came here to see if you could live with your aunt and uncle."

He grimaces, like he's not sure how to explain himself. "The first time I came here, that was why. That was last winter. While I was here, I met this . . . amazing girl." He looks into my eyes, and I pray he can't see the hurt there. "Then I had to leave for a while, and . . . she's the reason I came back."

"Oh." I try not to wince, but I'm not sure if I succeed entirely. "Where is she? Why haven't I seen you with her?"

He looks away and feigns interest in a pelican floating on the water. "Have you ever wondered how a bird that heavy can fly?" The question seems so random, but then I recall something he said two days ago in the chocolate shop. *When questions are like daggers, I dodge.* He's definitely dodging.

Like it's the most natural thing to do, I put my hand on his jaw and turn his face back toward mine. His skin is like fire in my palm, and it burns all the way up to my cheeks. But I can't seem to detach my fingers from his face.

"Please," I say in the most persuasive tone I can manage. "Talk to me, Kai." His face is so close to mine I can see the fine white hairs on his forehead and cheeks. I can see the gradations of blue and green in his irises, and the tears that are beginning to pool there.

"This is the one thing I can't talk about," he says in a broken whisper. "Please—don't ask me."

He looks so heartbroken that I don't even think twice when I slide my arms around his shoulders and pull him into a comforting hug. Whoever this girl is, she must mean the world to him. And whatever the reason he can't be with her, it's tearing him apart. I force my own feelings aside and focus on what he needs right now—a friend.

I feel his arms hesitantly slide around my waist, and his head sinks into my shoulder. My hand moves to the back of his head, and I become keenly aware of the softness of his hair on my fingertips. Silky, smooth, light. He's so warm, and it's a warmth I can't quite categorize as temperature. Whatever it is, it invites me in, and I draw him closer. I notice how we seem to fit together perfectly. My head falls into the place between his neck and shoulder, and I mold into him like soft caramel. The sun is hidden behind rain clouds, but my skin is tingling as though its rays are being redirected through Kai.

He tightens his arms around me, drawing me even nearer, clinging to me like a life preserver in a wind-tossed sea, and I realize just how much hurt he's been holding in all this time. I want to take it from him, to draw it out and absorb it into myself the way he seems to have done with all my pain. And at the same time, I want to raise his face to mine and kiss him. So many emotions are warring inside of me that I feel dizzy. Sorrow and compassion, intrigue and desire, swirling around and around.

My heart is pounding so hard against my ribs that I'm sure he can feel it through my surf tee. And then, like hearing a clarion call, I receive the message my body is trying to send me.

I love him. I love Kai. I love this boy who came into my life three days ago and changed me forever.

And he loves someone else.

But the way he's holding me makes me wonder if he's at least beginning to fall for me too. I search for a sign that he feels something more than friendship. I feel for his heartbeat against mine. I'm positive he can feel mine. But I don't feel anything. His heart is still.

The clouds have long since smothered the sun, and now something inside of me feels smothered too. The wind picks up, brisk and sharp, and a drop of rain splashes on my arm. Goose bumps rise on my clammy skin, and I reluctantly pull back, feeling like my heart is being torn in two.

I can't look at him, so I look at the sea instead. The waves are growing larger, wilder. Gusts of wind rip across the wave crests, turning them white. I'm suddenly uncertain about everything. As though I've taken a wrong turn and ended up in an unfamiliar city, and I'm not sure how to get back on the right track.

Unsure what Kai will see in my face, I step away and go gather our things. We load the car in silence, and even though I feel his gaze on me now and then, I don't dare meet his eyes. When I slide into the driver's seat, I see a text on my phone from Paige.

Movie night? Pick you up at 7?

I think about Kai, about the girl he loves. The more time I spend with him, the more it will hurt when things work out between him and this other girl. Suddenly a movie doesn't sound like a bad idea. I could definitely use the distraction. I text Paige back.

Sure. Pick me up.

21

avery

"hy didn't you tell me *he* was coming?" I whisper to Paige in the theater lobby. Tyler and Dillan are a few yards away, buying our tickets from a kiosk. When Paige picked me up, she said nothing about meeting anyone. But when we got here, Tyler and Dillan were waiting for us as though that was the plan all along.

"I thought you wouldn't mind," she whispers back, looking at me like I'm crazy.

I eye the glass doors of the theater. It's pouring outside, and people are rushing in and out with jackets over their heads or umbrellas bursting open. I fasten the top button on my rain jacket, seriously considering making a run for it. But then I remember that Paige drove, so unless I want to make the five-mile trip home on foot, I'm stranded here with a boy I never want to speak to again.

"I thought you guys were working things out," she says in a hushed tone. "I saw you kiss the other night at Dillan's. So what's going on?"

What's going on? I'm in love with a guy I met three days ago. And he loves someone else. I don't have it in me right now to face Tyler after what he said to me the other night. I just want to go home and hide under my blankets for the next twelve years. My stomach hurts. I hug myself, trying to squeeze the pain out. "We're not working anything out."

She tilts her head and offers a consoling look. "What happened?"

I don't want to get into it with Tyler so close, so I brush off her question and say, "I can't believe they agreed to come to a rom-com with us." And then I question why I agreed to come to a rom-com. As if watching people get all lovey-dovey on a seventy-six-foot screen is going to make me feel better. "I thought Dillan hated Zac Efron."

She shrugs. "He's just jealous because I once pointed out how blue Zac's eyes are. He insists the movie people Photoshop them or something to make them bluer than they really are."

After buying the tickets, the boys come over. Dillan slings an arm around Paige and kisses the top of her head, handing her a ticket. She looks down at it, and her mouth falls open, appalled. "What! Batman?"

Dillan gives an apologetic shrug. "Your movie was sold out."

She rolls her eyes. "Riiiight. Ugh. This is what happens when you let guys buy the tickets." She punches him in the ribs, and he laughs.

"Come on," he says, tugging her toward the concession stand. "I'll buy you some nachos."

That leaves me alone with Tyler, who up until this point I've been avoiding looking at. When I finally glance at him, he's watching me uncertainly, one hand in the pocket of his hoodie, the other in front of him clutching our Batman tickets. He looks incredibly handsome as usual, but the butterflies that used to go crazy in his presence are now lying dead in the pit of my stomach.

He takes a wary step toward me. "Hey."

"Hey," I reply. Because it's much more civil than the things I really want to say.

"I'm glad you came."

"Yeah, well . . ." I look at a poster on the wall of the movie Paige and I had planned on seeing—because eye contact feels too intimate with Tyler right now. "I didn't know you'd be here."

He inhales and exhales slowly, as though trying to calm himself. "Want some popcorn?"

The theater's buttery smell usually makes me want popcorn. But tonight, the thought of putting anything in my stomach makes me nauseated. I shake my head, keeping my eyes on Zac Efron. His eyes really are unnaturally blue. "I'm good."

His hand comes up and brushes the bridge of my nose, and I flinch at the unexpected touch.

"Sorry," he says, like he just remembered he's not supposed to touch me anymore. "You got some sun today. You're all pink."

"I went surfing," I say evenly, as though it's no big deal.

"You did?" He says it like I just told him I won the lottery. "That's great! I mean, seriously? And I missed it?"

I shrug. "I wasn't planning on it. It just . . . happened." I almost want to tell him *how* it happened, but decide to keep it to myself. Because if I talk about it, about Kai and what he did for me today, all these tears that are mounting inside of me will come bursting out, and Tyler will know. He'll know that I love Kai. I have to pull myself together if I'm going to make it through tonight.

"Right on," Tyler says. His hand drops to his side, and he lets out a long breath. "Look—I've been meaning to call you. I want you to know . . . I'm sorry."

I eye him, and his face is bordering on desperation. "Sorry for what?"

"For what I said the other night. It came out all wrong. I only meant . . ." He shakes his head and lets out a frustrated growl. "I know you've had a hard time, but this has been hard for me too.

I'm sorry I hurt you. And I'm sorry I broke things off the way I did." He sighs. "Sometimes I do stupid things. And . . . I guess I just got scared."

I shoot him an inquisitive look. "Scared of what?"

"I don't know, being needed so much. And scared that if I kept hanging around you, I'd lose myself, the way you seemed to have lost yourself. Don't look at me like that. I'm still figuring out this 'love' thing." He makes air quotes, like love isn't really a thing at all.

"I didn't know love was something that needed to be figured out."

"You know what I mean—like what it means to love someone. And love at the time felt so . . . heavy. There was so much responsibility attached to being with you. I didn't feel ready to carry that kind of burden."

"Nice," I say, smothering the word in sarcasm. "So that's what I am? A burden."

"No!" He throws his hands up in exasperation. "But at the time, that's what love felt like."

"And now it's different?"

"Well . . . yeah."

"Why?"

He scratches the back of his head and thinks for a moment. "I've matured, I guess."

I arch an eyebrow. "In a few days?"

He shrugs, at a loss for words.

"Does your accelerated maturation have anything to do with Kai?"

His head jerks back. "What are you talking about?"

"You started changing how you saw me when he came around."

"No." He shakes his head. "It's not like that."

I fold my arms and give him a look that demands the truth.

He sighs loudly. "I don't know—maybe. When I saw you with him, it bothered me. And things seemed to be moving pretty fast.

So I had to decide pretty quick if I was really prepared to lose you to some other guy. And . . . I'm not."

"Well . . ." Suddenly my throat feels tight. "You wouldn't have anyway."

His face lights up with hope. "What?"

"Kai doesn't . . ." I pause, swallowing back the huge lump in my throat. "He doesn't see me . . . in that way. He's in love with someone else." The words come out bitter, and I spit the last ones out. "Some *amazing* mystery girl." Saying it out loud hurts so much more than I expected, and I clench a fist around my jacket lapel as though it will make it easier to endure.

"Oh." His brow furrows. "Are you sure? He seems really into you."

"Yeah. In fact, he says you know her."

He points a thumb to his chest. "Me?"

I nod. And now that I think about it, if Tyler knows her, I probably do too.

"Come on, guys!" Paige is waving for us to follow her into the theater, so we do. Tyler hands over our tickets, and as we walk down the long hallway in silence, I start sifting through every girl I've ever met, trying to match her up with someone Kai would be in love with.

We find our seats in the dimmed theater, and without much thought I sit between Paige and Tyler. Even though the screen is huge and vibrant and the surround speakers are blaring, I don't see or hear any of the movie. Because a parade of girls is marching through my head, each one trying out for the part of Kai's love interest. None of them seem good enough for him. Whoever this girl is, she's undoubtedly beautiful and smart, capable of deep conversations and philosophical insights. She probably plays the guitar or a cute little ukulele, and she definitely has a sultry singing voice. But after searching through all my acquaintances, I come up short. I finally give up and turn to Tyler for help.

"Who did you hurt?" I ask in a loud whisper, immediately

realizing how random the question sounds. He answers with a blank look. I obviously need to start somewhere else. I try again. "Kai said you hurt the girl he's in love with. Who was it?"

His brows crash together, either because he's wondering why I would start a conversation like this while we're watching a movie, or because he really has no idea what I'm talking about. He shrugs and opens his palms, then turns back to the screen.

I know my quizzing should wait until later, but my curiosity is making me so antsy I can't sit still. "Have you dated anyone since we broke up?" This time I forget to whisper, and someone in front of us turns around and shushes me.

Tyler leans over, bringing his face an inch from mine. "Why are we talking about this right now?" His whisper is harsh, annoyed.

"I need to know who it was," I whisper back.

Then Tyler says the words that are just beginning to teeter on the edge of my subconscious. "Maybe he was talking about you. You're the only girl I've ever really hurt. And I'm sorry, okay? For the millionth time, I'm sorry!"

A handful of popcorn comes flying at us over the seat in front of us. Tyler picks a piece out of his hair and faces the screen, his jaw rigid. His hands clasp the armrests on either side of his chair as if he's in a roller coaster ride about to plummet down a hill.

Or maybe it's me who's on the ride, because suddenly my heart is rising to my throat. Is it possible that *I'm* the girl Kai was talking about? That *I'm* the girl he loves? That can't be. What about his fight with Tyler? That couldn't have been about me, because I'd just met Kai that day. Only, now that I think about it, the fight sort of had been about me. Tyler got upset with Kai because he was watching me.

But Kai said he met the girl when he came here six months ago. Was it possible that I met him then and don't remember? How could I not remember Kai? And if Kai does have feelings for me, why doesn't he tell me? Maybe because he thinks I'm in love with Tyler. Maybe he's protecting himself from getting hurt, from getting rejected after spending his entire life being rejected by those who should love him.

It all feels like such a stretch. And yet, there's something inside of me, something growing and gaining substance with each breath, telling me that Kai really does feel something for me. Even Tyler said that Kai seems really into me. Why else would he have done everything he has for me over the past few days? Why else would he look at me the way he does, like he never wants to look away?

As I allow myself for just a moment to believe that he loves me, a joy that I've never felt burns in my chest. I cling to the feeling, to the warmth, because if I let go, I'll be left in a place so cold and dark I may never find my way out. I let hope spread through me like flames on kindling. And then, I'm on fire.

I turn to Tyler. "I have to go."

He pulls his wallet from his back pocket and fishes out a wrinkled twenty, offering it to me. "Will you bring back some popcorn and a Fanta?"

"No—I mean I'm leaving. The theater. I need to leave."

He gives me a blank stare. "Why?"

I don't answer. Just turn to Paige and whisper hurriedly, "I need you to drive me somewhere."

She nods and keeps her eyes on the screen, not understanding the urgency of my request.

"Now," I whisper.

She gives me the *Are you crazy?* look again. "Can't it wait?" She gestures to the movie screen, like, *Duh, we're in the middle of a movie.*

I shake my head. "No." I grab her hand and pull her up, dragging her out of the theater. I don't look back, because I'm afraid of what I'll see on Tyler's face.

"What is going on?" she says when we make it to the lobby.

"I have to go see Kai. Right now."

She throws open her hands. "What's the big rush?"

"I have to tell him how I feel about him before he leaves."

She stares at me, blinking in shock for a few seconds, and then her face softens. "What about Tyler?"

There's nothing to say about Tyler. So I frown and shake my head.

She gives a heavy sigh. "Fine. I'll drive you there. But he'll have to give you a ride home because I'm not waiting."

I pull her into a hug. "Thank you."

"You're lucky I'm a hopeless romantic." I feel her cheek lift into a smile. "And that I hate Batman."

22

KAI

I don't know how long I've been lying on the floor of the cottage, staring out the window at the sky, but it's been long enough to watch gray clouds turn to black, and sprinkling rain turn to a downpour. The weight of untold truths holds me down, runs through my veins like poison, sapping every ounce of energy.

I came so close to telling Avery the truth this afternoon. It was the way she looked at me when I told her about the girl I love, like her heart was breaking. I came to help her heal, but instead I've injured her in a whole new way. But I couldn't tell her that she's the one Tyler hurt, the one I met last December and recently came back for. There was too much risk. Risk of her connecting me to the boy who saved her life. Risk of her finding out that I'm dead.

The last of the daylight has faded now, and I can't even see the rain anymore, only hear it drumming on the roof. There's a dripping sound somewhere, but it's too dark to see where it's coming from.

There must be a way to tell her how I feel without giving away my identity. I did see her once briefly in front of the chocolate shop before rescuing her in the ocean, so I could say that that is when we met. But even then . . . I don't know. My heart and mind are so muddled right now that I don't trust myself to make a good decision.

I drape my arm over my eyes, and now it's pitch dark. My body still thinks it's in the waves, because it feels like I'm moving up and down, up and down. The rain begins to sound like a pounding surf, and then I'm being pushed deep, deep under, and I'm drowning all over again. How is it possible to feel like I'm dying when I'm already dead? This separation from her will be so much worse than the first one, when I'd barely met her. Because now I know everything about her. I know the shade of blue her eyes turn in the setting sun. I know the scent of her hair after she spends a long day in the chocolate shop. I know by the curve of her lips when she's genuinely happy and when she's putting on a brave face.

I wish I didn't have to leave at all. I wish that I still had a mortal body, flesh and blood. If I did . . . The thought hurts too much to finish, and I let out a loud, frustrated groan. Then I call out to the only person I can speak the truth to right now. "Charles?"

Seconds later, I sense a presence in the room. I move my arm from my eyes. Charles stands beside me, the soft light of his aura filling the room.

"Things not going as you expected?" he asks gently.

I rub my bare foot along the grain of the wood floor. I love the sensation of it. Rough. Real. I have a body now. Isn't there a way to keep it? Isn't there some miracle to make that possible? What about those stories my first foster parents told me of all the people in the Bible who were raised from the dead? And what about all the people I've been assigned to heal? The power exists. I've seen it with my own eyes. Felt it flow through me like water from a spring. Why can't it be applied to me?

"Charles," I say quietly. "Has anyone ever been brought back to life?"

The look of pity that comes over his face is too hard to take. I have to look away. "You know the answer to that."

"Well, yeah. I've seen people healed who are on the brink of death, or barely dead. But what about those whose death has been sealed?"

He sits on the floor beside me, folding his legs beneath him. I never saw him sit that way when he was alive. His old body just wouldn't bend that way. And looking at his face now, he appears younger, as though he's been slowly aging in reverse without my noticing. His hair is fuller, the wrinkles around his eyes less pronounced. Instead of seventy-two, he looks maybe in his fifties. "Sure, it happens," he says. "But usually with those who haven't been dead for very long. I'm sure you've heard stories of people waking up in morgues or coffins."

"Has anyone ever been brought back to life after being dead for a long time?"

"A long time?" Charles asks carefully, because he knows why I'm asking. "Meaning, six months?"

"Yeah. Six months, fifteen days, and . . ." I glance at a clock on the wall. "Seven hours."

He releases a sad sigh. "I'm still learning about these things, like you. But from what I understand, it's not unheard of. Only extremely rare. I have never seen it done." He pauses, and a thin line appears between his brows. "But Jerick has."

I sit up and stare at him, intrigued.

Charles looks hesitant to tell me more. "In the two hundred years he's spent sealing people's deaths," he says, his voice laced with caution, "he has unsealed only one."

"Unsealed a death? How?" I try to sound casual, as though my very happiness doesn't hinge on his words.

He rubs the knee of his white pants, as though it's helping him gather his thoughts. It's something he used to do when he was alive, and it makes me recall all the evenings we sat in his living room together, when I'd tell him about some punk I fought with at school. He'd rub his knee for a minute, then say something like, "It takes the stronger man to walk away, and you're stronger than that boy. I believe in you, Kai. And I know you'll make a better choice next time."

And usually, I did.

Now, his hand goes still. "I don't know all the details. You know Jerick's job is to seal a deceased person's body so that their spirit can no longer enter. He mentioned one case where he was assigned to unseal the elements of someone's body after it had completely decomposed, so that the elements could be reorganized and the body restored. That's all he told me." He gives me a pointed look. "Once in two hundred years, Kai. Please don't dwell on the possibility. It hurts to see the hope in your eyes."

"But why not me?" I ask. "No one even knows I'm dead. My body has never been found. And I still have a life to live here. There are my sisters, and music, and . . ."

"And Avery," he says sadly. "We all leave something behind. But the most important things follow us in their own time."

"You mean . . . when she dies someday," I say weakly.

I must look like I'm going to fall to pieces, because he braces my shoulders with both hands. "If it were up to me, I would give you back your life in an instant. But you know it's not." He smiles sadly, then gives me an encouraging look. "There's another life for you, the life beyond here. It's time to accept it, to take it and live it. You've been telling Avery the last few days that she needs to live her life. Well, it's time for you to take your own advice and live yours."

His hands on my shoulders do nothing to stop my voice from coming out in a fractured mess. "That's what I'm trying to do."

"No . . ." He shakes his head, and then looks deep into my eyes. "The miracle isn't being raised from death, but living beyond it."

His words hang in the air, almost as if I can see them scrolling in front of me over and over. And then they slowly start to absorb into my mind. I mull them over, trying to understand and accept them. But everything in me wants to fight against them.

"You've done so much good for Avery," Charles says. "But it's time to let her carry on with her life, and for you to carry on with yours."

My chin sinks to my chest, and I take in a long, stuttering breath.

"Come with me," he invites gently. "Give me back my ring, and come to Elysium. See what awaits you there. There's more ahead of you than you can even imagine."

Maybe he's right. Maybe I need to let go of this place, of Avery, of the life I knew, and of this new temporary life I've just started to get used to. Maybe it's time to see what's next for me. And maybe whatever it is will heal this hole in my heart, will temper the pain that grows more and more every day at the thought of being separated from Avery.

But can I leave without saying good-bye? Without letting her know how much I love her? Now that I know how she feels about me, will I be able to live with myself for the rest of eternity knowing that I didn't openly return her affection when I had the chance?

The thought is unbearable. And it gives me the clarity I need to finally make a decision. I rise to my feet and pace the room. "I can't," I say to Charles. "Not yet. I still have one more day." One more day that can't go to waste. And every hour, every moment that she believes I don't love her, is a tragic waste. I grab a black hoodie from the couch and throw it on. I may not be able to give her the whole truth, but if I break Avery's heart, it won't be because she thinks I don't love her.

"I have to go somewhere," I say.

The room dims, and when I turn to Charles, he's already gone.

Avery is out with friends tonight. But that doesn't matter. I open the cottage door and jog into the rain. Wherever she is, I'm going to find her and unload this heavy truth.

23

avery

the rain showers down as I race through the vineyard, my sneakers splashing through muddy puddles and drenching my pant legs. My heart is racing too, soaring with hope in one beat, surging with fear the next. I don't even know what I'm going to say to Kai. I spent the entire drive telling Paige about the past few days, so I didn't have a chance to plan anything. I only hope that when I see him, the words will magically come.

As I cut the corner at the end of the vineyard row, I slam into something so hard it knocks the air out of me. I look up to see Kai, his hands clamped on my arms to steady me. He's breathing hard, as if he's been running too. His face is mostly in shadow, faintly brushed with the distant light on the cottage porch.

He doesn't say anything, just keeps gripping my arms like he thinks I'm still in danger of falling over. My mouth is open, waiting for me to fill it with words. So when I finally catch my breath, I say the first thing that comes to mind.

"What's her name?"

Through my jacket, I can feel the heat of his hands on my arms. It makes me shiver.

"Whose name?" he asks.

It's raining so hard we're practically breathing water. But somehow, my mouth is like a desert. I swallow. "The girl you love. The girl Tyler hurt. What's her name?"

Every part of him goes perfectly still, as though he's terrified to move or speak. Except his chest, which is rising and falling more rapidly with each breath. I look up into his face, all shadows and vague strokes of light, a fragile, crumbling night giving way to dawn.

"You can trust me," I whisper. "Tell me her name."

His hands loosen on my arms and slide upward, gathering the lapels of my jacket and tugging me gently toward him. My pulse leaps and skitters at his nearness, and there's no way my breath is going to slow down now. His hands move farther up, forming to my face and neck, setting my skin on fire.

He dips his head so close that I can feel his breath on my cheeks. And then he whispers the name of the girl he loves. "Avery Ambrose."

I inhale a sharp breath as the sound of my name sinks in. I was right. *I'm* the one he loves. The joy that floods me now swells my heart to the point of bursting.

Slowly, almost cautiously, he tilts his head and leans closer, then brushes his lips against mine, leaving a little trail of rain on my mouth. He doesn't pull back, though; he lingers there, his face a breath away and his hand on the back of my neck. I rise to my toes and he kisses me again, more confidently this time. As though whatever made him cautious a moment ago is gone.

Rain patters on the grapevines around us, and water droplets slide over my lips between his warm breaths and kisses. It's like butterfly wings and hot cocoa and rolling waves all together. Beautiful and succulent and scary woven into something divine.

When he pulls away, I clutch the front of his hoodie to keep him close. "Why couldn't you tell me earlier?"

His exhale is long and stuttered. "Because I'm not—" His voice breaks, and he pauses to regain composure, then tries again. "I'm not the one who can make you happy."

I reach up and touch his face, wishing that I could somehow make him feel just how happy he makes me. And wishing that I could make him happy too. "You already do. In fact, after these last few days, I'm convinced you're the only one who can. My happiness is in your hands."

"Don't say that."

"Why?" My throat is suddenly burning. "Even if I don't say it, it's still true."

He shakes his head slowly and his shoulders sink a notch. "You know I'm leaving."

"It doesn't matter." I find his hand at the small of my back and weave my fingers into his. "We can figure something out."

As I gaze into his sad eyes, waiting for him to respond, something taps at my memory like the rain on his face. Keeps tapping, tapping, tapping until a specific memory cracks open. Looking at Kai in the rain reminds me of the boy who drowned, as he clung to my surfboard in the rain and restless waves. But this time in my memory, I glimpse his face through the rain. And the longer I look at Kai, the more he doesn't just remind me of the boy, the more it's like I'm looking at the boy. The lines and details of Kai's face slowly fill in the gaps of my lost memories, and suddenly, Kai *is* the boy who saved my life.

I let go of his hand and step back, blinking through the rain at him. It can't be. It's impossible.

"What's wrong?" Kai asks, worry darkening his expression.

I open my mouth, but only a little whimper escapes. If I tell him what's going on in my head, he'll think I'm crazy. But I have to ask. "Kai," I say, my voice wavering with doubt. "If I'm the girl you were talking about, then you said we met six months ago." I shake my head in disbelief. "Where did we meet?"

He steps toward me, and his hand comes up to stroke my wet cheek. "You gave me a chocolate sample in front of your shop. I don't blame you for not remembering me. We were never . . . officially introduced."

I close my eyes and focus all my energy on recalling the day that boy drowned, on remembering the details of his face, or even a vague image. But all I see is Kai's face, Kai's eyes, Kai's wet hair. Only, it was a different color then.

Then I remember something else.

The scar.

I grab Kai's hand and lead him out of the vineyard and through the lavender field to his cottage. I pull him inside and shut the door, click on the table lamp, then turn to face him. "Take off your hoodie," I demand.

He gives an amused and slightly bewildered half-smile. He raises an eyebrow, but doesn't remove anything.

I feel my cheeks warm as I realize he's probably wondering what exactly I have in mind. "I . . . just want to see something," I explain. He stares at me for a moment longer, his face turning more serious, and then he peels off his soaked hoodie. The shoulders of his T-shirt underneath are damp where the rain soaked through.

Without warning or explanation, I circle to his back, grab the hem of his shirt, and hike it up. Surprisingly, he doesn't object. I hold my breath as more and more of his back is revealed. It's defined and sinewy beneath smooth skin. Not a single scar or even a mole or freckle. I run my hand up his spine and over his shoulder blades, searching for the texture of a scar. But it's like flawless satin. I shuck his T-shirt higher so I can see his shoulder blades. And still, his skin is perfect.

"Are you looking for something?" he asks, twisting to look at me over his shoulder.

I look up into his eyes. The teasing expression I expect to see isn't there. Instead, his face is grave. I let go of his shirt, and he lowers it back down.

I'm wrong. It's not him. And yet, it's Kai's face on the boy in my memory. Maybe I'm imposing it onto the faceless boy from last winter. It makes sense, seeing how Kai has rescued me too, just in a different way.

Or maybe I'm going crazy.

"Yes," I admit, looking at the floor as a hot wave of embarrassment makes its way to my cheeks. "I thought . . ." I shake my head. "Sorry. Just forget that happened."

He turns to face me. "What—"

"Please don't ask. You'll think I've lost it."

He gazes at me for a long time, a million questions in his eyes that sometimes toy on the edge of his lips. But he keeps them in and finally draws me into his arms. For now, I brush aside the confusing memories and instead breathe in deeply this warm and alive boy, as though it will somehow make him a part of me, fuse us together into something unbreakable. And then I whisper the words that have been burning on my lips all day. "I love you, Kai."

His arms tighten around me, and I feel his warm breath whispering in my ear. "I love you, Avery. Promise you'll never forget that."

I pull back to look into his eyes. They're the eyes of someone who's peered over a dark horizon and seen a tornado stirring. He's talking as if he's leaving tomorrow, and panic surges through me. I don't understand why he can't find a way to stay, especially now that I know how he feels about me. I open my mouth to voice my thoughts, but stop myself. Something tells me I need to be patient with him. I don't know everything he's been through, but he probably has a hard time trusting the permanence of anything. Whatever his circumstances are, I know we can work through them. With time, I can convince him to stay. For Isadora. For his sisters. For me.

I reach up and brush a piece of his white hair from his forehead, then whisper, "Some things last." I don't know how I know this, especially when I've seen my own parents separate. But I have to believe that it's possible for love to last, for two people to stay together through thick and thin.

He leans his forehead against mine, closing his eyes. For a few breaths, he says nothing, and then, "Can I take you somewhere tomorrow?"

I nod, and his smile widens, showcasing that adorable crease in his cheek. Instead of restraining myself like I have the last couple days, I rise to my toes and kiss it.

"I have some things to do in the morning," he says, opening his eyes. "But I can pick you up at noon. Do you think you can get off work?"

I nod affirmatively, figuring that with enough groveling, Paige or Sophie will cover for me. "Just pick me up at the shop. Or I can meet you here." It occurs to me that right now, my Cherokee is parked in the dry garage at home. "And by the way . . . can you give me a ride home tonight? Paige dropped me off."

He presses his lips to my forehead. "Of course."

I don't feel the rain as we walk to Isadora's truck, because all my nerve endings seem to have migrated to where his fingers are laced between mine. And when he drops me off, his kiss goodnight is full of the promise of more to come, and I feel a binding thread strengthening between us. I only hope it will grow strong enough to make him stay.

KAI

I stand in front of Ed's Guitar World, clutching the handle of my case. The instrument inside is so much more than a guitar. It's three months of hard work in Charles's vineyard. Thirty-two hundred dollars. It's my identity and self-worth. My sounding board and vent for things otherwise too hard or risky to express. But most of all, it's my dreams. And this morning, I'm going to trade it all in for cash.

I try to tell myself that it's not really a loss or a sacrifice since I can't take my guitar with me anyway, but my feet still refuse to carry me through the sliding glass doors. I don't want to let it go. Not yet. I still have a little more time, don't I? I catch my reflection in the glass. I look like a regular teenage boy. I can almost imagine that I am. Maybe for just one day, I can pretend to be.

My fingers tighten around the case handle, and my feet turn and take me down the sidewalk, away from the store.

Today, I'm not dead. I'm just a kid with a dream. I have a heart that beats and pumps blood through my veins. Today, I'm just a seventeen-year-old boy trying to impress a seventeen-year-old girl.

A girl I actually have a chance with. I'm a boy who has a tomorrow, and a day after tomorrow, and many days after that.

Just for one day, I'm going to pretend that I've earned this life that's finally worth living.

I stop at the corner and lay my guitar case on the concrete, unlatching the lid and opening it. I take out my guitar and sling the strap over my shoulder, then tune the strings and start playing. It doesn't take long for passersby to notice. They slow down, turning their heads to watch, then stop and come closer. When I start singing, a small crowd forms around me, heads nodding and feet tapping. Dollar bills and coins drop into my guitar case like rain in an empty well.

I play song after song, each followed by applause and whistles and enthusiastic compliments. I have the sensation of finding something that's been lost for a long time, relief and rejoicing and remembering why it was so important to me in the first place. Before I died, music was one of the few things that made me feel alive. Not much has changed about that.

By late morning, my guitar case is littered with bills and coins. I take the money and drive Isadora's truck to a department store where I buy some new shorts and a nice button-down shirt. Next, I go to the grocery store and pick up picnic supplies. And then, very discreetly, I leave what's left of my cash in an envelope in the office of the shop owner whose window I broke, along with a note of apology. At noon, I drive to the chocolate shop and pick up the girl I love.

On a grassy cliff overlooking the ocean, Avery sits across from me on one of Isadora's colorful woven blankets. She's wearing capris and a sleeveless blouse, and her freckled shoulders are making it really hard to appreciate the spectacular view. A warm breeze stirs her hair and the grass around us, and the sun hits her just right, making her edges incandescent. I can't believe she's really here with me, glancing at me between bites of her lunch with a little smile that says she's thinking as much about our kiss the night before as I am. Of all the things I thought might happen by stealing Charles's ring, this was the least expected.

She picks up a strawberry and bites it in half, studying the open flesh while chewing the other half. She looks so content, and I think how I've never seen her truly happy until today. The tense lines in her face are all smoothed out, and without the worry and pain in her eyes, she looks almost childlike. Innocent and carefree. She's never looked more beautiful.

I want her to always look this way. I know that's not possible, but this is how I want to remember her.

For now, I banish all thoughts of what tomorrow will bring, and allow myself to imagine a future with her. A lifetime of days just like today, at the end of which I'll have a million mental snapshots of her hair stirring in the ocean breeze, of her freckled cheeks turning pink, of her blue eyes rising to meet mine, of her soft lips parting to say my name. I see her hair pinned up and adorned with white flowers and a veil. I see her greeting me with a smile in the doorway of our little home. I see her in the ocean, laughing while teaching our kids to surf.

A flood of pain and joy and longing rises up inside me, and if I don't open the floodgates now, I just might drown all over again. So I pick up my guitar, and set the deluge free.

Avery watches in quiet appreciation as I strum a progression of chords in a swaying rhythm, like a boat rocking gently in undulating waves. It comes easy, like the song was already written and I'm merely reading the tablature. The words come effortlessly too, as though they've been floating around in my mind for months, and now I'm plucking them out of the air and dropping them into their rightful place in the melody.

"In this borrowed heaven, in this sliver of time . . . A lifetime unfolds where I'm hers and she's mine."

The way her blue eyes light up at my lyrics makes my lungs swell, making it kind of hard to get the next lines out.

"The sky is raining stars, four seasons intertwine. . . . She makes the tides reverse and the drums beat out of time."

She closes her eyes as though she doesn't want her vision getting in the way of the music. It seems to draw her in, and her body slowly leans toward me until she's so close I can see the individual eyelashes shadowing her cheeks.

"I'm lost in her embrace, tangled in gold hair. . . . Breathing in white petals, blissfully ensnared."

In all my attempts to escape the misery of my childhood by imagining a brighter future, I never imagined this. Never imagined her. How it feels to love her. How it makes me wish I were a better person. How it makes me want to find all the dark things inside of me and wrench them out and burn them. I almost feel unworthy of her love and vitality and beauty. I never could have imagined it, because it's a beauty that can't be seen with the eye.

"She's a black swan in the sea, an unexpected good charm. . . . My heart was buried alive, but it rises in her arms."

As the last chord resonates in the salty air, Avery gazes at me quietly with a look I can't quite discern. Every time I think I can define it, it changes to something else. Awe, reverence, and admiration all cross her face before her lips curve into a warm smile. She tilts her head and squints at me, then asks softly, "Where did you come from?"

I don't know how to answer, so I just give a breathy laugh.

She scoots closer until her knees are touching mine, and then she shakes her head. "I'm serious." She sighs, and I feel her sweet breath on my face. It makes me want to kiss her, but she's studying me so intensely that I figure it's probably not the right moment. "Where did you come from?" she repeats.

I set my guitar on the blanket so there's nothing between us. "Michigan, remember?"

"I've never met anyone like you." Her hand comes to my shirt collar, and she clutches it between her fingers. Now I really want to kiss her. But she keeps talking. "Four days ago, my life was something different. And then you come along, and now . . ." Her blue eyes slowly well up and she gets this worried look on her face as though someone just gave her bad news.

"What's wrong?" I ask, brushing her cheek with the back of my finger.

"Nothing. I'm just . . . dangerously happy." Her hand comes to rest on my knee, sending a shot of heat up my leg and into my abdomen. Her other hand is still on my collar, and she tugs me closer until her lips find mine. Her kiss is so soft and exquisite that for a moment the cliff and the ocean and the sky fall away, because there's only her.

She leans back and looks at me, the fear gone from her face. "So what do I need to do to get more answers from you today?"

I clear my throat, still reeling a bit from her kiss. "Nothing. You have a VIP pass now."

She raises one corner of her mouth and a skeptical eyebrow.

I'll probably never have an obituary, or a eulogy, or even a gravestone. Nothing to leave behind to tell people about my short and pathetic life. But I want to leave some of myself behind. I want someone to know and remember me, not only for who I was as a kid, but for who I've become. "I'm an open book, Avery Ambrose. I want you to know everything about me."

She hesitates, like she's unsure whether I mean it. "Really?"

I almost say yes, but there's one chapter in my book that will have to remain stapled shut—the one where I die. However, I'm sure I can avoid the subject easily enough while still remaining honest. I've had four days of practice, after all. "Ask me anything."

"Okay, then." She leans back on her hands and lifts her face to the sky, biting her lower lip while deciding what to ask me. She's wearing little aquamarine studs in her ears, and they catch a bit of sunlight and sparkle. I see her come to some sort of conclusion, and then she looks at me. "Why aren't you off pursuing a music career when you play and sing like that? And don't give me some lame, vague answer like 'life.'" She says the last word with a deep voice, attempting to impersonate my answer from a couple days ago. It makes me laugh for a second, until I realize that giving an honest answer as promised is going to be harder than I thought.

I roll onto my stomach and play with the grass at the edge of the blanket while formulating a reply. I'm tempted to make up some BS answer about how I realized there were more important things in life than music and fame and fortune and blah blah blah, but something tells me she'll see right through it. And then I find myself thinking that if music were the one thing I could have taken with me when I died, maybe my death would have been bearable. Charles urged me yesterday to accept and live my new life, but how can I when everything I love, everything that brings me joy, has to be left behind?

"Come see what awaits you in Elysium," he said. "It's more than you can imagine." Maybe things are different there. Maybe that's where the music is, and it's been my unwillingness to move on that's kept me from happiness in the next life.

Avery's hand falls lightly on my wrist, and I realize she's still waiting for an answer. "It's still the plan," I say. "I've just been delayed with . . . everything."

She must think I'm referring to running away and all the resulting complications, because she seems satisfied with my answer. "That's good to hear." She's lying on her stomach now too, and she scoots closer until the side of her body is pressed against mine. It's like hooking up to a generator the way it makes every cell in this body hum to life. She loops her arm under mine, and the ends of her hair tickle the skin on my forearm.

I turn and kiss her temple, leaving my lips there. "Anything else you want to know?"

She tears off a blade of grass and splits it down the center. "Yesterday," she says hesitantly, "you said you had a rap sheet." She makes an apologetic face. "What's on it?"

"Hm," I grunt. "Did I say 'open book'? I forgot to mention that some of the pages have been torn out."

She nudges me with her shoulder. "I won't judge. I just . . . I don't know. I want to know all of you. I trust you with my secrets, and I want you to trust me."

I let out a long sigh, and then look away so I don't have to see her reaction to my confession. "Vandalism. Theft. Assault. Jaywalking." I throw on the jaywalking at the end, hoping she won't dwell on the assault. But I hope in vain.

"Assault against who?" I feel her arm tense under mine, as if she's suddenly nervous to be here with me.

"I had a lot of emotions I didn't know how to deal with when I was growing up. Grief from losing my mom, stress from trying to protect and take care of my sisters, and dealing with my dad . . ." I don't want to go there, so I shake my head, casting the memories out. "And then being separated from my sisters and placed in strange homes with strange people . . . my feelings were all over the place. I looked for conflict, because it was an avenue to release all the frustration and anger and everything else inside me. That's no excuse, of course. But every time I hurt someone, my foster parents would get scared and I'd get sent to a new home. Over, and over, and over."

Avery rubs my arm consolingly, but I still can't look at her. I don't want to see the disappointment or judgment or pity in her eyes. So I roll on my back and gaze up at the lacy white clouds, and keep talking. "I went through more therapists than I can count, but fought against everyone who tried to help me because . . . I don't know. I guess I couldn't bring myself to believe that they actually cared. Maybe they did. But when they'd take out their little books and worksheets and assign me mental exercises and tools to work through my emotions, I couldn't help wondering how many other kids they'd given the same canned advice to. It made me feel like one more file in their cabinet that they'd pull out every now and then to work on." I close my eyes. I've never talked to anyone like this, so openly, so vulnerable. It feels scary and liberating at the same time. I open my eyes. High in the sky above me, a dark bird drifts on the headwind.

"You seem like a different person than the one you're describing," Avery says quietly.

"I guess that's because I am. Mostly thanks to Charles. I was placed with him when I was sixteen, and he was different than everyone else. Instead of trying to baby me or pretend to care about me, he put me to work in his vineyard. At first I hated it, but he was persistent and patient. There was this one day when all my pent-up anger came bursting out, and I took it out on one of his vines. I kicked and tore the thing apart. When Charles came over to see what was happening, I thought he was going to kick my can and throw me out."

I pause and smile at the memory. "But he just looked at me, and at the shredded vine, and at me again, and then said, 'Well, sonny, I guess now would be a good time to show you how to repair a vine.' And that's when I knew. Knew that he really cared about me. He was always patient with me, and eventually taught me better ways to vent my emotions, like through music and hard work. But then, like I told you, he passed away last winter."

And so did I. But I'm trying really hard not to think about that right now.

Avery is so quiet that I finally brave a glance at her. She's lying on her side watching me, head propped on her hand, and her expression is the last thing I expected to see. It's a medley of admiration and reverence, of tenderness and love. She slides closer and lays her hand on my cheek, stroking my skin with her thumb.

In the months since my death, it's been my job to heal dozens of people. But in Avery's touch, I feel more healing power than I've ever felt leave my own hands. It gathers up the dark things, capturing them and dissolving them like bleach on a stain. It's a cleansing feeling I've ached for my entire life, and her soft fingertips are the last place I would have expected to find it.

"You're a beautiful person," she says softly, and then her face gets all blurry because tears are suddenly flooding my vision.

I shut my eyes and try to swallow them back, but they squeeze through the cracks and trickle down my temple. I don't want to cry right now. I don't want to waste this day by turning into a mess. But healing, in all its warmth and light and grace, is also painful. There's a sudden void where all my sorrow once dwelled, and when the peace and warmth come rushing in to fill that space, it's a shock because I've never felt anything like it.

I feel her fingers brushing away my tears, feel her lips on my forehead, on my cheeks, on my lips. Her arm slides around the back of my neck as she pulls me close to her.

In this moment, I have no regrets. I don't regret dying for her. I don't regret stealing Charles's ring. And I don't regret letting her in to love and heal me. Because even if it's only for a little while, I now know what it is to love and be loved. And really, Avery is the one who has saved *me*. She's salvaged my life, taken something stained and damaged and transformed it into something valuable.

The waves crash into the rocks below, drowning out all other sound, and it feels as though Avery and I are the only two people on this Earth. If I could, I would stay here forever with her. But I can't, so the best I can do is leave a piece of me behind.

"I have something for you," I say, pulling away. I sit up and open my guitar case, retrieving the notebook of my lyrics. The edges are gray with dirt, worn from being laid out on sidewalks and street corners and truck stop tables. But the pages inside hold my heart and soul, the only parts of me I can leave with her. I hand it to her.

"What's this?" she asks, sitting up.

"Songs I've written."

She lets the pages fall open, then flips through, reading as she goes. Her face turns sad, and she shakes her head. "You can't give this to me."

"Yes, I can."

"But—"

"Please." My voice is strained. "It would mean the world to me if you'd take it. It's the only thing I have to give you."

She looks at me uncertainly for a long time, and then her face relaxes and she nods. "Okay. But if you ever need it . . ."

"I'll know where to find it."

She smiles, and then her gaze sweeps over my face, her expression turning perplexed as though she's looking at a sliding puzzle and trying to figure out how to move the tiles into their proper place. "Kai, I have to tell you something."

Maybe it's the serious tone in her voice, but my stomach tenses up. "What?"

"Something really weird is happening to me." She pauses, reaching up and playing with a button on my shirt. "I keep having these memories. Of the day that boy drowned. And . . . I've been getting glimpses of him."

It's a good thing she's not looking at my face, because my eyes go wide.

"And," she continues, "I know this sounds nuts, but the face that I see . . . is *yours*."

I pray that she doesn't lift her eyes, because if she does, she'll know the truth. It takes one, two, three seconds to wrestle my face into composure. I can play this off. She can't know it was me. I tilt my head, like what she said is the strangest thing I've ever heard. "Huh. That's weird."

She finally looks at me. "I know. And I know this is crazy to ask, but . . . is there any possible way that it could've been *you* that day?"

"Avery," I say without missing a beat. "If it was me, would I be sitting here now?" Her cheeks turn crimson, and then her ears too. I feel bad, but what else am I supposed to say? *Why, yes, it was me. I've been keeping my true identity from you for four days. And by the way, I'm dead.* No—there's nothing else to say.

"I know—you're right," she says sheepishly. "I think my mind is just playing tricks on me." She bites her lip and stands, walking toward the fringe of the cliff. She stops a few feet from the rim and looks out to sea. The wind is whipping the tops of the waves white and blowing her hair off her back and shoulders. She wraps her arms around her waist, obviously troubled.

I go and stand behind her, circling my arms around her shoulders and drawing her close to my chest. Dipping my head to her ear, I softly say, "You don't have to remember his face to remember *him*. Remembering what he did for you is enough."

She's quiet for a long time as she gazes out at the blue horizon, watching a sailboat slowly disappear into the seam between earth and sky. Then in a small voice she says, "Do you really have to leave?"

I should tell her that I'm leaving in the morning. But I can't bring myself to say it because it will crack apart this perfect day that I've so carefully constructed. There's more time. Not much, but enough to save bad news for later.

The mast of the sailboat is almost gone now, and I say, "When I do leave, I won't really be gone. I'll be just over the horizon." I bury my lips in her hair. "And it won't be good-bye forever." At least I hope with everything in me that it won't. I have to believe that. And I hope that long after I'm gone, she still believes it too.

She turns in my embrace and slides her arms around my waist, burrowing into my chest. I soak in the warmth of her body, the softness of her hair between my fingers, the tickle of her breath on my arm, and push away all thoughts of tomorrow.

Today, she's mine, and I'm hers, and nothing—not even death—can separate us.

When I walk Avery to her mom's porch at dusk, I don't want to leave. She must not want me to leave either, because before I can begin my half-baked this-is-goodbye-for-this-life speech, she grabs my hand and says, "You want to come in for a movie or something?"

I don't think, just nod, because I'm far from ready to say good-bye. She opens the door and I gladly follow her inside. It's pitch dark in her mom's condo, and ice cold. Avery fumbles for the light switch for a minute before she finds it and flips it on.

"Sorry for the mess," she says, looking a bit confused as she glances around at the magazines scattered across the living room floor. "Mom?" she calls out. There's no answer, and Avery gestures to the couch. "Have a seat. I'm going to check on her."

She disappears down the dark hallway, but I'm suddenly too anxious to sit. Something doesn't feel right.

Seconds later, Avery screams.

I rush down the hall, following the sound of her cry. I find her in a bedroom, curled over something on the floor. I flip on the light, and there's her mom, crumpled on the floor beside a broken wineglass.

For a split second, instead of Avery's mom, I see my own mom. Nine years earlier, lying on our dirty kitchen floor in the same position. Only, my mom had a needle sticking out of the crook of her elbow.

A deep voice comes from the corner of the room. "What are you doing here?"

My eyes snap up to see Jerick's towering figure by the window, his scepter burning like a saffron flame, his icy-blue eyes freezing me into stillness.

I don't answer him, don't even consider the implications of him seeing me, because Avery is kneeling over her mom and screaming, "Mom!" She's touching her mom's face, neck, stomach. "She's not breathing." She turns to me. "She's not breathing!"

Jerick is here to seal her mother's death. I can't let that

happen—not to Avery. Not when I know how it feels to have a loved one blotted from your life. And not when I'll be out of her life tomorrow too. I kneel beside her. She's already starting CPR, blowing breath into her mom's mouth.

I can stop this. With my wristband, I can save her. I haven't been assigned, but I've already broken so many rules. What's one more?

I look at Jerick. He's shaking his head as if to say, *Don't you dare.* I ignore him and touch Avery's shoulder. "I'll take over. Call 911."

She looks at me a brief second, searching for something. Maybe reassurance or confidence, or maybe she's gauging my ability to perform CPR. She must see what she needs, because she stands and moves out of the way. She finds her phone and hits three numbers, and I put my hands on her mom's chest and start pumping. It must be too much for Avery to see, because she disappears into the hall. As I'm pumping, I try to draw from the healing power the wristband gives me, but for some reason I feel completely drained.

Jerick steps forward. "What do you think you're doing?"

"Saving this woman's life," I say quietly between heavy breaths, hoping Avery won't hear. She's on the phone with dispatch in the hall, giving them information. Her tone threatens to fracture my already dead heart into pieces, and I increase my focus, trying to direct all my energy into healing her mom.

"Who assigned you?" Jerick asks suspiciously. "I was supposed to seal her death."

"Not today," I say, ignoring his first question. "There must have been a mistake."

He nods at Avery's mom. "But it was her mistake. So you need to stop what you're doing and let her go."

I don't stop. I can't let her go. I seal my mouth over hers and blow air into her lungs, then pump her heart with the heel of my hands, just like I did nine years ago with my own mom. Only then, my arms weren't strong enough to make any difference.

They're stronger now, but still may not make a difference. I need the healing power that I know is in me somewhere. I try to summon it again.

Just as I start to feel it build, Jerick asks, "Where did you get that ring?"

The energy drains, and I fight to get it back. Jerick knows I shouldn't be here. Knows I shouldn't be materialized. Shouldn't have the ring. I can't tell him where I got it, because Charles might get in trouble. "I'm here to help Avery," I say. "Just for a little while."

Jerick gives a dubious grunt. "On whose orders?"

I don't answer because I'm blowing air into Avery's mother's lungs. And then I feel more than air leave me. Energy, power, life, leaves me and goes into her.

A sick fear coils in the pit of my stomach. I've been caught. Jerick is going to tell someone. I look up at him as I continue reviving Avery's mom. "Please," I say contritely between pumps, hoping that somewhere in his apathetic soul is a sliver of compassion. "You don't understand."

Jerick says nothing, just takes a step back, and disappears through the wall without completing his task.

They could be here any moment now, to take me back to Demoror or someplace worse for breaking the rules. I'll never see Avery again. This can't be it. I only hope I have enough time to save her mom's life. Enough time to say good-bye. I hope Jerick says nothing. But I know that's too much to hope for.

I need to focus. I need to not think about what's going to happen to me or to Avery when they come for me. I need to heal Avery's mom, for Avery.

I stop pumping and breathing and instead let my hand rest on her stomach. I can feel her soul's warmth still in her body. I shut my eyes and concentrate, drawing not only from the power in the wristband, but from everything inside of me, all my sources of energy, and I let them flow into her.

"Stay," I tell her. "Stay here. Stay here." I feel it come from deep inside of me. Everything my soul is made of. Every thread, every watt of energy I've stored over the course of my existence. It comes from grief and anger, joy and love. It all pours out of me as energy and into her. But it isn't enough.

"Please," I cry out. I feel the word leave my lips like a bolt of lightning. It ricochets around the room and then shoots up, away to where such pleas go. In the same moment, the stone in the wristband lights up, and I feel a power surge inside of me and flow into Avery's mom.

I hear sirens outside, and soon paramedics burst into the room.

25

avery

My dad's been gone for a long time," I say to Kai. He's sitting beside me in the ER waiting room, his hand blanketed over mine.

"It's only been . . ." He glances at the clock on the wall. "Eight minutes since they took him back to see her."

"I just hate not knowing." I'm so tired of being in the dark. About the identity of the boy who saved me. About whether or not Mom will ever reconcile with Dad. About whether or not she's even alive. So much uncertainty. So much powerlessness. I feel like a boat in the middle of a stormy sea with a torn sail. The winds will do what they want with me.

I want to leave. I want to go to the chocolate shop and make five hundred truffles, each one exactly the same. I want to measure the cream and sugar and vanilla with precision, and have each truffle come out exactly the way I intend.

I glance at the clock again. It's two in the morning. "You don't have to stay with me," I say, even though I desperately want him to. "You look exhausted."

"I'm not going to leave you here alone." His voice is subdued, weak with fatigue.

"Maybe Sophie will be here soon." Dad asked her to come with him to the hospital, but she said she'd come later. I'm not sure what later means, but I wish she'd come now so Kai could go home and get some rest. His back is slumped against his chair, and deep shadows underline his eyes. What a way to end a day, walking in on your girlfriend's half-dead mother. I feel bad for dragging him into this. But I'm also grateful that he was there with me, and for what he did for my mom.

The way he reacted, the urgency with which he revived her, was almost as if it were his own mother on the floor. I wonder how his mom died. If he didn't look so exhausted right now, I'd ask him. And I wonder if seeing my mom like that brought back painful memories for him. He was saying strange things as he worked on my mom, almost like he was having a conversation. I didn't hear everything he said, but I caught a few words. He said there must have been a mistake. And that he was here to help me.

Just as I turn to ask him about it, the double doors to the ER open and Dad emerges. His eyes are red, his face pale. His hand trembles as he wipes his nose with the back of his hand.

I stand and take three long steps toward him, my heart sinking at the sight of his anguish. It's bad news. I just know it.

He stops in front of me and his hand comes to my arm. "She's going to be okay."

A breath of relief rushes out of me, and I fall into Dad's arms and release the tears I've been holding back for five hours. I cry into his chest for what seems like forever, soaking his T-shirt with my tears. He rubs my back, whispering soft reassurances in my ear. But soon my relief turns to sorrow. And in the next breath, my sorrow turns to anger.

"How could she do this? After everything I've gone through in the last few months?" I look up at Dad. "How could she do this to you? After all you've done for her?"

"We don't know that she meant to do it."

"But she knows what happens when she mixes alcohol with her sleep med—"

"Avery. She's going to be okay. Let's focus on that." He releases me and takes a small step back, running his hand through his messy hair. "She's awake. But she won't talk right now. You can go in and see her if you want." He looks me in the eye and gives me as stern a look as he's capable of. "Now is not the time for accusations or interrogations. Okay?"

I nod slowly and turn to see Kai standing behind me. His hair is a disaster, and once again, his face is so full of sadness and fear you'd think it was his own mother in the ER.

"I'm going to see her," I say. "If you want to leave, I'll ride home with my dad."

"I'll wait for you."

"Kai—"

"I'm not going anywhere." His expression is like steel, and I know there'll be no convincing him to leave.

I nod, then follow Dad through the double doors. The hallway is quiet, other than beeping noises coming from patients' rooms and the hum of fluorescent lights overhead. We enter Mom's room. She's lying in bed with her head turned away, slightly elevated with an IV in her arm. I slowly approach and slip my hand into hers. It's cold, and she doesn't respond to my touch. She keeps her eyes on the pastel curtains.

I don't know what to say. And yet, there are so many things I want to say.

Why? Did you do it on purpose? Or was it an accident? Please tell me it was an accident like last time. Please tell me you're not that stupid. Not that selfish. That you care about me and Dad and Sophie too much to remove yourself permanently from our lives.

But I don't say any of these things. Instead, I say, "I love you, Mom. I'm glad you're okay." The rest can wait until later, or maybe forever.

She gives my hand a featherlight squeeze, and I stay at her side for a few more silent minutes before it all becomes too much for me. I don't feel strong enough for this right now. Maybe tomorrow, or the next day, I can face her without feeling like my heart is being crushed in a vise. I withdraw my hand from hers and leave her alone with Dad.

As promised, Kai is still sitting in the waiting room. He stands, and I walk up to him. "Will you take me home?"

26

KAI

She's quiet on the ride home, facing the open window, wind whipping hair across her face. She's watching the darkened scenery rush by, her thoughts probably rushing even faster.

I don't want to tell her I'm leaving in the morning. It's such bad timing. But it's either say good-bye now or leave without saying good-bye. I wonder why someone hasn't already come for me. Maybe it's because I'm with her, and they don't want her to know. Maybe I can just stay with her. For tonight. And tomorrow. And the next night. It won't work forever, but it could buy me more time.

She straightens and turns to me. By the light of the dashboard, I see that her brows are pursed together, her makeup all cried off. She looks beautiful. "Kai, I heard you talking. When you were helping my mom. What were you talking about?"

I keep my eyes on the road and my face composed. I can handle this. I'm an expert liar. "Sometimes when I'm stressed out, I mumble things."

"It sounded like you were talking to someone."

"I was talking to your mom. Telling her to stay."

She pulls one knee up. Her shoelace is untied, and instead of tying it, she starts winding it around her finger. "You said something else too . . ."

As I wait for her to finish her sentence, I try to remember what I said earlier to Jerick. How can I explain myself?

"You said, 'I'm here to help Avery. Just for a little while.'" She releases the shoelace. "Why did you say that?"

"I was there to help you . . . with your mom. I mean . . ." How can I possibly explain? I can't. And from the skeptical look on her face, she's not buying what I already offered.

"But . . ." She shakes her head with her eyes closed. "That doesn't make sense."

"Avery," I say in a heartbroken tone that makes her straighten and look at me. She's not expecting what I'm about to tell her, and it's agonizing to say the words. "I'm leaving in the morning." And just like that, it's out.

Her mouth drops open a little. "Leaving? For good?"

This is it. This is good-bye. I feel something fracture deep in my chest. It starts to spread, like an earthquake dividing a continent in two. It makes it impossible to speak, so I just nod.

She stares at me. My eyes are on the road, but I can see the hurt in her face in my peripheral vision. "Why?" Her voice sounds small, fragile.

I can't answer honestly. So I don't even try.

"Is it because they know where you are?" she asks.

I know she's referring to earthly authorities and not heavenly ones, but I nod an affirmative.

"Are you ever coming back?" The sliver of hope in her voice is enough to shatter what's left of me.

No. Never. Now that they know what I've done, I doubt I'll be able to return to Earth with or without a body. But I don't say that. I just repeat what I said to her on the cliff. "This isn't good-bye forever."

I must not sound convincing, because the silence that follows is worse than anything I've ever endured. It's the sound of hopelessness, of her heart breaking. I want to comfort her. I want her to know that I have no choice, that I would stay if I could, that I'll be thinking about her for the rest of eternity. But I'm leaving. Anything I say now will sound insincere.

She doesn't say anything else. Maybe she's too emotionally exhausted from what her mom just put her through. But it kills me that she doesn't question me, that she accepts my plans without debate or further discussion. She goes back to looking out the window, and her hand moves to her arm, where she digs her fingernails into her skin.

She's back to square one. What was the point of my coming here to help her, if I was just going to break her heart anew? I reach over and unhook her hand from her arm, then lace her fingers through mine. Her hand feels lifeless in mine.

I wish I could convince her that I'll see her again someday, but I don't know that for sure. So I lift her hand to my mouth and kiss it. Then I say the only words I can say with certainty. "I love you, Avery Ambrose."

She says nothing in return. Doesn't look at me. Just keeps staring out the window.

When I pull up to her house, she doesn't say good-bye. She gets out and quietly shuts the door, then walks to her front door and disappears inside.

27

avery

As soon as the door clicks shut behind me, I sink to my knees and surrender to the tears I've been holding back. I can't believe he's leaving. Can't believe he couldn't wait a little longer, especially after what happened tonight. And if he knew he was leaving, why didn't he tell me earlier? Why wait until now? Maybe because he just made the decision. Maybe he's more like Tyler than I thought, and he doesn't want the burden of trying to console a grieving girlfriend.

Only, when I think of everything he's done for me over the last few days, I know that he wouldn't abandon me without good reason. I just don't understand what his reasons are.

I feel so alone. Like a castaway, drifting in the middle of a dark ocean without a lifeboat. The house is so dark and empty that I may as well be.

I hear a whimpering sound coming from the hallway. It takes all my strength to rise to my feet and follow the sound to Sophie's bedroom. She's curled up in bed still wearing her combat boots, arm over head. I kick off my shoes and lay beside her, draping my arm over her and pulling her close.

"She's okay," I whisper.

Sophie cries harder, her whole body convulsing. I know what she's feeling. She doesn't have to say it, because I feel it too. There's no point talking about it, because there's nothing to be done. There's only grief and anger and sorrow, churning around us, through us, over us.

I clutch her hand in mine, grateful that at least we don't have to drown alone.

My head is only an inch below the water, but I'm going to drown. And it's not my life that's flashing before my eyes, but a poster I once saw in my pediatrician's office warning that it only takes a couple inches of water for a child to drown. My fingers claw at the leash around my neck, but it's so tight I can't squeeze a pinky underneath. Just when I think my lungs might burst and the edges of my vision turn black, I feel a sharp sting, and for a second I think I'm being attacked by some sea creature. But then the pressure around my neck releases. A hand circles my arm and yanks me above the surface and onto my surfboard. I cough up the liquid in my lungs, and when I can somewhat breathe again, I follow the arm that's draped over my back to its owner. Through the rain, I squint at the boy who's hanging onto the opposite side of my surfboard. All I can really see is that he's shirtless, and I wonder what he's doing in the winter Pacific without a wetsuit.

"Are you okay?" he shouts over the roar of the rain and waves. We're traveling up and down from peak to trough, as if we're on some sadistic amusement park ride. I want to get off now, but the only exit is the beach.

"We need to get back to shore!" I shout back, as though he doesn't already know.

He moves his arm from my back to my surfboard, then turns

away and, holding onto my board with one arm, starts kicking and paddling toward shore. I join him, kicking as hard and fast as I can. With the rain falling in my eyes and splashing up into my face, all I can see is his arm on my surfboard and the upper part of his back and shoulders. I notice a long white scar running along his shoulder blade. Every now and then he looks back at me, like he's making sure I'm okay, and through my squinted eyes I catch little glimpses of his jaw and lips.

After a while, he stops and turns back toward me. He dips one arm into the water and pulls out what's left of my surfboard leash. He grabs my wrist and ties the leash around it, and for the first time, I see his eyes.

My eyelids fly open, and for a minute I don't know where I am. In the ocean? At the hospital? I glance around, and when I see the Astromotts poster on the wall, I realize I'm still in Sophie's room, lying beside her. I feel her warm body beside me, breathing deeply. As opposed to my own quick, shallow breaths.

For the first time, I saw his face in my dream. Only, it didn't feel like a dream. It felt like a memory. And once again, the face I saw was Kai's.

I sit up and quietly slide off Sophie's bed. I don't know what time it is, but no light is seeping through the cracks in her blinds. I go to Dad's office and turn on his computer, glancing at the clock while it boots up. It's just past five in the morning, and I feel exactly like I've had two hours of sleep. But there's something I need to do so that maybe I can prove to myself that I'm not losing my mind.

I type in "missing foster kids Michigan" in the search engine and hit enter. Up comes a link for an official Michigan website that says, "Help us find these missing children." I click it and find a database. I know Kai's picture will be in here somewhere. I don't know why I need to see it. Maybe I want to know if I've seen his picture before in another missing persons database. Because that might explain why he looks so familiar. Why I'm imposing his face on the boy who saved my life.

"Where are you, Kai Lennon?" I whisper, wincing at the ache that comes with saying his name out loud. With a pounding heart, I click on a link at the left of the screen for children whose last names start with L.

Three profiles populate the screen, two boys and one girl. No Kai though. Maybe he's not in the database after all. Or maybe . . .

I start clicking through the other letters, starting with A and moving down the alphabet. My palms grow moist as I anxiously search through each page for his face.

When I get to T, at least a dozen profiles pop up. I scroll down the list, scanning the pictures for his face.

Halfway down, my heart stops.

There he is. Looking at me from a thumbnail picture on the screen.

His hair is darker, a sandy blond. His face looks more tan, a bit more worn and angry. But without a doubt, it's him. And then I look at his name.

Zackai L. Turner.

L for Lennon.

Kai is a nickname. And Lennon is his middle name.

Why would he lie to me about his name? Maybe he was afraid I would report him if I found out he was a runaway. A shiver runs through me as I click his name to view his profile. The picture expands. There's absolutely no question now that it's Kai. I read the information on his profile.

Missing since December of last year. Last seen in the Upper Peninsula. Current age: 17. Six foot two. One hundred eighty pounds. Blond hair. Blue-green eyes. Other Distinguishing Features: Scar on back over left shoulder blade.

Scar. On his back.

Scar. Left. Shoulder blade.

Heat washes over me, and I push my chair back and stand up, staring at the computer screen in disbelief.

It's not possible. Is it? No. It's absolutely impossible. I looked for the scar on Kai's back that night in his cottage. His skin was flawless.

But the face on the computer screen is Kai's face. Either it was too dark in the cottage that night to see his scar, or I didn't look high enough. But how is it possible that he survived? And why wouldn't he tell me who he really is?

All I know with certainty is that he lied to me. He knows how much anguish it's caused me to not know who saved my life last winter. But he withheld the truth anyway.

I grab the mouse and click print. The printer spits out a copy of his profile, and I pick it up and stare at it as I pace the room.

Zackai L. Turner. L for Lennon. L for Lowlife. L for Liar.

I clutch my stomach, fighting the nausea that's climbing up my throat. Please don't let this be. Don't tell me he's capable of deceiving me like this, of withholding the knowledge that I've been chasing for months. Please let him have an explanation.

If I'm going to get any kind of explanation, I have to catch him before he leaves this morning. I throw on some jeans and a T-shirt, then grab my keys and rush out to my Cherokee. My hands are shaking so badly it takes me a few tries to get the key in the ignition.

Tremors rack my insides as I drive up the winding canyon road toward the vineyard. I squeeze the steering wheel, trying to ground myself to something. A battle between pain and fury wages inside of me. Between wanting to trust him and ask him kindly for an explanation, and wanting to knock down his door and clock him in the jaw.

With each curve of the road, I think of more names to attach to him. Cruel. Heartless. Creep.

Beloved. Soul mate.

Callous. Brute.

My everything.
Scum. Conniving.
Beautiful. Treasure.
Deceiver.

There's no answer. Maybe he's already gone. Or maybe I scared him by pounding so hard on his door. I knock again, a little gentler. The quaking inside of me is virtually off the Richter scale now, and I clutch the paper in my hand as though it can absorb some of the shock. I hear the lock unlatch, and very slowly, the door swings open.

Kai stands there in the same clothes he wore yesterday, his face pale in the pre-dawn light. He looks tired, but not the least bit surprised to see me, as though he knew I was coming. "Avery," he says softly.

"Zackai," I say, and his face goes slack. I push him back inside and step in, shutting the door behind me. Then I shove the crumpled paper at him. "Explain this."

He takes it, unwrinkles it, and studies it for a few seconds as he strolls over to a small dining table. He lays it down and leans over it, head hanging. "I couldn't tell you my real name because—"

"You think that's what I care about? Kai—Zack—whatever. That profile says you have a scar on your back in same place as the boy who saved my life." I'm short of breath, but the words manage to rush out anyway. "You've been missing since last winter. And you said we met before. And the memories I keep having . . ." I shake my head, my throat tight. "Tell me the truth. It was you that day, wasn't it?"

He doesn't answer, just straightens and looks at me, his face terrified.

I can't believe it. It is him. He's the boy who saved my life. The boy who I thought drowned. And he knew the last couple days that I suspected it was him, but he denied it.

"I thought you were dead!" The words burst from my lips with fiery outrage. "I've been carrying around the burden of your death for six months. And you lied to my face! I asked you yesterday if it was possible that you were the one who saved my life. And you said no." My whole body is shaking with fury, my heart galloping in my chest. I charge over to him and before I even know what I'm doing, my hand comes up to slap him. Before it reaches his face, he catches my wrist.

"I didn't lie to you," he says through clenched teeth.

"You misled me," I snap back, trying to twist out of his clutch. "Same thing." My throat is on fire, my eyes stinging. "Tell me why," I beg. "Why would you lie to me? You saw how much I was hurting. Why wouldn't you just tell me that it was you? Do you have any idea how much pain you could have spared me?" I can't see his face anymore, because my eyes are swimming in tears. "Let go of me," I demand.

His fingers unfurl and I fall back a step, swiping tears from my eyes. I hear him exhale, and then he says weakly, "I didn't tell you the truth because I couldn't. And you wouldn't have believed me anyway."

"Try me. How did you survive?"

His expression is defeated. Crushed. The charade is over, the game lost. His lips part, but no words come.

"They looked for your body for days," I say angrily. "And after everyone else gave up, I spent weeks with my mom on her sailboat, combing the shores."

"I know," he whispers.

"No—you don't." He has no idea. He doesn't know how many tears I've cried, how many nightmares I've suffered, how many hours I've wasted searching for his body and sifting through missing persons databases for his face. "Tell me. Did you swim back to shore and just leave?" Though, I still don't understand how that's possible when I saw him under the water, unconscious.

He turns away, gripping the back of a chair as though he needs support. "Avery." My name sounds like a mournful cry. "When I said yesterday that I wouldn't be here if I had been the one to save your life, it wasn't a lie. I shouldn't be here. Because when I went under the water that day, I didn't resurface. I didn't make it back to shore."

I stare at him in bafflement. "Well, you obviously did at some point, or else you wouldn't be standing right in front of me."

He turns and hesitantly reaches out to me, like I'm a wild horse, and he's afraid I'm going to rear back and gallop away. Maybe I will. I don't know. All I know is that beneath all this rage, I'm aching for his touch. I desperately want him to set things right. To explain everything in a way that will make it impossible for me not to forgive him. He inches closer and rests his hands on my arms as if to steady me. Then he leans down so that his eyes are level with mine.

"I died that day," he whispers.

The hair on my arms stand on end, and then I do rear back, shaking out of his hold. "Stop lying to me!"

His shoulders slump, then he closes his eyes and grimaces.

"Please," I beg, softening my voice and reaching out to touch his arm. "I just want to piece things together. I want to understand."

He opens his eyes and gives me a desperate look. "Why do you think you didn't find a scar on my back the other night? It's because this isn't my mortal body."

I stare at him. "Why are you doing this?" I whisper. "Don't you trust me enough to tell me the truth?"

He takes a step toward me, gently takes my hand in his, and raises it to his neck. "Try to find a pulse," he whispers despondently.

Only to get this ridiculous conversation over with, I press two fingers under his jaw where his artery is. But other than warm skin, I feel nothing. I move my fingers around, searching for a pulse, but find nothing. I look up at him for an explanation, but then realize he's already given me one.

I don't buy it. "Hold still." I press my ear to the left side of his chest, over his heart. "Shhh. Hold your breath." He does, and I listen closely. His chest is like a tomb. No sound. No vibration. Not the slightest sign of life. And then my own heart is suddenly pounding in my chest.

I look up at him again, my mouth falling open.

"I'm not lying to you," he says, his voice tattered. "I am dead."

I can't grasp it. Can't reconcile my disbelief with the undeniable evidence. But if it is true, it would explain everything. My legs start to shake, and then they buckle and I sink to the floor. I can't breathe, as though someone has their hands clamped around my throat. My head feels tingly. The room is spinning, the walls going in and out of focus.

I feel Kai's hand on the back of my head. "Breathe, Avery. Breathe." His voice is urgent, worried. The room keeps spinning, black dots popping into my vision. They fill the room until it grows darker and darker, until all I see is black.

"Avery." Kai's voice sounds so far away. I feel his warm hand on my forehead, my cheek, my neck. His fingers on my wrist, checking for a pulse. "Avery, wake up. We don't have much time."

My eyelids flutter, and then slowly open. I'm on a bed. Kai is lying beside me, propped on his elbow and leaning over me.

"You okay?" he breathes.

Am I okay? Kai is dead. And talking to me. I'm definitely not okay. I feel as lifeless as he is. I gaze at his face, at the same time recalling my memories of the boy who saved my life, and my mind slowly melds their faces together, uniting them into one person.

I can't move, can barely breathe with this heaviness pressing on me. The heaviness of finality. Of knowing the truth. The truth that Kai—Zackai—is the boy who saved my life. And because he saved my life, he did lose his own. And I love him. And he's here now, in front of me. But he's dead. He's dead, and here, touching me, speaking to me, looking at me. It's too much to carry, too much to take in, and every muscle in my body is drained and useless from the weight of it all.

"I'm so sorry," I whisper.

He brushes away the tear that's running down my temple. "I'm not." And then he leans down and kisses me, breathing life and energy back into me. I'm a sailboat in the doldrums, and he's the wind. He kisses me and kisses me, and I feel life come back into me, rushing through me, tingling and electric and humming.

He pulls away and looks in my eyes. My arm finds its strength, and I reach up to touch his face. "You," I say, in awe of his realness, his substance, his tangibility.

This boy who has been a ghost to me, a vague and elusive memory, is here in the flesh, in front of me. I pull him close and hold him tight, this phantom I've never been able to catch. He's mine now. In the snare of my arms, and I'll never, ever let go. I crush his body against mine and cry into his ear, rejoicing, marveling, at the miracle in my arms. "If you're . . . dead," I say brokenly, shaking my head in disbelief, "then why . . . how are you here? How can I see you, and hear you, and feel you?"

He leans away and trails a thumb down my cheek, his grief-stricken eyes taking me in as if it's the last time he'll ever see me. "It doesn't matter now." He glances toward the door as though he's expecting someone. Then he looks back at me. "I don't have time to explain. All you need to know is that I love you. In five days, you've given me all I could have asked for in a lifetime. So no regrets, okay? I've never regretted losing my life for you. And I don't want you to regret it either. Can you remember that? Promise me you won't forget." He's talking urgently, like he has one foot on the step of a departing train.

"Don't leave me," is all I can say, my voice desperate. "You're not leaving now. Not ever."

His eyes snap shut. Then he turns away from me and says, "Please don't. You don't understand."

At first I think he's talking to me, but then he opens his eyes and focuses on something across the room, like there's someone there I can't see. "A little more time," he says. "Please."

"Kai. Who are you talking to? Who's there?"

He grimaces and slips his hand out from under my neck, holding it in the air like someone hailing a cab. His wristband comes unclasped and flies off his wrist. Before it hits the floor, it vanishes into thin air. His ring comes off next, vanishing as well.

I sit up in a panic. "What's happening?"

He rolls onto his side, eyes squeezed tight, and groans in agony. "Kai!"

"My time here is up," he says weakly.

I clutch his shoulder. "No! Look at me! You can't leave. Please!" I lie at his side and slide my arms around him, clinging to him. I won't let him go. If I hold on tight enough, he can't leave.

"No regrets," he whispers in my ear. I feel his arms close around my waist. "Promise me."

His body feels strange in my arms. Less dense. I loosen my grip on him, afraid I'm hurting him. "What's happening?"

He doesn't answer. Just whispers, "Promise me."

My arm sinks into his side, and I move back, startled. I reach for his arm, but my fingers sift right through it. I can still feel him, but he's losing substance. I try to take his hand, and it's like running my fingers through fine sand. He doesn't crumble away, but there's no way to hold him anymore.

"Kai," I cry as though my heart is being wrenched from my chest. I try to touch his face, and it feels like the edges of a feather, or a soft breeze. My vision blurs again, but I swipe the tears away, knowing that I don't have much time left to see him.

The sunrise breaks through the window, and as though he's woven of gossamer, the warm light shines right through him. The texture of the pillow behind him slowly becomes more defined. I reach for him again, but I may as well be trying to capture the rays of a setting sun. I'm powerless to keep him here. So I gaze into his fading eyes through my tears and watch him grow more and more faint, until he's gone.

In a daze, I find myself at the beach where Kai rescued me last December. I stumble out of my car and shuffle toward the water to where the sand is wet and fizzing with the receding tide. A wave laps onto shore, and I step into the cold water. I sink to my knees and let it surround me like a mote, willing it to numb my pain.

This is his grave. The closest I can get to him now.

As the wave recedes, so does whatever energy remains inside me. Anguish presses down on me, and I have neither the strength or desire to resist. I lie down on the wet sand and close my eyes.

The sound of waves breaking roars in my ears. Cold water surrounds me, rising to my ears and filling them with sand and salt. I let it wash over me again and again, only because I can't move. I'm a forgotten sand castle, and I'm slowly disintegrating. Pieces of me are being swept out to sea, bit by bit, grain by grain, until there's nothing left.

28

KAI

In Demoror, it's silent on the shore of the silver lake. There's no breeze, no rustling leaves or singing birds, no sounds or smells of the earth. Only the weeping trees with their crystal blossoms surrounding the lake, and the fine white sand at my feet. I'm alone. Utterly alone. I'm wearing my white clothes again, and my feet are bare. My wrists and fingers are bare too, stripped of all my powers. And my hands are empty.

I think of Avery, of how I left her crying and terrified in the cottage. Desperate to see her, I kneel at the edge of the still, silver water. It's like a mirror that stretches as far as the eye can see.

"How is Avery?" I ask the water, my voice catching on her name.

I wait for the surface to ripple like it usually does before showing answers to my questions, but it doesn't even quiver. So this is my punishment for taking the ring. I can no longer receive answers from the lake.

And then I remember the consequence for revealing my identity as a dead person.

With dread, I stand up.

I try to step into the lake to enter the portal back to Earth. But my foot doesn't break the surface. It's solid now. Impenetrable. I take a few more steps to make sure. Then I jump, slamming my feet against the surface. But I may as well be standing on a sheet of steel.

There's no going back.

I sink to my knees and bow my head in anguish. What did I expect? I knew this would be my consequence, but I chose to break the rules anyway. She's lost to me now. I'll never see her again, not as long as she's on Earth. My chest seems to be caving in, and an emptiness spreads inside of me, a black hole consuming every speck of light. There's nothing more.

There's nothing more.

29

avery

omeone is stroking my hair. I want to open my eyes to see who it is, but my eyelids are too heavy. I don't know where I am or how I got here, but everything feels foreign. Something hard and bulky is stuck to my index finger, and I'm being smothered by warmth. It's on me and around me and shoved between every limb and joint. I try to place myself, to remember something. Anything. But it's like I'm standing on a beach in a thick predawn mist, and I can't see any landmarks to orient myself.

"Avery." A whisper breaks through the mist, gentle and concerned. More stroking on my head. The hand is trembling. And then I smell something like hand sanitizer and ammonia.

"I think she's coming around," someone else says. A female voice I don't recognize. And then I notice another sound. A rhythmic beeping, and a loud breath of relief.

"Avery?" This time I recognize the voice. It's one that always gives comfort. Dad.

My eyelids crack open, catching a glimpse of my surroundings before closing again. A hospital room. Just like Mom's. Pastel curtains and a purple upholstered chair by the window.

The woman speaks again, her voice close to me. "Her temperature is looking good, and her other vitals are stable. I think she's going to be okay."

Another sigh of relief from Dad. More stroking my hair. His warm hand on my arm. "I don't know what she was doing out there."

"Avery?" the woman says. "Do you remember what happened? What were you doing out there?"

Doing out where? My mind searches for something to ground myself to. For reality. I will the sun to rise, to burn off the mist, but it stubbornly stays hidden beneath the horizon.

I open my eyes. The nurse is pushing buttons on an IV pump, and Dad rubs my arm gently. "Sweetheart." He sounds exhausted, stretched to his limit. "What were you doing lying in the cold water at the beach?"

Water. And then I remember lying down in the sand. Bits and pieces of memories start surfacing in my mind. My fingers on Kai's neck, and no pulse. His hand under mine, feeling less solid than it should. Ocean water washing over my face, and my not having the strength to sit up. I squeeze my eyes shut and turn my face, burying it in my pillow. I don't know what's real and what's not.

"Let's give her some time," the nurse says. "Why don't you come out in the hall with me to discuss some things?"

Dad pats my arm. "I'll be back in a minute."

I hear their footsteps move across the room and the click of the door as it shuts behind them. Their muffled voices seep through the door from the hallway, and I catch words here and there.

Mom in the hospital too. Coping mechanisms. Hereditary. Counselor.

Maybe my worst fear is coming to pass, and I'm going crazy.

Maybe I imagined the last few days. It can't have really happened. Kai couldn't really be dead. He couldn't have disappeared in my arms. It's impossible. But if it didn't happen, that means I *am* losing my mind, and I can't accept that either.

Dad comes back without the nurse and pulls up a chair beside me, taking my hand in his. "Do you want to tell me what happened?" he says.

I shake my head. I can't piece it together in my mind, let alone put it into words. And even if I could, I would be sent straight to the psych unit because no one would believe me. I'm teetering on a fence between sanity and psychosis, between truth and delusion, and not even Dad's sturdy hand is enough to steady me.

30

avery

I've spent the last three weeks trying to make sense of everything that happened with Kai, and I've made only a small amount of headway. It's not like I can talk it out with anyone, and there's no one to ask the millions of questions crowding my thoughts.

It's drizzling today, and I sit curled up on a bench at the end of the deserted pier, watching swollen waves through the railing. Sitting in the rain helps me think. It shuts out the rest of the world, and the white noise drowns out the loudest of my thoughts and helps me focus on the quiet ones that are harder to hear. Usually the quiet ones are the most important.

I've been replaying the moments I spent with Kai, searching for clues as I see my memories in a new light. From the first time I saw him on the beach when he lent me his pocketknife to the moment he disappeared in my arms. I've read through his book of lyrics at least a dozen times, and I practically have all his lyrics memorized. And although I've slowly come to the conclusion that

Kai and everything that happened with him was real, the biggest questions, *how* and *why*, remain unanswered.

Everywhere I go, I see him. At the chocolate shop, at Mom's condo, on the beach, the pier, even in my car. I see the things he did, hear the words he said. Things that didn't make sense before make sense now. Like his reluctance to talk about himself. Or his efforts to get me back with Tyler. His parting words the first night we had dinner, *no regrets*, that at the time seemed so random. His abandoning a music career despite his incredible talent.

His still heart, when I hugged him close on the beach that day.

With numbered sunsets and bated breath, he sang to me at Tyler's party. *I'll swallow her tears; mend the unjust.*

And I heard him sing in the vineyard, *Forbid heaven to alter . . . for her, I would die but not falter.*

What about the words I overheard the night we found Mom unconscious? *I'm here to help Avery,* he said, *just for a little while.*

Slowly, all the pieces fall together like scattered stars moving into alignment. He knew me. Really knew me. He knew I was hurting, knew what I needed to be healed. To know that, he must have been watching me all along, ever since his death. He must have seen how his death affected me. And somehow, he found a way to return for a time to help me.

I'm suddenly filled with a love so immense I can't contain it. It grows and swells until it's ripping me apart from the inside out. Tears spill down my cheeks, mingling with the warm rain. I dip my head into my arms and let them come freely.

I wonder, if he saw me before, does that mean he can see me now? I go perfectly still, trying to sense any kind of presence around me. But other than the rain tapping on my head and arms, I feel nothing. I don't know how he was able to see me before, or how he was able to come back in the flesh for those few days. From some of the things he said and did, I get the sense he wasn't supposed to be here at all, that he broke some rule to come and help me. That his presence here was an anomaly, and he'll never be back again.

And then I do sense a presence. But when I turn around to see who it is, it's not Kai. It's Mom. She's huddled in her raincoat, her hair soaking up the rain and getting curlier by the second.

"Your dad said I could find you out here," she says, looking around and taking in our surroundings. She sits on the wet bench beside me. "I can appreciate the romantic setting, but what exactly are you doing out here, sitting alone in the rain?"

I shrug, sniffling a bit. "Just thinking. Trying to figure things out."

"What a great place for thinking." She says this with sincere enthusiasm, then closes her eyes and lifts her face to the sky, smiling as raindrops fall on her cheeks, forehead, and eyelids. It's good to see her back to herself. "So," she says, wiping the rain off her face and looking at me, blinking rapidly to keep the rain out of her eyes. "Let's figure things out together."

I've spent my whole life watching Mom trying to figure things out, so her offer doesn't give me much hope. She must know what I'm thinking, because her smile fades and she turns to watch the rain-pocked waves for a while. I watch too, not really knowing what to say.

Finally, she says, "I'm sorry for what happened last month. *So* sorry."

This is the first time either of us have brought it up. I've wanted to talk to her about it, but also wanted to wait until she was ready. That, and finding her lifeless body on her bedroom floor is one more thing I haven't quite processed yet.

"I know," I say.

She shakes her head slowly, then brings a hand to her forehead to shield her eyes from the rain. "I didn't intend for that to happen. You know, to end up in the hospital. To . . ."

"To almost die?" I finish for her.

She looks at me, eyes tormented. "I was just . . . hurting. *So* much. I took an extra pill. But it wasn't quite enough, so I took one more. And had a glass of wine. Or two. I don't remember. But the next thing I knew, I woke up in the hospital." Her hand falls on my knee. "You must be so angry with me."

I can't be angry with her. Because there's not much difference between what I did—lying in the cold waves and subjecting myself to hypothermia—and what she did. We were both just trying to numb our pain.

"I love you, Mom. No matter what. I'm glad you're okay. I'm glad you're still here with us."

She smiles sadly and wraps an arm around my shoulder, giving me a side hug and a kiss on the cheek. She lets out a sigh of relief, of finishing a difficult task. We go back to squinting at the waves through the rain, and then she says, "Life is precious, isn't it? It's sad that sometimes you have to almost lose it to realize that."

I think about Kai, how precious his life was. And how my life was so precious to him that he gave his up for it. My throat starts burning, and new tears prick my eyes. I glance over to the place where he stood beside me on this pier, where I felt his warm fingers brush my cheek, and heard him say, *Have you ever thought that maybe he doesn't regret what he did? That saving you was the crowning moment of his life?*

I bite down hard on my lip, but it doesn't stop me from bursting into tears. Mom pulls me into her arms, rubbing my back as I clutch her and sob into her neck. In all my reckless adventures, I've been injured countless times. Cuts, scrapes, bruises, sprains, broken bones. Some injuries take longer to recover from than others. But I don't think I'm ever going to recover from this.

"I'm so sorry, Avery."

She thinks this is about her. Maybe it is, a little. I don't try to correct her, because there's no way I can tell her what this is really about. So I just cry, and cry, and cry, putting the rain clouds to shame.

Finally Mom pulls back so she can look in my eyes. I take a stuttering breath, trying to calm myself.

"I want to live, Avery," Mom says. "I mean, *really* live." She looks at me as though she's about to offer a challenge. "But I can't do it alone. Help me? Embrace life with me?"

I recall all the times Kai pleaded with me to live my life to its fullest. *He gave his life so you could live,* he said to me on this very pier. *So live.*

That's all Kai wants from me in return. So I take Mom's hand and weave my fingers through hers. "Okay," I say. "I will." For my mom, for me, but most of all, for Kai.

31

KAI

There's no way to measure time in Demoror. No day or night, just a fixed sky full of stars that shine so brightly it's like a thousand small suns scattered across the sky. So I don't know how long I've been wandering the shores of Demoror. All I know is I've never seen so much of it. Like Earth, it's beautiful. Just in a different way. Where Earth is distorted and gritty and broken like a rock band, Demoror is flawless and smooth and clean like a symphony. The sand under my bare feet is fine and pure, no broken shells or fragments of trash like on Earth.

Up ahead, a man emerges from the silver lake. He looks disoriented, like most people do when passing from the living world for the first time. A handful of people are gathered on the shore to greet him, and he wades out of the lake into their welcoming embrace. It hurts to see, so I hurry past, tuning out their laughter and rejoicing. It makes me ache for my mom. Even now, no one can tell me where she is. So most of the time, I try not to think about her.

Since I was brought back here, I've seen countless people come and go through the silver lake of Demoror. Mostly people who've just died. Some head straight to the towering cliffs of Elysium, and some slink off to the Briar across the lake because for whatever reason, they're most comfortable in the dark. Others hang around the shore, waiting for something. Waiting to go back to Earth while their body is healed, or waiting to receive an assignment, or waiting until they feel ready to move on to Elysium.

When I first died, I never used Demoror as my waiting place. Because every time I was here, I felt restless and out of place, as though I'd stepped into a fine restaurant wearing board shorts. So I spent all of my time between assignments with Avery. She was my home base, my Demoror. I was her silent companion. Her invisible friend. The one she talked to when she thought she was talking to only herself. The one who talked to her even when she couldn't hear me. It made me feel like I wasn't alone.

Now I'm alone again, but I can no longer find comfort in her company. Maybe I shouldn't have done what I did. Maybe I made things worse for her. If I'd given her time, she probably would've healed on her own. She would have found happiness again. Instead, I gave her one more wound to heal from. And now I'm stuck here, with no connection to Earth, no access to the people I love. I can't even glimpse them through the silver lake.

So I keep strolling, not knowing what else to do while I wait for Avery and Helen and Jane for the next few decades. I watch the stirrings of the water as I go, the endless procession of comings and goings reminding me of a wooden plaque that hung in one of my foster family's living room that read in cutesy hand-painted lettering, *Life never ends. It just moves from one place to the next.* At the time I thought it was absurd. But who knew a stupid little plaque could hold so much truth?

And the truth is that in their own time, Avery and my sisters will move to where I am. The thought should bring me comfort, but for some reason it makes me feel like someone is twisting a knife in my heart.

The lake begins to curve after a while, and the fringes of the Briar slowly rise on the horizon like a storm cloud. I pause and look back the way I came, realizing how far I've traveled. When I began walking, I was near the cliffs of Elysium. Now from where I stand, their majestic height rises far above the gentle hills and crystal trees across the lake. I can just make out the shimmering, iridescent waterfall that souls pass through to enter Elysium. The one Charles always tries and fails to convince me to enter. The distance makes me feel a bit uneasy. But I can always quicken back in an instant if I want to.

Only, when I consider it, I find I have no desire to. All I feel like doing right now is moving farther away. Away from other people. Away from light. Away from anything that might require me to let go of the things I'm trying so hard to hold on to.

I look back at the Briar, feeling a strange sort of beckoning. Maybe it's curiosity. Or maybe it's the despair inside of me knowing it will feel more at home there than in Elysium. Whatever it is, I surrender to the pull and keep walking toward the Briar.

As I get closer, the land gets more barren. The grass grows more patchy and blanched, and I'm surprised to see rugged rocks jutting out of the sand. It's more Earth-like on this side of the lake. It's also colder, like late autumn in the Upper Peninsula.

I keep moving, and soon the sand turns hard and sharp, broken rocks littering the ground like shattered dishes. They jab the soles of my bare feet, and I welcome the pain. It's feeling *something*. Like being alive again.

I feel a particularly sharp pain, so I pause and lift the sole of my foot for a look. I'm surprised to see several cuts marking the bottom of my foot. Strange. There's no blood, of course. Not even the clear liquid of a materialized body. I shrug it off and continue.

But it occurs to me that maybe the soul is made of some type of matter, only too fine for mortal eyes to see.

The Briar's thorny vines begin encroaching on the crystal trees, like arms reaching out to capture anything light. I stop at the edge of a trench as wide as I am tall, and so deep I can't see the bottom. This alone should stop me from going farther. But I'm already dead, so I don't fear falling. I do wonder what would happen if I fell, but my imagination doesn't come up with anything bad enough to worry me.

I back up a few paces, run, and leap over the trench, landing hard on the opposite side. A few more steps, and then I'm standing at the fringe of the Briar. So close that if I hold out my hand it will be sucked into the shadows.

I gaze into the black and untamed thicket, thorny bushes and gaunt trees leaning on one another as though the darkness here saps even the vegetation's strength. Something in the shadows, in the thistles and tangled undergrowth, speaks to me. Tells me that my pain and sorrow is welcome here. That I belong here. It invites me to come in. To surrender to the shadows and dwell in them. From where I stand, it seems like such an appealing invitation.

But then I feel something else. Something rearing inside of me in resistance and objection. Experience and knowledge, gained from the life I lived on Earth. I lived in darkness as a child, and there was nothing comforting or appealing about it. Nothing that felt like *home*. The more I surrendered to it, the more painful it became. And I know now that there is something better than darkness.

I close my eyes and allow my thoughts to drift back to my last day with Avery. I feel her caring fingers on my face. The love, the healing that flowed from her and into me. And then I ask myself, *If that's the alternative to darkness, what am I doing here?*

I open my eyes and turn around to leave, and Charles is standing right behind me. I fall back a step in surprise.

He reaches out to catch me by the shirt, as though afraid I'll stumble backward into the Briar. When he's convinced I'll stay upright, he releases me. "You scared me for a minute there," he says. His face is worried, and has grown even younger since the last time I saw him. He looks maybe in his late forties now, and if I hadn't been observing his transformation over the past months, I wouldn't even recognize him.

"Don't tell me you've been watching me."

He gives a small guilty smile. "Only keeping tabs." He scowls over my shoulder at the Briar like it's a drug dealer who just tried to sell me crack. "Why don't you come with me and we'll have a talk. Like old times."

I shrug in agreement, and we quicken away from the Briar to where the lakeshore is smooth again, and find a place to sit under the branches of one of the weeping trees.

"You have a decision to make," he says when we settle on a patch of soft blue grass.

I'm sitting cross-legged, and I notice that the soles of my feet are already completely healed. "About what?"

"What to do next."

I let my eyes sweep over the expanse of the silver lake, from where it touches the rocky banks of the Briar to the other end where it holds a perfect reflection of the majestic cliffs of Elysium. "I've already decided. I'm waiting."

"Kai, you can't just do nothing until Avery comes. You could be waiting for decades. And by then . . . she may have—"

"Don't say it." I drop my head in my hands. "I know. I realize I'm being overly optimistic. But I'm waiting anyway."

"It's not just that she might not be . . . *available* when she comes. You're putting yourself in danger."

I lift my head. "How so?"

"Those who linger too long on the banks of Demoror tend to get . . . lost."

I know what he means even before he nods in the direction

of the Briar. I felt the darkness trying to lure me inside moments ago. I sigh. "If I leave the lake, what if I miss her when she comes?"

"You'll know when she gets here."

I raise a curious eyebrow. "How?"

"The same way you found her on Earth." He motions to his chest. "You'll feel it here. That connection, that pull, between you and those you love. You only have to be paying attention."

Maybe he's right. When I went back to Earth to help Avery, I could always sense when she was near. At least when I was paying attention. My chest aches now with the desire to see her again. "Charles," I say, "can I see her? Just once?"

He lets out a tired sigh. "Remember our deal, Kai."

"I only want to see if she's okay. She's got to have a million questions after what she saw."

He gives me a wary look. "What did she see, exactly?"

"Well, I showed her I didn't have a heartbeat. She passed out." I wince. "And then . . . I sort of disappeared in her arms."

He shakes his head slowly, maybe because he can't quite grasp the mess I've gotten myself into.

"Can't you just . . . show me one glimpse in the lake?" I ask.

"No."

"Then . . . can you pay her a visit and explain things so she doesn't think she's losing her mind?"

He rubs his knee for a long moment, and then shakes his head. "I can't do that. I broke the rules by letting you keep the ring those three days. Please don't ask me to do anything else."

"But this isn't a big deal. It's a little conversation. Please."

His mouth sets in a firm line. I know the look. It's the look of immovability. "No. You promised. I gave you three days, and you promised to let her go. I kept my end of the deal. Now it's your turn to keep yours."

My shoulders sink, and I shut my eyes and clench my jaw in frustration at my powerlessness. I know he's right, though. No matter how hard it is, I made him a promise, and it's time for me to keep it.

He pats me on the shoulder. "What you need is something to keep you busy. So, I have a new job to offer you."

I blink in surprise, hope rising in my chest. "I thought I couldn't go back to Earth."

He shakes his head. "It's not on Earth."

"Oh." I look down at the grass and run my toe through it, hoping he won't see how disappointed I am. "What's the job?"

He pulls something out of his pocket. A pendant attached to a fine silver chain. The pendant appears to be a raw crystal with a shimmering vein of light coiled inside.

"Wow," I say, fascinated by the glimmering thread inside the crystal. "What does that do?"

He hands it to me. "Here—put it on and you'll see."

I take it and hang it around my neck. As soon as it touches my chest, the crystal lights up like a halogen light, practically blinding me. I flinch at the unexpected brilliance and cover it with my hand so that I can open my eyes again. "Whoa. What is this job, exactly? Dental assistant?"

Charles smiles at my dumb joke, and then his face goes serious. "It's dark in the Briar. Sometimes all people need is a bit of light to find their way out."

I stare at him. "Weren't you just saying how worried you were that I'd get lost in there?"

He nods at the pendant. "You won't get lost as long as you're wearing that."

I look back toward the Briar, an eerie sense of dread coming over me. "And what's my assignment?"

"It's simple, in theory. You're a guide. The goal is to lead people out of the Briar and bring them back here to the lakeshore."

"What happens when they get here?"

"That's when a mentor will be assigned to them, like I was assigned to you. They'll be offered a job and more guidance."

I gaze at the Briar, considering. It seems like such a dreary job. Especially after standing at the edge of the Briar and feeling how strong the dark pull was. If I go in, I don't know if I'll have the strength to handle it, even with the pendant. What if I never find my way back out?

Charles must see my hesitation, because he says, "You don't have to accept the job, but if you don't, you'll need to come with me to Elysium. There are other things for you to do there."

I inhale a deep breath and exhale slowly, unsure what to do. "Charles," I say, "is there music in Elysium?"

He regards me a moment, pursing his lips. "Why don't you come there with me and see for yourself? You won't be disappointed."

"And if I do, I'll know when Avery gets here?"

"Yes. My wife was in Elysium when I came, and she knew right away."

Maybe it's time to stop resisting. I don't know why I'm so afraid to go there. Maybe I fear I won't belong. Or maybe I've gotten used to Demoror, and I don't like change. Or maybe it's one step farther from Avery. But as I consider the alternative, I can't imagine stepping inside the dark Briar. I stand and remove the glowing pendant and hand it back to Charles. I nod at him, wordlessly telling him that I've chosen to go to Elysium.

He stands and lays a hand on my shoulder, and we quicken away. At the place where we stop, the cliffs of Elysium rise from our feet to the sky. The pearlescent white rock is smooth like polished opal, and the waterfall entrance to Elysium appears to fall in slow motion. There's no mist or splashing when it hits the ground, no pool to collect the water. It simply vanishes into the ground, like a thread being pulled through fabric. I've never seen it from this close before, and I'm mesmerized by the strange movement of the water. Like a thousand-foot-long curtain gently undulating in the breeze. I tip my head back, following the waterfall to its source. But it's so high I can't see it. It just fades into a shimmering blur.

"You ready?" Charles asks. He's standing beside me, his face encouraging.

I look back the way we came, since I didn't really see any of it when we quickened here. We're in a sort of circular courtyard, closed in by a low rock wall. The ground is heavily sprinkled with little sparkling flowers the color of Avery's eyes. Beyond the wall, the land gracefully drops and expands into wide grassy fields and groves of crystal trees. If this is what's on the outside of Elysium, I can only imagine what I'll find inside.

I turn back to the waterfall, then reach out and hesitantly touch the hazy water. A surge of peace flows from the waterfall into me. I close my eyes, reveling at the warmth that fills my chest. It reminds me of the way I felt when Avery touched me. Or when I heard her voice say my name. It's the feeling I've ached for since returning to Demoror. Like touching the doorknob of a home filled with the people I love. Like hearing my little sisters laugh. Like my mother's embrace.

"Charles," I say, turning to him, "where's my mom? I . . . I can't move on until I know for sure."

His expression turns careful, then grave. He holds up a finger. "Wait here for a minute." He turns and steps into the waterfall, and it swallows him up. I want to follow, to hear for myself the answer to my question. But he asked me to stay, so I keep my feet planted.

A few minutes later, he emerges from the waterfall and steps up to me. "They said you're strong enough now."

"Strong enough for what?"

"To know where she is."

Something sinks inside of me, and I'm suddenly afraid to learn the answer. Because I already know where she is.

He dips into his pocket and retrieves the guide pendant, handing it to me. "If you want to find your mom, you'll need this."

32

avery

'i've been parked across the street from Kai's sisters' house for thirty minutes, trying to summon the courage to go knock on their door. It's a late July afternoon, and the sun filters through the big tree in their front yard, casting fluttery shadows on the white clapboard. It's also shining through my windshield, heating up the inside of my Cherokee, and beads of sweat are gathering on my forehead and making my palms slick.

I've known for weeks now who died saving my life, and I've yet to tell anyone. Sometimes I think it would be better if no one ever found out. But his sisters must know that Kai is missing, and the uncertainty of his whereabouts must torment them. They'll be devastated to find out what happened to him, but at least they'll know the truth.

I gaze at the lace curtains and bite my nails, wondering how on earth I'm going to get through this. More than anything, I want to turn my car around and leave. I could go to the sheriff's detective instead and tell him that I finally recognized Kai on a missing persons report. And then he can be the one to tell Kai's family.

I try to think what Kai would want. Would he want his sisters to hear it from a cop? Or from the girl whose life he saved, who can give the details of how their brother died a hero? Maybe that's why he left his aunt and uncle's address in the book of lyrics he gave me, because he wanted me to be the one to tell them.

But really, I don't know what he would want. I only know what I want. And as crazy as it is, I want to tell them myself.

With a trembling hand, I pull the handle and push the door open. It's a good thing I haven't been able to eat all day, because I would be losing the contents of my stomach right about now. With every step toward their house, I have to find my courage all over again. Every muscle in my body is tense and trembling. Except my heart, which is robustly throbbing in my chest. I cross the street and drift up their driveway past a navy SUV. And then I'm standing on their porch. The door is painted the color of rust and a heart-shaped wreath hangs on it. The lacy curtains in the window are drawn, and I stand there for a minute, stalling, listening for noises on the other side of the door as I try to remember what I'm going to say.

I knock on the door. I've practiced the words a thousand times in my head, yet I feel so unprepared for this. The door opens way too soon, and there stands Kai's sister. I know it's her because she has the same blue-green eyes, and her curious expression is the same one I've seen on Kai's face dozens of times. Suddenly my throat is closing up, and I have to bite the inside of my cheek to keep from bursting into tears. I can't talk, can't look away, can't do anything but stand there and try not to see Kai in her face.

Her brows pull together, and she takes a small step toward me. "Um . . . are you okay?"

I nod, swallowing hard, even though I'm far from okay. "Are you Hannah?" I ask, my voice a pitch higher than usual.

She tucks a piece of long hair behind her ear. Her hair is much darker than Kai's, like Dad's darkest chocolate. "Yeah. Why?"

I take a deep breath. "I'm Avery. I was wondering if I could talk to you for a bit."

"About what?" Her tone is impatient, and her gaze is wandering down the street. She probably thinks I'm a solicitor or something. And she's holding a pair of black socks, as though she's getting ready to go somewhere.

"About your brother."

"Kai?" She perks up, giving me her full attention.

"Yes. Kai." I wince when I say his name.

Her hand goes to her stomach, where it clutches her snug black T-shirt. "What is it?"

I peer over her shoulder into her house, but don't see anyone else. Just a shiny tile floor and a black upright piano. "Is Jane here?"

"No. She's at karate."

I want to tell them both. But I'm here, and Hannah knows I have something to tell her about Kai, so I can't say, "Never mind, I'll come back later." I gesture to the porch steps. "Can we sit down?" My legs are shaking, and there's no way I'm getting through this standing up.

She steps outside and shuts the door behind her, and we both sit on the top step. She turns toward me, anxiously picking at a frayed hole in her skinny jeans. "Is he in trouble?"

It's so hard to look at her. Not only because she reminds me of Kai, but because I can see in her eyes how much she loves him. What I have to tell her is going to hurt. But if I were her, I'd want to know.

"He saved my life," I say reverently. "I went surfing one day, and got into trouble, and he jumped in the water to save me."

She smiles, but her face is still worried. "That sounds like something he'd do."

I nod in agreement, knowing for myself how selfless a person

Kai is. I take a deep breath, because the hardest part is next. "It was during a storm." I'm trying so hard to keep my voice steady, but I'm failing miserably. "We were both hanging onto my surfboard, but then he got swept off by a wave and he . . . he didn't resurface." My voice is so small when I say the last part that I'm not sure she heard me. But then her hand comes to her mouth, and I know she heard loud and clear.

"What do you mean?" Her face goes even paler than her already milky complexion.

"I'm so sorry," I whisper, bracing her with a hand on her thin arm. "He didn't . . . he didn't make it back to shore."

"What?" Her eyes fill with tears, and she shakes her head in disbelief. "Are you telling me he's . . ."

I nod once, unable to say the words because my throat has closed up again. She understands my meaning, because she drops her head into her hands and starts crying. And then I'm crying too, and I blanket an arm over her, doing my best to comfort her, even though I know there's nothing that will ease her pain.

"When?" she asks between stuttering breaths.

"Last December. But I didn't find out who he was until recently, because . . . they never found his body."

She sits up straight, her mouth open as though she's astonished by something I just said. "December? Wait a minute." She settles a hand over her chest, seeming relieved. "I just saw him last month." In one breath, her expression has changed from anguish to elation.

"What?"

"Yeah—he came here in June." She wipes the tears from her cheeks. "It was a short visit, but he was here."

"Oh." Of course he came to visit his sisters while he was here. This is a complication I didn't prepare for, and now I have no idea what to say. I can't exactly tell her that he was dead when he visited her.

"Are you sure he was the one who saved you?" she asks. "You said you just found out who he was. So what made you think it was him?"

"I . . . recognized him in a missing persons database," I say numbly.

"Well then . . . he survived." She takes a big breath of relief, then clutches my shoulder and smiles. "He's a runaway. And supposed to be in foster care. At least for a few more months until he turns eighteen. So he probably took off when he got back to shore because he didn't want to get caught." She's looking at me like she's waiting for me to rejoice with her. I try to smile, but instead, my face crumples and I break down in tears. She wraps her arms around me and now she's the one rubbing *my* back. "I know. Geez, that must have been horrible for you these last few months, thinking the guy who saved you was dead."

This only makes me cry harder, and even though I'm a complete stranger to her, she lets me hold her and cry into her shoulder. It's so bittersweet to have his sister in my arms. They share the same blood, or did, when he was alive. She's the only person I've met that really knows him. I wish I could tell her how much I love him, just how much he means to me. I want to tell her everything he did for me, even after saving my life. And I want her to tell me everything she knows about him, to share all her memories of him. Because that would make him more real to me, more alive.

"Hey," she says soothingly, leaning away so she can see my face. "Do you want me to tell him you're looking for him? I can give him your contact info the next time I see him. I don't know when that'll be, but hopefully soon."

I take a deep, shuddery breath. "Sure." Because what else can I say? And then I realize that Hannah and Jane will never know what became of their brother. No one will know except me. And it doesn't matter what I tell the detective now. If I tell him that it was Kai who saved me, then they'll assume he survived when they talk to his sisters. I can never tell anyone the truth. This is a secret I'll carry with me until the day I die.

Hannah has her cell phone out, a blank contact screen open. "Okay. What did you say your name was?"

I indulge her and give her my contact information, not only to keep up the charade, but also because maybe this can be the beginning of a friendship, a meaningful connection to the boy I'll always love.

When she's done entering my information, I stand to leave, but then pause. "Hannah," I say, "can you tell me about your brother? I'd love to know something about the boy who saved my life."

33

KAI

The moment I step into the Briar, I'm swallowed up in shadows. I hold up my pendant like a lantern, but even then, the light reaches only a few feet around me before being absorbed into the dark. I'm reminded of the times I played Hide and Go Scare in the woods back in Michigan with my foster siblings. I always won because, not only was I not afraid of the dark, but a kid jumping out from behind a tree was nothing compared to the real terrors I'd already experienced.

Only, this place is darker than any earthly woods, and I *am* scared. Scared of the unknown, of things foreign and unfamiliar. Scared that I won't be able to find my mom, and that even if I do, I won't be able to bring her out.

Charles didn't say exactly where I could find her, only that I'd be able to feel where she was. So I pause and listen. Not for sound, but for direction. For the path that leads to her. I visualize her face and concentrate on my desire to find her, and after a moment, I feel a tugging in the center of my chest. Like I'm standing near a magnetic field and my ribs are made of iron. I don't know how far away she is, but she's somewhere off to my left. I'm tempted to quicken to her, but Charles warned me not to, saying that the thorns would slash into me, similar to how the rocks cut my feet.

So I move slowly toward her, stepping over fallen branches and around patches of twisted growth. Sometimes I have to backtrack when the vague path comes to a dead end. Every now and then, I see shadowy movements in the thicket, or ambiguous shapes slinking across my path. And sometimes through the trees, I see the glowing pendants of other guides. Eventually I cross paths with one of them, and we acknowledge each other with a nod. A man trails behind him, looking afraid and uncertain, his eyes darting about as if he's expecting a monster to leap out of the shadows. "Keep your eyes on me," the guide says, and the man refocuses and seems to calm a bit.

The sight gives me hope, so I forge on, constantly seeking the unseen path toward my mom. I wonder what she'll look like when I find her. Will she be renewed and young again, the way Charles has changed? Or will she look the same as the day she died—fragile and spent, like a quivering autumn leaf barely clinging to a tree? I shut the image out and instead think of the times I saw her happy. Like when I brought home some clothes for Hannah and Jane and told my mom that the neighbors donated them. My guilt over stealing them came the next day, but I never told Mom the truth because I didn't want to spoil her happiness.

Or like the time I was seven and came home from school with a note from the principal and a bloody lip. She sat me down in the bathroom to clean me up, and as she dabbed a moist washcloth on my lip, she asked, "You wanna tell me what this was about?" I told her the truth, how I tackled some fifth grader because he was making fun of Hannah's hair. Mom gently laid her callused fingers on the back of my neck and gave me one of those rare smiles that reached her eyes. "That's what I love about you most, Kai. You always look out for the people you love."

And then there was the time she rallied enough courage to leave Dad, and she packed me and my sisters in our old Plymouth

Duster and drove all the way to San Luis Obispo to live with my aunt. I still remember watching her from the backseat as we flew down the highway with all the windows rolled down. Her hair whipping in the wind, her face full of possibilities, like a prisoner set free.

It didn't last long though. Whether it was Dad she missed or the drugs he provided, three weeks later we were back on the road, returning to Michigan.

Even then, she had trouble untangling herself from the dark.

The land has been sloping downward for what feels like weeks. Or maybe it's been days or hours, I really don't know. That's the thing about forever—time is irrelevant.

The shadows have started whispering to me, not piercing my ears, but somewhere deeper and more fragile. *Turn back*, they say. *You'll never find her. This is where she belongs.* I try to tune it out, but there's nothing else to listen to. *Take off your pendant and stay here. This is where you belong.* Desperate to fill my mind with something else, I start singing quietly to myself. I sing the songs I wrote for Avery, picturing her smiling face and imagining the warmth of her hand in mine. I cling to the hope that I'll see her again someday, and for a while the thought chases away the shadows.

Until through the bushes, I hear someone cry out in pain.

It's a man, but the way he's crying sounds almost childlike. Then I hear laughter and another man's mocking voice. I can't hear what he's saying, but I follow the voices, my interest piqued.

Whoever it is, I don't want them to see me. So I tuck my pendant under my shirt and follow the wailing and laughing. A bit of light still seeps out, and I can see only as much as I could on a moonless night on Earth. The land continues sloping downward, and the ground begins to feel moist. My feet sink into it with each step, and the slope is so steep I have to hold onto shrubs and branches to keep myself from slipping.

Through a narrow window between the trees, I see the land dip into a swampy area. At the lowest point, there's an enormous dead tree, its sprawling, lifeless roots attached to their reflections in the murky, dark water. I stay hidden in the trees, watching from the shadows.

A thin, gangly man kneels at the water's edge, hunched over and moaning in agony.

The other person, a husky beast of a man with wiry hair sprouting from everywhere except his eyes and nose, stands beside him. "I told you," he says gruffly between jeering barks of laughter. "Not everyone can handle it. But if you want to go back to Earth, it's the only way."

This gets my attention, and without a moment's thought, I step out of the trees and slide down the slick hill to the level ground where they are. The man's laughter halts. He falls back a step, startled, like I'm a cop crashing his kegger. I step to the edge of the murky water, a few feet from the two men.

"Is this a portal to Earth?" I ask, my mind suddenly spinning with possibilities.

The big man regards me a moment, looks me up and down like he's sizing me up. His lips twist into a smile. "Sure is." He tips his bushy head toward the water. "Why don't you try it out?"

I'm not sure I believe him. I pull out my pendant so I can see the water better. Both men grimace and cover their eyes with their soiled hands.

"Put that thing away!" the big man shouts, spitting in disgust.

But I don't put it away. I hold it over the water. Beneath the glassy surface, the water swirls and writhes like smoke.

The man must see my wariness because he says, "What? You don't trust me?"

I look at him. "No. I don't."

"Here—I'll show you." Without hesitation, he steps to the water's edge and jumps in, vanishing beneath the surface. There's no splash, only a few small ripples circling his point of entry.

The other man, who is still on his knees, stares at the water fearfully as though it might reach up and grab him.

"Is it really a portal to Earth?" I ask, sensing that I can trust this man more than the other.

"It's not worth it." He drops his head and rubs his eyes with the heel of his hands, then cries, "I can't get the images out of my head."

"What images?"

The man doesn't answer, just rises and shambles away, scrubbing his eyes with his fists as he vanishes into the shadows.

The water ripples again, and the big man emerges and steps back onto the bank. His clothes are dry, and he dusts off his shoulders before looking at me. "See? Perfectly safe."

My curiosity winning over, I drop to my knees. The ground is spongy, and my knees sink in. I hold the pendant over the murky water again and watch the swirls of black weave into one another, snaking around and around. Fascination overrules my wariness, and I reach out a finger, hesitantly dipping it in the water.

Immediately, I'm jolted to a time and place entirely different, but nauseatingly familiar. I'm hiding under a sheet in a dark room. The smell of cigarette smoke burns the back of my throat. Dad's footsteps thunder across the room, and he growls my name before clamping his hand on my arm.

I jerk away from the swamp and stumble backward on my elbows as though I'm still in that room, ten years ago.

As though amused by my terror, the man bursts into laughter. It echoes off the trees, the sky, the hollowness of my insides.

I don't understand what just happened, and I look to him for an answer as though he might actually give me a straight one. But he just keeps laughing, so I stand up and step over to him. My pendant lights up his face like a flashlight under his chin.

Maybe something about me scares him, because his face clears and he stops laughing.

"What is this place?" I ask through clenched teeth.

He rubs his overgrown beard between his hands like it's a stick and he's trying to start a fire. "They say it's like a cesspool, where the worst memories drain to."

I give him a dubious look. "And it's connected to Earth?"

He laughs again, loud and raucous and sneering, like he thinks I'm the biggest idiot that ever existed. "Where do you think the worst memories come from?" He slugs me in the shoulder, and I fall back a step. "Not everyone can handle it," he says again. "But for most of us here, it's the only way back to Earth."

My thoughts go to Avery, to how it would be to see her again, even if she couldn't see me. Would being near her again be worth reliving the anguish of my childhood?

"Go on," the man says. "There's someone you want to see, isn't there? A girl, I bet, from the ache in your eyes. I bet she's pretty. Don't you want to see her again?"

I kneel at the water's edge again, gazing into the water. "How long does it take? To go through?"

"Seconds. Technically." He makes a raspy and gruff coughing sound, then points to his head. "But the perception of time is all in here. Depends on your memories."

How many memories would I have to relive to get to Avery? A handful? A dozen? All of them? However many, it would be worth it just to see her once more. I stretch out my hand again and lean forward, on the verge of diving in.

But something stops me. The same thing that kept me from stepping into the Briar before I had the pendant.

Experience. Discernment between darkness and light. And as I see my glowing pendant reflected in the black water, I remember why I came into the Briar to begin with.

I rise to my feet and leave the swamp behind, the man's laughter fading as I move farther away.

As I refocus my effort to find my mom, I feel a pull stronger than ever. Holding up my pendant, I move through a grove of enormous dead trees, their barren branches twisting into one another as if trying to tear the other down. A dark mist blankets the ground, swirling at my feet with each step.

She's close. I feel her presence like heat from a fire. I follow the warmth, peering into the dark spaces between the trees for a sign of her. "Mom," I mouth silently, so anxious to find her that I'm practically tripping over my feet.

From the corner of my eye, I see a streak of color. Pastel blue. But when I turn, it's gone. I stand still, watching the trees, waiting to see it again. And then I do, moving from behind one tree to another. It flows and ripples as it moves, like thin fabric. It beckons to me, the little bit of color in all this gray. And then it disappears behind a tree again. I move toward it, and when I see it again, I realize what it is. A woman's dress. She's striding through the grove.

Even without seeing her face, I know who she is.

"Mom," I whisper. I step toward her, and a twig snaps under my foot. She whips around, and I glimpse her face. Her eyes are full of fear, just like the last time I saw her alive. And then she turns and runs away.

"Wait!" I call out, rushing after.

She loses me easily, and I find myself deep in the grove, turning in a circle. I pause to feel for her, and then follow the pull to an enormous trunk. There's a jagged opening on one side, and when I lean down to peer inside I see the hem of her blue dress.

"Go away!" she cries, her voice shaking with terror.

I don't want to scare her, but there's no way I'm leaving now. I drop to my knees, the pendant's light pouring into the hollow. It's about as big as a two-man dome tent, and she's sitting in a nook, knees pulled up, head buried in her arms. Her dark hair spills over her arm like a waterfall.

It's been nine years since I've seen her, since I've felt her arms around me, since I've heard her soothing voice. The sight of her now, afraid and alone in the dark, shatters me. If I'd known, I would have come sooner. It occurs to me that maybe that's the reason they didn't tell me before where she was. Charles said I wasn't strong enough until now. Maybe he was right. If I'd come into the Briar to find my mom when I first died, I would have never found my way out.

"Don't be afraid." As I say the words, my mind is flooded with all the times I've heard others say those words in vain to her.

Don't be afraid to leave your husband.

Don't be afraid to go to school and make a better life for yourself and your kids.

Don't be afraid to battle your addictions, to find better ways of coping with your pain.

It was fear of pain that ultimately killed her. The need to numb it by any means. "I won't hurt you. I only want to talk. Will you come out?"

She doesn't budge, just stays huddled in her nook. "Leave me alone," she says, her voice muffled under her arms. "You're wasting your time."

Cautiously, I crawl inside and pause a couple feet from her. Rocking back on my knees, I say softly, "Mom."

Her head snaps up, and her eyes slowly widen as they travel over my face. She makes a sound of disbelief, and her fingers come to her lips. "Kai?" she whispers beneath her fingers. Then she reaches out to touch my face. Her fingers are cold on my cheek. "What are you doing here?"

"I'm here for you." I reach out, but she recoils as though my hand is a python.

For a long moment, she stares at me as though trying to decide how she feels about me being here. "You shouldn't be here," she finally says. "You don't deserve it."

"Neither do you. I came to take you out of here."

She shakes her head, then sinks farther into the shadows and goes back to hiding her face.

This isn't going to be as easy as I imagined. I slump back against the inside of the hollow, sitting on black dirt and wood shavings. My mom is so close I could reach out and take her hand, but for some reason she doesn't seem to want that. So I clasp my hands together and try to ignore the ache in my chest that's growing more intense by the second. "Mom," I say quietly, my voice pained, "don't you want to leave this place?"

In her hand, she clutches the fabric of her skirt and kneads it between her fingers as though it sooths her. "It's not that simple. If all it took to get out of here was desire, there would be no one in the Briar." Her hand goes still. "Though, for a long time after I came here, I didn't want to leave." She slowly lifts her head, but doesn't meet my eyes. "I was so . . . sad. I didn't want to face anyone. Especially you and your sisters, because of the pain I knew I caused you. But being here—there's nothing to do. Nothing to take my mind off things." Her eyes rise to a spot in the hollow, and I follow her gaze. Where the wood is smooth, faint images have been carved. I squint and lean closer, trying to see what they are. Faces. Round and childlike. Two girls and one boy.

"All I've thought about since I came here," she continues, "is you and Helen and Jane. I've wondered how you are, if you ever healed, or if you were still hurting. And if you were safe. And I've thought how, if I could just get out of here, then maybe I could find out." She looks at me then, and her eyes wander over my face, studying me. "Kai—how long have I been in the Briar?"

I know why she's asking. She wants to know how old I was when I died. "It doesn't matter," I say, not wanting to dampen her spirits even more with the details of my death. "All that matters is that I'm here." I grasp my pendant. "I can help you out of here."

She shuts her eyes and grimaces, then shakes her head. "It's not that easy. There have been others like you who've tried to help me out. But . . . even with the light . . ." Fear seeps into her eyes. "You don't understand." She lowers her gaze, suddenly looking detached. "You should go," she says without looking at me. "Get out while you still can."

"I'm not leaving without you."

As she meets my eyes again, her expression turns pleading.

"Don't ask me to go. You don't know how much it hurts when I try to leave. I'm not strong enough. I've never been strong, even when I was alive. If I had been, I would've made different choices. I would have made a better life for you. I wouldn't have died and left you alone with your dad."

I reach for her hand, and this time she doesn't pull back. She lets my fingers wrap around hers. "You were always stronger than you gave yourself credit for. I know you did the best you could. But all of that is in the past. What matters is *now*. This isn't the end. Your life isn't over. You have another chance here, to make a better life for yourself." I tug her gently toward me. "Come with me. I'll lead you out of here, to somewhere light and warm. You'll be given something to do. Something that will make you happy. You'll be able to help other people."

"I can't," she whispers, shaking her head. "I'm too afraid."

She doesn't have to tell me what she's afraid of. Because I don't think her fears have changed since she died. She's afraid that if she leaves the darkness, she'll eventually be pulled back in, and all her effort will be for nothing. For years I watched her try to quit drugs, or quit Dad, and it was like scaling a vertical mountain without a harness. She fell with every attempt, and the wasted effort, the pain of each fall, kept her from trying again.

A sort of longing spreads over her features. "I just want to know if you and your sisters are happy. If I can know that, then it doesn't matter if I'm trapped here. I'll be at peace. So tell me— give me that peace."

I feel my own hope dwindling. I can't save her now, just like I couldn't save her back then. I can't pick her up and carry her out of the Briar any more than my eight-year-old arms could carry her out of Dad's house. Because if she truly believes that this is where she belongs, she'll come back. Only she can decide to leave. All I can do is light the path, and try to convince her that she deserves something better.

"Do you know what would make me happy?" I say. "You

know what I or Helen or Jane have always wanted more than anything? It's for you to be happy. You to be free from pain and fear and sorrow." I take a deep breath. "If you come with me, I'll take you to Demoror, to the silver lake. And there, you can see Helen and Jane for yourself."

For a split second, her eyes brighten at the notion. But then a shadow sweeps over her, dimming her eyes again. I feel the darkness spread, filling the hollow, washing over me, through me. *It won't work*, the shadows say. *Give up.*

I dip my head, my shoulders sinking under the weight of discouragement. My eyes slide shut, and I have the urge to lie down and make myself comfortable here. But I fight it. I curl my fingers around the pendant and search deep within myself for something light. And what comes to my mind is a melody. I hum it softly to chase the shadows away, and soon the weight on my shoulders lifts. My back straightens, and I open my eyes and look at my mom, who's watching me with interest.

"What is that song?" she asks curiously.

"I wrote it," I say, and then an idea sparks in my mind. "Remember all those chords you taught me on your old guitar? They were the best gift anyone's ever given me. I've written dozens of songs with them. The one I was humming just now . . . I wrote for you."

Very slowly, the corner of her mouth tips up.

"Do you want me to sing the words to you?" I ask.

She nods once, a faint light returning in the depths of her eyes.

So I sing it to her, and the dark, empty space is filled with a melody that chases the shadows away. When I finish the song, she asks me to sing it again. And then again. As I sing it for the third time, she scoots closer to me, and when I finish, she sits quietly for a long moment. Then she reaches out and takes my hand, squeezing it gently. "Do you know what I love most about you, Kai?" she says quietly. "You always fight for the people you love." She purses her lips and sits silently for another long moment. And then something changes in her face. It reminds me of the day she packed us up to go to San Luis Obispo. The flame in her eyes grows brighter by the second, and she clenches her jaw as though gathering courage.

She looks in my eyes. "I'm ready to fight. For you."

Hope rises to a sharp and dangerous summit in my chest. I nod and squeeze her hand in return. "Whatever is out there that scares you, whatever causes you pain, I'll help you face it."

She brings my hand to her mouth and kisses it. "I know you will."

The Briar feels even darker on the way out, like it knows we're leaving and wants to hide the paths that lead back to Demoror. Even with the pendant, I can only see a couple steps ahead. So I navigate with my heart, thinking about all things light. About Avery and my sisters, about the silver lake and the peaceful falls of Elysium. And with every step, I know in which direction the next should be.

My mom follows close behind, and even with her hand in mine, she pauses or stumbles every now and then. But with encouraging words, she keeps going. The shadows are whispering again, louder than before.

You won't make it out, they say. *You're not good enough. She's not good enough. She'll just come back.*

As we're passing through a thorny thicket, my mom stops and lets go of my hand. I glance back, and she's huddled down, crying with her hands over her ears.

She can hear the voices too.

I drop to my knees in front of her. "Don't listen to the shadows," I say. "I'm here. Listen to my voice. You can do this. You're strong enough. You're worthy enough. This isn't where you belong." I help her to her feet, but when she tries to take a step, she can't move.

She shakes her head. "I'm stuck."

Her dress is tangled in a thorny vine. I grab a handful of her skirt and yank, but it doesn't come loose.

"I can't get out," she cries.

I take a deep breath. "Yes, you can. It'll just take time. Which is something we have plenty of." I set to work removing thorns from her skirt, one by one. Dozens of them keep her captive, jutting out from the vine twisted around a section of her skirt. It's a tedious and painful process, and she helps me by holding back the fabric as it gets freed.

When I remove the last one, she scoots away from the vine but doesn't get up. She looks at me, her face contorted in fear. "What if I don't belong where you're taking me? What if people look at me, and judge me for the way I died? I'm not good enough to be anywhere but here. I can't go farther. I want to stay. I want to stay here."

I kneel down and take her hands in mine, biting back the tears burning my throat. "All those things in your head—they're not true. Fight them. Fight for me. Do you remember the words I sang to you?"

She lowers her eyes, and I see her recalling the song. The fear slowly melts away, and she gives a determined nod before meeting my eyes and pleading, "Sing it again."

I pull her to her feet, and with her hand securely in mine, we continue on. As I sing, I think of all the times I wanted to take her hand when I was a little boy and lead her to safety. Lead her somewhere warm and secure, where she could be at peace. Never did I think I would actually have the chance to do it. Feeling the warmth of her hand in mine now, I'm filled with a love so bright it chases the darkness away, so intense that I don't even need the pendant to find my way.

34
avery

Sitting on the bow of Mom's sailboat, I lean on the lifeline and watch the sun dip into the west horizon. The mainsail is swollen with a southerly, and as we fly across the face of the sea, the wind rushes over my face and whips through my hair. The sound of laughter pulls my attention to the stern, and I glance back to see Mom grinding the winch to trim the sail while Dad pulls the line. She's smiling at him, and he says something that makes her laugh again. It's a contagious sound, one that makes even Sophie smile. She's at the helm, lounging lazily in the captain's chair while steering with her feet.

With Mom and Dad being separated, I wasn't sure if our annual sailing trip would happen this year. But the last week of July, Mom started planning as usual. Three weeks later, the four of us set sail for the Channel Islands. The last couple days have felt like we've traveled back in time. Like Mom never left. Like the only care or worry we have is staying afloat on the ocean. I've even seen Mom and Dad share a hug or two. I don't know what it means. Maybe they're working things out, or maybe it's just the romantic setting making her more affectionate. All I know is it makes me happy to see them together.

The light is fading fast as we anchor at the islands, so it's a scramble to get all our camping gear to a high plateau and set up camp. Dad cooks spaghetti on a gas camping stove, and he and Sophie are so beat after dinner that they go straight to bed. That leaves Mom and me, sitting in our camping chairs with half-eaten plates of spaghetti as we soak in the 360-degree view of the ocean around us. The moon is full, its silvery light spilling over the ocean like sapphires sewn into satin.

Mom seems distant and thoughtful, spinning spaghetti noodles around her plastic fork instead of eating them.

"You okay?" I ask after watching her spin her fork about forty times without lifting it off the plate. She looks at me as if just remembering I was there. Then she lays her fork on her paper plate, and her chest rises and falls with a deep breath.

"I'm good." She gives a sad and laborious smile that doesn't match her words. "Really good."

"Mom, did you forget to bring your med—"

"No—" Her hand curls around my wrist, and her lower lip quivers. "I mean it. It's been so long since I've felt so happy, so . . . so . . ." She motions to her chest, like she's feeling something there that she can't describe with words. She shakes her head and throws her hands in the air, giving up on verbal communication.

"Is it because . . ." I start carefully, not wanting to push her where she may not want to go. "Because we've been all together these last couple days?"

She picks up her water bottle and takes a sip, then sets it down and goes back to spinning her uneaten spaghetti. "What do you think he'd say . . ." She glances at me and shakes her head, as though she's not sure she should finish the thought. Or maybe she just doesn't want to say it out loud. But I know exactly what she's thinking, so I answer the question she's too afraid to ask.

"I'd think he'd say it's about time," I say quietly. "And probably, 'Welcome home.' "

She looks at me, then she's looking through me, as though visualizing the scene. The one where she comes home with a full suitcase and tells Dad that she's happier when she's with the people she loves. The scene where Dad pulls her into his arms and tells her that it's where she belongs. At least that's the scene I'm seeing in my own mind, and it makes my chest swell with hope.

She wipes her hands on a napkin and drops it over her spaghetti. "Well, we'll see what happens when we get back." She tosses her plate in a nearby garbage sack, then stretches her arms over her head. "It's late. The sack is calling."

"I'm going to sit out here a little longer."

"Well, don't stay up too late. Your dad has hiking plans for tomorrow." She stands and kisses the top of my head, then walks through the dry grass. I hear the zipper of her tent, and then the sound of her rummaging through her medicine bag to find her sleep meds. Before I can finish my cold spaghetti, I hear the soft rumble of her snoring.

I consider joining her, but even though my body is tired, my mind is restless. The island is quiet, save for the sound of waves rolling and crashing down on the shore, and so my thoughts turn to the sea, and to Kai. To the first time I saw him, when he pulled me out of the water and tied the leash around my wrist. As I close my eyes and try desperately to recall the feeling of his hand in mine, my fingers slide into my pocket and find the pocketknife there. Kai's pocketknife. It's been my constant companion for the last couple months, a tangible reminder that he really was here with me those few days in June. Reverently, as though unveiling an ancient and fragile relic, I pull it out and run my finger over the smooth metal.

I should really go to bed. But there's a hollow aching in my chest that I'm sure will make it impossible to sleep. So I rise to my feet and wander away from camp, following a moonlit path that runs along the edge of the cliffs. The music of the sea calls to me the way it used to, and I feel that tugging in my chest, that irrepressible need to go to where the water is. So when I come to a fork in the trail, I take the path that leads down to the beach. The grade is steep, and I use the cliff wall to steady myself.

At the bottom, there's nowhere to go but through a jagged archway, and when I come out on the other side, I find myself in an enormous cavern with an arched opening that faces a small cove. The tide is low, the sand exposed. Moonlight pierces through holes in the cavern, spotlighting little pools in the sand.

Treading to the middle of the cavern, I sink to my knees and hug my stomach, trying to squeeze the ache out. I always knew that love could hurt, but never knew it could hurt *this* much. Never knew that losing someone could carve a place inside of me so deep. I'm as hollow as this cavern, waiting for the tide to return and fill it back up.

But what if the tide never returns? What I'm never filled again?

As I sit there, still and silent, feeling the breeze play with my hair and tickle my cheek, listening to the surf echo off the cavern walls, it occurs to me that the cavern is not as hollow as I perceive it to be. It may not be full of water, but there is air—it fills my lungs as I breathe it in, keeping me alive. There is sound—beautiful and rich, saturating my ears. I may not be able to see these things like I can see the water, but the cavern is still full.

There may be a hollow inside of me left by Kai's absence, but there are other things to fill it. There's my family. My friends. This life and all the things I can learn and do here, even if Kai isn't with me.

And then I think how just because Kai isn't with me now, it doesn't mean I'll never be with him again. "When I leave," he said on the cliff that day, "I won't really be gone. I'll be just over the horizon." Until I meet him beyond that horizon, all I can do is live my life the way he taught me to.

Slowly, I rise to my feet and step through the sand to the

water's edge. The cove is circled by towering rocks, and although I can hear waves crashing into the rocks on the outside, the water in the cove is calm. I wade in and sway my foot back and forth. The water is cool as it glides over my ankle and between my toes. I move deeper, feeling it on my calves. The rhythm of the sea calms me. It hums with life, a lullaby that sooths me into tranquility. My body relaxes, sinks deeper to my hips, then my waist. The sea engulfs my shoulders, circles my neck like a strand of pearls. I lie in the water as though it's a bed, and the moon and stars are my blanket.

The dark water stirs the adventurer in me awake. I draw in a few deep breaths, then dive under, swimming down a good ten feet. To keep myself from rising, I grab hold of the edge of a rock that juts out of the reef. Gravity has no power over me down here. Even my cares seem to rise from my shoulders and drift away into the nocturnal underwater world. Colors are muted into shadow and light. Shafts of moonlight cut through the surface, slicing up the darkness. The light reflects off the white sand, painting the liquid ceiling into a rippling silver sky.

Being underwater like this, a piece of myself is restored. I am strong and courageous and fearless again. I am the girl who can free-dive to thirty feet and hold her breath for four minutes. A familiar thrill courses through me, a rush of adrenaline I haven't felt in so long. My skin tingles the way it does when I repel down the face of a mountain or slide across the perfect wave. Or when the boy I love brushes his fingers over my skin.

My chest burns, but not because I'm running out of air. It's the joy of finding myself again. It's gratitude for Kai, for all he did for me. And the aching desire to return the favor somehow. To make restitution. To tie that leash around his wrist the way I failed to before.

My lungs are begging for air, so I let go of the rock and push upward. But I only make it a few inches before I feel a sharp tug on the back of my head and then jerk to a stop.

My hair is caught. Tangled in something. I reach back to untangle it and feel the skeletal fingers of the reef entwined in my hair.

I yank hard, trying to free myself, but there's too much hair caught. My heart is pounding, burning up oxygen. *Calm down*, I tell myself. *There's a way out of this.* And then it comes to me. The pocketknife. My hand grapples it out of my pocket, and it takes me a few tries to unfold the knife. I swipe the blade behind my head and feel a lock of hair come free. I take another swipe. But this time my hand slams into the reef and the knife slips from my fingers. I fumble for it, twisting and sweeping my hand through the water as I watch it sink down, down, but it hits the sand before I can catch it.

It's only five feet below me. But my arm won't reach that far.

Calm down. I've been under longer than this. I think. Just relax. But I can't calm down when all I can hear is my heart throbbing in my ears. My lungs are screaming for air. My body gives a jerk, and then a shudder. *Calm down. Calm down. Calm down.*

My feet. I can grab the knife with my toes. I grab hold of the reef and bring myself vertical. But just as my toes touch the knife, I feel my hair come free and my body begin to drift upward.

I abandon the knife, turning and kicking toward the surface. As I get closer, it brightens as if the night has suddenly turned to day. When I break the surface and take a gulp of air, it *is* day.

And I'm no longer in the cove.

35
KAI

Beneath the crystal trees of Demoror, I sit beside my mother, listening to her soft voice. Starlight sifts through the crystals, scattering little specks of colored light all over her face. We've been having a lot of these long conversations since she came out of the Briar—about her new assignments, or my ongoing journeys into the Briar, or about my sisters. And with each conversation, she looks less like a withered grapevine long-deprived of water, and more like one after a few good rain showers. The longer she spends away from the dark, the more light she drinks up, and the more she stands tall and strong, stretching her branches toward the sun.

She's telling me now about a little girl she was able to heal. Her eyes are bright with enthusiasm, her hands resting peacefully in her lap, her healing wristband glinting under the sparkling sky. In her voice, I hear something I've never heard before. Something I've ached to hear ever since I was a kid. Happiness. Genuine happiness. It makes something rise from my chest and catch in my throat.

And then as she continues, a different sound breaks through. A different voice. One that sends a jolt through my chest like a shot of adrenaline. My hand falls on my mom's, and she trails off, looking at me curiously. "What is it?" she asks.

"Did you say my name?"

The crease between her brows deepens. "No. Why?"

I sit still a moment, listening for the sound again. "I . . . I could have sworn someone just said my name. It sounded like . . ." I scan the trees around us, searching for Avery. But of course she's not here. "Never mind. Whatever it was, I must have imagined it."

Maybe I want to hear Avery's voice so badly that my mind conjured the sound of it. I gaze through the trees at the silver lake, wishing I could see her through it like I used to. Over two months of Earth time have passed since I left her in Isadora's cottage, and it's torture to not know how she's doing. I take a deep breath and remind myself that it's better this way. Because if I could see her, I would watch her every hour of every day, and anytime she wasn't happy or had a problem, I'd want to fix it. No—it's definitely better that she live her life without me hovering.

"Is everything all right?" my mom asks, drawing my gaze back to her.

"Yeah. It's just—" Before I can finish my answer, I hear it again. "Kai." Avery's voice.

I rise to my feet. "There it is again. Did you hear it?"

"What?"

"Avery's voice. Calling me." I turn in a frantic circle, scanning the area for her or whatever is producing the sound of her voice. But I see nothing except the tree branches. "Something's wrong. I need to talk to Charles." I hold out my hand to her. "Come with me?"

She nods and takes my hand. I picture Charles in my mind, and then we quicken to him, finding him on a bench near the cliffs of Elysium.

He must see the worry in my face, because he stands. "What's wrong?"

"I keep hearing Avery's voice."

His lips part in surprise for a moment, and then he presses them together and braces his hands on my shoulder like he's about to deliver grave news. It makes my hands turn cold.

"I told you," he says, "that you would know when she came."

"What?" The word makes no sound, because all the air has been knocked out of me. I close my eyes and shut everything out, trying to sense her presence to see if what he's saying is true. It takes a minute, and then a riot breaks loose inside of me, shattering order and reason, obliterating the bit of peace I've scraped together over the last few weeks. Because there, in the center of my chest, I feel it. Feel her presence in Demoror like a new sun in the sky, bigger and brighter than any other, shifting my center of gravity so that suddenly I'm falling toward her. Without another word, I leave Charles and my mom and surrender to Avery's pull, quickening in an instant to where she is.

On the still shore of the silver lake, I find her. She doesn't see me because she's turned toward the water, gazing at something. Her hair spills down her back like a silk cape, shimmering gold under the sparkling sky. Her dress is like a white and iridescent moonflower, twisting at her waist and flaring at her calves. It reminds me of the one I pictured her in the day I sang to her on the cliff. Everything about her is *soft*. She is satin and snow, a lullaby and a whisper.

She's close enough to touch, but my hand is a dead weight at my side. The warmth of her nearness burns in my chest, but my skin is as cold as the Briar. Because she shouldn't be here. Not yet.

I feel a hand on my shoulder, and I turn to see that Charles and my mom have followed me here. Charles squeezes my shoulder and gives me a look that says, *Calm down*. But I can't. "No," I breathe, turning back to Avery as my vision blurs.

At the sound of my voice, Avery whips around. Before I can blink the tears from my eyes to see her face, she throws herself into my arms and cries out my name.

Her embrace softens the shock, and for a moment all the panic and questions take a backseat to the joy that's humming in my chest like an amplified guitar riff. I let my arms do what they've ached to do for weeks now, and I gather her close, breathing in her presence, feeling her warmth spread through me, completing me like missing lyrics of an unfinished song. I bury my lips in her hair. *This.* This is what I've been waiting for. To be made whole by the certainty and permanence of her love, never to be lost. It just came sooner than I thought. Too soon.

As much as I want to keep holding her, my need for answers nags me like the whistle of a departing train. Reluctantly, I pull back and cradle her face in my hands. Her blue eyes glisten with tears, and she is even more beautiful than I remember. I breathe a sad sigh and brush the tears from her cheek with my thumb.

"What are you doing here?" I ask in a broken voice.

"I . . ." She shakes her head. "I don't know. I was swimming, and then . . ." She seems confused and disoriented. I remember feeling the same way when I first came here. Even after Charles finally came to greet me, it took me a while to piece together the details of my death.

She swallows and blinks a few times. Then instead of finishing her sentence, she looks at the water near our feet. The glassy surface shows an image of her body. In the ocean, limp and entirely submerged.

"No," I whisper, only because I feel too weak to shout. I shake my head, unable to accept her fate. I have the impulse to jump into the lake to return to Earth to help her. But there's only one way for me to return to Earth now. And even if I went through the swamp in the Briar, I wouldn't have the substance or the power to save her.

I turn to my mom, almost asking her to go back to Earth to

save Avery's life. That's her job now, after all. But I stop myself. She hasn't been assigned, and I can't get her into trouble.

I cast a desperate look at Charles. "Why isn't anyone assigned to help her?"

"I've called to Jerick, and he's on his way. Maybe he can give us some answers."

"Grim?" I snap bitterly. "All he'll do is seal her death." As my panic shoots up like a rocket, so does my creativity. It takes only a split-second for a plan to form in my mind, though it's half-baked as usual. I don't know if it will work; I only know that the girl I love still has a life to live. And I'm willing to pay any price to make sure she keeps it.

I take a half step toward Charles, then say in a hushed voice. "Charles, all the times you've told me that you trust me, that you believe in me, did you really mean it?"

His brows pull together. "Yes. Of course I meant it." And then very slowly, he adds, "I *still* trust and believe in you."

I nod. "That's all I need to know." I give him a hug, patting him firmly on the back. At the same time, as quick and furtive as the practiced pickpocket I am, I slip my hand in his pocket.

But the ring isn't there.

"Other pocket," he whispers in my ear, and when I pull back, expecting to see disappointment in his face, all I see is love. His hand comes to mine, and he slyly passes me the ring. I drop it in my pocket, choking back a surge of tears.

I have the ring, but it alone won't be enough to save Avery. There's one more thing I need.

With hands trembling, I gather Avery in my arms and whisper in her ear, "Go back through the lake to your body. I'll meet you there." I kiss her on the forehead, then turn to my mom. I don't know how this is going to turn out, or what's going to happen to me. So I tell her I love her and that I'm proud of her. She doesn't even notice me feeling for the clasp on her wristband. Then, bracing myself for flight, I flick it open and swiftly remove it from her wrist.

She gasps and blinks in bafflement.

"I'm sorry," is all I say, and then, giving one last look at Avery, I turn and quicken away.

I go straight to the Briar, quickening through the bramble toward the swamp. Thorns slash and slice into me as I fly through them, but there's no time to waste on walking. Within seconds, I'm standing at the edge of the swamp, terror shaking me as I peer down into the black water. The thorns have torn me up, but that's nothing compared to what I'm about to go through for the chance to save Avery's life one last time. I shove my mom's wristband in my pocket with Charles's ring so I don't lose them. Then I conjure an image of Avery's body in my mind so that hopefully when I emerge on the other side, I'll be where she is. Then, bracing myself for the pain I'm about to feel, I dive in.

Not even the light of my pendant can ward off the dark. My hands over my ears do nothing to dampen the awful sounds. Screeching and breaking, an amplified train wreck. Metal scraping and glass shattering and lives being torn apart.

I'm in a dark room. The metallic taste of blood coats my tongue. A child screams. Helen's little figure runs through the doorway. Heavy steps follow.

Dad in an orange jumpsuit. A glass partition between us. He's pointing to the phone on my side, urging me to pick it up so I can hear his voice. But I've heard enough of his voice. Loud and clear and belligerent. I don't want to hear it again. His hand comes up and slams the glass.

I'm digging through a clothes basket. No socks. Only mildew. Something sharp stabs my finger. I jerk my hand back. There's a hypodermic needle stuck in my finger.

Huddled under a fern in the woods. Wolves howling. Helen and Jane crying. Running home in the dark. Dad in the doorway to meet us.

An open coffin. Mom in her blue dress. Eyes glued shut. Hair curled. Not like her. Only a shell now. My mouth is dry. I'm as cold and empty as her body. Sisters clinging to my arms. Aunt Laurel and Uncle Gerald lead them out of the room. I'm alone.

A boy lying flat beneath me, my fists pounding into his bloody face. I hate myself. But I can't stop. Because I hate myself.

Shoving my belongings into a black garbage sack. Being ushered out of a foster family's home. Again. And again. And again.

Standing in a crowded room, looking through a window, watching the girl I love kiss another boy. I want to die. But I can't. Because I'm already dead.

In Avery's arms. "Stay," she cries. But she doesn't have the power to keep me. And I don't have the power to stay.

I'm in the ocean. I can't move. My pendant lights up the water, but I'm still someplace very dark. Little particles float around me; the surface ripples above. I must be close to shore, because there's sand about ten feet below. It looks and feels so familiar that for a second, I don't know if I'm reliving my death, or if I'm actually in the ocean. The same fear that gripped me while I drowned grips me now. Only, I'm not struggling for breath. And this time, the fear isn't for myself.

It's for Avery.

I straighten and look around for her body, and find it a few feet below me, limp and suspended in the blue. She's facing down so I can't see her face. Just her long gold hair, half tangled in the reef, the other half slowly swaying in the current. Pain rips through me at the sight of her, and without wasting another second, I dig Charles's ring out of my pocket and slip it on my finger.

I reach for her, but my hand sweeps right through her. The ring isn't working yet. It's too soon. It will take a couple minutes for my body to materialize, and I pray it won't be too late. With my mom's wristband, I should still have time to save her. When I was a healer, I used it once to revive someone who should have been far beyond the point of revival.

The sand beneath me begins to swirl and gather into a cloud, and as the particles rise from the ocean floor and start clinging to me, I stay near Avery's body, trying every second to take hold of her as the pain of materializing sears through me. My hand starts to drag a little when it passes through her. Any second, and I'll be able to take hold of her.

When I try grabbing her again, my hand closes on the back of her neck. I've got her. I take a handful of her tangled hair and tug hard. Some of the strands break, but she's still stuck. As I dig my hands deeper into her hair and start yanking strands a few at a time, I see a flash of metal on the ocean floor. My hands freeze and my eyes go wide. A few feet down, there's a pocketknife lying in the sand. I push away from Avery and swim down to retrieve it just as these temporary lungs start to burn for want of air. I kick back up to her and cut her hair free, then clutch her arm and drag her upward.

My lungs gulp in air as I break the surface, and when I look around, the shore isn't too far off. I secure her to me with one arm as I paddle shoreward with the other, kicking my legs to keep us both afloat. If Avery dies now, it won't be because I didn't do everything in my power to keep her alive.

Soon I feel sand under my feet, and then I find my footing on the ocean floor. We're in a little rocky cove where the waves are mild. I carry her to a cavern with dry sand and lay her down.

The light from my pendant illuminates the cavern, and I see Avery's body with heartbreaking clarity. Her eyes are closed, her lips blue. I press my fingers under her jaw, checking for a pulse. Nothing.

I look around for Avery's spirit, but she still isn't here. It doesn't matter. Once I restore her life, her spirit will be brought back to her body.

I reach into my pocket and retrieve my mom's wristband. If Charles's ring works for me, then the power in my mom's wristband should too. I circle it around my wrist. But when I try to close the clasp, I can't connect the two ends. I try to squeeze them together. But her wrist is so much smaller than mine, there's no way to make it fit.

Maybe I don't need to close the clasp. I leave the wristband open and rest my hand on Avery's stomach, trying to summon the power to heal her. But I feel nothing. Not the faintest stirring inside of me. No warmth. No energy. No power. Only cold emptiness. My shoulders sink in defeat. I pound the sand with my fist, then lift my face to the sky and roar in frustration.

I tear off the wristband and toss it behind me. I don't have the power to heal her. But I have hands. And I have air in my lungs.

Wasting no more time, I lean over her lifeless body and put my hands and lungs to use.

36

avery

*e*veryone is looking at me. The dark-haired woman, the man named Charles, and the tall guy who just appeared and introduced himself as Jerick. But no one is giving me answers, and the looks on their faces have me panicking.

"Where did he go?" I ask again, my voice reflecting my rising anxiety. The anxiety of realizing I'm dead. Of imagining my family discovering my drowned body. And of Kai's sudden disappearance.

They all look at one another, like they're not sure who should answer my question. Finally, Jerick steps forward, holding some kind of scepter.

"Kai went exactly where we thought he would," Jerick says dryly, clearly unamused. His towering figure casts a shadow over me, but it's not the only thing about him that intimidates me. His icy-blue eyes seem to pierce right through me. And there's a troubling absence of emotion on his face. Like a stiff suit, ready to close a deal that's all business and nothing personal.

Lowering the scepter to his side, he comes closer. He settles a hand on my shoulder, heavy as a cannonball. "You'll need to come with me," he says grimly.

I don't argue, because he seems like the kind of person you can't win an argument with. I look to Charles for some kind of reassurance, and he gives a small but encouraging smile. "He'll take you to Kai."

I let Jerick take me by the arm, and he leads me back into the silver lake. We're swallowed up in the still waters and my vision whites out. In the next second, I hear the sound of the surf. Details start filling my vision. We've somehow traveled back to Earth, because we're now standing on a familiar beach surrounded by cliffs. I hear Kai's distressed voice, saying my name, pleading with me to *live*. I look over, and there he is in the cavern. On his knees in the sand, leaning over my body, trying to revive me.

So this is where he disappeared to. He came back to rescue me. Again. Some kind of light is shining from his chest, lighting up the scene. My hair and clothes are soaked. My eyes are closed, my skin pale. My limbs motionless. It's surreal and disturbing to see my own lifeless body, but I can't look away. At the sight of Kai laboring over my body, I'm filled with a myriad of warring emotions. Gratitude and love, and a little bit of anger and disappointment. He's already given so much for me. When will it be my turn to give him something in return?

"Live, Avery," he begs between labored breaths, so focused on his efforts that he doesn't notice us behind him. "Come back. Please. Come back."

"You have a choice to make," Jerick says quietly beside me. He leans down and picks something out of the sand at our feet, then straightens and opens his palm. He's holding the wristband that Kai took from the woman's wrist. It's like the one Kai wore when he was here with me those few days in June.

"What is that for?" I ask as the waves crash on the rocks outside the cove, drowning out my voice.

"It holds the power to restore mortal life. *Any* mortal life. So, should you choose to live, you'll need to put on the wristband and lay your hand on your body, and the power within it will do what Kai here can't do on his own."

I take the wristband from Jerick, marveling at the power it holds. Is this what I really want? To be returned to my body? To the living world? I feel just as alive in this world as in the one I came from. And if I don't use the wristband, I can stay with Kai. I look at him, at his hands beating into my chest, his face all torment and determination, and I know that it's not what *he* wants. As always, he wants me to *live*. And I realize now that I want the same thing. I want to return to my body. I want my skin to turn pink, want my lungs to expand of their own accord, want my eyelids to flutter open as much as he does. Not only for my family, or the life I've yet to live, but because if I die now, then Kai's sacrifices will be for nothing.

Slowly, I circle the wristband around my wrist and close the clasp. Then I step over to my body and kneel on the opposite side of Kai, facing him.

When he sees me, he doesn't stop his efforts, only proclaims through labored breaths, "I'm not giving up."

I hold up my wrist, showing him the wristband. "You don't have to."

He exhales heavily and rocks back on his heels, his chest heaving. "Well? What are you waiting for?" His hands are still over my body's sternum, ready to keep pumping if needed.

I extend my hand, then pause. Seeing Kai's hand there, so close to mine, sparks an idea. Jerick said the wristband could restore *any* mortal life. That all I had to do was lay my hand on the body. And in a way, in this moment, Kai has a body.

I glance at Jerick, who's twenty feet away, holding his glowing scepter over the lapping sea. I don't know what he's doing, but as long as he's nowhere near us, I don't care. I turn back to Kai. He's out of breath, anxiously waiting for me to take action. I don't know if this will work, but as I gaze into his blue-green eyes and see the beautiful life he never had the chance to live, I know I have to try. After all he's done for me, maybe this is how I can repay him, by setting things right for him. This may be the only chance I get to make restitution, and I'm not throwing it away.

"You don't always have to be the hero," I say, my voice catching. I lower my hand like I'm going to let it fall on my own chest, but at the last second I drop it over Kai's hand. He must not realize what I'm attempting, because he doesn't object like I thought he would. He must think I'm only giving him one last display of affection before I return to my body. His face softens and he surrenders to it, lacing my fingers through his and closing his eyes as he raises my hand to his lips.

I feel something warm blossom in the center of my being that has nothing to do with his lips on my skin. It feels very similar though. Like how I feel when Kai kisses me, or touches me, or looks at me. Like love. It grows and expands until I don't think I can contain it anymore. And then it rushes out of me through my hand and into him.

That's when he notices. "What are you doing?" His eyes fly open and he tries to wrench his hand away, but I grab his wrist and hold on with every ounce of strength.

"No!" he shouts, trying to twist out of my grip, but I won't let go. Not this time.

This time I'm tying the leash of my fingers around his wrist with a thousand unbreakable knots.

He stumbles backward into the sand, and I fall on top of him. I can feel the power surging into him at every point our bodies connect.

"Avery!" he cries out, his voice heartbroken. "What are you doing? You're going to die!"

The surge of energy weakens, and then I weaken. Kai wrenches my hand from his wrist and slides me off of him, and then he crawls back over to my body, where he restarts his resuscitation efforts with even more vigor. I roll onto my back, too drained to move. Something feels wrong. Incomplete. Fragmented. I'm slipping away, but I don't know where to.

Jerick's towering figure appears over us, his face as emotionless as ever. "She's made her choice."

"You can't seal her death," Kai growls. "It's not too late." He stops pumping for a split second to grab my hand and lay it on my mortal body, as if the wristband still has the power to save me.

But it's too late for that. There's a pulling sensation right in the center of my chest, as though I'm a hooked fish being reeled from the water. My vision goes bright, so bright I can't see anymore. And then it feels like I've turned to liquid, and I'm being sucked down a drain.

37

KAI

"Avery!" I search my surroundings frantically for Avery's spirit. She was here a second ago, lying beside her body, and now she's gone. I look at Grim. "Where did she go?"

"Right where you sent her," he says flatly.

I don't know what he means. But there's no time to interrogate him when Avery's lungs still aren't breathing on their own. I seal my mouth over her cold lips and blow air in her lungs. From the corner of my eye I see her chest rise with each of my breaths. It's not too late. I'm not giving up, not letting her die. Especially after what she just did—tried to give up her own life to restore mine. My throat tightens as I recall the look on her face as she circled her hand around my wrist. Fierce determination mixed with sorrow. She knew exactly what she was giving up. If only she'd known that it wouldn't work. That my mortality is far beyond the point of reclamation. I'm not any more alive now than I was before she laid her hand on mine. And if I don't revive her, both of our sacrifices will have been in vain.

Just as I'm about to go back to pumping her chest, all the energy drains out of me, like I'm a machine whose plug has been pulled. I haven't felt physical fatigue since the morning I left Avery in Isadora's cottage. But something is siphoning every last bit of strength from me, along with all my hope of saving Avery's life. I don't understand. I try to fight it, to fight for Avery, but I'm not strong enough. My limbs are shaking, my eyelids heavy, and I crumple into the sand beside Avery's body, unable to move.

"Well," Jerick says impassively, "I suppose my job here is done." He turns as if to leave, but then pauses and turns back. He steps over and crouches beside me. "You've really outdone yourself this time, Zackai Turner." He reaches behind my neck, where he unclasps the chain that holds my pendant. The light in the pendant slowly dims until the cavern turns dark. He stuffs the pendant in his pocket, then takes my hand and slides Charles's ring from my finger. I want to object, to get up and keep fighting for Avery's life, but my muscles are useless.

"Some have a talent for outsmarting death," Jerick says. "And others succeed out of sheer stubbornness. But only a few are self-less enough to surrender their lives to win someone else's." He pierces me with a fiery blue gaze, and then like a candle being snuffed out, he disappears.

Using my last ounce of strength, I turn my head toward Avery. It's dark now without my pendant, but by the moonlight seeping through holes in the cavern, I see her in deep shades of blue. Her eyes closed, her long eyelashes touching her cheeks. Her lips, slightly parted, but no breath breaking through. Her hair, wet and splayed out on the sand around her head.

My beautiful, brave girl.

Maybe I should have just been happy to be with her, no matter which realm she existed in. And now I don't know if we'll ever be together at all.

I'm losing substance fast, but I feel something warm under

my hand. Avery's arm. Avery's arm, which should be cold. But it's not. It feels like a flame under my hand. And then I smile. Because there, on the inside of her wrist, I feel a faint, rhythmic throbbing. And now I know where her spirit went.

38
avery

t's the same dream I always have. I'm in the middle of a wild sea on my surfboard, rising and falling over rain-pocked hills of water. I dive under the surface to find the boy who saved my life. And there he is, suspended in the dark water beneath me, face down. Only, he's not just the boy who saved my life. He's Kai. The selfless and gallant boy I love.

I swim down to grab his wrist, but I'm tugged back when I reach the end of my leash. His hand is so close that my fingertips brush his knuckles. But I can't get close enough to grasp him because the leash tied to my wrist is too short.

This time, instead of returning to the surface for air, I stay with him. I reach up to my tethered wrist and untie the knotted lifeline that Kai put there.

And I'm free. Free to save him.

I turn back to him, and the water goes unnaturally still, as if I'm in the deep end of a pool instead of a churning ocean. Rays of sunlight break through the surface like fingers of a glorious hand, reaching out for Kai and wrapping him in a golden embrace. I swim easily down to him and hook his wrist in my hand, then tug him toward the surface. We gulp air into our lungs as we break the surface, then drape ourselves on opposite sides of my surfboard, facing each other.

The sky is lit up in gold, a fiery sunrise that stretches from horizon to horizon. The water is a still sheet of glass, reflecting the sky. There's no sound, only the breaths moving in and out through our lips, whispering to us that we're alive.

Kai gazes at me across the surfboard, his blue-green eyes blazing with light and life. And something else. Something that makes my chest swell with warmth.

He loves me. And he knows that I love him. And through squalls and tempests, through life and death, nothing will ever change that.

"Breathe, Avery," he whispers. "Breathe."

I open my mouth to tell him that I am breathing, but I can't get the words out. Because there's water in my throat.

There's water in my throat. My mouth. My lungs. I roll to my side and heave it out, coughing and gasping until my airways are cleared. Then I lie there, breathing in and out, in and out. I don't open my eyes, because I'm not ready to leave my dream. But it's too late. The dream and Kai and the tranquil sea are gone, replaced with the gritty, cold sand that's grating against my cheek.

The air smells of brine, and I hear the pulsing of nearby waves. My head is throbbing, trapped in a thick haze, and my chest feels like someone's been using me as a punching bag.

My clothes are soaked, and I shiver. I need to change. Get warm. But where are my dry clothes?

Oh yeah—in my tent. I walked down to this beach last night. Went swimming in the dark. But I don't remember getting out of the water. So how did I get back on the beach? I blink blearily, trying to open my eyes. For a minute, my vision is as muddled as my head. The shore is cloaked in a fine morning mist, like clouds sleeping in on the beach. I'm in the cavern, the sifting sound of the surf echoing in the hollow space like a soothing whisper.

The subtle glow in the sky tells me dawn is near. I draw in a deep breath, filling my lungs with oxygen. It seems to clear some of the mental haze, and my gears start to turn. Or maybe I'm drifting back into dreamland. Because new images are spilling into my head that can't possibly be real. A silver lake, as still as the ocean I just dreamed of. A wristband inlaid with opal-like stone as brilliant as fire. Like the one Kai wore.

Kai. At the thought of him, pain rips through me, as real and raw as the morning he vanished in my arms. As though the wound of losing him has been slashed open again. And then for the quickest moment, I see an image of him on this beach, kneeling in the sand over a body. *My body.* I see my own hand reaching out to touch his, the stone of the wristband ablaze with light.

My hand goes to my wrist, where I can almost feel the weight of the wristband still there. And then I'm having trouble breathing again. Because it dawns on me that the things I'm seeing aren't dreams or illusions. They're memories of what just happened. And slowly, my fragmented memories link together to form a whole picture.

I was dead. Kai dragged me out of the water. And on a hopeful whim, I tried to sacrifice my chance at life to restore his.

I sit up, my eyes wildly sweeping the beach for him. Behind me, lying in the sand with eyes closed, I find him.

The mist hangs over him like a blanket, softens him like frosted glass. I slowly drink in the sight of him, as though he's the only water in a desolate, drought-ridden land. From his bare feet, to his tattered black shorts, to his rising and falling chest, to his shoulders, and then his face. Peaceful. At rest.

He's close enough to touch, but I can't move. And my own breath is lodged in my throat like a stone.

In the gray wash of predawn, he is everything but gray. He is light and color and life. Tousled wisps of tawny-gold hair frame and soften the hard angles of his face. His skin is flushed, his cheeks ruddy. There's more texture, more lines around his mouth and eyes. Stubble on his jaw. He's never looked more alive, more real, more beautiful.

Some quiet, detached part of me understands what all this means. The rest of me is screaming, *Delusion! Dream! Psychosis!* Because everything I'm seeing would mean that Kai is—no. He can't be.

But there's a small white scar on the top of his hand that wasn't there before. And beneath the frayed hem of his black shorts, his knees are callused. There are veins bulging in his hands. Purple veins. Veins full of blood.

He's turning blurry, so I blink to clear my vision. And then he stirs. His lips part as he draws in a deep breath. And then his eyes flutter open. For a few breaths, he gazes at the ceiling of the cavern, as though he still has one foot in a dream and he's reluctant to leave whatever he's seeing there.

In his eyes, I can almost imagine what he's seeing. A vineyard in the early morning light, broad green leaves spotted with dew. His sisters' faces, lighting up with smiles when they see him for the first time in months. A stage at his feet and an audience stretched out before him, a guitar in his hands.

A white beach, pale as ash in the morning sun. And me, in his arms.

His hand reaches out and finds me, his warm fingers curling around my wrist.

39

KAI

The air tastes salty on my tongue. The sand is cold on my back. But Avery's wrist is still warm, and her pulse is racing faster and stronger than ever. I breathe her name on a sigh of relief, then turn to look at her. Her hair is wet, strung around her shoulders and arms like ribbons on a gift. She's sitting close, looking down at me, trembling as though she's about to collapse. So I tug her to me. She falls into my arms easily, like a house of cards in a gust of wind. I gather her up, cradling her to my chest.

"I was afraid I was too late." My voice is hoarse and rusty, as though I haven't used it in months. "What were you thinking? I can't believe you almost threw away your chance to—" I trail off, because I notice that my ring finger is bare. Charles's ring is gone.

Avery lifts her head, and her eyes are wide. She finds my hand with hers, then guides it to my chest, where she spreads my fingers over my sternum. "Shhh. Hold still," she whispers.

We both go still. And then I feel it. Beneath my skin, behind my breastbone, a strong, rhythmic thumping. Like a bass drum, pounding out the beat to a song that has only just begun. I stare at

Avery, speechless, as my heart thuds faster and harder. In her eyes, I see the answer to the question I'm too afraid to ask.

"You're alive," she whispers, her eyes welling up.

It takes five steady heartbeats for the words to register in my mind, and then the truth burns through me like a fuse to dynamite, and ignites.

I suck in a sharp breath. It takes a minute to remember how to exhale, and then all the air whooshes out of my lungs with the word, "How?"

She shakes her head, unable to answer any more than I can. She's biting her lip, but it does nothing to keep the tears from spilling down her cheeks.

I pull her into my arms again, too shocked to do or say anything else. My heart and lungs are throwing a raucous party inside my rib cage, and I breathe in Avery's scent deeply, trying to calm myself. She smells like salt and sunbaked skin, feels like sunshine. When I say her name again, my voice splits. Fractures into pieces. And then so do I. We're both crying. Her hands are in my hair, on my shoulders, my face. She's shaking. Or maybe it's me. Or both of us. All I know in this moment is that I'm alive. And she's alive. And the possibilities of *us* are racing through my mind in a rapid-fire stream.

She burrows deeper into my embrace, and we stay that way for a long time, listening to the sound of the incoming tide. The ocean is sighing. It's the sound of relinquishment, of release. Of surrendering my body so that I could have it again. For how long, I don't know. But it doesn't matter anymore. Because I know that life is life, whether in this realm or the next. It's like the sea, fluid and always in motion. It brings us ashore, then sweeps us back out to where we came from. And sometimes, the seas surrender, and part, and bring us back again.

40

avery

One year later

A thin morning mist hangs over Isadora's vineyard, veiling everything in a cloud of gold light. As I make my way down a row of vines, I feel the moisture in the air clinging to my arms. Clusters of ripe fruit hang from the vines, practically begging to be plucked and eaten. What a difference Kai has made here. Not just for the plants, but for Isadora. He's gotten so close to her that I've occasionally wondered this summer if he'd actually be able to leave her to move to LA with me. But last month he finally found a new vineyard manager to take his place, someone he feels will take good care of the vineyard and of Isadora.

At the end of the row, Kai's cottage comes into view. I pass through the swinging wooden gate and stroll through the lavender field, inhaling deeply the sharp and sweet scent of the purple blossoms. The smell always reminds me of Kai, and of the first time I walked through this field to find him playing his guitar in the cottage. My heart is a little heavy knowing that it will be a long time before we come back here. But I'm also excited for the road ahead—the marine biology program at UCLA for me, and the serious pursuit of a musical career for Kai. I can't wait to see how it all turns out. And at the same time, I want to slow the days down so I can savor each moment with him.

On Kai's porch, I tap on his door, but don't wait for him to answer before letting myself in. The cottage is quiet and dim, the curtains still drawn, and the scent of the herbs growing in the window permeates the room.

"Kai?" I call softly.

He doesn't answer, so I stroll across the small living room to his bedroom door. It's cracked open, and I cautiously duck my head in, not wanting to wake him if he's still asleep. He's lying on his back, one hand resting above his head, the other on his stomach. Sunlight spills from the window onto him and his ivory blankets, turning them radiant. His eyes are closed, his dark lashes shadowing his cheekbones, and his chest rises and falls in a slow rhythm.

He should have been up a couple hours ago, but the sheet music, pencils, and guitar scattered on the floor tell me he was up late again writing music. At the thought, the corner of my mouth lifts. There are few things I enjoy more than watching Kai write music. Sometimes when he's working on a new song, I'll curl up on his couch and become absorbed in the sound of him humming and wrestling chords into just the right place and rhythm. And he's never more attractive to me than in the moment that he finally gets it the way he wants, his eyes burning with intensity, his hair flopping across his forehead as his head bobs in satisfaction.

On the floor at the foot of his bed, his suitcase is open and full of haphazardly folded clothes. At least he's already packed. Either way, I should probably wake him so we can get on the road. I slide through the doorway, then gingerly cross the room to his bedside. My hand reaches for his shoulder, but I stop before touching him. It wouldn't alter our travel schedule too much if I spent just a couple more minutes drinking in the delicious sight of a sleeping Kai.

As quietly as I can, I settle into the twig chair by the bed and prop my chin in my hands to watch him like a favorite movie. I let my eyes wander over his face—the stubble on his jaw, the curved slope of his nose, the smooth spot on the side of his mouth that is so ridiculously kissable. His dark blond hair is an adorable disaster, sticking up in tufts all over his head. And then there are his hands. His thick knuckles, his callused fingertips that somehow always feel so soft when they touch my skin. I find myself leaning closer and closer, until I'm on my knees and bent over him, his face only a foot from mine.

Sometimes even now, even after having him immersed in my life for a year, he seems like a mirage that will vanish if I get too close. Or like a mythical creature I can't take my eyes from, because of the feeling that his presence is a rarity so scarce that I'll only ever have the chance to glimpse him once.

Carefully, I reach out and lay my hand over the left side of his chest. Beneath his cotton T-shirt, I feel his heart beating slow and strong. Reassuring. Grounding him to my world, my reality. Maybe someday, my mind will accept that this is the way he'll stay. That this isn't a dream I'll wake up from. It all seems so incredible still. Everything that happened, and everything he's told me.

Whether it's my hand on his chest or my breath on his face that wakes him, his eyes blink open. He rolls to his side to face me, and as his eyes slowly focus on my face, a tranquil smile tugs at his mouth.

"Go back to sleep," I say quietly. "I'm not done stalking you."

His eyes close again and his smile broadens, stretching his full lips. Then he reaches out for my arm, and his hand slides down and closes around my wrist.

"C'mere," he murmurs in a sleepy voice, tugging me up onto his bed to lie beside him. Burying my head in the bend of his neck, my hand returns to his chest. Having him close like this feels like kindling has been stacked and lit in my chest. The warmth spreads through me, filling me with a peace I've become so familiar with. It's a meandering stream, a fiery sunset, a lullaby. It makes me want to close my eyes and go back to sleep, to forget that we have two hundred miles to travel today. I do close my eyes, and I feel his lips on my forehead, his quiet breaths on my cheeks.

When I open my eyes again, Kai is holding up his left hand, slowly turning it back and forth in the sunlight. My hand comes up to meet his, lightly tracing the lines of his fingers, weaving in and out, exploring every ridge and curve.

"What are you thinking?" I whisper.

From the way he's gazing at his hand, I can guess the answer. But aside from the interrogation I put him through the week after last summer's sailing trip, it's not often that we discuss our journey to and from the afterlife. Only because words never seem sufficient. We exchange a lot of unspoken words with our eyes, but most of the time, our experiences from the other side feel too sacred to voice. Almost as if we fear that some kind of spell would be broken, and the miracle would unravel.

He doesn't answer for a long time, just watches the shape of our hands as they move in and out of each other. "I was trying to figure out if the dream I had last night was a memory . . . or just a dream."

Part of the problem with not talking about our memories of the afterlife is that they are becoming more and more hazy. They come and go, rising and falling from our consciousness like the tide. Sometimes even when we compare notes, details are lost to us. But when we both remember the same thing, we know it's real.

I release his hand and prop myself on one elbow so I can see his face. He looks perplexed, his brows drawn together. "Maybe I can help," I say. "What was your dream?"

His chest rises with a deep breath, and the line in his forehead deepens as he tries to translate his dream into words.

"I was talking to my mom . . . under a weeping tree with crystal blossoms." His blue-green eyes move to mine. "Is that something I told you about before?"

I take a moment to search my own memories, starting with when I showed back up at my family's island camp with Kai in tow. He told them that he'd been so anxious to see me that he took a morning ferry to meet me on the island—and accidentally left all his things on the ferry. We got a strange look from my dad, an appreciative sigh from my mom, and a huge eye roll from my sister. But they all bought the story.

After we got back from the sailing trip, I spent days making Kai explain everything to me, from how he rescued me the day he drowned, to his own experience in the afterlife, to the wristband that had the power to heal people. And for weeks after that, I walked around in a mystified daze, trying to absorb and make sense of everything I experienced and everything Kai shared with me. He even told me all about Charles . . . and about his mom.

"Yes," I say, my eyes returning to Kai's. "You did tell me about that."

His features grow thoughtful and distant, as though he's reliving the memory. "I'm glad." After a long moment, a small, serene smile spreads over his lips and his eyes refocus on me. His gaze travels slowly over my face, ending up on my mouth, and his thumb comes up and brushes over my lips. I lean closer, and just as my lips graze his, there's a knock on the cottage door.

"I better get that," he whispers, his lips still touching mine as he speaks. "Probably Isadora."

Reluctantly, I sit up and slide off Kai's bed so he can get up. I follow him to the front door, but when he opens it, it's not Isadora standing on the porch.

His sisters stand there—Helen with her eyes like Kai's and her long dark hair, and petite Jane with her blonde pixie cut that makes her look like Tinker Bell.

"Hey," Kai says brightly as his mouth spreads in a wide grin. He steps out onto the porch and gathers them in his arms. "What are you two doing here?"

"I know we said good-bye at your going away party last night," Helen says, looking up at him, "but we wanted to see you one last time before you leave."

Jane holds up a blue envelope. "Plus, Aunt Laurel asked us to bring this to you."

He takes the envelope and raises an eyebrow. "What's this?"

Helen shrugs. "I think it's an apology."

Kai rubs the back of his head and quirks his mouth. "Would you do me a favor? Tell her I understand and that all's forgiven." Then he casts a glance my way. "And that I wouldn't have it any other way. Things turned out just the way they should."

Kai's sisters hang around and chat for a bit while he finishes gathering all his things, and as they leave, he promises to call them often and to visit whenever we're back in town.

With a couple suitcases and his guitar, we stroll away from the cottage through the lavender field. The morning sun has burned off the mist, and the view all around is breathtakingly clear. At the wooden gate, Kai pauses and turns west, where the land slopes downward toward the sea. Through a wide gap in the hills, the blue ocean stretches out to meet the sky. He sets down his suitcase and guitar, and as he takes the other suitcase from my hand and sets it down too, I see a ripple move across his chin. He draws me into his arms and holds me close, whispering into my hair the three words I most love to hear.

I return the words, then tip my head back to look at him. His eyes are shining and slightly troubled. "What's the matter?" I say softly, wondering if he's having second thoughts about moving away from his sisters and Isadora.

He shakes his head slowly. "Nothing. I'm just . . . dangerously happy."

I exhale a sigh of relief and clutch a handful of his shirt. "Me too." As I gaze into his eyes, I hear the faint sound of the sea in the distance, the eternal and constant movement of the waves.

When we kiss, his lips are soft and warm, welcoming like bathwater and charged like a summer rainstorm. Through his shirt I feel his heart pounding against my rib cage, and it only makes me want to kiss him more, longer. Because we have longer now. And in this kiss, unhurried and tender and humming with life, we drift away from the world and into a tranquil sea of our own, where the waves carry us into an endless horizon.

ACKNOWLEDGMENTS

I honestly thought my second book would be easier to write than my first. (You fellow writers can pause to laugh here). After all, I'd spent years learning the craft and fine-tuning my writing process. But about halfway into the first draft of this book, it occurred to me how wrong I was. And that was when I began habitually and exasperatedly asking my critique group, "What was I thinking writing a story about a DEAD person?" They would just laugh, probably because they didn't know how I was going to pull this story off anymore than I did. So as I continued working on it, I had to spend a lot of time listening. Listening to the voice inside me that told me this was a story worth finishing. Listening to my critique group whenever they insisted I was taking a wrong turn. Listening to instructors at writing conferences who gave helpful world-building and plotting advice. And most of all, listening to Kai and Avery as they revealed their true characters and stories to me. Their story stretched me to my limits and then beyond. It helped me grow tremendously as a writer and even as a person. It forced me to dig deep into the things that I fear and believe and hope for as I traveled in their shoes and carried their pain. At times, the journey was grueling and emotionally exhausting. But in the end, the joy I felt at having finally gotten their story right made it all worth it. So I want to thank all of the people who supported and encouraged me along the way.

First, to the lovely ladies of Critiki. Heather Clark, for your keen sense of story structure and character arcs. Sabine Berlin, for your killer editing skills, for swooning over Kai even before he became a likable character, and for threatening to hunt me down if I didn't finish the story. Juliana Ali, for your impeccable logic and problem-solving sorcery. Rebecca Scott, for being the cutest Dictionary Face in the world. Janelle Youngstrom, for sometimes turning my angsty romance into a comedy with your lively enactments. You girls put the fun and love in critiquing, and writing would be drudgery without you.

To the other girls of Real Writers Write, Nikki Trionfo, Caryn Caldwell, Amy Wilson, Shari Cylinder, and Teresa Richards, for always being there to offer support and advice. Also to Chris Weston (C. K. Edwards) for reading and giving feedback on a really crappy early version of this book, and other members of the Point Writers (Shauna Dansie, Kylee Wilkins, Terri Barton, Darren Eggett, Alyson King, and Garrett Winn) who helped me brainstorm when I first began this story.

The setting in this book was a huge deal to me, so I owe a big thanks to genuine surfer girl Ane May and her family, for introducing us to the charm of Avila Beach and providing us a lovely place to stay while visiting there. So many scenes were inspired while I explored your beautiful little town, and I couldn't have imagined a more picturesque setting.

Many thanks to the fiction team at Cedar Fort: Emma Parker for your enthusiasm for my writing and your thorough and insightful content editing. Michelle May, for the beautiful cover. Melissa Caldwell for removing all those extraneous commas and keeping my grammar in check. You all have been a joy to work with.

A colossal shout-out to all the readers out there who take time out of their busy lives to read my stories. I hope you know that your kind and generous feedback is what keeps me going on those hard writing days. You're always in my mind, and I have many more stories to share with you, so thank you for opening the covers of my books and letting your eyes travel along the path of my words.

My three boys are getting older and have started asking questions about the stories I write. They understand now what romance is and that I write about it, and so they've all vowed to never read anything I write (unless "there's no kissing and it has cyborgs in it"). But even though they don't appreciate my work (yet!), they do support me by giving me time to write and not being too annoyed when I sometimes get lost in my own little fictional worlds. So I want them to know how much I appreciate their support and their unending supply of hugs and kisses and hot sauce potions.

Last, I want to thank my sweetheart, Keith. For your eternal support, encouragement, and example in living a fearless and creative life. You're my everything, and I love you to Elysium and beyond.

ABOUT THE AUTHOR

Sarah Beard is the author of YA novels *Porcelain Keys* and *Beyond the Rising Tide*. She earned a degree in communications from the University of Utah and is currently pursuing an MFA in creative writing. When she's not writing, she referees wrestling matches between her three boys and listens to audiobooks while folding self-replicating piles of laundry. She is a breast cancer survivor, a baker of sweets, a seeker of good love stories, a composer of melancholy music, and a traveler who wishes her travel budget was much bigger. She lives with her husband and children in the shadow of the beautiful Wasatch Mountains.

SCAN TO VISIT

WWW.SARAHBEARD.COM